D1206071

CANADA
1874-1896

ARDUOUS DESTINY

A HISTORY OF CANADA IN EIGHTEEN VOLUMES

The Canadian Centenary Series is a comprehensive history of the peoples and lands which form the Dominion of Canada.

Although the series is designed as a unified whole so that no part of the story is left untold, each volume is complete in itself. Written for the general reader as well as for the scholar, each of the eighteen volumes of *The Canadian Centenary Series* is the work of a leading Canadian historian who is an authority on the period covered in his volume. Their combined efforts have made a new and significant contribution to the understanding of Canada and of Canada today.

W. L. Morton, Vanier Professor of History, Trent University, is the Executive Editor of *The Canadian Centenary Series*. A graduate of the Universities of Manitoba and Oxford, he is the author of *The Kingdom of Canada; Manitoba: A History; The Progressive Party in Canada; The Critical Years: The Union of British North America, 1857-1873*; and other writings. He has also edited *The Journal of Alexander Begg and Other Documents Relevant to the Red River Resistance*. Holder of the honorary degrees of LL.D. and D.LITT., he has been awarded the Tyrrell Medal of the Royal Society of Canada and the Governor General's Award for Non-Fiction.

D. G. Creighton, former Chairman of the Department of History, University of Toronto, is the Advisory Editor of *The Canadian Centenary Series*. A graduate of the Universities of Toronto and Oxford, he is the author of *John A. Macdonald: The Young Politician; John A. Macdonald: The Old Chieftain; Dominion of the North; The Empire of the St. Lawrence* and many other works. Holder of numerous honorary degrees, LL.D., and D.LITT, he has twice won the Governor General's Award for Non-Fiction. He has also been awarded the Tyrrell Medal of the Royal Society of Canada, the University of Alberta National Award in Letters, the University of British Columbia Medal for Popular Biography, and the Molson Prize of the Canada Council.

PETER B. WAITE

CANADA 1874-1896

ARDUOUS DESTINY

The Canadian Centenary Series

McClelland and Stewart Limited
Toronto/Montreal

0-7710-8800-0

The Canadian Publishers

McClelland and Stewart Limited
25 Hollinger Road, Toronto 374

ACKNOWLEDGEMENTS

We wish to thank the following sources for permission to use their material in the illustration sections of this book:

NOTMAN PHOTOGRAPHIC ARCHIVES, MONTREAL for the portrait of Sir William Van Horne; Saint John harbour, New Brunswick; Logging camp on the Nashwaak River, New Brunswick; bar of the Balmoral Hotel, Montreal; portrait of Sir Charles Tupper; Notre Dame Street, Montreal; Miss Legge of Montreal; Ottawa Post Office, Parliament Buildings, and Rideau Canal bridges.

PROVINCIAL ARCHIVES OF BRITISH COLUMBIA for C.P.R. heavy grade engine, 314, at the summit of the Rockies.

PROVINCIAL ARCHIVES OF MANITOBA for the arrival of the locomotive, *Countess of Dufferin*, Winnipeg; Hudson's Bay Company post, Grand Rapids.

PUBLIC ARCHIVES OF CANADA for the portrait of Sir John A. Macdonald; troops leaving Fort Qu'Appelle.

PRINTED AND BOUND
IN CANADA BY
THE HUNTER ROSE COMPANY

A History of Canada

W. L. Morton, EXECUTIVE EDITOR

D. G. Creighton, ADVISORY EDITOR

*1. *Tryggvi J. Oleson* The North to 1632

2. *Marcel Trudel* New France, 1524-1662

*3. *W. J. Eccles* New France, 1663-1701

4. *Jean Blain* New France, 1702-1743

*5. *G. F. G. Stanley* New France, 1744-1760

*6. *Hilda Neatby* Quebec, 1760-1791

*7. *Gerald M. Craig* Upper Canada, 1784-1841

8. *Fernand Ouellet* Lower Canada, 1792-1841

*9. *W. S. MacNutt* The Atlantic Provinces, 1712-1857

*10. *J. M. S. Careless* Canada, 1841-1857

*11. *E. E. Rich* The North, 1670-1857

*12. *W. L. Morton* The Critical Years, 1857-1873

*13. *P. B. Waite* Canada, 1874-1896

14. *R. Craig Brown and G. R. Cook* Canada, 1897-1921

15. *Roger Graham* Canada, 1922-1939

16. *Morris Zaslow* The North, Volume I, 1870-1905

17. *Morris Zaslow* The North, Volume II, 1905-1967

18. *D. G. Creighton* Canada, 1939-1967

VOLUMES STARRED ARE PUBLISHED

CONTENTS

Canada 1874-1896:

Arduous Destiny

MAPS AND ILLUSTRATIONS

FOREWORD

The Canadian Centenary Series

Half a century has elapsed since *Canada and Its Provinces*, the first large-scale co-operative history of Canada, was published. During that time, new historical materials have been made available in archives and libraries; new research has been carried out, and its results published; new interpretations have been advanced and tested. In these same years Canada itself has greatly grown and changed. These facts, together with the centenary of Confederation, justify the publication of a new co-operative history of Canada.

The form chosen for this enterprise was that of a series of volumes. The series was planned by the editors, but each volume will be designed and executed by a single author. The general theme of the work is the development of those regional communities which have for the past century made up the Canadian nation; and the series will be composed of a number of volumes sufficiently large to permit adequate treatment of all the phases of the theme in the light of modern knowledge.

The Centenary History, then, was planned as a series to have a certain common character and to follow a common method but to be written by individual authors, specialists in their fields. As a whole, it will be a work of specialized knowledge, the great advantage of scholarly co-operation, and at the same time each volume will have the unity and distinctive character of individual authorship. It was agreed that a general narrative treatment was necessary and that each author should deal in a balanced way with economic, political, and social history. The result, it is hoped, will be an interpretative, varied, and comprehensive account, at once useful to the student and interesting to the general reader.

The difficulties of organizing and executing such a series are apparent: the overlapping of separate narratives, the risk of omissions, the imposition of divisions which are relevant to some themes but not to others. Not so apparent, but quite as troublesome, are the problems of scale, perspective, and scope, problems which perplex the writer of a one-volume history and are magnified in a series. It is by deliberate choice that certain parts of the history are told twice, in different volumes from different points of view, in the belief that the benefits gained outweigh the unavoidable disadvantages.

In this volume Professor Waite reveals a gift for presenting history upon its own terms, history with its own shape and attitudes, and with its own lively personalities. The mode suits the period. In the years 1874-1896 the great experiment of Confederation, so long conceived, so hastily undertaken, was put to the test. It was freighted with enterprises whose scale was to daunt even some of the most robust minds of the time. The testing was, as Edward Blake felt and Professor Waite confirms, arduous indeed. Out of it were to come results not altogether foreseen, a Canada with a character not wholly intended by the makers of Confederation. This complex story Professor Waite tells with its many subtleties, and evokes colours and mutations not before perceived.

W. L. MORTON
Executive Editor
D. G. CREIGHTON
Advisory Editor

PREFACE

Arduous Destiny

This book is a survey; it is a waterbug kind of book, skimming across the surface. Much research is left undone; it is not possible to cover all the primary sources for these twenty-three years of Canadian history, except as the work of a lifetime. There are, for example, some four hundred Canadian newspapers, not one of which has been canvassed comprehensively for the whole period. Bits and pieces from here and there are the most that can be included. Even in the rich manuscript sources of the period, there are gaps I should like to have avoided.

I have tried to write a history of Canada between 1874 and 1896 on the assumption that there is more to that history than the political doings at Ottawa, fascinating as they often are. They cannot be ignored; indeed, they may have filled a disproportionate part of the book. Nevertheless, the history of Canada includes the great diversities of the provinces that make up Canada. Here there is much that is still unknown, and my research has not been comprehensive enough to fill the gaps. Whenever it seemed relevant, I have included "provincial" history without using that name, nor made excuse for doing so.

Past politics is not all of history. History ought to include politics as an important expression of the ideas and life of Canada, but I have not hesitated to introduce economics or poetry when it seemed right to do so, and have doubtless exercised rather cavalier choices. I have also made free with personalities; it is, after all, men who make history. The book is roughly chronological. There are no topical chapters as such; readers will have to endure some indiscriminate catholicity of narrative.

Some mention may be made of the provenance of the book. Dean John Saywell of York University was first asked to write this history; he had to give it up in 1963. I thought then, and often since, that he would have made it a great book had he been able to carry on. I was asked in November, 1963, if I would undertake it, and I have been working on it since.

During the summer of 1965 I worked in the Archives beside Ramsay Cook, the author of Volume XIV in this series, and am grateful for suggestions he, and other colleagues, have made. Professors Murray Beck and Alistair Sinclair at Dalhousie University have made helpful suggestions in their respective fields of Political Science and Economics. Professor Norman Morse has been kind enough to read and comment on Chapter 5. Professor K. G. Pryke has made available materials from his own research into post-Confederation Nova Scotian history. I am indebted to several graduate students, Kenneth McLaughlin in particular. Indeed, I have much reason to be grateful to the work of graduate students everywhere in Canada. Some of my obligations have been acknowledged in notes, others in the bibliography.

The original manuscript was a brute of 200,000 words. It is now about 145,000. In the process I have had to drop out some cherished topics (and stories), cut some pet quotations, but it was a salutary exercise in pruning a somewhat rambling narrative. Here I must thank Professor W. L. Morton, of Trent University, for his great patience and skill, and Dean John Saywell, who made a number of valuable suggestions, and had to read the manuscript in the midst of a press of other business. My most searching critic was Professor Craig Brown, of the University of Toronto, who went over the material inch by inch taking a sharp pencil to inconsistencies, irrelevancies and occasional demonstrations of sheer ignorance. I hope he will forgive my recommending him to other authors. Many of his and other suggestions have been adopted; I hope I have succeeded in reforming the book better than indifferently.

My thanks as well to the Canada Council for making possible a summer of research at Ottawa in 1965, and to both the Council and Dalhousie University for a sabbatical leave in England, 1967-68, when most of this book was written. My wife and daughters have lived with it all with wonderful understanding and patience.

P. B. W.
Halifax, N.S.
April, 1970.

CHAPTER 1

Canada in 1874: An Overview

Canada is a hard country. It is a hard country to govern, and for much of its history, it has been a hard country to live in. Its people have lived between a habitable, tractable south where, one might say, anything is possible, and an uninhabitable, intractable north where nothing is possible. Canadians live in the shadow of the great impossible. A Canadian has only to look northward from that hundred miles north of the American border, to see, either in his mind's eye, or in fact, *la lisière du forêt*, that edge of wilderness that is the beginning of humility. ". . . mais toujours derrière les champs nus la lisière des bois apparaissait et suivait comme une ombre, interminable bande sombre entre la blancheur du sol et le ciel gris." So Louis Hémon wrote, in *Maria Chapdelaine*.[1]

The interaction of man and nature, characteristic of all literature, is especially a theme in ours. The importance and popularity of the painters of the Group of Seven is surely because they touched something fundamental, as does that most beautiful of all English-Canadian poems, "Late November," written about 1886:

The hills and leafless forests slowly yield
To the thick-driving snow. A little while
And night shall darken down. In shouting file
The woodmen's carts go by me homeward-wheeled,
Past the thin fading stubbles, half-concealed,
Now golden-gray, sowed softly through with snow,
Where the last ploughman follows still his row,
Turning black furrows through the whitening field.

Far off the village lamps begin to gleam,
Fast drives the snow, and no man comes this way;
The hills grow wintery white, and bleak winds moan
About the naked uplands. I alone
Am neither sad, nor shelterless, nor gray,
Wrapped round with thought, content to watch and dream.[2]

We have made a glory of the brutality of our land, and triumphs from its vicissitudes. The Canadian hero is the explorer, the fur trader. The Canadian Pacific Railway was more than an act of faith; it was a conquest, and we have romanticized it, as we have the voyageurs.

Canada is a hard country to govern. Size and geography and history all emphasize regional identities; to superimpose upon these a national existence is political audacity that takes persistence, energy – perhaps faith. If Canadians do not indulge in loud professions of patriotism it is because the very existence of Canada takes patriotism enough. Edward Blake, for all his uncertainty, grasped this, as he painfully groped his way past a Canadian union with the United States and, instead, chose for Canada "that more arduous destiny"[3] of living alone. That is the challenge. It was difficult enough to put Canada together in a mere decade between 1864 and 1873; but making it work was the appalling task that faced Canada from 1873 to 1896.

"What a time! and what changes!" Alexander Campbell was sixty-three when he wrote this to Macdonald in 1885.[4] By 1896 many of the major technological devices we are now familiar with had come or were imminent. Ottawa had its first Bell Telephone book in 1882, with two hundred subscribers; Parliament was being planned for electric light; and even in 1884 there were complaints in Toronto about the ugly and graceless confusion of electric wires "perched at the top of hideous poles."[5]

But the old ways did not die easily. For all the inventions it was a different world from ours, in the most palpable things of every day life. The very sounds and smells were different. The sounds were of a gentler pace, of wind, rain, and horses. Some mechanical sounds had been added: trains and the loon-loneliness of their whistles. There were the great wagons grinding their iron-rimmed wheels on the streets. In winter the sound of sleigh bells was iterated and reiterated, and as *The Week* remarked in March, 1884, was apt "to pall upon the most imaginative after four months. . . ."[6] Canada in March! The sheer dreariness of that half-frozen landscape: the inexorableness of its poverty, the meanness of its details – tin and boards, half-decayed sheds and rotting piles, limping fences, untidy vacant lots, mounds of ancient half-thawed refuse, a welter of poles, boards, pipes and slush, and a tired tram-line straggling down a thoroughfare of puddles.[7] But then March is the time of year designed to remind most Canadians of the price of being Canadian.

Through the streets and lanes crept the smell of horses. The streets were swept, of course; notwithstanding, the dust of summer was mixed with horse manure, as was the mud in spring and fall; and the snow in winter merely accentuated the sight and mitigated the smell. Mud and dirt were everywhere. Winnipeg was notoriously the worst. Every turn of a wheel in spring or in a wet autumn ladled up that marvellous, viscous, slippery gumbo, "so heavy that the driver had frequently to stop and clean it off with a stick," which, duly trodden into the wood sidewalks, made them quite indescribable.[8]

Public places smelled of tobacco, often in a virulent, liquid form. Here is a political meeting in Newfoundland in 1896: "a bare barn of a hall . . . lighted by swinging kerosene lamps. . . . The odour of the place is reprehensible. Almost from the first, a dozen tiny streams of tobacco juice course tortuously between the seats, and by degrees reach the aisle; and a current visible to all, swollen from a hundred sources, courses silently toward the door."[9] Nor was this practice confined to Newfoundland. The grandeur of the Royal Lyceum Theatre in Toronto was coloured, one might say, by the tobacco chewers, giving "the floors, particularly in the gallery where the twenty-five-centers assemble, a pattern and an odor [*sic*] not to be experienced in modern theatres. . . ."[10]

Society was still rough and ready. It was a school of hard knocks because it was a world of hard knocks. It was a game, often bloody, where the human animal expressed his prejudices in a ruthless and direct fashion. Examples could be multiplied beyond necessity of the elemental crudeness of much of life. George Johnson, writing the life of Joseph Howe around the turn of the century, supplied the Reverend George Grant, Principal of Queens, with an account of Howe in Lunenburg from a "Dutch" woman that Howe knew. "Oh! yes Mr. Howe is just the nicest man I ever knew. No nonsense about him. He's just one of ourselves. He stands up with his back to the fire, puts his hands under his coat-tails and breaks wind (that's not the word she used) like one of the family."[11] Howe's sensational Detroit speech of 1865 was made after he had gone out of the meeting to get cool and had been drinking beer with the men in a nearby bar.

For drinking no apology was expected or given in a Canada where consumption of alcoholic drink was four gallons per annum for every man, woman and child in the country.[12] In 1873, of the twelve thousand arrests made in Montreal, fifty per cent were for drunkenness and another fifteen per cent for other offences, arising from it. The Chief of Police of Montreal, F. W. Fenton, put it more graphically:

> What is the cause of almost all larcenies? – drink! Of assaults? – drink! Fights, furious driving, interference with police? . . . Drink, drink, drink! . . . From these numerous hot-beds of all that is vicious [taverns] issue forth a host of rowdies and idle and disorderly individuals, always on the look-out for mischief, and whose chief and most relished pastime seems to consist of attacking the police, rescuing prisoners, and spreading terror in certain portions of the city.[13]

In 1874 Toronto had a tavern for every 120 of its population. Children and abstainers aside, it means that sixty people supported each tavern.[14] The effects of drink on society were sometimes deplorable and on Parliament occasionally disastrous.[15] There was a mighty drunk in the House of Commons in 1878 just before that august body passed the Canada Temperance Act. It had started during a long debate on the Letellier affair, a debate that Alexander Mackenzie, the Prime Minister, wanted to end, but with a provincial election campaign on in Quebec, Conservatives wanted to prolong. The Conservatives could not be turned off. Sir John Macdonald started drinking in the evening and by seven-thirty in the morning, after a final tumbler of whisky, was quietly stowed away by the Conservative whip in the rooms of the Deputy-Sergeant-at-Arms. Lt.-Col. C. J. Campbell, J.P., M.P. for Victoria, Cape Breton, known as "Tupper's goose," was worse, getting onto the floor in front of the Speaker, with his hat on, flourishing a stick round his head, stamping his feet on the floor, declaring his utter independence of Governments, Parliaments, Speakers, or any one else, daring the Government or any member of it to fight, and all at the top of his voice. He was taken away by friends before the Sergeant-at-Arms intervened. James Domville, M.P. for Kings, New Brunswick, following a colleague at eight in the morning, rose to be greeted with shouts of ribald laughter from friends and foes. " 'Button up your pants', 'Shame', and so on. Having buttoned up, Mr. Domville commenced to read. . . ."[16] In the 1880's *Grip*, the Toronto comic weekly, turned some striking cartoons to the purpose of prohibition; but drinking went on with ebullience. Only slowly did the idea of prohibition make its way.

In the 1870's society was still imbued with old-fashioned and long held tenets of self-help. The Halifax *Evening Express*, a Roman Catholic paper, made this point with vehemence:

> There must always be working men, men to work with their hands, to be poor, to be industrious, to be unfortunate, to suffer; it is the will of God and the destiny of the race. That will and that destiny are not to be counteracted by public meetings, by agitators, by speeches of demagogues, by public orations, or other foolish means.[17]

This was probably an extreme statement of a characteristic point of view. But there were changes already stirring in the direction of support for the working man, the printers in Toronto being the best-known example. Sir John Macdonald, who had been largely instrumental in effecting this recognition,[18] though he still insisted that the rights of property were paramount,[19] was already beginning to sense, in that uncanny way of his, that opinion seemed "more and more inclined to the idea that vested rights must yield to the general good."[20] In 1888 the Royal Commission on Labour and Capital was sympathetic, "To treat labour and wages as a simple exchange between equals is absurd. The labourer must sell his labour or starve."[21]

The Toronto *Globe* was less charitable. In 1881 when Dr. Bergin introduced in the House of Commons a bill to regulate the hours of employment for women and children, the *Globe* replied:

> . . . the less the state interferes . . . the better. The subject of the employment of women would be best regulated by leaving it to the factory owners. . . . As to preventing overtime work by young persons under eighteen . . . we fail to see that a strong girl or lad of sixteen or seventeen would receive any injury for an additional hour or two of well paid work occasionally.[22]

Child labour was still a better solution to the problem of street waifs than the rattan proposed by the *Globe*. What else could children do? Even the progressive Ontario Education Act of 1874 enjoining parents to have children between the ages of seven and twelve at school for four months a year, was not enforced. It was the opinion of the Commissioners of 1882 that children might very well be better off "spending a portion at least of their time at work rather than wasting it on the public streets."[23]

In Quebec and in the Maritimes, children were still worse off than in Ontario. The law in Nova Scotia stated that boys under ten could not be employed in mines, and those between ten and twelve were supposed to work no more than sixty hours a week. The Commissioners of 1889 considered the work they did easy – opening and closing the doors inside the mines for the passage of coal cars; but they could not approve of a system that permitted the continuous employment of children so young. In Montreal a boy's ordinary hours in the cotton mills were from 6:30 A.M. to noon, and from 12:45 to 6:15 P.M.

The slums were like all slums. St. John's, Newfoundland, in 1886 was probably no worse than many others, varying only in detail. The streets were narrow, tortuous, and rough, and the stranger frequently found himself

> in quarters of unimaginable filth, tumble-down hovels, windows with broken sashes, decrepit fences, streets paved with old rags and decayed cats and other animals. One's nostrils are assailed by nauseating odours, and one's eyes by loathsome sights and sounds. One gets glimpses of dirty faces at dirty windows, ragged children, slipshod women, men with evil faces and slouching gait.[24]

By 1874 Newfoundland felt more isolated than she had ever been. The last British troops had marched down from Signal Hill to the waiting ships in 1871, to the infinite chagrin of the Newfoundlanders who gloomily ruminated that Newfoundland, which had never gone up many steps in the world, had now gone down another.[25] The French shore was still a source of annoyance and concern, but Newfoundland's interest in her own west coast was growing, as was her determination to keep it. She even got permission from the Imperial government to appoint a magistrate at St. George's Bay. But there was no regular boat service from the west coast to Nova Scotia, and

Newfoundland's own coastal communications were at best capricious.[26] The Speech from the Throne in February, 1875 was to announce the beginning of the trans-Newfoundland railway, for which an early survey had already been reconnoitred in 1868. This mighty project was to take another twenty-three years, and was to contribute heavily to the crisis of 1894-95,[27] and to Newfoundland's last real attempt to unite with Canada until fifty years later.

The 1870's were the last big years of Maritime shipping.[28] Frank Killam, M.P. for Yarmouth, had doubled his own ship tonnage between 1866 and 1876 and the rest of Yarmouth County had done as well.[29] And although trade was down somewhat after 1875, shipments of Pennsylvania oil gave new impetus, and on the whole the ships prospered. In 1874 no fewer than 826 square riggers were registered in Nova Scotia, to say nothing of hundreds of schooners. In that year was launched the biggest Canadian square rigger ever built, the *W. D. Lawrence*, 2,500 tons. But by the 1890's, although big ships were still being built, the best years were over. It was the iron hull that killed the Canadian square riggers, not the tramp steamers, still twenty years in the future. Iron sailing ships were free from the curse of leakiness that affected most softwood ships, which meant the latter were relegated to the cheaper cargoes that wouldn't spoil.[30] Gradually the wooden ships were sold and by a kind of marine Gresham's law ended up doing the mean jobs in the mean places of the world.

Blaming Confederation for the decay of Nova Scotian shipping was still in the future. The complaints about Confederation in Nova Scotia in the early 1870's were different. The provincial government did not have enough to live on, not even after the better terms of 1869. There was still the memory of the press gang technique by which Nova Scotia had been brought into Confederation in the first place. But by 1873 prosperity had mitigated much of this feeling. In Nova Scotia ship owners, traders and merchants were prosperous, although they continued to grumble about Confederation. The West Indian trade was still good, and although the tariffs of 1867 and 1870 were mightily resented, Halifax, even in the leaner years of the 1880's retained its mixture of a busy harbour and its comfortable, if sometimes drab, merchants' houses.

Another mitigation of Nova Scotia's anti-Confederate agitation was developing by 1872: increased prospects for a Reform government at Ottawa exercised a surprisingly soothing effect on the refractoriness of some of the Nova Scotian newspapers. The Halifax *Morning Chronicle* which had been particularly conspicuous in the anti-Confederate struggle, had this to say in August, 1872, just before the federal elections:

> Our cause is the cause of those noble statesmen Mackenzie and Blake, the Reform leaders of Ontario. We cast our fortune in with theirs, believing that

> the time has now come when the Liberal party of the Dominion should unite its strength from all the provinces to ensure for United British North America an honest, economical, honourable and Liberal government.[31]

Similar comments were heard from this quarter two years later when the Mackenzie government took over the helm. Anti-Confederation was not dead in Nova Scotia; but it was being eroded by the inevitable acceptance of necessity and by prosperity.

By 1873 the New Brunswick school question complicated all existing political issues inside that province, and was destined to do the same outside. It upset the precarious *modus vivendi* arrived at in 1867. The irony was that the New Brunswick School Act of 1871 was against the spirit, but not the letter, of the British North America Act. It roused French Canadians over the educational privileges of their fellow Catholics in New Brunswick, and became a bone of contention in federal politics, splitting party lines. There is some evidence that it had already influenced the framing of the Manitoba Act of 1870.

The delicate checks and balances in the educational structure of 1867 had been rudely shaken by the gusts of opinion generated by the Vatican Council of 1870. The Council created great enthusiasm in many Catholic quarters, and real uneasiness in some others; it did inspire a new militancy in those quarters of the church naturally ultramontane. The 1870's were racked with religious quarrels, in France, in Great Britain, in Germany especially, and in Canada. Canada was decidedly vulnerable. Catholics comprised 40 per cent of the population of Newfoundland, 50 per cent of Prince Edward Island, 25 per cent of Nova Scotia, 35 per cent of New Brunswick, 90 per cent of Quebec, 17 per cent of Ontario, 30 per cent of Manitoba, 10 per cent of British Columbia. The population in 1871, about 3,700,000, was 43 per cent Roman Catholic. There were a number of peculiar and delicate compromises in education and in religion that could easily be upset. The New Brunswick school question was therefore not a small issue, although it seemed so when it began. On the contrary it could not be contained within the province any more than the Manitoba school question was to be.

The resolution of the difficulty might have been effected by George Etienne Cartier, but by the summer of 1873 Cartier was dead. Bright's disease had killed him in May despite all that London doctors could do. There was no one to replace him. He had been the head of the Conservative party in Quebec, and although his authority had been weakened by his quarrel with Bishop Bourget and some fine clerical sapping of his political foundations, there was no one else with the command over the jarring factions, the natural condition of politics especially in Quebec. After Cartier's funeral the French-Canadian Conservatives met in St. Lawrence Hall; federal members, provincial members, and a sprinkling of Senators and Legislative Councillors. Hector Langevin was made *chef*.

Langevin had been under a cloud since his disappearance from Canadian parliamentary life in 1896, but not without reason was he Macdonald's man until Macdonald's death in 1891. Langevin was a capable administrator; he had intelligence and a capacity for hard work. In Parliament he had finesse, good temper, discretion, *politesse*, quite unlike Cartier. But Langevin had no parliamentary *panache*; he had a monotonous voice, a pedestrian mind, and no gift at all for the pungent or striking phrase.[32] In Quebec particularly, which liked its politics and politicians vivacious, this weakness left him open to strong flanking movements from people like the meteoric Chapleau. And Langevin's difficulties were compounded by the fact that, unlike Cartier, he was from Quebec and not from Montreal.

Montreal could not be easily ignored. It was now a city of over 100,000, nearly double the size of Toronto. It had grown twenty per cent between 1861 and 1871 whereas Quebec city had grown by less than three per cent. Seven hundred ships a year came now to Montreal's lengthening wharves, already fifty-five per cent of the tonnage that came to Quebec city, and the proportion rising all the time.[33]

Montreal's prosperity was partly based on the market in the new Maritime provinces. The Montreal manufacturers had not expected Confederation to produce a strong market in the eastern provinces, despite all the fulsome talk about the vast market that Confederation would create. Businessmen heavily discount oratory. But from 1867 onward the Quebec and Ontario manufacturers found, developed, and exploited the eastern market. William Muir of Montreal, a wholesale clothing dealer, before a parliamentary committee in 1874, said, "Our business increases with the trade of the Dominion which has increased largely. But one of the principal elements of the increase has been our getting the Maritime Provinces as a market. Not less than one-third of my own trade is with Nova Scotia and New Brunswick."[34]

A serious problem in Quebec was where to settle the burgeoning population. That many were coming to live in Montreal is patent, as were the repercussions later on with the frightful small-pox epidemic of 1875-76; but not all were staying in the province. Many went to New England, to mill towns like Manchester, Nashua or Lowell. They were not looking for more land, but for more money. In consequence, Quebec's population between 1861 and 1871 went up only 7 per cent compared to Ontario's 23 per cent, though this changed by the census of 1881 to 15 per cent and 19 per cent respectively.

The great bulk of Canada's people still lived on the land. Of the 3,700,000 in the 1871 census, eighty per cent were described as rural, that is, living outside of any incorporated city, town or village, of whatever size. The predominantly rural character of the Canadian population in 1871, and in 1881 it was still seventy-five per cent, has to be kept continually in mind in considering the character and setting of Canadian life. The conservativeness of the French-Canadian countryside is well known, its resistance to social change as strong as its political allegiances; but so much of Canada was similar that the descriptions of town life in this chapter are misleading. Canada was rural. And this goes a long way to explain many of the characteristics of politics and politicians in Quebec and elsewhere.

By the 1870's the French Canadians were moving gradually into the English townships as they were to continue to do for a long time to come. Sherbrooke in 1871 had already a slight Roman Catholic majority, although a French-speaking majority appeared only in the 1891 census.[35] This quiet French-Canadian occupation of land in the townships was a curious process. Rather like the gathering of a hive of bees by the introduction of a queen, the symbol of French-Canadian expansion was the establishment of the parish church and a curé. It also suggests how difficult it was, given French-Canadian traditions of land settlement and the character of French-Canadian law, for French Canadians to move away from Quebec. The western land survey did not lend itself to French-Canadian ideas of cultivation and development.

Moreover, there had never been in Quebec anything resembling the enthusiasm of Ontario for the acquisition of the West. There was little confidence in the value of the land itself. This was the natural result of appeals of French-Canadian missionaries for help for "le pauvre colon de la Rivière Rouge" that had been made in Quebec for the last thirty years.[36] This Quebec view of a proverty-stricken west encouraged charity, but it discouraged emigration, and when French-Canadian emigration became desirable, Lacombe and others "found themselves defeated by their own earlier tactics."[37] Besides, not only was Manitoba far away, but the climate of opinion that swirled out of the events of 1869-70 in Red River could hardly encourage French Canadians to believe that their nationality had a strong future there. Not that a French west was impossible; Cartier's vision of a dualistic west had been embodied in the Manitoba Act. But it was a difficult concept to make viable. The Protestants of Ontario would find it easier to pull up their roots to make a living in the West.

Ontario in 1873 held the dynamism and the population that was to do much to develop the West. Its people represented nearly forty-five per cent of Canada's 1871 population. Largely Protestant, convinced of the desirability of material progress, setting its sights often from persuasive American examples, Ontario was expansionist and aggressive. Canada First was a characteristic expression of the idea "Ontario, Ontario." Canada First contained much that was bigoted and violent, but it also reflected the high-minded and exuberant patriotism of the young. More mature contemporaries may not have fully shared Canada First's sweeping desire to regenerate Canadian political life, but many, especially on the Reform side of politics, had immense faith in the moral and material improvement of

Canadian society. Boasting by far the largest railway mileage per capita, Ontario had already the basis for commercial and industrial growth; it was also ready to imagine a new Canada, one modelled in its own image, as its drive into the west would show. As early as 1881 Ontario-born living in Manitoba were more than double any other group in the province, save those born in Manitoba.[38] By then the West was already taking a shape that was quite different from that envisaged by Cartier a decade before.

By November, 1873 at the Stone Fort on the Red River the trees had already blazed into yellow and gone out. Snow had come and the river was now frozen over. With the temperature below zero,[39] the third and last contingent of the Mounted Police had come on sleighs down the twenty miles from the Forks (the City of Winnipeg it was called with becoming modesty), to the fort George Simpson had had erected – a monument to his aspirations and to his asperities – some forty years before. There it stood, on the high bank above that unpredictable river, facing alone the great stretch of prairie that opened to the west. Here the first of the western Indian Treaties had been signed with the Swampy Crees and Saulteaux two years before, and it was here that the North West Mounted Police really began.

Frank Oliver of Edmonton said many years later that "no more wildly impossible undertaking was ever staged than the establishment of Canadian authority and Canadian law throughout the western prairies by a handful of Mounted Police."[40] Few yet knew the magnitude of the task that lay ahead of the Mounted Police. Alexander Morris, Lieutenant-Governor of Manitoba, although he was sometimes dismissed in the East as an alarmist, had much to be alarmed about. The far west, the vast reaches of grassland in southern Alberta (it had no name then), was in American hands. This movement was both innocent and sinister; it was the same process by which the United States had acquired Texas and Oregon. Morris discerned the danger as early as 1867. "The people of the United States are . . . going in, and if they find no established institutions or organized Government, they will form an Association and commence a Government on their own."[41] The position in 1874 was that the American government officially recognized the forty-ninth parallel, but southern Alberta and Saskatchewan were unofficially the provinces of American traders from Fort Benton, on the Missouri. Southern Alberta is superb country; the great swales of grassland run in vast waves ten miles across. On these and the flatter grassland to the east and north lived the buffalo. The boundary survey parties of 1874 were held up for several hours on at least two occasions by the passing of enormous herds.

The Fort Benton traders had come in after the American Civil War and had moved steadily further to the north and west and east, until by 1873 they had establishments on the Red Deer River, the Bow River west of the forks, and in the Cypress Hills, and a trail from Benton to Edmonton.[42] Much has been written about these traders, often called whisky traders. They were not outlaws, though they have been so described. Probably there were some desperadoes among them, but mainly they were tough-minded traders doing business in the frontier fashion, in the fastest, most efficient, most ruthless way they knew. They therefore traded whisky for buffalo skins. Of course the American example infected the Canadian traders. Despite the Governor General's proclamation of 1870 against selling alcohol to Indians, it was brought into the Edmonton country from Winnipeg along the Carlton trail.

In 1873 a new Act gave power to any Justice of the Peace to seize and destroy liquor in the Northwest Territories with or without a warrant.[43] But there were as yet no means of enforcement. A lone magistrate who dared to apprehend a trader with liquor would discover that "swift revenge would be taken if not on himself personally – by the destruction of his property."[44] But the Canadian and American traders were not inherently vicious. The Chief Commissioner of the Hudson's Bay Company wrote that, ". . . with the exception of the liquor question and its results, I have found them [the American traders] whole hearted and generous fellows, always kind and ever ready to do us a favour."[45] The trade made them what they were. Like the Canadians, most of the Americans would accept law and order if it came; that would make trading conditions equal all round. As things were, no one was safe, neither the traders nor the Indians.

From Winnipeg the problem of the plains assumed formidable proportions. Southern Alberta lay across nine hundred miles of virgin prairie, far from supplies, and with little local fuel. No wonder Lieutenant-Governor Morris was uneasy. The Mounted Police force training at the Stone Fort was quite inadequate, in his opinion.

> . . . it may be possible to preserve order, though I do not believe the Privy Council have yet fully realized the magnitude of task that lies before them, in the creation of the institutions of civilization in the North West, in the suppression of crime, and in the maintenance of peaceful relations with the fierce tribes of the vast plains beyond Manitoba. . . . *I believe the difficulties of the position that Canada has assumed, have never been fully appreciated, by either Government or People. . . .*[46]

That last sentence was, indeed, the cold, hard truth.

It was even more apposite applied to British Columbia. Surely no province more belied its appearance on the map – a vast territory, the size of Oregon, Washington, Idaho and Montana rolled into one, yet with barely twenty-eight thousand whites.[47] The political and economic centre of British Columbia was the far south-west corner of it, Victoria. There the comfort of a salubrious and easy climate produced a delicious *dolce far niente.* As one visitor wrote, "Theirs was a happy, somnolent community, bathed in sunshine midst the fragrance of flowers. . . ."[48] J. H. E. Secretan, one of the first Pacific Railway engineers in British Columbia, remarked that the shopkeepers positively "hated to be bothered with business, especially if there was a cricket match on, and they would all shut up shop in the event of a horse race." Victoria had survived the trying days of the sixties and now, in 1873, prospects were that the Pacific Railway terminus would be established there. Upstart mainland talk of a terminus in Burrard Inlet caused some uncertainty, but this was dismissed as the natural pique of grubby mainlanders. Viewed from the perspective of the Island, British Columbia was Victoria and Victoria "still fancied herself a Crown Colony."[49]

This was the impression that unhappy and uncomfortable politicians in the east received from British Columbia or from Victoria. "The spoilt child of Confederation"[50] summed up the eastern reaction. It was not easy for British Columbians to see the eastern Canadian viewpoint, to picture the horror of easterners at building three thousand miles of railway across naked prairies and unknown mountains to nowhere; nor was it easy for easterners to appreciate the anxiety of British Columbians over being at the fag end of nothing in particular, stranded on the Pacific. British Columbians were British Columbians first and foremost; they were Canadians only by act of Parliament, and that but three years old.

In 1874 Canada was a conception rather than a reality. After six years the country was prosperous and the lines of inter-provincial trade – one might still have called it intercolonial – were starting to appear. The achievement of the late nineteenth century in Canada was considerable; the more one examines the realities of the time the more considerable the achievements become. But the problems were enormous. Canada was only seven years old; the only force that existed to link together these vast areas was a paper constitution, some real interests in common and a decaying fear of the United States. The Intercolonial Railway was already bogged down in politics as the Grand Trunk had been; it was now partly a colonization railway for eastern Quebec and northern New Brunswick, going the long way round to Halifax. It was a long, lonely way from Halifax to the coast of British Columbia. Where was the law, the moral force, the sense of nationality, to keep such centrifugal forces as these from flying apart? Only the thinness of the population prevented such forces from having more mass than they did. To keep the country going was to take enormous drafts of energy and persistence. And it was going to be far more difficult when the Government that had originally launched, sustained and expanded Confederation collapsed in the very act of trying to create that long line of iron that alone could nail the country together.

The collapse came on November 5, 1873.

CHAPTER 2

Mackenzie, Reciprocity and British Columbia 1874-1875

November, 1873 came to Ottawa, damp, dull and cold. Along the melancholy streets ragged fragments of the dead summer clung to naked branches that creaked in a low-spirited wind. Thick clouds and squalls of snow on November 1, "very dark and gloomy" on the 2nd, rain and wet and snow squalls all day on the 3rd: the days reflected the gloom of the government.[1]

It had been a bad autumn for the Conservative government and it was getting worse. Agonizing uncertainty haunted Sir John Macdonald. Were there more letters and telegrams yet unpublished? What *did* Blake know? Had all he had telegraphed in those fateful August days of 1872 come out? The dread of further exposures seemed to paralyse his action. After Parliament opened he put off the Address in reply from Thursday to Monday, and when the Opposition guns opened up that week he would not speak, hoping to drive Blake into speaking first. And he was drinking. During the whole session that fall, the Conservative government never had Macdonald's abilities deployed to full advantage.[2] Every day support melted away. The Government began with a probable majority of twenty; within eight days Langevin was anticipating defeat.[3]

Macdonald made his speech at last on the night of Monday, November 3, 1873, drinking steadily and copiously throughout. He arranged for Peter Mitchell, his Minister of Marine and Fisheries, and two members, each unaware of the other, to supply him with gin and water.[4] There was much home truth in the gin. "Was there any one gentleman on the opposite side," Macdonald asked, "who could say he had not only not expended money himself on elections, but had never got any from his friends? . . . these things were done and they would always be done. (Cheers and laughter.)" David Blain, M.P. for West York, interjected that not a cent went out of *his* pocket to pay for *his* election.

SIR JOHN MACDONALD – Well you know, if a man has not a pocket his wife has. (Loud cries of "shame!")

MR. BLAIN – How dare you? . . . You ought to be ashamed of yourself. (Cries of "order," cheers and much confusion.)

Macdonald, unperturbed, concluded in ringing tones that, ". . . there did not exist in Canada a man who had given more of his heart, more of his wealth, more of his intellect, and more of his powers . . . for the good of the Dominion of Canada. (Loud and prolonged cheering.)"[5] But no one who knew Sir Hugh Allan, cynically indifferent to politics, and notoriously not lavish of his money, could believe that he would contribute nearly a fifth of a million dollars to any cause without strong expectations of something in return.[6]

Macdonald's speech enormously cheered his followers. Some of the Cabinet seem to have believed that the Government might yet survive. It was a very full House of Commons; of the 206 members, only Riel, member for Provencher, was absent. In a letter of November 4, Langevin anticipated that the 205 members might split with the Speaker casting the deciding vote.[7]

That same day Donald Smith, M.P. for Selkirk, was persuaded to go to see Macdonald.[8] The two men were no longer on good terms; Macdonald was furious over Smith's reluctance to support him over the Pacific Scandal, but mutual friends thought that in this desperate contingency peace might be patched up. However, Macdonald was either too drunk or too angry to make it up with Smith, and spent the twenty minutes of their interview abusing him.

Macdonald was not in the House the night of November 4, when Smith rose to give his earnest plain-spoken speech. He began by condemning the Opposition for using stolen correspondence to establish their case against the Government. He did not believe that the money was taken by Macdonald with any corrupt intention. He would be quite willing to support the Premier – a pause punctuated by Ministerial cheers during which several Tories cheerfully headed for the bar[9] – "if he could do so conscientiously. (Vociferous applause from the opposition benches.)" Smith then proceeded to accuse the Government of grave impropriety. With his weight thrown into the scales against the Government, the last hopes of most Conservatives vanished. A little later, Hector Langevin, the Acting Leader, moved adjournment.

The next day, November 5, was cold and clear, a kind of anti-hangover morning. At three o'clock the House met, and Macdonald rose quietly, as if nothing at all were happening, and announced amid utter silence, that the Government had resigned. Pandemonium! The press vanished to the Centre block telegraph offices. The crowd came down from the galleries. James Macdonald of Pictou County was the first government member out and he headed for the bar. The more experienced members, however, rushed across the House to secure the best seats they could on the other side.[10] "Members arrived with their stationery piles, blue books, and constitutional reading, stamped through the crowd and lighted down on a heretofore Grit desk, taking possession and stamping their names."[11]

Alexander Mackenzie, the new Premier of Canada, was a Highland Scot, born and raised in Perthshire. Perthshire comes with a burr in it, and all his life Mackenzie retained that burr. His education had stopped at thirteen and his grammar (written) always revealed a slight uncertainty of spelling and occasionally of syntax. One of the family breadwinners when he was fourteen he was subsequently apprenticed to a stonemason.[12] Goldwin Smith's unkind jibe of 1877, "a stone-mason he was, and a stone-mason he is still" was unfair, but true. Mackenzie was impatient with the subtleties of human nature and frequently surprised at the malleability as well as the venality of men. "The attribution of evil motives," he wrote rather pathetically in 1872, when he was fifty, "is new to me. . . ."[13]

Like many self-made men, Mackenzie had a profound distrust of class structure. Every man is equal "and has the same opportunity, by exercising the talents with which God has blessed him, of rising in the world. . . ."[14] It may be unfair to put too much weight on this remark, but it was characteristic of Mackenzie and the older members of the party, most of whom were self-made men of modest education. Any humble man could succeed in life given hard work and good habits. Mackenzie and Brown had been humble men; they had succeeded. Mackenzie and those of his party like him had a basic intolerance for the have-nots of the world. The have-nots had come from the same background, and, presumably with the same opportunities, had failed. There was little pity in Mackenzie or Brown; they were tough-minded. And here lay the germ of the split between "Reformers" and "Liberals."

Yet, lacking a good education himself, Mackenzie never had sufficient confidence to overcome an instinctive diffidence toward those who were better educated than himself; this partly explains the ambiguity of his attitude to Edward Blake. Beyond his immediate family and close friends, the impression he left was of a narrow, graceless man not without humour but devoid of charm. He could be stubborn and wilful, when he had a mind to be, impervious to argument. But he seems to have lacked the capacity, intuitive or intellectual, to know *when* to be stubborn. He yielded to party pressure on at least two disastrous occasions. Mackenzie's political instincts were not unsound, but he would never fully give them their head, and would defer to others who were less sure judges than he was.

Few ever had reason to doubt Mackenzie's tremendous capacity for work. John A. Macdonald said Mackenzie gave more time "than the country could claim or had a right to expect."[15] In 1874, when, as Minister of Public Works, he had become dissatisfied with Sandford Fleming's accounts for the Pacific Railway survey, he decided to look into them himself. Orders were given; the accounts arrived in his office – a trunk four feet long, two feet wide, two feet deep, filled to the brim with vouchers. Mackenzie took one look at it and even he had to admit that checking that mass of material personally was out of the question.[16]

Hard work was his substitute for those arts he dimly knew he lacked. Free from an interest in or a taste for intrigue, it was easy for him to condemn it. His administration, almost at once, struck a ring of probity it never entirely lost despite desperate Conservative attempts to hang something, anything, on it.

Mackenzie became Prime Minister because he had been prominent in the Reform party of Ontario. He had served as Treasurer under Edward Blake, when Blake became Premier of Ontario in December, 1871. One of the acts they passed abolished dual representation between the House of Commons and Ontario, effective in 1873. Both men preferred Dominion politics; in the autumn of 1872 Blake turned over the Premiership to Oliver Mowat, and Mackenzie gave up the Treasurership.

In the spring of 1873 the various elements of the Opposition in the House of Commons came together to select a leader. Mackenzie was by no means an obvious choice. Blake was clearly preferred, a preference that Mackenzie himself endorsed. A. A. Dorion, the leader of the French-Canadian wing, was another possibility. Blake did not want the job; Dorion thought the leader ought to be an Ontarian; and Luther Holton of Montreal appears to have been largely influential in persuading a committee of caucus, and later caucus itself, to accept Mackenzie.[17] Mackenzie reluctantly agreed to serve, and so led the party, variously named "Reform," "Grit" and "Liberal," through the hectic events of the summer and fall of 1873. But it was still a group, not a party, an uncemented amalgam of diverse interests thrown together by the nature of the political system.

The Mackenzie government was sworn into office on Friday, November 7, 1873. Making that Government was an appalling task. "... I was sick, sick before it was done," Mackenzie admitted.[18] Edward Blake would only come in without portfolio, and then only at the last minute, and it took the whole Liberal caucus to get that. A. A. Dorion became Minister of Justice, an acquisition expected and needed. Luther Holton refused office for personal reasons. Mackenzie was hoping he would at least come in as President of the Council, but Holton had refused even that. Instead Lucius Seth Huntingdon, who had launched the Pacific Scandal, was appointed President of the Council in January, 1874; but he was notoriously imprudent, as his Argenteuil speech of October 1875 was to show.

The Maritime members of the Cabinet were not much better. Isaac Burpee, hardware merchant and M.P. for Saint John, was appointed Minister of

Customs, and kept his portfolio through to the end, in common only with four others of Mackenzie's Cabinet.* Burpee, honest as the day, was hard-working and knowledgeable in his own Department, but able to offer little Parliamentary or Cabinet help outside Customs. A useful acquisition might have been Timothy Anglin of Saint John, editor of the *Morning Freeman*, and M.P. for Gloucester. Mackenzie found that the New Brunswick Liberals would not have him at any price, and was forced instead to recommend him for Speaker when the new House met.[19] Thomas Coffin, M.P. for Shelburne, Nova Scotia, was foisted on Mackenzie by the Nova Scotian members; Mackenzie himself would have preferred others; it is, perhaps, evidence of his attempts to win the Nova Scotians that he consented to the arrangement. Coffin was useless; he turned out to have "neither talent, tongue or sense."[20] Albert Smith, Minister of Marine and Fisheries, M.P. for Westmoreland, had been Premier of New Brunswick and had had considerable administrative experience. He too was useful, but being hypercritical and of a combative disposition, he was thorny to get along with. David Laird, from Prince Edward Island, as Minister of the Interior, was an undistinguished speaker, and seems to have carried little weight. Altogether the Atlantic provinces were not very fortunate in their ministerial timber in the Mackenzie government;[21] nor was it to improve later, although Alfred Jones of Halifax was an exception.

So far the Cabinet was distinctly ramshackle; Blake, even without portfolio was useful, but he was to resign shortly after the 1874 election. One can hardly imagine Mackenzie's government without Richard Cartwright, his Minister of Finance. Cartwright had been ten years in Parliament, elected in 1863 when he was twenty-eight to the old Province of Canada Assembly. Cartwright had the advantage of being from an old Loyalist family in a part of Ontario where that counted. He was the president of the Commercial Bank of Kingston when it collapsed in 1867, as much because of bad luck as bad management, having too much money tied up in Great Western Railway, and Detroit and Milwaukee Railway bonds.[22] Up to this time Cartwright had been a Conservative. In the Commercial Bank failure, Macdonald, acting perhaps on biased Bank of Montreal advice, refused to bail him out, as much to the chagrin of A. T. Galt, the Finance Minister, as to Cartwright's; and Cartwright's disillusion with Macdonald probably began then. The bent of his politics finally changed when, in 1869, Macdonald appointed, as Finance Minister to succeed John Rose, not Cartwright, but Sir Francis Hincks. Cartwright was not the only Conservative who resented Hincks; Mackenzie Bowell of Belleville admitted to Cartwright that Hincks could hardly be swallowed with a thick coat of sugar, and "even if the operation don't choak [*sic*] some of us I shall be mistaken."[23] Bowell did

* The others were Mackenzie, A. J. Smith, Cartwright and Coffin.

not choke, but Cartwright did. He voted more and more with the Liberals. In the summer of the Pacific Scandal he met the Liberal caucus for the first time, and by November was in the inner councils of the party.[24]

Bankers do not necessarily make good finance ministers. There is a narrowness, possibly inevitable, about the fiscal and financial views of bankers, which comes doubtless from the rigidities of debit, credit, loans and balances that they are brought up in. Cartwright was one of these. He was not a financial wizard, like John Rose, or George Stephen; he seems to have been timid and unenterprising, financially speaking. But it is easy to be unfair to Cartwright. He faced continually declining revenues throughout his ministry, and could bring to bear on his problems only the conventional financial wisdom of the time. Still, what strikes one about Cartwright is his hard, narrow orthodoxy. His apocalyptic utterances on Canadian prosperity, or the lack thereof, began with his first budget speech in 1874, and it was a tone he never altogether lost. While he had things to complain of, the position of Canada in 1874 and to some extent in 1875, was not altogether unhappy, though it was to get more difficult in 1876 and 1877. No, Cartwright seemed to enjoy his gloom and doom. *Grip* made fun of him, some years later, January 28, 1893:

> Photographer (to sitter): "Now do try and look pleasant."
> Subject: "Impossible, sir. I am Sir Richard Cartwright."

Cartwright was quick and hard-hitting in debate; perhaps opposition suited him better than did the Treasury benches. He would rather strike than build. His speeches made much of the sins of his predecessors. John Cameron, of the London *Advertiser*, once remarked, "powder is not good for much when it has once been shot off. . . ."[25] Stale scandals have relevance only if they can be applied to new conditions. Cartwright doubtless thought that they always could; that there were moral lessons to be derived, endlessly, from the contemplation of the wickedness of Sir John Macdonald. In 1878 George Brown, himself a good hand at denunciation in his time, suggested to Cartwright that however delicious damning Sir John was, a more positive tone was, perhaps, to be preferred.[26]

Mackenzie's cabinet was short on talent and experience. Cartwright was wholly new to office; Mackenzie had had ten months as Treasurer of Ontario; of the Maritimes men none but A. J. Smith had been in office before; of the Quebec men, only Dorion, and he only briefly. An unfriendly London, Ontario, paper remarked with truth, "The whole thing is as green as a cucumber."[27]

Green, no doubt, they were; but not naive. Within a few days of taking over the Privy Council files they became overwhelmingly aware that Macdonald's government left office never expecting to be in power again.[28] Even a Conservative paper, which knew a lot less than either Mackenzie or Macdonald, concluded this when Leonard Tilley was appointed Lieutenant-Governor of New Brunswick. Welcome as he was in New Brunswick, Tilley was, in the view of the *New Brunswick Reporter*, needed in the Conservative opposition in Parliament. "We almost conclude that the outgoing government look upon their case as a lost cause, which they will never attempt to regain."[29]

The appointments made between October 21 and November 5, 1873, were indeed one manifestation of the state of mind of the former government. The great majority were patronage appointments, rewards to party officials and others for their work and energy, before the power to bestow such rewards was gone utterly. Tilley had been gazetted on November 5 the very last day, and it was easy for Liberals to protest that he was sitting on the Treasury Benches with the appointment in his pocket.[30] Tilley's appointment Mackenzie found impossible to cancel,[31] but most of the others made after October 21 were cancelled by the new government on November 13.[32]

Mackenzie was urged to go even further. Why not a general sweep of the civil service? Jones of Halifax continued to remonstrate about this until he joined the Cabinet in 1878, and, presumably, after.[33] Mackenzie admitted, after just five days in office, "All the offices are crammed with hostile people so that we can trust no one."[34] "Hostile" is perhaps too strong a word. A few of the civil servants were actively hostile, and did play the spy. In some cases proposed measures were known to Conservatives before the Cabinet knew about them. But what was just as bad was the passive resistance to the Government. Skilfully done it was hard to catch. A favourite device was to enforce the full rigour of the law against Reformers and interpret it liberally for Conservatives.[35] Of course it could happen the other way, and did. But the civil service was strange to the Ministry and it would take time to concert the activities of a body that was something less than politically neutral. Blake was compelled to admit in 1878 that "untold difficulties had beset the Government . . . from the strong active partisan feeling of the servants who were nominally under its power. . . ."[36]

Wholesale dismissal of civil servants, or the "spoils system" was indeed an answer to a problem like this. And it was a real enough problem to get policy administered by officials who had some interest in the success of the Government and its measures. Mackenzie was opposed on principle to the idea of a purge of civil servants; "I am no believer in a retaliatory policy at any time, nor would I for the world do an unjustice to the humblest official";[37] it was something he had been denouncing for years;[38] still, he might have been more ruthless had he not had considerable electoral support from Conservatives and he was reluctant to antagonize them unduly.

The idea of a politically neutral civil service was still unformed. George Casey of Elgin County was the great supporter of a non-partisan civil service, and sought at various times to implement it; but to be unpolitical in a political age was still regarded as quixotic. Macdonald caustically called it trying to put Canada back to "the age of Adam and Eve before the apple."[39]

The new ministers took their elections late in November and all but Cartwright were returned by acclamation. Although a general election was clearly in the offing, some in the party wanted to establish new election laws first. But in December there was a bye-election in West Toronto to replace J. W. Crawford whom Macdonald had made Lieutenant-Governor of Ontario. The Liberal, Canada First candidate, Thomas Moss, won so decisively[40] that it was decided shortly after Christmas to hold the general election at once and deal with electoral reform in the new Parliament. The writs were issued on January 7, 1874. In the meantime Mackenzie tried as far as he could to institute one reform: having the election on one day across the country. It did not quite work, but there was no manipulation of the timing to suit party preferences.

The election turned on the Pacific Scandal. A party already weakened in the 1872 election was slaughtered in 1874. As the editor of the Ottawa *Citizen* wrote to Macdonald, "We have met the enemy and we are theirs."[41] Macdonald held his seat in Kingston by thirty-eight votes, to be unseated on petition in November, 1874, and re-elected in December with a majority of seventeen. T. N. Gibbs and his brother went down in South and North Ontario, John Carling in London, Langevin in Dorchester; J. J. C. Abbott, in Argenteuil, with a majority of four, was unseated on petition and defeated. In the Maritimes the Liberals took twenty-nine of the thirty-seven seats in Nova Scotia and New Brunswick, and all of Prince Edward Island's six seats. In Quebec they took thirty-five of sixty-five, a modest increase from the twenty-seven in 1872; in Ontario they took sixty-six seats of eighty-eight, against fifty in 1872. Even in Manitoba the Conservatives lost two seats. Only British Columbia remained true to the authors of the Pacific Railway. Altogether, of the 206 seats in the House, the Liberals had 138, the Conservatives 67, with one Manitoba independent.[42]

Before one dilates too much on the Conservative disaster of 1874 it is salutary to recall the figures of the popular vote. What produced Mackenzie's thumping majority was a popular vote of 53.8 per cent. A swing of only 4.2 per cent from one side to the other was to produce an equally resounding victory for the Conservatives in 1878. In all the elections of the period the swing of popular votes was narrow. The biggest spread showed in 1874, and it dwindled steadily till 1896. The uncommitted vote or defections from one side to the other were sufficient to tip evenly balanced scales.[43]

But there was no denying the reality of that seventy-seat majority for Mackenzie.[44] The Grit side of the House could not contain them all. *Grip*, which had contributed not a little to the Reform cause,[45] offered a cheerful George Brown:

> . . . I have all
> My Rivals endways knocked! Lo! CARLING lies
> Supine among his beer-tubs; mighty GIBBS
> Is but a gibbering phantom; stout SIR JOHN
> Trembles, a fleeting shade. . . .[46]

George Brown was the great panjandrum of the Reform-Liberal party. No longer in the House, he was still very much in politics, and had built the most formidable newspaper in Ontario. The power of the Toronto *Globe* is partly explained by its being a metropolitan daily; but other metropolitan dailies could not call down the wrath of the heavens the way the *Globe* could. The *Globe* was well run and well written, if one may substitute force for finish. Its range of reports from Newfoundland, Manitoba, the North-west Territories, earned it an audience in English Canada outside of Ontario; but the fact that its founder and owner* had been the leader of the Reform party of Canada West undoubtedly contributed much to establish and confirm its authority, an authority more than once described as tyranny. There is a core of truth in the hatred of the *Nation*:

> [The *Globe*] swaggered and dictated, blustered and controlled, set up and pulled down, threatened and abused – all without apology or excuse. . . . Reputations oscillated nervously between its black letter and its small pica. It professed to be above party interrogatory, for it constituted itself a court of first and last resort. "What will the *Globe* say?" was the pitiful enquiry of many a Reform candidate before he dared to creep into notice.[47]

In December, 1873, Mackenzie appointed Brown to a vacancy in the Senate. The question of Brown's influence with Mackenzie is difficult. They were close friends; they liked and trusted each other; they shared confidences, sorrows, difficulties. Their attitudes to society and government were similar; make government economical, efficient, honest; let the individual be given equal rights and equal chances. They were certainly different in temper and manner; Brown big, hearty, hot-tempered, earnest, outspoken; Mackenzie in most of these respects more diminutive than Brown, a head shorter than Brown to start with and four years younger. Mackenzie was less volatile than Brown, and, one suspects, less vulnerable. Brown could talk himself (and others) into enthusiasms; Mackenzie had none of that in him. There is a characteristic exchange between them after the defeat in 1878, when Mackenzie was deciding whether to resign. Mackenzie asked, "Would you be good enough to write me (by return mail tonight so that I may get it to-morrow evening) what you think. The crisis is a serious one." The reply to that letter is not extant, but a few days later Brown wrote again, cheer-

* The Globe Printing Company was incorporated in 1866. The shares were held within the family until after Brown's death in May, 1880.

fully and exuberantly, "Don't mope – I wish I were beside you now to poke you up." Mackenzie replied in his dogged way. "I assure you I'm not given to 'moping'. . . ."[48] Not for nothing did Lord Dufferin describe Brown, as "the protector of my Prime Minister."[49] The bronze statues of Brown and Mackenzie stand about a hundred feet apart on Parliament Hill; and one can see Brown's stern glance fastened, still, upon Mackenzie.

Why was Brown not in the Government? Possibly he had no mind to be. More likely Mackenzie could not afford to have him in. Brown's presence would have made co-operation with the diverse elements that must make up a Canadian Cabinet difficult, perhaps impossible.[50] That so many important elements in the party were missing in the government suggests Mackenzie's difficulties.

Before the new Parliament met Senator George Brown was off to Washington as joint Commissioner with the British minister for negotiations with the Americans about a Reciprocity Treaty. It was something Brown had sought ever since the Americans had abrogated the old one, in 1866.

Reciprocity is a word that begs a lot of questions. Reciprocity of what? and to what degree? The Treaty of 1854-1866 had been a free exchange of "the growth and produce" of British North America.* This meant not only grain and lumber and fish, but farm products that had been processed like butter and cheese. As with any treaty, the details are everything, and details include the way a treaty is administered. The Treaty of Washington of 1871 had given Canada free admission to the United States of her sea fish; but the effect of this clause was certainly restricted by the ruling of the American customs administration that canned lobster was subject to duty, on the manufactured metal of the cans.[51] The complicated balances of the Treaty which came into force on July 1, 1873 had given Canada the use of the American inshore fisheries to Latitude 36 north in return for American use of the Canadian (and Newfoundland) inshore fisheries. The difference in the value of the fisheries was considerable, and a commission was to be appointed to adjudge the extra value of the Canadian fisheries for the twelve years the articles were to be in force. Since 1871 the United States had made a number of unsavoury efforts to avoid this responsibility. By 1874 nothing had been done by the Americans toward appointing such a commission. Paying hard cash for the use of the Canadian fisheries, which Americans still believed it was their right to use, was highly distasteful. Why not, thought Brown, substitute a trade agreement for the hard cash? Mackenzie agreed, and Brown was in Washington early in February, 1874, to test the ground.[52] It proved favourable; Brown was back in two weeks, reporting that formal negotiations could be started with some hope of success.

* BNA did not include British Columbia or Vancouver Island. Newfoundland was given the option of coming in.

These negotiations began in March, 1874. Meanwhile Washington had turned sour. Brown spent much time trying to catch the elusive and slippery Hamilton Fish, the American Secretary of State, and working to rally support for the trade treaty in the American Senate.

One problem was Fish's insistence that Canada keep her tariff against British goods. British machinery, for example, would pay the Canadian duty while American machinery would come in free. This kind of discrimination was revolutionary for Brown and Mackenzie; Brown insisted that whatever American goods came free into Canada so also would British. In the end he seems to have been unable to make this stick, and the Canadian Government were prepared, albeit reluctantly, to accept discrimination against Britain, for three or four years, at least.[53]

The terms and impact of the draft Treaty that emerged are interesting. The treaty was to include everything of the 1854 Treaty and added a wide range of manufactured goods: agricultural implements; wood; iron and steel manufacturers of a great variety; paper; manufactured cotton, rubber, leather; boots and shoes.[54] Mackenzie estimated the implementation of the treaty would cost Canada three million dollars a year in lost customs revenue.[55] Even more interesting was the opposition that developed against the Treaty in Canada. When Brown, in the Senate, moved for the papers to be brought down, the debate revealed protectionist sympathies among Conservative Senators, even from Nova Scotia. Senator Henry Kaulbach of Lunenburg, who knew New England well, quoted the Boston *Post* for reasons why Canada ought to be careful of Reciprocity.

> [A Reciprocity Treaty] would prevent Canadian manufacturers from expanding. We will throw our hooks for grappling objects, conquer and compel them to make their abode with us. We will break up their Union and prevent their trade from growing in the north and west. We will have all the advantage.[56]

For the same reasons Ontario manufacturers were uneasy. They received cold comfort from Mackenzie. "It is quite evident," he wrote to one, ". . . that you want protection simply for your own interests. . . ."[57] The Manufacturers Association of Nova Scotia, meeting in Halifax in March, 1874, asked the Dominion government to inaugurate not reciprocity, but protection.[58] Manufacturers complained that a Reciprocity Treaty would close Canadian factories. Canadian nationalists, like William Caniff, complained it would crush Canadian nationality, and Caniff added that if the old Reciprocity Treaty had existed in 1867, Confederation would not have been possible.[59]

Probably the Mackenzie administration would have carried the treaty in the session of 1875, but they did not have to try. After interminable and apparently deliberate delays by Hamilton Fish, the draft Treaty went to the American Senate on June 18, 1874. It disappeared into the maw of the

Foreign Relations Committee; Congress adjourned on June 22, and the Treaty was never seen again.[60]

The first session of the new Canadian Parliament met on March 26, 1874, to deal notably with electoral reform. Drafted carefully by A.A. Dorion, the new election law[61] stated that general elections were to be held on the same day in all constituencies except Manitoba, British Columbia, and the more distant parts of Ontario and Quebec. The franchise was still based on those in each province qualified to vote in provincial elections. Furnishing drink of any kind by candidates for election purposes was prohibited; so were favours, ribbons and flags; bars were to be closed on polling day. Detailed statements of election expenses were to be submitted two months after election day. Any proved violation of these provisions constituted corrupt practice and voided the election.

The most far-reaching change in the Act was, however, the introduction of the ballot. Before 1867 the secret ballot existed only in New Brunswick; in the other provinces open voting prevailed, which often meant open bribery, sometimes open intimidation. Federal Liberals had been urging since 1869 that elections be conducted by ballot. Nova Scotia had introduced the ballot in 1870. Oliver Mowat in Ontario brought it in in 1873. In Quebec it was brought in by the de Boucherville Government in 1875.

There were misgivings on both sides. The Conservatives had talked about it in 1873, but it was swamped in the Pacific Scandal. Mackenzie, who might have been expected to be an enthusiast, was not. He introduced the ballot only because, characteristically, he thought the public wanted it.[62] Basically a conservative, he remarked, "I dread anything like a revolutionary measure unless there is the greatest necessity for it."[63] Some Conservative papers supported the ballot believing it would help them, as its introduction in 1872 had allegedly done in England.[64] But both parties were uneasy.[65] What would happen when the voter, released from the moral (or immoral) pressures of a vote in public, got into a booth, all by himself, to declare, clandestinely, his political belief? The first federal election with the ballot was another bye-election in West Toronto in November 1875 which the Liberals lost decisively. George Brown was quite definite about the cause.

> The ballot has stripped us of the moral controul [*sic*] we had over electors & has I fear inaugurated a lower form of political warfare than before. We fought roughly in past times, but it was principle that in the main guided the electors. [!] But now to a little principle there goes a great deal of concealed sectional sectarian and personal motive of the pettiest kind.[66]

W. B. Vail, defeated in a Digby bye-election of January, 1878, told Mackenzie, "The fact is no election can be considered safe under the Ballot; while the system was new to our people they voted as they agreed to, now they are fully up to the dodge of talking one way and voting another. . . ."[67] One thing was likely: much of the old blaze of colour and triumph and mayhem surrounding voting would go. No more would early rushes to the poll inspire one party and make gloom for the other. So at least thought the *Nation*, January 22, 1875.

The most controversial aspect of the session of 1874, and for at least two sessions afterward, was the Pacific Railway. That the immediate construction of a railway to the Pacific coast was vital may seem obvious now; it was by no means so then. When the Union Pacific-Central Pacific was finished in 1869, California had a population of two million in a country of thirty-nine million. By 1874 that railway was a financial disaster. British Columbia's white population was twenty-eight thousand in 1871, in a country of three and a half million. The size of the enterprise, the enormity of the expense, seemed out of all proportion to the population it was designed to serve.[68] When the commitment to British Columbia was made, government revenues were growing, and the economy as a whole was buoyant, even expansive. The terms Canada offered to British Columbia in 1870 staggered the British Columbians themselves.[69] "The Government of the Dominion undertake to secure the commencement simultaneously, within two years from the date of Union [*i.e.* by July 20, 1873] of the construction of a railway from the Pacific towards the Rocky Mountains, and from . . . east of the Rocky Mountains towards the Pacific . . . and further, to secure the completion of such railway within ten years from the date of the Union [*i.e.* by July 20, 1881]."[70] In 1871 the resolutions passed the Conservative caucus only with J. W. Trutch's assurance that British Columbia would not expect literal fulfillment of the terms, and further assurance from Cartier that the construction was to be managed with no increase in taxation. These soothing words were repeated in the House with the British Columbia delegates in the gallery. In 1876 Senator R. W. W. Carrall, one of the delegates, emphasized, "that that *ten years was* NOT *put into the terms of Union as an absolute limit for the construction* of the railway, but it was put there as a *bona fides* that the Government would commence the road and carry it on to completion as quickly as could be without injury to the interests of the country. He appealed to the reporter to take down his words correctly. . . ."[71]

From the very beginning, Canada's apparently generous terms to British Columbia were opposed strongly by the Liberals, principally the Ontario members. Cartier was a strong supporter of the railway, and a glance at the map will suggest why. The Pacific Railway would arrive in the east via the Ottawa Valley; and it was probable that Montreal would derive the benefit rather than Toronto. The Pacific Railway project was always to have in it the seeds of a Quebec-Ontario quarrel, and it is a matter of no surprise that Ontario members of Parliament, especially those southwest of Toronto, on both sides of the House, were uneasy or hostile to it, dragging their feet even at the best of times.

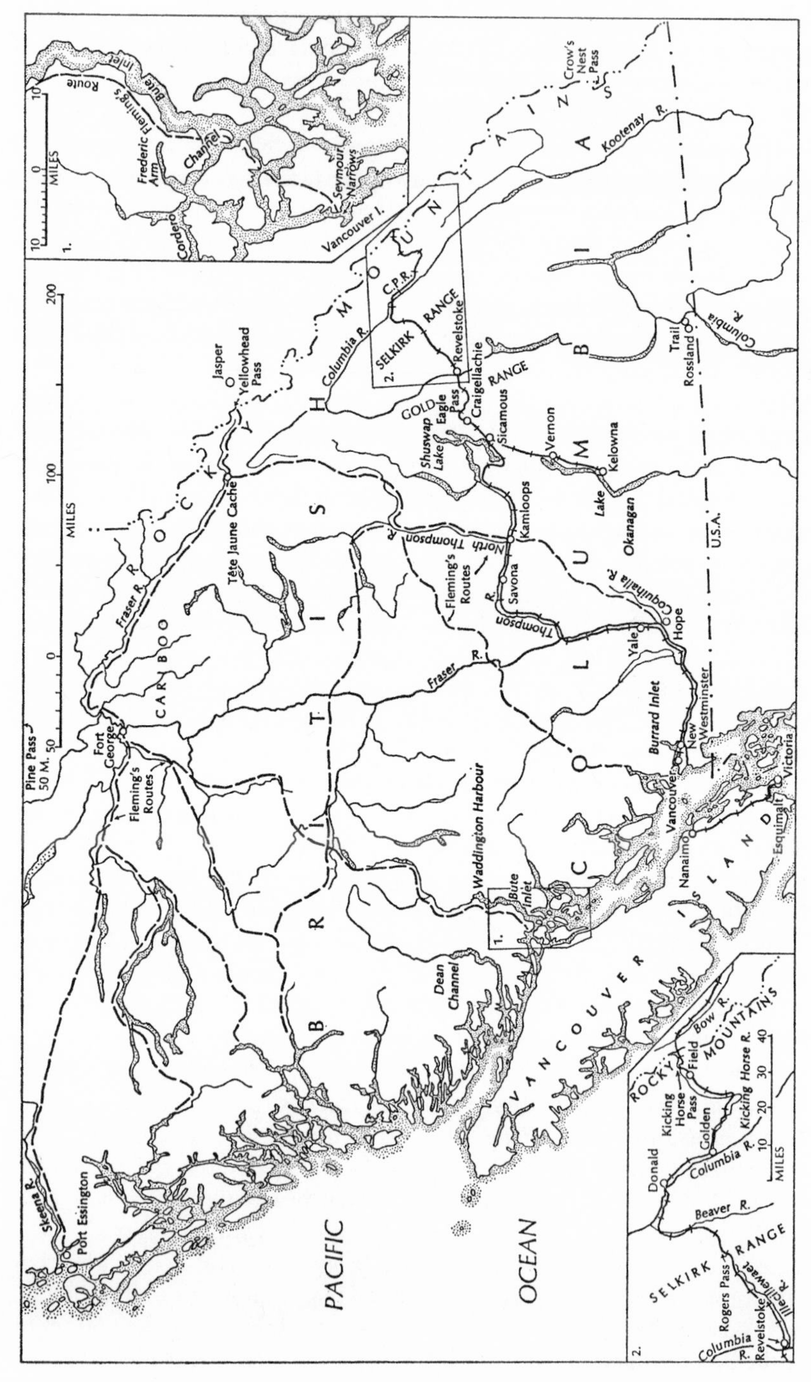

Canadian Pacific Railway Routes, 1872-1886

On the other hand, the British Columbians soon got over their surprise at having their own terms for union improved by the Canadians, and came to accept immediate construction of the railway as an absolute necessity. By 1874, the railway was everything. By then it was possible for British Columbians to say (and to believe) that British Columbia joined Canada for the Pacific Railway, and the Pacific Railway alone. H. P. P. Crease, judge of the British Columbia Supreme Court, wrote his friend Langevin that he wanted "a real live confederation with Canada instead of a paper one. . . . Confederation means with us . . . *the through line of Rail* across the continent to make us as nothing else will, an integral part of Canada. . . ."[72] That British Columbia was excessively sensitive on the subject of the Pacific Railway is not surprising; equally, it is not surprising that Ontario which paid the most taxes should blanch at a three-thousand-mile railway into nowhere, at the thought of Ontario money poured into those enormous and interminable surveys, into those rocky and profitless gorges on the Fraser 73, or the fabulous line along the cliffs of Bute Inlet to reach Frederick Arm.[73] There, seven bridges were needed over the islands of Seymour Narrows; no piers were possible in those depths of water – forty fathoms in most parts of Cardero Channel – and there were ferocious tide rips where Seymour Narrows shoaled to a usable depth. The words of Fleming's 1874 Report sounded horrifying: Fraser Canyon, "formidable difficulties . . . the work would be enormously heavy and the cost proportionate"; at Bute Inlet, especially from Waddington Harbour, at the head, to Vancouver Island, works "of a most formidable character."[74]

Could private enterprise be induced to take up the road? Most Liberals preferred this. There is no reason to suppose Mackenzie had changed his mind from 1867, when he remarked the proper way to deal with government railway enterprises was to get rid of them altogether.[75] Government construction, or operation, was especially unwelcome after the experience with the Intercolonial.[76] If the Intercolonial, through territory that had been settled for fifty or sixty years, was losing substantial sums of money (Cartwright reckoned over a million a year), how much more would a railway six times as long, through virtually uninhabited territory, lose? That was Cartwright's agonized arithmetic in his 1874 Budget speech. Luther Holton of Montreal put it succinctly:

> The Pacific Railway is our Elephant. It would be easy to devise a scheme for constructing it or sections of it if we had any faith in its merits as a commercial enterprise either now or within a moderately distant future; but in the absence of such a faith any scheme which does not contemplate the provision of entire cost by our government in money or lands must be a mere speculation on the credulity of foreign capitalists.[77]

Macdonald had attempted to arrange with a private company to build the line at a price of thirty million dollars and fifty million acres of land. The company had failed to secure capital in England and had folded. What Macdonald had done was to establish, by Order in Council, Esquimalt, on Vancouver Island, as the western terminus. He had also issued peremptory instructions, on July 13, 1873, for a Dominion officer in Victoria to "begin the railway by survey planting stakes and otherwise," that is, to fulfil the terms of Union through a form of beginning construction before July 20, 1873.[78] The Canada Pacific Railway having failed to come off, the Macdonald government had largely given up its plan for an immediate transcontinental line, and had gone back to its original plan of working through American lines as far as Manitoba, leaving the Northern Ontario section to be completed later. The line from Winnipeg to Pembina on the American border had been contracted for, the aim being to have it in operation by December 1, 1874. But the arrangement was cancelled just before Macdonald's defeat.[79]

Sandford Fleming, who had been appointed Engineer-in-chief of the Intercolonial Railway in 1867, was asked, in 1871, to become Engineer-in-chief of the Pacific Railway as well. Prior to the failure of the Canada Pacific Railway Company there had been no need for him to prosecute the work actively, but that position had been substantially altered with the Pacific Scandal and the accession of Mackenzie. From the first Mackenzie reluctantly conceded that the railway would probably have to be built by public resources. He proposed to develop settlement in the prairies as rapidly as possible, trusting to this means to justify a railway there, and thereby encourage development progressively further west.[80] This also emphasized a policy of communications with the prairies, and of surveys northwest of Lake Superior. The surveys were important in the east for real railroading reasons; the surveys in British Columbia were important mainly for political reasons.

Fleming was a Scot who had come to Canada in 1845 at the age of eighteen. He was an engineer with an itch for exploration. He liked his surveys; he worked hard, and with care and dedication. One of his surveyors working out from Prince George remarked afterward, "I cannot help reflecting upon the thorough, accurate and complete manner in which all the surveys were made.... No matter how remote and inaccessible the district to which we were sent, the procedure was just the same. The regulations laid down by Sir Sandford Fleming were always religiously observed."[81] Not the driver Van Horne was to be, he believed that a railway the size of the Pacific Railway was not going to be built in a day or, for that matter, ten years of days. The Macdonald government had asked him in 1871 whether the line from Lake Nipissing to the Pacific could be finished in ten years: he replied that it could not be done, or, if it could, ought not to be done. In his view it would take nearer twenty years.[82]

By early 1874 the Yellowhead Pass had been established as the probable route for the Pacific Railway.[83] From Tête Jaune Cache, forty miles further west, a number of different routes diverged; the southern route being the present C.N.R. route down the North Thompson, the Fraser to Burrard Inlet, with an alternative via the Coquihalla valley; the central route to Bute Inlet, to Dean Channel; the northern route to Port Essington (opposite present-day Prince Rupert). These were all highly tentative. Fleming seems to have sheered away from the Burrard Inlet Route; he had made that journey himself in 1872, and Marcus Smith's reports were against using the Fraser Canyon.[84] Fleming, like Smith, leaned instead to Bute Inlet, even though there, in the last fifteen miles to Waddington Harbour, the grades ran 110 feet to the mile.

Mackenzie was too honest and forthright to allow the ambiguity between the terms and his prospects for their performance to stand. Even had he been disposed to accept the terms as a statement of hope rather than of realities,[85] his hand was forced by members of the Cabinet like Cartwright, and others outside the Cabinet like Holton and Blake, who were still more refractory about British Columbia than he was. A more experienced Mackenzie might have prefaced, as Lord Dufferin recommended he should, all his criticism of Macdonald's commitments to the Pacific Railway by a profession of the binding character of the Canada-British Columbia arrangements. By the time Mackenzie realized this, the damage had been done.[86]

The delicate task of persuading British Columbia to accept a relaxation of the terms was first offered to A. T. Galt.[87] When Galt refused, Mackenzie chose J. D. Edgar, a young Toronto lawyer, the Liberal whip in 1873, and a defeated candidate in the 1874 election. He was to explain to British Columbia that it was impossible to build the railway within the time allotted, that the surveys would be energetically prosecuted, that mainland construction would begin immediately upon completion of surveys, and that for the time being a wagon road and telegraph line would be built. If that failed to satisfy British Columbia, the Canadian government was ready to consider building a railway from Esquimalt to Nanaimo, which would be part of the main line if the Bute Inlet or Dean Channel route were chosen.[88]

The approach was wrong. British Columbians did not want to go back to the wagon road and telegraph line; they had proposed that in 1870 and the ante had been raised by the Canadians themselves. As for the Esquimalt and Nanaimo line it would have been better not to have even suggested it, for that implied compensation. Compensation for what? There could only be one answer: delay. What British Columbians really wanted was simply that the work on the railway go forward as rapidly as possible.[89]

Edgar arrived in Victoria, March 8, 1874. He encountered a tangle of British Columbia politics with no clear end to begin with except that unravelled strand, the Premier, George Walkem. Edgar's interview with the Premier was a touchy one. Walkem would go to elections on any alteration of terms. Adjustment was difficult. Walkem tried to prevent too close relations between Edgar and the Lieutenant-Governor by saying Trutch disliked Mackenzie and that he (Walkem) was the best man to deal with.[90] That Trutch disliked Mackenzie and his policies was only too true.[91]

Edgar was young and inexperienced; before he knew it he was fairly entangled in Victoria politics.[92] Many of the local politicians were holders of property in Victoria or Nanaimo,[93] with a standing interest in increment, earned and unearned. Walkem, though representing Cariboo on the mainland, had been long enough in Victoria to acquire Victoria interests himself.

The Esquimalt and Nanaimo proposal was thus a complication of all the other issues. On the Island it was regarded as an acceptable compensation for disagreeable delays, acceptable, that is, if it was to be part of the main line. The mainland hated the idea of compensation – to the Island! – disliked the proposed Bute Inlet route, and even more disliked proposed delays. Walkem was no fool. He played for time crudely but effectively, finally questioned Edgar's powers as Dominion plenipotentiary, infuriated both Edgar and Mackenzie, and the whole negotiation was abruptly broken off.[94]

It was a bad start. Walkem appealed to the Imperial government in person, stopping in Ottawa on his way to London, and proving to Mackenzie that Edgar's difficulties were not entirely owing to inexperience.[95] In London the Colonial Secretary, Lord Carnarvon, suggested arbitration of the British Columbia difficulty, and after some hesitation from Walkem, and much more from Mackenzie,[96] the offer was accepted. Carnarvon's terms struck a balance. The time limit for the completion of the Pacific Railway was extended to the end of 1890. In return for this British Columbia was to receive the immediate building of the Esquimalt and Nanaimo railway, the expenditure of two million dollars a year on the railway when the surveys were finished, and active prosecution of the surveys in the meantime.

The surveys were being actively prosecuted. Sandford Fleming told Lord Dufferin in the summer of 1874 that it would be impossible to cram another theodolite on most of the proposed British Columbia routes. Some five hundred surveyors were at work, and Fleming was now under instructions from Mackenzie to spare neither men nor money.[97] Enough was already known by the end of the summer of 1874, however, to suggest grave difficulties with the Bute Inlet route. This in turn threw a shadow over the Esquimalt and Nanaimo railway, an essential part of a Bute Inlet route, but of no use whatever on a Fraser valley route. Yet Mackenzie was committed to the Esquimalt and Nanaimo, albeit reluctantly, as part of the Carnarvon terms.

The dilemma was resolved in a curious way. Mackenzie proposed the Esquimalt and Nanaimo railway bill to Parliament late in the session of 1875; it came up for second reading on March 28, just ten days before the end of the session. The bill asked for approval to proceed with survey and railway contracts without further parliamentary reference. Still the Esquimalt and Nanaimo Bill passed, 91-64. It came to the Senate for second reading on April 6, two days before prorogation. The Government leader in the Senate, R. W. Scott, made an extraordinarily inept speech, less than a column of print in length, delivered so limply as almost to suggest the measure was not seriously being proposed. Conservative Senators moved the six months' hoist, which the Bill duly got.[98] Still more curious, two of those voting for the hoist were staunch Liberal Senators, who had regularly supported the Government through the session. One was Edward Goff Penny, editor of the Montreal *Herald*, who had actually seconded the Government motion for second reading! Penny did not vote against the Bill by accident, either; he said in 1876 that he would vote against the Bill again if it were re-introduced.[99]

The defeat of this major bill clearly took the Government aback. The Government did not intend to accept defeat by the Senate but planned to re-introduce the railway bill in the next session. Steel rails for the railway were shipped to Victoria after the prorogation of Parliament. But the Esquimalt and Nanaimo railway bill was never re-introduced. The line was finally built as part of the general settlement of British Columbia-Canada affairs in 1884, and completed in 1886 with Macdonald himself driving the last spike.[100] As for the Carnarvon terms as a whole, they were never passed by Parliament, and remained a dead letter.

The reason was simple. The quietus of the project was the price exacted from the Government for the return to the Cabinet of the man behind whose steel-rimmed spectacles glowed the whole moral force of the best of Protestant Ontario, Edward Blake. Blake joined the Government as Minister of Justice on May 19, 1875.

CHAPTER 3

Blake, Religion and Laurier 1873-1877

Edward Blake was born in 1833, in a log cabin, at Katesville, on the fat lands west of London, Ontario where his father had taken a parish church. In 1834 the family moved to Toronto where his father took up law and became head of the Chancery Court. Young Blake received the best education old Canada West could give – Upper Canada College, and the University of Toronto, where he took the silver medal in Classics, and in 1856, his M.A. (Hence the occasional, usually pejorative, references to "Master Blake.")

Everything about Blake was remarkable; his powers of application, his range of knowledge, the subtle and powerful logic of his mind; and an ego wound up like a sensitive spring. He never really learned the easy give-and-take that would have dismantled his vast egocentricity. Shut up in that great brain he was unable in his groping, clumsy shyness to reach the people around him. He was outrageously sensitive to slights, real and imagined. He would also sleep or read a newspaper through the speeches of his political friends[1] and be hurt when anyone commented on the frequent prolixity of his own.

His speeches appealed little to emotions; they were addressed to the minds of men. The House of Commons is an odd place. It will tolerate even intellectuals, but it feeds on humour and the cut and thrust across personalities and power. Blake commanded the Commons because he knew so much; he bored the Commons because he said so much. "The very abundance of his knowledge was his weakness," wrote G. W. Ross, "Evidence that would have been sufficient to his audience was not conclusive to his mind, and so he piled Ossa upon Pelion and threw Parnassus above them both. . . . I have often watched from a public platform the dazed look of many of his hearers."[2] When forced by time or circumstance to be brief and blunt, he could be very effective, but his bent was otherwise. He liked to lay bare a subject: the essence of any matter was the details of it. Blake had little use for gross simplifications. Generalizations distorted; they were illusions. Blake would tell the truth. And out the truth came, in never-ending prose that drugged its listeners, so that after five hours they ached for a few sentences of simplicity or laughter. Blake had little patience with easygoing ways. His reactions to life were cerebral rather than physical.

Over six feet tall, broad-shouldered, sturdily built, towering over Mackenzie, nearly as tall as George Brown, Blake was to all appearances invincible. But he lacked the brute strength to carry on when things got difficult. He was always questioning; he lacked nerve to commit himself utterly to a cause. He was taunted by John Beverley Robinson in the West Toronto election of 1875 of being afraid of the "great muskrat," George Brown:[3] an unjust remark, but one not without relevance. As Goldwin Smith put it, referring to the *Liberal*, having crossed the Rubicon he ought to have had the nerve to have gone on to Rome.[4] Short-sighted, his health strung on his nerve ends, Blake was a lonely, neurotic man.

It also made him seem glacial. P. D. Ross, part owner of the Ottawa *Journal* in the later 1880's, was walking near the Russell Hotel with Arnott Magurn, Ottawa correspondent of the Toronto *Globe*, when Blake, then leader of the Opposition appeared – he had not been in Ottawa for a while – his hands clasped behind his back (as usual), looking absent-minded (as usual). Magurn stopped and held out his hand. "How do you do, Mr. Blake! Welcome back!" Blake looked blankly at him, and without shaking hands, said stiffly, "How do you do, sir," and walked on.[5] But the glacier in Blake could melt unexpectedly. He was sitting in the Commons reading room in solemn abstraction over the newspapers when a colleague from the front benches came in from dinner, with a bottle or two of wine visible in his manner. He lurched against Blake, brought his hand down with enthusiasm on Blake's bowed shoulders and gurgled, "Come – come 'long you – you old hulk, and have some fun." The old hulk put his arm affectionately round the back of his unsteady friend and fairly shook with laughter.[6]

In 1874 Blake was well on his way to making a fortune at the Bar, as senior partner in Blake, Kerr and Boyd, Toronto. Strong pressure from relatives and a fear of being short of money kept him from withdrawing from the firm. But the reason he left the Cabinet that year seems to have been his feeling about Brown's role. His resignation from the Government broke his party allegiance; he was now free to join the yeasty groups of the younger generation, hitherto either critics on the sidelines or simply youngsters growing up.

An attack on the existing party system necessarily affected the new ruling party with its top-heavy majority. The forces that combined for the attack were Blake, Goldwin Smith, the Canada First movement,[7] and sympathisers from both old parties. It was mounted in the press in three publications; one monthly, the *Canadian Monthly and National Review*, 1872-8;[8] one weekly, the *Nation*, 1874-6; and one daily, the *Liberal*, January-June, 1875. The popular success of the publications is indicated by their duration, but their influence was considerable; the *Nation* enjoyed an influence in English Canada as far as Halifax, the *Canadian Monthly* reached even further and lasted longer. They were different in tone and purpose, the *Canadian Monthly* a literary journal, and the *Nation* political in the style of the English weeklies. Both were immensely refreshing. The Hamilton *Evening Times* wrote, "We consider it a public boon to have, at least one man in the country who is not afraid to give praise where praise is due and censure where censure is due, even though his political theories may be thought Utopian and antagonistic to our own."[9] That man was Goldwin Smith.

Goldwin Smith was a former Regius Professor of History at Oxford, who had moved to North America, first to Cornell University and then to Toronto in 1871. He was well-to-do himself, and in September, 1875 married William Henry Boulton's widow and lived serenely in the comfortable Boulton House, with its ten acres of grounds, on Dundas Street.

Serenity did not characterize his public life, however. From his secure private base, he could exercise freely his remarkable gift for critical journalism. Smith was as much a controversialist as George Brown, and a far more efficient one. His weapon was lighter but sharper; he had a turn of phrase and a range of information that was the envy of every political writer in Canada. Who but Goldwin Smith could have found in Dryden a comment on the British North America Act?

> Got while their souls did huddled notions try
> And born a shapeless mass like anarchy.[10]

Goldwin Smith wrote for the *Canadian Monthly*, almost from its first issue, as "Bystander." In the spring of 1874, when he returned to Canada from England, Edward Blake and Canada First friends (doubtless with Smith's knowledge and some financial support), had already started the *Nation* and Smith also began writing for it.

Much has been made of Canada First. It saw the light of day in Henry Morgan's corner room in Matthews Hotel, Ottawa, in the spring of 1868. It was a direct outgrowth of the enthusiasm of D'Arcy McGee, whose assassination in 1868 gave the group its first martyr. Thomas Scott, its second martyr, was more questionable. The group fused together in the heat and fury of the "Canadian" cause in Manitoba. The shooting of Thomas Scott, March 4, 1870, by order of Louis Riel and Métis court-martial, did more for Canada First than McGee and Confederation had done. By 1874 it had grown up somewhat. Nevertheless, without Goldwin Smith's talent and money, without Edward Blake's talent and political influence, Canada First was merely a congeries of young nationalists with little to hold them together but a rather callow, English-Protestant nationalism. Without

Smith and Blake they did not last long. Still, the movement generated a great deal of enthusiasm among the generation that had been growing up in the seven years since Confederation. Old issues, wrote one young enthusiast from New Brunswick, are dead. "The young men of Canada on every side are beginning to feel that neither New Brunswick nor Ontario, nor any of the other Provinces, contains the limit of their country; and, in the glow of a new enthusiasm, are proud to call Canada their home and to acknowledge themselves Canadians."[11]

Canada First sought to regenerate, if possible to supersede, the old parties. The first step was to make newspapers less abusive and more constructive. Independent journalism was a more serious question for Liberals than Conservatives. This is one reason why the *Globe* went at the Canada Firsters. It wanted to smash the *Nation*, drive off Goldwin Smith. It did not want, however, to quarrel publicly with Blake. Blake, for his part, refused to lay the cornerstone of the new National Club because it would compromise the Liberal party.[12] He did, however, want to make clear where he stood.

The Aurora speech was given on a beautiful autumn afternoon, October 3, before a large crowd. Blake set out his ideas on imperial relations, the Senate, and summed up the credo of Canada First:

> The future of Canada, I believe, depends very largely upon the cultivation of a national spirit. We are engaged in a very difficult task – the task of welding together seven Provinces which have been accustomed to regard themselves as isolated from each other, which are full of petty jealousies, their Provincial questions, their local interests. How are we to accomplish our work? How are we to effect a real union between these Provinces? Can we do it by giving a sop now to one, now to another, after the manner of the late Government? . . . Do you hope to create or preserve harmony and good feeling upon such a false and sordid and mercenary basis as that? Not so! That day I hope is done for ever, and we must find some other and truer ground for Union than that by which the late Government sought to buy love and purchase peace.[13]

This speech was not the passionate and embittered utterance of a man estranged from his party. Some of his expressions may have had the ebullience of a Member of Parliament out of the ministry, but he was not out of the party or even estranged from its leaders. It was the talisman of a man trying to replace Alexander Mackenzie as Prime Minister, to replace old Grittism with new Liberalism. And it did bring him somewhat closer to the Prime Ministership as the events of March and April, 1875, were to show.

Moreover, the Aurora speech was not a temporary efflorescence of Blake's independence, dropped when he entered the Government again. The philosophy of his speech, and its tone, came through again and again in the years that followed. His speech in the House six years later, given just ten days before he took over as leader of the Opposition shows the same spirit:

> Hon. gentlemen opposite affirmed, with great warmth, in 1876 and for years afterwards, that it [Confederation] was but a union on paper, and that the reality and permanence of the connection were yet to be established and secured by a careful policy, and by a practical experience on the part of the people of its benefits. . . . I want to know what has been done to cement it, to make it real and permanent, to make it a union of hearts and interests, to give it vitality and strength?[14]

The Aurora speech was a landmark in Blake's career and in his thought.

On the whole the press reaction was temperate and judicious.[15] A few extreme Conservative papers, such as the Toronto *Mail* and the London *Free Press* happily saw it as a Liberal party split; but the more moderate Conservative papers, like the Montreal *Gazette*, treated the speech with conspicuous respect and consideration.

> We prefer to regard the [Aurora] speech as another added to the many evidences which surround us of the advancement and prosperity of this country. . . . All the old practical questions have been settled. There is not at this moment in Canada a single political grievance, felt to be so by the people at large, and demanding reform at the hands of Parliament. . . . The questions of party discussion are mere matters of administration. . . . There is leisure for speculative politicians to air their doctrines, and there is fortunately culture enough to appreciate and weigh their value. That to our mind, is the significance of Mr. Blake's speech; and . . . by drawing men's minds away for a moment from the mere personal controversies which too much characterize our politics, tend[s] to elevate the tone of political thought and debate, and thus help us on in that career of national advancement upon which we have so worthily entered.[16]

The *Globe* praised the speech generously, but took issue with parts of it, making the point – a good one – that "nations, institutions and sentiments *grow*, and grow slowly. They cannot be called into existence. . . ."[17] The *Globe* did not want to split the party into Mackenzie and Blake camps but to assert Mackenzie's direction, which it did by hitting hard at Goldwin Smith and his ideas (many of which were then also Blake's). The truth was, said the *Globe*, "Canada is *not* a nation," and did not yet have enough strength to stand alone. If she did, she would at once be captured by the United States. To propose Canadian independence of Great Britain was equivalent to treason.[18] And with that effortless shift from principles to personalities, so characteristic of the *Globe* (and of much Canadian journalism), it added that the Canada Firsters, with Goldwin Smith in the lead, "were simply mischief makers, whose insignificance and powerlessness were their sole protectors, as these made the community feel they were not important enough for either the traitor's trial or the traitor's doom."[19] When Goldwin Smith protested against such personal language in a political discussion, the *Globe* labelled him a coward.[20]

Brown did not say so in the *Globe*, but privately he felt that Blake had ruined his chances by his outspokenness at Aurora, and that in consequence, Mackenzie's position was much strengthened and with it "the safe policy of the old line Reformers."[21] That was precisely the kind of thinking that Blake and Goldwin Smith felt was utterly outdated. "There is no reactionary," Goldwin Smith once remarked, "like the exhausted Reformer."[22] Increasingly Brown and Mackenzie left an impression of Reformers with nothing left to Reform – an impression strengthened by the Speech from the Throne in 1878, which began, "... I am glad to be able to say that nothing beyond the ordinary business of the country requires your attendance."[23]

Blake followed up his Aurora speech by launching, early in 1875, a new daily newspaper in Toronto, the *Liberal*.[24] But it was an expensive business, more expensive than either Blake or his editor, John Cameron, expected. The paper was losing about seven hundred dollars a week by May, 1875.[25] The arithmetic was inexorable. Goldwin Smith stepped in with as much money as he could afford, but a month later Blake had joined the Government and the *Liberal* had folded.[26] Smith said in the *Bystander* with bitterness at Blake's having given up so soon, "He saw a giant armed in the path [the *Globe*] and turned aside."[27] Still more, Goldwin Smith lost hope for Canada. He wrote to Blake in May, 1876, "My dream, at all events, has fled through the ivory gates."[28] In the *Fortnightly Review* of London, in the spring of 1877 he wrote, "Canadian nationality being a lost cause, the ultimate union of Canada with the United States appears now to be morally certain ..."[29] From that position Smith never really shifted.

Nor did Canada First survive as a movement.[30] There had been no real agreement about a positive program. Riel had supplied the lack for a time, and then in 1874 Blake and Goldwin Smith had come along. Charles Mair, in particular, had resented Brown's opposition to Canada First, and being labelled, with Goldwin Smith, as a traitor; but Blake's and Goldwin Smith's embrace had been strangling. Canada First's pure stream of nationalism (as Mair thought of it) was choked with constitutional projects, the imperial connection, proportional representation, reform of the Senate. Moreover Blake's dislike of British Columbia tended to embrace the Northwest as well, while Mair, though originally from Ontario, more and more identified himself with the Northwest, and resented the narrow provincialism of Mackenzie and the whole Liberal government at Ottawa. "... the very name of Ontario stinks throughout the Northwest, and its [Ontario's] scattered natives are fain to hide their shame. ..."[31]

Blake's re-entry into the Government was a complicated business. That the party wanted him there was no doubt, but at what price? Blake preferred to be Prime Minister; if not, he would serve under Luther Holton as Prime Minister. A tortuous correspondence developed between A. G. Jones of Halifax (who was the most anxious to get Blake in as Prime Minister), Mackenzie, Holton and Blake, a correspondence which went on from early March to May, 1875. By the end of March the issue had become serious. Most of the Quebec Cabinet members and members of the House wanted Blake as Prime Minister. Brown was in the middle trying to tidy things up, and still keep Mackenzie in office.

The major stumbling block was the Carnarvon terms. Blake found these impossible to accept, and Mackenzie found them impossible to give up. The Senate defeat of the Esquimalt and Nanaimo Bill early in April did not remove this obstacle, but it suggested ways out: perhaps, a money compensation to British Columbia for the loss of the Esquimalt and Nanaimo railway. As far as Blake was concerned delays with British Columbia would continue into the future as well.[32]

So the split between Grits and Liberals was papered over. Blake was not Prime Minister either. But he could scarcely "sink into a common Grit."[33] At his re-election on taking office, he said, "I have no sympathy with a so-called Reform Party which says there is nothing to reform, with a so-called Liberal Party which says there is nothing to liberalize, with a so-called Party of Progress which is determined to stand absolutely still."[34] When the *Nation* gave up in September, 1876 (Goldwin Smith being simply fed up with writing it), its own valedictory said, "We believe that the seed of national sentiment . . . has taken root if not in minds of old politicians, cast in the narrow mould of existing parties, in those of a generation which is destined soon to rise to power."[35] Blake was one of the new generation.

One of Blake's particular themes in the Aurora speech had been the freeing of Canada from what he regarded as imperial thraldom. Blake had already tangled with transatlantic opinions several times. He supported the Oaths Bill of 1873, only to find it disallowed in Britain; he opposed Lord Dufferin's prorogation of 1873 only to find it was held quite constitutional in Britain.[36] About constitutional law he had things to learn, and he was piqued enough to set about learning them.

As Minister of Justice Blake immediately became interested in the new Supreme Court of Canada, established in the session of 1875 after a number of false starts. Blake asked Macdonald as early as 1868 if the Conservative government were going to establish a Supreme Court. Macdonald said, "Yes, certainly," and that he hoped a bill would be introduced in the session of 1869.[37] A bill was introduced in 1869, but it was deferred; in 1870 Blake was again asking questions. The Conservatives never did bring it in because the French-Canadian wing of the party, led by Cartier, Langevin and Chapais opposed it, saying that only two of the proposed seven judges would be French Canadian, and the others would be unfamiliar with French-Canadian civil law. Chapais at least was not opposed *à outrance*, and rather than upset the Government he would have accepted the Supreme Court;[38] but Macdonald never pressed the issue this far.

Mackenzie proposed such a bill in 1874, and although there is no indication that A. A. Dorion was opposed, the bill did not appear that session. Dorion was appointed Chief Justice of the Quebec Court of Queen's Bench, June 1, 1874. While it benefitted the Bench of Quebec, which had been sinking lower from year to year, it was an irreparable loss to the Liberal party's Quebec wing.[39] There was no real leader to succeed him – Télésphore Fournier certainly not; but it was Fournier, who as Minister of Justice introduced the Supreme Court Bill in February, 1875. The bill was based upon extensive work done by Macdonald, as Fournier himself admitted.[40] It was opposed by French-Canadian Conservatives, but the French-Canadian Liberals, led by Fournier and Rodolphe Laflamme, felt that a Supreme Court with two judges of six familiar with French law was better than the Privy Council none of whose judges knew very much French-Canadian law.[41] The discussion of the Privy Council's role led to an amendment by Irving and Laflamme, that appeals to the Privy Council, saving the Queen's prerogative to accept them, be abolished.[42] This was accepted at once by Fournier in the name of the Government, in circumstances that looked rather like collusion. Here Sir John Macdonald, who had supported the measure, objected. It would lead straight to disallowance, he said; even if not disallowed, the Bill must be regarded as evidence of "growing impatience" with the British connection. Those, Macdonald said, "who disliked the colonial connection spoke of it as a chain, but it was a golden chain, and he, for one was glad to wear the fetters."[43] There was evidence, referred to by Fournier, of abuse by the wealthy who used the threat of a Privy Council appeal to intimidate financially weaker, but hitherto successful, opponents.[44] Blake averred later that there was a legal clique in England who promoted Canadian law suits to the Privy Council.[45] The Irving-Laflamme amendment passed 112-40 with twenty-seven French-Canadian members voting for it, and nine against it.[46]

In the Supreme Court debate Blake had not played a conspicuous role, though he had spoken several times, and he had voted for Section 47. His interest in the whole subject was general rather than specific. His nationalism led him to champion Section 47. It was the kind of subject that suited him and he set out to master the whole question of Privy Council appeals.

The Colonial Office was largely convinced by Blake's argument that Canada did have power to restrict appeals to the Privy Council as of right; but the Lord Chancellor, Lord Cairns, one of Disraeli's principal colleagues and himself a great equity judge, opposed Blake's view categorically. The argument in 1876 was a long, hot, summer's work. Blake was three months at it, and sick of it all before he was through. He wondered how on earth he would make up the time that British officialdom, with its interminable delays, had stolen from him.[47] The upshot was that the offending clause was left untouched, but the whole question of the regulation of appeals to the Privy Council was left in a limbo of uncertainty. Blake summed it up in 1880, when there was a proposal to abolish the Supreme Court. He moved, and with Macdonald's support carried, the six months' hoist on the proposed abolition, by a vote of 148-29.

> The whole British system is in contradiction to the Federal system. . . . Now, a Constitution like ours, complicated and delicate in its adjustments, requires for its interpretation that measure of learning, experience and practice which those who live under it, and work it, and who are practically engaged in its operation are all their lives acquiring. The British North America Act is a skeleton. The true form and propositions, the true spirit of our Constitution, can be made manifest only to the men of the soil. I deny that it can be well expounded by men whose whole lives have been passed, not merely in another, but in an opposite sphere of practice. . . .[48]

There, indeed, spoke Canada First.

None of these constitutional problems cut very deeply into political life. Right from the start of his administration, Mackenzie faced two much more emotional issues that cut clean across party lines and deep into federal-provincial relations. These two issues were the New Brunswick school question and the Riel amnesty. The first was not solved at all, and the second only by the fiat of the Governor General, with the help of the British government.

The background of the New Brunswick school question has already been sketched in.[49] The French-Canadian wing of the Conservative party wanted to guarantee to New Brunswick Catholics, French and Irish, the specific rights guaranteed to Ontario Catholics, and to Quebec Protestants, by Section 93 of the British North America Act. In Nova Scotia, New Brunswick, and in 1873 in Prince Edward Island, the British North America Act guaranteed only the educational privileges that existed *by law* before the Union.

There were four ways of giving the New Brunswick Catholics what they wanted. The House of Commons could ask the Legislature of New Brunswick nicely to please give back to the Roman Catholics the educational privileges of which they had been deprived in 1871. That was tried in 1872. The second was outright disallowance of the offending New Brunswick School Act. That was short and quick. A resolution praying that this be done passed the House of Commons in May, 1873. But for French Canadians it was too dangerous a precedent, especially when the Law Officers of the Crown had indicated that the Act was within the competence of the New Brunswick legislature.[50] The resolution of the Commons was never acted upon. The third way was by a constitutional amendment. A French-Canadian attempt to have the British North America Act changed failed in 1872. The fourth way was to appeal to the courts to definitively test the law on the subject. Another resolution to the Commons in May, 1873 authorized the spending of five thousand dollars to cover the cost of appealing to the Privy Council one of the two cases recently before the Supreme Court of New Brunswick.

The question was most clearly set forth in the case Ex *parte* Renaud *et al.*, a 5-0 decision, delivered by Chief Justice Ritchie of the New Brunswick Supreme Court in 1873. The case turned upon the privileges the New Brunswick Roman Catholics had by law before July 1, 1867 under the Parish School Act of 1858. No one denied that New Brunswick had had publicly supported denominational schools. But had such schools existed by law? Justice Ritchie said no. And to counter the tortured argument used by counsel for the applicants* Ritchie added, "it is a well established canon of construction, that an Act is to be construed according to the ordinary and grammatical sense of its language. . . ." There was no doubt, in Ritchie's view, that the New Brunswick Roman Catholics had had privileges before Confederation, but they did not exist by law; hence damage to them was something the law could not take cognizance of. He was sympathetic. ". . . hard cases," he said, "are apt to make bad law; . . . if there is a general hardship . . . it is a consideration for the Legislature, not for a Court of Justice."[51] It was another case that went to the Privy Council, *Maher vs. Town Council of Portland*. This case the Privy Council dismissed on July 17, 1874, with costs, on precisely the same ground that Ritchie had taken.[52]

In 1874 New Brunswick held a general election, and the King government, which had passed the 1871 Act, was returned with an overwhelming majority. The Caraquet riots of January 14, 1875, over the attempt to fight off the school legislation, in a French-speaking part of New Brunswick, were one unfortunate result.

Consequently in 1875 the New Brunswick Roman Catholics, led by the Irish Catholic Conservative M.P. for Victoria, John Costigan, had only one forlorn hope, the Parliament of Canada. French Canadians urged caution, but Bishop Sweeney was determined to go ahead,[53] and go ahead Costigan did. His aim was to get a resolution through the Commons praying for an amendment to the British North America Act. Hitherto neither party had wanted to interfere with the British North America Act as it was, though it had been tinkered with already, with the better terms of 1869 to Nova Scotia and the general increase in the debt allowances in 1873. Still, Costigan would probably not have got very far but for the success of Mills motion against the Senate on March 1. Costigan rallied his friends and proposed his

*Renaud and others were applying for a writ of *certiorari*.

motion on March 8. It was such a success that had a division been taken that night, the Government, who opposed it would have been beaten.[54] But the debate was adjourned for two days, and in the meantime the Liberals held a hectic caucus to straighten the matter out. What emerged was curious. Mackenzie's motion, made the next day, stated that any amendment to the British North America Act encroaching on powers reserved to the province was dangerous, and ought not to be proceeded with.[55] Joseph Cauchon proposed that the House regret that its motion of May, 1872 (asking the New Brunswick government to please change its mind) had not been acted upon. The Queen was then requested to use *her* influence. This extraordinary combination carried the House on virtually a party vote.[56]

And there the New Brunswick school question ended. As to the moral right of New Brunswick Catholics to their privileges there is little doubt; but legal right they had none. The remedies, as Justice Ritchie had laid down, as Mackenzie had urged, lay with the Legislature of New Brunswick. *La Minerve*, run by Arthur Dansereau, in March 1875, commented,

> On avait cru qu'après avoir trahi sur la question du Manitoba, . . . ils tiendraient à se racheter au moins sur la question religieuse des écoles pour réparer leur lâcheté sur la question de l'amnistie.[57]

The question of the Manitoba amnesty goes back to the events of the Riel provisional government in 1869-70. Riel had been congratulated by the Lieutenant-Governor of Manitoba for helping to put down the Fenian threat of 1871. But the Ontario Government's reward of five thousand dollars for his capture still stood; Riel's home had actually been invaded by a group of armed men in 1871 because of that reward; Riel just happened by luck not to be there. In consequence, he had gone to the United States early in 1872, with four thousand dollars furnished secretly by the Government of Canada and Donald Smith, for his own upkeep and the support of his family in St. Vital. He drifted back to Manitoba in the early summer of 1872. Attracted, moth-like, to the flame of power, when the nomination for Provencher in Parliament was offered him, he accepted. On advice, he gave way to Cartier, who had lost Montreal East. Then a year later, a warrant was quietly sworn out in Winnipeg for his arrest,[58] on the initiative of several Canadians who had their eye on Ontario's five thousand dollars. Riel could not be found in St. Vital. But Ambroise Lépine, his right-hand man, arrested at his farm, surrendered quietly, and was taken to Fort Garry. Riel was hiding in a haystack on a friend's farm. Shortly afterward he replaced Cartier as Member for Provencher. He was spirited out of Manitoba and sent on his way to friends in Montreal late in 1873.

Riel was met in Montreal by Honoré Mercier and was taken to Parliament at Ottawa – it must have been just in the last days of Macdonald – but would not go in. Despite A. A. Dorion's advice to the contrary, Riel was re-elected in the January, 1874 general election, and just before the opening of the Parliament that year in the company of Dr. Romuald Fiset, M.P. for Rimouski, he entered the Parliament buildings and was sworn in routinely by the Clerk of the House, Alfred Patrick. He never took his seat.

The question of the amnesty is a tangled one. When Archbishop Taché went home to Red River, from meetings with Cartier and Macdonald in February 1870, he carried with him the assurance of an imperial amnesty. But did this assurance apply to all acts which happened up to the Archbishop's arrival in Red River? Thomas Scott had been shot on March 4, four days before the Bishop arrived. The Archbishop was confident that his assurance covered all eventualities; Cartier, he said, had been positive on that point. As a result he persuaded both Riel and Lépine that the slate was now wiped clean.

But Macdonald found the agitation that swirled out of Ontario over the shooting of Scott impossible to resist. Whatever amnesty had been promised, it was wise to postpone its official application until things had calmed down in the East. When they had, Macdonald maintained that he had never promised the kind of amnesty that Archbishop Taché proclaimed when he arrived in Red River; specifically, that the amnesty was never intended to cover the shooting of Scott. To this the Archbishop remarked in a letter to Bishop LaFlèche of Trois Rivières, "le Très honorable John-A. Macdonald a menti (excusez le mot) comme ferait un voyou.*"[59] What Cartier had promised Taché was uncertain but by the summer of 1873 Cartier was dead, and there was only Taché's word, the word of the Manitoba delegates, and Sir John Macdonald's to go on.

The French Canadians had been sympathetic to the cause of Riel, and when Ontario had expressed its outrage over the Scott shooting, French Canadians naturally added a lively resentment against Ontario to their sympathy for the Métis. The issue had rapidly become intractable, as the events of 1870 showed, but by 1872 and 1873, with Riel drifting back to St. Vital, it was dying down. Then, in the fall of 1873 had come the arrest of Lépine and the flight of Riel to Montreal. Alphonse Desjardins, owner of *Le Nouveau Monde*, an ultramontane paper close to Bishop Bourget, opened the columns of the paper to Riel and his sympathizers, and the French-Canadian Conservative press began to use the issue to belabour the Mackenzie government.

This was not difficult to do. Mackenzie had been Treasurer of Ontario when that Government had offered the five-thousand-dollar reward for Riel's capture. The federal government was now said to be dominated by Ontario,

* The expression comes through best as "lied like a trooper." "Voyou" is a street tough.

a charge that became weightier after A. A. Dorion, the only strong French-Canadian minister, was known to be leaving the Government.

Lépine's case did not help. The trial began on October 13, 1874, a year after his arrest.* He was tried, as by Manitoba law he could be, by six French-speaking and six English-speaking jurors. Adolphe Chapleau and Joseph Royal (founder of *Le Nouveau Monde* and now editor of *Le Métis* of St. Boniface) defended Lépine, the former in French, the latter in English. Chapleau was perhaps the most brilliant politician of his time; with what the French call "tendances boulevardières," he had verve, passion, *brio*, and was loved by crowds and by women. He had "le talent le plus souple, le plus varié, le plus complet, le plus séduisant que le pays ait produit peut-être. . . ."[60] Like Laurier he was a superb actor and like Laurier he had immense charm. With the cheers of the crowd at Bonaventure station still in his mind, he spared nothing in Winnipeg, spoke of the spectacle "de l'honnête homme honteusement suspendu au gibet d'ignominie, de la veuve inconsolable, des pauvres orphelins. . . ."[61] The mixed jury found Lépine "guilty with a recommendation to mercy."[62] The Chief Justice imposed the death sentence.

What followed in Quebec was a dress rehearsal, so to speak, for the events eleven years later, except that the positions were reversed. The Conservatives in Quebec were fiery supporters of amnesty; the Liberals were embarrassed. The Quebec legislature passed a unanimous resolution asking the Governor General to grant amnesty to Lépine, *and* Riel. To make matters worse for the Liberals, in the middle of this came the Privy Council decision in the Guibord affair. And there was a provincial election coming up in 1875.

The Conservative press of Quebec was thus in full cry. *Le Canadien* of Quebec City, edited by Israël Tarte, led the pack. Tarte was amazing: vibrating with intelligence, he had a style of writing that was nervous, mordant, and deadly. And what he was to do with Langevin in 1891, he did with the Liberals in 1874, turning them neatly over on the grill.

Lépine's condemnation put the Liberal government fairly on the spot. Had Lépine never been arrested the whole matter would gradually have died out. As the Toronto *Liberal* pointed out, the amnesty promised through Archbishop Taché, whatever quarrels may subsequently have arisen about its range, contributed a great deal to the pacification of Manitoba and the general acceptance of the new Canadian order of things.[63] But now action of some kind was imperative. Lépine awaited execution (set for January, 1875), and the Liberal ministers from Quebec threatened resignation unless something were done. Lord Dufferin wrote, "This is the most thorny business I ever had to deal with, thanks to the imbecility of almost everyone who has

* The delay was due to questions about the jurisdiction of the Manitoba court for crimes committed before Manitoba came into existence.

hitherto meddled with it."[64] Mackenzie had forced Riel's expulsion in April 1874 over Fournier's and Geoffrion's resistance, but it was altogether unlikely he could force them to knuckle under a second time over such an issue as Lépine's life.

It was Dufferin who removed from the government the responsibility for the odious decision that they would not, or could not, take themselves. The decisive fact in Dufferin's mind was the behaviour of Riel (and Lépine) in the Fenian crisis of 1871, and more to the point, that the Queen's representative in Manitoba had personally thanked them for it. That could not be ignored, or explained away, nor could the apparently strong assurance of complete amnesty given by Cartier through Taché. "No argument," wrote Dufferin, "will ever persuade the French population that the promises of the Government to Riel and Lépine were not most absolute explicit and complete."[65] At the same time, it was impossible to ignore Thomas Scott. He had been shot, in a calculated, ruthless way, not only for what he had done, but as a deliberate act of policy.[66] So Lépine's sentence was commuted to two years in prison and permanent loss of civil rights.* The whole decision was delayed until the Ontario provincial elections were out of the way – at Mackenzie's request – and the Governor General's proclamation was issued in the *Royal Gazette*, January 21, 1875.

With this lead from the Governor General, it was possible for Mackenzie to follow. On February 11, 1875, Mackenzie moved an Address granting general amnesty for events in the Northwest five years before. Riel was given amnesty on condition of five years banishment. The Address was carried on February 12, 126-50, with some of the fifty opposing Conservatives being against the amnesty because it was not complete, and others, like Bowell, against the amnesty because there was one at all.

The amnesty question may have hurt the Liberals in Ontario and in Quebec – Macdonald believed it hurt them badly[67] – but moderate opinion was prepared to accept any reasonable solution, and the whole issue gradually died away. When Riel visited Manitoba in 1883 he was badgered, not by Ontarians or by police, but by newspaper reporters.[68] It took courage to face the amnesty issue, but the Governor General's independent power certainly helped, and in 1875 the ineluctable necessity of dealing with it gave the Mackenzie government the courage of desperation.

"Courage of desperation" describes the position of the Liberal party in Quebec for peculiarly difficult ecclesiastical and religious reasons. Ultramontanism places the church over the state; liberal Catholicism places state over the church. The ultramontane urges that the moral law is the supreme

* Lépine lived on, through 1885 and after, until 1923. Some years before he died, his civil rights were restored to him.

law; the liberal Catholic says the world is the world, and there are duties both to Caesar and to God.

Liberalism, allied with socialism, fought the Church openly in the 1840's, and the liberal Catholics were caught between. In Quebec the Church was both nationalist and conservative, buttressing French-Canadian life and, at the same time, refusing to countenance violent change of the established political order. Since the Church in Quebec had always been a powerful force toward the preservation of the French-Canadian way of life, it was more than usually difficult for a true French-Canadian patriot to criticize it. Notwithstanding, a movement developed among the young and liberal or socialist-minded intellectuals who moved into politics on the left and became known as Rouges.

Conflict between Rouges and the Church was natural. Some of the Rouges were strongly anti-clerical or agnostic; others were practising Catholics who felt religion had nothing to do with politics. Both positions the Church deplored, the latter almost more than the former. The anti-clericals were out in the open and could be fought as such; but practising Catholics who believed in the separation of church and state were much more dangerous. Conflict began over the Bishop of Montreal's attempt to suppress the clubs and reading rooms that nourished Rouge ideas, the Instituts Canadiens. In 1869 Bishop Ignace Bourget succeeded in having the Institut banned as long as it continued to harbour perverse doctrine and kept prohibited books in its libraries. The Vatican Council of 1870 strengthed the hand of the ultramontane side. The war was on. One aspect was the celebrated case of Joseph Guibord.

Guibord, a member of the Institut, died after the Bishop's 1869 decree. The Church insisted that Guibord be given only a civil burial, that is, buried in unconsecrated ground. This ruling Guibord's widow and his friends, most of whom were practising Catholics, attempted to have rescinded, but in vain. Guibord was placed in a Protestant cemetery for the time being, and a law case ensued. Judgment was given on May 6, 1870 in favour of the widow, condemning the Catholic cemetery to pay costs. It was appealed, and thrown out at the Appeal Court on the ultramontane ground that civil courts had no jurisdiction in ecclesiastical causes. After a further appeal to the Court of Queen's Bench, it was taken to the Privy Council. There, on November 28, 1874, judgment was given that the parish and the cemetery bury Guibord in consecrated ground, and that the parish pay the costs – now $6,000. Joseph Doutre, and Louis-Amable Jetté who had argued the case for the Guibord family, returned triumphant to Montreal, exploited their advantage and alienated friends[69] by going a stage further and asking for religious exercises to accompany the re-burial. Altogether it was more than the ultramontane press, or the bishop, were prepared to take, and an aroused population forcibly prevented an attempted re-burial on September 2, 1875.

Many of the crowd were quite out of control. "No bloody xxxxxx will pass this gate! God damn Guibord!"[70] So the corpse and coffin were rattled back through the Montreal streets to the Protestant cemetery once again.

Pressure was brought to bear. Lord Dufferin intimated quietly that the Queen's judgment had been given and ought to be respected. Mayor Hingston, a courageous and cool man, then saw the Bishop of Montreal. What was needed, he said, was a letter from the Bishop to be shown to the curés of the parishes, and the mayors of the municipalities through which the procession was to go. With this *laissez passer* the curés could tell their congregations about the impropriety of further resisting the law. Bourget hesitated and finally consented.[71] On the day of the funeral, November 16, 1875, hardly a Catholic put his nose out of the door. The grave in Côte des Neiges cemetery was dug directly above Madame Guibord's (she had died in 1873 and was buried satisfactorily). All was peaceful. The coffin was put in, the grave filled up with cement and scrap iron, while a cold November drizzle beat steadily on the snowy muddy ground.[72]

In principle, the Guibord case was a triumph of the civil over the ecclesiastical power. In practice, the ecclesiastics still won. No civil power could prevent the bishop's exercise of purely sacerdotal functions. He de-consecrated the particular part of the earth where Guibord rested. Madame Guibord, underneath, was not, presumably, included. And, oddly enough, in the six years between Guibord's death and his final burial, no less than six members of the Institut Canadien had been buried with full ecclesiastical honours, four of them in Montreal.[73]

It is easy to accuse the ultramontane movement of bigotry and intolerance. No doubt elements of both existed, as they existed in sections of the Protestant Church. But the ultramontanes, like the Calvinists, touched much of what was best in the Church and society – dedication, zeal, purity. The lay supporters of the movement, such as Senator F.-X. Trudel, one of the authors of the Programme Catholique, were notably free from the corruption associated with both political parties in Quebec and elsewhere. Indeed, ultramontanism looked beyond the Conservative party to making politics pure and, of course, Catholic.

The Programme Catholique of 1871 was a translation of the ultramontane position to political, lay terms. The ultramontane program, authoritarian, devout, and high-minded, was suitable for a society with a preponderant Catholic population, which indeed Quebec had, and an authoritarian political tradition which Quebec had not. Moreover there was a highly vocal and powerful minority who were not Catholics and who were strongly opposed to Catholicism, the Quebec English Protestants. Even in the French-Canadian community, however, ultramontanism was disrupting. It was supported by Bishop Bourget of Montreal, Bishop Laflèche of Trois Rivières, and the Church orders that Bourget had brought to Canada, notably the

Jesuits who were now restored to grace and favour. But other elements in the Catholic Church took a more flexible attitude to political society. These Catholics, while subscribing to the doctrines of the Syllabus of 1864 and Papal Infallibility, did not draw from them the hard conclusions that the ultramontanes did. The head of this more flexible group was the Archbishop of Quebec, Elzéar-Alexander Taschereau (1820-1898). With him stood the bishops of Rimouski, St. Hyacinthe, and Ottawa. In some ways the differences between Bourget and Taschereau reflected the difference between Montreal and Quebec, between a city where the Protestants were powerful and a city where they were not. But there was more to it than religion. Bishop Bourget had long wanted to establish a Jesuit university at Montreal. When he applied to Rome for sanction of the project, it was refused, at the instance of the Archbishop of Quebec. The matter went from Rome to the Quebec legislature, and back to Rome again, gathering bitterness as it went.

The Quebec bishops were briefly united on the Guibord affair. They all signed a pastoral letter with strong warnings about Catholic liberalism, which differed from ultramontanism mainly in its political neutrality. But the word "liberalism" had different meanings. Emotionally charged in a clerical context, it had quite a neutral meaning in a political one. Was it possible to be a good Catholic and a good Liberal, in a Canadian political context? Given the Programme Catholique, it was a proposition easy to deny. So good Catholics who were good Liberals found the *programmiste* position impossible to live with. In Bishop Lynch's analogy, the basic difference between a liberal Catholic and a Catholic Liberal, was the same as that between a horse chestnut and a chestnut horse.[74]

That was all very well, but the distinction was easy to blur with voters, especially since the Quebec Liberals had been associated with the strident anti-clericalism of the Rouges in the 1850's, and especially when it was in the interest of the Conservative party to promote confusion. The practical effect on the programmiste-ultramontane position in politics is best illustrated by the Charlevoix federal bye-election of 1876.

Despite the support of the Church, the Conservatives in Quebec had not had an easy time since 1873. The odium of the Pacific Scandal had fallen on them. Then, in July, 1874, the provincial Conservative government, intimately associated with the federal Conservatives, was caught out in the Tanneries scandal, broken by the Montreal *Herald*. The details are complicated (scandals are never simple), but it involved the exchange of a piece of land owned by the province near Montreal, at St. Henri des Tanneries, worth perhaps, $135,000, for another at Lachine worth about $40,000. As Rummily puts it, it was a case of "un boeuf contre un oeuf."[75] In the process of this exchange some of the money got loose; Arthur Dansereau of *La Minerve* acquired fifty thousand dollars in his bank account, and it was easy to conclude that it was part of the general distribution of a *pot-de-vin* (that happy

French expression). At least two of the Quebec provincial Cabinet were involved; the Premier, Gédéon Ouimet, and the Solicitor-General, Adolphe Chapleau, the real power in the Government. The scandal apparently got out because some of the English supporters of the Quebec Conservative government were not given any of the *pot.*[76] The Tanneries scandal ousted Ouimet and the rest of his Conservative Cabinet (except for J. G. Robertson, the Treasurer), and a new, but still Conservative, Cabinet came in under Charles de Boucherville. Much of the change was engineered by Hector Langevin, for the good of the party.[77] Charles de Boucherville was a thoroughly honest, dedicated *programmiste,* on excellent terms with the Church. In the Assembly the real power was in the hands of the bright, talented Auguste-Réal Angers.[78]

In the provincial election of 1875 the Conservatives were able to set against the Tanneries scandal a Liberal public works scandal on the Lachine Canal – much to Mackenzie's chagrin. And with clerical support for Charles de Boucherville, the Conservatives carried forty of the province's sixty-five seats. Langevin now decided the time had come to get back into politics. He had been urged by Sir John Macdonald to do so.[79]

Charlevoix was back country, its people, as Charles Langelier described them, "illettrés et profondément religeuses."[80] The sitting member, Pierre Tremblay, had won handily in 1874, but was unseated after a long court case, and a bye-election was called for January 22, 1876. Enormous efforts were made by both sides to take the election. Langevin posed as a pillar of the Church. And although the ultramontane papers were noticeably reticent about Langevin, other Conservative papers were much less scrupulous about exploiting clerical influence to the advantage of an important Conservative candidate.

Langevin's campaign was supported financially by Thomas McGreevy, and was directed by Israël Tarte. On the day before the election, according to Cauchon,[81] the parish priest at La Malbaie called meetings of the habitants at the schoolhouses, and then had the children kneel "as they were pure before God and to pray that their parents should not be damned in voting for Tremblay."

Cauchon was managing Tremblay's campaign. He had just fought Tarte in Quebec Centre, in the bye-election on Cauchon's elevation to Mackenzie's Cabinet. It was not a good appointment. Cauchon's maxim was, "Celui gouverne mal le miel qui n'en goute et ses doigts n'en lèche."[82] After a year and a half Mackenzie and Blake could take no more and Cauchon was shipped off as Lieutenant-Governor of Manitoba. *Grip* published a vivid cartoon showing Mackenzie leaving the grubby baby in a basket with a label, "Please keep him," at the door of the province of Manitoba; then walking away, holding his nose.[83] Cauchon was not that bad; but he brought no kudos to the Ministry and precious little talent; what he did bring was a reputed working relationship with the Archbishop of Quebec.

Langevin won the bye-election, 952-741.[84] It was protested at once under the Dominion's Election Act of 1874, for undue influence. The hearing was delayed a year, perhaps deliberately, by Judge Routhier who was a friend of Langevin's. During the interval Archbishop Taschereau drew back from the position the Quebec bishops had taken in 1875, and issued a new, personal *mandement* in May, 1876, in which he forbade his priests to give political advice.[85] In November Judge Routhier decided for Langevin, and the case was appealed to the Supreme Court of Canada. In February, 1877, the decision was handed down unseating Langevin, and charging him six thousand dollars in costs. The verdict was written by Justice Taschereau, the Archbishop's brother. A new election was set and Langevin won in 1877, 1,185-1,129.

The Protestant reaction to the clerical pressures in Quebec was considerable. The Protestant press, especially the Montreal *Witness* and Reform papers in Ontario, tended to present the more extreme utterances of the ultramontanes as indicative of the Church's views as a whole. Equally, they assumed the Church was a monolithic structure, conveniently forgetting the congeries of orders, and intra-Church conflicts of jurisdiction that the government of the Church, like any other government, has to endure. Moreover a current of fear ran through all Protestant utterances. In Britain two of the finest minds in the Church of England, Cardinals Manning and Newman, had gone over to Rome; others, it was thought, were in the process of going.[86] The Vatican Council of 1870 accentuated these fears and seemed to give them authority.[87]

Behind the scenes, direct and useful efforts were afoot to cure the difficulty. The Bishop of London, Ontario, Dr. John Walsh, and Sir Edward Kenny, went to Rome in the autumn of 1876. According to Kenny's report to Mackenzie, a false impression had been built up at the Congregation of the Propaganda about the Liberal party of Canada, equating it with Liberals in France, Belgium and Italy – an impression built up, Sir Edward alleged, by Quebec sources. Dr. Walsh did not mince words with the Cardinal Prefect. The whole visit was sufficiently successful that orders were issued, virtually at once, to the Quebec bishops to stop public opposition to the Liberal party, and the Irish Bishop Conroy was ordered to come out in the spring.[88] His visit coincided with Laurier's famous speech on Political Liberalism to the Club Canadien in Quebec City in June, 1877, and together they mark the fact that the high point of the ultramontane cause had passed.

Laurier deeply felt the strain between the Liberals and the Church. On the eve of the Charlevoix election, he was depressed and gloomy. As he wrote to James Young in Galt, Ontario,

> Political strifes are bitter enough in your province, but you have no idea of what it is with us. The people is ignorant, the priests are prejudiced and arrogant, and we liberals are put down like enemies of the church, of society, of mankind. . . . To tell you the candid truth, I am rather dejected at the prospects before us. . . .[89]

Laurier was thirty-six in 1877. He was born at St. Lin, about thirty miles north of Montreal. He was a graduate of L'Assomption College and McGill University, and set up for a time an unsuccessful law practice in Montreal. Then, at A. A. Dorion's request, in 1866 he took over J. B. E. Dorion's practice and newspaper at L'Avenir, a little lumber town in Arthabaska County. Later he moved to the county town, gave up the paper, and settled down to acquiring a practice. Within five years he was in the provincial Assembly, and in 1874 was elected to Parliament for Drummond-Arthabaska, a Liberal in a constituency old with memories of J. B. E. Dorion. And his presence in Parliament was early noted.[90]

It was in Parliament that he made his first speech in English. Laurier had picked up English when, as a boy of eleven, he had been sent to board with a Scotch family ten miles from St. Lin. Laurier used English with a flair and a finish perhaps uncharacteristic of the feel of the language, but which carried very well – better on set occasions than on casual ones.

Laurier disliked authority; he disliked coercion; he disliked bigotry. He had an almost morbid distaste for violence. His fastidious nature abhorred dirt, and arrogance, and stupidity. And he hated to give pain as he hated to endure it. He disliked the vulgarity and corruption of politics, and English liberalism came to him, therefore, as ready-made doctrine. Nor was his elegance a pose; it was a clear expression of the man within.

His speech on political liberalism at Quebec City in June 1877 illustrates this as well as anything in his career. It was a courageous utterance, notwithstanding the pains he had taken to ensure that it would be acceptable. He consulted Abbé Benjamin Paquet of Laval, whom he knew to be sympathetic; Mackenzie, Blake, and Charles Pelletier, of the Cabinet, were uneasy but entered a *nihil obstat*. Bishop Conroy, the papal Legate, was staying in Ste. Foy, and Laurier may have known that Rome would probably moderate episcopal disapproval. The speech was given in a city sympathetic to his ideas, for he would have had a much sterner reception in Montreal. In spite of all that, it was a difficult speech to give.

Laurier took his theme on the differences between Conservatives and Liberals from Macaulay's *History of England*.[91] Conservatives were those who were attached to old institutions and who accepted change with reluctance and distaste. Liberals were those who, strong in ideas and hopes, saw the imperfections in the present and expected that change would improve the human condition. This duality, Laurier insisted, was apparent in everything human, for in everything there was the charm of custom and the allure of novelty. More significantly, Laurier tried to define the role of a Roman Catholic in what was, after all, a pluralistic society. He was justified in feeling uneasy; he was making a direct attack on the ultramontane position of the bishops and the *programmistes*.

What gave this speech its *éclat* was its timeliness, its force, its frankness, its absence of party feeling, its elevation of thought, its elegance and its judiciousness. Charles Langelier, thirteen years afterward, recalled the impression it made. "Le succès fut immense, éclatant. Jamais depuis les grand jours de Papineau, on avait entendu une si mâle éloquence . . . il avait, d'un souffle, d'un coup de maître, dissipé tous les vieux préjugés, terrassé l'hydre du fanatisme. . . ."[92] It made Laurier's reputation at once, as indeed it was intended to do.

Laurier was sworn in as Minister of Inland Revenue, October 16, 1877, and his bye-election in Drummond-Arthabaska was set for Saturday, October 27. A few days before, from the pulpit in Arthabaskaville, a general pastoral letter from the Bishops in Quebec was read declaring that Catholic liberalism had nothing to do with any Canadian political party. Monseigneur Conroy had been at work. In addition, the priests were privately instructed never to teach that it was a sin to vote for one candidate or the other.[93] This was not the end of the religous difficulties of the Liberals in Quebec, but it heralded the end.

Laurier's real difficulties in Drummond-Arthabaska came from the Conservatives determined to make a party triumph, and, incidentally, to cut Laurier down before he got fairly started. It was a frequent custom to give Ministers an acclamation election when coming up for re-election; Laurier got a savage battle. The Conservatives moved in their big guns: Israël Tarte of *Le Canadien*, Arthur Dansereau of *La Minerve*, Louis-Adélard Sénécal, at Chapleau's special instructions, arrived at the last minute with money; and Drummond-Arthabaska, which had given Laurier a 1,786-1,548 victory in 1874, elected a Conservative by twenty-two votes.

The defeat of Laurier came as a stunning surprise.[94] John S. D. Thompson, a budding Conservative in the middle of a bye-election fight for the seat of Antigonish in the Nova-Scotian Assembly, remarked, "Laurier's defeat has made all our friends here as bold as lions and converts are dropping into our camp every day."[95] Mackenzie and Brown shared the suspicion that Laurier had been too confident. Whether that was true or not, it was certain that there had been bribery and intimidation on a gross scale. The election could certainly be protested, annulled, and a new writ issued, but that would take a long time, judging by Langevin's experience in Charlevoix. Instead, Quebec East was offered to Laurier, and he accepted. The new bye-election was set for November 28, 1877.

The Conservatives, of course, would not give up that easily. "No pains should be spared to beat Laurier in East Quebec," wrote Macdonald to Langevin, "See all our friends. Explain to them how much depends on the victory."[96] McGreevy was asked by Macdonald to help prime the pump.[97] Chapleau was set to work in Montreal to drum up funds, "la besogne la plus ingrate," as he put it.[98]

Nevertheless Laurier took Quebec East, 1,863-1,548. He was to hold that seat until his death, in 1919. But just ten months away was the general election of 1878 that was to take him out of power until 1896. And Laurier's health, never robust, broke down that winter leaving him virtually useless to the Government in the session of 1878.[99]

CHAPTER 4

Railways, Manitoba and the Northwest 1873-1880

Building railways is expensive, and difficult for a young country with chronic shortage of capital. Meagre local savings are often either used for local improvements or invested in something promising faster return. Given this, railways in Canada could be built in three ways. One: import capital, and surrender the profits (and risks) to a company outside Canada, as with the Grand Trunk Railway, 1853-60. Two: make the railway as cheap as possible, with maximum curves and grades (and often narrow gauge to exploit both), and build a local line with local savings. Much of the Toronto, Grey and Bruce, 1868-1875, was built this way.[1] Three: use government construction and, possibly, government operation, as with the Intercolonial Railway, 1864-1876.

The financing of government construction differs from the financing of private construction. Government funds for railway construction derive either from annual taxation to meet continuing costs, such as construction over a period of years, or from the marketing of bonds, guaranteed or otherwise, to provide large amounts of money for construction that would be too heavy a drain on the Government's current income. Funds for private railway construction derive first of all from the sale of stock in the railway company itself. There is a calculated gamble by the purchaser that the company will make a profit and pay dividends. Private companies also issue bonds, which are ordinary long-term debts paid at a rate of interest determined by the standing or prospects of the company.

Governments and private companies thus had different approaches to railway construction. Governments could afford to take a leisurely pace. Sometimes they had to. The Intercolonial Railway is a case in point. The surveys were actively prosecuted from 1864; construction began in 1868 under a £4,000,000 issue of Dominion of Canada bonds ($20,000,000) guaranteed by the Imperial government. When that proved insufficient, current income was used. However private companies could not wait. The private railway had to be operational and earning income in the minimum time consistent with efficient construction. Income depended upon the size, efficiency and commercial viability of the railway. Big through lines, like the Canadian Pacific Railway, could be, and were, opened in sections which earned some income. But real income to provide dividends, to pay interest on bonds and amortize the debt they represent, depended, in the C.P.R.'s case, on rapid completion of the full line from Montreal to Port Moody, British Columbia. Until that was done capital was locked up, earning little income. This accounts for the rapid pace of C.P.R. construction, in direct contrast to the Intercolonial Railway, and to the sections of the Pacific Railway built by the Government. The C.P.R. could not afford to be slow; the Government could not afford to be speedy.

The difference between the railway policy of the Macdonald government and that of the Mackenzie government was largely determined by these principles. It is too crude to say that the Conservatives favoured private railway companies and the Liberals favoured publicly-owned ones. There are few indications that the Liberals ever seriously wanted government ownership. The railway policies of both were determined by what was possible. In 1872 it was possible to get a private railway company to agree to build and operate a Pacific railway. In 1874 it was not. Mackenzie tried in 1878; Macdonald tried in 1879. It was not possible again until 1880 when Macdonald had been two years in office. In short, both political parties preferred railways operated by private companies. If they could be *built* by private companies so much the better, provided the fiasco of the Grand Trunk construction could be avoided, where a private company continually had to be bailed out by the Government.

One reason why governments disliked building, and especially disliked operating railways was the inefficiency inherent in nineteenth-century government. They simply did not have the necessary flexibility in hiring and firing. Macdonald found it quite possible to condemn government roads as refuges for political hacks, and at the same time to use the Intercolonial Railway for that very purpose. Governments were not always enthusiastic dispensers of patronage, but their supporters expected it and insisted upon it. In the age of the impartial civil servant we forget to what degree Canada was run by patronage. It was not all bad; Charles Sangster, the poet, got a job in the Post Office in 1868, as did Archibald Lampman in 1883. They were good poets; whether they were good for the Post Office is not known. The worst side of patronage is the obvious one. But it kept the party together; it created and sustained party loyalty; it was the reward for the otherwise unrewardable party services.

Government enterprises were therefore notoriously inefficient. Patronage inevitably involved the use of local as against outside talent; and resentment was often acute if an official were appointed who did not come from the province in which he was serving. Of all of Canada the Maritimes exhibited the sincerest devotion to patronage, and the most unblushing concentration on its many forms and variations. In this respect there was nothing to choose between Conservatives and Liberals, equally hungry, equally vicious, and equally squalid.

Still, the Intercolonial possessed some better features. Its Chief Engineer, Sandford Fleming, and under Mackenzie at least, a government prepared to back him up, were two of these. The route of the Intercolonial had been fought over since its inception especially in New Brunswick, where there was a tug of war between the Saint John valley and the North Shore. The Saint John valley had many real advantages, population and political power; but the North Shore had Peter Mitchell and George Etienne Cartier. As far as Cartier was concerned, the Intercolonial was a colonization road for eastern Quebec. He was supported by Sandford Fleming for quite other reasons; Fleming envisaged it as part of a grand transcontinental route beginning in Newfoundland, and coming via Shippegan harbour and Montreal to the West.

The early years of the Intercolonial were a continual struggle between Fleming and the Board of Railway Commissioners, a political body appointed by Macdonald to supervise the work for the Government.[2] Fleming wanted an efficient, well-constructed railway; the Board wanted patronage and cheap construction. What was lost in patronage and bad contracts, could be made up by cutting corners and by cheap methods of building, such as iron rails and wooden bridges. Fleming, fortunately, got his way, steel rails and iron bridges, but it took a major battle. He also got, in 1873, a decision to convert the line to standard gauge.

Fleming's difficulties with local contractors were notorious. Not all were the result of speculation; Fleming seems to have had a too trusting nature and a general distaste for accounting procedures, characterized by Mackenzie as "most unbusiness-like."[3]

When Mackenzie took over the Department of Public Works, he abolished the Board of Railway Commissioners, took the Intercolonial under the Department and had C. J. Brydges, a former member of the Board, and recently Managing Director of the Grand Trunk, make a report to the Government. Brydges was then appointed General Superintendent of Government Railways and proceeded, as far as he could, to make the line efficient. Mackenzie insisted, through Brydges, that appointments be made on the basis of efficiency; if that was consistent with the recommendations of members of Parliament Brydges could accept them, otherwise not.[4] This annoyed numerous politicians, since the Intercolonial traversed no less than fourteen constituencies between Rivière du Loup and Halifax.

But the railway went ahead and the last section, between Mont Joli and Campbellton, was completed in June, 1876. The first through train from Halifax arrived in Lévis on July 6, 1876 carrying Leonard Tilley in a richly elaborate private car. The distance from Halifax to Rivière du Loup was 561 miles. The 125 miles from Rivière du Loup to Lévis was owned by the Grand Trunk, though it was acquired in 1879 by the Intercolonial for $1,500,000, about half the original cost.[5] In 1876 the journey from Halifax to Rivière du Loup took seventeen hours, at an average speed of thirty-two miles an hour.[6] The line was clearly in good working order.

As of June 30, 1878, the railway had cost $36,100,000. Its gross revenues for that fiscal year were $1,400,000, its working expenses were $1,600,000.[7] Although in the year ending June 30, 1881 gross earnings slightly exceeded working expenses, this was clearly not the arithmetic of financial success; but the obvious political, and many of the commercial advantages, could not be measured in balance sheets. Perhaps that is why the Conservative Government found it difficult to resist tinkering with freight rates.[8] Traffic grew steadily, except for a drop in 1879. Sugar volume from Halifax to Montreal doubled from 1878 to 1879 and doubled again in 1880.[9] The lineaments of trade were developing: flour, agricultural machinery, manufactured woolen and cotton goods eastward; coal, sugar, and imported fruit westward. The Grand Trunk, for example, used Nova Scotian coal as far west as Brockville, though Belleville, the next main divisional point, used American coal.[10] The gradual shift from the familiar ports of New York, Boston and Portland, began toward Halifax. The American ports continued to get Canadian trade, and always would. But the new management of the Intercolonial was efficient enough to go after business, and to get it.[11]

The Liberals could finish the Intercolonial quickly; the line was well under way when they came into power and they had to find only thirty-five per cent of the cost from general funds. With British Columbia it had been another story. Distance and the absence of detailed surveys made easterners reluctant to mortgage their souls for a railway through "trackless" mountains. The Northwest was, however, much more fundamental to the Government's purposes than was British Columbia. Mackenzie tried to bridge the gap between the Great Lakes and Red River. Here too the lack of sufficiently detailed information made immediate construction impossible. When Mackenzie came to power no part of the Pacific Railway, from Lake Nipissing to Vancouver Island, could have been put under contract. A great mass of exact data in the Surveys Office in Ottawa was destroyed by fire in December, 1873.

The Pacific Railway Act of 1874 was predicated on a 430-mile through line from Lake Superior to Red River. Within a year, as a result of dwindling government revenues, Mackenzie had changed his view in favour of the Dawson "road." It had been a Canadian government project, based upon a survey by S. J. Dawson, in 1859 and built after 1870. Road it was not; route it was. In 1873 some sixteen hundred people had made their way to Red

River by this route, and at full capacity in summer it could handle fifty travellers a day, each with a baggage allowance of two hundred pounds.[12]

In good weather and with good luck it was possible to get to Red River in nine days.[13] A more standard performance was three to four weeks. From Port Arthur's Landing the first stage was a wagon road of fifty miles to Lake Shebandowan; thence by boat to Lac des Milles Lacs, a lake described in high summer by one ecstatic Ontarian:

> [there] are tall and slender birch of snow white bark, and foliage of livid green, shading with an amber hue myriads of . . . coves; an endless variety of islands . . . some extending for miles, and others like gems of green in a watery bed of crystal clearness; some almost submerged, others towering boldly up by inaccessible cliffs. . . .[14]

But there was another side to these glories. Over the whole route there were some seventy loadings and unloadings. It was impossible to keep things dry. Boats leaked. But it was small wonder that real immigrants with real baggage would be tempted by Duluth, where the Lake Superior steamer docked

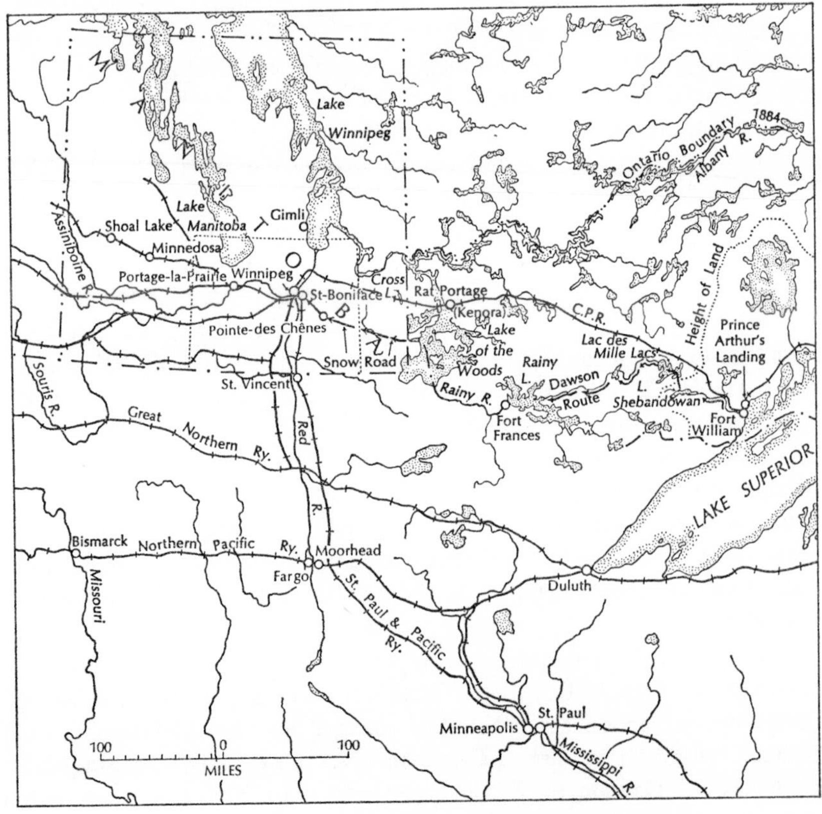

Manitoba Railway Complex and the Dawson Route

and where the Northern Pacific took one straight to Moorhead, Minnesota on the Red River, and so north to Winnipeg by Red River steamer.

Mackenzie's 1875 policy was to build railways at either end of the Dawson route, 45 miles westward toward Lake Shebandowan, 115 miles eastward from Red River to Rat Portage (called Keewatin, and later Kenora). Between Keewatin and Lake Shebandowan was that 270 miles of "virtually" continuous water navigation. Why not use the water? The rub lay of course in the "virtually." Either a water passage is continuous or it is not. Mackenzie did build locks at Fort Francis, but that left the seventy portages. However, government policy did not change until near the end of Mackenzie's régime.

On Mackenzie's insistence, Sandford Fleming had given up the Intercolonial early in 1874,[15] and confined himself to the Pacific Railway. His surveys in the Lake Superior-Red River section were far enough advanced by early 1875 to put the two end sections under contract for grading and bridging. The first, from Selkirk (the best place in Fleming's view to get a railway across the Red) to Cross Lake, just west of the present Ontario-Manitoba boundary ran seventy-six miles. The second ran northwest from Fort William thirty-three miles along the Dawson route. At Fort William, on June 1, 1875, the first sod for the Pacific Railway was officially turned. A year later track laying started. By 1876 and 1877 influences of the East were evident. Peterborough canoes were everywhere.[16] Nitro-glycerine was now used along the right of way. Dangerous stuff it was, carried through such country in fifty-pound cans:

> One poor lad who was carrying a can . . . tripped, and was blown to atoms, part of one foot, stuck in the fork of a tree about a hundred feet off being all that was found of him. A man lost his sight and one arm from merely striking a rock where some of the horrid stuff had been spilt.[17]

By the time Mackenzie went out of office in 1878 track at the western end had been contracted for the 112 miles from Selkirk to Keewatin, and at the eastern end 113 miles from Fort William to English River. The "water stretches" policy had fallen into utter discredit, and Mackenzie had already advertised for tenders for the remaining 185 miles between English River and Keewatin. Much work had been expended, and nothing very usable had so far emerged. Emigrants to Red River went mainly by Duluth, and there American land agents subjected them to all sorts of temptations and misrepresentations to persuade them to go elsewhere than to Manitoba. Hanging out "Information for British emigrants," and a British flag, was a favourite device.[18] Even the official visits of Scottish and English tenant farmers, sponsored by J. H. Pope under Macdonald in the early 1880's, went by Duluth. All that can be said for the "water stretches" policy is that it postponed the necessity of completing a difficult railway line at a difficult time. And postponement of such necessities was what Mackenzie was after.

The Pembina branch from St. Boniface to Emerson on the border was more useful. The Macdonald government had cancelled a contract just before it fell.[19] A new contract was made and grading began in 1874. But that too took an interminable time; it was October 9, 1877 before Hill and Kittson's stern wheeler appeared off Winnipeg with a locomotive, the *Countess of Dufferin*, six flat cars and a caboose towed on barges. Even that did not put the railway into operation. In 1878, Mackenzie tried to pass an act allowing the leasing of the Pembina branch to George Stephen (acting on behalf of Hill, Kittson, Donald Smith, and himself of the St. Paul, Minneapolis and Manitoba Railway), with which the Pembina branch was connected in November, 1878.

Mackenzie's attempt to lease the branch produced an interesting debate in the Commons. Macdonald protested that Stephen would thus acquire a monopoly of Northwest traffic, and prevent any other line reaching Manitoba. Freight rates would be wholly uncompetitive. Mackenzie in turn defended Stephen and the lease.[20] Macdonald disliked Donald Smith, and as far as he was concerned the lease was a reward for Smith's having supported Mackenzie one momentous night in November, 1873. The Senate defeated Mackenzie's bill, and all Stephen got was running rights. Macdonald's crowing over that defeat led to the shameful scene at prorogation that year.[21]

Finally, on December 3, 1878, the first train steamed out of St. Boniface for the border. The *Guelph Herald* was exuberant:

> Three days from Winnipeg! In mid-winter too! . . . The iron horse has opened up a new era for the Manitobans, and the blessings of civilisation will flow upon them in car loads. . . . Oysters will tumble from $1 to $3 a can to a price at which as many as two may be used in an ordinary stew without bankrupting the restaurateur. Apples will cease to be objects of curiosity, and will be banished from private museums. . . . Bachelors will be enabled to import and marry their "Ontayreo" girls at all seasons of the year. . . .[22]

The Pembina branch was not very grand. There was not a water tower in the whole sixty-three miles and for lack of a turn-table at St. Boniface, the engine was compelled to make one of the trips backwards.[23] The train was scheduled to leave St. Boniface at 4:30 A.M., (it more often did not) and the traveller left his hotel in Winnipeg by horse-bus at 3:00 A.M. C. J. Brydges went over the line in 1879 as passenger and found himself very uneasy indeed on the three large trestle bridges.[24] Nevertheless, the Pembina branch made money. The section from Emerson to Selkirk and on the main line eastward to Cross Lake were opened to traffic in February, 1880. Within five months gross earnings were running thirty per cent over working expenses, despite the fact that the *Countess of Dufferin* could not cope with the snow drifts and had to be reinforced with four Intercolonial veterans from Moncton.[25] A year later, on a section of line that now included Keewatin (Kenora) and Portage la Prairie as well as Emerson, gross earnings were running twenty-five per cent over working expenses.[26] However, even under government auspices, the Pacific Railway clearly could not afford competition from prospective local lines. Fleming spoke firmly against allowing it early in 1879:

> Applications are now being made to Parliament for Private Bills . . . to construct railways in various directions in Manitoba and the North-West Territories . . . it will prove to be a grave mistake if railway companies receive the necessary power to establish lines as they have been constructed in other parts of Canada; without forecast; without due consideration of the actual requirements of the country as a whole. . . . I conceive that the prudent course will be not to allow the passage of Private Railway Bills for Manitoba and the North-West, until a general railway scheme be deliberately and carefully matured.[27]

On April 30, 1881, this government railway, its prospects for profit, its hope for monopoly, were all turned over to the new Canadian Pacific Railway Company.[28]

By then Manitoba was doing very well. Winnipeg's population in 1873 had been about 2,500 and grew to 8,000 in 1881. In July, 1874 the Toronto *Globe's* correspondent reported that rents in Winnipeg were such as to realize the cost of a building in three years.[29] Some of this real estate boom was undoubtedly the result of speculative fever aroused by the beginning of work on the Pembina branch; but population growth accounted for much more. Consequently, Mackenzie's railway policy only aroused general irritation in the province, especially in Winnipeg. The ponderous progress from the east, the interminable time to get the Pembina branch going, and the choice of Selkirk, twenty-three miles north of Winnipeg, for the important crossing of the Red River, all caused concern. No wonder in 1877 a Conservative association was formed in Winnipeg. A meeting was held at the California Hotel, run by a redoubtable figure called Old Man Wheeler. Judge D. M. Walker and G. H. Ham, the organizers, arrived early and decided to find out what the old man's politics were. The Judge asked,

> "Wheeler, what are your politics?"
> "Oh, I don't mind," he replied, "I'll take a little Scotch."

Winnipeg was a cheerful, yeasty place in those years.[30]

In 1881 Manitoba's population reached 63,000, based in part on the enlarged boundaries of that year. The character of the population had also changed as was reflected in the shift in constituency representation in the Manitoba Assembly. In 1874 there were ten Catholic constituencies and fourteen Protestant ones in the Assembly; in 1878, six Catholic and eighteen Protestant. Of the twenty-four members of 1878, six were born in Red River, seven were born in Ontario, three in Quebec, five in England, and one each in New Brunswick, Scotland and Ireland.[31] The immigration of French Canadians from Quebec and New England could not begin to keep pace with the immigration from Ontario. And non-English immigrants, the Mennonites, the Icelanders, changed still more the character of the province from what Cartier and Ritchot had envisaged.

In March, 1873 a volcanic eruption in the mountains of northern Iceland laid pumice two to three inches deep over an area of twenty-five hundred square miles.[32] Gimli, on the western shore of Lake Winnipeg, was established late in 1875, and a large group of Icelanders arrived in the summer of 1876. They did not have an easy time of it, first with scurvy and then with small pox, despite $80,000 assistance from the Mackenzie government – to be repaid at six per cent interest.[33]

The Mennonites, German-speaking settlers from the Ukraine, had done rather better. They had first settled in 1875. The total Mennonite population was seven thousand by 1877, with a large colony at Rat River, east of the Red, about half-way to the American border. The account of this sober, industrious people given to the House of Commons Committee in 1878, is heartwarming:

> ... these people were put down on the naked prairie in the middle of the summer, barely three years ago, about 14 miles distant from any wood, and at a still greater distance and out of sight of any human habitation. They had to dig wells for water for their daily use on their arrival, and sleep, with their women and children, under the shelter of their waggons. They broke a little sod for the beginning of a crop the first year, and built temporary huts or houses . . . the first winter. They subsequently built the substantial houses and outbuildings of the villages we saw . . . besides carrying on the large farming operations . . . and besides furnishing the Winnipeg market with eggs, poultry and other farm produce. . . . The secret of this result I found to be that every man, woman and child in the settlement is a producer. We saw women ploughing in the fields as we drove into the settlement. We next saw a woman thatching the roof of a building . . . a girl plastering the outside of a house. . . . We saw very young children take out and bring in the cattle . . . we saw men, women, and children going out into the fields to work before the morning was grey.[34]

Despite substantial increases in population the administrative establishment was too elaborate for the revenues or the needs of the province. Mackenzie suggested confidentially to Lieutenant-Governor Morris that the whole provincial apparatus be dismantled, so great was the disparity between expenditures and revenues.[35] That Manitoba would not accept. Instead in 1876, Legislative Council was abolished on condition of a $100,000 increase in Manitoba's annual subsidy. But Manitoba was nothing if not ebullient. The University of Manitoba was chartered the following year!

The land of Manitoba was not Manitoba's. The Federal government kept it until 1930 for Dominion purposes, for railways, for colonization and immigration. The Manitoba Act of 1870 granted to the half-breeds, French and Scottish, as their share of the Indian title, 1,400,000 acres of Dominion land to be allotted to the children of the half-breed families. At the same time the Act confirmed existing half-breed, and white, titles in the river lot farms along the Red and Assiniboine. One can still see the result coming to Winnipeg by air, the strip farms surrounded on the west bank, and on the east, by the great square blocks of the Canadian survey.

The half-breed children attempted so far as they could, to take their acreage behind these river lot farms, where there was some woods and contiguity with their parents. But that land was valuable, some of it already alienated, and hundreds of claims and counterclaims ensued, both about river lot farms and new grants. Nothing much was done about these claims until Mackenzie's time, and it was 1880 before most were settled, and claims continued to come in after that. In the meantime the land was tied up.[36] Altogether the half-breed children got about 240 acres each.[37]

In 1874 the half-breed heads of families were given $160 in land scrip toward the purchase of additional Dominion land. The children had not received scrip; but the heads of families who did get it, tended to sell it to speculators.*

The Dominion Lands Act of 1872 was a homestead act. Every applicant could acquire one-quarter section, 160 acres, of free Government land for a ten dollar registration fee with title conditional upon three years' residence. It was said that the Government was betting the settler ten dollars that he could not live on 160 acres for three years! But free government land was only available in the even-numbered sections of the township. The odd-numbered sections were government lands available for sale, and in later years were often used as railway grant lands. There were other exclusions also. Sections 11 and 29 in each township were set aside as school lands, that is, the capital sum acquired from their sale would be used as endowment to support schools in the province or territory concerned. Section 8 and three-quarters of Section 26 were Hudson's Bay Company lands, part of the 1869 arrangement by which the Company acquired one-twentieth of the land of the fertile belt.[38] Mackenzie had tried to buy this back for Canada in 1876.

* I have simplified here. The half-breed children who made supplementary claims were given scrip, presumably because their claims were now sufficiently old (as doubtless the children themselves were) to be treated as were the half-breed heads of families.

All this says nothing of the quality of the land or of the difficulties of farming it. The Métis and Scotch half-breeds had not taken to farming. It gave them food and hay, but their way of life was the buffalo hunt or later, as packers and boatmen for the Hudson's Bay Company. Easterners who first came to the prairie were appalled at being so far from wood and water. Poplar and cottonwood were available, and though it worked well enough for house-building and for fuel, there was not enough of it, particularly in the districts farther west. Settlement at first therefore shied away from bald prairie toward the wooded areas to the north.[39] There were a variety of natural ills to cope with: periodic visitations of grasshoppers – a bad one in 1875, when some settlements in eastern Manitoba lost not only wheat but even potato plants; the usual spring danger of flood along the Red River valley; and hordes of insects that came with late May. Mosquitoes arrived in clouds, especially in the Red River valley. It was bad enough for men; it was worse for animals. "The tender skin around the eyes of horses and oxen gathers moving crusts of torment; a rider rubbing a hand across his mount's face brings up a pulpy mess of crushed insects and blood. And horseflies, . . . a horse will flinch from the bite of one as if he has been nicked by a knife blade."[40]

The boom in Manitoba land, as distinct from Winnipeg real estate, began after 1875. Basically the cause was new milling methods. The sober, blunt words of Ontario millers before the Mills Committee of 1876 mark a revolution.

> They [the Americans] have educated their people to use a very superior article which they are making from their spring wheat, which is giving better satisfaction than any flour they can make from fall wheat. . . . [It] is called Minnesota Spring Wheat.[41]

James J. Hill remarked in 1877 to the Immigration Committee that that wheat was so popular it was impossible to over-produce it.[42] As early as 1876 the preference for hard western spring wheat in the east was enough to threaten the sale of Canadian flour, still made from soft Ontario winter wheat.[43] What Minnesota could do, Manitoba could do better. The superb harvest of 1876 was the first in Manitoba to yield a real surplus. The variety, Red Fife, yielded about twenty-five bushels to the acre, and, though the straw was useless, the grain was plump and hard. In 1880 one expert observer from England reported the crop that he saw – an average one – had been sown on May 22 on virgin soil imperfectly plowed, and was dead ripe within 105 days.[44] The soil of Manitoba is pure vegetable loam, black as ink, and feet thick. Hill, with only a touch of exaggeration, told the Committee in 1877 that Manitoba land was the richest he had seen in North America.[45] Manure was pointless; the farmers used to trundle it out onto river ice in the winter, until Manitoba law prohibited it.

Agricultural machinery grew in sophistication. By 1880 self-binding reapers had already made their appearance, and chilled steel plows, first from John Deere, then from Massey, from Harris, and other implement manufacturers in Ontario, soon became essential. In 1877 a shipment of Manitoba wheat went to A. W. Ogilvie's mill at Goderich, Ontario, via Duluth. St. Boniface got its first grain elevator in 1880. By 1877 Red Fife had at last replaced brown beaver as the great Manitoba staple.[46]

The Northwest Territories of Canada were set up in the Act of 1869. They were called Territor*ies* because they included Rupert's Land, the watershed of Hudson's Bay, and the whole watershed of the Mackenzie and other Arctic rivers. In 1869, the new Northwest Territories were very large indeed, from the Labrador boundary to the British Columbia border, northward from the height of land in Quebec and Ontario and from the forty-ninth parallel in the West, to the Arctic. The Northwest Territories Act was designed as a temporary arrangement to replace the Hudson's Bay Company rule. Because the Macdonald government was utterly in the dark about the needs and problems of the area, details were to be thought through later. The system was due to commence upon the Hudson's Bay Company surrender, scheduled for November 30, 1869. But Canada refused to accept it then, and it was not till June 22, 1870 that the surrender was accepted by the British Government, and the territory turned over to Canada on July 15. The delay was caused by the Red River Rebellion, 1869-70.

The Rebellion altered the Government's legislative arrangements for the Northwest Territories in only one particular: it created the postage-stamp province of Manitoba. Without Riel's rebellion it would not have come into existence at that time, and was not intended to. Manitoba being created, however, the rest of the vast Northwest Territories remained under the Act of 1869, that "temporary" arrangement. It was re-enacted in 1871 as permanent without any alteration whatever.[47]

The Northwest Territories were governed by a Lieutenant-Governor and Council. Inevitably perhaps, the Lieutenant-Governor of Manitoba simply added his Northwest duties to his other functions. The Council was not constituted until the end of 1872, and was composed mainly of Manitobans, owing to the difficulty of arranging meetings. By the time Mackenzie came to power, the marvellous vacuity of the 1869/1871 Act had been amended, and the Northwest Council was given explicit power to establish ordinances for the peace, order and good government of the Territories, provided that these were approved by the Dominion Cabinet.

In the first session of the Northwest Council, March, 1873, three ordinances were passed. Nothing was heard from Ottawa. Finally it was discovered that the proceedings of the Council had been mislaid in Macdonald's office for six months, and at the end of October, 1873, Lieutenant-

Governor Morris learned that only one of the ordinances had been approved.[48] Nor was the Mackenzie régime much better, as the Council had reason to complain in a stern protest in December, 1874. Since the Dominion government was so unconscionably dilatory, the Council led a frustrated existence. Mackenzie seems to have felt that Macdonald's commitments to the West, to British Columbia, to Manitoba, to the Northwest Territories, were altogether disproportionate to their present value. Future they had, no doubt; that was old Grit doctrine; but present realities were another matter.

A belated attempt to deal with these was made in the Act of 1875, to come into force in October, 1876. The old, appointed Council was replaced with a new, smaller one, with provision to acquire elected representatives on the basis of one member per thousand voters per thousand square miles. The Council could now pass ordinances without prior approval from Ottawa. It had no power to impose taxes, and school districts depended entirely upon local support. The Dominion government followed the prescription laid down for Manitoba, and separate schools for Roman Catholics or Protestants were allowed. This was followed in 1877 by the official use of both French and English in Council proceedings.[49] More dramatically, the capital was shifted westward, from Winnipeg, along the line projected by Fleming for the Pacific Railway, to Battleford, now in communication by telegraph (more or less) with Edmonton and Winnipeg. The Lieutenant-Governorships of Manitoba and the Northwest Territories were separated and David Laird became the Northwest's first separate Lieutenant-Governor (1876-1881).

The new Council's appointed members were three English-speaking stipendiary magistrates with some experience of the Northwest. Despite the urging of Lieutenant-Governor Morris no Métis or English-speaking half-breed was appointed. Laird took this up on his arrival at Battleford, and appointed Pascal Breland. But Breland was old and ineffective, for he had spent most of his time in Manitoba. Amedée Forget was Clerk of the Council, but he could hardly count politically. There was a point in Morris's private letter to Langevin in 1878, "It is a crying shame that the half-breeds have been ignored. It will result in trouble and is most unjust."[50] The half-breeds were, as Lord Dufferin said during his official visit to Manitoba in 1877, "the ambassadors between east and west."[51] The absence of really savage struggles between whites and Indians was due in great part to their influence. They were indispensable at Indian treaty negotiations. The American consul at Winnipeg, J. W. Taylor, said as much in 1878 in a letter to Washington:

> . . . the extensive intermarriage of the English, Scotch and French residents – prominently the officers and employees of the Hudson's Bay Company – with the Indian women, diffusing over the whole country in the lapse of several generations a population of Métis or mixed bloods equal in number to the Indians and exerting over their aboriginal kindred a degree of moral

and physical control which I find it difficult to illustrate, but which I regard as a happy Providence for the Dominion of Canada.[52]

In the 1870's there were about 145,000 Indians in Canada; 4,000 in the Maritime provinces, 26,000 in Quebec and Ontario, 34,000 in the Northwest Territories, Manitoba and Keewatin, and 82,000 in British Columbia.[53] Seven treaties, all western, were negotiated between 1871 and 1896, and for convenience they can be listed:

Treaty No. 1	Stone Fort	July 25, 1871	Swampy Crees, Chippewas
Treaty No. 2	Manitoba Post	Aug. 17, 1871	Chippewas
Treaty No. 3	North-West Angle	Oct. 3, 1873	Mainly Ojibways
Treaty No. 4	Qu'Appelle	Sept. 15, 1874	Part of Crees and Ojibways
Treaty No. 5	Lake Winnipeg	Sept. 24, 1875	Swampy Crees and Chippewas
Treaty No. 6	Fort Carlton	Aug. 23, 1876	Plain and Wood Crees
Treaty No. 7	Blackfoot Crossing	Sept. 22, 1877	Blackfeet (Blood, Piegan, Sarcees, Stoney)[54]

The Treaties were the formal cession of Indian title to the government of Canada, with reservations kept for the Indians' own use, and with Indian rights to hunt over the ceded land retained, except where land had been privately acquired. Payments were made at $12 per head, plus an annual payment of $5 for every man, woman and child, with special grants of $25 for the Chiefs and $15 for the Councillors. Lands allotted for reserves in the agricultural areas were about one section for each family of five, with some agricultural implements provided, as spelled out in detail in the various Treaties. It was a system of band reserves, not always small, but scattered. In the woodlands of Keewatin similar arrangements were made, but the Indians there preferred to hunt and fish. The Government agreed to prohibit all liquor, and the Indians agreed to respect the Queen's peace.[55] The whole was then duly executed in full ceremony, with silver medals and elaborate uniforms for the Chiefs and Councillors.

Such treaties were not easy to negotiate; they took infinite patience, understanding, and time. The Fort Carlton Treaty took from August 18, 1876, through the day of the signing, August 23, to August 26 when there was a final celebration. Lieutenant-Governor Morris and the Mounted Police were in continuous attendance, often in full regalia. The supplies of food, clothing, money (usually in uncut sheets of one-dollar bills) were enormous. In short, the logistics of treaty-making were monumental.

At Fort Carlton there was a new departure. It was Morris's last treaty before he stepped down, and it was negotiated with some skill. The clue to Morris's success was the inclusion of seed grain, and other provisions, in the event of Indians' being afflicted with pestilence or famine. In 1876 there were good reasons for the Indian insistence on the new clauses. They were very conscious of their increasing vulnerability owing to the dwindling of the buffalo. David Mills, Minister of the Interior, objected to the new clauses and censured the Commissioners. Morris was angry; he pointed out that Treaty No. 6 dealt with new problems, that there was "no cast iron form of Treaty which can be imposed on these people." Further, any real calamity among the Indians "has ever been regarded as the duty of the State to alleviate." The Hudson's Bay Company had acted in this paternal fashion; the Canadian Government could hardly do less.[56] It was accepted by Ottawa, as it had to be, but with the poor grace symptomatic of a general attitude of easterners who had never seen the West and who knew nothing of it at first hand.[57] Morris, on the other hand, had negotiated every Indian Treaty since No. 3, and had helped revise the first and second. He had a great deal of knowledge and *savoir faire* on Indian subjects. Mills' viewpoint was characteristic not only of the Mackenzie government, but, even more, of the Macdonald government. There was short-sightedness and downright miserliness in Ottawa's attitude, but it is fair to add that in the East the problem was wholly new, and the orbit of political thinking scarcely included the West as yet. Moreover, the West had little real political power. In 1874 Manitoba had four seats, British Columbia six; even with the four members that the Northwest Territories received in 1887, the West in 1896 had only seventeen members in a House of over two hundred.[58] And the prospect of having to feed twenty-five thousand prairie Indians for any length of time was one before which any Canadian government in the late nineteenth century might have balked.

More spectacular than Treaty No. 6 was the great Blackfoot treaty of 1877, concluded at Blackfoot Crossing September 19, 1877. It was a glorious day: a great arch of blue sky, air like crystal; the cottonwoods and aspens along the Bow River blazing yellow in the sunshine; the river itself still milky from the mountains, with the golden uplands lifting behind it; the great camp, the lines of smoke-browned tepees, the ubiquitous kettles tended by dark Indian women, the smell of the cottonwood campfires; and the mingled sounds of Indian drums and the Mounted Police band.[59]

The North West Mounted Police had had an eventful four years since the first groups had arrived at the Stone Fort in 1873.[60] The Commissioner was Lt.-Col. G. A. French (1873-1876), a British officer seconded to the Canadian militia after 1871. His designation was a clear indication of the civilian front the Force was to present; instead of Colonel, Major, Captain, Lieutenant, Sergeant, the names Commissioner, Superintendent, Inspector, Sub-Inspector, and Constable were used. The Force was not subject to the Queen's Regulations and Articles of War; its strong discipline was enforced by virtue of powers conferred by statute, and strengthened in 1875. The criminal jurisdiction of the very senior officers was that of stipendiary magistrates; they could hear, determine, and sentence in summary fashion, without jury, charges for theft or assault. The Force had formidable powers for the maintenance of public order. Much depended upon their reputation for honest dealing and fair justice.

French soon saw that the 150 men would be inadequate. Two hundred additional recruits were gathered over the winter of 1873-74 in the east, and the whole force assembled on June 20, 1874 at Fort Dufferin. They were uniformed with the scarlet norfolk jacket, dark cavalry breeches with a scarlet stripe down the side, white helmet, cavalry boots and spurs. Revolvers were carried, and in a bucket holster on the saddle, Snider carbines* (later Winchesters). The men were nearly all easterners, often farm men, young and fairly fit; but they were tenderfoots by prairie standards, unfamiliar with the ways (and the tricks) of the prairie. That they were easterners was not wholly a disadvantage however. Their views of the Indian, doubtless coloured or distorted, were basically uncommitted and unprejudiced. This dispassionateness was to be the great asset of the Force, an asset it never really lost.

The North West Mounted Police were to establish Canadian control of, and police, the western plains, particularly what is now southern Alberta. Few trails headed that way; most routes went northwest from Winnipeg, Por-

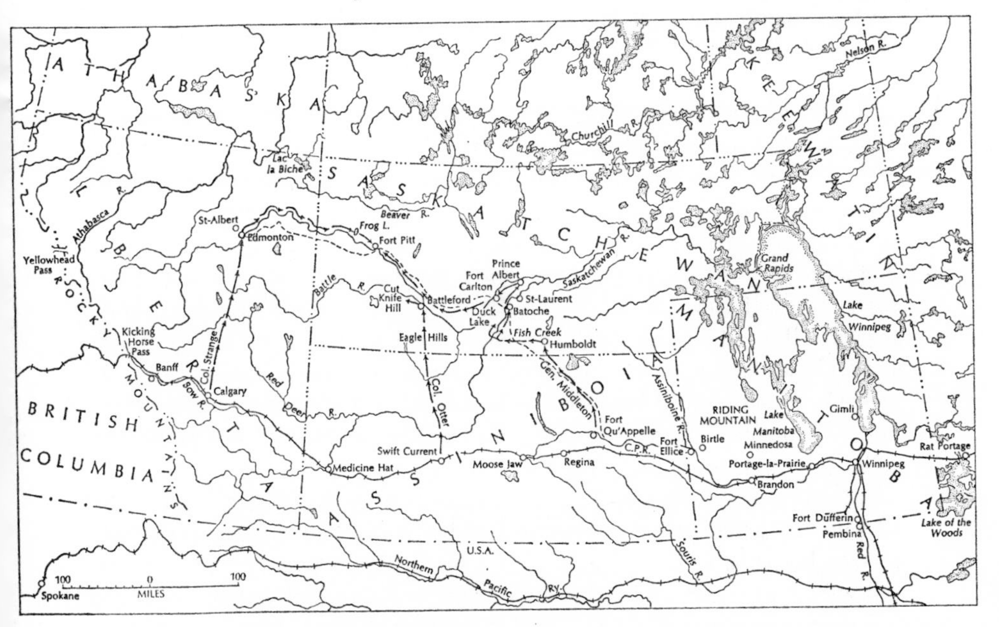

Western Trails and Treks, 1872-1874

* A carbine was a short rifle designed for cavalry.

tage, toward Fort Ellice (at the junction of the Qu'Appelle and Assiniboine) and Fort Carlton. The southern route lay through virtually uncharted country. The Force left Fort Dufferin July 9, 1874 and headed due west, just north of the border, 318 men with horses, carts, and supplies. 1874 was a very dry summer, and grasshoppers had reduced what pasturage there was. The expedition made about eighteen miles a day. By July 24, 270 miles west of Fort Dufferin, near the upper reaches of the Souris, the horses were tired out from heat, bad water, and a shortage of oats. A prolonged rest was called to help horses and men recover from dysentery. But the going got worse; by early August the Métis guide had gone beyond the country he knew.

By mid-September they had reached the country south of present-day Medicine Hat, but were in desperate condition. The weather had by now turned cold; and a blizzard would have decimated animals and men alike. Ice covered the sloughs, and if snow came and covered up the buffalo chips (dung) there would be no fuel either. In his diary Sub-Inspector Denny entered a laconic, "Can't go much farther," on September 16.[61] Luckily, two days later a sheltered camping ground and pasture were found beyond the Milk River, close to West Butte, almost on the forty-ninth parallel. The Police had seen no forts, no whisky traders, nothing. The nine hundred miles behind them were strewn with broken carts and abandoned horses and oxen. Yet everyone knew they were coming and had marked their progress (often enough inaccurately) – the Indians, the whisky traders, even the Americans in Fort Benton.

What the Mounted Police needed in September 1874 was supplies and accurate information. Colonel French got both in Fort Benton, Montana. I. G. Baker, a substantial and reliable merchant began, there and then, an association with the Mounted Police that continued until the C.P.R. came to Alberta in 1883. Supplies and guides were acquired. One guide remained with the Mounted Police until his death in 1895. The son of a Scots trader and a Piegan woman, he was Jerry Potts, the most famous guide and interpreter the Police ever had. He read the prairie like a book, this short, bow-legged half-breed, and the Mounted Police were grateful to him to the end.[62] Potts chose the site of Fort Macleod (named after the Assistant Commissioner), on a sheltered lowland on the Old Man River, twenty miles from Fort Whoop-Up. There, with winter drawing on, the log fort was built. Fort Whoop-Up was found to be "as innocent of whisky as a temperance hall."[63] The man in temporary charge of the fort even gave the officers dinner. The first whisky arrest was made late in October, 1874: two wagons of alcohol, sixteen horses, a variety of guns, and a hundred and twenty buffalo robes. All were confiscated under the law of the Dominion Parliament.

So came the North West Mounted Police to the West. The whisky traders vanished. The presence of the Police as the embodiment of the law was virtually all that was needed. Americans left their gun law cheerfully behind them when they found the country well policed. They took out Canadian brands, paid for Canadian grazing leases, and conformed to Canadian customs. They were all but indistinguishable from Canadian ranchers to whom they can fairly be said to have taught the whole business.[64] The problems of the Mounted Police, then, were not the Americans, but learning to live with the West and the Indians, to be disciplined, cool-headed, strong, uncompromisingly self-reliant, to contain within oneself the skills and adaptability to survive.

The Mounted Police came at a critical time in the life of the prairie Indians. Whites and half-breeds, with the Winchester repeater, had taken a terrible toll of buffalo. Even the Métis took buffalo for their tongues or hump ribs and left the rest of the carcass to the sun and the prairie wind. Warnings sounded from 1873 onward. John Schultz told the House of Commons in 1876 that the Government of Canada could expect to deal before long with "a race of paupers rendered dangerous from want of food."[65] Father Lacombe believed the buffalo would be extinct by 1885. The burden of the problem fell upon the Indian affairs branch of the Department of the Interior and especially upon the Mounted Police.

Several posts were established. Fort Walsh on the southern side of the Cypress Hills controlled one of the main routes to the south, as did Fort Macleod. It was started in June 1875, and while it was being built an incident took place that showed the importance of uniform. Sioux arrived, driven over the border by American cavalry. They were friendly until they noticed two Mounted Police constables wearing parts of United States uniforms, purchased from American traders to replace worn-out parts of their own. The Sioux became excited; the Union Jack flying above notwithstanding, the Mounted Police were clearly Americans in disguise. Superintendent Walsh put on a brave front, but the position was tense until a large band of Crees arrived, and in the face of these old enemies the Sioux made off. The red uniform was an inspired idea. The instant impressiveness of the scarlet tunic was one major reason that the slim force of Mounted Police was so spectacularly successful. "One of the most visible aspects of the International boundary [in the west] was that it was a colour line: blue below, red above, blue for treachery and unkept promises, red for protection and the straight tongue."[66]

A post between Forts Macleod and Walsh in the south and Fort Edmonton in the north was needed, and after some reconnoitring, Fort Calgary was built in the fall of 1875. Cecil Denny, then a Sub-Inspector, described his first view of the Bow River valley in September, 1875:

> The view from the hill on the north side of the Bow . . . amazed us. Before us lay a lovely valley, flanked on the south by rolling hills. Thick woods bordered the banks of both streams [the Bow and the Elbow]; to the west towered mountains with their snowy peaks. . . . Buffalo in large bands

> grazed in the valley, but of man there was no sign. . . . Our first sight of this enchanting spot was never to be forgotten . . . by far the most beautiful we had seen since our arrival in the West. . . .[67]

Fort Calgary was a good site for trade, just sixty miles west of Blackfoot crossing, and in 1876 some twelve thousand buffalo robes were traded there.

By the end of 1876 the North West Mounted Police had established themselves in several key positions across the west, a total of 309 men and 287 horses; 112 officers and men at Fort Macleod; 102 at Fort Walsh; 37 at Fort Calgary; 22 at Fort Saskatchewan; 33 at Swan River; and sprinklings of other detachments at a few smaller posts. But what a territory and how few men!

With the gradual disappearance of buffalo it became possible to turn cattle loose on the open range.* Southern Alberta was as well suited for cattle as it had been for buffalo. The country in summer was a vast pasture and the grasses cured themselves in the wind and sun of fall; the few inches of snow that came in winter were just enough to keep the grass moist and cattle could easily graze through it.[68] A blizzard might cover up the grass, but it was usually conveniently followed by a chinook to melt the crusted snow. It was a precarious balance, but it worked more often than not.

The Mounted Police thus stablilized an otherwise dangerous position. In later years Canada took pride in her Indian policy, especially in the light of American experience; but that was owing more to history and luck than to foresight. The Hudson's Bay Company had co-operated with and looked after the Indians who supplied them with their trade. At once a Company and a monopoly, it could afford to do so. Then too, the accidents of history brought the Mounted Police just three years after the Hudson's Bay Company had been bought out of its proprietory commitments. Finally the Canadian Shield provided a superb buffer between the burgeoning white population of the east and the Indians of the west. By the time western expansion began in the later 1870's, the Indian treaties had been made, and some attempt to systematize their change of life had begun. Canadian pioneers in the west moved into a land already partly stablized. And if the Ottawa government had not been so niggardly and thoughtless in handling western issues, the Saskatchewan rising of 1885 – very much connected with Indian unrest – would never have happened.

For the problem of controlling the American West lay less in controlling the Indians than in controlling the whites. "How do you keep your whites in order?"[69] David Mills was asked by Carl Schurz, the American Secretary of the Interior, when the two met in Washington in August, 1877 to discuss the crisis with the Sioux. Mills was astute enough to seize upon that question as the nub of the American problem. But the problem was never, to any degree, a Canadian one.

* Buffalo would have taken cattle into their herds, with the bulls being killed.

As white settlement developed Indian life deteriorated. The years 1878-1880 were probably the worst of all in western Indian history. At Fort MacLeod seven thousand Indians were fed in 1879 on what scanty rations the police could find. Treaty stores were broken into at Fort Qu'Appelle in June, 1879. In the desperation of these starvation years, in the fear of an Indian rising, the Canadian government, on the basis of the Treaty provisions in Numbers 6 and 7, sent supplies to Fort MacLeod and Fort Walsh. Edgar Dewdney was made Indian Commissioner of the Northwest Territories and given broad discretionary powers. But this was only the beginning; the main problem still remained to plague the Macdonald government in the 1880's. The conditions that brought that government to power were not of course western at all, but were embedded in what was still the political and economic core of Canada, the east.

CHAPTER 5

Depression, Protection and the Resurgence of Sir John Macdonald 1874-1878

The picture of the period 1874 to 1896 as one of economic stagnation relieved by a few bright years in the early 1880's, is distinctly misleading, and in several significant respects probably wrong. In the absence of detailed statistics, the concept Gross National Product is difficult to apply to the late nineteenth century; but, although O. J. Firestone's figures are necessarily tentative, they give a quite different perspective. Between 1873 and 1896 the G.N.P. of Canada rose from $710 million to $1,800 million. In other words, in 1896 it was 2.5 times what it was in 1874. Canada's population increased from 3.7 million in 1871 to about 5.1 million in 1896. Putting the figures another way, the output of goods and services, *per capita*, increased by 83%.[1] Savings deposits in Canadian chartered banks increased 2.5 times between 1874 and 1896, from $77 million to $193 million.[2] And the purchasing power of the dollar increased 13% from 1870 to 1900.[3] From 1870 to 1896, exports rose from $65 million to $116 million; imports from $67 million to $105 million. Railway mileage in operation grew from 2,600 to 16,400 in the same period, and manufactures went from $217 million per year to nearly $500 million.

In this perspective the growth of the country in terms of the means of production and internal growth, was substantial.[4] We think of present-day Canada as growing rapidly; the G.N.P. is growing at about 4% to 5% per year; between 1873 and 1896 G.N.P. rose 4% per year. Canadians at the time, however, measured the growth of their country by that crude but convenient yardstick, the census. By that standard Canada's growth was only modest, about 40%, especially compared with an American population increase in the same period of 100%. The other available yardstick was trade, imports and exports. These too gave a modest overall increase, and in certain periods, notably the Mackenzie years, they showed a positive decline. It was easy at the time to conclude that the country was not progressing very quickly; some Canadians decided eventually that it was not progressing at all, and reinforced their conclusions by citing the movement of Canadians to the United States.

The American transcontinental nation dated, however, from 1847 when California was acquired; the Canadian dated from 1871. The Americans got their transcontinental railway in 1869; Canadians got theirs in 1885. Canada developed later than the United States; Canadians at the time expected too much too soon. They were forever looking to the south, and wanting to realize at once what the United States had done, or was doing. Given this perennial juxtaposition – they are still at it – it was understandable that some Canadians at the time should have been restless and dissatisfied.

The whole position was grossly distorted by partisan jeremiads. The Conservatives had been rather discreet in the 1870's about criticizing the difficulties of Canada; after all, they had, between 1867 and 1873, committed the country to substantial expenditures for railways and other forms of national enterprise, and could not afford to utter cries of woe. The Liberals, who inherited it all in the face of declining government revenues, could, even in office, bewail the outrageous burdens that the Conservatives had placed upon the country; and in the eighteen years of Conservative rule from 1878 to 1896 the Liberals had an open field for all kinds of criticism, justified and unjustified, temperate and intemperate, responsible and irresponsible.

Liberal views had one justification in that the federal government's revenues depended heavily upon import duties. In 1873, 75% of Dominion revenue came from customs; in 1896, 70%.[5] This proportion continued until the introduction of the income tax – really until 1918. Consequently, revenues were controlled not by the internal business of the country but by what the country imported. In earlier years there was a substantial correlation between the state of business within the country and imports; but as the country's business and manufacturing developed, the correlation between business and imports weakened. To determine the economic condition of Canada by means of import duties was a good enough rule in the 1850's and 1860's; it was less accurate in the 1870's and 1880's.

It is not surprising that historians, who must rely heavily upon contemporary documentation, should have concluded that in the period 1873-1896 the economy was in trouble most of the time and that prosperous years were infrequent. But all that period manufacturers and businessmen quietly went on making money. The absence of really comprehensive studies makes generalization treacherous, but chapter headings in a new business history of the John Northway Company of Toronto point out the contrast between the old concepts and the realities of business: "Steady growth in a depression, 1873-1888," "Anticipating the Laurier boom, 1889-1895."[6] Massey, Harris, Frost and other agricultural implement manufacturers also grew steadily. In Merrill Denison's words, "The depression [of 1874-79], however, seems to have had little or no effect on the implement firms with which this narrative is concerned."[7] Iron and steel and their products were a good general indicator of the growing sophistication of Canadian industry. In the 1870's Canadian production equalled imports; in the 1880's it was nearly double imports; in the 1890's the ratio was three to one.[8] William Kilbourn's history of the Steel Company of Canada makes the same point that the others do, if anything more forcefully.[9]

Central Canadian business owed its prosperity to its successful conquest of the market in the Maritimes between 1867 and 1874. One agricultural implement manufacturer in Ontario said in 1874 that seven-eighths of the scythes, forks, and other tools used in Nova Scotia and New Brunswick came from Ontario and Quebec. A. S. Whiting, of Oshawa, in the same business, denied that figure, saying it was only one-half.[10] But even that meant a revolution. Testimony before the Mills Committee of 1876 showed clearly that in some lines central Canadian manufacturers were able not only to drive Maritimers out of business but also to force the Americans out of the Maritime market. F. T. Frost's evidence is revealing:

> The principal [agricultural] machines imported [into Canada from the United States] are in the Maritime Provinces. They come there from Boston, but for the last three years we have been establishing agencies there, and wherever we have gone the American manufacturers have retired from the field simply for the reason that we can undersell them. They make a very nice machine; it is the same [type of] machine . . . that we sell . . . there was one firm at Worcester, Mass., which took machines into Nova Scotia to Halifax from Boston. They sold there for $95 to $100 gold. We sent our machines of the same class down by Gult Port steamers to Pictou and sold them for $75.

Alfred Dymond, M.P. for North York asked D. McCrae, a Guelph manufacturer of woollen knit goods, "Confederation has practically given you the market of the Maritime Provinces?" McCrae's answer was short. "Yes," he said.[11]

Maritime members frequently complained. In the Senate, A. W. McLelan of Nova Scotia described the trade in 1875:

> Hon. Mr. McLELAN – I wish Hon. gentlemen could sometimes see in Nova Scotia the army of commercial travellers coming down from Ontario and Quebec,
>
> "Like a wolf on the fold,
> Hungry and hunting for 'gold.' "
>
> (Cries of oh! oh!)
>
> Hon. Mr. SIMPSON – It's poor pickings they find.
>
> Hon. Mr. McLELAN – Poor pickings indeed! Does the hon. gentleman know anything of the result? Has he ever seen the stream of agricultural produce and manufactured goods that all summer long pours down by steamer and sail on the Gulf and by the Grand Trunk *via* Portland to

> Halifax and St. John, and distributed all over the Provinces; and all paid for mainly by the expenditures in our ship yards and from the earnings of our ships.[12]

Undoubtedly much of the prosperity enjoyed by some central Canadian manufacturers came from the very fact of Confederation itself.

To proceed from here and label the cyclical depressions of 1874-9, 1884-7, 1893-5, as largely illusory would of course be a profound mistake. But the incidence of depressions (and booms) fell unevenly; some businesses failed, others flourished; some sections of the country thrived, others did not. Seen against the substantial growth of Canada over the whole twenty-five year period, the cyclical phenomena take on rather different proportions. They were associated with similar movements in the United States. The depression from 1873-78 in the United States, was reflected from 1874-79 in Canada. Any serious economic difficulty in the United States was bound to affect Canada, especially its export staples like lumber and wheat.

Exports to Britain developed markedly: the bad harvests in Britain and in Europe – owing to an unprecedented series of wet summers – gave a tremendous impetus to grain exports from the United States and Canada by the end of the 1870's. Rinderpest (a virulent cattle disease) hit British cattle in 1877; liver-rot in sheep in 1879; and in 1883 a terrible epidemic of hoof-and-mouth disease. All this produced a remarkable increase in Canadian export of live-stock to Britain in the later seventies. British agriculture never recovered economically from these disasters. Britain and Belgium, the two most heavily industrialized countries in Western Europe, did not impose duties on imported produce, they had become so dependent upon it. North American grain and cattle were cheaper than British, and moreover shipping rates dropped steadily owing to great improvements in marine engines.

There is thus an important distinction between long term economic growth and recurrent financial and trade depressions. The financial structure of Canada was not ill-designed for riding out cyclical economic storms, rather better designed perhaps than the institutions of the United States. There were two interrelated aspects to the Canadian financial structure, monetary policy and the operation of the banks.

The issue of Canadian money was governed by the Dominion Note Act of 1870 and the Currency Act of 1871. These established the basic framework of Canadian monetary policy until Canada went off the gold standard in 1914. Chartered banks were restricted to issuing notes of $5.00 and above. The Dominion government could issue notes below $5.00 up to a total of $9 million, with a reserve of twenty per cent of that amount in gold. Any issue of notes above $9 million had to carry with it an equal reserve in gold. In 1880 the Act was amended and the Government was authorized to issue $20,000,000 secured by fifteen per cent in gold and ten per cent in bonds guaranteed by the Imperial government. Except for a minor change in 1895, the basic structure remained essentially unchanged from 1871 to 1914.[13]

The system of banking had evolved under the sharp eye of the Colonial Office, and financial experimentation was not encouraged. The centralized banking principles of Hamilton's First Bank of the United States were a formative influence.[14] Canadian banking's association with staple production in lumber and wheat also encouraged a considerable degree of central control. Control of banks and banking was a power of the Dominion government, not of the provinces. The Bank Act of 1871 was the first permanent legislation on the subject, but even it was a consolidation of former practices.[15] One of the most interesting provisions of the Act was its ten-year charter principle, with simultaneous renewal of all bank charters, which kept even centrally operated chartered banks sensitive to public opinion.[16] Minimum capital was set at $500,000, at least one-fifth of which had to be subscribed before operations could start. Note issues were not to exceed paid-in-capital.* Stockholders were liable to double the face value of their shares in the event of failure. The banks survived the difficulties of 1874-79 remarkably well. In 1873 there were fifty chartered banks with 230 branches, in 1879 forty-four with 295 branches.[17] In 1896, there were thirty-seven banks with 533 branches. Some banks failed: in the main these figures represent growth and consolidation.

The revenues of the Canadian government had grown rapidly after 1867: from $11.6 million in 1867 they reached $20 million in 1873. At their low point in the Mackenzie years, in 1876, they declined only fifteen per cent from 1873. But the 1876 low had occurred even with a 2.5 per cent increase in the tariff in 1874; and with government commitments predicated upon continued growth, it was a hard enough row for Cartwright to manage.

To the declining revenues were added refinancing of maturing commitments, and some financing of new ones.[18] Canada's net direct debt in 1873, $134 million, cost nearly $6 million a year in interest. This meant that a sizeable 27 per cent of the government's tax revenues were required just to stand still. (In 1960 it was about 16 per cent.) However modest the decline in revenue was, the size of Canadian commitments made the Liberals fearful. Moreover, given their general sympathy with free trade doctrine, a substantial rise in the rate of the main source of government revenue, customs duties, was highly distasteful. The government faced an agonizing decision in 1876. Revenues were going to be down from 1875, even with the new 17.5 per cent tariff; James Young, Holton and some others had urged an increase to 22.5 per cent. Cartwright and Mackenzie reluctantly decided that the Government had no choice but to raise the tariff to 20 per cent.[19] So certain were some Liberal supporters that this would be done, that Thomas

* The ratio of note issues to capital was usually about 1:2.

Workman, M.P. for Montreal West, allowed himself to give his constituents the following masterpiece:

> Of course I am not at liberty to state – in fact, I do not know – what the proposed change will be, but I might say, that there will be an increase in the tariff and that the increase will tend to the protection of the manufacturing industries.[20]

At the last minute, however, strong pressure from the free trade side of the party, especially from the Nova Scotians, swung Mackenzie, uncomfortable anyway, and Cartwright, away from a tariff increase. The change of heart (unlike the increase) was a well kept secret. Everyone has heard the story of how Tupper came into the House on February 25, ready to damn Cartwright's new tariff rise as an extravagance, and was forced to produce from his sleeve another speech damning Cartwright's unraised tariff. Sir John Macdonald, who before 1873 had never been particularly suspected of protectionist sympathies, produced, two weeks later, a motion which deplored the lack of a tariff that would encourage and protect "the struggling manufacturers and industries as well as the agricultural productions of the country."[21] Here at last was the gauntlet thrown down for the Liberals to pick up.

By 1874 some American manufacturers were using Canada as a slaughter market. The Wood Committee of that year reported that American manufacturers found it convenient to dump their goods in Canada "at prices less than the cost of production. . . ."[22] Edward Gurney of Hamilton stated before the Mills Committee of 1876 (which had been established to justify the existing tariff level), that his Buffalo competitor was laying down stoves in Canada at half the American price. This was done to drive Canadians out of business, but it was also owing to American anger over Canadian stealing of American patterns, and probably patents too.[23]

Another example of this intermixture of slaughter-selling and patent-stealing was given by G. Boivin, a Montreal boot and shoe manufacturer. A shoe sewing machine had been patented in the United States around 1865, and Boivin went to Boston to buy one. The owner of the patent, McKay, a shoe manufacturer, asked $500 and a royalty per pair. So Boivin set up a plant in Montreal that made the machine for $400, whereupon McKay dropped their price to $160. Boivin went again to Boston where the following conversation took place:

> McKay's Manager: "There are two courses of dealing with you, the first is to buy you out, and the second is to kill you."
> Boivin: "Which would you prefer?"
> McKay's Manager: "It is a matter of dollars and cents."
> Boivin: "Buy us out. I will make an inventory."

Boivin's sewing machine enterprise was then closed down.[24] Certain manufacturers in Canada were strong enough to ignore competition from the United States, notably the Ontario manufacturers of agricultural implements. F. T. Frost, at Smith Falls, admitted frankly that he could undersell American machines and with as good a product. These manufacturers were sufficiently strong that a protective tariff did not interest them. C. A. Massey of Newcastle, Ontario, would even have accepted a lower tariff, though the present one was satisfactory.[25]

Broadly speaking, however, Canadian manufacturers felt the pinch of American competition and were disposed to make themselves heard. They were not yet a powerful political voice – that had to wait till 1879 – but they were listened to with increasing sympathy by the Conservatives. Saturday, February 26, 1876, the day after the Budget, a deputation of Montreal manufacturers arrived in Ottawa. "There is the devil to pay among the Montreal manufacturers," wrote Charles Belford to T. C. Patterson of the Toronto *Mail*. "They had an interview with Sir John today and left greatly pleased with him. They go down to Montreal tonight to hold indignation meetings. There is to be a caucus of our friends Monday evening. Sir John distinctly told the deputation today that moderate protection was part of the policy of the opposition."[26] That was the provenance of Sir John Macdonald's protective tariff motion of 1876.

The Liberals, on the other hand, were disposed to keep to what they felt was the greatest good for the greatest number. Cartwright described a higher tariff as a tax on 95 per cent of the public for the sake of 5 per cent.[27] He refused to rob the Canadian public, he said, "and in particular I decline to do it on behalf of the poor and needy manufacturers who occupy those squalid hovels which adorn the suburbs of Montreal, Hamilton, and every city of the Dominion."[28] But Liberal views covered a broader spectrum than that. On the right, A. T. Wood of Hamilton, Thomas Workman and Louis Jetté of Montreal, and others were outright protectionists.[29] More moderate, James Young of Galt, had no objection to incidental protection, or even to a 20 per cent tariff, to encourage manufacturing.[30] Laurier sympathized with Young, but was content that 17.5 per cent satisfied his "moderate Protectionist" ideas.[31] On the left was David Mills, a convinced free-trader, who in 1877 denounced the protective tariff as "plunder."[32] His views had wide currency in the party. The position of the *Globe* was characteristic:

> The only bonuses worth much are those which nature supplies. The only protection which is ultimately effective lies in the busy brains, the skilled hands . . . combined with a reasonable international system of trade and commerce, which will enable one out of his fulness to supply what another lacks . . . protection is . . . the devil's lie that nations are and ought to be each others' enemies. . . .[33]

Mills and John Charlton could be described as doctrinaire; Mackenzie and Cartwright were close behind.

Cartwright's philosophy was really *laissez-faire*. It was not in the power of a Canadian government, nor of any government, to make a country prosperous by act of Parliament.[34] The present Liberal government must practise "prudence and economy until this present trial be passed."[35] The people had to "atone for past extravagance and folly by the simple recipe of thrift and hard work. . . ."[36] The country simply had to submit as patiently as possible "to the needful and necessary privations which must always follow the reaction from such an extreme expansion."[37] To say that the Liberal government was to blame for the depression was as absurd as to argue that the late Macdonald government was responsible for the prosperity from 1870-1873. The latter had about as much to do with that prosperity as "any other set of flies on a wheel and no more."[38]

That was the locus of Cartwright's famous "fly on the wheel" figure. It proved impossible to prevent the Opposition from misusing the metaphor. It passed into general currency,[39] and continued to haunt him for years to come. *Grip*, with some justice, satirized the Liberal position:

> Little Canadian Manufacture had become very sick indeed, having been fed on imported diets. . . . So one day . . . he crawled up to the house of his guardian, Mr. MACKENZIE, and begged him to let him have some Protection diet. . . . Now MACKENZIE was not an ill-natured fellow, but very much afraid of his chief doctor. "Puir callan," he said, "ye suldna want for Protection parritch, whilk is cheap aneuch. We maun ca' the doctor." So Dr. BROWN, a tall cross-looking person with a long nose, came in, and looked very severely at poor little Manufacture, and looked at his tongue, and felt his pulse and said:—"It's joost a muckle fat lazy loon. Pit him to wark . . . on a fairm." . . . [He] went to see Dr. CARTWRIGHT, who had big whiskers and thought he knew everything. So he patted the little boy on the head, and said that it was not his productive but his distributive organs that were out of order. . . .[40]

Clearly, in the National Policy – Mackenzie protested against that title – the Conservatives were on to a good thing. There was some sympathy in non-party journals for a protective tariff.[41] Macdonald in 1877 teased the Government by saying that every anti-protection speech they and their supporters made strengthened the Conservatives.[42] Macdonald's motions became more comprehensive after 1876, but they all reflected the same general theme: the concerting of a tariff policy that would benefit manufacturers, labourers and farmers alike.[43]

Macdonald was on good ground in including the farmers. There is no reason to assume that the Canadian farmers were free traders, and some evidence that they were not. In the right circumstances they could be as protectionist as manufacturers. The Grange, an American organization that appeared in Canada in the 1870's, sounded out its members on the subject of protection for agriculture during the winter of 1875-76, and got five thousand signatures – about one-third of the membership – answering for protection. It was only in the 1880's that the farmers drew away from protection, and then mainly in the west,[44] where the wheat farmers were clearly dependent upon world markets.

There was no doubt that the protection issue was a good one. The more pertinent and difficult question is, was there a real case for protection? There have been a number of powerful criticisms against it recently, as there were criticisms at the time. The Americans had established their high tariff during the Civil War, and had found it a convenient umbrella under which to shelter native industry. But it began a tariff debate in the United States that lasted into the 1930's. Canada did not escape these influences, and the anti-tariff arguments from south of the border were often conveniently packaged for use in Canada. The opponents called it legalized robbery, skinning the consumers for the benefit of the rich. There can be no doubt that the tariff was abused. It raised prices for the consumer to the benefit of industry and its workers and to the disadvantage of the rest of society, and continued after it had ceased to be of significant value to the industries it had once fostered. But the main question remains.

A case can be made for a protective tariff to get industry started. Industry just starting may need time to overcome its shortage of capital, lack of experience, and the difficulty in establishing markets. In a young country with young industry the tariff can undoubtedly produce useful results in the short term; it can do much of what its advocates say it can.[45] But the heart of the matter is the long term; and here one must sympathise with Richard Cartwright. Unless barriers in the long term come down the standard of living must suffer.[46] And bringing the tariff barrier down was to prove very difficult to do. The tariff was a warm comfort, easy for industry to become accustomed to, hard to give up for the cold blasts of competition.

In all this Macdonald had moved cautiously and carefully, feeling out the ground as he went. He was no doctrinaire; ideas invariably dissolved before the realities of human beings. If ideas were useful they could be picked up quickly enough, and adapted as need be. It was so with Confederation, and with the tariff. From Macdonald's point of view the provenance of the name "National Policy" was nearly irrelevant. He had picked it up from Rose or Hincks or Tupper; it appears in his writing for the first time in 1872,[47] and then was only in the form of private advice to the editor of the Toronto *Mail*. It was an instinctive attempt to steal something from both Canada First and the protection movement, for the good of the Conservative party. But Macdonald never took much stock in "mere newspaper articles" as he once put it.[48] If one really wanted to attack something the House of Commons was the place. The National Policy became an articulated policy only four years later when, in Macdonald's view, the time was ripe. "We must watch events – and make the best of them. . . ."[49] He had an instinct for when it was time to lay out lines toward new policies, and so warp the ship along to a new berth.

Macdonald seems to have felt his age after November, 1873. Despite his support in caucus, he felt his fighting days were over.[50] He seems to have felt his political disability strongly all through 1874 and after, although he never quite got to actually resigning. Most Liberals thought him finished, and it seems likely the feeling was shared inside the Conservative party, though they may not have said so. After the election of 1874, the party was a shattered wreck that few expected to see rally until after a further election. Macdonald was himself unseated for bribery, and in November 1874 won Kingston by only seventeen votes, narrowly escaping disqualification even to sit in Parliament.[51] He was obliged to lie low politically and to ask his followers to do the same. Party discipline grew rather lax. A badly defeated party had to be guided in the House with an easy rein,[52] and he merely tried to prevent them from being factious. His policy of avoiding party opposition to the 1874 Reciprocity Treaty, and allowing opposition in Canada to develop of itself illustrates the point.[53] In the House Macdonald was temperate and judicious, and won praise from non-party journals for his consummate tact.[54] Even two years later the *Canadian Monthly* remarked how he was using his knowledge and experience for the general good: sober suggestions, calm amendments, offered cordially and unostentatiously.[55] This tact was deliberate policy. "The Opposition," he wrote to Langevin in 1874, "are displaying a spirit of fairness which is telling in the country."[56] Country first, party second, was Conservative policy, he told Tupper.[57]

But he was run down in spirit and in health. He went as little as possible to the House in 1874 and spoke infrequently. By that time he was already settled in Toronto, operating his law practice, and seemed to be drifting out of public affairs. However the quarrels within the Liberal party that developed late in 1874 seemed to revive him, and in 1875 he enjoyed flicking at the sensitive relations between Blake and Mackenzie. A little carefully fostered jealousy was, as D. G. Creighton has remarked, "a wonderful solvent in politics."[58] The turning point for Macdonald came with two events in the autumn of 1875, the "big push" letter, first published in the Toronto *Mail*, September 25, 1875, and the West Toronto bye-election won by John Beverly Robinson (the younger) in November. The "big push" letter was nothing more than a letter from Brown to Senator John Simpson, President of the Ontario Bank, soliciting campaign contributions for the 1872 election.[59] However unimportant, it was just what the Conservatives needed to paint the Liberals just a little black. Straight from Robinson's election Macdonald went to Montreal and gave a rousing speech at a consolatory dinner for Thomas White who had narrowly lost (by fifty votes) a bye-election in Montreal West. *Grip* pricked up its ears. "There's life and spirit in the old man yet."[60] There was indeed. And though Macdonald referred again – on his sixty-fifth birthday in January 1877 – to giving up and retiring,[61] from 1876 onward he was probably committed to coming back into power again.

The Liberals felt the difference. In 1876 Macdonald proposed his tariff resolution, and on July 1, began the round of political picnics in Ontario at the little park in Uxbridge.[62] One can see the charm of political picnics: countryside, trees, sunshine, men, women, politicians all mellowed over cakes and ale; or, to put it less gorgeously, "cakes and sandwiches washed down with weak tea or dubious lemonade. . . ."[63] Political picnics may often have been inane and foolish, but they could not be ignored. The Liberals were forced into that game too. Macdonald was better at it than Mackenzie, or Mowat, or Cartwright, or Blake. It suited his style; he was good-humoured, quick at repartee and remembering names, "a happy soul whom everybody likes." The picnics proved, if it needed proving, that Macdonald and no one else could lead the party. In the summer of 1877, the *Canadian Monthly* commented:

> Age or infirmity may compel Sir John to retire; but so long as he has the required physical power depend upon it he will not leave his party, nor will his party, if it can help it, let him go. He, its life, soul and all! . . . The hope of the Opposition is in its leader. . . .[64]

Another cogent contemporary was Leonard Tilley. There are few more prescient letters about the position of both parties than those from the Lieutenant-Governor of New Brunswick. The Government, he wrote to Macdonald in 1875, are doing your work for you; but there will not be an election soon. They will hold on for two more years until an election is compulsory.[65] That election "will then, in my humble judgment, leave them in as hopeless a minority as our friends have been left after the election of 1874." Don't defeat the Government now, Tilley urged Tupper. There were too many difficult questions to be solved, and the Conservatives should not try to come in before commercial matters improved. Let the Government "wallow through their difficulties. . . ."[66]

Macdonald's principal lieutenant in Parliament was Charles Tupper of Nova Scotia, whose reputation for parliamentary blather and for exaggeration was notorious. *Grip* advertised a new book in 1879: *India rubber in relation to public discussion*, by Charles Tupper, M.A., M.D., F.S.A. (Factus Stretcherus Assolutus).[67] Tupper had no sense of humour; he was impervious to the shafts of an opponent. He spoke always at full tilt as if determined to win no matter what the subject.[68] He would bear down an opponent by sheer weight of armour, argument, noise and *bravura*. He was a parliamentary bully boy who could be depended upon to defend anything or oppose anything the party interest (or Tupper's) required to be defended or opposed.[69]

But Tupper was an undeniable asset. Possessed of a good memory, he could on the spur of the moment marshal facts and improvise arguments with considerable facility, and stretch both facts and arguments when it suited. He had a copious vocabulary, and serviceable bad temper, and some real capacity for finance and for administration. That he had a taste for patronage, and for looking after his family and friends is understood; he was not a Nova Scotian for nothing. The rule to be remembered when dealing with Tupper was suggested by the Halifax *Morning Chronicle* in 1896. It gave the derivation of the word "Tupper" from the French, "Tu perds," you lose.[70]

Tupper had one great advantage; he had been quite outside the Pacific Scandal. Had Macdonald given up the leadership in the 1870's it would undoubtedly have devolved upon Tupper. The scandal had been a warning to all politicians to keep their papers safe, or better, burn them. Cartier's papers were probably burned by arrangement with Macdonald by John Rose, in 1873; there were going to be no revelations from that source. Langevin remarked a month later to his brother, "Je te demande tout spécialement de brûler toutes mes lettres. . . ."[71]

The sessions of 1877 and 1878 reflected the increased energies and hopes of the Conservative party and its leader. Country first and party second were all very well when the party was under a cloud. But the bye-elections of 1875, 1876, and 1877 resulting from the 1874 Election Act proved the Conservatives had a real following. By the beginning of 1878 the Mackenzie government had lost something like twenty seats to the Conservatives and their majority of seventy in 1874 was closer to thirty.[72] In 1877 want-of-confidence motions were served up, as Mackenzie put it, for breakfast, dinner and supper.[73] That session left the whole Liberal front bench drained of energy. Mackenzie looked like "a washed out rag, limp enough to hang upon a clothes line."[74] Blake's health was broken by excitement and overwork, and his debility, a kind of neurasthenia, grew markedly. He tried to keep going, but in November 1877, he told Mackenzie he would have to retire. "I *cannot* remain a useless hulk. . . ."[75] Early in January 1878 Blake cleaned out his office, pigeon-holes and all, and left.

The session of 1878 started, continued and ended with fireworks. Mackenzie warned Anglin that the Opposition leaders would be "as offensive as possible all through the Session so that we may expect very nasty work."[76] Nasty work it was. The atmosphere was tense, the Conservatives smelled an election coming, and they wanted to give the electorate plenty of thunder and lightning. The Letellier business made the Session still more heated, especially with the recriminations arising from the vast drunk that followed the debate.[77]

At prorogation there was the resounding clash between Donald Smith on the Government side and Macdonald and Tupper. Both Cartwright and W. T. R. Preston saw fit to republish the closing debate with denigration in mind.[78] But the report gave only a pale version of the real scene. The debate stopped when Black Rod appeared. The scene did not. In the lobby outside the Chamber, Macdonald, still beside himself with fury, went at Smith, "I could lick him quicker than hell could scorch a feather." A. H. Dymond (North York), and Joseph Rymal (South Wentworth) intervened in time.[79]

It was like a bar-room scene. Parliament could get like that. There was a complaint in 1874 that Tupper had had a Blue Book thrown at him; the Hamilton *Times* made light of the charge, saying that it was only the Supplementary Estimates![80] Parliament was only a reflection of society. After all, duels had been fought within the memory of Tupper, Macdonald, and Smith.

The machinery for enforcing law in Canadian society was still primitive. In Edmonton vigilante tactics had appeared briefly; in the East there were equally informal ways of dealing with law and order, through organizations like the Orangemen, the Irish Society or even labour unions, who made sure their own were not harmed, or, if they were, that there was suitable retribution.

Labour unions in Canada had been in existence for a generation in one form or another. The nine-hour day agitation of the early 1870's had brought the printers of the Typographical Union into conflict with the Toronto *Globe*. Under colour of law, Macdonald secured a party victory in 1872 by repealing application of the common law of conspiracy in restraint of trade against the union, and duly got his reward in working class support in the 1872 election.[81]

The Toronto Typographical Union was part of an international union, that is American, as were the bricklayers and masons, the railway men, the iron moulders, and the coopers. In 1871 the leaders of the coopers union had organized the Toronto Trades Assembly, which did yeoman work in helping the printers. The value of a united front had been so abundantly proved in the printers strike and the Dominion legislation that followed, that in September 1873 the Toronto Trades Assembly had called a general convention from which emerged the Canadian Labour Union. Its main purpose was to "obtain the enactment of such measures by the Dominion and Local legislatures as will be beneficial to us, and a repeal of all oppressive laws which now exist."[82] But interesting as the Canadian Labour Union was in conception and organization, within two years its annual convention had only a bare quorum.

The depression of the mid-seventies inhibited trade union attempts to capitalize further on their position, and they had difficulty surviving at all. Difficulties were severe over the winter of 1876-77, and on December 7, 1876, the Grand Trunk Railway issued an order reducing train staff and other employees by twenty per cent, as of December 23. The Grand Trunk said they had to cut expenses; the engineers claimed it was because they were members of the Brotherhood of Locomotive Engineers. This union was an international one, founded in 1863, and by 1876 an estimated ninety per cent of Canadian railway engineers belonged to it.[83]

They struck for the sake of their brothers that had been fired, beginning 9 A.M. Friday, December 29. The Grand Trunk proceeded to break the strike, by attempting to run trains with additional hired help. The Brotherhood resisted, especially in Belleville and Brockville. Consequently, Joseph Hickson, the Managing Director of the Grand Trunk, asked the Mayor of Belleville to call out the Hastings Rifles in aid of the civil power. The militia was a weak and awkward weapon to use.[84] Being called in aid of the civil power was a task they thoroughly disliked. The militia seem to have spent the night of December 30 replacing the cars on the track, and as fast as they could replace them the strikers got them off again.[85]

The federal government was then asked to step in, by ordering more disciplined troops from Kingston or Quebec. But Blake and Mackenzie answered with a *non possumus*. Local authorities, that is, municipal authorities with the help of the provincial attorney-general, were responsible for the preservation of the public peace. Only in case of war or insurrection could the federal government order out regular troops. Mackenzie was sympathetic, but helpless. ". . . I have no more power than you have, . . ." he telegraphed to Hickson, "I entertain the strongest possible desire to aid you in resisting the monstrous usurpations of the engine-drivers, but can only give you moral assistance."[86]

Such was the power of the Prime Minister of Canada. The Grand Trunk strike was settled, with the new men installed, though the railway agreed to hire as needed engineers who had struck.[87] Still, the weakness of the Dominion government in the face of civil disturbance was obvious and the remedy was not in sight in 1877 or until much later.

The helplessness was illustrated also in the Hackett affair of 1877 and its consequence in 1878. The Loyal Orange Association of British America, to give it its proper name, had in 1878 a membership of about 200,000, heavily concentrated in Ontario. That 200,000 was equal to roughly one-third of all Protestant males over twenty-one in Canada. Without precise figures it is difficult to calculate their voting strength, but it was clearly formidable. The Orange Order was as exclusive and dogmatic as the Catholic Church and a good deal more ruthless in habit and tendency. Its members were sworn enemies of the Catholic Church. If an Orangemen married a Catholic or sent any of his children to a Catholic school he was thrown out of the Order. In Ontario especially, the Orange Order gave to Protestantism its strong anti-Catholic tone. Its ideas permeated Ontario society as in no other province, and explains much of the intractability and querulousness of Ontario's attitude to Catholics, both Irish and French.

In an age of direct action, the Orange Order often had been, and could still be, an engine of intimidation, before which governments, being representative, were bound to be circumspect. The Orange parade in Montreal was organized in the middle of a good deal of local unemployment and a past history of incidents reaching back beyond Guibord. According to Bernard Devlin, there had never been, within his recollection, any attempt to have an Orange procession in the streets of Montreal.[88] To avoid incidents the Catholic and Orange societies negotiated an arrangement that the parade would take place without banners. But hot-heads could not be stopped, and banners appeared. It is not known if there was a band; if there were, the usual Orange tunes, "Kick the Pope," "Croppies (Irishmen) lie down," and that rollicking, exuberant triumph "Lillibulero" could hardly help.[89] Thomas Hackett, one of the marchers, perhaps because he was provocative and armed (his pockets were found stuffed with shot) was assaulted by an Irish-Catholic mob and killed. That was on Thursday, July 12, 1877. Hackett's funeral the following Monday was transformed into a vast anti-Catholic demonstration with Orangemen brought in from Ontario, who threatened dire vengeance upon Montreal if they had occasion to return there. And the murderers of Hackett were never found.

The Orangemen had applied to Mackenzie for military protection before the parade had started but were assured it could only be provided locally. The same problem arose, in more formidable proportions, a year later. After Hackett's death, Orangemen were angry. Special trains carrying Orange supporters from Toronto to Montreal were to arrive before daylight on July 12.[90] The House of Commons had passed in the 1878 session the Crimes of Violence Prevention Act aimed at preventing, after due proclamation, the carrying of dangerous weapons. Any citizen might arrest an armed person and present him to the custody of a constable.[91] Armed with this power, and with a large number of special constables sworn in for the occasion (some of them decidedly dubious), Mayor Beaudry of Montreal swooped down at eleven-thirty on the morning of July 12, 1878 and arrested the Orange leaders for violation of the Act. The Militia, who had been called out, were not needed. A vast crowd of Irish and French who had happily prepared for a pitched battle reluctantly dispersed. But the Orangemen did not easily forgive Mackenzie and the Liberal Government at Ottawa, or, for that matter, the Liberal Government of H. J. Joly at Quebec.

Mackenzie also succeeded in 1878 in alienating one other interest – the tavern owners – with the Canada Temperance Act.* Temperance was a

* At prorogation it was called the Intoxicating Liquors Act, but before being officially enrolled in the Statutes the name was changed. It was popularly called the Scott Act.

misnomer for it was not temperance but prohibition that was sought. Prohibition had developed strength in the 1870's in the Maritime provinces and in Ontario and the West. In the heartland of Mackenzie liberalism – Southwest Ontario – Methodists, Baptists, Congregationalists, Free Kirk and Presbyterians were strongly prohibitionist; the great bulk of this vote was Liberal.[92] It was a cause to which Mackenzie was basically sympathetic although he had mellowed somewhat from his outright stand of twenty years before. There was evidence that drinking was a sufficiently palpable social evil that it might be met by more stringent controls than the provincial licensing practices that already existed. The answer was devised by Senator R. W. Scott, the Secretary of State: prohibition on the basis of local option, and it was partly based upon G. W. Ross' Select Committee of 1874.[93]

The Temperance Act of 1878 was a re-application and a re-drafting of the Dunkin Act of 1864 to apply to all of Canada. Local option voting used existing electoral lists and machinery. One-quarter of the eligible voters had to petition for a local option election. The election itself had to carry only a majority for prohibition to go into effect.[94] But was a man not to drink wine because fifty-one per cent of his neighbours disapproved of wine? Speaker T. W. Anglin, down from his Chair when the Bill was in Committee, denounced it. "Tyranny more gross than this it is impossible to conceive. . . ."[95] There was active but cautious interest in the Bill; few cared actually to oppose it outright. Macdonald was prepared to come from sickbed and speak to it, or at least to be there.[96] It was evidence of the tender susceptibilities on both sides of the House, that, notwithstanding the determination of Conservatives to make political capital at every opportunity, there was no roll-call division.

It was one of those genuine attempts to reform society that get imposed upon the country by a vociferous minority, sufficiently small to be able to elect only a handful of members, but sufficiently large to persuade a government that they might hold power over a large number of constituencies.[97] The truth was that prohibition, like all deeply felt causes, was a source of vast inconvenience and embarrassment to any government. Canadian political parties were not held together by principles or by hard causes, but by generous concessions on points of principle, compromises, with loyalty and patronage as the glue to make it all stick.

A blistering attack on the Scott Act was made in the Commons in 1887 by Dr. Darley Bergin, M.P. Cornwall and Stormont. His constituency was by then dead against the law it had once adopted. It simply could not be enforced. Worse:

> We never knew what drunkenness was until the enactment of the Scott Act. We had in the town where I lived [Cornwall] twelve licensed hotel keepers previous to the introduction of the Act, and every man of them – to their honor be it said – was a sober man. . . . But, to-day, we not only have not

> twelve respectable hotels, but we have from 100 to 150 unlicensed places dealing out poison morning, noon, and night, Sabbath day and week day.[98]

Although the Canada Temperance Act lost ground in the later 1880's, in 1896 thirty-one counties and municipalities in five provinces continued prohibition under its aegis; thirty-four counties had by that time repealed its operation.[99] Whether owing to the Act or not the consumption of spirit was halved between 1871 and 1896, though beer consumption doubled.[100]

The Ontario government had already passed a tavern licence act in 1875, known as the Crooks Act. It transferred the power of granting tavern licences from municipalities to a provincial Board: it also raised the fees and limited the number of taverns to a per capita scale.[101] There were strong protests by Conservatives in the Ontario Assembly against the Act; and one of their charges was borne out in subsequent years: that it placed the granting of licences in the hands of a partisan, though more efficient, provincial Board. The officials of the Ontario Licensing Board were active agents for the Liberals in every electoral contest. It was dangerous for a tavern licenceholder to be an active Conservative in provincial politics. Inactivity was tolerated; some display of zeal for the Mowat government was likely to assure the renewal of the licence.[102] Here was at least part of the reason for Mowat's twenty-five year reign in Ontario – not exactly corruption – but administrative control of patronage in the party interest. The result was unmistakeable. One Conservative wrote from Toronto in 1880, "Formerly we had a host of tavern keepers who worked earnestly and well for Conservatives. Now I doubt if we have even one who will dare to work openly . . . lest he should lose his license [*sic*] next year. They tell us their bread and butter depends on their doing nothing hostile to the Grit party."[103] This was one significant reason why Macdonald wanted control of liquor licences placed in Dominion hands, which he attempted to do in the Intoxicating Liquors Bill of 1883. Mowat's control was not of course established at once, not in time to prevent five or six thousand tavern keepers in Ontario being unsympathetic to Mackenzie in 1878.

The election of 1878 was to have been held in June. Had it been held then, it is possible that Mackenzie might have been returned. Macdonald was said to have admitted as much in 1879.[104] He also knew the writs were being made ready for a June contest. "The elections are sure to come off at once," Macdonald wrote to Langevin, on May 18, "So you have not a single hour to spare. . . ."[105] It was nearly true. Ontario supporters wanted an election at once. The whole Cabinet did. Holton was "raving for an early election."[106] All wanted to get it over before that twelfth of July in Montreal, and before the Conservatives spent another summer picnicking. But Joly was unhappy; a provincial election on May 1, 1878 had rendered his position precarious, and he wanted to avoid a federal election just then. Also opposed were the

Liberal governments in New Brunswick, Nova Scotia, and Prince Edward Island all of whom were to have elections themselves within the next nine months.

In the end Mackenzie decided for September 17, 1878. That gave Macdonald and the Conservatives the time to talk up the National Policy at their picnics. "There has risen in this country," said Macdonald on August 26, "a CANADIAN PARTY, which declares we must have Canada for the Canadians – (applause).... You cannot get anything by kissing the feet of the people of the United States ... England, gentlemen, was the greatest Protectionist country in the world until she got possession of the markets of the world ... in fact to give a sprat to catch a mackerel."[107] On September 17, using the secret ballot in a general election for the first time, the people of Canada crushed Mackenzie and the Liberals. Only in New Brunswick did he win a majority of the seats, eleven of sixteen. For the rest it was a sad tale. Nova Scotia, only 7 of 21 seats; Prince Edward Island, 1 of 6; Quebec, 18 of 65; Ontario, 26 of 88; Manitoba, 1 of 4; British Columbia, 0 of 6. In all, 124 seats went to the Conservatives and 64 to the Liberals.

The victory, to say nothing of the extent of it, was unexpected by the public at large. Both Liberals and Conservatives were surprised.[108] Mackenzie was stunned. "Nothing has happened in my time so astonishing. It is impossible to understand how wide a defection existed among our own friends without our knowing it."[109]

He was also bitter. "Canada," he lamented to a friend, "does not care for rigid adherence to principle in the government. I administered her affairs with a more scrupulous regard to economy and justice than I would shew in my own affairs but one who shamefully and shamelessly abused the trust has been preferred before me."[110] But there had been complaints about Mackenzie's rigidity in public administration. Charles Pelletier wrote in November 1877, that in Quebec they felt that "the Government is too scrupulous."[111] It was true elsewhere as well. An "intercepted letter" in *Grip*, 1880, said what no one would say. "The next time we get in we want to make something by it – that's the fact, and MAC is not the man to wink hard."[112] Cartwright's jeremiad on the Canadian people turning an honest man out of office had some justification. There was more to the election than that, but clearly honesty had not gone down well with the supporters of the Liberal party who were looking for rewards during a difficult time.

In Nova Scotia, Jones blamed the hard times for the defeat of the Government; in London, Ontario John Cameron blamed the Orangemen, the cry of Scotch domination, and the feeling of the public that "George Brown was the real leader of the Reform party and that the policies of the party first saw the light in the *Globe* office &c."[113] This feeling placed Mackenzie at a disadvantage in Quebec. Indeed, Mackenzie himself thought he would lose

Quebec and the West but would manage nicely to hold Ontario and the Maritimes.[114]

Mackenzie had to resign. He could not wait until defeated in Parliament, though this course was urged by Brown. Mackenzie replied that they had discovered there was no money, and there had to be refinancing. That could not easily be done by a defeated government. Even Brown admitted, "there is of course no option."[115] Mackenzie resigned office on October 9, 1878.

Mackenzie's administration might have been accepted in other circumstances, and from someone who had more electoral appeal. There was something hectoring and schoolmasterish about Mackenzie. He enjoyed his rigid canons of administrative ethics, and being the scrupulous administrator – making the fat run out of a corrupt department. He was hard on his colleagues as well; he judged them by the amount of work they did, or how well they were posted on their department's affairs. His own fatal handicap was the Public Works portfolio. He often talked about giving it up; it was urged upon him time and again. But he could not stand seeing it done less well than he could do it; he was determined that the country should see how a department should be run, and run it he did. But in effectively running the Department he effectively ruined his Government. *Grip* was jocular, but right.

> He was sitting, you remember, like a clerk; slaving, I may say, as he always would do, when it would have been better for the party had he been seeing people and wining, dining and poking bartenders in the ribs, jovially, like John A. But he could never be taught these little arts. . . . There was no gin and talk about MAC. . . .[116]

What finally lost Mackenzie the election was a run of bad times; indeed, there was a bad harvest in Ontario and Quebec while the election was being held. Against that was set the persuasive promise of the Conservatives that they could remedy what the Liberals had so decisively said was irremediable.

CHAPTER 6

Macdonald, Letellier and the National Policy 1878-1880

Almost the last official act of Lord Dufferin in Canada, in October, 1878, was inviting Macdonald back into the office that Macdonald had left five years before. The new Governor General, Sir John Douglas Sutherland Campbell, Marquis of Lorne, heir to the dukedom of Argyll, and his wife, the Princess Louise, arrived at Halifax with all the panoply that the old city, the government of Canada, a rather unsteady Macdonald,[1] and a blowy November 25 could supply. Lord Lorne, at thirty-three, reputed to be something of a prig, turned out to have none of Dufferin's jovial fulsomeness – blarney is the word – but he was intelligent and willing. He was also the husband of Queen Victoria's daughter. The senior Dominion was to have a Royal Highness in Rideau Hall. The Princess Louise is best remembered for the ethereal and haunting lake named after her, or for Alberta, her third name. She had all of her mother's imperiousness, some of her looks, much of her temper, and her progress through Canadian society was a succession of shocks both to her and to the society. One of the funniest letters Alexander Mackenzie ever wrote was his description of a vice-regal presentation in Toronto in September, 1879. It was a terrible crush; 1,150 people.

> Lady Howland went through in grand style curtseying so low that every one wondered how the whole of that 300 pound woman ever got up again. Another stupendous woman a head taller than me and three times as thick went through with the preliminary movement to a curtsey. The officer immediately behind stepped back hurriedly evidently seized with a sudden apprehension of what might become of his family if the curtsey should fail in the recovery. Some one whispered, "is that whole woman to be presented at once. . . ."[2]

Nor did the Princess care for Canada. The old pines of Rideau Hall were much more attractive than pompous Senators in sealskin coats. Her interest in Canadians "was entirely picturesque . . . much the same as she felt for a Cascapedia salmon." Canadian society she found odious, and Canadians unpleasantly forward. One worthy at a ball was said to have laid his hand familiarly on her shoulders and congratulated her on the plumpness of her figure.[3]

On October 17, 1878, at the age of sixty-three, Sir John A. Macdonald was sworn into office. He was to be Prime Minister until he died. He was a curious figure, "a rum 'un to look at, but a rare 'un to go," as one old lady remarked.[4] He was tall with curly hair clustered mainly at the back and sides, and a long large nose "que faisait toute sa gloire" as Langelier said, a nose that acquired ripeness, as it matured, from years and whisky. A blaze of blue eyes suggested a temper to be watched. He also had a rich, soft voice,[5] one of the more amiable legacies of years of drinking. In the House he was carelessly nonchalant, leaning his head on the desk behind him; or pulling his knees up against the edge of his desk; or twisting his legs under his seat; or turning to listen to the speakers of his party behind him; or exchanging glances and witticisms with those around him.[6] He could step into a debate bogged down in details and acrimony, set a problem in perspective, warm it with a bit of laughter and common sense, and not infrequently restore the House to good humour and purpose.

He would support his own followers as they supported him. When one of his backbenchers addressed the House, even if the speech were bad, the struggling speaker was sure of Macdonald's attention. Not for Macdonald that happy oblivion of Blake's. He would listen, even turn in his seat and interject, "Hear, hear!" to some awful platitude while the rest of the House waited impatiently for the end.

Macdonald had a marvellous memory for names and faces, a knack only Lord Dufferin could match. The stories about this faculty are legion; it was the stuff that made and kept his great following loyal to the end. He cultivated his talent, he used it, he never forgot that popularity was power; yet his liking for human beings was genuine. But, "there is no gratitude to be expected from the public," he wrote Stephen in 1888, "I have found that out years ago."[7] Macdonald was in fact a shrewd judge of people. When John S. D. Thompson of Nova Scotia was being solicited, through Charles Hibbert Tupper, for the post of Minister of Justice, a letter arrived that seemed to young Tupper a definitive no. Macdonald looked at it and quietly said, " 'Whispering she would ne'er consent, consented.' He is our man when we want him."[8]

He was not to be pushed too far too often. Votes were one thing, and he could be excessively flexible in yielding to them; but he was impatient with importunities within the Cabinet. Few were more importunate than the Tuppers, both father and son. "Dear Charlie," he once scribbled on one of the younger Tupper's obtrusive letters, "skin your own skunks."[9]

Macdonald did not, as a rule, nurse grudges. What he found hardest to forgive was disloyalty, and by that he meant not supporting the party or Macdonald when the going got rough. He felt that an independent or objective position in politics was the refuge of the intellectual, the visionary, the timid – the Goldwin Smiths, the Galts, the Donald Smiths.

There was resilience and toughness of fibre in Macdonald and a great deal of experience. In the Cabinet he assembled in the fall of 1878, the only person who could match him in experience was Tilley, his Minister of Finance, whose political life went back to the New Brunswick Assembly in 1850. Leonard Tilley (Sir in 1879, with Tupper, Cartwright, and some others) was sixty years old, a wily politician, who had been brought into Dominion politics as part of the general skimming of the cream of colonial legislatures in 1867. By financial expertise he had earned a serviceable reputation in New Brunswick. A quiet, decent, shrewd fellow, with no claim to being a parliamentary lion, he had a reputation with both sides for tact. But he was not a strong man in the House. In the 1883 Budget debate under cross-questioning by Blake, he was very much on the defensive, fending off the insidious questions rather lamely, when Tupper arrived upon the scene.

In his own characteristic style Tupper at once carried an attack into the Opposition's camp, causing Blake to remark, almost sentimentally, "I am sure we are all glad to hear the old voice singing the old tune, delivered with some of that old time vigour, not to say vehemence. . . ." Poor Tilley was reduced to explaining, somewhat plaintively, that Blake's pre-eminent abilities as a lawyer made it difficult for mere ordinary mortals to cope with him.[10] He was not a brilliant finance minister; Tupper would probably have been a better one; but Macdonald needed Tupper in Public Works. Galt was brought in in 1879 to help Tilley with the new tariff, for the work of seeing delegations and overseeing the new schedules was exhausting him. But he retained the finance portfolio for seven full years until he went again to New Brunswick as Lieutenant-Governor.

For the same period the Minister of Agriculture was John Henry Pope, from the Eastern Townships, as salty a figure as ever came into a Macdonald Cabinet, and one of the most likeable. He had a plain, lined face, and had neither style nor manners to adorn his presence. He once replied to an Opposition charge by saying, "There ain't nothin' to it."[11] Lord Lansdowne found Pope disagreeable at first, then discovered his sagacity, and "how much kindliness burned beneath that rugged shell. I remember chuckling when I found he not only succumbed to an invitation to our house, but shewed a disposition to flirt with Lady Lansdowne."[12] Pope was strong, tough-minded, sure-footed, a man upon whom Macdonald relied increasingly and with whom he developed an intimacy that ended only with Pope's death in 1889. Pope was one of those men designed by nature to think, plan, direct; he let those more nimble of tongue do the defending or the advocating.[13] He had sat for Compton since 1857, knew his way around the business circles in Montreal and was to become a tower of strength in the Canadian Pacific Railway Company. It is owing to Pope, more than to anyone in the Cabinet, that the

Canadian Pacific survived as a private company through the vicissitudes of 1884 and 1885.

Pope had little use for the three undistinguished representatives of Ontario in the Cabinet, whom he considered "smaller than the little end of nothing." Senator J. C. Aikins was Secretary of State which is about all that can be said of him. Senator D. L. Macpherson was in the Cabinet because, as was so often the case, of long association, of gratitude, and because of his considerable business connections in Toronto. He joined only in 1880, as Minister without Portfolio and took over as Minister of Interior when Macdonald gave that up in 1883.

Mackenzie Bowell was Minister of Customs for the full thirteen years from 1878 until 1891, where his principal preoccupation was patronage. His correspondence reveals a faithful, plodding administrator. He seems to have enjoyed the small change of politics, and to have been good at it. Bowell was Grand Master of the Orange Order from 1870 to 1878, and did much to keep the Order aligned to the Conservative party afterward. And his knowledge of the petty details of Ontario politics was so considerable that although the Gerrymander of 1882 was not drawn by him, it was done largely under his direction.

With Alexander Campbell, Macdonald's old friend and colleague, as Receiver-General, James McDonald, the uninspired but judicious Nova Scotian as Minister of Justice, James C. Pope from Prince Edward Island as Minister of Fisheries, there remained the French-Canadian members. The most important was Hector Langevin who became Postmaster-General, an important patronage department. After some changes it was taken over in 1882 by John Carling from London, Ontario. In May 1879 Langevin moved into Public Works where he remained until August, 1891, when the McGreevy scandal rudely unhorsed him. Louis F. Rodrigue Masson who represented Terribonne from 1867 to 1882 came in as Minister of Militia. Masson was wealthy, courteous, a true member of "la noblesse du pays," ultramontane in sympathy, and had been mainly responsible for giving Chapleau his start in politics. L. F. G. Baby from Joliette, Inland Revenue, was one of the "old guard" from before 1873. Chapleau was apparently asked to join the Cabinet – he could not be ignored – but as the ex-provincial secretary of the ousted De Boucherville administration he wanted to stay in Quebec and turn out the Joly Liberal government, while the federal Conservatives would remove Lieutenant-Governor Letellier. The French-Canadian Conservatives, starved by the difficulties of living without power at Ottawa, had not had an easy time. They had been wounded by the Tanneries affair of 1874. And the ultramontane movement, although it had given some of them a strong sense of purpose, had weakened the party as a whole with its inability to agree with the more secularly-minded section. Charles de Boucherville, Premier of Quebec from 1874 to 1878, was a good example of the ultramontane side as Chapleau represented the secular side. Their strained relationship was crossed by the strands of the Montreal-Quebec antipathy, obvious in the bishops, but also in the working relations between Chapleau and Langevin, *le chef-en-titre* of the French-Canadian Conservatives.

In the midst of this was the question of the north shore railway. The line began in Quebec City, ran up river through Trois Rivières toward Montreal. Called by a number of names as it developed, it became at the end of the 1870's the Quebec, Montreal, Ottawa and Occidental Railway (Q.M.O.&O.). It was to go north of Montreal Island, cutting into the city by a spur, through Ste. Thérèse, along the north shore of the Ottawa to Hull, thence across to Ottawa. The route was less quixotic than might at first appear. At Ottawa it would connect with the Canada Central, running from Brockville to Ottawa, and projected through Renfrew and Pembroke to Lake Nipissing, where it, in turn, would connect with the Pacific Railway. The Q.M.O.&O. had two functions. It was to bring the western traffic to Montreal and Quebec and service local traffic on the north shore as well as act as a colonization road west and north of Montreal. But a good deal of opposition developed. When it was first proposed, nine-tenths of the existing railway mileage in Quebec was on the populous and prosperous south side of the river, and the ten-million-dollar enterprise offered no *quid pro quo* to the south shore. Furthermore, the Grand Trunk ran by the south shore, and did not welcome the prospect of competition from the north shore route. The private companies that sponsored the project could not raise money, and in 1875 the whole project had been taken over by the Quebec government, the cost to be shared between the province and the north shore municipalities.

The government project was soon in difficulties. In 1877 Chapleau and Masson, the provincial and Dominion members for Terrebonne, had drawn the Quebec-Montreal route through Terrebonne and Ste. Thérèse, giving these towns the main stations and workshops,[14] whereupon Montreal refused to give its promised $1 million to the railway. Engineers were changed, routes were altered, and recriminations began. In short, it was a mess.[15]

In this situation sat a new Lieutenant-Governor, appointed by Mackenzie early in 1877, Luc Letellier de St. Just. His predecessor, René Caron, had allowed de Boucherville to do things himself and use the Lieutenant-Governor pretty much as a rubber stamp. Letellier, a former Liberal tribune of some popular appeal who had helped the Liberals in their battles with the Church, was a *gaillard* who was not going to be a fifth wheel to anyone's coach, least of all to that of an ultramontane Conservative like de Boucherville. It was unwise at best to juxtapose a veteran Rouge with an extreme Bleu.

In 1878 the de Boucherville government passed a bill compelling municipalities to pay the promised money to the Q.M.O.&O. But Letellier was not consulted, not through deliberate neglect, but rather out of the habits de Boucherville had acquired. Letellier reserved the bill, certainly a controversial bill anyway. De Boucherville might have accepted that, but before he could, Letellier used the opportunity to dismiss his Government.[16] And out they went, on March 2, 1878. The leader of the Liberal opposition, Henri Joly de Lotbinière, was asked to form the first Liberal government in Quebec since Confederation.

On the eve of a Dominion general election the Conservatives believed that Letellier was playing the most outrageous party politics, that he had acted as the instrument of the Mackenzie government to overturn the provincial Conservatives. A Liberal régime in Quebec City was a great step toward securing Quebec. But the evidence is all against connivance between Mackenzie and Letellier. For one thing it was not Mackenzie's style; for another there is Letellier's evidence that he consulted no one in the Ottawa Cabinet at all. Whatever Letellier's motives – perhaps the making of a centre party was one – he seems to have acted on his own, except to ascertain that Joly would form a government if asked.

To put it mildly, the Quebec Conservatives, Dominion and provincial, were furious. King Luke I he was called, and worse. Chapleau invoked the spirit of Papineau: "Que dirait donc Papineau . . . ? Que dirait-il? Il ferait un de ces accents terribles . . . et s'écrierait: Faites taire la voix de Spencer

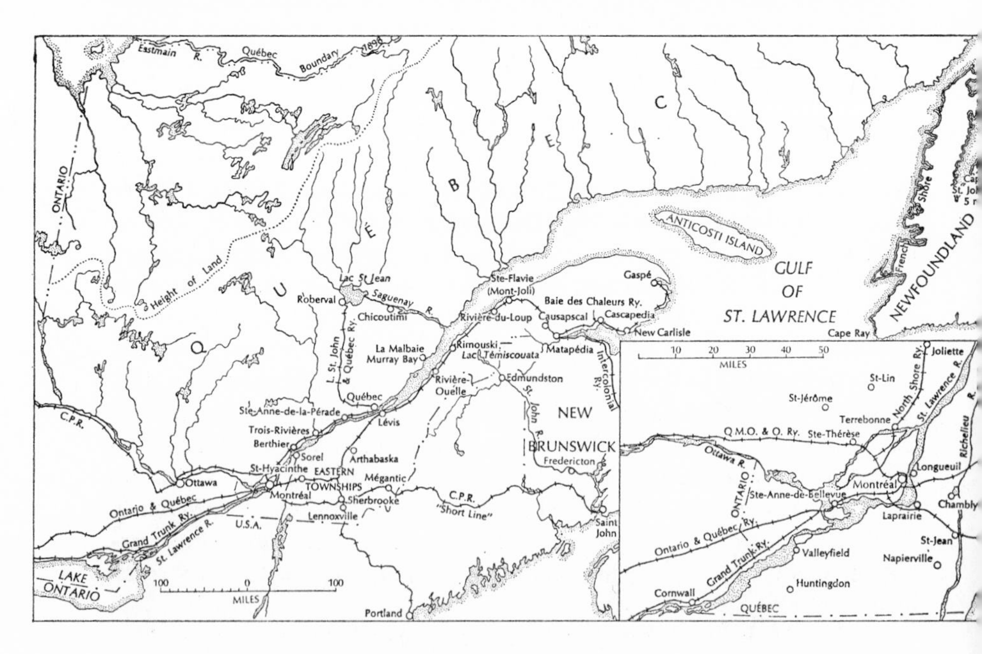

Railway Lines in Quebec

Wood, et laissez parler la grande voix du peuple!"[17] Nor were the Liberals very comfortable. Laurier admitted privately to Ernest Pacaud that Letellier's action was quite indefensible, certainly unconstitutional.[18]

Henri Joly, in a minority of about 22-43 got the election he required, and was returned with a majority. It was the thinnest majority possible – the casting vote of the Speaker – but there it was, and it made the Conservatives even more vicious. In the Dominion campaign of September, 1878, the Quebec Conservatives vowed to have Letellier dismissed if they won. And they made great efforts to win, asking for money from Ontario, and using whatever help they could still get from the bishops.[19] With 45 of 65 seats from Quebec going to the Conservatives, Macdonald was thus fairly put to it.

Macdonald would have preferred to leave Letellier alone however much he had protested against the Lieutenant-Governor's action during the 1878 session; Letellier would be out of office in 1881 in any case. But his Quebec supporters would have none of it. Accordingly a resolution of censure was proposed by Joseph Mousseau, M.P. Bagot. Both sides argued the question on the basis of provincial autonomy, the Liberals saying that Letellier's dismissal would be a gross violation of provincial rights, and the Conservatives pointing out (the ground was carefully chosen) that Letellier himself had violated provincial autonomy in dismissing de Boucherville. Mousseau's resolution passed with a substantial majority.

There remained the task of convincing Lord Lorne that dismissing Letellier was an appropriate use of Dominion power. Lord Lorne was opposed. But in the end the Colonial Office accepted, and got Lord Lorne to accept the right of a Dominion ministry to dismiss a Lieutenant-Governor for any cause the Dominion Cabinet thought sufficient. Letellier himself, ironically enough, had supported such a position in 1868.[20] With much reluctance, and in spite of Letellier's appeal, the Governor General dismissed him on July 25, 1879. A Conservative successor was appointed the very next day.

That was not the end of it. The new Lieutenant-Governor, Théodore Robitaille, used the Conservative majority in the Legislative Council to turn out Joly's government. The Council refused to accept a supply bill; Robitaille refused Joly an election; on October 30, 1879, Joly resigned, and Chapleau was called to office as Premier. The brief and hectic ministry of Henri Joly, the first Protestant French premier of Quebec, was over after a year and a half. Letellier died in January 1881, and was buried at Rivière Ouelle in Kamouraska, in a blinding snow storm, his life tempestuous to the last.

It was an extraordinary illustration of all the ordinary things that go into Canadian politics – railways, personalities, perquisites, religion – showing the interrelations between federal and provincial parties, and how party loyalty ignored distinctions between the Dominion and the provinces. Voting one way in a provincial election and another in a Dominion was still in the future, a product of special conditions in one or two provinces in the

1880's; it was as yet something no party in power in Ottawa saw fit to encourage.

The effect of Luther Holton's death is another example of the interrelation between provincial and Dominion politics. Holton was sixty-three in 1880, a parliamentarian of considerable experience. He had been a key figure in the Liberal party of Quebec for years, influenced the Montreal *Herald*, spoke French fluently, and was a tremendous source of strength in and out of Parliament. He was taken suddenly with a violent pain Saturday night, March 13, and was dead within a few hours. Poor Mackenzie could not finish his tribute to Holton in the Commons on the Monday. "What shadows we are, and what shadows we pursue"; Macdonald, in a philosophical moment unusual with him, quoted Burke.[21]

Holton's death also weakened Mackenzie, whose health had deteriorated. Even in 1879 it was clear that the great draught he had made upon his energies between 1873 and 1878 had prematurely aged him. Then, ten days after Holton's death, George Brown was shot at the *Globe* office by a ne'er-do-well employee. The flesh wound became infected; gangrene set in; the rest was inexorable. Brown was dead within seven weeks. As Brown lay dying, so too was Mackenzie's leadership of the Liberal party. The stinging defeat of 1878 had made the party unhappy and uneasy, and Mackenzie's failing health in 1879, his palpable lack of vitality in 1880, Holton's death, all stirred the cabals against him. But it is a curious comment upon Brown's influence, that Mackenzie was still leader until it was irrevocably certain that the "great muskrat" of King Street, Toronto, was dying.

A change of leadership had been mooted since Blake's re-entry into political life in 1879. The Montreal *Gazette* predicted that "poor Mr. Mackenzie is likely to be left like Athanasius, *contra mundum*. . . ."[22] There was talk in and out of Parliament about the imminence of a change. Mackenzie said nothing. No caucus was called. He sat beside Blake all through the session, feeling the conspiracy gathering around him. The evidence on how he was actually turned out is conflicting. According to Laurier, Joe Rymal, the chairman of caucus, called a caucus without Mackenzie, and got a resolution asking him to consider the question of the leadership. Mackenzie got wind of it, but seemed to have thought it a conspiracy of a few of the party, and said so to a small group who came to see him. Laurier stepped forward. It was a more general movement than that, he said, "it is only human nature that a defeated army should seek another general. There is not a man who has not high regard for your services, but there is a general feeling. . . ."[23] Mackenzie was hurt and bitter. Later that same night, April 27, 1880, just before adjournment, he announced his resignation of the leadership to the House.[24]

Mackenzie's presence continued to be felt in the early 1880's; he was even acting Leader for a while in 1882. He did not waste words, and his parliamentary remarks have more than his usual toughness, bite, and relevance. He was well worth paying attention to. Still, as the *Bystander* rather unkindly remarked about a dinner where Mackenzie spoke, "Through the speech of Mr. Mackenzie there ran an undertone of sorrow over the inability of the old shrivelled wine-skin of Gritism to hold the new wine of Liberal opinion."[25]

Blake himself denied that he sought the Liberal leadership in 1880; rather that it was *vice versa*. But his speeches in the 1880 session, particularly later on, show strong echoes of Aurora, and bolder utterances on general policy than had been heard from Blake for some time. Just ten days before the change of leadership he produced an enormous speech, highly critical of many aspects of government policy, especially the unprofitable application of capital fostered by the new 1879 tariff. It lasted all of one evening and all the next afternoon – a full forty-five pages in the *Debates*. Blake concluded:

> Such is your reckless, your inconsistent, your vacillating, your unpractical policy! Do you ask for mine? I will tell it. Set free the springs of legitimate revenue.... Open the avenues of legitimate trade, by lowering the legislative bars designed to close them. . . . Return to a moderate revenue tariff, the only practicable plan in our circumstances, and a necessary incident in whose operation is to give some of the so-called advantages of protection to some of your native industries. . . . Complete the railway to Red River; go on with the prairie section as fast as settlement demands. For that, risk something. . . . Postpone meanwhile, the western work, and do not, by your present action, based on airy dreams and vain imaginations, risk the ruin of your country.[26]

Those were not the words of a man uninterested in the leadership of the Liberal party.

The 1879 tariff had been in operation a year, and it was still early to judge its effects. Its structure was put together between Jannary and March 1879 with a great deal of trouble. Deputations innumerable presented their case for (or against) tariff changes.[27] Charlton pitied Tilley, the victim of bores of every description. "They have waylaid them by night, taken up his time by day. . . ."[28] It was even said that Tilley had engaged an assistant from the United States Bureau of Statistics to help him construct the Canadian tariff.[29] The Budget was brought down on the evening of March 14, 1879, the new rates to go into effect the next day.

Consistent with the principles of protection, the schedule admitted some things free, unmanufactured wool, raw cotton, machinery for woollen and cotton mills, steel (not iron) until January 1, 1881 (later extended to 1883), and animals for stock. The dutiable list included: agricultural implements, 25 per cent *ad valorem*; bricks, 20 per cent; carriages, wagons, and railway cars, 30 per cent; iron, ranging from 15 per cent on rails to 35 per cent on screws; paint, 25 per cent; refined sugar (several varieties here), 30 per cent and one-half cent a pound; woollen clothing, 25 per cent and ten cents per pound. Agricultural products were also protected by specific duties: wheat, 15 cents a bushel; butter, 4 cents a pound; cheese, 3 cents a pound.[30] Many of the rates on manufactured goods had gone straight up from the 17.5 per cent of the 1874 tariff.

The tariff debate lasted till nearly the end of April. David Mills had opportunity to ventilate persuasive free trade doctrine. The Government, he declared, was now telling the taxpayer:

> "Why, bless you, my dear sir, you do not know what is good for you. Do you not know that the way to make you prosperous is to take the money out of your pocket? People are made rich by what they pay. You have been well nigh ruined by getting too much for your money. Cheap tea and cheap sugar, cheap coal, and cheap furniture, cheap food and cheap clothing, have well nigh made you a beggar. . . ." I am sure the workingmen will understand this.[31]

Everyone had a go at it; arguments that had been dished out in 1876, 1877, and 1878 were re-warmed – with spice (and water) added – in 1879. The Conservatives were once more accused of being the cause of such a wicked rise in the tariff, by inflicting vast and ruinous public works on the country. Arthur Gillmor, member for Charlotte, New Brunswick, lit into British Columbia, "that incubus of British Columbia, that excrescence of British Columbia, that cancer, financially, of British Columbia, that was eating into our vitals. . . ."[32] The tariff was now, as Charlton noted, into politics for fair; it was to be the same kind of political issue it had already become in the United States.[33]

For the essential feature of the 1879 tariff was that it was intended to be "permanent." A tariff for protection could not be introduced one year and repealed the next. In the view of its supporters the protective tariff ought not to be repealed at all. No real investment could be made in industries so fostered without some reasonable assumption of a long running start. Whatever was meant by permanent, Macdonald was quite insistent about it. During a discussion in 1881 about giving the beet-sugar industry an eight-year exemption from customs duties on machinery they needed – a concession the wool and cotton manufacturers had received in 1879 – Macdonald made this point perfectly clear.

> Sir, there is a great danger before us in connection with this matter. There is the danger that capitalists who are now with some degree of trembling and hesitancy investing their capital in new enterprise . . . will be turned aside from their purpose if they find us tampering with the integrity of the National Policy. . . . In all the discussions which took place upon the National Policy, if there was one point which was laid down and argued almost *ad nauseum* by the majority [of the manufacturers], it was that we must make

> the policy a permanent policy, and we must adhere to that principle of permanency. . . . That is the principle upon which the National Policy has been adopted. . . . The principles of that policy were, first, moderate and reasonable protection, and, secondly, permanency.[34]

This necessity of permanence inevitably made the manufacturers permanent supporters of the Conservative party.

Before 1878 the manufacturers had not been a political force of much significance. Now a new relationship emerged between politics and manufacturing. John Willison remarked in 1903 that every Dominion election since 1878 had been controlled by manufacturers.[35] The free trade doctrine of the Liberal party in some of its most outspoken leaders – Mills, Cartwright, and Mackenzie – was a great handicap, unless the doctrines were altered, or some issue arose to swamp mere matters of trade policy.

In its political effects the tariff was a little like a railway: once track was laid and trains running, it was not easy to undo. Accommodating themselves to that fact was the greatest problem the Liberal party had, and they found it extraordinarily difficult. Many sincerely believed that a protective tariff was incurably wicked. They consistently underestimated the power the manufacturers could exercise. It took years to change Liberal doctrine, and then only after they had experimented with various alternate proposals. All of this of course was in full public view, and the manufacturers, who depended upon the tariff (or thought they did), could hardly be expected not to support the Conservative party. In fact the Liberals got into power only after they had definitely revised their tariff policy. Whether that revision, in 1893, was the reason they did return to power in 1896 is a nice question.

Of necessity the new tariff improved government revenues. Customs revenue rose from $12.9 million in 1878, to $14.1 in 1879 and to $18.4 in 1880. And, fortuitously, by 1880 business began to pull out of the doldrums. However, 1878-1880 were lean years. With uncertainties in the capital market, and no signs yet of any substantial increase in revenue, the Macdonald government went cautiously with railway expenditure. In 1879 the House passed a resolution authorizing one hundred million acres of western land for the purpose of subsidizing further expenditures on the Pacific Railway. A Commission was to be appointed to administer the program. But this proved to be no answer. Macdonald's and Tupper's attempts to interest private capitalists in the railway were no more successful. It was tried on an official visit to England in the summer of 1879. The Railway would still have to be wrought the hard way with Government energy and Government funds. One important gesture to British Columbia was made, however. The section from Yale, on the Fraser Canyon, to Savona's Ferry, at the west end of Kamloops Lake, 127 miles of the most difficult terrain in the whole system, was placed under contract at the end of 1879. At Yale, on May 14, 1880, the first blast of dynamite was touched off, and the construction of the Fraser and Thompson River section began. The Government had hesitated about the terminus; it had been put at Victoria by Order in Council in 1873; Mackenzie had established it at Burrard Inlet by Order in Council in 1878. Macdonald, now member for Victoria, put it back at Victoria in April 1879, but it was returned to Burrard Inlet the following October.[36]

Behind the scenes Macdonald's problems with British Columbia were almost as severe as Mackenzie's. The position regarding the railway lands was, originally, straightforward enough. In return for getting the Pacific Railway, British Columbia had agreed in 1871 to give to Canada a belt of land not to exceed forty miles in width along the whole length of the British Columbia section. At the same time Canada agreed to pay the province $100,000 a year, because such a belt, comprising so much – presumably – of the agricultural lands of the province, would deprive the British Columbia government of a major source of revenue.[37] In the long interval between 1871 and 1880, however, many things had happened. There was no clear indication until 1878 where the railway would go; and by the time the Burrard Inlet route was established many of the choice lands in the lower Fraser had gone. The announcement of that route only increased public pressure on the Fraser railway lands.

British Columbia claimed that the railway belt was to be taken as it was, mountains and all. Canada claimed, with some justification, that since nine-tenths of the land now available was worthless, a grant of land outside the railway belt ought to be made in compensation for the remaining poor lands within it. Walkem was as slippery as ever. He made excuses; he said that when he was in Ottawa in January, 1880 he had heard nothing from Macdonald about this aspect of the land problem. Taxed with this Macdonald was astonished. "You say," he wrote to Trutch, "that he [Walkem] expressed surprise that I did not speak to him about the lands. We did speak about them and about their comparative value, and he never intimated in the slightest degree to me that he was going to ask us to find our farms perpendicularly between the valley and the sky."[38]

Given such ways of doing business, negotiations between Victoria and Ottawa were long and tortuous. Walkem was clearly working toward some *quid pro quo*, such as the Esquimalt and Nanaimo railway. But Macdonald did not want to mix the Terms of Union with the Carnarvon Terms. The latter, he said, had never been accepted. They were now dead and gone. Macdonald talked of stopping $100,000 per annum; Walkem talked of seizing the Customs House in Victoria. Both threats were mainly talk.[39]

Over the question of the Pacific Railway in its new 1880 form, and some other issues, Tupper and Sandford Fleming were forced to part ways. The Fleming papers reveal much bitterness between himself and Marcus Smith, the engineer in charge of the western division, over the choice of the Burrard Inlet route; Smith was a great advocate of the Pine River Pass.[40] Macdonald had been unwell during the latter part of 1879, and the private breach between him and Tupper had developed political overtones.[41] Fleming had always had close relations with Tupper, and the railway was an opportunity for the anti-Tupper elements in the Cabinet to oust Fleming and curb Tupper.[42] The Cabinet agreed that the office of Engineer-in-chief of the Pacific Railway be abolished, and Fleming was removed by Order in Council. He could now be Consulting Engineer, and, if he wished, reappointed Engineer-in-chief of the Intercolonial. But Fleming refused, and departed the government's service, June 7, 1880. His departure was the occasion for a Royal Commission, to examine the whole question of government construction of the Pacific Railway. Its report, in 1882, confirmed what many on both sides of the House, and outside of Parliament, expected. Construction of the railway as a public work was a waste of "money, time and efficiency," and the whole enterprise would have been more effectively conducted by a private company.[43] Macdonald himself maintained, in 1881, that it was impossible for a government to build and run a railway satisfactorily.

There was no easy solution. On the contrary, the railway produced questions at every turn. The twists of Conservative policy after 1878 suggest that for all the drawbacks and slowness, Mackenzie's methods of tackling the Pacific Railway had something to be said for them. The broad truth was that by 1880 the Government, Parliament, and people were fed up with the Pacific Railway, fed up with the interminable discussions that swirled around it, tired of ten years of bickering with the British Columbians, and ready to take any reasonable way out of it all. To turn the whole railway over to a private company had been the first aim of the Government, Liberal or Conservative, and never ceased to be so. But heretofore no one had wanted to touch it with a barge-pole. Then, just about the time of Fleming's resignation in June 1880, a group was found that was interested.

CHAPTER 7

The Beginnings of the C.P.R., Ontario and the 1882 Election

The genius of the Scots, wrote Sir Walter Scott, lay in discretion, prudence and foresight.[1] They had done well in Canada: the roster of Canadian business was strewn thick with Scottish names. One of them was George Stephen. He had begun in 1850 as an assistant to a cousin who was a dry goods merchant in Montreal. He had a nose for business: an aptitude for thoroughness, a scrupulousness about money (his own and other people's), and the courage to take gambles. He was soon junior partner in a prosperous firm. From dry goods it was only a step into manufacturing, and by 1868 he was vice-president of the Paton Woollen Mills of Sherbrooke. In 1872, with Donald Smith, his first cousin, he established the Canada Cotton Company at Cornwall. He had become a substantial shareholder in the Bank of Montreal and was elected director in 1871, vice-president in 1873, and president in 1876. He was then forty-seven years old.[2]

Stephen was something of a financial genius. Few men of his time were as resourceful or had his skill to know when to take the plunge. He had trained himself to be cautious, but he was instinctively impulsive, and it was part of his success. He could not take things casually; it was all or nothing. It was the same with friends, those who were not with him were against him. "I can stand anything but suspicion when I think I am entitled to confidence."[3] On the whole, overly sanguine though he often was,[4] Stephen was to be trusted. "Do not forget," he told Macdonald three days before the signing of the C.P.R. contract, "we are contracting to build and operate a road from Lake Nipissing to Port Moody . . . and having once entered into the contract we mean to execute it to the letter."[5] These were fair words, fairly said and fairly meant.

By 1876 Donald Smith had been talking about railroading opportunities in the Northwest, and especially about one railway, the St. Paul and Pacific. James J. Hill and Norman Kittson, of the Red River Transportation Company, both of whom Donald Smith knew well, had been quick to see the possibilities, and they combined with Smith and Stephen. The idea was to buy the $28 million in bonds out from the unfortunate Dutch bondholders at a sharply depreciated price, foreclose, acquire the controlling stock, and put the whole operation in working order. Broadly, that was what was done. In March, 1878, the bonds were purchased for $6 million, mostly on credit from the Bank of Montreal. By 1879 the four had control of the stock, fended off a raid from the Northern Pacific Railway, and, as bondholders, had foreclosed and got the property. Holding $28 million of indebtedness against a bankrupt railway is one thing; holding it against a railway in operation and in full possession of a substantial land grant is certainly another.

The partners incorporated their railway as the St. Paul, Minneapolis, and Manitoba Railway, with Stephen as President, and issued $8 million in new bonds, many of the old Dutch bondholders taking these for what was still due to them in cash. They then issued themselves $15 million in common stock. The bond issue was used to complete the building to St. Vincent, on the border south of Emerson, Manitoba, in time to link up with the Pembina branch at the end of 1878.

By the beginning of 1879 the St. Paul, Minneapolis and Manitoba Railway was in working order, and was soon selling its lands in the rapidly expanding market that developed in Minnesota (and in Manitoba). It made money both on the lands and on the railway. The Bank of Montreal was paid off, leaving each of the group a substantial personal fortune in the stock of a well-run and personally controlled railway, whose value would appreciate considerably as the years went by. It was a classic coup in the best tradition of North American railroading, a legitimate business enterprise, a little sharp with the Dutchmen perhaps, for Stephen and the others tended to depreciate the prospects with them,[6] but no worse than ordinary canons for business technique.[7] Indeed the Dutch bondholders seemed grateful to Stephen for rescuing them. The St. Paul, Minneapolis, and Manitoba eventually metamorphosed into the Great Northern, which was completed to Seattle in 1893, with Stephen, Smith, and others of the original group still holding substantial quantities of the stock. It was the only trans-continental American road that did not go under in the American railway crash of 1893, a tribute to the care and solidity with which James J. Hill had built it.

By 1880 Stephen was reputedly the richest man in Montreal. It was John Henry Pope who suggested the Conservatives approach Stephen. "Get their money for your Canadian Pacific before they have time to invest it somewhere else," he advised Macdonald.[8] The Stephen group approached the Government through Duncan McIntyre, president of the Canada Central. Negotiations began; then on July 2, much to Pope's annoyance, broke down over the amount of cash subsidy, the Government offering $20 million and Stephen insisting on $26.5 million. Stephen's broad view was put in a letter to Macdonald on July 9, from the salmon fishing on the upper Matapedia, where he and R. B. Angus had talked little else but the Canadian Pacific. There were two ways the railway could be built by a private company, Stephen said. In the style of Jay Cooke and the Northern Pacific, one could float a large issue of bonds with a handsome prospectus, pocket the proceeds at once and build the railway as may be. This transferred the real responsibility to the bondholders, precisely what had happened to the St. Paul and Pacific when the Stephen group found it. Stephen himself would have borrowed as little as possible, built the line from the cash subsidy and from the Company's own resources, and looked for return from the land grant as the country developed, and possible profits on working the line. Angus and Stephen were both confident they could build the Pacific Railway "without much trouble." One thing was sure: the railway could not be profitably run out of Lake Nipissing: it would have to be firmly connected, perhaps through subsidiaries, with eastern traffic or it could not survive as a working proposition.[9]

In Ottawa, on October 21, 1880, the Canadian Pacific Railway contract was signed. That contract did two things. First, it engaged the Canadian Pacific Company – whose incorporation was a schedule of the contract – to build the Pacific Railway from Callander, near Lake Nipissing, to Port Arthur, and from Winnipeg to Kamloops. For that purpose the government paid the Company $25,000,000 and 25,000,000 acres of land. The only available government land at that time was in the Northwest. Ontario land was Ontario's, and British Columbia land for the purpose was still in the limbo of discussion with British Columbia. The land was first to come from a belt forty-eight miles wide from Winnipeg to Jasper, or, as it turned out, Winnipeg to Banff, with the Company getting every odd-numbered section not already sold. For acreage that was lake, swamp, or "in a material degree . . . not fairly fit for settlement," the company would get land elsewhere in the fertile belt, along with the extra acres needed to make up the 25,000,000. Macdonald estimated that the railway belt from Winnipeg to Jasper would yield 11,000,000 acres.[10] But the Company changed the route, and as it turned out the main line belt yielded the Company about 5,300,000 acres.[11]

The "not fairly fit for settlement" clause was inserted in the Allan charter of 1873, probably at the behest of the Northern Pacific group who stood behind Allan and who had had considerable experience with land grants. The clause appeared, again without much comment, in Mackenzie's standing offer to capitalists in 1874.[12] The Stephen group knew all about land grants from their experience in Minnesota. But it was sufficiently unfamiliar to Canadian parliamentarians to have passed without much comment.[13] In the West they were shrewder. The Manitoba legislature passed a resolution on December 21, 1880 asking that the Company be required to take lands regardless of quality.[14]

Second, the Canadian Pacific Railway agreed to operate the complete line when finished. The main line was to consist of the sections the C.P.R. itself, built together with the sections that were under construction and to be completed by the Government. The Government sections ran from Port Arthur to Winnipeg, still unfinished but operating in 1883; from Kamloops to Yale, now extended to Port Moody on Burrard Inlet, which the Government completed in 1885; and finally the Pembina branch, already finished. Altogether the C.P.R. received about 730 miles of government-built railway, worth at cost, without interest on investment, about $31,500,000, and by no means the easiest sections of the line to build.

The Government gave the Company land for stations and roadbeds, where such land was still in government hands. Where it was not, the Company would have to purchase its own land. All materials used in building were exempt from duty, although steel products were exempt for everyone anyway. The Canadian Pacific Railway Company property, and its capital stock, were declared forever free from taxation. The lands were exempt from taxation for twenty years, or until sold. The railway was to be finished and running by May 1, 1891.

One of the most controversial clauses of the contract, No. 15, stipulated that until October 1900, no line of railway was to be authorized *by the Dominion Parliament* south of the main line except in the compass direction southwest around toward west; and even then no line was to come within fifteen miles of the American border. This was clearly designed to protect the monopoly of routes to the United States that the C.P.R. already enjoyed in the Pembina branch, and thus to prevent the traffic of the main line from being tapped off by any other railway. But it remained perfectly possible, by the terms of the contract, for Ontario, or Manitoba, or British Columbia, to charter lines to the border, even if the Dominion Parliament could not. Macdonald admitted it. "... we cannot check any other Parliament; we cannot check Ontario, we cannot check Manitoba...."[15]

Parliament was called for December 9, 1880 in order to get the C.P.R. contract through before Christmas. Macdonald seemed confident that Parliament and country would welcome this solution. It had long agitated Parliament and had raised apprehensions that the railway as a Government enterprise was just a bottomless pit into which government revenues were being poured. There seemed indeed to have been a general sigh of relief. Even the waspish *Bystander* was disposed to be cheerful. "It is always something to have the strongest man at the head of affairs.... Like a powerful horse, if he gets you into a scrape [the terms of Union, 1871], he pulls you through."[16] Even the Liberals, at least in Quebec, were disposed to accept it.[17] But that was before the terms of the contract were announced.

When they were, the Conservatives were taken aback at the range of concessions to the C.P.R. The caucus met before Parliament opened, and

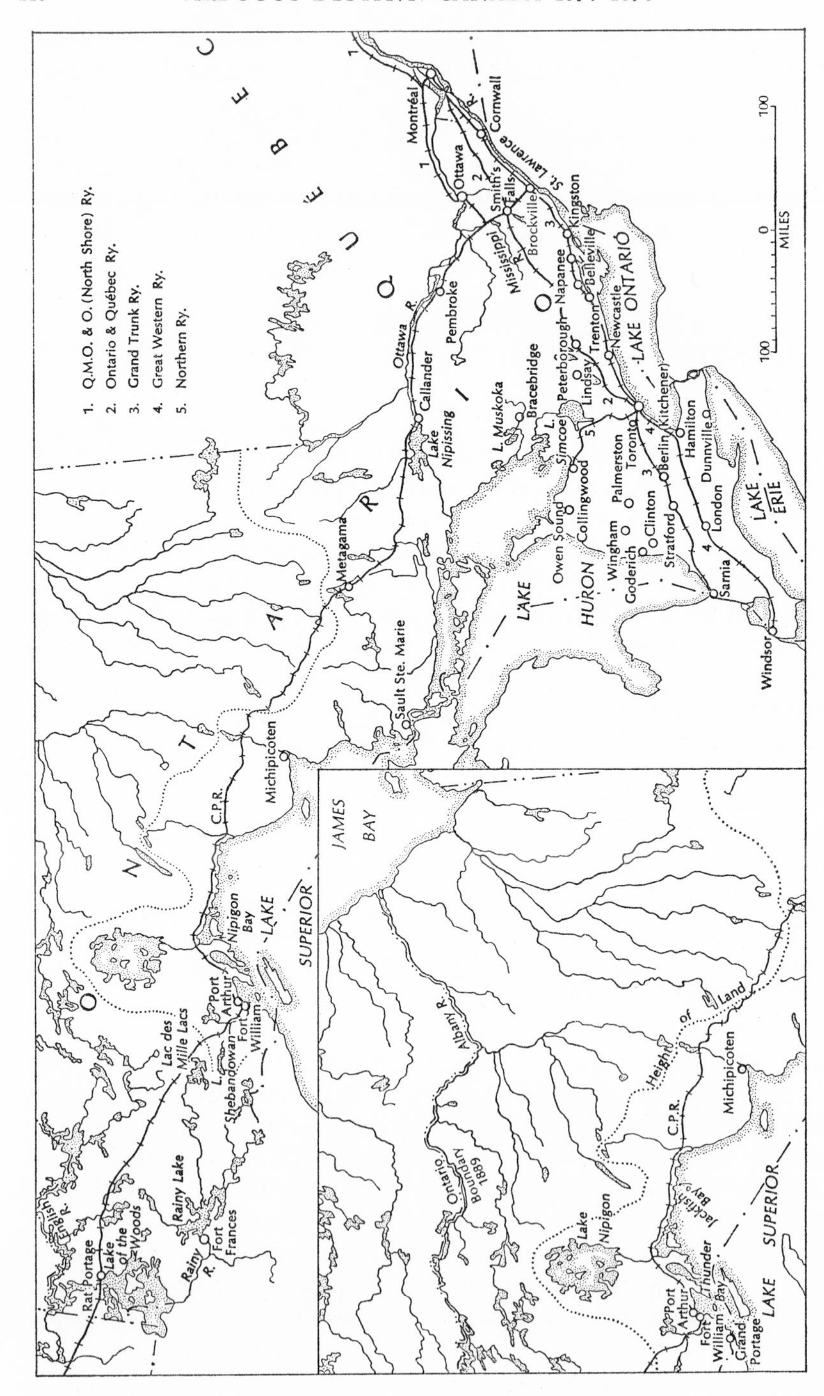

Main Railway Lines in Ontario

according to G. W. Ross, was so shocked that not a single member approved of the contract.[18] The next day it met again; Tupper explained the negotiations and persuaded caucus that the terms were reasonable.

The Liberals moved heaven and earth against it, putting forward two arguments. First, government construction had now proceeded so far that it was absurd to hand it all over to a private company to make money on. Frank Oliver's new Edmonton *Bulletin* put it neatly.

> If the credit of Canada is good enough to raise $17,000,000 to build the road from Lake Superior to Red River, through a country which is not worth a yellow dog, or raise $9,000,000 to build 127 miles in British Columbia, beginning in nothing and ending nowhere [i.e. Kamloops to Yale], surely it is good enough to build the road through 1000 miles of fertile country.[19]

Laurier asked in Parliament, "What great calamity has befallen this country that the Government should be compelled to surrender unconditionally to the [C.P.R.] Syndicate?"[20] Edward Blake's view was roughly the same, although he covered so much ground it was difficult to tell. He acted as if he, as leader of the Opposition, had a standing brief against the government in a court of equity.[21] His C.P.R. speech lasted five mortal hours: Mackenzie fell asleep, a copy of the *Globe* over his head;[22] even Cartwright, no saint when it came to short speeches, remarked, as he rose to follow Blake, that it was not easy for anyone to follow after Blake without repetition. But, he added with cheerful determination as he plunged in, "this is a case in which we should not be afraid of repetition. . . ."[23]

"We all know," said Blake, "where the grain from the North-West will go. It will not go to the Province of Ontario, but it will go *where it ought to go, to the port of Montreal*. . . ."[24] He was too big a man to indulge in envying Montreal, but his words suggest a second reason for the bitterness of lesser Ontario Liberals of narrower vision. The Canadian Pacific Railway Company was a Montreal company. The trade from the Northwest would pass, so to speak, over the heads of Ontarians, through Callander far to the north, and via the Canada Central and the Q.M.O.&O. to Montreal. This was the substance of a memorandum from the Toronto Board of Trade, December 21, 1880.[25] The Toronto opposition to the C.P.R. was the same as had developed to Sir Hugh Allan's company of 1872; and as in 1872, there was an alternative group, with an offer forthcoming.[26] A syndicate, mainly from Ontario, was put together with three or four respectable figureheads, Sir W. P. Howland and A. R. McMaster among others, who offered to do the work for less. It was regarded by Conservatives, and not a few Liberals as a "p.u.j." – to use Thomas White's expression – a put-up job.[27] It was a political engine concocted in Ottawa and Toronto; J. H. Plumb claimed to see Blake's logic sticking out of every clause in its proposed contract;[28] but it reflected the unhappiness of some Ontarians. As *The Week* put it in 1884, all that Ontario had to gain from the Pacific Railway was "the gratification of staring like a cow at the passing train."[29]

After some twenty-five amendments were proposed by the Opposition, and systematically voted down by the Government, the C.P.R. bill went through the Commons on January 27, 1881. It was given royal assent on February 15, 1881, and the very next day the required deposit of $1,000,000 was placed with the Minister of Finance. The day after that, in London, England, the Canadian Pacific Railway Company was organized, with Stephen as president, Duncan McIntyre as vice-president, who, with Angus and Hill, formed the executive committee.

Western reaction, felt less in Parliament, was no less outspoken and rather more knowledgeable. The Edmonton *Bulletin* claimed that the C.P.R. was being put through Parliament

> by men who know no more about the geography of their native land than they do of that of Patagonia; who think the sun rises in Halifax, shines all day straight over Montreal and Ottawa, and sets in Toronto – whose hymn book is the praise of England and whose Bible is the example of the United States.[30]

In Manitoba the principals of the C.P.R. were only too well known. The Westerners were delighted with their railway connection with St. Paul, and with Port Arthur, but to have both in the same hands was unwelcome, particularly since the freight rates on the St. Paul, Minneapolis and Manitoba were so steep. Freight rates were everything to Manitobans, as C. J. Brydges, now Land Commissioner with the Hudson's Bay Company in Winnipeg, pointed out to Macdonald. With wheat as the cash crop, freight rates dictated the profit of the farmer. Manitoba wheat in December 1880 was selling in Toronto at $1.10 a bushel. The freight from Portage la Prairie to Toronto via St. Paul took up forty-four cents of that. Of that forty-four cents, about twenty-five cents went to pay the freight just between Portage la Prairie and St. Paul, Minnesota.[31] Blake made a similar and equally damaging calculation in the *Debates*.[32]

The monopoly clause of the C.P.R. contract when added to this history of high freight rates nearly explains the attitude of Manitobans to the C.P.R. It certainly does when one remembers that the monopoly clause, as far as Manitoba charters were concerned, was enforced by a private agreement between Norquay and Macdonald, and ultimately by the executive authority of the Cabinet at Ottawa through the power of disallowance.

In August, 1882, J. H. Pope, though closer to the C.P.R. than anyone in the Cabinet, raised the question of the public interest. The Government would complete the Port Arthur-Winnipeg section of the railway early in September, 1882; but, said Pope, the C.P.R. do not want to operate it yet.

> I fear Stephen and Hill would rather it [the Port Arthur to Winnipeg section] would not be open, but the fact is, they are charging such exorbitant rates from St. Paul to Emerson, that it is almost ruinous to shippers, and operates very much to prejudice the public against our policy. . . .[33]

A revealing letter; not without reason did the Manitobans complain about the C.P.R.

Then there was the question of the section between Callander and Port Arthur. Stephen said the commitment to this section north of Lake Superior went into the contract at Macdonald's insistence. At this stage the C.P.R. accepted it, not because they really believed in it, but because they felt Macdonald had had to insert it for political reasons, and the building of it could be perhaps limited to a colonization road, postponed, or perhaps given up altogether. James J. Hill was opposed to building this section under any circumstances; he said it was an utter waste of good money.[34] This attitude on the part of some of the Syndicate was public knowledge.[35] The C.P.R. was to acquire control of lines in Northern Michigan and Wisconsin, which made a far more acceptable route. At the second meeting of the Company, authority was given for building from Callander to Sault Ste. Marie and bridging the St. Mary's River to connect with the Duluth, South Shore, and Atlantic, drawing western traffic into the territory of the St. Paul, Minneapolis, and Minnesota Railway.

By the end of the summer of 1881 Stephen had drawn away from his early antipathy to the line north of Lake Superior. Apparently, visiting Winnipeg and seeing the building and the business there had helped materially to change his mind. He wrote Macdonald that with the Lake Superior route the C.P.R. could take lumber from Ottawa and lay it down in Winnipeg for ten dollars less per thousand than it was being presently marketed from Lake of the Woods.[36] One can sense Stephen's view shifting with the prospect of profits. His colleagues on the Executive Committee probably did not share his views yet; certainly J. J. Hill did not; and a divergence of interest between the Canadian Pacific and St. Paul, Minneapolis, and Manitoba was clearly in the making. The ST.P.M.&M. made money from its Canadian traffic; that was one good reason why the directors had wanted the control of the C.P.R. But the C.P.R. was getting to be too big to handle as an offshoot of the ST.P.M.&M., and the beginning of the separation, the change that would send the two lines diverging across the United States on the one hand, and across Canada on the other, lay in the question of the route north of Lake Superior.

Besides the Canadian Pacific Railway Company, the Conservative party had another trick or two in the bag before risking a general election. Perhaps it was the Liberal outcry over the C.P.R. that persuaded Macdonald his control of Ontario was not as safe as he hoped. Mowat had, after all, won the provincial election of May 1879 despite the thumping majority that Ontario had given the Conservatives in the Dominion election nine months before. The opportunity to make Ontario more secure lay ready at hand. The census of 1881 showed Canada's population up eighteen per cent to 4,300,000. Accordingly, a redistribution of seats in the House of Commons was due, using as base the ratio of Quebec's population to her sixty-five seats. By this calculation Ontario was entitled to four more seats, and Manitoba one, making a House of 211.

Redistributions of seats have been a decennnial agony. Those unversed in the ways of the House of Commons may think it largely mechanical process; it is anything but. It touches members where they are most vulnerable, or where they think they are most vulnerable, in their constituency – its make-up, traditions and loyalties. Tinkering with the size and shape opens a Pandora's box. So it was in 1882.

Redistribution could have been done by committee with some semblance of honesty. Instead it was an unblushing attempt to weaken the Liberals by engineering out of existence wherever possible some of their electoral support. "Hiving the Grits," Macdonald called it, putting as many Liberals as possible in the same hive. "Every new constituency," he said with simple cynicism, "is a Grit constituency."[37] For example, three constituencies which had returned three Liberals by slim margins, could be re-arranged to return two Liberals and one Conservative, or even, with luck and ingenuity, one Liberal and two Conservatives. The name for this delightful process is gerrymandering. It can be managed where the vote is not too disparate between parties, and spread through several constituencies that are fairly populous. Ontario suited these requirements nicely.[38]

The Redistribution Bill was introduced late in the 1882 session – a habit of Macdonald's, increasing now as he grew older, especially with controversial legislation. It was presented for first reading on April 28. When it came up for second reading on May 6, Blake quickly noted it was substantially different from the first bill. The Speaker ruled, rightly, that the process had to begin all over again. Even before first reading there had been a great spate of representations from Ontario Conservative members and those who hoped to be Conservative members; between first and second readings there had been another flood from those who wanted this township taken off or added. The meeting at which these were sorted and settled was stormy and violent, and one member averred he had not heard so much profanity since the caucus on Letellier's political execution.[39]

That the Gerrymander of 1882 was bitterly resented by the Liberals is an understatement. G. W. Ross, Liberal M.P. Middlesex West, whose constituency was one of the many operated upon, suggested that the Redistribution Bill be replaced by one more frankly worded, "An act to bull-doze the Liberal Party of Canada and for other purposes." Part of Ross's bill read:

> . . . And whereas it is desirable to secure, if possible the defeat of the Liberal Party of Canada. . . . Therefore, Sir John Macdonald, by and with the advice of party wirepullers and Tory deputations from the Province of Ontario . . . enacts as follows:— 1. The House of Commons shall consist of 211 members, of whom a majority shall belong to the Conservative party.[40]

Macdonald's bill was aimed especially at the Liberal leaders. Cartwright's constituency just disappeared; Mackenzie was known to be shifting from Lambton to York East, and York East was engineered against; Bothwell was re-arranged so that Mills was defeated, though he subsequently won on petition; Joseph Rymal, not a leader but a great wit and much enjoyed in the House, had sat for Wentworth since 1857; he was driven from Parliament for good. Almost his last words in Parliament was his speech against the bill. He added that Macdonald had told him privately, on the floor of the House, "We meant to make you howl."[41]

It was a bad bill, bad in principle, clumsy in execution, and nearly useless in effect. Constituencies disliked such arbitrary and partisan outrages on their *esprit de corps*, and were the more disposed to vote Liberal out of sheer resentment. Macdonald, although he clung to the principle that constituencies in Ontario were to be as nearly equal in population as possible, was not by any means abashed to own to the real purpose of the bill. The Gerrymander of 1882 brought a tone into the Debates and into public life that had not been there since the great adventure of the double shuffle in 1858.

Was the danger from Ontario in 1882 such as to warrant it? Was it Macdonald's anger with little Oliver Mowat, the Cromwell of Ontario? Or was it just the corruption of that great re-conquest of 1878? The Act made the Conservative party resented in Ontario, a resentment cast against not only Ontario Conservatives but against the Quebec ones. David Mills' paper, the London *Advertiser*, talked of the dismembering of Ontario by the French Bleus.[42] This kind of talk predated 1882, of course. It went right back to before Confederation, but it had been largely quiescent until 1879, when the Conservative party, despite the fact that they had more supporters from Ontario than from Quebec, was labelled by the *Globe* as an engine of Quebec domination.

> When Ontario joined the Confederation, her supposition was, by doing so, she had escaped from Lower Canadian domination. . . . The Tories follow the lead of their precious chieftain and would put Ontario, which they know they cannot either cheat or control, back again under the rule of the Frenchmen, whom Sir John can humbug and swindle if he cannot control.[43]

This was absurd. But at the same time it has to be said that the Ontario Conservatives, except for Sir John Macdonald himself, were singularly devoid of strong leaders. The ministers were a weak lot: Bowell, Carling, O'Connor, in the Commons, Aikins, and Sir Alexander Campbell, a rather stronger figure than the others, in the Senate. None of them were in the great spending departments, unless Macdonald in Interior might be so reckoned. Langevin had Public Works; Tupper, Railways; Caron, Militia; Pope, Agriculture and Immigration; all Quebeckers and Maritimers, battening, as the *Globe* and some other Liberal papers saw it, upon the Dominion government in order to spend Ontario's fat tax contributions.

Two other issues had sharpened Ontario's attitude to Ottawa by 1882: the disallowances of the Rivers and Streams Acts, and, closer to the feelings of Ontarians, the Ontario boundary question.

The Rivers and Streams issue was originally a personal and legal issue between two lumbermen. Peter McLaren of Perth had acquired control of a central section of a river in eastern Ontario called the Mississippi, running roughly parallel to the Rideau, north and west of it, and into the Ottawa near Arnprior. McLaren had bought a number of properties along the stream, and had put in some $200,000 (estimates vary) into making it passable for logs. The Mississippi was not a big river and McLaren's improvements were the only reason that the reaches of the stream near Perth were passable. Another lumber company in the area, Boyd Caldwell & Son of Lanark, asked in the spring of 1878 if it could run logs over McLaren's slipways, and it was apparently agreed on payment of a charge per piece. Caldwell did not pay up, or did not pay up completely. In 1879 Caldwell ran his logs through on a Sunday when McLaren's lumbermen were off for the day. In 1880 Caldwell requested permission, offering to pay a reasonable toll. McLaren said no, that neither Caldwell nor anyone else would be allowed to do so.[44] Caldwell apparently threatened to run his logs anyway, whereupon McLaren obtained an injunction to prevent it. Caldwell fought the right of the courts to issue such an injunction. *McLaren vs. Caldwell* went to the Ontario Court of Appeals where Caldwell's right to use the improvements was upheld; to the Supreme Court of Ontario where McLaren's right to prevent him was upheld, and finally to the Privy Council where Caldwell's right was sustained, late in 1883.

Notwithstanding litigation, the Ontario legislature in 1881 passed an "Act for protecting the public interest in rivers, streams and creeks," by which all persons would have the right to transport logs down Ontario streams, subject to the right of any improver to levy a toll. The toll was to be set, however, by the provincial Cabinet.

This Act was disallowed by the Ottawa government as was its re-enactment in 1882,[45] and again in 1883. Finally, in 1884 it was enacted a fourth time, this time giving the right to decide the toll to the county judge, and this time, at long last, it stood. In its final version the Act was reasonable, preventing lumbermen under the pretext of a private right from establishing a private monopoly inimical to the public interest; but Mowat was probably wrong in seizing the initiative while the case was still before the courts. His

Comment by Grip, February 25, 1882, on the C.P.R. *monopoly*

Basilica, Quebec City, in a snowstorm, 1882

Winnipeg and Toronto troops leaving Fort Qu'Appelle, April 1885

Richmond Street, London, Ontario, 1882

William Van Horne, 1886

C.P.R. *heavy grade engine, 314, at the summit of the Rockies*

A distant view of Toronto, from the Kingston Road, 1882

Montreal harbour in the early eighties

Saint John harbour, New Brunswick, in 1870

Logging camp on the Nashwaak River, New Brunswick, 1871

The bar of the Balmoral Hotel, Montreal, about 1890

action made the Rivers and Streams Bill into a political issue in the Ontario legislature, the Dominion parliament and even in the election of 1882. It had no business there.

Still more was this the case with a sensitive issue like the Ontario boundary. What were the western and northern limits of the province of Ontario? The old Province of Canada in its dispute with the Hudson's Bay Company had pushed its claim to the Northwest back to western explorations in the French régime, and refused to admit the validity of the Charter of 1670. When the new Dominion of Canada acquired the territory of the Hudson's Bay Company in 1870, the Dominion naturally took up the old Company position about the boundaries. The old quarrel between the Hudson's Bay Company and the Province of Canada was transmuted into a new quarrel between the Dominion of Canada and the province of Ontario.

Boundary disputes are legal questions that have usually become entangled with political ones. In 1871 Ontario and the Dominion agreed to appoint two commissioners to decide upon the north and west boundaries between Ontario and Dominion territory. Before it was actually accomplished however, the Conservatives lost control of the Ontario government, and the new Premier of Ontario, Edward Blake, declined to agree with the arrangement.

There the matter rested until 1874 when it was agreed between Canada and Ontario – both governments now being Liberal – that there should be a three-man commission, the determination of a majority of which would be "final and conclusive."[46] The case was heard August 1-3, 1878. The Commissioners made a unanimous award giving Ontario virtually all she had contended for, the western boundary at latitude 95° 14′38″, at Lake of the Woods, and the northern along the line of the Albany River. It more than doubled the area of the province. Ontario accepted the award and passed in 1879 an act to ratify it;[47] but before Alexander Mackenzie had an opportunity to confirm it for the Dominion, his government was out of office.

The result of the Conservative victory was the appointment of a select committee in 1880 upon which the matter was "pitchforked," to use Blake's words.[48] They duly reported that the Award was wrong in law and fact.[49] In 1881 an adroit move of Macdonald's complicated the question still further; Manitoba's boundaries were extended on the east to the western boundary of Ontario, wherever that was. That brought Manitoba and Ontario into direct contact, perhaps conflict. Then in April 1882, the Dominion Parliament authorized a reference of the whole question either to the Supreme Court of Canada or to the Judicial Committee of the Privy Council. And that was where matters stood at the time of the election.

Mowat claimed that the proposed reference to the Privy Council was merely an excuse to delay, more or less indefinitely, any settlement whatever. Manitoba, egged on by Macdonald, incorporated Rat Portage (Kenora) as a Manitoba town in the summer of 1882; Ontario insisted this was illegal, that Rat Portage had been nominally under Ontario jurisdiction since 1871. The ground was laid for the three-way quarrel that culminated in the celebrated Rat Portage affair, in the summer of 1883.

In 1883 Ontario gave its police magistrates at Rat Portage power to add to the police there, and a series of wild reports issued forth in the dog days that year about the clashes between the newly appointed Ontario constables, and the newly appointed Manitoba ones.[50] There was no lack of inflammatory material available; one hopeful lumber baron offered to supply the Dominion government with three hundred men if a timber limit were given to him.[51] But when all was said and done, Manitoba was unwilling to press hard. At the height of the "war" on the classic field of Rat Portage the effect of feverish telegrams was rather spoilt when it was learnt that the chief of the Manitoba war machine, Premier John Norquay, had gone fishing.[52]

Manitoba did not really care, not then at least, about the disputed territory. The land was owned, like all Manitoba Crown Land, by the Dominion. Manitoba had gone into the dispute at Macdonald's urging, but it had no wish to spend money or time fighting Ontario. "To Manitoba," wrote the *Manitoba Free Press*, "no possible good can result. . . . She has everything to lose and nothing to gain. . . . We have a common interest with her [Ontario] in opposing the centralizing proclivities of the Macdonald clique. . . ."[53]

There was a conference in Toronto between the Attorney-Generals of Manitoba and Ontario; still more fruitful was an accidental encounter at the end of October, 1883 in Montreal between Alexander Campbell and Oliver Mowat. They met over a late breakfast, and in two hours nearly settled the whole question of interim arrangements and a reference to the Privy Council.[54] There were further hitches, from Macdonald,[55] but the argument of the case took place in London, England, in July 1884, with McCarthy for the Dominion and Mowat for Ontario. Virtually the whole of the Commission's award of August 1878, was accepted by the Privy Council. Despite McCarthy's and Christopher Robinson's expostulations, legally, it was not a bad decision. But it flew in the face, as W. L. Morton remarks, of both history and geography;[56] and its practical effects were perhaps unfortunate. Rat Portage and even Port Arthur were more properly eastern outlets of Manitoba than western outposts of Ontario, and it would have been more sensible, if sense may be obtruded into such a matter as this, to have made the whole territory part of Manitoba. In 1884 Manitoba however heaved a visible sigh of relief. "Do you object," telegraphed Macdonald to Norquay early in March 1885, "to an imperial act confirming boundary award –" "No," came the reply, "will be glad to have the question settled beyond revival."[57] But there was life left in the issue yet, and it was four more years before the matter was settled.

The Gerrymander of 1882, the Rivers and Streams issue, and the boundary dispute had all reached the boiling point at about the same time. And from the mish-mash of fact and prejudice that surrounded all three issues, arose the song, "Ontario, Ontario." In May, 1882, dissolution of Parliament had been announced, and the election was called for June 20. One rainy afternoon in May, at a committee meeting of Toronto Liberals, a well-known baritone, E. W. Schuch, who had been singing in a political campaign in Ohio, suggested a similar technique in the Dominion elections, if there were a suitable song. J. W. Bengough, of *Grip*, went behind the counter in the grocery store where the meeting was held and penned the lyrics in half an hour. They were sung to the tune of "Tannenbaum," or "Maryland, my Maryland":

> Ontario, Ontario,
> May surely claim her rights to know,
> But now her foe's enslaving hand,
> Has Gerrymandered all the land.
> Ontario, Ontario, etc.

There were several more verses all equally lugubrious. The song was sprung as a surprise at a great Liberal rally in Toronto in June, where Blake was the chief speaker. Blake, on the platform, heard the song and whispered to his neighbour, Peter Ryan, "Who is responsible for this damned rubbish?" Ryan did not know. "Well, these smart gentlemen have cost us the province of Quebec." Blake would have left the platform there and then, but was dissuaded and spent part of his speech eulogizing French Canadians.[58] It is hard not to admire Blake for his wonderful impatience with bumptious bigots, but his proposition that the song cost the Liberals the province of Quebec is doubtful.

Adolphe Chapleau had won the Quebec provincial election of 1881, fifty-three seats to twelve, almost the same as the Dominion elections were to produce. But the striking victory was won on extraordinarily narrow margins. Twelve of the Conservative seats were carried by less than one hundred votes. Henri Joly told Blake "We have never been so near to carrying the province. . . ." Joly complained of lack of organization and too much money on the other side. He confessed also that his political ideas differed from those of other Quebec Liberals; "they deal with men as they are, I try to deal with men as they *ought to be*."[59] Honoré Mercier put it another way. "Joly est *estimé*," he wrote Blake, "mais *ne commande pas*. Il manque de sens *pratique* et *dédaigne les intrigues légitimes*."[60] Joly was already considering stepping down as Liberal leader, and did so early in 1883.

Laurier was disturbed at the accessibility of politicians and electorate to bribery. "I tell you my heart sinks within me at the sight of what is going on," he wrote to Blake. "We cannot get candidates . . . unless we promise thousands of dollars to each. . . ."[61] The lack of independence was due as much to ignorance as to religion, in Laurier's view.

> The great mass of the electors are ignorant, and a great majority of them never read, and remain as much in the dark as to what is going on in this country as if they were residing in Europe.[62]

The educated class in Quebec, said Laurier, was trained in *collèges classiques*. Conservatism, social and political, was bred into the very bones of the class from which Liberals ought to have the most to hope. The strong liberalism of Ontario came from the schoolrooms across the province where the great majority of children learned at least to read, if not to think. The two electorates reflected two profoundly different social systems. It was a nice question which was the easier to influence. Ernest Pacaud and Laurier thought that the Quebec electorate was thoroughly corrupt. Pacaud wrote to Blake:

> Le voici, suivant moi: notre population est essentiellement vénale et corrompue. Or nos adversaires gorgaient d'argent & nous n'avions pas le sou. Les électeurs se sont rangés du côté de l'argent.[63]

Chapleau's victory had occurred in spite of great Liberal efforts to expose Conservative scandals in Quebec, and he was riding high at the beginning of 1882. He was, surely, the greatest power the Conservatives had in Quebec. Langevin seemed dry, dull, a mere bureaucrat of patronage, beside the *panache* of Chapleau. Chapleau had mastered every oratorical trick in the book, and a few outside of it. When, for example, he returned to Montreal after a winter in France, to prove to the crowd at his first public meeting that he had gone abroad for health, not pleasure, he coughed into his handkerchief and showed it, marked with blood, to the crowd.[64] Not without reason did Liberals say, alluding to Chapleau's early interest in becoming a priest, "Que d'âmes il aurait pu sauver, et qu'il a perdues!"[65]

In the Quebec session of 1882 the Q.M.O.&O. came up for sale. Chapleau would have preferred to sell it all to the C.P.R., but the C.P.R. was only interested in the Montreal-Ottawa section. Chapleau then decided to sell this section to the C.P.R. for $4 million, and the eastern section to Sénécal for $4 million. The solution was not liked in Quebec City, for it was suspected that the eastern section would degenerate into a second class road if split off from its western connections. The main source of opposition, however, was the fact that the railway had cost the people of Quebec twelve to thirteen million dollars; and it was going for eight million dollars. The sale went through, but it scraped through the Legislative Council by only twelve votes to eleven.[66] Even this seems not to have affected, for the time being at least, the hold of the Conservatives in Quebec. As in Ontario, prosperity made the electorate ill-disposed to change. The standing of the Quebec members of the House of Commons before the election of 1882 was 52 Conservatives, 13 Liberals; after the election it was 52 Conservatives, 13 Liberals.

For the second time in four years, Nova Scotia held her provincial election the same day as the Dominion. For the Conservatives in 1878 this had been lucky; the Liberal régime in Nova Scotia, in power since Confederation, was defeated resoundingly. The Holmes administration – sometimes called the Holmes-Thompson – had come to power as a reaction to the difficulties of provincial finance, much of it involving railways, and concomitant problems of the later 1870's. Simon Holmes, editor of the Pictou *Colonial Standard*, was the undistinguished Premier. In the first flush of its vigour the Holmes government passed the Counties Incorporation Act of 1879 that transferred to the counties constituted under the Act, the administration of roads and bridges. It was partly an economy measure, but it was also an important step in making local authorities assume the responsibility of taxing themselves for their own local improvements, something that had existed in Ontario and Quebec for over thirty years. In Nova Scotia, however, throwing fiscal responsibilities on local authorities required courage and determination; that came from the one strong member of an otherwise weak government, the Attorney-General, J. S. D. Thompson.

John Thompson was thirty-five years old in 1879. A Methodist, in 1870 he had married a high-spirited and ambitious young Roman Catholic girl, under special dispensation of the Halifax diocese. In 1871 Thompson became a Roman Catholic himself, perhaps as much owing to the influence of Archbishop Connolly as that of his wife. In Nova Scotia this was easier and less horrendous than in Ontario, but such was Thompson's integrity that he was able to wear his Roman Catholicism, even in Ontario, without giving offence. He was a short, burly man, but even his enemies admitted his power and his dignity. No one trifled with Thompson.[67] He looked out on the world with the confidence of a strong mind at ease with itself, and perhaps a little impatient of those less self-confident than he was. Thompson had no patience with the heart-burnings and anguish of Blake over moral issues. He never seemed too inclined to question, as Blake would have done, the ultimate right or wrong of the party cause he supported;[68] and he lacked Blake's massive and versatile mind. Not that Thompson was devious or tricky, or that he would defend or oppose anything on five minutes notice, as Tupper would, rather there was about him "a steady sagacity and a clear-headedness."[69] Thompson would simply bring his right-mindedness to bear, the way a well-engineered warship, cleanly, efficiently, beautifully run, would be brought to bear upon the enemy in war.

Simon Holmes was a dogged, dictatorial and ineffective Premier who alienated most of his Cabinet before his administration was over. His Government was also hampered by the actions of a Legislative Council dominated by the opposite party. W. S. Fielding, editor of the Halifax Liberal daily, the *Morning Chronicle*, and only two years away from the Premiership of Nova Scotia, admitted frankly to Blake that the Legislative Council had been used by the Liberals to block measures passed by the Conservatives in the Assembly.[70] For the same reasons, Joly, Holmes, W. W. Sullivan in Prince Edward Island – all newly installed – made a number of attempts to rid themselves of the incubus; none succeeded. Quebec was to keep her Legislative Council until 1968; Prince Edward Island got rid of hers in 1892; Nova Scotia only in 1929.

Holmes resigned before the provincial election of 1882, and Thompson carried a weakened party into the provincial elections of June and lost. The Conservatives returned only fourteen in the thirty-eight-seat Assembly. Thompson was appointed to the Supreme Court of Nova Scotia, amid general acceptance, on July 27, 1882 by the Macdonald government. He then went on to take a leading part in the formation of the Dalhousie Law School.

On the same day they defeated the provincial Conservatives, the people of Nova Scotia voting in the Dominion election, elected fourteen Conservatives and seven Liberals. The phenomenon of a province voting two ways on the same day illustrated a growing tendency in the 1880's for voters to distinguish provincial and Dominion aspects of political allegiance. In 1879 Ontario had returned Mowat to power despite having elected a majority of Conservatives in the Dominion election of 1878; but there is no better illustration of it than in Nova Scotia on June 20, 1882.[71]

None of the Liberal high command in Dominion politics had a strong following in Nova Scotia or in New Brunswick. Mackenzie was no match for Tupper, especially on Tupper's home ground. Even Liberal sympathizers admitted that.[72] In Saint John, Mackenzie was described (by a Conservative paper, it is true) as a "cold, metallic speaker with a shrill tone of querulousness. . . ."[73] Blake gave a series of addresses both in the summer and in December of 1881. They did not catch fire. In free trade country, Blake was weakened by his own misgivings about free trade. During a three hour speech in Saint John, on December 15, it became quite clear that Blake was not a free trade man at all. He had in fact never been one. He was an "incidental protectionist," in favour of a revenue tariff that would incidentally protect Canadian manufacturers from the worst of American competition. A Toronto lawyer, Blake could understand perfectly how free trade was impossible for the manufacturers. On this question he never really changed and he carried his policy with him until in 1891 he was virtually forced out of the party.

Tupper in Saint John made mincemeat of Blake's eminently judicious approach. Blake, claimed Tupper, had laboured for three hours to convince the people of Saint John that Conservative policy was utter disaster. And what did Blake end up saying? "Why, Sir," said Tupper, "he actually swallowed our [tariff] policy holus bolus. (Cheers and laughter.) I was glad he did, for the moment he had gulped it down I felt he had more principle and policy in him than ever before."[74]

Clearly Blake would have liked to change the whole front of the Liberal party on the tariff question, but the party were by no means agreed. Blake had tried to understand the manufacturers' point of view, and personally solicited some of them for their opinions. F. W. Glen of Oshawa told him that the majority of manufacturers of stoves and machinery in Ontario had begun their business in the later 1860's and from a start with little or no capital, most of them were now worth between $40,000 and $500,000. A. G. Whiting was an example.[75] He had started in 1863 with a scythe and fork works in Oshawa, borrowed $20,000 at twelve per cent from an American friend, some more from the bank, and died in 1877 worth $100,000. McClary's began as tin pedlars and were now worth a quarter of a million. ". . . . our manufacturers," wrote Glen, "have done very much better than the average of business men."[76] In the 1882 session, the Liberals avoided diatribes against the National Policy. Mercier told Blake, as Laurier had, that protection was popular in Quebec, and many Liberals were protectionist in sympathy.[77]

The election of 1882 gave the Conservatives much the same parliamentary majority they had had in 1878, 139 seats to 72, as against 142 seats to 64. The Liberal percentage of the popular vote increased slightly, 46.4 to 46.8, and the Conservatives dropped from 52.5 to 50.7. There was danger for the Conservatives if that trend were to continue, but for the moment the Liberals found it a little dispiriting to find things so much the same. Still, it was not unexpected, and Blake's hopes lay in the next election. "The good times was the only thing against us," wrote William Paterson to Blake.[78] "Electors of the Dominion!" cried the Conservative broadsheet, ". . . VOTE IN FAVOUR OF PROSPERITY!"[79] Prosperity had done the Conservatives' work for them, both in the factories and in the countryside.[80] Alexander Mackenzie, looking at the farms as he usually did (and as many others still did too) observed, nine months before the election, "between good harvests here for three years, and very bad ones in England, these rascals have had the devil's own luck."[81]

CHAPTER 8

The West and the Building of the Canadian Pacific Railway 1882-1885

The Winnipeg land boom of 1881-1883 was the most feverish example of a general Manitoba phenomenon, where prairie hamlets like Portage la Prairie and Brandon were rapidly escalating into towns. It occurred especially in urban real estate. Town lots were turning over at 100 per cent and 150 per cent, and Ontario and Quebec money poured west to finance it. "Elliot [Galt] made a capital sale of part of my Winnipeg lots," wrote Galt cheerfully in March, 1882, "if the rest do as well I shall make some $15,000 profit."[1] George Casey, Liberal M.P. for Elgin West, and his friend James Coyne, put whatever money they could scrape up into Winnipeg.[2] Richard Cartwright bought heavily in Manitoba lands, and in Assiniboia territory he bought some ten thousand acres of C.P.R. land at three dollars an acre, south of what is now Broadview.[3] Knowledgeable easterners, especially if they were on the spot, seem to have made money, but in the fall of 1883, the boom ran down, as it had to, to the dismay of more ardent speculators.

The word "speculator" reflects eastern prejudices. But much in the West, farming not least, was in the nature of a speculation. Farming was risky in a way quite different from Ontario where there was always a good crop of something. The Ontario farmer could afford to ignore exigencies of freight rates. He had, a generation earlier, been nearly self-sufficient, and he could in a pinch get down to it again. But in the West that was nearly impossible, especially as one moved westward from Winnipeg. Lumber had, increasingly, to be bought; clothes and fuel were paid for by a cash crop that was itself a speculation. Farming was a gamble, a gamble that heat and rain would come at the right time and in right proportions, that frost would not linger too long in the spring, or arrive too soon in the fall. And upon freight rates, elevator rates, access to railways, upon the whole nexus of transportation facilities, the farmer's profit utterly depended. In the prairie, the stakes were higher, and the risks greater. So was the grumbling. Nicholas Davin, the meteoric editor of the Regina *Leader*, described westerners in 1889 as just wanting "to do something – kick – bring about impossibilities &c. – which distinguishes the North-West man."[4] In the variety of western agitations, in Manitoba's dislike of C.P.R. policies, in the annoyance with the slowness of land patents, in a hundred other sources of friction between the prairies and Ottawa, there was much of the frustration of the gambler-farmer.

The swings of prosperity and catastrophe on the prairie were like the prairie weather that determined so much of both: never normal. Never normal, that is, by eastern standards; prairie weather could only be readily understood by someone who had been there. Unfortunately, many ministers, and especially the Ministers of the Interior in the first eight years of Macdonald's government, had not been west, not Macdonald himself, nor his successor, Senator David Macpherson.

Then there was the question of agricultural machinery. The 1879 tariff had not raised the prices of Canadian agricultural machinery much, if indeed at all; by 1885 Canadian machines were competing with American in terms of price, in fact under-selling them. But at this stage they had not yet been completely adapted to western conditions, while the American ones had been. In the West the harvest came on with a terrible urgency. Everything depended upon speed, and the machinery was worked full blast from dawn at five o'clock to dusk at nine-thirty. One large Ontario manufacturer, who also handled Deering binders in the Northwest, found he could sell an American machine for thirty dollars more than he could a Canadian one of the same type. For the westerners wanted the best and most reliable machine; a flaw or break in it at the wrong time, far perhaps from available repairs, could be disastrous at harvest time. No one willingly risked it.[5]

Another difficulty in the West was the gradual decline in the price of wheat as the country continued to open up and farming techniques became more effective. In the 1860's eastern wheat fluctuated between $0.85 and $1.80 a bushel; in the 1870's between $0.86 and $1.36; and in the 1880's between $0.83 and $1.34. In the 1890's with western wheat commanding ten per cent premium over eastern wheat, the price range fell to between 61 cents and 93 cents a bushel.* Of course the lower prices of the 1890's reflected a generally lower cost of living; an 1890 dollar brought about ten per cent more than an 1870 one. Still, the decline was very real, and freight rates did not decline proportionately. Meanwhile, wheat production grew, erratically, but grew, from 30 million bushels in 1878, to 48 million in 1882, through a low of 31 million in 1883 to 43 million in 1885; then to another low of 31 million in 1890 to 61 million in 1892 and 56 million in 1895.**

* These are wholesale prices of No. 2 white, Toronto, until 1888; then No. 1 Northern, at Winnipeg.

** These figures are for all of Canada. See Urquhart and Buckley, *Historical Statistics of Canada* (Toronto, 1966), 360, 363-4. Figures are given for crop years, ending in the spring; I have put them back to the year in which they are grown.

Western problems reflected the increases of western population. Manitoba jumped from 62,000 in 1881 to 156,000 in 1891 and to 255,000 in 1901; the Northwest Territories from 56,000 in 1881 to 91,000 in 1891 and 214,000 in 1901. In the House of Commons Sir Charles Tupper wryly noted the change in 1884:

> Why, I was amused when I heard the hon. gentleman [Alexander Mackenzie] talking about a great public meeting at Moose Jaw. How did that happen? Why I was at Moose Jaw two years ago, and there was not a house to be seen within the whole range of vision from the Canadian Pacific Railway to the horizon. . . . How is it that in that great wild and unpeopled portion of the desert . . . as if by magic, [it] is transformed into a place in which a great public meeting can be held? Why it is the policy of this Government. . . .[6]

It was unwise for the Government to have been that complacent about northwest grievances, but Tupper's point was not without relevance. The government policy he mentioned, of course, turned upon the Canadian Pacific Railway.

The first Superintendent of construction in the West was A. B. Stickney, of the St. Paul, Minneapolis, and Manitoba Railway. But someone more dynamic was needed, and William Cornelius Van Horne, then thirty-nine, was made General Manager and Engineer-in-chief as of January 1, 1882. Born and brought up in the American Midwest, in 1880 he was general superintendent of the Chicago, Milwaukee, and St. Paul, where his path crossed that of James J. Hill. Van Horne's energy, his knowledgeable (even ferocious) command of means, his Napoleonic *daemon*, recommended him to the chiefs of the C.P.R., who wanted to get the railway built before the Northern Pacific drained off too much western traffic. Van Horne was a brute of a man with a huge leonine head, and shoulders and chest hard as a hammer.[7] He radiated energy; he gloried in it; and he had an enormous zest for work and living. Inside this gargantuan furnace, as if strenuosity had failed to be a wholly satisfying principle of life, lay a sensitivity of taste still largely unexpressed, which in later years was to find utterance in his collections of Japanese art and old masters.

Van Horne was not an engineer; he was a telegrapher metamorphosed into a railwayman; he distrusted engineers. One of the best locating engineers in the business, J. H. E. Secretan, described one of his encounters with Van Horne at Winnipeg. A tunnel had been put in on the line east of Banff, along the Bow River. How long would *that* take to build? Van Horne asked. Twelve to fourteen months, said Secretan. Take it out! said Van Horne.

> He was not there to build fool tunnels to please engineers. . . . "Mind you go up there *yourself* and take that d—d tunnel out. Don't send anybody else." I asked for the profile, and when I reached the door, paused for a minute and

said, "While I'm up there hadn't I better move some of those mountains back, as I think they are too close to the river." The "old man" looked up for a second, said nothing, but I could see . . . his corporation shaking like a jelly. He was convulsed with laughter.[8]

The Bow River points to the major decision of the company, made before Van Horne came on the scene, to abandon the northern route that Fleming had so carefully worked out through Battleford, Edmonton and the Yellowhead Pass. The route that was now chosen lay much farther south, through Swift Current, Calgary, and the Kicking Horse Pass. Lacking C.P.R. sources, little is known precisely, but the reasons for the change must have been strong ones, for the C.P.R. wanted to change the route before they knew what pass they would use.[9] They opted for the Kicking Horse Pass knowing it was eleven hundred feet higher than the Yellowhead, and without knowing whether they could get through the Selkirks. They were thus willing to risk taking the line around the Selkirks by the Big Bend of the Columbia, building an extra 150 miles on the Columbia, the only offset being the 100 miles saved by the southern route.

The reason for the C.P.R. decision was probably the Northern Pacific Railway. In 1880, just when the C.P.R. charter was being presented to Parliament, the Northern Pacific issued a new series of bond arrangements to launch its transcontinental line from Fargo to Spokane and Portland. Finished in 1883, already in the summer of 1881 it was threatening the C.P.R.'s control of Manitoba.[10] The territory between Fleming's route and the Northern Pacific was a vast area into which both the Canadian Pacific and the Northern Pacific could move with branch lines. It was much simpler, and far more effective, to avoid such a contest altogether by running the C.P.R. main line two hundred miles to the south, blocking off the Northern Pacific, and putting in branch lines to serve the northern prairies.

Another aspect of the C.P.R.'s decision was coal. C.P.R. coal, until 1883, came from Ohio. On much of the prairie they were burning wood. The first train into Calgary in August, 1883 burned wood. In 1879, young Elliott Galt had told his father about coal prospects along the Belly and Oldman rivers in southern Alberta. Sir Alexander was then Canadian High Commissioner in London, but as the Pacific Railway got nearer he became more restless, and wrote Macdonald of responsibilities for eleven children, eight of whom were daughters, all of whom, it appeared, depended upon this rotund, mercurial financier of sixty years of age.[11] Galt got leave and spent part of the summer of 1881 with Elliott and Col. J. S. Dennis, the Surveyor-General, going out to the coal areas from the end of track. The result was the Northwestern Coal and Navigation Company, organized in London in April, 1882. Galt had acquired a good opinion of the coal, but a bad opinion about southern Alberta land, and, with his Grand Trunk connections apparently intact, was uneasy about the C.P.R.

The commercial exigencies that dictated the C.P.R.'s change of route carried with them some disadvantages. The wrenching of the railway suddenly to the south pulled the rug from under long established expectations of settlers in the Saskatchewan valleys. At one stroke were destroyed the hopes of a string of settlements, in good land northwest of Portage la Prairie, Minnedosa, Birtle, Humbolt, Prince Albert, Battleford, to say nothing of Edmonton itself. And despite all Stephen's talk, the land of southeastern Alberta was not the equal of land farther north. Galt's impressions, the utterance of which annoyed Stephen so much, were accurate.

The headlong rush of the C.P.R. to build the line astonished both Parliament and public. The speed was dictated by the fear of the Northern Pacific, and Stephen's natural instinct to avoid tying up capital unprofitably any longer than he could help. That the railway would be profitable when completed Stephen never had a doubt. The main thing, as far as he was concerned, was to get it built and get it operating. The longest journey that a railway can take, said a shrewd and practical engineer, Thomas Keefer, is "the journey from the charter to the rolling stock."[12] So Van Horne was determined, with the Company backing him to the hilt, to get the line across the prairies and through to the Rockies to Kamloops by the most expeditious route and as quickly as possible.

In 1882 Van Horne had set his mind on a full 500 miles, instead of the 275 of 1881. He organized a special construction gang of his own to push the contractors and follow them up. The logistics of the operation were immense: rails from Great Britain and Germany, ties from Lake of the Woods and Rat Portage; the stores branch had checkers strung out between New York and Winnipeg reporting daily on the arrival and movement of C.P.R. supplies.[13] The location engineers were followed by the ploughs and the scrapers, and these by the great construction gangs, working in assembly-line fashion. The bridges were built at night under lights. In this way the line moved steadily west from Oak Lake, just west of Brandon, at the rate of two or three miles a day. It was not jerrybuilt; it was intended to be, and was, a first-class line. Materials were as good as the C.P.R. could get. The rails were the best German and British steel. P. T. Bone, walking through the Calgary yards in 1945, found some of these original rails still in use, stamped KRUPP C.P.R. STEEL 1883.[14] "We cannot afford to build a cheap road," Stephen told Macdonald, "A poor road could not be operated in winter."[15]

Along this new line the capital for the Northwest Territories was re-established in July, 1882. Edgar Dewdney, Indian Commissioner since 1879, was appointed Lieutenant-Governor of the Northwest Territories in December, 1881. Dewdney is difficult to assess. Macdonald seems to have thought well of his administrative capacities and his cool head with Indians, and he was, ostensibly at least, a good choice for Lieutenant-Governor.[16] But it was not difficult for any Lieutenant-Governor of the Northwest Territories to make enemies. Liquor permits granted, or refused, were a fertile source of feuds. Dewdney was also criticized for his brusque and discourteous manner, and even Conservative papers in the West disliked the way he seemed to acquire money. "He is," said the Winnipeg *Times*, "in this great country, the most signal exemplar of the science of how to get along regardless of the means or methods of locomotion."[17]

Dewdney was already pre-disposed to a site at Pile of Bones Creek; he knew the country well enough by this time, and he found the land there "magnificent." Donald Smith and Angus McIntyre had already bought into Hudson's Bay Company lands there.[18] Van Horne and Dewdney met at Qu'Appelle early in June, 1882, went westward together, and Pile of Bones Creek was agreed upon early in July.[19] The choice was formally confirmed by the Government in 1883 and the name Regina substituted for the unlovely but honest old name.

At the end of the 1882 season Van Horne's line had reached to within twenty-five miles of Medicine Hat, and it was in that summer that the Rogers Pass was re-discovered. Rogers Pass was first assayed in the 1860's by Walter Moberly. It was in 1865, as Assistant Surveyor-General, that he discovered Eagle Pass through the Gold Range, between Shuswap and Revelstoke. That superb pass – the only one through the range – he was said to have discerned by watching an eagle make its way through it. On the east Eagle Pass opens upon the Columbia River at what is now Revelstoke. Fortuitously, directly across the river, can be seen another promising opening, up the Illecilleweat River into the Selkirk range.[20]

Major A. B. Rogers came sixteen years later. Rogers was a New Englander and J. J. Hill was instrumental in getting him made Engineer of the Mountain Division of the C.P.R. in February, 1881. He was a rough and ready little fellow, a master like Van Horne of picturesque profanity, whose idea of provisions seemed to be a plug of tobacco in one pocket and a sea-biscuit in the other.[21] As a consequence of the decision to move the main line south to the Kicking Horse Pass, Rogers was instructed to look at the Selkirks for a line through. From reports available and from talking to Moberly, he saw at once that he had to begin where Moberly left off years before. After great difficulties he reached the pass from the eastern side on July 24, 1882. He got back to his base at the mouth of the Kicking Horse River so badly bitten and swollen from black flies and mosquitoes that he declared his ears shook like pieces of raw liver when he walked.[22] Rogers got a cheque for $5,000 from the C.P.R. for that effort.

Rev. George Grant of Queens and Sandford Fleming, with Rogers himself as guide, made a trip over the pass in the late summer of 1883, emulating their more daring adventure by the Yellowhead of 1872.[23] There was a trail up from the Beaver River Valley, that Columbia tributary that is the key to the Rogers Pass from the east. Grant's description of this beautiful pass in its pristine glory is worth quoting:

> The ascent was so easy that I rode the whole way. On both sides of the trail grew an extraordinary variety of high bushes laden with berries, hanging so conveniently that we could pick handfuls without dismounting; blackberries . . . raspberries. . . . High above these bushes towered huge, stately forest trees; one cedar having a diameter of eight or nine feet, and a spruce being the largest any of us had ever seen . . . flowers, such as asters, the hardy blue-bell and the well known fire-weed . . . and a rich abundance of ferns. . . . After three hours of this, we emerged from the forest into an open saucer-shaped valley covered with tall rich grass, and flanked on both sides with mountains that rose high above the snow line. "There," said Major Rogers, pointing to a streamlet, "is Summit Creek, and there" – pointing to the other end of the valley, "is the summit where our zero stake is located." . . . We took our seats on a moss-grown rockery beside the creek. . . . A grander and lovelier scene could scarcely be imagined.[24]

After cigars, the Canadian Alpine Club was constituted on the spot, with Fleming as President, Grant as Secretary. The first duty of the new executive was to resolve that Major Rogers be the first honorary member, and that the pass be named Rogers Pass.

There was more to Fleming's trip than just the delights of the Rogers Pass. He had come over from London at Stephen's request, to inspect the work that Onderdonk was doing on the Government section from Kamloops to Port Moody.[25] In Fleming's opinion to Stephen the Onderdonk section was by no means up to C.P.R. standard, and Stephen promptly went after Pope for trying to "palm off on us a road such as you [Fleming] describe."[26] There was to be considerable difficulty and eventually arbitration, over the quality of that Government section from Kamloops to Port Moody. Probably with the great expense of building it, especially in the Fraser Canyon, the Government was sorely tempted to skimp the specifications.

Rail reached Calgary early in August, 1883. Père Albert Lacombe was then at a mission at Calgary.

> I would look long in silence at that road coming on . . . cutting its way through the prairies; opening up the great country we thought would be ours for years. Like a vision I could see it driving my poor Indians before it, and spreading out behind it the farms, the towns and cities you see to-day [i.e. 1909].
>
> No one who has not lived in the west since the Old-Times [1860's] can realize what is due to that road – that C.P.R. It was magic . . . changing the face of the whole country.[27]

At the end of the 1883 season, November 24, the line was at the summit of the Kicking Horse Pass. Just three weeks after that Stephen wrote

Macdonald, "Things have gone to the d--l in New York & I am off there tonight. . . . Something must be done at *once*. . . . The stock has gone down to 54 and the idea is becoming general that the Coy has not the money to go on & must stop. . . . Our enemies here and elsewhere think they can now break us down & finish the C.P.R. for ever."[28]

The three years of operations had cost the C.P.R. enormous draughts of money. The company had been prodigal both with energy and with funds. Van Horne had been told to build the railway and Stephen would find the money. In 1883, the Montreal *Star* interviewed Van Horne who opined in his usual reckless language, "The Canadian Pacific Railway has never estimated the cost of any work; it hasn't time for that; it's got a big job on hand, and it's going to put it through." The reporter asked, if the C.P.R. had not estimated its costs, how did it know it would have sufficient funds to do the mountain sections? "Well," said Van Horne, with frightening ebullience, "if we haven't got enough, we'll get more, that's all about it." Blake quoted that interview in the House in 1884 and added, "So it is getting more. We are providing for it tonight."[29] The prairie building of 1882 was enormously in excess of estimates. A first-class road cost double what a poor road would have cost, and although the prairie around Regina was flat enough, there were sections of broken rolling country in western Manitoba that occasioned very heavy work.[30]

The C.P.R. had also acquired eastern lines, and was in the process of acquiring more. Stephen had learned from J. J. Hill that a railway must build its own traffic and it was essential to develop a system of eastern feeders. And, of course, it had never been C.P.R. policy to stop at Callander. The Canada Central for Callander to Ottawa and Brockville had been acquired outright in 1881, as was the western section of the Quebec, Montreal, Ottawa, and Occidental in 1882.[31] On January 4, 1884 came the biggest acquisition of all, the lease of the Ontario and Quebec Railway. Its president was E. B. Osler; Stephen and McIntyre had been on the Board since 1881.[32] The Ontario and Quebec brought other lines, principally the Credit Valley Railway from Toronto to London and St. Thomas, and the Toronto, Grey, and Bruce from Toronto to Owen Sound, both lines of great value. The Ontario-Quebec parent line was still incomplete, but it was projected from Toronto to Perth, Smith's Falls, and Montreal via Peterborough. These important Ontario acquisitions were in Stephen's view "the right arm of the C.P.R."[33] They were also evidence of the failure to work out any arrangements with the Grand Trunk.

Impending competition from the C.P.R. had already forced the Grand Trunk to swallow the Great Western in 1882, and Stephen's substantial holdings of Credit Valley Railway stock did nothing to lessen Grand Trunk unease. The Grand Trunk's ill-will toward the C.P.R. was natural enough, and its expression not likely to be charitable in an age when railway buccaneering was a fact of life. The Grand Trunk network ran from Chicago through Montreal to Portland. The C.P.R. ran from the Canadian prairies to Montreal with the possibility, never really denied, of getting to the seaboard. Preference for the C.P.R. claims over those of the Grand Trunk was discernible in several important members of the Cabinet: Tupper, J. H. Pope, Frank Smith (a Minister, without portfolio, since 1882) and, to no small degree, Macdonald himself. On the Grand Trunk side there was Bowell, perhaps Tilley, with Campbell and McLelan both being uneasy about excessive commitments to the C.P.R.

Naturally, the Grand Trunk used its established position in London to make things difficult for the Canadian Pacific. It did not take much doing. Canadian railways were not enjoying an enthusiastic press. In Sir Alexander Galt, Stephen found no help at all, and he strongly suspected Galt's old Grand Trunk connections were responsible for his indiscreet public remarks about C.P.R. land in the west. Macdonald had succeeded in persuading Galt not to resign in 1882, and reminded him early in 1883 that the Grand Trunk still owed the Canadian government fifteen million dollars from 1857, and that Canada would not "mince matters if forced to act. . . ."[34] But Galt's position and attitude toward the Canadian Pacific were changing. In August, 1883 the first coal from the Lethbridge mine came down the Oldman River by boat to Medicine Hat and was given a triumphant test run on the C.P.R. In 1884 Stephen placed a five-year contract for coal with Galt's company. Almost certainly its duration was designed to win Galt's goodwill.[35] A railway was built from Lethbridge to Medicine Hat and Galt was, so to speak, in clover. By 1890 they were mining five hundred tons a day, all of it taken by the C.P.R.[36] In 1884 he was replaced in London by a much more ardent C.P.R. man, Sir Charles Tupper.

As of December 31, 1883, the C.P.R. had spent $59 million making its railway, and had received from the Government in cash and in land sold some $21 million. That left $38 million to be provided out of its own pocket.[37] This had come mainly from the sale of stock, though also from land grant bonds. The authorized stock had been raised from the $25 million under the original contract, to $100 million in 1882; and a surprising amount of this increased stock issue went to the directors. Stephen's holdings, for example, increased from $500,000 (5,000 shares) to $3,100,000 (31,000 shares). Whether the Company actually got full value for these extra shares is doubtful; rumour had it that Stephen and other Directors paid only $20 per share.[38] The whispered suggestion that the directors had awarded themselves handsome bonuses for their hard work and their risks did not help. Were the assets to warrant $100 million? In other words, was C.P.R. stock watered?

Nor could Stephen go to the Bank of Montreal much longer. The Bank itself was in danger from a bear raid on its stock; "heavy advances to the C.P.R. without adequate cover" as he succinctly stated it.[39] The Government was the only resort, unless the C.P.R. were to stop operations altogether. That was indeed the question. It was confidently expected in New York that the Canadian Pacific Railway would go under, that it had simply run out of money and would have to stop. This solution was distasteful to the strongest members of the Canadian cabinet, to say nothing of what it was to the Company; but the alternative, a massive government loan, was an awful dose for the Conservatives to swallow. The Canadian Pacific needed about eight million dollars at once. It could not even wait for the Parliament to meet and it went, hat in hand, to the Bank of Montreal. The Bank stepped in only with greatest reluctance; and then only upon assurances that the Government would absolutely back the Canadian Pacific, and after beating down strong opposition in its own Board of Directors.[40]

The Canadian Pacific estimated that $27 million more would finish the road, and it asked the Government offically for a loan of $22,500,000, which, with the down payment of $7.4 million for a government guarantee of three per cent on its stock, made $30 million. If Macdonald were sure of his majority in the House, the Opposition, certain to make an enormous fuss, could be beaten down. But Macdonald was by no means sure. Such a loan, coming on top of "such privileges as have never before been given by a free self-governing people," as *The Week* put it,[41] was certain to unhinge allegiances. Indeed, a "cry of dismay," in Macdonald's words,[42] went up when Conservatives were told what they would have to swallow.

Parliament met on January 17, 1884, probably because the C.P.R. could not wait. Blake began the attack in the debate on the Address. "I attribute a great portion of the difficulties in which the Canadian Pacific Railway Company are now confessedly involved, to the circumstance that they have engaged in matters not contracted for in their contract, and . . . with the capital which was directly due to the performance of the contract. . . ."[43] Davies of Prince Edward Island ridiculed the C.P.R.'s continual cries about the Grand Trunk:

> . . . whining like a spoiled child . . . that this scheme of theirs has gone astray . . . and all because there are some naughty people in this House and some naughty rivals out of it, who will not do exactly as they want. . . .[44]

Tupper's resolutions were brought in on February 5 for second reading. The terms for the government loan had become progressively stiffer as resistance in caucus made itself felt. The loan was to be secured by a lien on the whole main line and on all the land grant proceeds. None of the $35 million of unissued stock could be sold without the Government's consent. If the Company failed to pay interest on the loan for more than six months, statutory foreclosure ensued. These were hard terms. It was a fair measure of the C.P.R.'s necessity that it accepted them, as it was a fair measure of the Government's necessity to have to propose them.[45] The Company was tied hand and foot, and everything would depend upon getting the work completed expeditiously and reasonably, perhaps being able to sell an additional few millions of stock still unissued, or marketing the bonds or stock of one of its ancillary companies, like the Ontario and Quebec. On the other hand, as Tupper said, trains were running on nearly fourteen hundred miles of main line. Moreover, its difficulties, common to all North American transcontinental lines at that time, were compounded by a determined effort on the part of other railways to get the C.P.R.

A devilish combination of Maritime and Quebec Conservatives insisted upon concessions as the price of their support. As soon as a C.P.R. loan was mentioned the French-Canadian Conservative press became unfriendly to the company. *Le Monde* which often reflected Langevin, began early in the year to print anti-C.P.R. editorials, as did *La Minerve*, the official Bleu organ in Montreal. There were some fifty Conservatives from Quebec, of which forty were French Canadian, and from Nova Scotia and New Brunswick there were twenty-seven Conservatives. Both groups were powerful; and the French Canadians, even without the Quebec ministers, were sufficient to bring down the Government if they so chose.

Rumours were rife. Apparently the day after Macdonald put the C.P.R. resolutions down for precedence, Ouimet, Amyot, and Houde were delegated by the Quebec Conservatives to see Langevin. The whole provincial government of Quebec, with the exception of the Premier, J. J. Ross (who was ill), came to present their views to the Dominion Cabinet.[46] Ranks of French Canadians vanished from the House, and took up their debates in Committee Room No. 8. It was rumoured[47] – and denied on both sides[48] – that Blake and Ouimet had had *pourparlers* about a coalition between Liberals and Bleus, reminiscent of the great coup of 1854. Macdonald resisted the blackmail from Maritimers and Bleus as long as he could, but the pressures were considerable. Behind the Bleu opposition was the Grand Trunk. Hickson published correspondence early in February, protesting against further bolstering of the great Canadian Pacific monopoly, and Sénécal and other "Grand Trunk" Bleus helped stiffen the ranks. Macdonald and Langevin met the caucus to offer terms. But were they satisfactory? Monday evening, February 18, the discussion in Room 8 went on until the small hours, and broke up with no agreement. The next day the House, due to meet at 3:00, met only at 3:45, with every French-Canadian Conservative but the Ministers absent. Macdonald had sworn the C.P.R. loan would go through that day. At the six o'clock supper break the Bleus were still out; the debate droned on after supper. Blake assumed his characteristic recumbent attitude, his head on his arms, and his slouch hat on the back of his neck; Macdonald himself was drawn and weary, but determined now to stick by what he had offered. Only when the division bells rang about midnight did the French-Canadian Conservatives file in, sullen, unenthusiastic, to vote second reading. But vote they did.[49] It was law on March 5 and just in time. Stephen had been on tenterhooks, trying to keep the Company alive for the past three weeks.

It would not do, of course, to have the arrangements for passing the C.P.R. bill mixed with the bill itself. The fulfilment of the February agreements with the French Canadians and the Maritimers did not come until late in the Session. On April 7 Tupper moved an omnibus resolution granting subsidies to railways. First of all there were the Maritime subsidies, the most important of which was the subsidy to the "Short Line," from Montreal to the sea, via the shortest route. New Brunswickers had become uneasy in 1881 over the possibility of a C.P.R. winter terminal at Portland, Maine. Tilley said categorically that nothing of the kind was being considered.[50] But the question rose again in 1883, when Stephen, McIntyre, and Abbott, invited to Portland, made some generous remarks that were a lighted match to the inflammatory material available in New Brunswick. A storm of protest followed about even the suggestion that Portland might be thought of as a winter terminus.

Then there were the eastern townships of Quebec. J. H. Pope was President of a railway called the International that ran from Lennoxville to Megantic, and a Maine company of the same name and auspices had already been chartered. This involved anxious questions about a route, whether through Maine – by-passing Quebec city, with all that that involved – or using an all-Canadian route via Edmunston. Tupper's resolution authorized a subsidy of $170,000 a year for fifteen years to any railway connecting Montreal to Saint John (Halifax was added for good measure) by the "shortest and most practicable route," and, significantly, "after the report of competent engineers."[51] This was still a far cry from building the railway, and there was considerable uneasiness among members from Quebec City and beyond. There the matter rested for the moment. The subsidy was laid out; it remained to be seen whether it would be taken up.

The subsidy to Quebec involved principally the Quebec, Montreal, Ottawa, and Occidental. The C.P.R. judged its price for the western section reasonable, but for a political railway, it was a substantial loss. The eastern end, sold to Sénécal, was resold a year later to the Grand Trunk for an estimated one million dollars' profit. That too was a loss for the Quebec government. Both sections had been expensive provincial experiments in Government construction, and having lost about five million dollars, the Quebec government had for some time since been asking for a subvention of $12,000 a mile. Had not the Canada Central got that much between Callander and Pembroke? Was not a railway from Ottawa to Quebec entitled to the same? Laurier pointed out that the Quebec railway went through a populated and well-settled countryside, and did not need such a subsidy.[52] Blake was convinced that such wholesale subventions were a pernicious form of centralization, the more so since in the most inviting, that is to say material, form. Ontario municipalites had put over three million dollars into subsidies for lines that were now part of the C.P.R.: should not there be compensation for them?[53]

To these points Macdonald's reply was entirely characteristic. Blake, he said, condemned the resolutions as corrupt in spirit, but said at the same time they didn't go far enough. He was like the preacher in the western isles of Scotland, where, said Macdonald, they pray as much for a good season of wrecks as they do of oats. During a Sunday sermon, someone slipped quickly into church, and a pronounced restlessness went through the congregation:

> The parson twigged at once that there was a ship in distress in the offing, so he said, "my friends, keep your seats; listen to the words of wisdom, do not be carried away by feelings of love for filthy lucre"; but he unbuttoned the door of the pulpit, and making a dash towards the door, said: "but let us have a fair start at all events."[54]

The upshot was that Quebec was given $12,000 a mile for the 120 miles from Ottawa to Montreal, and $6,000 a mile for the 159 miles from Montreal to Quebec, the other $6,000 going to the C.P.R. to help it build another line should the Grand Trunk decide not to sell. Altogether, the Q.M.O.&O. subvention came to $2.4 million. This was not what the Quebec government wanted; they wanted the extra $6,000 a mile. But it was all Macdonald was prepared to give.

So, in 1884, the C.P.R. went on, hobbled by the Government's stringent terms, but still intact. And the Government was justified in sustaining it given the prevailing assumption that the only railways a Canadian government would take over were ones that were unprofitable. The C.P.R. profit for the nine months from April, 1883 was nearly one million dollars.

The strong Liberal opposition to the loan and to the Government's support of it forced the C.P.R. to become more politically minded. Macdonald had suggested in 1883 that in its war with the Grand Trunk the Canadian Pacific had better look to its friends and, more to the point, had better arrange to have friends to look to. He reinforced this at the very time of the loan's going through:

> We are going to have a regular quarrel & fight with the GTR – & they will oppose us politically all along the *line.* To meet this the CPR *must* become political & secure as much Parliamentary support as possible. The appts to the Ontario & Quebec [railway] should all be made political – There are plenty of good men to be found in our ranks.[55]

Stephen agreed. Macdonald then turned to H. H. Smith, the Conservative organizer for Ontario.

> He [Stephen] says that you had better see Mr. Van Horne who is fully aware now of the necessity of not appointing anybody along the line who has not been fully "circumcised" – to use his own phrase.[56]

There were hints from Macdonald later in 1884 that in the event of a dissolution early in 1885, the C.P.R. would be expected to pitch in so that the Government would not have to "fight at a disadvantage," as he delicately put it.[57] By such means as these was the C.P.R. gently introduced into nice arts of Canadian politics.

From Callander westward to Port Arthur there stretched 650 miles of most intractable terrain, wild, remote, with a few pinched and thin acres of usable land, country in its own way majestic. This the C.P.R. called its Eastern Section, and it had been a source of some contention within the Board.[58] As Stephen's determination to build the Eastern section as a full scale part of the main line had crystallized, so also did J. J. Hill's reluctance to accept it. The engineering problems east of Port Arthur were enormous; one mile of line near Jack Fish Bay cost $700,000 and several other miles half a million each.[59] Over the whole 650 miles ten per cent of the total cost of construction went for dynamite alone. The C.P.R. was forced, as Onderdonk was in British Columbia, to set up its own dynamite factories.

J. J. Hill resigned from the C.P.R. Board on May 3, 1883. The two railway systems, he said, were too great and diverse to be operated effectively under a form of common control. His real meaning he had spelled out to R. B. Angus eighteen months before:

> It seems to me that the entire Dominion of Canada, which is paying so large a bonus for a Canadian Pacific Railway, has a direct interest in preventing the business of this new North-west from being diverted to our American lines, to American markets.... If Canada does not use its Canadian Pacific Railway to bind together commercially the older with the new provinces, they will have made a poor bargain and will have difficulty in maintaining a permanent political bond between the sections.[60]

That was the nub of the matter. Whatever Blake may have felt about the route north of Lake Superior, it was a political necessity. Without it Canada was fractured into an East and a West, and inevitably the western traffic, tipped down into the United States, would have ended in the orbit of St. Paul and Chicago, not of Fort William and Montreal.

The pace of construction in 1884 was still mighty, although it was bound to cover the ground less rapidly from the top of the Kicking Horse to Kamloops than it had across the prairies; but the gap narrowed, and north of Lake Superior the two ends, one westward from Callander, the other eastward from Port Arthur, closed steadily. In an oddly prophetic thought Stephen told Macdonald that the gaps in Northern Ontario at the end of 1884 will be small enough that, "Troops *could* be sent over the line in sleighs &c any time this winter. . . ."[61] Of the 2,550 miles between Callander and Port Moody, rails had been laid for all but 480 miles by the end of 1884. Alexander Mackenzie, making his first trip west, wired enthusiastically from Mt. Stephen, British Columbia, "I heartily congratulate you on the wonderful work accomplished."[62] That did Stephen's heart good. He was going to need it.

For the stock market had gone from bad to worse. At the end of 1884 C.P.R. shares stood at forty-three in New York. The Ontario and Quebec railway tried to market an issue of five per cent debenture stock* with a C.P.R. guarantee: it got nowhere. It merely proved (as if Stephen needed proof) "the powerlessness of the C.P.R. to fund money on any kind of security they have to offer of, in short its utter want of all credit."[63] There was a threatened strike on the Eastern Section for pay, in December 1884, which was somehow stalled off until the arrival of the next consignment of government money, paying for work done.

Early in January Stephen submitted suggested relief proposals to Macdonald, but the Government was now fed up – or too many members of it were. Stephen had hinted at difficulties and the possibility of new legislation as early as July 1884, but even at that time Macdonald was frighteningly firm. "You must not look for any more legislative assistance for the C.P.R. and 'must work out your own salvation' by your own means."[64] Stephen's hot letters, his periodic bouts of hysteria, had caused him to be read at a certain discount. "I confess to a painful impression," he told Macdonald in 1885, "that all I have said as to the position of the Coy & the straits it is in, is only partially believed [.] I feel that *my* ability to save it is gone."[65] Tilley seemed to feel quite cheerful at the prospect of the Government getting its hands on such a good property so cheaply. That made Stephen no happier.

> I kept my temper because of the interests involved. It is as clear as noon day Sir John unless, you, yourself, *say* what is to be done, nothing but disaster will result. The question is too big for some of our friends & nothing but your own authority & influence will carry anything that will accomplish the object. Please put this in the fire.[66]

Smith and Stephen borrowed $650,000 themselves to pay the usual amount of extra dividend expected in New York and London in January, 1885 and they borrowed another one million dollars for the C.P.R., all on securities of their own. This was, up to a point, sensible. They knew the commercial possibilities of the C.P.R.; but Stephen pointed out to Macdonald that what he and Donald Smith were doing was not business but foolhardiness, risking substantial personal fortunes to save a failing business from receivership. Their attitude was almost a kind of personal immolation. It may be that the

* Debenture stock is stock the interest on which is guaranteed in perpetuity.

C.P.R. will go under, Smith told a gloomy C.P.R. board, but it must not happen "as long as we individually have a dollar."[67] There was to be no cut and run. So the railway stumbled on, ekeing out a precarious existence with promises and hopes, but drawing steadily near bankruptcy. On March 13, 1885, the Toronto *Mail* announced editorially that the C.P.R. had defaulted and the whole property had been forfeited to the Government.

Macdonald's position was nearly as desperate as Stephen's. He felt sure he could not carry Council for another C.P.R. loan, and certain he could not carry caucus. Alexander Campbell warned him:

> I dare say with your "many-sided-ness" that most of the points will have occurred to you. . . . As far as I can judge we had better face the evils which the fall of the company (if it must fall) would undoubtedly entail than those which lending them 10 millions more would bring about. . . . Whatever measures were needed to enable you to complete the road [by Government building] would be freely given and the conservative party would remain uninjured – The other course I believe presents graver danger than we have ever encountered.[68]

On February 9, in the House, Blake asked Macdonald point blank whether the Government intended to bring in legislation on the C.P.R. Macdonald said no.[69] True, perhaps, but the official application came on March 18, and Macdonald was gloomy. Tilley did not want to loan the C.P.R. a dollar. "God knows how it will all end," Macdonald wrote Tupper despairingly on March 17, "but I wish we were well out of it."[70]

The Opposition by now were complaining that everything in the Session was still left undone. Everything was late. Tilley's budget was brought in five weeks after Parliament opened. And where were the government measures announced in the Speech? Blake asked on March 10. "*In medio tutissimus*," replied Macdonald.[71] (In the middle, safety.) Was that the reason that on March 19, 1885, the day that police reinforcements were sent to the Saskatchewan, Macdonald, that superb tactician, chose to introduce, in the seventh week of a do-nothing session,[72] the most controversial and bitterly opposed piece of legislation of his whole career (and which he knew to be so) – the Franchise bill? The Franchise bill might pull the party together; a C.P.R. bill could only have divided it.

The C.P.R. was going to go down. Macdonald told Stephen on March 26, that it was unlikely Council could agree to the proposals to be put before them officially in the afternoon. In the evening Stephen returned to the Russell House from Earnscliffe, his worst fears confirmed. Macdonald had finally refused the C.P.R. loan. Stephen packed his bags and went to pay his bill. There he encountered Frank Smith, and probably John Henry Pope. They appealed to him to stay over, and themselves drove out for a midnight talk with Macdonald. They returned about two in the morning, defeated too. There was no way out. The C.P.R. was finished.[73]

Then the unexpected happened. The next day, a telegram came announcing the disastrous encounter of the Mounted Police with the Métis at Duck Lake the day before. At once in Macdonald's ingenious mind the possibility arose: "He could use the railway to defend the west. He could use the west to justify the railway."[74] The Franchise bill could be a smoke screen for both.

The offset of troops and a C.P.R. loan was due to Van Horne who had the brilliant idea of offering to move troops, were that to be necessary, from Ottawa to Qu'Appelle in eleven days, given forty-eight hours notice.[75] Van Horne got that notice on March 27, 1885, the day the news of Duck Lake came. Thus, by an extraordinary combination of circumstances, C.P.R. relief, the Franchise bill and the Northwest rebellion, all landed on Macdonald's desk at the same time. From here on it was a question of tactics. The Franchise bill would be used to block awkward questions on the Northwest rebellion; the Northwest rebellion would be used to aid the C.P.R. and the C.P.R. relief would benefit from the Opposition's preoccupation with the first two. *In medio tutissimus*, indeed. As tactics it was masterly: as government it was desperate. Macdonald might have conceded this; he would have been the first to admit that the Government was a mess.[76]

A Franchise bill had been hovering about Parliament Hill since Confederation. Macdonald had talked of it in 1867, it was read a first time in 1869, and got to second reading and committee in 1870. It was announced in the Speech in 1873 in the spring, and again in the fall. It then dropped out of sight until announced in 1883 and read a first time. This was done again in 1884. It was announced in 1885 and read for the first time on March 19. The astonishing aspect of the bill was that there had been almost no agitation for change. Its various introductions in the past seem to have elicited little reaction. Few believed it would be enacted this time.

The bill was to establish Dominion qualifications for elections to the Dominion Parliament. Since the right to vote had been determined by each province there were seven different franchises, roughly as follows: in Prince Edward Island and British Columbia, virtually a manhood franchise; in New Brunswick and Manitoba, ownership of real property worth $100; in Nova Scotia, property worth $150; in Quebec, property of $300 in cities, $200 elsewhere; in Ontario, the property was $400 in cities, $300 in towns, and $200 elsewhere, with the addition that farmers' sons could be assessed for their share of a farm and thus be entitled to vote.[77] There was not much disposition by the provinces to tinker with these franchises, but, in 1885, Ontario broadened its franchise to $200 property in cities, $100 elsewhere, and added an income or wages franchise of $250 per annum.[78]

The idea of a Dominion franchise was, on the face of it, a reasonable one, but it looked more reasonable than it was. A farm of twenty acres in Prince Edward Island might have a radically different valuation than one of the same size as Ontario. A property franchise imposed by the Dominion was bound to be basically inequitable. "So long as this diversity of values exists to the extent it does exist at present," said one sensible M.P., "it is an utter impossibility."[79] The bill as originally brought down set a property qualification of $300 in cities, and $150 elsewhere, with provision for giving the vote to properly qualified women who were widows or were unmarried. Indians similarly qualified could vote. Women and Indians presumably would vote Conservative, but in other respects the proposed Dominion franchise, roughly equal to that of Quebec's, was a distinct restriction of the existing franchise. By a still more extraordinary arrangement, voters' lists were to be compiled by government appointees, in effect, henchmen of the Government of the day.

It was handled with such extraordinary ineptitude that it seemed deliberately designed to provoke the Opposition. Macdonald introduced its second reading on April 16, with a speech of eight and a half minutes, occupying exactly one page of the *Debates*. He seemed, either deliberately or inadvertently, to have failed to master its details, and the bill got a very rough time. Cartwright was indignant:

> The First Minister deliberately precipitated a measure on this House which he knew would meet with the most intense opposition, which he knew involved an almost interminable discussion, and he did that mainly for the reason that he desired, by the introduction of that measure, to deprive my hon. friends and the other gentleman of this side, of the opportunity of calling him and his friends to account for that misgovernment which has set this country in a flame.[80]

The bill got past second reading on April 22, and was at once bogged down in Committee of the Whole. There it stayed for six mortal weeks, to the exclusion of nearly everything else, and punctuated now and then with telegrams from the Northwest that Caron or Macdonald would read to the House. While the great events in the Northwest went on, Parliament was busy with kazoos behind the Speaker's chair, noises "like the utterances of an emaciated tom cat,"[81] desk scraping, a sophisticated technique with the bottom of the shoe applied deftly against the side of the desk, the whole gamut of machinations that occur when, as Macdonald delicately put it, "an hon. member has not the ear of the House, and the House is disinclined to hear him, [and] the House allows it to be known by unmistakeable signs of inattention. . . ."[82] The whole spirit of the Opposition was summed up in the remark of the Liberal whip, James Trow, "The Bill will not pass the House if we have to sit six months."[83] Their bitter resistance is explained by the bill itself, but there was method in it, as the Toronto *Globe* described:

> The Administration of Sir John Macdonald is bleeding at every pore. . . . Every province, not excepting Ontario, is in a state of dangerous discontent.

> . . . Under these circumstances, a dozen resolute men could "hold the fort" at Ottawa, and it will be a disgrace to the Liberal Opposition if it is surrendered now. Had the Gerrymander Bill of 1882 been dealt with in the way referred to it would never have been passed.[84]

Blake apparently did not share the enthusiasm of his party for this method of proceeding.[85] Macdonald nursed his strength, but was resolute. There were hints of closure; Macdonald remarked that he hoped it would not be necessary to do what Gladstone had felt compelled to do in 1881.[86] The Government did not bring in closure but Parliament did almost nothing else but talk the Franchise bill until June 10. By then even Macdonald was fed up.

It finally passed third reading, much amended, much improved, and much more complicated, on July 6, 1885. Votes for widows and spinsters and certain classes of Indians were dropped, the property qualification was lowered and, in particular, appeals were allowed from revising officers' voting lists to a judge. Macdonald, in fact, agreed to use judges for revising officers wherever possible. That clause was by no means shorn of its power: it was still an effective weapon against the Opposition in the hands of a determined and ruthless government. Like the Gerrymander Act of 1882, however, the Franchise Act probably did less damage, and less good, than feared by its opponents or expected by its friends. After the smoke of battle had cleared off, it was obvious that the Dominion franchise was more extensive than the seven provincial franchises it had replaced.[87]

While this vast debate had been proceeding, the Canadian Pacific Railway teetered from crisis to crisis, living by its wits, Stephen's nerves and money, Smith's determination and money, Shaughnessy's ingenuity with suppliers, and a good deal of luck. The Government backed a Bank of Montreal loan to forestall immediate collapse at the end of March. But Macdonald was in no hurry to bring in legislation: as far as he was concerned, the longer that was put off the better. The C.P.R. bill was to be given no priorities; it would come on when the Government was ready, and not before. There was to be none of that public demonstration of blackmail that there had been in 1884; the Maritime and Quebec members would be pacified, and at C.P.R. expense, but quietly with the whole matter arranged to Macdonald's satisfaction. And nothing was going to interfere with the Franchise bill. The C.P.R. was going to be used to strengthen the Government's hand with its supporters; it would have to pay for its own exigencies. Stephen moaned often enough about his troubles; Macdonald sharply reminded him that the Government had its own:

> You have sometimes told me that I did not appreciate your difficulties. Your note of the 24th[88] shows that you have not yet grasped mine. . . . The majority of our friends in Parlt and *all* our & your foes were in favour of the Govt assuming possession of the road, and my personal influence with our

> supporters and a plain indication of my resignation only got them into line – This was done by personal communication with every one of them – Now any change of the arrangement will upset the cart. . . .
> I showed your note only to one colleague and his immediate reply was that as fast as we got you out of one trouble, you tried to plunge us into another & we had better break up the whole arrangement.[89]

The main elements present in the 1884 loan were present in the 1885 one; the difference was that the C.P.R. had to take over, and operate, what had only been subsidized in 1884. The legislation of 1884 had not solved the north shore problem. Quebec City wanted to be an ocean terminus of the C.P.R.; but the north shore line was still owned by the Grank Trunk. Stephen had not been interested in acquiring it; he did not think it would pay. Nor did the Grand Trunk want to sell it. Giving the C.P.R. running rights over it would not satisfy the Quebec members. Stephen was made to agree to buy it, and if the sale were not accomplished, to agree to build a third railway from Montreal to Quebec. The negotiations attending this arrangement were long and messy; Macdonald, Pope, Langevin, Abbott, Stephen, and Hickson of the Grand Trunk were soon all hip-deep in it, and its attendant issues like the McGreevy Round House at Quebec, or the Jacques Cartier Railway at Montreal.[90] Ultimately the Grand Trunk sold the line to the Government, who re-sold it to the C.P.R., as of September 21, 1885.[91]

The "Short Line," Montreal to Saint John, was also up. The subsidy of 1884 had not solved that problem either, and the C.P.R. was made to take that on. Tupper in London and Pope in Ottawa both persuaded Stephen that the C.P.R. stood to gain, not lose, by acquiring a winter outlet in Saint John, with connections to Halifax. Pope had both political and personal advantage to gain; and since Stephen was fond of Pope, the latter consideration weighted quite as much as the former.[92] Stephen said except for his desire to relieve Pope of his personal load in the International Railway, it was doubtful if the "Short Line" would ever have been built.[93] Pope and Tupper assured Stephen that the Intercolonial Railway, in government hands still, would be run as a local line, and that the "Short Line" would absorb most of the through traffic.[94] The Maritime members, like those from Quebec City, insisted that the "Short Line" be part of the Canadian Pacific system, and would listen to no other arrangement. At the same time members from Quebec district, Laurier among them, fought hard for a line to the Maritimes via Edmunston;[95] but all they got was an increase in the subsidy offered for such a line.

As for the C.P.R. loan, Macdonald proposed the resolutions on June 10, 1885. The $35 million of C.P.R. stock held by the Government was replaced, and the stock cancelled, by an issue of $35 million first mortgage bonds. These were the first bonds the Canadian Pacific Railway had issued on the security of the line. The Government were to hold $20 million of them as security for the $30 million loan of 1884, and held land grant bonds for the rest. The remaining $15 million of the mortgage bonds was to be marketed through Government trustees; $8 million was security for a $5 million temporary loan from the Government, and the remaining $7 million given out as needed to the C.P.R. The marketing of this $15 million bond issue, to run thirty years at five per cent, was the first real success the C.P.R. had had in some time. It was handled, successfully, through Baring Brothers of London, who took half at ninety and the rest on option at ninety-one. When that news was cabled to Montreal, Van Horne and Angus capered around the C.P.R. boardroom like children, kicking the furniture joyfully as they went.[96] The bonds were offered to the public at ninety-five. Ostensibly the whole of the $15 million was accepted, but in actual fact only about $9 million was actually placed. Barings held the rest and fed the market slowly and carefully over the following months, selling the bonds at ninety-six or so.[97] Stephen was grateful to Barings ever after for their confidence at this critical stage. When Barings were on the brink of collapse in November 1890 from bad Argentine railway investments, Stephen and Donald Smith helped to bail them out.[98]

The log jam in C.P.R. affairs was now broken. The eastern section north of Lake Superior was finished in May 1885; the government section, Kamloops to Port Moody, was finished at the end of July 1885, and formally handed over to the C.P.R. on June 30, 1886; Lord Lansdowne, the Governor General, went west in September 1885 to visit the western prairies and British Columbia, and was to drive the last spike near Eagle Pass. But the work was held up by bad weather; Lansdowne, who would have liked to stay on in British Columbia, was by October, 1885 needed in Ottawa. "C.P.R. rail will not be laid before end of month. Should return?" Yes, was the reply from Macdonald.[99] So it was Donald Smith who drove the last spike.

Craigellachie is at the western end of Eagle Pass, where the valley opens out to the westward. There is nothing there now but an ancient disused little station house, a sign with "Craigellachie" painted on it, and a cairn. There it was that the two C.P.R. gangs met, one working eastward from Kamloops, and the other westward from the Kicking Horse Pass. Saturday, November 7, 1885 was a misty, unattractive day, the clouds low, the great spires of spruce and cedar swaying in the damp wind. A camera recorded the last spike of iron being driven by Donald Smith. The next week Stephen wrote to Macdonald from London that C.P.R. bonds were at par (Barings would make a good profit on those), and the stock was now up to fifty-six, and headed, Stephen hoped, for seventy-five.[100]

The stock of the Government was headed the other way. It had had a bad year and a half. There had to be new men; the Government was too old, too sick, too weak in power and talent. Tilley was ill and feeble and had been getting progressively more so for the past two or three years; he gave up completely in mid-session and was operated on for kidney-stones in London, in June 1885. Langevin was well enough, but had been too preoccupied with the administration of Public Works and only recently was beginning to help with the general work of the government.[101] Bowell and Carling were not much help, though Bowell took over Tilley's duties at Finance while Tilley was in London. Chapleau brought only his perennial quarrel with Langevin to the Government, and he had been away ill; Macpherson was sick and so was Pope for part of the session. Costigan was hopeless in the House, even in his own Department, and too often drunk.[102] McLelan of Nova Scotia was better, he did not get drunk, and he knew his Department, but was fearful and uncertain in the House. A. P. Caron was not very effective either, easily needled and utterly devoid of tact. Macdonald was congratulated by the Liberal whip on how healthy he looked at the end of that awful 1885 session;[103] but he seems to have been the only one. Alexander Campbell had told him on March 22, that he wanted to be out at the end of the session. Macdonald appealed to him in August to stay on in the Cabinet, and Campbell agreed. But, he added,

> As I am writing, let me say how much I hope that, we may get on without this eternal yielding to every one who has, or thinks he has, control of a few votes. . . .[104]

Macdonald admitted that the work was being ill done; so much of it fell upon him. "If we don't get Thompson I don't know what to do."[105]

Campbell was still more critical, privately, to friends. From Newport, Rhode Island, he wrote his old friend T. C. Patteson, now the Postmaster of Toronto.

> . . . things have been going badly in the Ministry for a year or more – Macdonald has lost his grasp, and does nothing he can help. Putting off, his old sin, has increased upon him, until it has become an irritation to have relations with him. . . . He retains his old power of dealing with his followers and his keen insight into motives of action – but for the work of government and of legislation he is gone I think – his franchise bill as he presented it, was a remarkable instance of his incapacity for the work of legislation – all the really able men in Parliament appreciated the confused jumble in which he had placed the whole subject. . . .[106]

It was conditions like these, at the very heart of the Conservative government, that bred the neglect, the delays, the exacerbating frustration, that had by March, 1885, inflamed a Northwest agitation into open, and armed, rebellion.

CHAPTER 9

The Saskatchewan Rebellion and After 1884-1886

"A huge cloak-bag of pomposity and conceit";[1] that was Charles Mair's unrepentant description of Sir David Macpherson, appointed Minister of the Interior in October 1883. Macpherson had been a Senator since Confederation and, although there was talk of having him run for a Commons seat,[2] it never came to anything. A Toronto business man with some highly laudable Montreal connections, he was not a robust or energetic minister, and now, at sixty-five, coasting came easily. His appointment, considering the importance Macdonald attached to the office, was curious, and is part of the pattern of Macdonald's appointments in the early 1880's. Macpherson was a political friend with whose habits Macdonald was long familiar, and whose loyalty he trusted.

In the spring of 1883, and again in 1884, Charles Mair took the 250-mile wagon road from Prince Albert to Winnipeg, and the 1,700-mile train journey to Ottawa. He pleaded with officials to make concessions to the whites and Métis of the Saskatchewan country, before blood was shed. Ottawa proved to be indifferent. George Denison recalled:

> He told me each time he went down that there would be trouble; each succeeding visit he became more and more alarmed. He begged of the Government to make some concessions. . . . I could not help laughing at the picture he gave me of Sir David Macpherson, a very large, handsome, erect man of six feet four inches, getting up, leaving his room and walking away down the corridor, while Mair, a short, stout man, had almost to run along side of him as he made his final appeal to preserve the peace and to prevent bloodshed.[3]

Mair moved his family back to Windsor, Ontario, in September 1884.

The Department of the Interior, when Clifford Sifton came to the office in 1896, he described later as "a department of delay, a department of circumlocution . . . a department which tired men to death who undertook to get any business transacted with it."[4] But in 1884 Sifton was twenty-three, practising law with his brother in Brandon, and disposed to be less sweeping in his criticism. His complaint in 1884, and that of many others, was that the numerous changes in land laws produced such confusion that few settlers knew, or could find out, what the land regulations really were. The prospective settler was left in the toils of the discretionary power of the Land Board officials in Winnipeg, or agents thereof, and there was a strong suspicion that this power was abused. Even when it was not, the conflicting construction placed upon the regulations by different officials encouraged such suspicions. Altogether the system, if that was the name for it, "to our certain knowledge had a most disastrous effect in deterring persons . . . from taking up land. . . . it has become the conviction of many intending settlers that it is impossible to procure eligible homesteads." The changes Sifton suggested were simple enough: that the land laws be changed only by act of Parliament, and not by Orders in Council; that the discretionary power of officials be strictly limited and defined. With reforms such as these dissatisfaction with the Department of the Interior's land policies would soon come to an end.[5]

The local officers in the Northwest, in the Indian Department especially, were often dedicated and hard working men, on little pay, and subject to the great difficulties produced by vacillations of government policy. But there was also a strong political taint to many of them. Not all political appointments were bad; Elliot Galt was a conspicuous success, and won golden opinions wherever he went; but too many officials aroused the same feeling that the Northern carpet-baggers gave the Southerners after the American civil war. In fact, "carpet-baggers" was the expression often used to describe eastern political appointees battened upon the West.[6] Rev. John McDougall, of the Stoney Mission at Morley, complained of Indian Department officials who were expected to teach the Indians habits of thrift and industry from the cocoon of their own laziness and incompetence.[7]

The Superintendent-General of Indian Affairs was Macdonald himself from 1878 to 1887, but he left administration largely in the hands of Lawrence Vankoughnet, the son of an old political friend, appointed Deputy in 1880. Vankoughnet was narrow and niggling in administration, and unimaginative in policy. "Imbecile" was the word the editor of the Toronto *Mail* used to describe him and he added that A. M. Burgess, Deputy Minister of the Interior, was in a position he was not capable of filling, and ought never to have been put there.[8]

The Northwest rebellion papers include a long letter, August 1884, from Edgar Dewdney, summarizing some of the problems of the Northwest at that stage, and particularly critical of Vankoughnet, who had made a trip through the Northwest the summer before. Dewdney hit hard at the departmental penny-pinching that resulted from Vankoughnet's recommendations to Macdonald, which merely exacerbated an already bad situation.[9] The letter is endorsed on the back in Macdonald's hand, "Discuss situation with Vt. after session. *JAMD 30 June 1885*."[10]

With the heavy deficit on current account on the Government's books for 1883, and another deficit forecast for 1884, Macdonald felt compelled to shorten sail. The Indian Department suffered with the rest. But the $140,000 reduction in the Indian Department was an ill-chosen saving. There were dismissals of clerks indispensable to the Indian agents if they themselves were to spend time on the reservations working with the Indians. The agents were now restricted both in authority and in initiative. C. E. Denny of Fort Macleod was told to limit his visits to the reserves to once a month. Denny, who had licked his agency nicely into shape with hard work and perseverance, resigned in January, 1884.[11] This line of government policy was fundamentally wrong, Dewdney told Macdonald. "The bulk of Indians, require constant supervision, you have to talk with them, think for them, advise them, *work for them* at the same time let them think they are doing their share of it. . . ."[12]

What was worse, Indians rations were cut down. John Rae, Indian agent at Battleford, wrote in despair to Macdonald over the head of Vankoughnet, his proper senior authority. Vankoughnet, Rae said, had nearly precipitated an Indian outbreak by his handling of Big Bear whom he ordered to take his reservation within a month or get no rations. It was general policy now that Indians were to work to receive rations, which, said Rae, was reasonable for Indians who were well settled, but would not work with the newcomers "who have always been either warriors or horse thieves."[13]

There was, moreover, some Indian resentment over the Treaties and what they really meant. The idea of selling their land to the Canadian government seems never to have been in their heads. "Owning" land was a concept foreign to their thinking. They used land, and it was this usufruct that they believed they had conveyed to the white man. What they had imagined, as one Indian pointed out, was usage similar to that of the one white authority they had known, the Hudson's Bay Company.[14]

On the other hand, it was the purpose of Canadian Indian policy to make self-sufficient, and presumably to civilize, the Indians, the former being of the most immediate urgency. This meant converting the Indians from hunters into farmers. It was far from easy. Hunting is poor preparation for farming. Prairie hunting required collective discipline, but farming required the heroic self-discipline and sustained effort of individual labour. Nursing food out of rocks and earth was ill-suited to the Indian nature.[15] Vital Grandin, Bishop of St. Albert (near Edmonton), who had lived in the West since 1855, remarked:

> Les sauvages . . . ne peuvent se résoudre au travail; ils ne savent s'y résoudre que pressés par la faim, et la raison en est qu'ils ne voient pas en cela comme dans la chasse, le résultat immédiat de leurs efforts; cela les décourage.[16]

Even at the end of 1882 many Indians had not given up hope that the rich, free days of the buffalo would return.[17]

Still, there was real success in the arduous process of change, exaggerated perhaps, in the government reports to facilitate next year's appropriation. Four hundred bushels of potatoes were sold by Little Child's band in Treaty No. 4 to a Broadview firm in August 1883, at one dollar a bushel, and there were frequent reports of good crops on reserves.[18] But there were perennial problems arising from the fecklessness of the Indian. Denny, for example, reported in 1883 that wire fencing would have to be substituted for wooden fencing on the Indian farms, since they found the wood too convenient in winter, and burnt up the fences for fuel.[19] Denny wrote, many years later, that the Indians had been a free and happy race, "knowing no law or restraint but their own will or the tribal rule, and were now like people suddenly shut off from light, having blindly to grope their way towards a new and unknown condition of which they had no conception. Their faults, many of them as we saw them, had been virtues to themselves."[20] Goldwin Smith wrote, after a trip west in 1884, "The Indian is manifestly doomed. There he sits in the sun gazing listlessly at the railway train. . . ."[21] It was this fate that some of the great Cree chiefs, Poundmaker, Big Bear, Little Pine, Lucky Man (though the last two had been prevailed upon to sign Treaty No. 6) were fighting against in 1885.

The population of the Northwest Territories, white, half-breed, and Indian was, in 1885, as follows:

	Whites	*Half-Breeds*	*Indians*	
Assiniboia	16,574	1,017	4,492	= 22,083
Saskatchewan	4,486*		6,260	= 10,746
Alberta	4,878	1,237	9,418	= 15,533
Total	25,938	2,254*	20,170	= 48,362

Among the white population there were grievances in plenty, many of them the kind that occur in any pioneer community, but all aggravated by a bad frost in 1883** and a wet harvest in 1884. Prince Albert suffered more than any other district of the Northwest. Even Dewdney, always willing to keep the worst of the bad news to himself to spare Macdonald, had to admit that at Prince Albert the crops in September were a total failure, and seed grain would have to be provided to make a fresh start in the spring.[23] The whites in the northern Saskatchewan valleys were particularly unhappy over the change in railway route and the failure of the land boom. Thus farmers looking for a good crop and speculators looking for a fat increment – often

* The Saskatchewan figure includes whites and half-breeds.[22]

** Frosts are always uneven on the prairies, but the frost of September 7, 1883 was generally very damaging.

one and the same person – were both dissatisfied.[24] The Assistant Indian Commissioner reported the feeling in Prince Albert in November, 1883:

> A strong feeling is being fostered against the Govmt & all officials relative to the nonissuing of patents . . . the people are egged to the belief that nothing short of a rebellion is necessary in order to obtain their rights – this is mainly brought about by the hard times which give the merchants & others little to do or think about. . . .[25]

It was a long way to Ottawa from Prince Albert. There was no representation of the Northwest Territories in Parliament; that did not come until 1886 as a direct result of the events of 1885. Few Northwest grievances, especially those from the territories, got onto the floor of Parliament. The North-West Council at Regina – now six official and eight elected members – proved powerless in fighting for Northwest demands. It was, said the *Prince Albert Times*, a "wretched farce . . . whose pitiful powers are controlled by Government officials."[26] The North-West Council passed a long memorial in 1883, and a sharper one in 1884; they disappeared into Ottawa pigeonholes until, two months after trouble had broken out, a report was prepared upon them by Macpherson.[27]

The attitude of some of the elected members of the Council and some of the newspapers to Ottawa was similar to the attitudes of the opposition of Lower Canada and Upper Canada just fifty years before toward London. To Ontario newspapers that counselled perseverance and fortitude rather than lawlessness, there was a sharp answer from that fire-brand, Frank Oliver. There were few more powerful arguments, *ad captandum vulgus*, than this from the Edmonton *Bulletin*:

> If it was not by – not threatening, but actual – rebellion and appeals to the British government for justice that the people of Ontario gained the rights they enjoy today and freed themselves from a condition precisely similar to that in which the North-West is being rapidly forced, how was it? Was it not by armed rebellion coupled with murder, that Manitoba attained the rights she enjoys today from the very men who now hold the reins of power at Ottawa. If history is to be taken as a guide, what could be plainer than that without rebellion the people of the North-West need expect nothing. . . .[28]

This is the familiar story of a country controlled by a distant government, unresponsive, or responsive only at several removes, to local exigencies.

How much more did these difficulties apply to a group that lacked any effective means of expression, neither newspaper nor effective representatives, nothing except the ubiquitous petition; a group which, while it had little to lose by crop failure or the ruin of land speculation, was both vulnerable and nearly helpless – the Métis. The Métis in the Saskatchewan valley had established the parish of St. Laurent in the 1860's and early 1870's, when it was a buffalo camp. Many more had come from Manitoba in the later 1870's having sold the land scrip they had received, and new offshoots from St. Laurent (also called Grandin) appeared, the parishes of St. Antoine de Padoue (later called Batoche), and St. Louis de Langevin. The oldest and largest of the Métis settlements in the West was St. Albert, near Edmonton, where in 1883 they had acquired the land patents for their strip farms. St. Albert seems to have played little part in the Northwestern agitation.

The Saskatchewan Métis had some real grievances, and some not so real. They claimed the same amount of land as the Manitoba Métis had got – 240 acres – based, in both cases, on the Métis share in Indian rights. The Manitoba Métis had found it had taken a long time to secure and patent their land and many, despairing of patents, and finding their way of life altered beyond recognition by white settlement, had sold out for what they could get and gone west, many to the Saskatchewan country. Thus, of Saskatchewan Métis, some were genuinely entitled to land, and many were not. Macdonald told the House of Commons in 1885 that nine-tenths of the Métis who had claimed scrip had had it already.[29] This figure is too vague to be given much weight; but Macdonald was right in saying that any Métis was entitled to 160 acres under the Homestead Act. Gabriel Dumont himself was officially entered for homestead, as of March 1, 1883, on the southwest quarter of Section 20, Township 42, Range 1 west of the 3rd Meridian, with a pre-emption right on the southeast quarter of the same section.[30] Isidore Dumont, his brother, had been given 240 acres in Manitoba. Macdonald was not far wrong:

> The half-breed . . . was not cultivating the land he had. Giving him more land was giving him nothing. The nomadic half-breed, who had been brought up to hunt, having had merely his shanty to repair in the dead season, when there was no game – what advantage was it to him to give him 160 or 240 acres more? It was of no use to him whatever, but it would have been of great use to the speculators who were working on him and telling him he was suffering. Oh! How awfully he was suffering, ruined, destroyed, starving, because he did not get 240 acres somewhere else, or the scrip for it, that he might sell it for $50! No, Sir, the whole thing is a farce.[31]

What the Métis resented was having to pay for land on the odd-numbered sections. Homestead lands were the even-numbered sections; the odd-numbered sections, if the township were not in a railway belt, were government sections for sale, at two dollars an acre. The Government could not see why the Métis should try to get around these regulations; the Métis could not understand why the regulations should apply to them at all.

The problem was made rather more intractable by the survey. The standard Métis river lot was ten chains, or 220 yards, along the river, and two miles deep. This was precisely the same area as a quarter-section, 160 acres, but it crossed several lines of the square survey. The square survey was certainly susceptible of adjustment by arrangement of subdivisions of quarter sections,[32] but it was not easy for the Métis to understand the tricks in laying it out, or the conveyancing involved in titles laid out in such a fashion.[33]

Memorials, letters, petitions, made their way eastward to Ottawa from 1877 on. The Department of the Interior proved to be most unresponsive. In 1882 it took six months to turn down the suggestion from the land agent in Prince Albert about making river lot surveys at St. Laurent.[34] A petition from St. Antoine de Padoue (Batoche) in 1882 had asked that the Métis be allowed to occupy odd-numbered sections without paying the two dollars an acre for government land, and that the lands so granted be set up on the Métis river lot principle. This was by no means unreasonable, and one of Edward Blake's most devastating hits in the House in July 1885, was the fate of some of the signers of that unanswered petition of 1882; Gabriel Dumont (wounded), Baptiste Rochlot (prisoner), Caliste Touron (killed), François Touron (prisoner).[35] The end of Métis frustrations was deliverance through violence.

It was nine years since the Canadian government had banished Riel for a five-year term, and he had had a difficult time. Near Washington, D.C. in November, 1874 he had had a vision in which he was visited by a spirit in a burning cloud, who told him he was God's instrument for the regeneration of the Métis. Within eighteen months he was in Longue Pointe Asylum in Montreal, "in the throes of psychotic disintegration." He was later moved to Beauport, near Quebec, where he was released early in 1878. Riel's illness has been classified by modern psychiatrists as manic and paranoid psychosis. In this type of illness, for reasons not even now well understood, the synthesizing and defensive functions of the ego break down. The origin of this trouble in Riel's case is obscure, perhaps the death, in 1864, of his father whom he idolized. If the causes are obscure, the results are not. When confronted with disappointment or frustration, Riel found release in delusions, an attempt on the part of the impaired ego to maintain contact somehow with external reality, though in a warped and sometimes dangerous form. In this state the resulting megalomaniac may seize upon "grandiose political or religious schemes which are designed to . . . recreate a new world to replace the one which has been lost. . . ."[36] This is the explanation of the overwhelming impression of intense personal vanity that everyone who met him, from 1869 to 1885, seems to have remarked upon.

Riel had quieted down by 1878, and was living on the charity of friends and the Church. He moved west later that year, and finally joined Métis near Fort Benton. He kept his hand in politics. In the Sioux troubles of 1879 he was in touch with Crowfoot of the Blackfeet, trying to persuade him to join the Sioux and the Crees to hold the West for the Indians and

Métis. In 1881, he married a Métisse; by 1883 they had two children, and Riel became an American citizen. His period of exile from Canada over, he returned briefly for a rather happy visit to St. Boniface in June 1883.

By 1884 he was quietly teaching at a mission school at Sun River, southwest of Fort Benton, and making a thin but respectable living. But teaching school, for a man who had once had all Manitoba at his feet, was boring and unsatisfying. He had never given up his conviction of his destiny to lead the Métis, though he had had singularly little success with the ones in Montana, who were nearly as demoralized from whisky as the Indians. Then on Sunday, June 4, 1884 Gabriel Dumont, two other Métis, and an English half-breed rode into Sun River. They had come seven hundred miles from the Saskatchewan country to see him, bringing letters from white settlers in Prince Albert, who urged him to come,[37] and who had provided the funds to bring him. Even Charles Mair, who had no sympathy for Riel, confessed that if a rising should take place he might become a rebel himself, "so scandalously mismanaged by Eastern politicians" had Northwest affairs become.[38] Riel agreed to go to the Saskatchewan, and he and his family arrived at Batoche early in July 1884, moving in with a cousin, Charles Nolin. Riel played his cards with uncanny skill. The welcome he received from the Métis was enthusiastic, for he was already invested, for them, with the touch of the Messiah. He was received with equal enthusiasm by the English half-breeds. Still more important, he was warmly supported by the whites of Prince Albert. Riel spoke there on July 19, 1884, when nearly the whole town turned out to hear him, many from curiosity, more from sympathy. He spoke with studied moderation, as if conscious that he must gather momentum slowly and carefully. There was to be no violence, he said; the settlers ought to have free title for their lands, representation of the Northwest in Parliament – perhaps even provincial status – and more land made available for homesteading. Riel's strength grew surprisingly rapidly, and with it his own conviction of his mission. "Not long ago," he wrote about this time, "I was a humble schoolmaster . . . and here I am today in the ranks of the most popular men in the Saskatchewan. . . . What has brought all this about? . . . you know that it is God."[39]

Riel's political support tempted him to be rather more firm with the Church. His growing impatience with Father André, the curé at Prince Albert, demonstrates his conviction of his own importance. He was irritated by criticism from the Church and was beginning to be irritated even by neutrality. He wanted active support, and that the Church would not, indeed could not, give.

Much preparation was made by Riel for Langevin's visit during his trip west in August 1884. Unfortunately, Langevin never came north, nor was Riel informed that he would not. The Métis watched the roads from the south in vain for the great man who never came. Instead, Riel was later interviewed by Amédée Forget, Secretary of the North-West Council, visiting the settlement with Bishop Grandin of St. Albert. "What are you aiming at?" Forget asked. ". . . Suppose the half-breed question is settled?" Riel answered that if the land issues were settled, some appointments made, including Riel's to Breland's seat on the North-West Council at ($1000 per annum), the half-breeds would be satisfied. Riel himself was not sure he would give up his American citizenship to go on the Council; if not, then he would want money.[40] In December it was clear that about $5000 would, provided settlement of the Métis claims were made, "cart the whole Riel family across the boundary." But the price went steadily upward as his support, and his exasperation, increased. In January 1885, Father André admitted that $35,000 was too much, but that it was perhaps better than leaving Riel loose in the Saskatchewan country. Macdonald was contemptuous of this kind of blackmail. But Riel was living again, as he had for so much of his adult life, on the charity of the Métis and whatever whites would help. He was utterly without means himself and it was galling to him.

By mid-December, 1884, a great petition had been prepared, in French and English, signed extensively, with something in it for whites, half-breeds, and Indians.[41] It was sent to Chapleau, the Secretary of State, and receipt duly acknowledged. Nothing happened. January came and went. Early in February, the Cabinet agreed to investigate the claims of half-breeds. But the Government had promised investigation since 1879. That was no answer to the Métis leaders. By the end of February, Riel had been forced to think of more drastic measures, egged on by his more military-minded general, Gabriel Dumont. Dumont apparently told Riel that he had accomplished nothing in the six months he had been in the Saskatchewan country, that the course he had followed in the summer and autumn of 1884 was too mild, that the Canadian government would ignore such methods and would only give in, as in 1870, before sterner measures. "I assure you," Riel told Rev. Charles McWilliams the day of his execution, "that three weeks before the Duck Lake fight I had no idea of rebellion. . . ."[42] What Dumont and Riel had in mind was not a real war. They thought a little obtrusive coercion would do the trick, as it had done in 1870. This meant armed blackmail. The proclamation of a provisional government, supported by the Métis and English half-breeds, and with the threat of Indian support, would bring the Dominion government to a more tractable frame of mind.

History never repeats itself. Macdonald had no intention of submitting to blackmail, or threats, from Louis Riel a second time. And the C.P.R. and the Mounted Police were two goods reasons why, in 1885, Macdonald did not have to. Nor could Riel hold the English half-breeds to his policy, as he had in 1870. They were sympathetic to Riel and to his cause, but they had not, in Professor Stanley's words, "bargained for rebellion."[43] They were opposed to the use of force of any kind, especially to Riel's idea, formulated by mid-March, of taking and holding Fort Carlton, a Hudson's Bay Company post with a Mounted Police garrison, as he had taken and held Fort Garry fifteen years before. Riel could not win over the Church either. Father André, Father Fourmond at St. Laurent, and Father Moulin at Batoche, all were opposed, in varying degrees, both to Riel's measures, and to the religious spirit with which he now invested them. Riel was a mystic: to the Métis he spoke with a voice now more religious than the Church itself. There was one God; there was a new Pope; and Riel was the prophet for both.

North West Mounted Police reinforcements were ordered northward to Fort Carlton on March 15. When the news of this move reached Riel, as it soon did, he was furious. With his supporters he seized as prisoners, on March 18, an Indian agent and some other government officials. It was the first overt move, as Riel himself recognized. On coming into Batoche that same day, he seized the church and Father Moulin, went to the local store for supplies, and said, "Well, Mr. Walters, it has commenced."[44] The telegraph line from Prince Albert to Regina was cut, and the provisional government, which Riel called the "exovedate," formed the next day. It was March 19, St. Joseph's day, the day of the patron saint of the Métis.

Fort Carlton is on the south bank of the North Saskatchewan, lying some distance back from the river, and overshadowed on the south and east side by a steep bank that virtually commands the whole interior of the fort. Had Fort Carlton been on the north bank of the river, much might have been different. But it was just twenty miles from Batoche and vulnerable. On Saturday, March 21, Riel demanded the surrender of Fort Carlton. The alternative was a "war of extermination," to begin on Monday.[45] Superintendent L. F. N. Crozier, in command, was not to be intimidated by threats like that. He refused to surrender the fort and Riel did nothing.

Then on March 26, Crozier unwisely decided to secure some provisions and arms at Hillyard Mitchell's store at Duck Lake. He had been warned by Mitchell that it would be best to leave well enough alone for the time being, and not wave a red rag at a bull; the small party that Crozier sent out was turned back by Gabriel Dumont and mounted Métis. Put on his mettle it was easy for Crozier to justify an immediate move, even though Commissioner Irvine, with reinforcements, was now only a few hours away. So one hundred men – fifty-three of them Mounted Police, the rest volunteers from Prince Albert – set out that same day for Duck Lake. Predictably, they clashed with the half-breeds, at a place the half-breeds themselves chose. Crozier's force had a very bad time of it: twelve dead and eleven wounded in the space of a quarter of an hour, casualties of twenty-five per cent. Riel, armed only with a crucifix, stopped the pursuit of the retreating police, and thus saved an even worse massacre. As the defeated column came into Fort Carlton, Irvine arrived on the scene with 108 men.

It was now considered vital to evacuate the Fort. The Prince Albert volunteers, who had been so brazen before the battle, wanted to go home and look after their families, not to be cooped up in Carlton fighting off an imminent Métis attack or, still worse, an Indian rising. The night of March 27, the fort was evacuated, and with all the supplies they could carry the joint force set off for Prince Albert, which they reached safely late on March 28, thanks mainly to Riel's restraint. Dumont had wanted an ambush.

The evacuation of Fort Carlton unhinged the remaining Government control of the North Saskatchewan; Batoche was in the ascendant, and the pressure now fell against Battleford, seventy miles to the west. Moreover the Métis victory at Duck Lake, which Riel lost no time in proclaiming, set the Indians in motion. Late March was always a bad time for them, with supplies running out after a hard winter. The news of Duck Lake ran through the whole valley of the North Saskatchewan, as if by telegraph. Indians from the Poundmaker and Little Pine reserves pillaged stores in Battleford and forced the population behind the stockade in the Mounted Police barracks. By the end of March some five hundred settlers and police were pinned down in barracks, while the Indians were in virtually full control everywhere else in the vicinity.

The news of Duck Lake reached still further westward, to Fort Pitt, a hundred miles up the North Saskatchewan, by March 30, just four days after the battle took place. The Mounted Police inspector there, Francis Dickens, the son of Charles Dickens, made preparations for a siege. Of food there was plenty; but of ammunition precious little. There were negotiations with the Indians, and the threat to the civilians forced Dickens to accept the Indian offer to allow the fort to be evacuated, and the whole group set off in a leaky scow down the Saskatchewan to Battleford, where they arrived cold and wet a week later.

Such were the consequences of Crozier's ill-advised asperity on March 26. Fort Carlton evacuated, Battleford invested, Fort Pitt evacuated, within four weeks the whole of the North Saskatchewan from Prince Albert west to the Alberta border and even beyond, was in Indian or Métis control. All this was spontaneous rather than planned. Although Riel urged the Indians on, an Indian war had not been his intention. He had wanted to use the Indian threat to extort concessions. But he lacked the communications, the skill, the stability, for so delicate an operation. He had wanted to capture Crozier at Duck Lake, and was forced by circumstances into a battle; so too with his use of the Indians. Fate played Riel's hand for him. It is hard not to retain a certain sympathy for the Métis and half-breed position. If agitation produced no remedy to their grievances, how were results to be achieved?

One weakness of responsible government is responsibility without responsiveness. The union of administration and representation in the cabinet system has great advantages. But both civil service and Parliament must be sensitive to public feeling if cabinet government is to be effective. A party a few years in power, with a civil service centred upon Ottawa, with a Parliament eastern in members and in thinking, could easily ignore what appeared to be a small group of noisy, ill-natured, feckless westerners. Nor was the press much help. *The Week* was exceptional in its coverage of news from the various parts of the country. A. W. Ross, Liberal M.P., Lisgar, and an Ontarian until he went to Manitoba in 1877, had some telling remarks on eastern ignorance of the West:

> Both political parties are to blame for the manner in which they obtain their information . . . filtered through partisan channels. . . . The people of the North-West object to having their country used as a foot-ball by the two parties, with the Treasury benches as the goal. . . . Our country is too much divided and hedged in by sectional feelings, in fact, there is a Dixie line around each province. . . . Our press is thoroughly sectional and provincial, and we have no papers that have yet been able to write for the whole Canadian people. Take the two leading papers in Canada, and along each column of their various editorials the water lines read: Ontario, Ontario.[46]

Between the Cabinet and the West was a great gulf of mutual ignorance that neither the civil service nor Parliament was in a position to remedy.

Once shooting started, however, the system worked admirably. One tradition of government the Canadians had inherited from Britain was a dislike of violence and killing. The law had nearly always come first and, whatever grievances existed, the law was the law. The breaking of the law had to be stopped; it could not be justified. Yet, in another sense it was justified. For most of the grievances that had caused the outbreak were remedied. Nothing in Parliament at the time was more telling than Laurier's point here:

> When the seeds of discontent have long been germinating, when hearts have long been swelling with long accumulating bitternesses, and when humiliations and disappointments have made men discontented and sullen, a small incident will create a conflagration. . . . Then the Government moved, but it was too late. [Here Laurier raised his hand and pointed at the Government, "Too Late! too late!"[47]] . . . In ten days, from the 26th of March to the 6th of April, the Government had altered their policy and had given what they had refused for years. What was the cause? The bullets of Duck Lake; the rebellion of the North-West. The Government had been refusing for years, and at last these men took their lives and liberties in their hands, and at last the Government came down and gave them what they were entitled to.[48]

The Saskatchewan rebellion raised up a Canadian militia army. The rebels would be put down by men from Nova Scotia, Quebec, Ontario, Manitoba, and the Northwest Territories; some 8,000 in all. It was organized and dispatched with uncommon celerity, much of it due to the Minister of Militia, Adolphe Caron (who seems to have surprised everyone), and to William Van Horne who improvised brilliantly from his experience in dispatching civil war troops at Joliet, Illinois. On March 23, three days before Duck Lake, Major General Frederick Middleton, General officer of Commanding Militia, was ordered to the West, and the Winnipeg Militia was put on alert. By March 25 one company was already at Qu'Appelle (which was to be Middleton's headquarters), and on March 27 Middleton himself arrived there with the rest of the battalion. The news of Duck Lake that arrived that day very much altered the scale of the military operation. Neither the Mounted Police nor the militia from Winnipeg were sufficient to deal with the general Indian rising now threatened, and requisition for militia from all of eastern and western Canada were sent out. The two permanent artillery batteries from Quebec and Kingston arrived in Winnipeg on April 5. Militia followed at intervals, in a surprisingly short time. The C.P.R. track west from Sudbury ended near Metagama, west of the Spanish River, and for the next four hundred miles there were awkward gaps. Guns and stores had to be unloaded from flat cars onto sleighs and back again, sixteen times, in very cold weather and deep snow. The gaps, graded but devoid of tracks or ties, made a good road for sleighs. On the railway the men rode on benches inside flat cars with the sides boarded up five feet around. It was a cold business at fifteen below, from ten in the morning to midnight. Within a week of Riel's proclamation of a provisional government there were troops at Qu'Appelle, and within two weeks, enough that General Middleton could set off northward.

The plan of the campaign was well conceived. The C.P.R. provided a transport baseline, with three points of departure. A column was to set off northward from each: from Qu'Appelle, Middleton against Batoche; from Swift Current, Colonel Otter to relieve Battleford, from Calgary Major General Strange to go north to Edmonton, and then east to Frog Lake, Fort Pitt and finally to effect a junction with Otter. Middleton left Qu'Appelle on April 6, reaching Clark's Crossing, just north of Saskatoon on April 17. Here he was joined by reinforcements. He split his eight hundred men into two groups, one on either side of the Saskatchewan for the march forty miles down river to Batoche. On April 24 the group under Middleton, on the eastern bank, nearly ran into an ambush at Fish Creek devised by Dumont, and were saved the worst of it only by the Métis firing precipitately upon Middleton's scouts.

Gabriel Dumont has been overshadowed by Riel, but he was much the more attractive man of the two. He had no head for politics – that he left to Riel – and he had the fecklessness and extravagance of the Indian, but his good qualities far outweighed the bad. He was a great hunter and horseman,

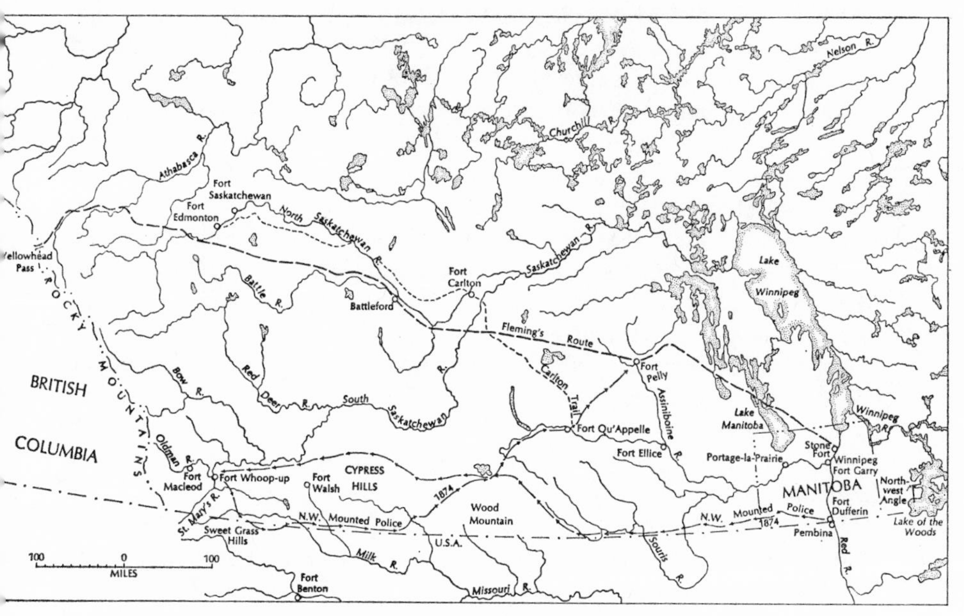

The Northwest Campaign of 1885

and knew the plain as if it were his own backyard. Those who knew him well never had an unkind word to say of him. Dumont had wanted to harass Middleton's advancing army, like the buffalo, as Dumont put it; but Riel would have none of it.

Fish Creek was a stalemate; Middleton was uncertain how strong the Métis were, and the respite gave Dumont a chance to slip away, taking his dead and wounded with him to Batoche. Middleton then halted for nearly two weeks, gathering the reinforcements that kept coming up from the south, pulling his troops over from the west bank to the east, organizing his supplies, and sending his wounded south.

Colonel Otter, with a combined Mounted Police and militia force, left Swift Current on April 13 with 550 men. The ice was out of the river – its precariousness late in March had prevented a Mounted Police attempt to move north in strength – and it was with some difficulty that the troops effected a crossing of the South Saskatchewan at Saskatchewan Landing (Matador). Only five days later was Otter able to move northward in earnest. His column was provided with wagons and it covered some thirty miles a day. On April 24 it marched into Battleford amid the shouts of welcome from the inhabitants who had been cooped up in the stockade for a month. In an attempt to prevent Poundmaker's Crees from joining Riel, Otter launched a surprise move against them at Cut Knife Hill, thirty miles west of Battleford. It failed, not ignominiously, but failed, and the Indians began to move toward Batoche, well over a hundred miles distant. Poundmaker was too late, however. He was at Eagle Hills, still a long way from Riel, when he received the news of the fall of Batoche.

Calgary was in a potentially dangerous position, with the powerful Blackfoot confederacy so close. Here Father Lacombe was invaluable. Macdonald telegraphed him on March 24 asking him to ensure if possible the loyalty of the Blackfeet. C. E. Denny was brought back, and these two experienced and able hands went from camp to camp trying to pacify the Blackfeet with government promises, to keep the restlessness of the Crees from infecting them. It was not easy. For one thing, Poundmaker was Chief Crowfoot's natural son by a Creewoman,[49] and Crowfoot was feeding many Cree families who fled down from the north. Crowfoot's promises to be loyal could not be relied upon absolutely. Although his promises extracted much food and other useful supplies for his tribes, the victories of the whites in the north were more important. The Blackfeet were clearly disappointed at the turn of affairs.[50]

Strange and his troops were welcomed in Calgary with considerable enthusiasm, as if eastern Canada – still referred to in the Northwest as Canada[51] – cared after all. Prior to their arrival most people there did not believe the Dominion government would send troops at all:

> When the train containing troops came in sight of the station at Calgary hundreds of the populace went to the Depot, and could scarcely believe their eyes when they saw the 65th's [Carabiniers', from Montreal] officers and men debarking. . . . Before the arrival of the troops the Canadian Government was freely sworn at. Many did not know there was a Government, and a number who were aware of it did not desire to cultivate its acquaintance; but the fact that it was sending troops here to protect the people and relieve Edmonton struck a responsive chord. The officers and men had come a long way. . . .
> The arrival of Col. Osborne Smith's Winnipeg Light Infantry shortly after the arrival of the Carbineers was followed by a total disappearance of anti-Canadianism. Here were men who had come from one distant part of the North-West to protect another part. . . . Even Calgarians are human, and if anything touched their hearts more than this fact it was not easy to find it. . . .
> A great number of the inhabitants of Alberta are not Canadians, and until very recently they had a very faint conception of what the Canadian Government and Canadian people could do. The military has swept away hostiles and rebels alike.[52]

Major General Strange moved north with the 65th Carabiniers and the Winnipeg Light Infantry. Father Lacombe, and Rev. John McDougall went ahead reassuring the Indians who were still peaceable. Like Otter's column, Strange's had difficulty with the western rivers, then in spring flood, and the Red Deer posed a formidable obstacle. Notwithstanding, the first part of Strange's column reached Edmonton on May 1, having covered 210 miles in ten days. A few garrison forces were sent out, but the bulk of Strange's force turned east toward Fort Pitt. Most of the troops had left Edmonton on May 14.

Middleton began to move toward Batoche again on May 7, and by May 9 was before the village, engaged in a full fire from the Métis who were neatly entrenched in the wooded reverse slope above the river firing on troops as they came along the horizon, almost unprotected except by the covering fire of Gatlings. These tactics went on for three full days, while the Métis ammunition ran rapidly down, as did militia patience with Middleton's rather ponderous military operations.

A flanking movement on May 12 broke down under a mix-up of orders, and the morning was wasted. While Middleton and many of the troops were at lunch, the men holding the line in front, the Midland Regiment and the Toronto Grenadiers with their Colonels, Williams and Grassett, impatient doing what they had done for three days, went at the Métis rifle pits full tilt. The Métis, weakened by shortage of ammunition – many of them had been firing nails for two days and some were now even out of powder – could only resist as best they could. The trenches were carried in bitter fighting. The shouts of triumph from the soldiers brought Middleton to his feet, and reinforcements, dispatched at once, arrived in time to take part in the final rush.[53] In a few minutes Batoche had fallen, and the Métis had taken to the woods. Gabriel Dumont and Michel Dumas, two of the Council, got clear away to Montana but Riel seems to have had no intention of doing so, despite Dumont's offer to escort him and his family out of the country. Middleton offered Riel protection until the Canadian government had decided what to do with him and he may have considered that safer than falling in with trigger-happy militia. He was alleged to have said, "Politics will save me."[54] On May 15 he gave himself up to Mounted Police scouts. At Battleford, on May 26, Middleton took the surrender of Poundmaker, that reluctant warrior, dragged into war on the heels of his more aggressive braves. Big Bear failed to effect a junction with him.

With Big Bear's surrender on July 2 the Northwest rebellion was over. It had cost the Government about five million dollars. It had cost the settlers much. The Battle River Valley was very hard hit; herds of cattle and horses disappeared during the month the Indians were in control;[55] by the time it was possible to work in the fields it was very late for seeding. Batoche and the Métis and half-breed settlements were shattered.

The Minister of Justice, Campbell, was informed that Middleton was sending Riel and all the other prisoners to Winnipeg for trial.[56] This move caused much unease at Ottawa. The Government had already been studying the relative advantages of trying Riel under Manitoba or under Northwest law, and they had concluded that Riel must under no circumstances go to Winnipeg. There he was entitled to a twelve-man jury and, much more important, had the right to insist that half the jury be French-speaking.[57] Furthermore, once the prisoners were in Manitoba, the Canadian government had no power, short of new legislation, to take them out again to the Northwest Territories. If the prisoners were tried in Manitoba, Campbell told Macdonald, "there will be a miscarriage of justice, I think beyond question. . . . I wish very much you would tell him [Caron] absolutely to send them to Regina. Do not, pray, send this letter to Caron, as I have written as strongly as I can, but send him a note from yourself."[58] From the Government's point of view the advantage of Regina was that a jury of six only was needed by Northwest Territory law, and the prisoner, although he had the right to challenge the choice, was not entitled to a mixed jury. So on May 23 Riel and his escort left the C.P.R. not at Winnipeg, but at Regina, where he was placed in the jail of the Mounted Police barracks.

There were in all 129 prisoners: forty-six half-breeds, English-speaking and Métis; eighty-one Indians; and two whites. A major effort was made by the Government to arrest some of the Prince Albert whites who had been behind Riel.[59] But the whites had covered their tracks too well; any incriminating correspondence they had already burnt.[60] Most of the Indians were charged with treason-felony, a crime defined by an Act of 1868, during the Fenian scare. Forty-four Indians were convicted, most of the proceedings being heavily biased by the feelings of the jurymen. Poundmaker's trial was a mockery of justice. G. T. Denison, a police magistrate himself, said that Poundmaker was "convicted on evidence that, in any ordinary trial would have ensured his acquittal without the jury leaving the box. . . ."[61] Poundmaker himself told Judge Richardson, "Everything I could do was done to stop bloodshed. Had I wanted war I should not be here now. . . . You did not catch me. I gave myself up. You have got me because I wanted peace."[62] That was all true, though it was not the whole truth.

Most of the half-breeds were released without trial, but eighteen were charged with treason-felony, eleven of whom were discharged upon a recognizance of four hundred dollars to take trial if called upon. Proceedings under this head were subsequently abandoned in 1886 by John Thompson, then Minister of Justice.

Riel was not charged with treason-felony. Macdonald had grave doubts that he could be convicted upon such a charge, for Riel's circumstances fitted none of the categories of the 1868 Act.[63] Instead, he was charged with treason, under an ancient British statute of Edward III, the Statute of Treasons of 1352, that is, that Riel "most wickedly, maliciously, and traitorously did levy and make war against our said Lady the Queen . . . and [did] endeavour by force and arms to subvert and destroy the constitution and government of this realm. . . ."[64] This statute had been used by the Crown in 1837-38, and Macdonald, a young lawyer then, was able to drive a coach and horse through parts of it. He confessed as much to Campbell.

With treason a subject was declared to have violated his "allegiance, fidelity and obedience" to the Queen. Riel was legally an American citizen; obedience, while in British territory, he may have owed, but certainly neither allegiance nor fidelity.[65] There was another difficulty with the 1352 Statute: the procedure for treason was perhaps not consonant with the summary procedure and jurisdiction for the territorial courts, there being no bill of indictment, or grand jury.

The judge was Magistrate Hugh Richardson, Stipendiary magistrate, appointed by the Mackenzie government in 1876. Unlike the judges in the rest of Canada, the Northwest Territory stipendiary magistrates did not have tenure on good behaviour, only at the Queen's pleasure.[66] He had a reputation with Edgar Dewdney for having no backbone.[67]

Riel's trial did not turn upon whether he was guilty of treason. Given that treason was within the jurisdiction of the court, a point by no means established beyond doubt, given that Riel's American citizenship was irrelevant, it was virtually *prima facie* that he was guilty of treason. But was he sane? W. H. Jackson, Riel's secretary, was tried for complicity in treason; he got off on grounds of insanity. Jackson's jury, incidentally, included some French names; there were no French names in Riel's jury. Riel's lawyers argued he was insane; Riel, like Jackson, protested he was not.

The trial concluded on July 31. The jury were out an hour. There is evidence that the foreman, Francis Cosgrove, was sympathetic to Riel; but all five of the other jurors agreed that he was both guilty of treason and sane, and the foreman was unable to persuade them to the contrary. But they all agreed to recommend Riel for mercy. While his acts of rebellion could not be justified, the Government were responsible, so the jury felt, for the rebellion's occurring in the first place. If the Government had done their duty there would have been no rebellion and no prisoner to condemn.[68] But Richardson was obliged by law to condemn Riel to death, on September 18, 1885. The jury's recommendation was forwarded to Ottawa.

Riel was insane by any present-day definition. That he was often rational, cogent, clever, is true, but on the very subjects upon whose authority he was so often to act, politics and religion, he was not merely unreliable, but dangerously unstable. Israël Tarte was right:

> I have known Riel well when he was locked up in our lunatic asylums, and I give you my word of honor that he was then completely demented. He was not an idiot, quite the contrary. He spoke with an eloquence many could envy. . . . He wrote Latin and Greek, but he was mad, mad of the folly of honors and religious reforms. I have seen him in telegraphic communication with Napoleon the third, with Bismarck, and Pius the Ninth.[69]

A. E. Forget told Honoré Mercier the same. "Oui[,] malgré son génie, Riel était fou, incapable de résister à la voix intérieure qui le poussait de l'avant. Il se croyait appelé à remplir une mission divine, et jusqu'au dernier moment il a cru sincèrement qu'il était prophète."[70] Riel's own writings carry Forget's view to the point of conviction.

The rule in English criminal law governing the applicability of a plea of insanity to a criminal charge was a straitened one: whether the person knew the nature and the quality of the act he was doing, whether he could distinguish right from wrong.[71] It was a poor test. As Dr. Daniel Clark, of the Toronto Lunatic Asylum, said at the trial, "a large minority of the insane do know right from wrong. . . ."[72] Still, the McNaughten rule, as it was called, was the legal test of the time, and unfair though it was, its application might be at least justified had it been applied to others. It is impossible to tell whether Jackson was more, or less, insane than Riel, but the careful construction and application of the McNaughten rule that was so conspicuous during Riel's trial was quite absent from Jackson's. The Government clearly took a great deal of trouble to prove Riel was sane; they seem glad to have found Jackson insane, as if his case were not important. What is most bothersome about the Riel trial was not its unfairness. It is possible even to agree with the *Manitoba Free Press* that "Riel was fairly tried, honestly convicted."[73] Laurier privately said the same:

> I never saw any fair ground of attack against the tribunal. It was an exceptional court, so organized from the exceptional nature of the country. . . . There is no fair ground for imputing partiality to anybody connected with the trial. The judge was hasty, severe, harsh. . . . Yet, in his rulings, the most supericivilous [*sic*] must acquiesce. The prosecutors and jury seem to have discharged their duty manfully and impartially.[74]

No, what was disturbing was the impression it gave that the Crown pressed the full rigour of law against Riel, and failed to do so against the others, and that it did not give the accused every benefit he might have had, such as one or two French-speaking jurors, or possibly a French-speaking judge. The Government were going to get Riel. They would do it openly, squarely, by every process of law, but they were not going to give him an opportunity to wriggle away. They hired the best lawyers they could get, they formulated the charge against him with great care; they had netted their bird and they were going to keep him.

No one really knows what was in Sir John Macdonald's mind. Evidence around the question of Riel's execution tends to be thin; letters were destroyed, probably deliberately, and officials were being extremely careful not to write too much. But there is nothing to suggest that Macdonald ever considered anything else but hanging. His thought from first to last seems to have been that Riel had been rightly convicted and rightly deserved to hang. And even the resignation of Caron, Langevin, and Chapleau would probably not have altered that.[75]

Riel's execution was postponed from September 18 until October 16, then again until November 10, and finally until November 16. The first two postponements were owing to appeals by Riel's lawyers, the first for leave to appeal the case to the Court of Queen's Bench in Winnipeg. This was turned down; if Riel's leave to appeal to Winnipeg had been granted, he would almost certainly have been acquitted or had a hung jury. The second postponement was over leave to appeal to the Judicial Committee, which was also refused. The third postponement was owing to the medical commission on Riel's sanity.

Langevin, Caron, and Chapleau, all felt their hands would be strengthened by a definite report on Riel's sanity. It was manifestly difficult to determine what it had been during the rebellion, but it was possible to consider what it was in November 1885. Three doctors were asked to see Riel, Dr. Jukes of the Mounted Police, Dr. Lavell of Kingston Penitentiary, and Dr. F. X. Valade of Ottawa. All three seem clearly to have been impressed with Riel, both as a character and as a man. Lavell wrote privately to Macdonald, "I confess I should be well pleased if justice and popular clamour could be satisfied without depriving this man of life."[76] Jukes and Lavell, operating within the narrow conventions of the McNaughten rule, found, publicly at least[77] Riel did know right from wrong. But Valade believed him insane. A. E. Forget reported privately to Honoré Mercier that Valade "l'a déclaré complètement aliéné et incapable de discerner entre le bien et le mal."[78] Dr. Valade's report to the Government actually read:

> After having examined Riel in pte conversation with him & by testimony of persons who take care of him I have come to the conclusion that he is not an accountable being that he is unable to distinguish between wrong & right in political and religious subjects which I consider well marked typical forms of a kind of insanity under which he undoubtedly suffers but on other points I believe him to be quite sensible & can distinguish right from wrong.[79]

The version published by the Government was heavily and misleadingly abbreviated:

> After having examined carefully Riel in private conversation with him and by testimony of persons who take care of him, I have come to the conclusion that he suffers under hallucinations on political and religious subjects, but on other points I believe him to be quite sensible and can distinguish right from wrong.[80]

Macdonald does not seem to have been very comfortable about it all. November 15 he wrote Dewdney, "I am anxious for tomorrow passing over."[81] The next day, at 8:30, on a bright cold morning, Riel was hanged in Regina jail. Almost his last words with Father André were,

> Sir John Macdonald is now committing me to death for the same reason I committed Scott [in 1870], because it is necessary for the country's good. . . . I was pardoned once for his death, but am now going to die for it.[82]

The hangman was Jack Henderson, imprisoned by Riel in 1870.[83] Dewdney telegraphed Macdonald in cipher, the words "Hindrance carabine avenged dissipating. . . ." Hanged, buried as directed, is what it said.[84]

There was great enthusiasm in the East on the return of the troops from the western wars. Parades, receptions, gala dinners were held in the cities that had sent the soldiers forth. Dense crowds greeted the arrival of the 65th Carabiniers, on July 20 in Montreal; to the battle honours of Monongahela, Carillon, and Chateauguay, was now added Saskatchewan.[85] While sympathetic to the Métis, Quebec had made her contribution to quelling the Northwest rebellion. Quebec was divided, as Ontario was, but the Conservative party in Quebec was peculiarly vulnerable, split between Langevin and Chapleau, with ultramontanes on the right being very severe with the Government over Riel. When Riel was sentenced, on July 31, the Quebec Liberals were handed a gift on a platter. It was an opportunity to make the Liberal party what it had never before been with the Quebec electorate, a *parti national*. The experiment had been tried by Louis Jetté, Mercier, and others in 1872. Then it had failed owing to the opposition of the clergy, and the dislike of the older liberals, like Henri Joly, for the precarious liberalism inherent in such a program. When the news came from Ottawa in November 1885 that the law would take its course, Montreal Liberals were alleged to have said, "Eh bien! tant mieux . . . cela nous vaut vingt comtés dans le Bas-Canada."[86]

The régime of Joseph Mousseau, arranged by Chapleau in 1882, had decayed all too soon. Chapleau had gone to Ottawa, probably believing he could supplant Langevin. Macdonald and Langevin doubtless suspected that well enough; but Chapleau, restless and dissatisfied, was too dangerous to be left in provincial politics. Chapleau did not achieve at Ottawa what he dreamed of when he went. Macdonald never really trusted him, brilliant, even magnetic, as he was. He was too much a creature of his impulses; he revelled in intrigue; indeed, he seemed to John Willison to have "a positive enjoyment of factional infelicities."[87] As Secretary of State, he had no spending department from which to find the means to reward his friends and develop his Quebec control. His seat in the second row of the Government desks, behind Macdonald and Langevin, was galling to him, as it was revealing of his true position in the government at the time.

Mousseau was but an understudy of Chapleau, having capacity neither for administration, nor for the role of *chef*.[88] He had been in office only three months, when there appeared, in October 1882, a broadside against Chapleau and his role in the Conservative party, by "Castor": *Le pays, le parti et le grande homme*, with some mighty shots from ultramontane armament against the whole Chapleau-Sénécal-Dansereau régime.[89] Something of the animosity of the right-wing Conservatives toward Chapleau is demonstrated by Langevin's son-in-law, Thomas Chapais, editor of the Quebec *Courrier du Canada* in 1884:

> Je le [Chapleau] vois lié avec des gens que je méprise et dont je hais les idées et les habitudes. Gens de lettres mal formés, gens de bourse, gens de coulisse, journalistes sans honneur et sans conviction, violà ses familiers, ses intimes. . . . S'il devient jamais le chef suprême du parti conservateur où nous conduira-t-il? . . .[90]

When Castor's pamphlet came out the triumvirate, and Israël Tarte (où n'était-il pas? Rumilly remarked)[91] were all in Paris for Chapleau's health, eating and drinking to help, presumably, Chapleau's chronic and serious bronchitis.

Besides the opposition from the ultramontanes and their sympathizers, Mousseau and Chapleau faced the Liberals and were thus subjected to fire from the right, and from the left. Mousseau found it impossible to carry on, resigned on January 10, 1884 and went to the Bench with a sigh of relief. J. J. Ross, with some ultramontane support, was made Premier.

In 1885 Honoré Mercier was forty-five years of age. He had been leader of the Quebec wing of the Liberals since Joly resigned in 1883. Along with several other Liberals of the same vintage, he had been educated at the Jesuit Collège Sainte Marie in Montreal. He was brought up in St. Hyacinthe, married and had a law practice there, but moved to Montreal in 1881, where his office quickly became a Liberal centre. Mercier was rather a showman like Chapleau, but possessed a much greater capacity for work. Even when the House was not sitting, he was working. In this, he was like Blake. But, unlike Blake, he was exceptionally adept at translating his homework in government documents into pungent and deadly shafts on the public platform. He was a clear, even elegant speaker, who followed the line of his argument to the end, using the touches that Chapleau knew so well, vehemence, laughter, or tragedy. Mercier was irresistible before a crowd; he could instruct them, interest them, and, still more, get them to love him. "Je ne connais pas," wrote Charles Langelier, "un homme politique, à l'exception de Papineau, qui restera autant que lui ancré dans le souvenir des foules."[92] Yet, there was something unreliable, slippery perhaps, about Mercier; he was one of that genre of politicians who seek power first, and worry about the principles to be applied to its use after. The two successive leaders in Quebec, Joly and Mercier, were poles apart. Joly would have none of the ultramontanes or the Conservatives; Mercier was willing to work with either, if the right terms were met. Joly deplored the use of the Riel issue to foster a nationalist agitation and resigned his seat in the Assembly over it. Mercier, or to put it more correctly, *La Patrie*, the Liberal organ of Montreal, virtually led such an agitation.

But the whole Riel agitation needs careful examination.[93] There is, for example, the famous quotation from the *Toronto Daily Mail* about smashing Confederation into its original fragments if exceptions to the law were to be made in favour of Riel. Usually it is quoted without its conceptual framework, and without the knowledge of the general position of the *Mail*, which was in fact most judicious, like that of its Conservative Montreal counterpart, *La Minerve*. There was a considerable degree of good sense displayed by the more responsible Conservative newspapers. They had, of course, every reason to dampen the agitation: as much reason as the Liberal papers had to try to fire it.

The *Mail*, as the leading Conservative paper in Ontario, was bound to assert Riel was guilty of fomenting rebellion – two rebellions, it did not fail to note – and that the law must take its course. That was in August 1885.[94] But agitation it left severely alone. There is hardly a single word editorially about Riel in the *Mail* for two months after the trial was over. It took for granted that if the Privy Council appeal failed, and no good reason for interfering with the law were discovered, the law would be carried out.[95]

The Toronto *Globe* was as reserved as the *Mail*, not so much from lofty motives as from the intrinsic difficulties of its position. It did not like Riel much, but it liked the Government less. The *Globe* said little, indeed almost nothing, beyond its statement of August 14, 1885, to which it was constrained once or twice later to refer:

> No one who had read the evidence can doubt that RIEL richly deserves death; nevertheless to have him executed by a Government which sat supinely still while the insurrection was brewing . . . would send a thrill of horror through the community.

After Riel's execution the *Globe* continued to preach moderation. Canadians, it said, should "keep their heads cool"; they should ignore the inflammatory appeals of some Ontario papers, that used the Quebec agitation to whet anti-French prejudices:

> We would ask every good citizen, whatever be his party . . . to do bare justice to our French-speaking fellow countrymen at this time; to consider impartially the causes of their wrath against the Ministry. . . . The man [Riel] represented a cause.[96]

The Conservative press of Quebec, both English and French had exercised a good deal of restraint on the Riel question; *La Minerve*, which represented Chapleau, remarkably so. It was a hard test for Bleu loyalty. *La Minerve* maintained it was not Riel who deserved sympathy; it was the Métis. Riel on the contrary was an apostate; and *La Minerve* laid great stress on the gap between Riel and the Church. A letter from six western Catholic missionaries, which it published in August 1885, made this point. "Riel ne mérite pas les sympathies de l'Eglise Catholique Romaine et des membres de cette église, ayant usurpé notre mission de prêtres. . . . Il a fait tout cela [rebellion] dans son intérêt purement personel."[97] *La Minerve*, the most widely circulated of all the Conservative French papers, set the official line, and it was followed by Québec *Le Courrier du Canada*, *Le Journal de Québec*, and some others. *Le Monde*, Langevin's paper in Montreal, was not unwilling to apply pressure upon the Government, which it did as it had done over the first C.P.R. loan, by openly indicating the expectations of French-Canadian Conservatives. *Le Monde* asserted again, with increasing emphasis, that Riel would not be hanged; and this right up to and including Friday, November 13.[98] Tarte later asserted that the whole Riel storm in Quebec was first raised by *Le Monde*.[99] It is hard to know what the real feelings of the French-Canadian Conservatives were in the face of such vehement agitation, but privately some of them, clerics especially, seem to have been quite unsympathetic to Riel. Abbé F.-X. Gosselin, close to the Cercle Catholique and to Jules-Paul Tardivel, wrote to his old friend Thomas Chapais, editor of *Le Courrier du Canada*, congratulating him on his moderation:

> Le plus qu'on puisse dire, c'est que le gouvernement a fait un acte impolitique. Il aurait peut-être mieux valu ne pas provoquer ce soulèvement de toute une province. Mais, même sur ce point, j'hésite à condamner mes chers. Car je crois que Riel, interné dans un asile ou dans une prison, n'aurait pas été oublié. A chaque session du parlement, ç'aurait été une pluie de motions . . . pour demander l'amnistie de Riel, et cela jusqu'à on l'ût obtenue. . . .
> Dans tous les cas, que le gouvernement ait bien ou mal agi dans son intérêt, j'entends, car il n'a commis aucune injustice – Riel méritait son sort et le méritait dix fois. Son exécution n'affectait nullement notre foi et notre nationalité. Mais l'agitation qui s'en suit, c'est la mort probable du parti conservateur. . . .
> Nos Patriotes de 1837 avaient certainement entrepris une lutte inégale, inconstitutionelle et surtout téméraire. . . . Mais au moins ils combattaient pour une belle, grande et sainte cause. . . . Mais Riel![100]

Israël Tarte, who had always the courage of his convictions, objected to making Riel a hero, and said so in *Le Canadien*.[101] Tarte was present with political leaders of both parties at the meeting in the offices of *La Presse* which drafted the resolutions the Champ de Mars assembly was to adopt.

He thought them too extreme, and said so, but "autant eût valu tenter d'arrêter le cours des rapides de Lachine."[102]

The spirit of the mass meeting at the Champ de Mars, Sunday, November 22, was of virulent mass protest by French Canadians of various political persuasions, against Riel's execution. It was a mood of genuine anger against the Government. Most French Canadians were disposed to share this sense of outrage, as if they had been, in *La Minerve's* words, humiliated.

It was here the Toronto *Mail* stepped in. Whatever its attitude to the Ontario Roman Catholics, it had never said "down with the French." The execution of Riel had never been, the *Mail* said, "intended to be an insult to, much less an attack upon the rights of the French Canadian people." If Riel had been English Canadian, the result would have been the same.[103] What the *Mail* did argue, a few days later, in those too often quoted words, was that the law should not be suspended from its operation because a French Canadian, Métis, or anyone else, was caught in its toils:

> . . . rather than submit to such a yoke, Ontario would smash Confederation into its original fragments, preferring that the dream of a united Canada should be shattered forever, than that unity should be purchased at the expense of equality.
>
> If the French desire to destroy Sir JOHN MACDONALD, in GOD'S name let them do it on grounds other than the execution of RIEL. The Dominion is not bound up in the fate of any one political leader or party. But if he should be overthrown simply because he has upheld the majesty of the law . . . then Canadian institutions cannot survive him.[104]

This was frank talking but it was not unreasonable.

The Liberal strategy in handling the Riel agitation was well planned and ruthless. Edward Blake was in England, having left Canada in the early autumn, broken in health and energy after the 1885 session, and already talking privately of giving up the leadership.[105] Thus Blake's judiciousness and fairness were absent, and the Ontario wing of the party was led by Cartwright and Edgar, both of them fire-eaters. Cartwright's views to Laurier about letting loose the tigers,[106] were supported by Edgar, who told Laurier, "I am writing to Langelier and to Mercier about this. I feel that by bold and vigorous action the tory party in Quebec can be split in twain before Blake gets back. What say you, mon frère?"[107]

The agitation was handled neatly on two levels, Mercier, the provincial leader, would take the lead. It suited him, and the Quebec Liberals had everything to gain provincially by so doing. Laurier, leader of the Quebec Liberals federally, could act as Mercier's senior officer, approving, smiling, but taking a cooler and more detached position. This was very convenient to him politically, for it would mitigate any harm done to him or to the federal wing of the party in Ontario.[108] There was even talk that a substantial number of French-Canadian Conservatives would bolt the party, and support the Liberals in a vote against Macdonald. The Liberals were suspicious of this, especially since the Conservative bolters promised nothing for the future.[109] As Alexander Campbell wrote laconically, "They will all come back; there is nothing else for them to do."[110] Mercier went to New York in December to concert strategy with Blake, who had arrived there just before Christmas.

Blake's position was made public in mid-January, 1886 in a speech at London, Ontario. It was one of his most statesmanlike utterances. Without avoiding the opportunity to condemn the Government, he attempted to keep the Riel debate as cool and honest as possible:

> . . . we are to strive for a just and statesmanlike judgment by the House of Commons. (Hear.)
> We must endeavour to eliminate, as factors in the decision, race and creed; and cause the Commons of Canada to speak with a voice and in a sense which posterity, after these heats have cooled and these mists have cleared, shall ratify and confirm. (Hear.)
> I believe we cannot, if we would, make of this a party question. (Hear.) . . . I do not desire a party conflict on the Regina tragedy; I do not propose to construct a political platform out of the Regina scaffold; or to create or cement party ties with blood of the condemned. . . . I do not care
> "To attempt the Future's portals
> With the Past's blood-rusted key."[111]

Blake's speech did tone down the more volatile members of the Ontario party, and he tried hard to persuade Laurier to try to do the same in Quebec. But that was too much to expect of Laurier, with a provincial election due in 1886, and with the Liberals having so much to gain there by keeping the agitation going.

Blake never lacked political courage; he was always ready, intellectual that he was, to take a hard position against the transient rages of the public. He would willingly brave the outrage of the public, but found direct confrontations difficult, and in the tone of speeches against Blake there was always the suspicion that his opponents felt he was a coward.

There was none of this in the man who became Blake's leading opponent in the House; a man who wore the kind of armour Blake would have liked to have had, and did not. That Blake was a greater man than John Thompson is true, but Thompson gave the impression of being a better armed parliamentarian who could, as was to appear in the 1886 session, unhorse Blake, and who, one senses, Blake feared. John Thompson reciprocated Blake's dislike. Few men could be more caustic when they chose to be than Thompson. He wrote his wife in Halifax, in May 1886, "Blake came back last night and was 'awfully clever' for about half an hour & then went up on the back benches and picked his nose and cut his nails for the rest of the night."[112]

Thompson had been appointed Minister of Justice in September 1885, rather to Campbell's chagrin. He brought a strong personality and a sobering influence into the Government. For the first time since 1881 the Minister of Justice was in the House of Commons, and from the start he made himself felt quietly and firmly. The 1886 session was to show him flexible, accommodating, with the right instinct for parliamentary footwork, without losing his control of the House or his capacity to hit and hit hard when he chose to. Unlike most of the Cabinet, he was quite without awe of Macdonald, never having been brought up in his shadow. The following letter is dated January 23, 1887, to his wife:

> Tupper [Sir Charles] will be here in a day or two. His coming will do us no good and do him much harm. It is the old man's work. He is showing some of the failings of age in being very suspicious. He has had something in his nose against me for a little while past – but instead of submitting like the others do I shewed fight and treated him to considerable impudence. I ignored his opinion on a legal question and talked to the other members of Council over his head. . . . I kept up the ?? by not speaking to that mole catcher of a wife of his at the dinner at Gov't house. Of course the poor old fellow is worried to death but I do not care for him and I am so determined to let him see it that I could insult him at every turn while he keeps it up. This is unheard of heresy here because the practice is to worship him from afar even when he is ugly.[113]

When Thompson sat down after his reply to Blake in the debate on the Landry motion, March 22, 1886, it was clear there was a new force in the Commons. Parliament is a peculiar place; it is not easy to deceive. It distrusts metaphor and rhetoric that does not grow from the strength of the argument itself. Thompson wanted most to be understood; he gave an impression of directness, simplicity, and integrity, and in Parliament these are the qualities that are apt to prevail.

A. G. P. R. Landry, M.P. Montmagny, President of the Quebec Conservative Association, moved two weeks after Parliament opened,[114] that the House express its regret that Louis Riel was executed. There is reason to suspect that this motion was concocted for the purpose of helping the Government.[115] It was so very convenient for the Government, since the full force of the Liberal party could never be brought to support it. It was especially neat after Langevin had moved the previous question, thereby blocking all amendments to it. This last, at least, had been carefully arranged. So the Riel debate of 1886 turned upon whether Riel ought to have been executed or not, and nothing else.

It was a sober debate, one of the best in the history of the House. Blake's speech was the most comprehensive, Laurier's the most moving, Thompson's the most skilful, and Macdonald's non-existent: an interesting parallelogram. It was hard to disagree with the conclusion of Laurier's speech,

> Had they [the Government] taken as much pains to do right, as they have taken to punish wrong, they never would have had any occasion to convince those people that the law cannot be violated with impunity, because the law would never have been violated at all.[116]

Altogether, the French-Canadian Liberals spoke with little heat and much good sense, as if their passion had gone and only the conviction of their rightness remained. Charles Langelier was especially judicious. Blake remarked that the "crowning proof of French domination" was Laurier's speech, in English, bearing off the palm of eloquence from the English-speaking members.[117] Blake's speech angered some Liberals, as being too sympathetic to Riel, but it was a reflection of his London spirit; and it marked the fact that a home now existed for moderate French Canadians within the Liberal party.[118] It was also resented, and bitterly, by some friends who felt he was not being high-minded at all, but was playing a very canny game of politics. Blake, in England, had not said a word about Riel's fate before he was executed; and there always remained the bitter suspicion that he had waited to see what would happen.[119]

The Landry motion was defeated, March 24, 1886. Of the fifty-two who regretted Riel's execution half were French Canadians, fifteen of them Conservatives, and half English Canadians, all Liberals, including Blake, Edgar, and Mills. With the 146 who did not regret it were twenty-three Liberals, including Cartwright, Charlton, Davies, Alexander Mackenzie, Mulock, and Paterson, and twenty-five French-Canadian Conservatives. Twenty-five of forty French-Canadian Conservatives supported the Government; it was a good measure of their real feelings, for the Landry motion was virtually an open vote. The Opposition mustered their forces in a pitched battle on most difficult terrain, and came off worsted. Never before had they had such tremendous possibilities in a plain issue: the results of Conservative administration in the Northwest. They were out-manoeuvred and were quite unable to do anything effective with it.

A few changes were proposed in Northwest arrangements; the territories were given representation in the Commons, Assiniboia two members, and Alberta and Saskatchewan one each, and in 1887 they were to get two members in the Senate. Land transfer regulations were made more flexible; Thompson brought in a bill to simplify registration of deeds in the Territories, to avoid hunting each land grant, as it changed hands, back to the original Crown grant.[120] Parliament prorogued early in June, and at last summer came. The first transcontinental C.P.R. passenger train left Montreal at 10:30 P.M. on Monday, June 28, 1886. There were nine cars; two baggage cars, two sleepers, a dining car, two first class and two second class coaches. For more than a mile outside of Winnipeg, people gathered to see it.[121] It arrived in Port Moody, B.C., greeted by excursion crowds from Nanaimo, Victoria, and New Westminster, at noon, Sunday, July 4, 1886. That first

C.P.R. train from Montreal to Port Moody was a greater contribution to pulling the country together than any other single event since the first Intercolonial train from Halifax to Montreal just ten years before. Canada was now stitched down and the effect transcended all acts of Parliament or after-dinner talk. The C.P.R. was. It could not be undone; at long last the east-west rationale behind 1871 was on the way to being a reality. In Toronto in 1888 a leading merchant and manufacturer said,

> Things were depressed last year in Ontario. What should we have done but for the North-West? In Toronto we can [could] hardly get a bill paid; Ottawa at stagnation point; London comes next. We are glad and surprised when we receive $150 from an Ontario shopkeeper. But it is a common thing to receive a letter with $500 from a customer in the North-West. We look, I can tell you, with great interest for our Western mail.[122]

The world was changing as one watched. The typewriters now often used in Ottawa and elsewhere symbolized the growing complexity of both government and business, and the growth and ramifications of the managerial skills common to both. In 1882 Toronto and Hamilton were linked by long distance telephone, and in 1885 so were Montreal and Ottawa. Electricity and telephones had already cluttered city streets with their ghastly cribbing of wires and poles. Canadian society would adjust, though only slowly, to new ways of living and of doing. The summer of 1886 was not that much different from many that had preceded it and many that were to follow, as the people made holiday. The Sand Banks on the Prince Edward peninsula on Lake Ontario on a July Sunday that year were full of visitors from morning till dark, with trim buggies, weather-beaten democrats, comfortable family carriages, all with loads of bashful youths and blushing girls. Farmers, bank clerks, all sorts and conditions of people came, to keep cool somehow and disport themselves.[123] Ottawa was slowly baked into its usual comatose laziness, to revive only in the long evenings. Muskoka, Murray Bay, Rivière du Loup, Dalhousie, St. Andrew's, Halifax, all came into their own. Then came autumn. Sara Jeanette Duncan has a haunting description of that October, 1886 in eastern Canada:

> The sunlight falls lazily through the haze that possesses the land; there is no stir among the crisping leaves; the great bursting horse-chestnuts hang motionless in the quiet air. . . . It is the time of times when no Canadian should have any distracting occupation which should prevent him from lying full length among the dropped spoils of some gnarled Spitzbergen, and staring up through its sun-gilt brown leaves at the fathomless blue of the deep above him. . . .
>
> All else is vanity and vexation of spirit, and dwindles insignificantly away beside the supreme joy and necessity of drawing in the golden fulness of this autumn weather. . . . All the sovereign largesse of glorious dishevelled October communicates a sudden, subtle thrill of triumph, a splendid sense of strength that shall endure. . . .[124]

CHAPTER 10

Toward a Federal Canada 1886-1888

In 1886 Canada was nineteen years of age. In the memory and experience of a mature man nineteen years is not a long time. Who yet knew whether Canada would work or not? It was too early to tell. Even the ultimate shape of the country was still partly undetermined. Macdonald conceived a centralized government overseeing the operations of seven provinces and three territories in the best interest of the country as a whole. It had this to be said for it: in the early years of Confederation, it fostered the idea of the country; the central government at Ottawa was, at first, the only meaningful content in the expression, "Dominion of Canada." There was little affection or understanding between the sections of the country in 1867, or in 1873. But as Canada developed, as the provinces acquired, so to speak, more mass, they acquired consciousness of each other and themselves. They had their own ideas about the political shape the country might take; they were even ready to discuss whether it was to take any at all.

Thus "the revolt of the provinces" was not a revolt in the accepted sense of that term. It was a debate about what Canada ought or ought not to be. It also expressed a basic dissatisfaction with the view that Ottawa, and Ottawa alone, represented the country. Canada was, after all, a federal state, or it was alleged to be. It was too naive, in 1886, to identify Canada with the Dominion government. Provinces had begun to think of their own individual identity, and felt their ideas about themselves and about Canada were entitled to something more than the cavalier treatment they were wont to receive from Ottawa. Not only did Macdonald have the understandable habit of identifying Canada with the Dominion government, but more perniciously for the four Liberal governments of the original four provinces, Macdonald also had the habit of identifying Canada with the Conservative party.

By 1886 the provinces had acquired, legally, support for their view of Canadian federation from the Privy Council. The Supreme Court of Canada had tended in its early cases to support a broad interpretation of federal power. In *Severn vs. the Queen*, 1878, the Supreme Court threw out an Ontario Act on the ground that it infringed the Dominion's power over trade and commerce. Here the two French Canadian justices voted with the majority.[1] The Supreme Court also supported the Canada Temperance Act in an 1880 case, *Fredericton vs. the Queen*, basing its support on the trade and commerce clause. But the city of Fredericton gave to Canada a better known case, *Russell vs. the Queen*, 1882, which went to the Privy Council. That body sustained the validity of the Dominion statute, not upon the grounds of the trade and commerce clause, but on the residual power of Section 91.[2]

But the trade and commerce clause of Section 91 had already come under Privy Council scrutiny in *Citizens Insurance Co. vs. Parsons*, 1881. The details in this case do not matter; the Ontario Court of Appeal, the Supreme Court of Canada, and the Privy Council all agreed on the verdict. But in the course of reaching its decision, the Privy Council, in what amounted to an *obiter dicta*, placed serious limitations upon the Dominion government's power over trade and commerce. As it stood in the British North America Act, this power could cover anything from arrangements for foreign trade to rules for the operation of, say a plumbing business in Yarmouth, which, said the Privy Council, was clearly not intended. The Dominion power for the regulation of trade and commerce "does not comprehend the power to regulate . . . a particular business or trade . . . in a single province."[3] This initiated a trend that was to give the provinces interpretations of their powers and of Dominion powers, that strengthened the whole conception of province, of a federal Canada, and, necessarily, weakened the centralist conception of the Confederation of 1867. The trend was to last for nearly fifty years. And while it has been much deprecated by constitutional lawyers and political scientists, it at least squared with the reality of a big country, with big provinces and strong regional identities.

Then came the celebrated *Hodge vs. the Queen*, 1883. Like many famous law cases it began from minute, almost ludicrous particulars: Archibald Hodge's billiard tables. One of the rules laid down by the Liquor Licence Commissioners of Toronto was that no games were to be played in licensed taverns when such taverns were closed for drinking. After 7 P.M., Saturday, May 7, 1881, Hodge's tavern, the St. James Hotel, was closed for drinking. Notwithstanding, a game of billiards went merrily on. This horror was duly apprehended, and Hodge was fined twenty dollars. This judgment was appealed, first to the Court of Queen's Bench, then the Ontario Court of Appeal, and finally to the Privy Council, Hodge's lawyers arguing that the Ontario government had no power to confer the authority it did upon the Toronto Licence Commissioners. The Privy Council upheld Hodge's conviction, and the Ontario Act of 1877 under which it was made, on grounds that suggest an opening for the future: that the question of liquor regulation had two aspects, the general power of prohibition operating via local option in the Canada Temperance Act (confirmed in *Russell vs. the Queen* of 1882), and the local power for making police regulations and licensing taverns. The provinces were, said the Privy Council, within the limits of their powers conferred by Section 92, "supreme." This aspect doctrine, as it came to be called, was direct descendant of the construction of the British North America Act proposed by the Judicial Committee in *Citizens Insurance vs. Parsons.*

Thus the constitutional groundwork was laid for the growth of the consciousness of provincial power, itself a product, in part at least, of the material growth of the provinces themselves. Nowhere was this more obvious than in the development of the factory system, and the problems that came with that development – urban growth, labour difficulties, factory evils – all of which, it soon became apparent, might have to be solved by provincial legislation. Associated with them were problems of business monopoly and railway rate discrimination which the Dominion government would have to deal with.

In December, 1886, the Dominion government appointed a Royal Commission to consider the relations of labour and capital in Canada. The Commission worked for two years, and the report was made public in 1889. It dealt first of all with labour and working conditions. Real wages, it concluded, had gone up but working conditions were bad, in some cases frightful. For the past ten years there had been a slow growth of money wages, a gradual drop in the price of groceries, and thus a palpable rise in real wages. Flour which in 1877 had been $5.40 a bag was in 1887 $3.70, and many other provisions likewise. In 1877 Nova Scotia coal in Montreal was $4.50 a ton, in 1886 it was $3 to $3.50 a ton.[4] As a New Brunswick informant remarked, "I can scarcely think of anything that is not cheaper now [than ten years ago]."[5] There was, however, one marked exception: rents. These had advanced in all the major cities, and "to such an extent that a serious burden has been added to those borne by people struggling for a living."[6] In Halifax, Saint John, Montreal, Toronto, rent absorbed one-quarter of working class income, in Quebec city one-fifth.[7]

The vulnerability of the working classes to sickness, improvidence, drunkenness, or just plain bad luck, is well known, but an example from Montreal cited by the Commission, though doubtless extreme, puts the point home. A poor family ran into debt for $11 for groceries. $7 of the debt had been paid off when the wife became ill. Time was asked for, and refused, and a judgment for the $4 plus $15 costs was rendered against the husband. His wages were garnisheed, and finally the despair of it all drove him to suicide. The Commission pointed to a sinister Montreal practice – doubtless prevalent elsewhere – for certain lawyers to canvass retailers and wholesalers for their outstanding accounts to collect, making a percentage on the collections, and taking the debtor, if necessary to court.[8] Doubtless the $4 judgment was extracted that way.

The work day was generally ten hours, but there were many exceptions. In Ontario the exceptions were on the side of shorter hours. In Nova Scotia and New Brunswick, ten hours was general. In Quebec the exceptions were toward longer hours, where "much evidence of long-continued labour came before the Commission."[9]

The worst evil was child and female labour, especially the former.[10] The introduction of machinery on a large scale made physical strength no longer essential in many routine factory jobs. It was mainly persistence and drudgery that were needed, and children, who could be paid depressed wages, filled the bill admirably. The Commission recommended that laws be passed, by the Dominion or the province, preferably the former, forbidding continuous employment of any kind for children under fourteen. Associated with child and female labour were an infinite variety of devices to keep production up and costs down. In one Quebec factory if the machinery were stopped during the day from accident or breakdown, the women had to stay at night to make up the time caused by the stoppage.[11] In boot-making there were examples of girls being paid one cent for every sole they made, and mulcted a fine of four cents a pair for each defective one. The fines, managed properly, could be very effective in keeping down wages. The worst working conditions were in the cigar factories.

> Here in stifling air foul with odors of tobacco, machine oil, perspiration, and a thousand other evil-smelling substances, are seated the slaves of the leaf. Young and old, women and men, boys and girls, from seven o'clock in the morning until six o'clock at night, with one short hour for dinner, they toil for three dollars a week and sometimes two. There are no toilet appliances, no fire escapes, no facilities for ventilation: there is nothing but work and a brutal foreman to enforce it.

So *Montreal by gaslight*, 1889.[12]

There were various attempts to combine labour's forces. Unions were well established among the railwaymen, the printers, and other trades, but they were overshadowed by an American secret labour society called the Knights of Labour. "The Noble and Holy Order of the Knights of Labour of North America" began in Canada in 1881, in Hamilton. It received guarded support from the church in Quebec, did well in Ontario, and by 1882 had forty lodges and 16,000 members. The Knights included in their ranks all kinds of labour, even small business men. One of their first encounters in Canada was the Toronto Street Railway strike of 1886, where Senator Frank Smith, the president, said no union men would be hired by the Railway. The settlement that emerged was based upon the tacit acknowledgement of the right of the men to belong to the union.[13] The views of the Knights of

Labour were heavily laced with Henry George (*Progress and Poverty*, 1879) and some quasi-Marxism. The Knights had an interesting disposition to resent the way that workers in Canada thought it perfectly natural "that a man should scrape together by hook or by crook a few thousand dollars, put the money out on mortgage, or salt it down," live on the interest afterward, and give a wicked "heritage of idleness to his children."[14]

They survived well into the 1890's, and in fact lasted longer in Canada than in the United States. Their idealism, the emphasis upon education and debate, the wide-ranging inclusiveness of their point of view, combined virtues not possessed by many of the more pragmatic but narrow-minded international trade unions.[15] And the trades unions themselves found some kind of central organization necessary. The Toronto Trades Assembly in 1883 provided the germ of a more lasting organization, the Trades and Labour Congress, which became definitely established in 1886. It was then mainly Ontario in character, but unlike the American Federation of Labour founded in the same year, the Trades and Labour Congress included not only trade unions but Knights of Labour assemblies as well.

Nova Scotia provided the most interesting example of unionism at the provincial and local level in the Provincial Workmen's Association. Both an industrial and a general labour union, it had grown out of the coal industry. It was concerned not only with labour conditions but also with output, and it enjoyed a considerable measure of good will both with the government and with the mining concerns. The strength of the miners in provincial elections partly explains the willingness of the Nova Scotia government to listen to them, but the paucity of strikes and the union's emphasis on conciliation procedures, as well as its sound knowledge of local conditions, largely explains why they managed so well over a period of forty years to maintain the good will of the public and of the press, and even to some extent of management.[16]

The factory system had been developing slowly for some years before Confederation, but the tariff of 1879 brought it on with a rush. ". . . it sprang into existence almost at one bound, and was the creature of the legislation adopted ten years ago."[17] Factories concentrated near transportation, rail or water, best of all both. To survive they had to supply a national market, not a local one. In the process, as railways became steadily more efficient and more pervasive, the big factories slowly choked local industry. In the immense collection of papers on Peel County in the Ontario Archives,[18] one can observe this process at work. Village wheelwrights, coopers, carriage makers, and other artisans were gradually destroyed by the factory products of Toronto and Hamilton brought in by railways.

Factories not only changed society, they changed the quality of the demands placed upon the workers. Factories must have a firm routine and must impose internal discipline on their workers. Punctuality is not merely a virtue, it is a necessity. That these powers would be abused, that workers would be forced to battle for wages and shorter hours of work, that the whole business of maximizing profits by both sides would bring ugliness and brutality was nearly inevitable. Still, it was admitted in 1885, even by those who proposed factory legislation to Parliament, that the system was not all bad. "The factory system as it exists in Canada has not, I must confess Mr. Speaker, up to this hour been productive of very great evils," said Dr. Bergin.[19] But evils there were, in the nature of the system itself, and in the new city that the system fostered. The new city, "where nothing rests and no man is,"

> And toil hath fear for neighbour,
> Where singing lips are dumb,
> And life is one long labour,
> Till death or freedom come.[20]

The Commission deplored the absence of any sense of obligation in most employers toward their workers. "The one fixed and dominant idea" was to pay as little in wages and get back as much work as possible. To do this, the mills and factories were "filled with women and children, to the practical exclusion of adult males."[21] Between 1880 and 1886 there were three Government bills and four private bills proposed in Parliament controlling hours of work, rules for women and children, factory safety. They were all finally dropped owing to considerable doubt about the constitutionality of such legislation after the failure of the McCarthy Liquor License Act of 1883 before the Privy Council. And if the Dominion government had not dropped the factory legislation, it would certainly have been taken to court by the Canadian Manufacturers Association.

Monopolies, rings and combines were well known in the United States where trusts were in part a response to the difficulties of interstate commerce in a country where the central government had no power to charter companies. In Canada all that was needed was incorporation under an act of the Dominion Parliament. Attempts to control competition, also implied in the idea of the trust, were common on both sides of the border, however. Dr. G. T. Orton, Conservative member for Centre Wellington, raised the question of a coal-oil ring in Parliament in 1881. He claimed the ring sold coal oil at thirty-five cents a gallon when it ought to have been about eighteen cents.[22] By 1890 there were a range of accusations from responsible and irresponsible periodicals, from *Bystander* on the one hand and *Grip* on the other, alleging combines in agricultural implements, plate glass, salt, indeed, that combines were "the order of the day."[23] But the existence of pools and combines was easy to allege, harder to prove. To argue, as Cartwright and some Liberals did, that the National Policy produced combines, was simply to say that combines were a natural development of industrial growth under a protective tariff, not less pernicious for that.

There were enough comments on combines to warrant the Government's striking a Select Committee in 1888, "to examine and report upon the nature, extent and effect of certain combinations said to exist with reference to the purchase and sale or manufacture and sale in Canada of any Foreign or Canadian products. . . ."[24] This was comprehensive enough. The Chairman was N. C. Wallace, M.P. West York, who said he believed that the National Policy had "reduced the price of everything manufactured in this country."[25] The committee produced a 743-page return to Parliament, 733 pages of it evidence from sixty-three witnesses. The main abuses the committee uncovered were practised in the distributing side of business; the Dominion Grocers' Guild of Montreal, the coal dealers of Toronto, the undertakers of Ontario, the Fire Insurance Underwriters' Association, and the oatmeal millers. In these diverse areas systems of price fixing and control of distribution existed. These associations had begun in order to arrange methods of business, terms of credit, but were now rapidly developing more ambitious ideas. To quote the committee, "The power used, cautiously at first was soon grasped with a firmer hand, and at length, 'the simple plan that they may take who have the power,' governed the operations of these associations."[26] Clarke Wallace successfully sponsored an anti-combines act in 1889, which was mainly a statement of the common law on conspiracy in restraint of trade.[27]

A monopoly was also alleged in railway freight rates. After the Grand Trunk absorbed the Great Western and the Northern Railway, and after the Canadian Pacific Railway had acquired its Ontario feeders, the Canadian railway business was largely in the hands of two giants. Some arrangement between them about freight rates would have been mutually advantageous. There is, however, no evidence that their rivalry was ever mitigated to that point. What caused more serious concern in Parliament was discrimination, of a great variety of kinds. Every railway was in itself a kind of monopoly and possessed the power to make or break shippers and communities. In the east the Grand Trunk bore the brunt of such accusations. They were raised as early as 1881 in the Senate, when the Grand Trunk was accused of giving a rebate of fifty per cent from its published freight rates to the Imperial Oil Company. Others complained that through freight was given much lower rates than local freight and that railways changed rates for different points depending upon whether the point were competitive or not.

Such complaints moved D'Alton McCarthy to propose a Court of Railway Commissioners with the power to settle freight rates. From 1882 onward McCarthy proposed his bill, and in 1885 it actually went before the Railway Committee of the House where it met determined resistance from

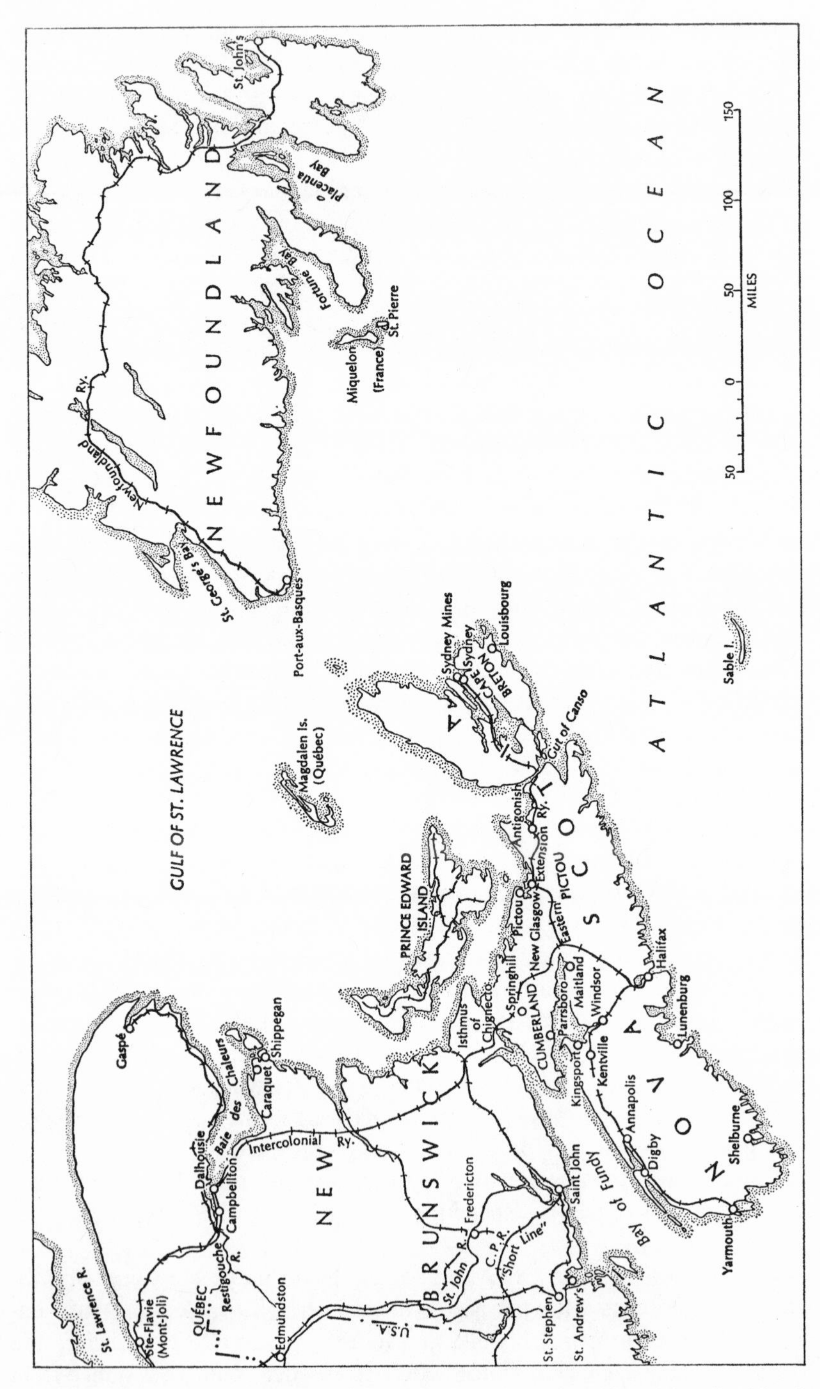

Railway Lines in the Maritime Provinces and Newfoundland by the 1890's

the railways, and also, interestingly enough, from numerous influential shippers. It was impossible to deny that railway rate discrimination was widely practised. But what was legitimate government regulation? The *Monetary Times* of Montreal put the problem neatly, in June 1885:

> There ought to be some limit to discrimination . . . but in trade the laws of competition can seldom be safely interfered with. Where to draw the line is a difficulty that has puzzled the wisest legislators in the world.[28]

Walter Shanly, a veteran railway builder, made a similar point when McCarthy's bill came up for second reading in 1886:

> There are duties and powers entrusted to the three members of the [railway] commission that no thirty men in the Dominion – or on this continent . . . could discharge. The effect of the Bill will be to place in the hands of those three Commissioners all that is now being done by the regular management of the railways, and those men are expected to do that which it takes fifty men working almost night and day. . . .[29]

The Bill was dropped on the understanding the Government would appoint a commission to investigate railway freight rate structures. It was appointed in 1886 under A. T. Galt, and reported in 1888.

Galt rejected McCarthy's idea, but recommended that the powers of the Railway Committee of the Cabinet be strengthened in order to end, if possible, rebates or secret rates of any kind.[30] The truth was that the Conservative government was not prepared to quarrel with the two major railways, and given the great intrinsic difficulties in rate regulation, McCarthy's proposal was not revived. Besides, there were good party reasons why the Conservatives felt it inadvisable to antagonize the railways to no really effective purpose. Both the Grand Trunk and the Canadian Pacific had contributed handsomely to the Conservative party in the general election of 1887.

Prior to that election, between April and December 1886, every province in Canada had held one. In Prince Edward Island the Conservatives were returned, as they had been in every provincial election since 1873. In Nova Scotia the Liberals, in power since 1882, were returned with five more seats. In New Brunswick the Liberals clung to office with independent support and in Quebec the Liberals won a narrow victory – if they could count on independent votes. In Ontario the Liberals won sixteen more seats, to solidify the control they had enjoyed since 1871. In Manitoba the Conservatives were returned as they had been since 1870, but with the narrowest majority so far. In British Columbia party divisions on eastern lines were still meaningless, but the Davie government that was to assume power in 1887 was, like all British Columbia governments so far, profoundly conservative in social attitudes, if not always Conservative in party allegiance. British Columbia had returned six Conservatives to Ottawa from 1872 until the election of 1896. So much had Mackenzie and Blake done for the Conservatives west of the Rockies! Thus the four original provinces of Confederation, comprising the populous, wealthy, and by far the most powerful section of the Dominion politically were by the beginning of 1887 in Liberal control.

The two most significant provincial elections in 1886 were in Nova Scotia and Quebec. Nova Scotia in 1886 had a population of 445,000, ten per cent of Canada, a little less than the proportions of 1867. It was about the mid-1880's when the proportion started to drop more steeply. (In 1969, it was four per cent.) This time, interestingly enough, coincided with the period F. W. Wallace ascribes as the beginning of the end of the square-rigged wooden ships.

But there were other industries in Nova Scotia that helped to counterbalance the slow dying of the ships and their trade. Coal mining in Cape Breton had begun in 1785; by the 1840's sales averaged 153,000 tons a year; by the 1860's this had trebled; in the 1870's it was 738,000 tons; and by the early 1880's sales of Nova Scotian coal were well over one million tons a year. In 1885, an average year, 1,255,000 tons were sold, representing about 95 per cent of total Nova Scotia production, and 65 per cent of the total Canadian.[31] The coal mines in Cape Breton had been leased in 1828 to a British consortium, but there had been new collieries opened since. There were three main coal areas, Cape Breton County, Pictou County, and Cumberland County, with production by the mid-1880's divided more or less evenly between them. The Cape Breton fields were the most extensive, but the important ones were largely under the sea bed at Sydney, and nearly three tons of water had to be pumped out from those mines for every ton of coal that was hauled out.[32] Still lacking a railway – it was built in 1887 – coal mining in Cape Breton was largely confined to late spring, summer, and fall, owing to ice in the Gulf of St. Lawrence. The Pictou and Cumberland mines operated the year round.

There was a large market for Nova Scotia coal in Quebec, forty per cent of the total production. Three-quarters of the coal used in Montreal was from Nova Scotia.[33] Nova Scotia absorbed thirty-five per cent of her own production, New Brunswick took twelve per cent, Newfoundland six and Prince Edward Island five. By 1886, the Ontario market for Nova Scotia coal was negligible. So too was the American market. American railways had cheapened American coal in New England so much that, with the American tariff on coal, it was nearly impossible for Nova Scotia to compete. 1885 was the lowest year for coal exports to the United States since 1850. It was an illusion to assume that New England was the natural market for Nova Scotian coal. Failing a system of reciprocity with the United States, Nova Scotian markets for coal lay within Canada, or in Newfoundland. Thus in 1887 Sir Charles Tupper, Minister of Finance, kept the duty on soft coal.

The duty on anthracite was repealed to develop the Canadian steel industry.

Iron rails had been made in Canada in the 1860's, but with the rapid increase in the use of steel rails, Canadian imports of iron and steel rose steeply. There was a nascent steel industry at New Glasgow in Pictou County, using local ore and coal; steel castings were already made in Montreal and Hamilton. Before 1887 Canada had a bounty of $1.50 a ton for pig iron made in Canada and a modest tariff of $2 a ton for imports. In 1887 the tariff was raised to $4 a ton, and lower grades of steel were given protection at 30 per cent *ad valorem*. This gave the steel industry in Nova Scotia, Quebec, and Ontario protection nearly equal to that of the steel industry in the United States.

On July 1, 1885 the Nova Scotian market for free fish in New England came to an end, with the termination, at American instance, of the fishery clauses of the Washington treaty. Between July 1884 and July 1885, there was a drop of seventy-five per cent in pickled fish and lobster exports to the United States.[34] The market for fish in the West Indies held up well (until 1899 in fact), but there was a sharp twelve per cent drop in 1886 and 1887, though this proved only temporary.

The changes in markets and in production were not all against Nova Scotia, but broadly the effect was to strengthen the prosperity of the northeast of the province against the southwest. It is not surprising that both Cape Breton County and Pictou County elected Conservatives in the "repeal" election of 1886.

The Nova Scotia government had had a difficult time; it complained in 1866, and in 1886, and at various times in between, that revenues were insufficient to meet expenses. Being traditionally a Liberal government, it had found railway subsidies from Ottawa light and unsatisfactory. The Eastern Extension Railway, from New Glasgow to Louisburg – at this stage extended as far as the Gut of Canso – was subsidized by the Nova Scotian government at $5000 a mile, and had eventually to be taken over by the Intercolonial Railway. Railways proved easier to subsidize with federal funds in counties where there were Conservative M.P.'s and Conservative M.P.P.'s than in the southwest or the Annapolis Valley where Liberal members had been generally predominant since Confederation.

The great bulk of Nova Scotians thought of the Dominion of Canada in a way instinctively federal. Nova Scotians were Canadians, all right, but some felt, in Jones' words, "I am a Canadian by Act of Parliament."[35] This local sentiment was substantially mitigated in the northeast by the Intercolonial Railway and the associated coal trade. The dispatch of Halifax troops to Saskatchewan in 1885 had done more than anything since Confederation to make the province feel part of Canada. So, at least, believed Robert Borden.[36] This ambivalence allowed Nova Scotians to elect a Liberal provincial government and still elect a majority of Conservatives to the

House of Commons. The allegiance to the Conservatives federally was a bread-and-butter allegiance. The Conservative party was, so to speak, the husband, while the Liberal housewife ran the local home.[37] And they not infrequently quarrelled.

The Liberal provincial government elected in 1882 was headed by W. T. Pipes, but he gave up in 1884, and W. S. Fielding, after some difficulty, constructed a government and became Premier.[38] Fielding was then thirty-six years old, a newspaper man with little actual political experience. He had been on the Halifax *Morning Chronicle* since 1864, and its editor since about 1870. Fielding was given the chief credit for the overthrow of the Holmes-Thompson government in 1882, no mean achievement for a newspaper editor. He was to remain in office until 1911, Premier of Nova Scotia to 1896, and in Laurier's Cabinet until Laurier's defeat. For all his glibness in the *Morning Chronicle*, for all his sweet reasonableness in the Assembly, Fielding was a canny, costive politician. Beckles Willson wrote many years later,

> . . . in the long years of our acquaintance I never heard an original or lofty remark pass his lips. . . . He was always the cheery, bustling merchant, the shrewd provincial politician, who never had any deep convictions on policy which he was not prepared to modify or even abandon for expediency's sake, although he could always justify his action on the highest grounds.[39]

There was no mention of repeal of the B.N.A. Act in the 1886 Nova Scotian Speech from the Throne, nor during most of that session. True in 1884 both branches of the legislature had appealed to Ottawa for a substantial increase of the debt allowance, and in 1885 Fielding had threatened that unless some relief were obtained Nova Scotia must of necessity consider the possibility of repeal.[40] Then, two days before the end of the 1886 session, Fielding proposed the following:

> . . . the feeling of discontent with regard to the financial arrangement [by which Nova Scotia entered Confederation] is now believed by this House to be more general and more deeply fixed than before . . . that the financial and commercial interests of the people of Nova Scotia, New Brunswick, and Prince Edward Island would be advanced by these Provinces withdrawing from the Canadian Federation and uniting under one Government. . . .

If this union of the Maritime provinces were to prove impossible, Nova Scotia would ask for a return to her original status as a Province of Great Britain. The motion was carried 15-7.[41]

It was, however, simply a resolution of the Assembly. No similar resolution passed the Legislative Council. Fielding seems to have devised the repeal issue partly as a way of forcing Ottawa to pay tribute, and partly as a way to be sure of winning the election. There had to be one before the end of June 1886, and given the circumstances of 1886, repeal was as good an issue as any other. Better, in fact, for it produced a target that all knew, all recognized, and which many did not mind shooting at. But it had never even been alluded to in any communication between Fielding and Lieutenant-Governor Richey. Richey quite sensibly decided the best way to handle the repeal issue was to let it alone, to ignore officially what he had never been officially cognizant of.[42]

The election was called for June 15. Federal ministers and members were sent down from Ottawa; Thompson, A. W. McLelan, and C. H. Tupper were instructed to do what they could. They could not do much. The result of Fielding's gambit was to increase the Liberal majority in the Assembly by five, giving the Liberals twenty-nine in a House of thirty-nine.[43] It was much more decided than anyone had expected, including Fielding himself. In many counties the issue was not taken seriously, but in some the old feelings of 1867 were in evidence again. The Nova Scotian Conservatives were in something of a panic, for they feared Fielding's use of that big majority. What would the Lieutenant-Governor do, or the Dominion government devise, if Fielding were to call an immediate meeting of the Assembly to deal with repeal and Maritime union? One thing was certain: "Nova Scotia must not get one cent of financial help as better terms upon the threat of repeal."[44]

What was Fielding going to do about it? He had, as the cartoon in *Grip* showed, called the genie out of the bottle.

> Genie: "And now what, master?"
> Fielding: "I-er-um-I find that-aw-really I have
> no power to do anything after all!"[45]

And nothing at all happened. It was obvious that the Dominion government would go to the polls soon, and it was deemed necessary to see how far the repeal issue would carry over into the federal election. *The Week* remarked, with its usual good sense, that no one could take the repeal agitation seriously as long as Nova Scotia continued to return thirteen members in support of the Macdonald government and only six opposed. This was no evidence of a wide-spread or deep-rooted agitation.[46]

If the Nova Scotians had wanted repeal in June 1886, they had changed their minds by February 1887. Of Nova Scotia's twenty-one seats in the House of Commons, only seven went to the Liberals, and of these only two were specifically for repeal. This defeat, which Fielding may have anticipated, left the repeal movement stranded high and dry. "I think it would be well," Longley wrote Blake, "if we should lay the Repeal cause on the shelf and go in for honest government."[47] The Nova Scotia Liberals decided, after much haggling in convention, that it was useless for the provincial government to proceed further.[48]

So the Speech from the Throne in Halifax in 1887 was silent on the subject of the repeal, and the whole issue was consigned, if not to oblivion, at least to the cupboard. Fielding proposed that it was now "inexpedient" to pursue the question of repeal, but that unless an improvement in the finances of the province took place, Nova Scotian discontent would continue, and it might then be necessary to take repeal from the cupboard and dust it off once again.[49] In the metaphor in the Conservative Halifax *Herald*:

> the legislature of Nova Scotia [has] consigned the repeal jackass to the silent tomb. . . . While many praised the beast, – some even doubting that he was dead – none doubted the expediency of burying him. Succeeded he will doubtless be by some other donkey with a different name . . . mayhap "Commercial Union."[50]

Quebec's election of 1886 was a more complex matter than the repeal election in Nova Scotia. It was not simply, as has been so often said, the victory of Rielisme. Politically, Riel was a myth, though a very successful one. What had bothered French Canadians most was not so much Riel, though certainly he cannot be excluded, as the feeling that something nearly all of them wanted was not given to them. Yet, pervasive as that feeling may have been, it accounted for surprisingly little of Mercier's narrow victory.

For one thing English-speaking support was important to Mercier, and there was some evidence to show he wanted it, and acquired it. In 1886 English-speaking voters were in a majority in eight counties, and were an important factor in at least six others.[51] The Liberals had been the main hope of the English for a pure and economical provincial government, on the model of Ontario's. Joly had been the kind of man who had drawn independent English-speaking support.[52] The Quebec Conservatives were tainted; the English-speaking community felt that the Quebec Conservative government, now nearly twenty years old, was a conspiracy of French and Irish to milk the province.[53] We must have, as one English Liberal wrote to Laurier, "leaders sans reproche."[54]

But Mercier also had an observable lean toward the "Castors," which bothered some English-Liberal voters, and his crusade of 1885-86 put a strain on English-speaking support from Liberals and independents; this was a risk that some French-Canadian Liberal newspapers, like *La Patrie*, were apparently willing to take. Mercier admitted to Cartwright in December 1886 that much of his success was due to the support of the "Castors."[55]

Mercier had won his greatest support in the counties just south and east of Montreal. The main focus of his campaign had been the Montreal-St. Hyacinthe-Sorel triangle, where a considerable shift in the popular vote turned seven counties over from the Conservatives to the Liberals. It was an area where new social complications, the development of labour and urban interests, were the long term source of what the Riel agitation effected in the short term. The nationalist sentiment swirling around Riel was a much stronger emotional outlet for French Canadian labour than the more rational, but more distant labour programs.[56]

It was not clear for some days after the voting what Quebec had actually decided. For a time both sides claimed victory. But it gradually became clear that the J. J. Ross Conservative government had elected only twenty-eight supporters out of sixty-five, against Mercier and twenty-nine of his supporters. That still left seven seats, and there was some controversy over these. Five were National Conservatives whom the Conservative government hoped might yet be won over; Langevin believed so. Two were Independents.

L. F. R. Masson, the Conservative Lieutenant-Governor, put off the day of reckoning until the Assembly met, January 27, 1887. The Assembly supported Mercier and on January 29, 1887 Quebec's second Liberal government was sworn in. It was to last, through a provincial election in 1890, just five years. Israël Tarte warned in *Le Canadien* that if Mercier was the cure for the evils of Conservative government, it would be worse than the disease. Mercier he said, would ruin the province.[57] Castors and English Liberals supported Mercier's *parti national* to get good and honest Government:[58] it was precisely this that Quebec was not to get. The cartoon in *Grip* of November 20, 1886 by L. Côté was timely:

Mme. Quebec. – "Now, Mr. Mercier, take care that you don't give me too decent a government – for I won't stand it!"
M. Mercier. – "Don't worry, Madame; there's not the slightest danger!"

The Dominion election of January, 1887 was preceded by a short picnic season in June, 1886, and a longer autumn campaign in Ontario. Picnics, Macdonald's forte, were often disliked by his ministers. Thompson complained that a Catholic picnic near Ottawa, on June 29, was "nothing but a lot of people walking about a field and some nasty provisions spoiling on a long table in the sun."[59] However much the public may have enjoyed themselves, the politicians got back to Ottawa "tired, sunburnt & billious [*sic*]." By the end of October, the Cabinet had decided upon a dissolution and an election in January 1887, all but three of the Cabinet preferring an election before rather than after the next session of Parliament.[60] Besides, there was that Ontario election in December. The campaigning began in earnest. The pace was ferocious; Macdonald went through meeting after meeting with ease, almost gaily. Perhaps it was the relief of escape. Thompson sardonically noted – his humour had always a cutting edge – Macdonald's "daily life at home is of itself tormenting enough. . . ."[61]

There are few more vivid accounts of what political campaigning was like for the campaigners themselves than Thompson's periodic letters to his wife about Macdonald's whirlwind campaign in south and west Ontario in mid-

November, 1886. The Dominion ministers, Macdonald, Thomas White, and Thompson, together with W. H. Meredith, leader of the Conservative opposition in Ontario, installed themselves in a special Grand Trunk car, lived there and slept there. Thursday, November 18 found them travelling from Palmerston to Goderich via Clinton in a perfect blizzard of snow. At every station there was a crowd, sometimes large, with a brass band, and always cries for "John A." Thompson would watch Macdonald go out, "shake hands everywhere with everyone & kiss all the girls and . . . come back to the car covered with snow."[62] On the Friday there was a town meeting twelve miles from Goderich, reached by carriage. It lasted five long afternoon hours. That night back at Goderich, there was another huge meeting until one in the morning. "I am beginning to be fearfully abused," wrote Thompson, "because of course I say very wicked things. You cannot hold such crowds as we have had unless you give them your best & your worst."[63]

They felt as Thompson said, like minstrels, from railway car to meetings, and back, often in dirty clothes, and in spite of "the exhaustion of one's brains of anything to say we are supposed to be quite up to the boiling point of excitement which prevails among the audiences."[64] Tough they were on the politicians. But to the voters it was different. Political meetings were entertainment, the translation of newspapers into life. And what else was there to break the daily round, and take men briefly outside the little worlds in which they moved?

Despite Conservative efforts, Oliver Mowat won a resounding victory in the provincial election increasing his majority, which had been 48-36 in 1883, to 64-26.

Chapleau set to work upon a series of negotiations with the Grand Trunk Railway for support in the Dominion election, due February 22, 1887. The Grand Trunk were popular in Montreal, and "they alone can control the vote of the Knights of Labor," Chapleau wrote. A war with the Grand Trunk was unthinkable, and would cause panic among Conservatives.[65] The railway had its own requests to make, but Joseph Hickson was prepared to be reasonable. Macdonald gave in on some and not others. He was frantically busy with campaigning and so dead tired he told Chapleau, "I can scarcely sit up to write you."[66] Chapleau also asked that fishery regulations along the St. Lawrence be "adjusted," to yield twenty-five or thirty votes in Boucherville; Macdonald endorsed Chapleau's letter over to the Deputy-Minister of Fisheries:

> Private and confidential
> My dear Tilton –
> Will you see to this & destroy this letter or as it is from a Minister return it.
> Yours al. JAMD.[67]

On the other hand the Liberals derived some funds from American sources or so Macdonald alleged to Lord Lansdowne. Chicago pork packers, who at one time controlled the Canadian market, were said to have sent $100,000 into Montreal alone; heading the list was W. D. Armour.[68] The Liberals probably expected the election after the session of 1887, not before. That is one explanation for the timing of Blake's attempt to persuade Oliver Mowat to assume the leadership of the Liberal party, early in January, 1887.[69] Mowat was willing to consider it. He suggested that Blake might lead the party nominally; alternatively, if Mowat himself led the Liberal party, he would want Blake in the government. Blake here proved to be his old self; he would stay in a Mowat cabinet if pressed, but without portfolio. In the middle of these negotiations Blake received word from Mulock that the election was called for February, and the negotiations fell to the ground. Blake took up his burden, "and will carry it with what strength may be given me."[70]

Blake tried to present the Liberal party as a legitimate alternative government, and his Malvern speech in particular said to the manufacturers, "Don't be afraid of us. The Liberal party does not want to abolish the protective tariff; only to adjust it. Sir Richard Cartwright does not really mean what he says."[71] The real issue was whether the present tariff system was not defective. He proposed to reduce duties on necessities – fuel, bread, sugar, cottons – and levy a heavier duty on luxuries. Such an arrangement would help curb monopolies. But, and Blake emphasized this, the most ardent free trader, whatever his principles, had to face the fact that Canada had substantial commitments, that the bulk of Canada's revenue was derived from the tariff, and that any substantial reduction in the tariff was quite "removed from the domain of practical politics." The whole purpose of Liberal policy was "to subserve the real interests at once of manufacturers and of the public at large."[72]

Despite the Malvern speech, the campaign of 1887 was largely devoid of national issues; it was fought on local problems. The Conservatives made no great effort to promote the National Policy in the election; the years 1885-87 had not been brisk commercial years anywhere in North America. Rather, they stood on the status quo, which, with the Gerrymander of 1882, and the Franchise Act of 1885, was no bad place to be. The Liberals seemed unable to seize the initiative, and the most surprising element in the election was not the weakness of the Conservatives, but the ineffectiveness of their opponents. The Liberals needed something more than mere opposition to the government, more than their insistence on purity of government. Maladministration of the Northwest was all very well, but the Riel issue was as awkward for them as for the Tories. Lacking a leader of charismatic quality, they needed an issue to energize and enthuse the electorate. They did not have one and they could not seem to find one.

The total vote in the election of 1887 was 723,000 as against 516,000 for the election of 1882. Much of this increase was clearly owing to the operation of the 1885 Franchise Act. The effects of this are difficult to assess, but the new voters may possibly have saved the Macdonald government from defeat.[73] The Northwest Territories were voting for the first time and, despite their vicissitudes, they returned four Conservatives. Macdonald had had a comfortable margin of sixty-eight seats after the 1882 election; it was now down to thirty-seven in a house of 215. In Nova Scotia the Conservatives got fourteen seats to seven. In Ontario, despite Mowat's resounding victory, Conservatives were 55 to 37. But the Quebec members presented the most accurate reflection of the provincial election, 33-32. It had been 51-14. A purely party division in the new Parliament was won by the Conservatives 105-85.

Laurier now acquired a substantial Quebec following. Not unnaturally he emerged from the election cheerful and buoyant. Given the 1885-87 depression, he felt it was really better to be out of office.[74] But Blake was crushed. He had been wounded by the failure of the influential parliamentary Liberals, Cartwright, Mackenzie, Charlton, Mulock, Davies, and others, to follow his lead on the Landry motion. His overture to Mowat may have been partly the outcome of his resentment. His Malvern speech had certainly been submitted to a party conference beforehand, and approved even by Cartwright; but in Cartwright's election speeches there was no evidence of his having accepted Blake's ideas or absorbed Blake's policy. Attacking manufacturers was an instinct with Cartwright, like attacking the National Policy; it was not a duty, but a positive pleasure. Given that, and his unruly tongue, discretion was quite too much to expect.[75] "Politics," said Cartwright, "is war and many things are lawful. . . ."[76]

Blake had, moreover, gone into the campaign with reluctance, having talked about giving up the leadership as early as the autumn of 1885. In fact, it is difficult to say that Blake had any strong wish to be leader at all. Whatever feelings he had on that subject had been directed toward the leadership of the party by others. There was something quite striking, and for the Liberal party demoralizing, in Blake's constant references, in little speeches here and there in the House of Commons, especially when needled by a member of the Government, about how much he did not want to be in power, how much he did not want to be leader of the Opposition, and how he was where he was from a sense of public duty.[77] No one can doubt Blake's sincerity. But for his party there was no joy in it either. He gave the impression of never having thought of himself as Prime Minister of Canada, or what he would do with the position if he got it.

There is a saying in politics that a party never gives its whole heart to a leader until he has led them to power; but there is no evidence that it was ever true of the Liberal party's attitude to Blake. He broached the idea of resigning to a few close party friends early in March 1887 and the result was consternation. "If we could penetrate the secrets of the Liberal caucus between 1880 and 1887," writes Willison, "we would discover an opposition on its knees in passionate pleading against the sudden decision of the leader to relinquish the command."[78] But Blake had had enough. And his resignation, postponed by a protesting, despairing party during most of the 1887 session, came finally in June, and this time with the advice of Blake's doctors to back him up.

The party tried to pull itself together and consider a successor. No one but Blake, and possibly David Mills, seems to have thought of Laurier, and Blake seems to have thought of no one else but Laurier. Cartwright was hopeful for himself, though he would not have relished it with Blake still in the House. Cartwright believed there was no one else but himself to lead the party.[79] But he would not have been accepted easily by the now important French wing, and he was completely at odds with the manufacturers. Mills was not popular; Mowat, Blake's original choice, was no longer available, it seemed. Who was there? Laurier. And he was the most surprised person in the party. Laurier passionately reasserted his unfitness for the leadership: on personal grounds, his indifferent health, his lack of money; on public grounds, that the party should not have a French-Canadian leader, now of all times. Blake insisted that Laurier was the man.[80]

Blake chose Laurier with the same absence of bigotry that had characterized his attitude upon the Riel question. Blake may have been ready on occasion to play politics, but the judiciousness of his mind, and the integrity of his purpose remain; it is difficult not to admire the bent of his mind that made him love Laurier. Laurier for his part could be very winning and accommodating when he wanted to be, but his admiration for Blake was genuine. In the short term it was an improbable, even difficult choice for the party; some Ontario Liberals consoled themselves that Blake's illness and incapacity was temporary, and that someone had to lead for the time being. The Toronto *Globe* asserted that there was no prospect whatever of Blake's return;[81] nevertheless there was a definite air of uncertainty in the party and outside of it about the permanence of Laurier's leadership, which Laurier was never at pains specifically to deny. He too felt tentative, as if the shadow of the great Blake still lay across his path.

Laurier had the mind of a scholar, the fastidiousness of a gentleman, and the inertia of a dilettante. Not for Laurier those blinding weeks of brutish work that Blake would put in, and get others to put in, to lay the solid foundations for a five- or six-hour speech in Parliament. Laurier did not take hold of issues that way. He knew little or nothing of finance or tariffs; he cared little about the ruck of business. If something moved him, then it was a real issue; if not, it wasn't. There is something naive in Laurier's search for a program that would appeal to the public after his assumption of the leadership, as if a program could be invented. Commercial Union touched no part of Laurier's real nature. What moved him was stupidity, arrogance, brutality; the plight of the Métis in 1885 or the plight of Liberalism in Quebec in 1877. Problems like these crackled across the polarities of his sympathy. With Laurier instinct answered for issues, a state of mind for policy. Real, hard answers to real, hard, issues he never found easy. No one would find it easy to solve the problems of the Manitoba school question. For Laurier it was less easy; his instinct, that treacherous jade, placed him on the side of the oppressed; first, the Manitoba Roman Catholics wickedly oppressed by the Manitoba government; second, the Manitoba government wickedly oppressed by Ottawa. There was always something of the anarchist in Laurier; not the anarchist of the caricature, but the scholarly anarchist who distrusts rules, dislikes authority, and ends, when in power, finding both rules and authority decidedly convenient.

Laurier was not a great House of Commons man, though he could on the right occasion give great speeches. He was lazy, and every first class House of Commons man has to do his homework before he commands attention. Moreover he disliked fighting and had no basic love for parliamentary sword-play. What made him a great political figure was the transparent honesty of his libertarian convictions, his wonderful capacity for expressing them, and his inimitable talent for charming people. That he espoused a cause made it seem the better; it was nearly as if the world were a better place because he was in it.

It was commonly thought at the time that Laurier had no iron in him, that his dislike of fighting betrayed a weak man, an absence of will and determination. That was the opinion of Cartwright. But it depended upon what Laurier wished to be determined about. Aroused he could be very effective. Willison recalled a meeting at Cannington in the summer of 1887, when an Anglican clergyman, with that discourtesy often common to low church and evangelical divines, rose during one of Laurier's speeches and shouted that no one could learn the true way in politics or in religion from a Roman Catholic. This hit Laurier in the right (or the wrong) place. In a few sharp sentences he proceeded to flog the interrupter into humiliation and silence.[82] There was no iron in Laurier; it was steel.

When Laurier became leader in June, 1887 his Quebec colleague, Honoré Mercier, had already proposed an interprovincial conference at Quebec. It was cleverly devised, a sort of league of provinces against the Ottawa view of Confederation. Yet there was a curious absence of any real stir about the Interprovincial Conference of 1887. Laurier and other Liberal leaders on the federal scene seem to have left it alone. Blake and Cartwright had denounced better terms too often for them to support it without embarrassment. Mowat was forced to be interested but, in his usual fashion, approached the project crabwise. There was a rumour in August that he would not even attend, and send someone to represent him. Ontario suspected any grand proposal to raid the federal treasury. British Columbia was ready to do whatever Macdonald wanted done.[83] Macdonald, of course, had no intention of having anything to do with it. "No good purpose," he said in his reply to Mercier.[84] And so A. E. B. Davie, the Premier of British Columbia, duly wrote to Mercier that there were no matters of difference between British Columbia and Ottawa that could not be solved by ordinary negotiations in the ordinary way.[85] That was a long way from the position a decade before! Prince Edward Island, after consideration by W. W. Sullivan and his Conservative government, deemed it "inadvisable" to go.[86] That was probably accurate enough.

So it was Quebec, Ontario, Nova Scotia, New Brunswick, and a dissatisfield Manitoba that came to the second Quebec Conference, which opened October 20, 1887. It sat for eight days. The group comprised twenty members from the provincial cabinets. Mowat was made chairman. They passed twenty-three resolutions unanimously, and one with New Brunswick dissenting. Resolution No. 1 proposed the abolition of disallowance; No. 4 asked that Senators be chosen by the provinces. There were protests against the Franchise Act of 1885 (No. 7), against the delay in settling the boundary question (No. 16), and in particular, in No. 17, there was an attempt to suggest a re-ordering of the financial arrangements of Confederation. The constitutional reforms were urged by Mowat; the better terms were the special interest of Mercier, Blair, Fielding, and Norquay. They all supported each other.[87]

When it came to ratification by the provincial legislatures it was not quite so simple. The legislative assemblies of all five provinces approved the resolutions by good majorities, though in New Brunswick it was felt that the 1887 Quebec Resolutions were simply being consigned "to the Archives of exploded transactions. . . ."[88] In the Legislative Councils of New Brunswick and Nova Scotia the resolutions were heavily defeated, and they were not presented to the Quebec Legislative Council at all. The attempt by the Conservatives to brand the Conference as a Grit-Rouge conspiracy was easy and successful; the federal Liberal leaders did not take up the proposals in Parliament, and the whole Conference slipped into the limbo of obscurity. For some time, as J. A. Maxwell points out, it was "completely forgotten."[89]

The one resolution that was not agreed to unanimously supported Manitoba in her determination to charter the Red River Valley Railroad in spite of Ottawa. This was the culmination in the story of her struggle over the disallowance of whatever of their railway legislation conflicted with the C.P.R. charter.

The issue really turned upon the control over east-west traffic. The C.P.R. were fearful of traffic being tapped off southward by a series of conduits leaving the pipe from Winnipeg to Fort William and, still more, from Winnipeg to Montreal, with too little to sustain the enormous expense of the line east of Winnipeg. Two lines already ran southward to the border on either side of the Red River. But both of these were in C.P.R. hands and both connected with the St. Paul, Minneapolis, and Manitoba Railway. C.P.R. interests still controlled that traffic. But they could not control an independent line in rival hands, especially in those of their arch rival, the Northern Pacific.

Manitobans were aroused long before that. The key to the problem was freights rates and the fear, endemic in western communities where railways were so vital to farm profits, of monopoly. The C.P.R. rates were not low, and it was easy to charge monopoly and set the stage for allegations that rates were too high. Nor was the issue unique to Canada; the western United States fought railway rates with every legislative expedient they could devise.

Macdonald and Thomas White had both stated in the House in the C.P.R. debate that the twenty-year monopoly clause was only in respect of Dominion legislation, that it in no way affected the right of a province to charter provincial lines that might conflict with C.P.R. interest. But C.P.R. pressure forced Macdonald to disallow railways that Manitoba chartered. He justified his action by a curious bit of administrative footwork:

> I said we could not interfere with the Manitoba Legislature. I said they can legislate in any way they please, and we can only pledge ourselves as to what the Dominion Parliament would do. . . . But what does not interfere with, it has no connection with, the executive power given to the central authority to exercise the power of disallowance as regards any Act passed by any Legislature which is detrimental or injurious to the interests of the whole Dominion.[90]

Much of the disallowance agitation in Manitoba was just agitation. Fuel was being stoked regularly into the newspaper boilers by politicians and anyone interested in railway manipulation. Herbert Holt, then one of the contractors for the Hudson's Bay Railway, remarked to a Winnipeg reporter in October 1887, "You people up here talk entirely too much to get a railway. It's a surprise to me if you ever succeed, in view of the way you must talk, talk, talk. . . ."[91] Altogether, the agitation helped drive the C.P.R. stock down to fifty in 1887, from seventy-six the year before. Stephen remarked ruefully that the shrinkage was "more than Winnipeg is worth with all the people thrown in. . . ."[92]

No Manitoba government could ignore the agitation. It was too convenient a weapon. If the Conservative government did not seize hold of the agitation, the Liberal opposition would. So Norquay's government had a tiger by the tail. A. A. C. LaRivière, Norquay's Minister of Agriculture, told Stephen in June 1887, that it was all just agitation. But what else could the Government do but go along with it? Capital development was wanted, and a new railway would effect that and kill the monopoly cry at one and the same time.[93] The Manitoba government had "either to yield or go out & they could not afford to go out."[94] So the legislature chartered the Red River Valley Railway in the early summer of 1887, to be built as a government work. One million dollars was voted to support it, to be realized through the sale of provincial bonds.[95] The Act went to Ottawa, nearly certain to be disallowed.

More effective in blocking the Red River Valley Railway was C.P.R. influence in London, persuading the province's financial agents, Morton Rose and Company, that they should not sponsor the bond issue. The first sod of the railway was turned on July 2, 1887. Two weeks later the Red River Valley Railway Act was disallowed. Manitoba went on looking for money anyway, in New York, and in Winnipeg itself. Then winter came and everything stopped, including John Norquay's Conservative government. It was forced out in December over another railway transaction, the Hudson's Bay Railway.

The Hudson's Bay Railway was by no means as chimerical as it sounds, and its story is a long and curious one.[96] Norquay had not been very careful; he had handed over provincial bonds, held as security, to Herbert Holt, contractor for the railway, though the authority for the transfer had been highly dubious (the Cabinet being against it for a start). It was but an example of Norquay's desperate financial expedients. He attempted to use trust funds as ordinary revenue, though this was blocked by the Lieutenant-Governor. Finally his colleagues resigned, and his resignation followed, just before Christmas.[97] The new Conservative government failed in their bye-elections, and when the Assembly met, in January 1888, Lieutenant-Governor Aikens was compelled to call in the Liberal leader, Thomas Greenway.

It was thus Greenway, not Norquay, who got the credit for bringing an end to disallowance, though the man really responsible was George Stephen. Stephen was now convinced that Dominion control over Manitoba railway charters in the C.P.R.'s interest, would have to go. Macdonald was reluctant; there was much haggling over terms; but the legislation went to Parliament in April 1888, giving the C.P.R. the guarantee of three and a half per cent interest on $15 million worth of land grant bonds. Manitoba at last got the unhindered privilege of chartering any provincial railway she pleased.

So the Red River Valley Railway was to go forward, if money could be found. Manitoba was not able to market a bond issue. Instead an arrangement was made with the Northern Pacific to build the third line for a $6000 a mile provincial subsidy. It would then be leased to a company called the Northern Pacific and Manitoba. This arrangement produced a furore nearly equal to the debates on the C.P.R. monopoly. There were allegations of a corrupt bargain between the Northern Pacific and the Greenway government. The colour of suspicion deepened when it was learned that Joseph Martin had become a director of the Northern Pacific and Manitoba Company. But the contract was ratified by the Manitoba legislature, and the line was begun.

Western feeders to it soon became essential.[98] It was over one of these that a dramatic quarrel with the Canadian Pacific Railway blew up, in October 1888. South of Headingley, a town about one-third of the way from Winnipeg to Portage la Prairie, the Northern Pacific and Manitoba had to cross the tracks of a C.P.R branch line running southwest toward Souris. No arrangements had been made and the C.P.R., now under Van Horne, was not prepared to be very accommodating. The Railway Commissioner of Manitoba, its Attorney-General, and a director of Northern Pacific and Manitoba, was that hotblooded fire-eater, Joseph Martin. Then Martin, as Attorney-General of Manitoba, decided that Martin, as the Commissioner of Railways, had the right to ignore the injunction, and proposed to Martin, the director of the N.P. & M., to go ahead and make the crossing anyway. The C.P.R. resisted. It had already taken out the diamond crossing laid in by the other railway and hung it up in the C.P.R. yard with a flag over it. An engine was ditched at the point of crossing and special C.P.R. crews were detailed to keep guard. Martin swore in special constables. The C.P.R. had justices of the peace available and they swore in special constables. Martin called out the soldiers, who camped serenely near the field of battle, *Fort Whyte* as the ditched locomotive was now called, after the C.P.R.'s western Superintendent. Then the whole thing slowly fizzled out.

The whole incident showed the absurdity of ignoring the law. The Dominion Parliament had prescribed certain formalities for all railways, Dominion or provincial, when they were crossing Dominion railway lines. The C.P.R. insisted on these formalities being observed, as they were entitled to, however impolitic it may have been. The question was really one for the railway committee of the Dominion cabinet. This was the sober second sense of most Manitobans.[99] But the incident did no particular good to the C.P.R., and it showed how unscrupulous Martin could be when crossed. It was war, and like most wars, no one won. The N.P. & M. got its crossing and eventually arrived at Portage la Prairie which was, incidentally, Martin's constituency. But the rates between the C.P.R. and the N.P. & M. soon showed very little difference.[100] Manitoba broke the C.P.R. monopoly and got another new railway. Otherwise, *plus ça change, plus c'est la même chose.* Macdonald told Stephen that he was "laying pipe" to blow up Greenway and Martin, [101] and, going into 1889, the Manitoba Liberal government was shaky and shaken, looking for another issue to help them stay in power. They were to find it in their school system.

There had been a series of bad years in the West between 1883-86, either frost or rain or drought, unevenly spread and unevenly felt, but felt none the less; but the harvest of 1887 was superb – so bountiful that at one bound it compelled the formation of the Winnipeg Grain Exchange. Prairie farming was becoming more knowledgeable; techniques of dry farming were now being developed – especially summer fallowing – and the land was a little less vulnerable than before. Much of it was good land. Nicholas Davin described a farm west of Riding Mountain, sixty-five acres under crop, with cattle, horses, pigs, hens; and bread, butter, eggs, bacon, all manufactured, so to speak, from the land itself, the sunny pastures, and the rich earth. A summer evening there was a scene,

> grateful to the soul and sense – the hen with her chickens, the calves graceful as fallow deer lying in the grass . . . a blue sky flecked with clouds of grey and shining fleece, not a house nearer than four miles in this beautiful fruitful land . . . a vigorous pioneer couple near, and the little fair-haired girl of a year and a half that toddles down towards the stables, and looks back and smiles. . . .[102]

CHAPTER 11

A Question of Identity 1888-1891

Between 1887 and 1891 a fundamental disparity developed between Canada's growing self-awareness and her political condition. The federal solution was not unworkable, but the federal idea was still difficult for Canadians to make into a meaningful measure of their nationality. The increasing awareness of French Canada in Ontario, for example, made Ontarians wonder if a country so conceived could endure. Could the country exist with one-quarter of it French, with a non-conductor, as Goldwin Smith called it, between the Martime provinces and the rest of English Canada? Cartwright insisted that only with the promise of a more spacious framework for Canadian nationality would Canadians be satisfied that the sacrifices of Confederation were worth the cost.[1] He meant that Canada needed a more systematic political form, something resembling independence. But was independence a conceivable goal, with Canada still a congeries of regional identities? That was the question.

In this context, Imperial Federation was a not unreasonable conception. Many Imperial Federationists accepted the idea of a Canadian nationality; but it was convenient for some, and necessary for others, to subsume it within the broader idea of the British Empire. There, of course, it was easily possible to lose the conception of Canada, especially when questions were accentuated by the racism characteristic of the Anglo-Saxon, German, Slavic and, to a degree, the French worlds of the later nineteenth century. There was talk of the Anglo-Saxon mission, of a British Empire grander than just the sum of its parts, of service to lesser breeds without the law. Imperialism was a kind of glory that could not be obtained at home. So Imperial Federation drew to it an interesting cross-section of high-minded English Canadians of Conservative bent who could not yet find the Canadian identity sufficiently satisfying. It was as if they were looking for some sovereignty, broad, noble and coherent enough to be loyal to.

The idea was one thing; its practical implementation was another. Imperial Federation was dogged from the beginning with a basic split between the idea and its application. Perhaps its surprisingly long life owed much to the Anglo-Saxon capacity for divorcing heady ideas and practical action. The program had three main planks, all of them difficult to implement: first, the possibility of colonial representation in the Imperial Parliament; second, the construction of an imperial tariff, affecting particularly the British commitment to free trade; and finally, contribution by the colonies to some scheme of imperial defence. The last, was of greatest interest to Imperial Federationists in Great Britain, and the one of which the Canadians were the most wary.

The Imperial Federation League was founded in 1884, and its first great triumph was the calling of the Colonial Conference of 1887 on the occasion of Queen Victoria's golden jubilee. There, much to Britain's surprise, the topic of most resounding interest to the colonies was not imperial defence but an imperial tariff structure, and it was this that was to undermine and ultimately to break up the League in 1893. The ideas that the League engendered, however, appealed to many on the Conservative side of Canadian politics, not the least among them being D'Alton McCarthy, M.P. Simcoe, who proposed a resolution on the subject of an imperial preference in April, 1888. "Change," said McCarthy at the formation of the Toronto branch of the League, in 1887, "was in the very air."[2] But the changes Imperial Federation envisaged were regarded with scepticism by others, including Sir John Macdonald.

The nearest Macdonald came to that subject had been the appointment of the first High Commissioner to Great Britain, in 1880. The idea, the choice of the name, had been mainly Canada's, the outgrowth of Macdonald's conception of Canada as an auxiliary kingdom of the British Empire. Sir A. T. Galt, the first High Commissioner, was a political, quasi-diplomatic representative with all the advantages of close contact with both the Colonial Office and the Foreign Office. Under Galt, and more especially under Sir Charles Tupper (never one to take an insignificant view of his position), the office became important and useful. The High Commissioners were, by 1890, virtually members of the *corps diplomatique*,[3] despite Sir John Thompson's robust assertion that the Canadian High Commissioner was "nothing but the agent of this Government living in London."[4] But representation in the Imperial parliament, contributions to Imperial defence, and a common Imperial tariff, both Macdonald and Blake in practice opposed. Macdonald was willing to make polite speeches – "the last man and the last shilling in defence of the Empire," he said in 1886 – but his private opinion was nearly as firm as Blake's, and Blake's was that "we should not be called upon to expend our blood and treasure in carrying out Jingo schemes whether of Tory or Liberal politicians on the other side of the water."[5].

More realistic, closer to home, fraught more with changes for the future, and carrying real electoral power, was the obverse of Imperial Federation,

Commercial Union with the United States. This movement had support in the United States, and in Canada drew into its orbit a wide range of opinion, from outright annexationists, like J. V. Ellis, M.P. for Saint John City, to secessionists like J. A. Kirk, member for Guysborough, through to more powerful figures who were genuinely interested in a free trade association with Canadian identity left intact, like Sir Richard Cartwright. There were also those who wanted unrestricted reciprocity, and those who preferred reciprocity restricted to natural products. As to the last category, both Conservatives and Liberals were ready to accept, at any time, free trade in natural products with the United States.

The whole question of Canada's commercial relations with the United States was brought to the forefront by the American tariff struggle of the 1880's, and in a more immediate sense by the North American Atlantic fisheries question. Much has been written on the fisheries from the diplomatic side.[6] One would like to know more of it from the practical side, about the technological and economic changes that governed the fishing industry both in the Maritime provinces and the New England states. The fishermen themselves were little different in Yarmouth, Nova Scotia, or in Gloucester, Massachusetts, and both had the same canny ways with governments and rules. "Fishermen," said Sir Charles Tupper with some feeling, "perhaps, are the most intractable and uncontrollable people in the world, and when a fisherman gets on board his little smack he thinks he is monarch of all he surveys, and he can go where he pleases and do what he pleases."[7]

Once upon a time the North Atlantic inshore fisheries were all one: Labrador, Newfoundland, Prince Edward Island, Nova Scotia, New Brunswick, Maine, Massachusetts, were all British. Then with the Treaty of Paris in 1783, the new United States obtained the right to use the British North American inshore fisheries without any substantial restriction save that of giving the local British inhabitants priority on the shore for drying and curing of fish. The War of 1812 abrogated most of these concessions – however reluctant the Americans were to accept the fact – and the Convention of 1818 replaced the 1783 Treaty. This Convention very much restricted American fishing privileges. First, it closed off the inshore fisheries from American use "forever"; second, it gave the Americans special shore areas on the coasts of Labrador, the Magdalen Islands, and part of the south, west and northeast coast of Newfoundland. On this "American shore" Americans could use the inshore fisheries and the coast itself, where uninhabited, to dry fish. Finally, in return for the concession of the American shore, American fishermen were severely restricted in using the commercial facilities of British North American ports and harbours. This last condition is of some importance, for it was the one most misunderstood and most resented by the Americans. Emergency use of British North American ports was allowed for purposes of getting wood, water, repairs, and shelter, but for no other use. There were to be no purchases of bait, or supplies, and no rights of transhipment. Thus American fishermen in British North American ports were in quite a different position from Canadian fishermen in American ports, because the United States had signed away the privilege of commercial use of Canadian ports, in return for that "American shore."[8]

As part of the Reciprocity Treaty, 1854-1866, the Americans got full use of the inshore fisheries and the free use of British North American ports. These arrangements were renewed under the Treaty of Washington. The offset for American use was not reciprocity, which the Canadians would have preferred, but the Canadian use of American fisheries, free entry of Canadian fish, and a money compensation for the difference in value. The compensation was set by an international commission sitting at Halifax in 1877 at $5,500,000, a figure that staggered the Americans, and was rather a surprise to the Canadians. It was to cover the twelve years in which the fisheries clauses were in force. As early as 1883 the Americans indicated they would not renew the clauses, and the whole arrangement ended on July 1, 1885.

By this time American fishermen had been using the Canadian fisheries and port facilities for nearly twenty-five years, and had become accustomed to accept them as part of their way of life. But by 1885 the inshore fishery was of less importance to American fishermen than being able to buy bait in Canadian ports; they wanted also to be able to buy supplies, and to ship some of their catch by rail. One American schooner captain summed it up in October 1886:

> If we had "free fish" it would give the Canadians some recompense for what our fishermen want, viz., the right to go anywhere and everywhere, use their harbors, ship men, get provisions, land and mend our nets, buy salt and barrels, and ship our catch home by rail or steamer without expense or annoyance, the same as we have heretofore.
>
> If we had had this privilege last year, myself and vessel would have been $5000 better off this season. . . . I do not say that I am too honest not to fish within the three-mile limit, nor do I believe there is a vessel in the fleet who would not, if the cutter was out of sight.[9]

All of this the Canadian government, and the customs collectors at every port in the Maritime provinces, were bound legally to prevent, unless the value of the Convention of 1818 was to go by the board. The Americans found the loss of their commercial privileges in Maritime ports extremely inconvenient, if not crippling, and the American shore was no compensation, indeed now of little interest. In short, the arrangements of 1818, which applied after July 1, 1885, were anachronistic. This was admitted privately on both sides, but difficult for either to give up. The American government was not unwilling to negotiate, but Cleveland's position with a

Congress, particularly a Senate, that was opposed to him, made the ratification of any treaty with Great Britain-Canada a touchy, indeed, doubtful, business.

The Canadians were ready to negotiate the question in 1883, but there was no similar disposition in Washington until the Treaty was about to expire, when it was too late to do anything about the summer season of 1885. Canada agreed to let American fishermen take fish in return for the promise that a Joint Commission would be recommended by the American President to Congress. That recommendation was thrown out by the American Senate. So, in 1886, Canada passed an Act authorizing measures to enforce the exclusion of American vessels from the commercial use of Canadian ports. The Act was reserved by the Governor General and approved by Great Britain only when the 1886 season was over. In the meantime the Canadians fell back upon the 1868 Act with its measures to protect the inshore fisheries. During the 1886 season some seven hundred vessels were boarded and some seized; in 1887, under the new Act, some 1,362 vessels were boarded.[10]

The seizures aroused much resentment in the United States where the details of the 1818 Convention were badly understood, interpreted differently, or ignored. In a spirit of general punitiveness, Congress passed a non-intercourse resolution in the spring of 1887, empowering the President to cut off all commercial relations with Canada, if satisfactory redress for the seizures was not made. Word of this was sent informally to the Canadian government by Erastus Wiman, pointing out the serious implications (though they were more serious for American interests than Canadian). Sir Charles Tupper went down to Washington in hot haste in April, for private talks with T. F. Bayard, Cleveland's Secretary of State, which ranged over a wide area of Canadian-American relations, including the fisheries. Broadly the Canadian position was to exchange the inshore fisheries for a reciprocity treaty; the American position was to avoid anything that touched tariff issues at all.

The Americans found Canada's diplomatic position curious and awkward. Canada's status technically was that of a British dependency, and the United States could not have anything but consular relations and then only through accreditation in London. Negotiations at the diplomatic level had to be managed through the British Minister in Washington and the Foreign Office. For instance, an urgent despatch from Bayard in 1886 reached Macdonald through the British Minister in Washington, the Foreign Office in London, the Colonial Office in London, the Governor General in Ottawa. As Bayard wrote privately to Tupper,

> In the very short interview afforded by your visit I referred to the embarrassment arising out of the gradual practical emancipation of Canada from the control of the mother country. . . . The awkwardness of this imperfectly

> developed sovereignty is felt most strongly by the United States. . . .
> It is evident that the commercial intercourse between the inhabitants of Canada and those of the United States has grown into too vast proportions to be exposed much longer to this wordy triangular duel, and more direct and responsible methods should be resorted to.[11]

The outcome was the Joint High Commission which met in Washington in November, 1887, the British-Canadian side being Sir Lionel Sackville-West, the British Minister in Washington, Joseph Chamberlain, and Sir Charles Tupper. The solution that emerged was that the United States would give up the use of the Canadian inshore fisheries, but Americans would have full commercial use of Canadian ports in return for free entry of Canadian fresh fish into the United States.

The Treaty embodying these conclusions could not be ratified before the 1888 fishing season began, and arrangements were made for a *modus vivendi* pending ratification which could be implemented by executive action. The Americans were given the commercial privileges of Canadian ports in return for payment of a licence fee levied by the Canadian government. Canada ratified the Treaty in April 1888, but the American Senate rejected it in August. So the *modus vivendi*, by mutual agreement, lasted until the whole question went to arbitration at The Hague in 1910.

Canadians had, of course, hoped for much more than this from the fisheries issue in 1885-87. Liberals in particular wanted a wide commercial agreement, suggested in the idea of commercial union. The origin of this idea is variously attributed. The meeting of younger members of the Liberal party in Toronto, in September 1885, raised the issue; there was a full article on the question by J. W. Longley of Nova Scotia in *The Week*, and in the paper he influenced, the *Acadian Recorder*, that autumn. J. S. Willison said that commercial union was probably born in the office of the Toronto *Mail*;[12] probably not, but it was to take it up, and thereby mark its final break with Conservatism and Macdonald.

Commercial union implied an arrangement not unlike the present European common market. Canada and the United States should have one tariff structure in common against the outside world, with all customs lines between themselves obliterated. The revenue thus derived would be shared on some proportionate basis, probably per capita.[13] There were at least two difficulties with commercial union; one was that the Canadian government, by surrendering its tariff on goods imported from the United States, would not have enough revenue to meet existing commitments. Blake anticipated this in his Malvern speech. The answer was not very satisfactory: the imposition of a direct tax, either an inheritance tax, as the *Globe* suggested,[14] or an income tax, which was a British solution.

But much the more serious difficulty was the shadow of political union that lay behind commercial union. It was possible to deny that if the main source of Canadian revenue, the tariff, were determined in Washington, political policies would follow; nevertheless, some American newspapers on this subject were devastating:

> No scheme which would give Canada an equal voice in the determination of federal taxation could be considered. She would have to accept the position of a State in the Union, with only such power in the determination of the tax rate as her comparative population would entitle her to. How this could be effected without representation in Congress is a matter hard to determine. [Philadelphia *Record*]
>
> Unless, therefore, the Dominion is prepared to make a complete and unconditional surrender of all control over its own tariff and accept whatever tariff our Congress may choose to enact from time to time, the scheme of commercial union . . . is entirely out of the question. . . . [Chicago *Times*][15]

Nor was commercial union helped in Canada by the knowledge that some of its enthusiastic supporters were known to be sympathetic to political union with the United States, and were usually called, with all the pejorative overtones of the expression, annexationists. J. W. Longley, leader of the movement in the Maritime provinces, did not hesitate to apply the word to himself at a banquet in Boston on December 28, 1887. He was bold and indiscreet, and his articles in *The Week* in the autumn of 1885 were written under the full conviction that the Canadian experiment was a failure, and that commercial union, followed by political union, should now be substituted for the National Policy.[16] The Halifax *Acadian Recorder*, a paper he was connected with, took up the idea in December 1885. Goldwin Smith followed with an outspoken article in *The Week* in January 1886, urging the hundred-year schism in the English-speaking population of North America be ended.[17]. The *Globe* took up the idea from the *Mail*, mainly because it was afraid of the effect of the advocacy of the *Mail* upon the Liberal constituency in Ontario, since it was by then clear that the *Mail* was an independent paper in search of party.[18]

Within four weeks of Laurier's acceptance of the Liberal leadership he was circulating a confidential letter asking for opinions on trade relations with the United States. His Quebec wing was much less enthusiastic than the Ontario wing. "Mais devons-nous nous livrer ainsi entre les mains des Etats et abdiquer nos pouvoirs? . . .frère Jonathan veut tout ou rien."[19] The Montreal *Star*, independent and now boasting the biggest circulation of any Quebec paper (28,000), considered that "protection is absolutely necessary to the development of the country."[20] There was some uneasiness even in Ontario; a fear – Cartwright described it as "mortal terror" – lest the cry of disloyalty be raised against those advocating commercial union.[21] James Young of Galt, perhaps the furthest to the right of the prominent Liberals, put his objections in a letter to the *Globe* on September 17, 1887. They were the loss of seven million dollars in annual revenue, the control of the Canadian tariff in American hands; altogether, for Canadian circumstances, commercial union represented "AN IMPRACTICABLE NATIONAL POSITION."[22] Alexander Mackenzie was quite opposed, believing that too large a number of the commercial unionists were annexationists. Annexation, with the adoption of the full American tariff, would only make protection far worse. "My feelings revolt at the proposal," he wrote to Cartwright, "As a party move, I daresay something could be made of it by careful handling, but on the other hand I dread to see the mess some of our fellows will make of it."[23]

Cartwright did not think such objections mattered. It was precisely as a party move that he was most interested in it. The Liberal party had to have a policy. And a policy like commercial union had one great advantage: it would help to draw the party away from the demoralization of the Ontario wing caused by the split over the Riel issue. "You and I know well," Cartwright wrote to Laurier, "that we cannot go through another session in the fashion we did the last, with half our men seeking by any & every miserable pretext to shirk a vote on the simplest & plainest questions."[24] As for Laurier, he was French enough to dislike compromising on the question of commercial union. He wanted, as he put it to Edgar, "at once casser les vitres," to plump for the whole policy and risk the consequences.[45] Nevertheless the outcome was a shift, perceptible as the 1888 session began. A motion was put on the order paper for commercial union, but it was subsequently withdrawn and Cartwright's motion for "full and unrestricted reciprocity" was substituted. It came up for debate on March 14, 1888.

Unrestricted reciprocity was the Siamese twin of commercial union: they were distinguishable but difficult to separate.[26] Unrestricted reciprocity, unlike the reciprocity of 1854-1866, meant that everything Canada produced would be admitted free into the United States, and *vice versa*. The advantage of unrestricted reciprocity to the Liberals was obvious. Canada would retain her present tariff structure except *vis-à-vis* the United States. It had not the horrendous implications of commercial union, and could be adopted without having to apportion joint revenues. It was a very good theory, but there were several things wrong with it in practice. What was to prevent smuggling? Canada admitted British woollens at from 25 per cent to 30 per cent; the American tariff on British woollens was nearer 50 per cent. What was to prevent a Montreal wholesaler from importing them and sending them to New York? The answer – it is by no means easy to find the contemporary answer – was that goods crossing the border would have to carry certificates of origin. Goods of Canadian origin would cross into the United States free, others would not. But it was both clumsy and ineffective as a solution.

A much more serious weakness of unrestricted reciprocity was that the Americans would have none of it. Their interest, such as it was, was wholly confined to commercial union. They had no intention of opening a hole in their tariff wall with such a nebulous scheme, and were willing to include

Canada within their wall only in commercial union. Doubtless most Liberals who adopted and supported unrestricted reciprocity knew this perfectly well. Equally, it was not difficult for Conservatives to run a coach and four through the proposal. Moreover, the very recent adoption of the program made it look precisely what it was: Liberals reaching for a policy. George Foster took this up:

> . . . I think the House and the country may be a little excused for doubting at the present time whether it is really a serious issue or not. Hon. gentlemen opposite have had within the last ten years or so so many issues, that they have become a sort of Chinese puzzle to the community at large, and when they spring a bran [*sic*] new issue within a few months upon Parliament and upon the people, Parliament and the people are quite excusable if they hold their breath for a little and watch in patience as to whether these gentlemen are in earnest. . . .[27]

Thus in the debate of 1888, the Government met the commercial union-unrestricted reciprocity issue (its advocates did not always distinguish) head on. The Government could with confidence show that manufacturers were opposed. Even Hart Massey was now unwilling to give up the high tariff.[28] It was much too comfortable.[29] And it was doubtless true, as Laurier said, that some of Canada's infant industries were little monsters, *lusus naturae*, their appetite insatiable, never strong, and having to be kept on the feeding bottle all the time. ". . . if you put them on their legs they moan piteously and are too weak to stand."[30]

The vote was decisive. The Government could well afford to be cheerful with 124-67, with some twenty Liberals abstaining or absent. The debate, a long one in which members on both sides took much interest, was not a conspicuous success for the Liberals. But Laurier had never expected otherwise. It was a policy Laurier was after. Whatever can be said about unrestricted reciprocity as a practical possibility, it had much to be said for it as a popular move. Willison told Laurier in July 1888, "Our young men are largely *Canada First*, not quite commercial unionists, but loyal to Unrestricted Reciprocity, kindly disposed toward the States, and partial to clean, honest politics, and while perhaps not quite against the British connection still in favour of our exercising full national rights."[31] There is a ring of solid substance about that assessment. Unrestricted reciprocity was thus a good shibboleth, good to talk about, popular with a number of voters. It was also quite worthless.

Nor was Blake very helpful. He had grave doubts about commercial union when Laurier had first proposed it, and his doubts had grown while abroad. He had spent a lonely and wet winter in Tuscany, from where he assured Laurier there was no hope of his coming back to the leadership and it was folly in Laurier, however generously meant, to think otherwise.[32] Blake returned to Canada in the summer of 1888, to Murray Bay, where Laurier had long talks with him. But Blake was against commercial union, against unrestricted reciprocity, and all he asked for was to be allowed to keep out of things, and not have to speak publicly against what was now accepted party policy.

It was impossible for the Liberal party to drop unrestricted reciprocity now. They had to keep it going. But they found it convenient to add another string to their bow. Cartwright on February 18, 1889, moved that Canada should acquire the right of negotiating commercial treaties for herself. It was one of the best speeches Cartwright ever made in Parliament. More than any other single speech of the later 1880's it expressed the feeling of many Canadians that something more had to be added to their sense of themselves; or, to put it more correctly perhaps, to give that sense a more spacious and clear-cut form. Cartwright's sharp tongue was for once turned upon something other than his eternal verities. The present status of Canada was "but a low one."

> . . . there are questions of great gravity now engaging the attention of the public, and more particularly of the younger portion of the community. Men are beginning to ask themselves on all hands whether this Confederation is to be a political *cul de sac*, or whether it is to be, what the hon. gentleman [Macdonald] says it never should be, a stepping-stone to a higher form of political existence. Sir, they are asking this, further: if we are to remain forever in a state of dependency, whether Confederation was worth all or half the sacrifices we made to obtain it?[33]

It was Cartwright's version of the ideas of Aurora, fifteen years later. And it was voted down by the Government in the evening. A month later Cartwright proposed his unrestricted reciprocity resolution again, and though the Liberals mustered a better vote, the debate was flatulent and stale. Laurier did not even speak. Unrestricted reciprocity had run into shallows; and what more the Liberal party could do with it was at least doubtful.

Then four days later, on March 23, 1889, W. E. O'Brien, M.P. Muskoka, moved his resolution asking for disallowance of the Jesuits Estates Act ot Quebec. A new chapter in the history of error and stupidity was launched.

It is not easy now to recover the intensity of the Protestant convictions of Ontario. It was obscurantism, hatred, fear, all a legacy of Protestant history, Protestant prejudices. The most potent of these was fear. The Roman Catholic religion was a conspiratorial engine, designed to dominate, and ultimately to destroy Protestantism. The refusal to tolerate Protestantism in some Catholic countries, the insistence upon control of the children in mixed marriages, the enthusiasm of the Roman Catholic Church for large families: all of this could be taken and was taken, then and later, by Protestants as hard evidence that they could never rest in safety. If they flagged, they would soon be overwhelmed. In the back counties of Ontario this attitude passed effortlessly from one generation to another. In some areas Roman Catholics were so few it was possible to wonder what a Roman Catholic looked like. In others, little boys on the streets would say in hushed tones, "There goes a Roman Catholic!" and all would turn and stare at the phenomenon who, upon inspection, *did* look different. Many of the thirteen M.P.'s who voted in 1889 for disallowance of the Jesuits' Estates Act came from backgrounds like this; McCarthy from Barrie, Tyrwhitt from Bradford, both in Simcoe County, Barron from Lindsay, Wallace from Woodbridge, McNeill from Wiarton, O'Brien from Shanty Bay in Muskoka, Peter Macdonald from Wingham, Bell from north of Napanee. These communities had Protestantism bred into their very bones, many of them strong Orange allegiances.

The Jesuit Order, like many orders of the Church, had acquired considerable lands by the time of the cession of Canada in 1763. These lands they kept; but in 1773 the Jesuit Order was dissolved by the Pope. They held their property until the last Jesuit died in 1800. By French civil law, the lands might then have reverted to the various dioceses in which they were situated. In fact, upon reasonable legal ground, they escheated to the Crown. In 1831 they were turned over to the Government of Lower Canada, to be used to endow public education in the province. They were duly acquired by the province of Canada, and in 1867 they became the property of the province of Quebec. In the meantime the Jesuit Order had been reconstituted in Rome, and soon Jesuits reappeared in Canada. There were various claims against the Jesuits' Estates, as they had come to be called. The Roman Catholic Church, through the bishops, advanced some. So did the Jesuits themselves, and these were sufficient to throw effective legal impediments upon any sales of the land. So they languished, some of them valuable property. It had been one of Chapleau's ambitions to solve this ecclesiastical tangle, but it was not resolved when he left the premiership of Quebec in 1882. J. J. Ross picked up the negotiations again in 1885; then in 1886 Mercier came along. Mercier had been educated at a Jesuit college, and he determined that the question should be settled, not by giving the Jesuits back their land, but by giving the Church and the Order compensation. The Jesuit Order was incorporated in 1887 and in 1888 the Jesuits' Estates Act came before the Quebec Legislature.

Some Liberals, both Quebec and federal, were not very comfortable. To compensate the Jesuits seemed rather too much. Were the Liberals now to abandon their friend Laval University, in favour of the Jesuit college at Montreal? Such was the question that Louis Jetté raised with Laurier, when Mercier pushed the Jesuits' Estates bill through the Quebec Liberal caucus.[34] The unease was exceptional. The general view was that an old and tangled issue was well out of the way. Discussion with the hierarchy on the one hand, and the Jesuits on the other, had been long and complicated. In the end Pope Leo XIII, through Cardinal Simeoni of the Propaganda, was to adjudicate. The Jesuits claimed the property was worth over two million dollars. But Mercier made it quite clear that there was no question of full compensation. Their title had gone long since. What remained was a moral obligation, in consequence of which the Quebec government agreed to pay the Church $400,000 to be apportioned by the Pope,* and to pay the Protestant Council of Public Instruction $60,000 as the English share of the Crown property. The bill went through both houses of the Quebec legislature with hardly a ripple of dissent. Two of the fifteen Protestant members raised some mild objections, but not to the point of dividing the House, so it was carried unanimously, both there and in the Legislative Council.[35] The text of the Act arrived in Ottawa in August 1888, and it was almost certain, in the ordinary course of events, to be allowed. That autumn Sir John Macdonald was visited by Mercier on financial business and a meeting of the Cabinet was called. Mercier, frock-coated and very formal, was shown into Macdonald's office; as the two men made their way down the corridor to the Council room, Mercier asked Macdonald, half-jokingly, "Sir John, I wish you would tell us whether you are going to disallow our Jesuits' Estates Act or not." Macdonald suddenly unbent, looked back at Mercier with a sparkle in his eye, and said, "Do you take me for a damn fool?"[36]

The Act itself was seven short sections occupying less than a page of print. More comprehensive was the preamble, some twenty-one pages of correspondence, going back to 1885, between Mercier and Simeoni, Mercier and Reverend Father Turgeon, Procurator of the Jesuits. It was printed to justify the measure, but with a certain over-comprehensiveness perhaps designed to be provocative. Nevertheless there the Act was, perfectly constitutional, and accepted generally in Quebec as a reasonable settlement of an issue too long outstanding.

It was disliked, however, in some quarters in Quebec. Robert Sellar's *Huntingdon Gleaner* was uneasy, and there were unfavourable comments in some of the English papers, including the Montreal *Gazette*, immediately after the Act had passed. By the autumn of 1888 the Protestants were making noises, and the newly formed Evangelical Alliance openly asked for disallowance late in October 1888.[37] Then, a few weeks later, the *Toronto Daily Mail* got hold of it.

The *Mail* was now disenchanted with its flirtation with commercial union, especially since the American election of 1888, and out the *Mail* editorials came, brilliant, savage, unrepentant, a deliberate set at the Jesuits, the Roman Catholic Church, and the province of Quebec.

* The Pope gave $160,000 to the Jesuits, $160,000 to Laval, and $10,000 each to the Catholic dioceses of the province.

> If the British and Protestant element in Quebec will not save itself, we must try to save it for our own sakes. That the abandonment of Quebec to the Ultramontane and the Jesuit will be the death of Canadian nationality is clear enough. But Ontario will not be safe. Our eastern gate has already been opened by the perfidious hand of the vote-hunting politician, and the French and Roman Catholic invasion is streaming through.[38]

To conjure rubbish like this into a fearful spectre would ordinarily be ludicrous; but after the events of 1885 and 1886 it was not only possible, but easy. And there were other ingredients that made the issue inflammatory, such as French-Canadian migration into eastern Ontario. It was harmless, doubtless useful, but it seemed to old-line Protestants as a distinct threat. More important was the attitude of the Orange Order. They had not forgotten the Hackett affair of 1877 and the failure of their revenge of 1878. In 1884, after a number of earlier attempts, they pressed hard to get incorporation of their order through the House of Commons. The real purpose of Dominion incorporation was to secure them the right to hold property in the province of Quebec. There was a debate of the kind the Commons liked to avoid, ill-tempered, hard, and passionate. It was on this occasion that Blake spoke sternly against incorporation and won himself the undying enmity of every Orangeman in Ontario:

> I do not care how good their purposes, or what their objects may be. . . . I think secret oath-bound societies . . . are contrary to the spirit of English law. . . . It is in the nature of these societies to become tyrannical and despotic.[39]

French Canadians and Roman Catholics left the debate alone. They voted against the bill, and Orange incorporation was defeated, with Sir John Macdonald in the happy position of being able to vote with the minority with impunity.*

Thus the provincial incorporation of the Jesuit Order and its subsequent endowment with public funds was a red rag to a bull. The *Mail* was followed by other newspapers, and by Protestant ministers. Soon the "drum ecclesiastic," as Macdonald put it,[40] was beating all across Ontario. The *Globe* was very uneasy; it did not want to lose Protestant support to the *Mail*, and it shifted and wobbled under the enormous public pressure for disallowance. Blake strongly objected to the tone of the *Globe*,[41] to which Jaffray, its President replied:

> I don't think you can be aware of the desperate struggle the *Globe* is having to maintain its hold upon its Protestant and liberal readers. Un-

* The order was incorporated in 1890, by a vote of 85-69 on second reading with very little fuss, and mainly in the character of a benevolent society. The Act is 53 Vic. c. 105.

A fine portrait of Sir Charles Tupper in 1893

Hudson's Bay Company post, Grand Rapids, Saskatchewan Territory, 1890

Clearing snow, Notre Dame Street, Montreal, about 1887

Arrival of the *locomotive*, Countess of Dufferin, *Winnipeg, 1877*

A Victorian beauty of 1876: Miss Legge of Montreal

Ottawa Post Office, Parliament Buildings, and Rideau Canal bridges, 1896

Sir John A. Macdonald, 1888. "The Old Chieftain"

THE RED RAG; OR, AGGRAVATING THE BULL.

"It is the intention of the Government to continue its Policy of Protecting Native Industry, and it will continue to protect the Canadian Workman rather than the Foreign Workman."—*Sir John Thompson, at Ottawa.*

From Grip, Toronto, February 24, 1894

THE BABES IN THE WOOD.

Sir Hector (*the Bad Ruffian*)—"They Must and Shall be Slain. Stand Aside, I Say!"
Sir John (*the Virtuous Ruffian*)—"Nay, Not So! I am a Hard Cruel Politician, Yet I Cannot, I Dare Not Permit That!"

From Grip, Toronto, April 18, 1891

MADAME QUEBEC'S WILD BOY.

MME. QUEBEC.—"IT'S SO KIND OF YOU TO TAKE HIM, SIR JOHN! HE'S NEARLY BROUGHT ME TO RUIN!"

SIR JOHN.—"HAVE NO FEAR, MADAME; UNDER *MY* TUITION HE SHALL LEARN PRUDENCE, ECONOMY, INDUSTRY AND THRIFT!"

From Grip, *Toronto, August 12, 1882*

> fortunately on a number of questions – although I believe it has been in the right – it has been on the unpopular side in Ontario [.] the *Mail* is threatening and making heavy inroads upon its circulation. . . .[42]

The contention of the *Mail*, and of the legion of Ontario Protestants who followed it, was that the Jesuits' Estates Act endowed with public funds a religious organization, and that it invited the arbitration of an authority unknown to the British Crown, the Pope. Therefore it ought to be disallowed, not only as unconstitutional, but as against the public interest of the people of Canada.

It was inevitable such a hot issue would get into Parliament. It was also inevitable that members on both sides of the House would shy away from it. Parliament's instinct with really divisive issues was to avoid them; it was the natural reaction of parties constituted from a broad segment of opinion. Neither Conservatives nor Liberals could afford the luxury of strong sectarian or religious passion. In a country with two million Roman Catholics and three million Protestants it was, as Mills remarked, "in the last degree mischievous to invade the political arena with religious discussions." O'Brien's motion for disallowance, made in the name of toleration and no special favours to any faith, was in effect, Mills said, "a demand for intoleration. . . .[43] Everyone who spoke against the motion in this memorable debate recognized how dangerous an issue it was. No one doubted O'Brien's sincerity, or that of his more powerful ally, D'Alton McCarthy, or of the other eleven who supported the motion. They were probably moved by genuine conviction of the rightness of their cause.

Whether genuinely right was another matter; as Laurier said, "it is always in the sacred name of religion that the most savage passions of mankind have been excited, and some of the most shocking crimes committed."[44] The vote came after three days of debate. O'Brien's motion was voted down, overwhelmingly, 188-13. Of the thirteen, eight were Conservatives, five Liberals. Even Alexander Mackenzie came down to the House and recorded his vote against disallowance at 1:45 A.M. March 29, 1889.[45]

Macdonald tried hard to placate McCarthy. He was not, by any means, read out of the Conservative party. The party would try to cope with the embarassment he and his friends offered as best they could. McCarthy was adamant. Was the country to be English or French? It was an absurd question, like one of those impossible questions in logic, to which any answer was wrong. He took his views from E. A. Freeman,* whose ideas on modern nationalism had, for McCarthy, suddenly lit up the whole contrived and awkward Canadian compromise, its dual languages here and

* E. A. Freeman was appointed Regius Professor of History at Oxford in 1884 and had already published widely. See especially his *Comparative Politics* (London, 1873).

there; its separate schools, here and there; the illogicality of such a structure; its failure, as McCarthy saw it, to establish a true national amalgam. All this was illuminated in the bright clarity of Freeman's principle that language always had, and always would, determine nationality. McCarthy quoted Freeman at the beginning of the great debate in 1890 on the Northwest language question: "where there is not community of language, there is no common nationality in the highest sense."[46] Switzerland was therefore an artificial community, created by the pressures of the big nations around her. Canada could never, by these terms, become a nation until English triumphed.

The Equal Rights Association was formed in Toronto, in June 1889. "Equal rights" was an absurd statement of what McCarthy was after. Not equality of rights, but supremacy of English was his aim. Equal rights of all religious denominations before the law, special privileges for none, sounded fine. But it would ruin the delicate compromises that gave the Catholic minority in Ontario its separate schools and, for that matter, the Protestant minority in Quebec its privileges. "Equal rights" was a shibboleth. It obscured, it did not clarify. McCarthy's real bent was revealed in his speech at Stayner near Georgian Bay on July 12, 1889. It was in part a repetition of what he said in the House in March, but perhaps because of a sympathetic audience, it was sharper and more ruthless. McCarthy was by now questioning the value of separate schools and the dual language system in the Northwest Territories, in Manitoba and, by open implication, in Ontario.

> Let us deal with the question of the dual language in the North-West, and let the people deal with French in the schools of the English provinces; and when these two questions have been dealt with, we will have accomplished something, and paved the way for the future. . . . Now is the time when the ballot box will decide this great question before the people; and if that does not supply the remedy in this generation, bayonets will supply it in the next.[47]

Using Tardivel's paper, *La Vérité*, as evidence, he claimed that French Canadians saw Confederation simply as a means to establish French-Canadian independence. Canada must have the St. Lawrence. Tardivel's proposition could not be sustained, and the sooner that the pretensions upon which these ideas were based were destroyed, the better. The place to begin this process was the Northwest Territories.

Yet, for all that, D'Alton McCarthy was one of the nobler figures of English Canada. He resembled Vaughan, in Tardivel's novel, *Pour la Patrie*, before Vaughan's conversion, looking to a great Canada, a strong central government, a united people speaking one language.[48] He was ultramontane, like Tardivel, in his dedication to principle, in his scorn of political trimming, in his uprightness, in his utter conviction of the rightness of his views. He and Tardivel were struck from the same mould. They were coloured differently, and were bound to be enemies, but doubtless each would have respected the other. It was impossible not to respect, even perhaps to admire, McCarthy. It was equally impossible to agree with him. His cause, like Tardivel's, led only to disruption. It was characteristic of McCarthy that he did not break with Macdonald personally. He broke on an issue of principle.[49]

McCarthy soon had more invitations to speak that he was willing to accept. He seems to have been unwilling to go as far as he could have in 1889; perhaps he did not want to take himself out of the party. If this is so, Macdonald's policy of refusing to read him out was justified. McCarthy went west in August 1889 and spoke only twice, in Portage la Prairie and in Calgary. He refused opportunities in British Columbia, Winnipeg, and elsewhere.[50] His Portage speech, August 5, combined an attack upon the French language with one upon provincial rights.

> The excuse of the Opposition gentlemen [Liberals] was that they were provincial rights men; and whatever a province did, good, bad or indifferent they would stand by. If this heresy be not eradicated, CANADA WILL GO TO PIECES. Carry out provincial rights to its legitimate conclusion and where is the Protestant minority [of Quebec]? No. This is a nation; the provinces have great powers for local government, but all these must be subject to unwritten laws which must regulate the whole Dominion. . . .[51]

It is doubtful if the fiery Joseph Martin, who was on the platform, approved. But he did approve of McCarthy's attack on the French language, and his presence made it look as if the Manitoba government approved. The Manitoba government was already concerned about a parallel question that had arisen out of the excitement over the Jesuits' Estates Act, the abolition of the dual school system. That had been raised in the *Brandon Sun* in May, 1889[52] and had not evoked much public response. But when the language issue was combined with the school issue, the result, like nitro-glycerine, was highly volatile. Moreover, it suited the Greenway government to have a lively issue to distract the electorate with. And it was one which, if Protestant sympathies were fairly engaged, they could not help but win. The Manitoba school question thus had local origins; but the elements that made it explosive were put together by McCarthy.

His Calgary speech had much less effect. The French language was not an important issue in the Territories. The Northwest Legislative Assembly was much more preoccupied with wresting full financial control, indeed full panoply of responsible government, from Ottawa, than it was with a minor question. Abolition of French was generally favoured, but it aroused little heat.[53] Davin in the Regina *Leader*, in September 1889, counselled moderation; "it is not necessary to be violent or offensive or to rail at this or the other section of the community. . . ."[54]

Parliament opened on January 17, 1890. Five days later McCarthy introduced Bill No. 10, to amend the Northwest Territories Act by expunging clause 110 allowing the use of French or English in the debates of the Northwest Assembly, in proceedings before the courts, and enjoining the use of French and English in the journals, and in the ordinances of the Assembly. Its use in this latter fashion had cost the vast sum of four hundred dollars a year since 1877,[55] and in the Northwest it had long been accepted as inoffensive, though increasingly less useful as French migration to the Northwest had failed to develop. Since 1870 only ten in every hundred who came to the Northwest were Roman Catholics, and the French-speaking among them rather less than that. In 1889 Bishop Grandin of St. Albert wrote despairingly to his fellow bishops in Quebec: "If even one-fourth of those [French Canadians] who emigrated from your Province during the past ten years had come to us, we would still constitute the majority, or would at all events be a powerful minority. . . ."[56]

McCarthy commented on the origin of this section of the Northwest Act. He said, rightly, that in 1877 it had originated as a Senate amendment, made by Senator Marc Girard of St. Boniface. It was at that time accepted by the Mackenzie government through Senator R. W. Scott. David Mills, Minister of the Interior at that time, admitted this. But he also added that it had been a prudent provision, "infinitely cheaper than gunpowder and police."[57]

The proposal to expunge the section could not have been debated on its merits; for no one could forget the ideas behind it, and no one was intended to. McCarthy's preamble was, "It is expedient in the interest of national unity in the Dominion that there should be community of language among the people of Canada. . . ."[58] The proposal put the Macdonald government in a dilemma. English-speaking Conservatives felt the people of the Northwest were entitled to make their own decision on the subject. French-speaking Conservatives felt that even *that* was a betrayal of vested rights. Macdonald did the only thing he could do: he made the issue an open question.[59]

McCarthy was shot at by members from both sides of the House. Blake, Laurier, and Macdonald all agreed that even if McCarthy's aim were acceptable (which all hastened to say it was not) he was surely going about it in the wrong way. History and human nature both showed, said Blake, "that impertinent interference, still more that threats of coercive interference" were certain to produce resistance. Macdonald was succinct. "I believe it would be impossible [to throttle the French language] if it were tried, and it would be foolish and wicked if it were possible." Cartwright's vigorous words carried the strongest castigation of McCarthy by any English-speaking member of the House:

> I say that no good has come of this Bill; I say that no good can come of it, and I am sorry to have to add that, in my judgment, speaking without

> prejudice or malice, I cannot but believe that no good was intended to come out of the proposal. . . .[60]

Under all this fire and shot McCarthy remained cool and controlled, and his precise and dispassionate reply elicited, even among those who opposed him, some admiration. It was a high point in his career. His "effect upon a hostile Parliament was singularly pervasive and profound."[61] His cause was clear and hard and wrong. *The Week* put it firmly down. "A chronic, exasperating sense of injustice and harsh treatment fermenting in the breasts of two-fifths of the whole population of the Dominion would be a more fatal obstacle to national consolidation than the use of half-a-dozen official languages by as many sections of a contented people could possibly be."[62] Confederation was a delicate system of mutual concessions. The school rights of minorities, as Mitchell noted, had been critical at the London Conference of 1866. "Confederation," said James Edgar, "is a compromise in itself, and without Confederation what is Canada, where is it, or where would it be?"[63]

There was hardly an answer to questions like that. In the end Sir John Thompson's amendment prevailed: the Northwest Assembly could regulate the language in which it published its proceedings, but the rest of the arrangements stood as they were. The Ordinances would still be published in French, and French could still be used in the courts of the Territories. This passed, February 21, 1890, by 149-50, with a few refractory French Canadians opposing it with McCarthy.

The debate had been a searching one, and though agonizing for the Government, is still one of the best in the turbid (and turgid) history of the House of Commons. Everyone tried hard to keep their language and temper under control. Altogether, George Foster was right in telling Leonard Tilley, "The debate was admirable in its temper – but the elements were very inflammable. . . ."[64]

George Foster was now Minister of Finance, having succeeded Tupper in May 1888. Foster had come on the scene in the 1882 general election. He had been Professor of Classics and History at the University of New Brunswick for seven years, and he brought to bear upon politics a cool, well-furnished mind. Foster's first speeches in the House did not endear him to that critical body. He produced orations which, members complained, had been well polished by frequent delivery elsewhere. He earned a rebuke in 1884 from Sydney Fisher, M.P. Brome, himself in the House only as long as Foster.

> . . . I trust I would remember the difference between a country schoolhouse audience which might be instructed and edified by those high sounding and rolling sentences and this honourable House, composed principally of business men who wish to discuss in a practical way a question of importance to the public.[65]

There was, and always would be, something singularly unappealing about Foster. He had no bonhomie. He despised liquor, had no other comfortable vices, nor any attributes of character to compensate for their absence. He was, as Augustus Bridle later remarked, "inexorably and fervently serious";[66] he looked the pessimist that Cartwright really was. But he had a schoolmaster's knack for making sense of his material and conveying it to his audience. He was a man of the utmost probity, whom it was good to have on your side; but he was also an individualist, hard, aloof, repellent, and perhaps even unassimilable,[67] reminding one rather of Eeyore in *Winnie the Pooh*.

In the 1890 session the Rykert scandal, which had been brewing underground for some time, erupted. John Rykert, M.P. Lincoln, was one of many Conservatives who in the palmy days of the 1880's, went into the West and set happily to work to make money as fast and as efficiently as possible. Rykert devised one scheme: acquire a timber limit, preferably near a railway that needs timber. He got one in the Cypress Hills, in April 1882, just before the C.P.R. had changed its route southward – one hundred square miles at five dollars per square mile. Of course there were other expenses in the acquisition of the limit, perhaps $10,000, apparently to ministers who would expedite the matter and keep it from the C.P.R. Within a year of its acquisition the limit had been sold for $200,000 to a Michigan lumberman. The profit was divided between John Adams, in whose name the limit had been taken out, and Mrs. Nannie Rykert. The proceeds to each were about $90,000.

The Opposition had soon got wind of this transaction. There were allegations in 1883, and in 1886, which Rykert denied. Then the Opposition got hold of solid evidence from some source, perhaps S. H. Blake,[68] and on March 11, 1890, Cartwright moved that Rykert's conduct had been corrupt and scandalous. In the end it went to a Select Committee which, as expected, refused to support Cartwright's charges. But the evidence was incriminating, and Rykert was driven to resigning his seat in May 1890. Lincoln-Niagara unblushingly returned him in the bye-election and he remained in Parliament until the 1891 dissolution. This transaction, said Cartwright, was but the "peak below which lies a . . . mountain range of undiscovered, but well developed rapacity."[69] In the 1886 Debates Charlton served up an enormous list of timber limits and land grants acquired by members for themselves and friends, amounting to: 17 Senators and M.P.'s who got Orders in Council for timber limits for themselves; 45 Senators and M.P.'s who got them on behalf of themselves and friends; 56 Senators and M.P.'s who applied; 115 Orders in Council passed upon the recommendation of Senators and M.P.'s.[70] Rykert was certainly not alone.

Then came more serious intimations. Thomas McGreevy, M.P. Quebec West since 1867, had for years been the Conservative Party Treasurer in

Quebec and was an important contractor and entrepreneur, president of a large steamship line on the St. Lawrence, a director of another, and of the Union Bank. He was related through a family marriage to Hector Langevin. The McGreevy brothers, Thomas and Robert, had been able, for a decade or so, to wangle rewarding government contracts for a firm they were associated with, Larkin Connolly and Company. The *quid pro quo* was campaign contributions and other perquisities for Thomas McGreevy and Langevin. All this was conducted with decent circumspection, until late in 1888 Thomas McGreevy took his brother to court over the division of the firm's profits. It was a disastrous case. It was impossible to keep things quiet, though really detailed evidence came only when Robert McGreevy, angry at his brother's action, compiled a fat dossier of correspondence which he sent, through Senator Theodore Robitaille, to Sir John Macdonald. Macdonald, after talking to both Thomas McGreevy and Langevin, refused to countenance the charges of Robert McGreevy, who then took the correspondence to Israël Tarte, with strict injunctions for secrecy. Tarte too approached Macdonald; but Macdonald still remained adamant, and fascinating bits began to appear in *Le Canadien* in April 1890.[71]

What M.P.'s might properly do, and what they ought not to do, was a question raised more and more frequently since Hincks had got into railways in 1853. Should an M.P. use his position, and the knowledge that he acquired with it, for private gain? A debate on this point took place in 1886 between Foster and Cartwright:

> Mr. FOSTER. If my hon. friend will say in his place that I took one single step toward corruption by applying in a legal way for a timber limit, let him do so.
>
> Sir RICHARD CARTWRIGHT. I do say so. I say no member of parliament has a right to ask for favors of that kind from the Government. . . . I say that members of Parliament are trustees; that no trustee has the right to speculate in the property of his ward. . . . That is my doctrine. . . .
>
> Mr. FOSTER. That is fine doctrine, but it will not stand the test. When a man applies under a law passed by Parliament, and in a strictly legal way for what the law allows him on legal conditions, he is applying for no favor.[72]

Timber limits, land grants, railway charters, public works contracts, were forms of patronage; and there were several others. On the general question of patronage Macdonald was consistent, both in opposition and in power. If a man had no confidence in the government, he had said in 1878, he could not expect to receive any benefits from such a government.[73] Again, twelve years later, he said, "a Member of Parliament in opposition, having no confidence in the Government, is [in respect of recommendations for patronage] in the position of any other Canadian."[74] Mackenzie Bowell had been rather more explicit.

> Everything in the whole system of Government, in connection with patronage, is carried on upon this principle: You consult your friends when anything is to be done in a constituency, and it is the merest hypocrisy to preach or lay down any other doctrine as being practiced by any political party in this country.[75]

In practice Cabinet ministers usually solicited recommendations from the local Conservative member; if the constituency were held by Liberals, recommendations were received from the Conservative who had fought most recently in the Conservative interest. But any attempt on the part of M.P.'s to assert a categorical right to recommendations for patronage, Macdonald sternly resisted.[76]

There could also be sharp clashes between a minister defending his deputy-minister against a tough-minded M.P. or another minister on the prowl for patronage. Pictou County was a hard and greedy constituency to manage, and Charles Hibbert Tupper was just the man to fight for patronage for his riding. When Macdonald became Minister of Railways after Pope's death, he had to defend Collingwood Schrieber, his deputy-minister, against the younger Tupper's impatient desire to get coal contracts for friends in Pictou County. Young Tupper could write hot letters:

> As a member of the Cabinet [Minister of Fisheries] I think I should expect a little better treatment at the hands of your Chief Engineer regarding matters in my county, than I receive from him. In my opinion he is being permitted to ruin us politically in the Maritime Provinces without doing a particle of good [to] the Intercolonial Railway. His inattention and sharp replies to business letters is only excelled by more discourteous treatment of matters sent to him by members of the Cabinet.[77]

Macdonald was forced to remind Tupper that he was young and inexperienced, and that furthermore he had yet to learn that his local interest in Pictou County had to be subordinated to the general good of Canada as a whole. Macdonald put in jocularly, "I see we must find you a seat where there are no coal mines, or we shall have annual trouble."[78] The truth was that too often young Tupper went off at half-cock.[79]

He was bent on departmental reform from the day he took over Marine and Fisheries, May 31, 1888. At first Macdonald was philosophical; ". . . it is like the measles," he said, "You will get over them. I was the devil of a departmental reformer when I began public life!"[80] Tupper's *bête noir* was pollution of fishing rivers by sawdust and fish offal, especially of the salmon rivers in British Columbia, New Brunswick, and Nova Scotia. His efforts were mightily resented, even in Tupper's own province. C. H. Cahan, editor of the Halifax *Herald* told Thompson that Tupper's vigorous administration of fisheries regulations was destroying the Conservatives in Nova Scotia.[81]

In the fall of 1890 he had wanted an injunction raised against some influential British Columbia canners. Macdonald in Cabinet said he thought it would be useful if Tupper wired his B.C. officials to hold off for a while. Tupper replied that he could not do this without authority from Parliament. At that Macdonald lost his temper, kicked the table, and said he would see whether the telegram was sent or not. But the Cabinet supported young Tupper. Next day, at Council, Macdonald made amends, saying, "Charlie, I want to say that you were quite right yesterday, and I was wrong. I cannot tell you just now what influence was moving me, but I can quite see that you have a statutory duty to perform, and your position is correct." And he repeated the explanation in Council. When dissolution came early in February 1891, Macdonald looked across at young Tupper and said, "Now, you will understand what was in my head when I asked you to suspend the enforcement of those regulations. . . ."[82] There is a whole world in that incident; as if Macdonald's whole political *métier* were summed up.

The election of 1891 has been widely discussed, in genesis, results, and significance. Unrestricted reciprocity had largely dropped out of sight despite valiant efforts by the *Globe* and other Liberal papers to keep it going. The prosperity of the later 1880's had weakened the Liberal argument, and they were seriously embarrassed by Butterworth's peaceful annexation resolution in the United States Congress in December 1888. The Republicans were the party most opposed to any moderate tariff concessions, but their territorial appetites were whetted by the implications of commercial union.

Given the high-tariff bias in the new Harrison Republican administration, and given a surplus of American agricultural produce, it was not surprising that the new McKinley tariff inaugurated protection for American farm products. The bill was introduced in Congress in April 1890, and put into effect on October 6. The tariff was almost wholly based upon domestic considerations, but it was widely believed in Canada that the purpose was to starve Canada into annexation, as Macdonald put it in October 1890.[83] Sir John Thompson, in a speech the next day added, "What is the use of talking about natural markets [in the United States]? . . ."[84] They were to all intents and purposes closed. And even if they were open there was no guarantee Canadian products could compete. American railways had done this for Nova Scotia by making American coal too cheap in New England.[85]

So unrestricted reciprocity, commercial union, or annexation, all labels that could cover the same thing, was back in Canadian politics. But there were other elements as well. The Langevin scandal was coming. *Grip* had a cartoon, November 29, 1890, showing a wild cyclone blowing out of the east, McGreevy's head at the top of the black cloud, with Macdonald and Langevin fearfully clutching their coats:

Sir Hector: It's coming this way, Sir John but if we can manage to reach the General Election before it strikes – that's our only hope!

A week later Langevin was pictured by Côté (also in *Grip*) holding his stomach in pain; "Too much Tart(e)!"[86]

Yet, Macdonald was not disposed to rush into an election. It was not required before February 1892, and there seemed to have been genuine disagreement within the Cabinet. As late as January 16, Macdonald anticipated an election only in the coming summer.[87] As to issues, there were two possibilities: one was to brand the Liberals as annexationists; the other was to produce a Conservative brand of reciprocity.

The first card, and what seems to have determined Macdonald to dissolve, was the discovery, through William MacDougall, of the famous proof sheets of Farrer's pamphlet,[88] probably between January 16 and January 21 when a tentative decision to dissolve was made. The Governor General was not very comfortable about using Farrer's proofs; "were I engaged in the Election contest, I must say, that I should not like to depend on this. . . . Of course, however, you know best. I don't venture to express an opinion one way or the other, as to the policy of using this unpublished paper as a weapon of political war."[89] Lord Stanley and Edward Farrer agreed. ". . . intelligent men," wrote Farrer in the *Globe*, "will feel sorry that Sir John should have been driven by the stress of the battle . . . to resort to so poor a subterfuge."[90] But that affidavit sworn out by C. St. George Clark, a compositor with Hunter Rose & Co., Toronto printers, was too good not to use.

The story was this. The brash and mercurial Farrer, had been brought over to the *Globe* from the *Mail* by Cartwright and others, and had begun to write for the *Globe* in August, 1890 under the nominal editorship of John Willison. Willison was new, Farrer was new, and the former confessed that, admitted or not, Farrer was "head of the table" in any paper he chose to be associated with. On November 15, Farrer had gone to Hunter Rose with an ordinary business proposition, to print, privately, a pamphlet he was writing for an American friend for possible use in the American Senate. The pamphlet, in the best Farrer style, summed up the arguments on how American politics could best be devised to weaken Canadian policy and drive Canada into annexation.[91] He suggested, for example, cutting off Canadian bonding privileges through the United States, and cutting the C.P.R. connnection with its American subsidiaries at Sault Ste. Marie, Michigan. Farrer himself admitted that he felt that "political union with the United States was the manifest destiny of Canada. . . ."[92]

The use of the Farrer pamphlet was made indispensable by the loss of what would have been a better card, had it been possible to play it. This was the hope that the Canadian Government could make public its private discussions on reciprocity with the United States. These Conservative overtures had grown out of the successful Newfoundland negotiations with James G. Blaine, United States Secretary of State, early in 1890, negotiations which embarrassed the British government, annoyed Canada, and made the Newfoundlanders chuckle with satisfaction. Canada blocked ratification of the Newfoundland-United States Treaty, to the great indignation of Newfoundland. Canada then proposed a full joint commission on Canadian-American problems. Blaine was reluctant to touch anything resembling moderate tariff concessions. But he was willing to hold private talks with the British Minister in Washington, provided no public reference was made, a condition that was apparently not known to the Canadians until January, 1891. So when Canada sought permission to make public the fact that there had been talks on reciprocity, Blaine, apparently on the insistence of President Harrison, categorically refused. Much worse, he stated, apparently at the instigation of Edward Farrer and Canadian Liberals, that "There are no negotiations whatever on foot for a reciprocity treaty with Canada."[93] Blaine had never been an enthusiast for reciprocity with Canada on terms the Conservatives could have accepted.

> Beyond the frontier, across the river, our neighbours chose another Government, another allegiance. . . . They do exactly as they have a right to do. I neither dispute their right nor envy their situation. . . . But I am opposed, teetotally opposed, to giving the Canadians the sentimental satisfaction of waving the British flag, paying British taxes, and enjoying the actual cash remuneration of American markets. They cannot have both at the same time. If they come to us they can have what we have, but it is an absolute wrong . . . that they shall have exactly the same share of our markets and the same privileges of trade under our flag that we have. So far as I can help it, I do not mean that they shall be Canadians and Americans at the same time.[94]

Nevertheless, after the broad hints in the Conservative papers in Canada that reciprocity negotiations *were* going on, Blaine's denial completely dished the Conservatives. There was nothing for it but to sail into Farrer, the *Globe*, and the Liberal party as a whole, and brand the whole lot of them annexationists, with the marvellous aid of the Farrer proofs.

That American money was sought and used by the Liberal party in that election is undoubted. Longley was in Louisville, Kentucky, when the election was announced, and rushed home to Halifax "with some means from the States, but not *enough*."[95] There were strong indications that the Toronto *Globe*, through Robert Jaffray, got some $50,000 from S. J. Ritchie, a mining industrialist in Cleveland, for campaign funds.[96]

For the Liberals the Grand Trunk Railway was just as important. Conservatives had made valiant efforts to get Grand Trunk support; Sir Charles

Tupper, who arrived in Canada early in February in response to Macdonald's earnest invitation, went to see the General Manager, L. J. Seargeant, at his house in Montreal. He asked for the moral and financial support of the Grand Trunk in the campaign. The Grand Trunk had many good reasons not to like the Conservatives. It was especially anxious to avoid giving the anti-Canadian lobbies at Washington any case for withdrawal of bonding privileges. So Seargeant said no. The Grand Trunk would be neutral. Tupper was angry.[97] The neutrality of the Grand Trunk was probably an illusion, given Canadian politics as they were. Evidently it decided the Liberal party was safer for its interests, and threw its support behind Laurier. Tupper alleged that Grand Trunk employees were ordered to vote Liberal, and that Canadians resident in Indiana and elsewhere were brought at Grand Trunk expense back to Canada to vote.

Mutatis mutandis, the Canadian Pacific Railway and the Conservatives. "It is the Tory Government on wheels," said the *Globe* of the C.P.R.[98] "Our canvass is nearly complete," wrote Van Horne to Macdonald just before the election, "and the C.P.R. vote will be practically unanimous. . . ."[99] Then there were the manufacturers, who were almost certainly dunned for campaign contributions. Not all manufacturers were staunch Conservatives, some would have liked to remain Liberal, and would have accepted a position within the party approximately like that of James Young of Galt. But the party's apparently unrepentant commitment to unrestricted reciprocity, which had made Oliver Mowat uneasy, and quite alienated Blake, made equally impossible the position of manufacturers with Liberal interests. For example, J. H. Fairbank, the leading producer of crude oil in Canada, had been a Liberal backbencher under Blake but refused the Liberal nomination in 1891. Laurier and Cartwright's policies would have wiped out the Canadian oil industry. Fairbank remarked, "Many of us Grits will take to the woods. 'I am a political orphan.' "[100] The Conservative standard-bearer in Lambton East, George Moncrieff, was to more than treble his 1887 majority in 1891. Much of the responsibility for this kind of alienation lay with Charlton and with Cartwright. Charlton was always regarded as American anyway, but Cartwright was as Canadian as Laurier. Laurier's statements were usually couched, even on the public platform, in ways that did not put people's backs up. Cartwright could not do that; and his fluency, his vigour, and what Laurier called his "nature batailleuse" made him difficult, indeed impossible, to hold in.[101]

Thus when Macdonald's published election address came, to the surprise of many there was not a syllable about reciprocity. "Not for many years," said the Toronto *Week*, "have the people been called upon to decide between two policies so broadly distinguished."[102] Macdonald opened the campaign in Toronto, February 17, 1891. He accused the Liberals of having been bought up with American gold; if this were to prevail, then "*finis Canadia.*"

> I believe that this election, which is a great crisis and upon which so much depends, will show to the Americans that we prize our country as much as they do, that we would fight for our existence. . . .[103]

Macdonald's famous remark "a British subject I was born, and a British subject I will die," falls into place, correctly, not as an expression of Imperial sentiment, but of Canadian nationalism.

It was strong stuff. J. V. Ellis, M.P. Saint John, wrote to Laurier after the election, "But the main thing was the loyalty cry. The changes were rung upon it in every way. All the Farrer business, all the Wiman talk, all that Sir Cartwright [*sic*] said in Boston. . . . It really surprised me in the end we had any votes left."[104] L. H. Davies, a better judge, was more succinct. ". . . it was not *boodle* that carried N.S. & N.B. (the boodle had its own influence), but sentiment – the sentiment of loyalty fanned into a flame by the clergy and others and the fear of annexation."[105]

The loyalty cry in 1891 was evidence of a difficult battle. Those two old and experienced party veterans, Sir Leonard Tilley and Mackenzie Bowell agreed it had been "a hard fight."[106] Patriotism is the last refuge of a weak cause. It has often been noted how close the election of 1891 was; Macdonald's margin was only about twenty-seven seats. The popular vote was 51.1 per cent to 47.1 per cent. But in 1891 Macdonald won a larger share of the popular vote than he had in 1887. What made the election of 1891 less successful in terms of seats was the change of seats in central Canada. There was no doubt the Conservatives had done well in the three Maritime provinces. They picked up two seats in Nova Scotia, two in Prince Edward Island, and three in New Brunswick. In Quebec, however, although the Conservatives had the majority of the votes cast, Laurier took five seats from the Conservatives. The Conservative votes were hived in traditional seats, while the Liberals exploited their advantage in areas that had swung to Mercier in Quebec provincial elections. In Ontario also Macdonald lost ground, losing seven seats to the Liberals. Here it was probably the rural vote that told against him. In the West only fifteen seats were at stake, and these came in exactly as they had in 1887.

Richard Cartwright, the *Globe*, and Liberals generally, with a majority of seats in Ontario and Quebec, seemed to feel, in that blind-eyed way they sometimes had, that they ought to be in power. Cartwright was furious that this Liberal millenium should be blocked by the riff-raff outside of central Canada:

> Our opponents' array . . . is most literally a thing of shreds and patches, made up of the ragged remnants from half a dozen minor provinces, the great majority of whom do not even pretend to be actuated by any principle save that of securing a good slice of booty for themselves. . . .[107]

Cartwright's contemptuousness did the Liberal party no good either, as Davies pointed out to Laurier. "Do we want to array N.S. & N.B. against us for ever?" It was easy for Cartwright to fling insinuations around, and they might bring temporary rewards in Ontario, "but they are treasured up by our opponents and used with terrible effect. . . ."[108]

But there was one man still more devastating than Cartwright. That was Edward Blake. One old Liberal, at a political meeting in Colchester County, Nova Scotia, just before the election, asked, "Where is Mr. Blake? We have heard nothing from him!" It was gently explained that "Mr. Blake is not just with us in our policy this time." "Neither am I then," said the old man, who reached for his hat and stick and made for the door.[109] Despite all Laurier's efforts to persuade him, the best Blake could do was to remain silent on the issue, and even at that he was restless and uncomfortable. He had returned to the House in 1890, still unwell, and he retained much of his old power there. But he fell easily into his habit of acting for himself. As Laurier put it, "Blake will neither lead nor be led."[110] Ostensibly Blake supported Laurier's leadership fully. He denied any desire to replace Laurier, and doubtless believed he had no such desire. But what Blake believed were his feelings, and what those feelings actually were, were sometimes different things.[111] There was often this neurotic juxtaposition in Blake, a constant strain between what he believed he ought to feel, and what he did feel. This private agony had considerable public significance.

Early in January 1891, believing an election coming, the Ontario Liberals had called for a provincial convention in Toronto in February. The call was issued by Laurier, but it came from Cartwright. Blake was not consulted, and was much annoyed. A few days after the convention was announced, J. S. Willison received from Blake a letter that denounced Liberal trade policy as wrong, unwise, impossible. Willison was thunderstruck. There was no doubt that Blake intended the letter for publication, and Willison moved heaven and earth to persuade him not to. Blake, outraged by the convention proposal, was determined. The upshot was that Laurier was summoned to Toronto to deal with Blake. Laurier begged Blake to put the letter in a drawer and forget it.[112] In the end Blake agreed to withhold publishing the letter until after the election, on condition the convention was called off. And it was called off. That in turn made Cartwright so angry that he never again spoke to Blake.

On March 6, 1891, the day after the election, out came Blake's celebrated letter to the electors of West Durham.[113] He refused, with a bitter pang, re-nomination in the Liberal interest for West Durham. It was a long letter argued with all Blake's unrelenting intellectuality. The logic ran thus. Unrestricted reciprocity could not be usefully distinguished from commercial union. Commercial union led inevitably to political union with the United States. The Canadian public ought to be told what they were letting themselves in for before they voted in the Liberal party with a blank cheque labelled Unrestricted Reciprocity. The lack of any positive content in the letter, which Laurier had remarked upon, made it possible to draw various conclusions from it. Pressed by newspapers and public to be more specific, Blake answered, at his oblique best:

> The contradictory inferences to which a sentence in my Durham letter, detached from its context, has in several quarters unexpectedly given rise, conquers my reluctance to trespass again so soon upon your columns, and I crave space to say that I think political union with the United States, though becoming our probable, is by no means our ideal, or as yet our inevitable future.[114]

Grip portrayed the Sphinx (Edward Blake's face of course), with Macdonald kneeling in front asking, "Speak! Tell us! What do you think *is* our ideal or inevitable future, then?"[115] All correspondence between Blake and Laurier for the time being stopped. Laurier believed that Blake had been "wrong, absolutely wrong in the position he has taken,"[116] but, whatever may be said in defence of Laurier and the party, Blake was close to being right. "The events of the last two or three years," he wrote to Longley a year later, "have placed the party in a position from which it will take a very long time to recover."[117] His real answer to the problems raised by this whole anguished debate came in 1892:

> I cling to the hope of a higher though more arduous destiny for the great Dominion. I look for the regeneration of my own country. I cling to the hope that – sooner or later, and rather soon than late – there may be born into the world an independent Canadian Commonwealth, nerving itself to solve, after its own fashion, the many . . . problems which confront us. . . .[118]

Blake was now out of Parliament for good. He was missed when it opened at the end of April 1891. "The tired head resting on a pair of outstretched arms and almost lost under the historic slouch hat"[119] was now gone. Carling was in the Senate, Alonzo Wright's wit was gone, even Rykert with his endless scrapbooks – the butt of interminable jokes – was gone, scrapbooks and all. A. G. Jones and Weldon were gone. So was Peter Mitchell. Israël Tarte, in the House for the first time, "the mildest mannered man that ever scuttled a ship or cut a throat,"[120] made his charges against McGreevy on May 11 amid profound attention, and gradually the House's interest swung over to the Committee on Privileges and Elections. The Government seemed to have had little legislation ready.

Macdonald had been unrepentant and cheerful in the Throne Speech debate. But his words had no longer the old ring to them. They depressed his followers and saddened his opponents. Macdonald had been through much in the election just past, too much. Laurier watched him in these opening days of the 1891 Parliament, as so often in the past he had watched and had learned. Now he watched and was sad, feeling that an old institution in the land was gradually sinking. In spite of all Macdonald's efforts the hand of fate was everywhere visible. Thus Laurier wrote, sadly, to Emilie Lavergne, *la maîtresse en titre* of his mind, "Pour réparer les ans, l'irréparable outrage."[121]

That came in the warm days of late May. On May 12 Macdonald had had a slight but ominous stroke during an interview with the Governor General. Lord Stanley suggested he lie down and rest. "Oh," murmured Macdonald, "that is no use, the machine is worn out."[122] He was back in the House a week later almost his old self, but he had another slight stroke on May 27. Recovering from it, he was overtaken by a third and far more devastating one two days later, that deprived him of all speech. It was announced in the House on the evening of Thursday, May 29 by Langevin in a shocked and tremulous voice. All debate stopped. That Saturday there were no games on Parliament Hill. All social events seemed to stop nervelessly. He slowly sank and on Saturday, June 6, 1891, died.

It was almost as if public life had suddenly ended. "It is now seen," said *The Week* soberly, "that . . . [he] had a hold not only upon the popular intellect and imagination, but upon the popular heart, to a degree which few, probably, had believed, or imagined."[123]

He was the archetype of Canadian prime ministers. His *métier* seemed to pass to Laurier – who had learned so much from him – and through Laurier to King. Each in his own way translated it. Unabashedly partisan as Macdonald's method was, the policies administered by it were large policies; if they were adopted and implemented as political convenience suggested, they were nevertheless conceived in no narrow spirit. And Macdonald learned as he grew older. He was not without the slow hardening of mind that comes with years, but his native flexibility, the empirical and practical cast of his mind, the richness of resources of spirit he could draw from, were a splendid endowment; his long political life, and his remarkable popular following, show the vitality and the verve with which he had deployed them.

CHAPTER 12

The Years of Thompson 1891-1894

Macdonald was not dead before awful rifts in the Conservative party began to open up. He had been, so to speak, the only political principle Conservatives had. James Edgar, watching them with amusement from the Opposition benches, wrote to his wife, "They are canvassing and caballing in an insane way.... If Sir John doesn't die in a day or two he will have half-killed his party with suspense."[1] The Liberals were lively and aggressive with only twenty-seven seats separating them from power, and with the McGreevy scandal hot and ready to serve. As Macdonald's illness began to look serious debate in the House had been upon the role of Sir Charles Tupper who so distinguished himself in the recent election as a vigorous – the Liberals used "shameless" – partisan of the Government.

Tupper was one possible choice as successor to Macdonald, though the *Globe* alleged that Macdonald would have sooner seen the Liberals in power than have Tupper become Prime Minister.[2] And although there were rumours about Tupper, he knew how serious the McGreevy charges were, and that for the moment he was well enough where he was. Eighteen months earlier Langevin would have been the obvious choice; but now, that was impossible. "I *know*," wrote Edgar, "that it was the Tarte business alone that prevented the Governor from sending for Langevin."[3] Who was left? Macdonald's own views were uncertain in his last days. At first he thought of J. J. C. Abbott, and then gave it up.[4] A month or so before he had told T. C. Patteson, "The best thing I ever invented is Thompson." He said it a little sadly perhaps, for he was thinking of D'Alton McCarthy, and what he might have been.[5] The Governor General sent for Thompson, who may even have tried his hand at a Cabinet.[6] Certainly he was pressed by Lord Stanley to take the premiership in ways that made refusal very unpleasant.[7] But his inclination was against it. He said the day Macdonald died that he was unwilling to lead the party, then or in the future.[8] And he stuck to his refusal, one reason being McCarthy. The Protestant section might have followed Langevin – even in June, 1891 – but not Thompson, the man who had abandoned Protestantism for the Roman Catholic Church.[9] This left as the most likely possibility a man who had not been, up to this time, conspicuous.

Sir John Abbott was not without attractiveness. Venerable and well-mannered, fond of whist and cribbage, an expert in railway legislation and a leading C.P.R. counsel, he was well suited to the Senate. But Abbott hated politics. "I hate notoriety, public meetings, public speeches, caucuses and everything I know of that is apparently the necessary incident of politics – except doing public work to the best of my ability. . . . My own impression is that Thompson is the man to be sent for. . . ." This on June 4, 1891.[10] So Abbott wanted Thompson, and Thompson preferred Abbott, and in the end Thompson got his way. Abbott's condition was that Thompson should lead in the House of Commons, while he remained in the Senate. It was in some ways a good solution. Thompson acting as House Leader could be a kind of deputy Premier, while Abbott saved the uneasy consciences of Ontario Protestants by serving as Prime Minister from the Senate. Abbott admitted he was a Prime Minister *faute de mieux*, but he was not without admirers in the House, among them Sir Richard Cartwright.[11] And he was soon installed in Earnscliffe, giving dinners in full style. But his guests felt odd, as if Macdonald were still there.[12]

Yet, all was not well. The Langevin question was making the Conservative party increasingly uneasy. Only Thompson's determination to have it all out saved the party from worse demoralization. Better to risk what the inquiry would bring forth than the greater risks in trying to cover up. The facts were bad enough.

On the afternoon of Monday, May 11, 1891 Israël Tarte came into the House with his black bag under his arm.* He spoke in English, with his marked accent, as though the gravity of his charges required that every English-speaking member of the House understand him. McGreevy's voice, when he rose to deny the charges, was barely audible. Langevin rose from beside Macdonald to deny them also, and the charges were ordered sent to the Select Standing Committee on Privileges and Elections. The Committee was composed of forty-two members, twenty-three of them Conservatives, with a small working sub-committee of five, both committees under the chairmanship of Désiré Girouard, Conservative member for Jacques Cartier. Tarte's charges were formulated in sixty-three paragraphs. From the moment the Committee met, May 15, it was clear that the Government, especially Minister of Justice Thompson, were determined that the inquiry would be fair, full, and as expeditious as possible. It was also obvious that the charges were going to cover a great deal of ground and take some time to unravel.[13] A month later, B. B. Osler, the leading criminal lawyer in Canada, was

* That black bag was locked away every night in a safe in Hull.

brought to Ottawa by Thompson as counsel for the Public Works Department.[14] This was not so much to defend, as to get at the truth. Osler and Henry were even sent by Thompson to see Tarte and offered their assistance to get at the facts.[15] And the nearly fifteen hundred pages of proceedings and evidence that we now have is indicative of the importance of the Committee in Thompson's view, and the scrupulousness with which he was determined to proceed.

Like all scandals the McGreevy-Langevin one is complicated, and by no means all the evidence wanted, or witnesses required, were available. The Public Works Department, inexplicably, was unable to find certain documents. Important books of several firms disappeared; a number of people seemed to have the remarkable habit of destroying their business correspondence soon after they received it; several witnesses, not least Sir Hector Langevin himself, had amazing lapses of memory; and others found it convenient to take a respite from the hot Ottawa summer in the United States. The story that emerges from this long enquiry – it lasted until September 16 – is roughly as follows.

In 1876 and 1877 Langevin had had some hard elections to fight on the hustings, and some hard election cases to fight in the courts. All this cost money, so he borrowed $10,000 from Thomas McGreevy, giving notes for the debt. These Thomas obligingly renewed every quarter year or so up to and including 1891; it was always a useful reminder to forgetful politicians, of favours rendered. When Langevin became Minister in 1878 and set up house in Ottawa, McGreevy, M.P. for Quebec West, used to stay there during sessions of Parliament and at other times. He also used Langevin's room in the Parliament Buildings, and kept some of his papers there. Altogether these arrangements were convenient. McGreevy was Conservative party treasurer for the Quebec district and Langevin, being the political chief of the district, could direct funds where they were most needed. (He denied, later, having had the slightest idea about their disposition.) Then in 1884 Langevin needed a newspaper in Montreal. His son-in-law, Thomas Chapais ran *Le Courrier du Canada* in Quebec City, but Langevin felt his role as *chef* in Quebec required a Montreal organ. The Conservative paper there, *La Minerve*, was Chapleau's. So *Le Monde* was acquired, with McGreevy's money (no notes this time), for about $25,000.

McGreevy was also a member of the Quebec Harbour Commission, established under an 1873 Dominion statute with a majority of its members appointed by Ottawa. By virtue of parliamentary legislation authorizing improvements, the Dominion government paid money to the Harbour Commission on the recommendation of the Department of Public Works. There were several contracts let by the Commission to the Quebec firm of Larkin, Connolly and Co., the shares of which were held by four working principals and one non-working one; Patrick Larkin, Nicholas Connolly,

Michael Connolly, Owen Murphy, and the non-working principal, Robert McGreevy. The firm received contracts for work at Quebec and at Esquimalt over the period of 1878-91 totalling $3.1 million. Of this the trading profits of the business were just under $1 million. Net profits for the five principals came to $735,000, with salaries $48,500, and "donations" to political purposes $170,000.

Robert McGreevy's share of the profits was $188,000, the largest of the five, despite the fact that he neither put capital into the firm, nor did much work for them. His contribution was his influence with his brother in securing contracts from the Public Works Department, and obtaining useful modifications and extensions. Thomas McGreevy did not go unrewarded either. Robert said that Thomas had received $114,000 directly from the firm's political funds, and that he had also received, as his share of the profits, another $58,000 through Robert. By the end of 1888, Thomas wanted more. The brothers' estrangement and subsequent law suit probably arose from a bitter quarrel over the division of spoils, especially out of the Esquimalt dry dock contract, which Thomas believed, rightly, had been very lucrative. Apparently Robert also owed money to Thomas for past loans and was not paying up rapidly enough, and Robert doubtless told brother Thomas what he could do if faster payment were insisted upon.[16]

Of course all Public Works contracts and Quebec Harbour Commission contracts were awarded after public tenders. But with Thomas' access to the Department of Public Works, it was not difficult for Larkin and Connolly to devise tenders that were publicly acceptable. For the cross-wall contract for Quebec harbour in 1883, which Larkin, Connolly were awarded, the *quid pro quo* was $25,000 paid by the firm to Thomas McGreevy, all signed and arranged in a picturesque office under a trap-door in the floor of Thomas McGreevy's regular Quebec office. Occasionally when Larkin, Connolly got a contract that they did not really need, they would offer to sell it. In 1882 Peters, Moore and Wright tendered for a government contract, but it was awarded to Larkin, Connolly. Soon afterward, Owen Murphy went to Edward Moore and offered to decline the contract for a price of $10,000.[17]

As to Sir Hector, he did not resign from Public Works. He insisted that Tarte's charges were vague and did not involve him.

> Q. . . . when a charge is made that a member of Parliament procures from the Minister of Public Works, alterations in a contract which cost large sums of money, do you understand the Minister of Public Works to be charged?
>
> A. I had nothing to do with this and don't know anything about it at all. . . .
>
> Q. I put the question directly to you. Did you understand that it [charge 63] charged you with corruptly receiving money?
>
> A. I did not consider it in that way. It was vague and undeterminate.[18]

From the time Langevin had first come before the Committee, he maintained this extraordinary air of injured innocence, knowing nothing, nothing of what was paid for *Le Monde*, for example; and he made desperate efforts to save himself. Poor Henry Perley was dismissed (though all he had got, it seems, was $1,800 worth of jewelry for his wife) and, along with other officers in the Department of Public Works, was freely blamed by Langevin. But as the awful inquiry went on, the Government became increasingly unhappy about Langevin himself. Owen Murphy's testimony of June 26 implicated Langevin directly. Murphy, an unlovely, unscrupulous, but interesting character, admitted straight out that he had given $10,000 in cash to Langevin's son, Laforce.[19] Both Abbott and Thompson began to consider ways of getting Langevin out of the Government. Thompson said ruefully to his wife, "his scandals are dragging us under every hour."[20] Sir John Abbott wrote Langevin at the end of July, saying that the charges about Langevin's acceptance of public money probably could not be proved. (Owen Murphy's testimony was denied by others as bad as he was.) Nevertheless, the inquiry had generated strong doubts about the efficiency of Langevin's department. The danger for the Government was in a motion of censure being put on going into Supply, or in the House refusing to vote the Public Works estimates. Either motion would be supported by some Conservatives, "and would be most disastrous to us. . . . I would ask you to consider the position anew, and endeavor to find a solution of this difficulty. . . . I think we are on the eve of a serious defection from us if something is not done – & we are not strong enough to stand it."[21] Langevin sent in a provisional resignation, though not yet to be accepted. Thus before his appearance before the Committee, on August 11, 1891, his resignation was at least in hand. What seems to have happened was a saw-off. ". . . if your resignation were accepted," wrote Abbott on September 5, "there would not be so strong a desire by the opposition to make the report of the committee so injurious to you, as they now wish to do."[22] On September 7 Langevin's resignation as Minister was accepted; the majority Committee report on September 16 simply said that the conflicting evidence "does not justify them in concluding that the Minister knew of the conspiracy . . . or that he willingly lent himself to its objects."[23] It was accepted by Parliament on September 24, by a thin margin, 101-86.[24] The irony of it all was that McGreevy was left penniless; he failed to give evidence in order to save, not himself, but his political friends.[25] McGreevy was prosecuted on a criminal charge and sent to prison early in 1894.

Unfortunately, that was not all of the scandals. There were several others, which went to the Select Standing Committee on Public Accounts at the same time as the McGreevy one was being heard. These were principally the contract for the Langevin Block, the Government Printing Bureau inquiry,

inquiry over payments for extra work in the Department of Interior, and the Post Office.

The Langevin Block contract, dated September 1883, for additional office space opposite the Parliament buildings on Wellington Street, was awarded to A. Charlebois & Co. (less roof, iron joints, and elevators) for $295,000, the work to be finished by May, 1886. It was finished in 1888. Extra claims filed by Charlebois came to $214,000. However it was not so much the extras, as Charlebois' insistence on kick-backs from the other contractors, failing which he would refuse access to the building or site. For example, in 1886 Charlebois lost the contract for the iron roof to Rousseau & Mather of Montreal. The Government however insisted that Rousseau & Mather make their own arrangements with Charlebois for access to the site, which, in effect, meant buying the privilege. Antoine Rousseau was angry, went to Langevin and said, "If the building belongs to you, you had the right to call for tenders. If it does not belong to you, you had no right to call for tenders." Langevin's reply is not known, but Rousseau "saw that Sir Hector was held by the throat by Mr. Charlebois."[26] Rousseau & Mather were compelled to withdraw. The working principle is quite clear from the evidence of John Fensom, of Toronto who got the contract for the elevators. The charge Fensom would have made for the elevators was $32,000; Charlebois wanted a kick-back of twenty-five per cent ($8,000) – for insurance, planking, and the use of his tackle! So the tender went in at $40,000 and was so accepted.[27]

Ironically the Public Accounts Committee made no comment. They simply presented the evidence to the House. It was the same with the others. Brown Chamberlin, Macdonald's old friend and former editor of the Montreal *Gazette*, had been Queen's Printer since 1870. André Sénécal was Superintendent of the Printing Bureau. Here the issue was presents of cash by successful contractors. P. T. Perrott, vice-president of Barber-Ellis of Toronto, admitted that ten per cent of the value of gross sales was given in presents to Sénécal. "Yes: after each order was completed he would insist upon having something."[28] Brown Chamberlin went aboard Sénécal over rumours he had heard. "Now, Mr. Sénécal, whatever commercial people may do, a civil servant taking a commission is a dead man officially. Put that down in your book." "Bosh," said Sénécal.[29] When the Committee called for him, he was unavailable.[30] On August 13, 1891, Cartwright moved in the House that acceptance of gifts by Ministers was wrong and tended to demoralize other officials. It was accepted *in toto* by Sir John Thompson.[31]

Ottawa was hot. The committee rooms were stifling, and some of the scenes in them beggared description, with epithets and insinuations hurled back and forth, and in at least one case, that of Henry Perley, tears, and later fainting.[32] When at long last the session came to end and the awful revelations ceased, there was a sigh of relief. The Government was still in power despite the terrific assaults upon its morale. What spared it from worse was the uneasiness among the Liberals with their own house in Quebec. There were problems there as devastating for them as for the Conservatives in Ottawa, the most important thing being the Baie des Chaleurs railway scandal. Mercier had already been accused privately, in the most scathing terms, as early as 1889, by Calixte Le Boeuf, president of the Club National of Montreal:

> Here they accuse the Mercier government of being made up of people who are incapable, ignorant, and hare-brained. Everyone agrees with that. And they add, "there is no government: there is only Mercier." Now . . . they find that Mercier was poor, and has become rich too quickly. . . . They say out loud that this administration is the most corrupt that has ever disgraced the halls of the legislature; that everything can be bought; that there is no principle, no honesty, no sincerity, no honour.[33]

The Baie des Chaleurs Railway begins from Matapedia, on the Restigouche River near the New Brunswick border at the head of Baie des Chaleurs. It winds eastward along the north shore of the bay, and a hundred miles from Matapedia reaches New Carlisle or Paspebiac Bay. This is the southermost point of the Gaspé peninsula; the railway and the coast now turn northeastward toward Percé and Gaspé village, at mile 202.

The scandal is a tangled story. Suffice it that even with subsidies from Quebec and the Dominion the railway had a hard time getting started. After it did, the contractor and a vital sub-contractor fell out; there was a law case, and into the trouble stepped the Quebec government. The contractor, C. N. Armstrong, kept his wits about him, and in effect bought off the Quebec government with $100,000 of their own $175,000 subsidy. Members of that government used the money mostly for paying off election expenses. But it all got out; the sub-contractor, through Toronto banking connections, initiated an inquiry in the Senate, August 4, 1891, a particularly useful antidote to the McGreevy-Langevin inquiry.[34] Some witnesses refused to appear before the Railway Committee of the Senate; but the inquiry produced enough to damage the Mercier government seriously. As early as August 17, Laurier said that the Baie des Chaleurs affair had lost the Liberal party the political value of their work on McGreevy and Langevin. "Il n'y a plus à espérer maintenant," he added to Beaugrand of *La Patrie*, "de faire de brèches sérieuses dans les rangs de la majorité."[35] Davies of Prince Edward Island was more outspoken. "The cursed luck of these Tories has been with them all thro this Mercier-Pacaud scandal. The fact is it saved the Ottawa Govt."[36]

The Conservative papers in Quebec made all they could from the scandal, and that was a good deal. Even Langevin's scandals had not been quite so brazen. Mercier, now back from Europe, did not deny the transaction; he simply said it had happened in his absence, and even so the money had gone only for election expenses. What was wrong with that? The Lieutenant-Governor of Quebec, A. R. Angers, thought there was quite a bit wrong with it. Angers was a Conservative but he was an honest man, and shocked at misuse of public funds.[37] He insisted, in the absence of an Assembly sitting, on an inquiry by Royal Commission. Mercier wanted to wait and get a committee of the Assembly. Angers stuck to his guns. The Royal Commission was appointed and opened hearings on October 6, 1891. Pacaud appeared on October 20, and at once shouldered most of the blame. Had he not done so the Government would probably have crashed at once. By December 14 the preliminary conclusions of the Commission were sent to Angers.

Angers took it all very seriously. Mercier was acquitted by the Commission of direct connivance, but Angers believed his government was badly, irretrievably damaged, and on December 16, 1891, he was dismissed. He was furious, and threw bitter accusations of partisanship at Angers; "vous recevrez bientôt de M. Abbott votre maître, le prix de votre trahison nationale."[38] Anger's appointment to the Senate and his concurrent entry into the Thompson government, in December, 1892, made Mercier's charge look good, but there was probably nothing in it. His appointment to the Cabinet had been urged before this, both by Macdonald and by Abbott.

Charles de Boucherville, now nearly seventy years old, was asked by Angers to form a government. And he had to have an election, despite the rule in the B.N.A. Act that said there had to be a meeting of Parliament or Assembly first. The election was held on March 8, 1892. The Quebec Conservatives, broken and scattered by *l'affaire Riel*, now happily joined together in *l'affaire Baie des Chaleurs*. Laurier himself was hard put to it to support the Mercier régime publicly. He was fond of Mercier, of Langelier, especially of Pacaud, for they were all part of that wonderful salon of Emilie Lavergne, where the mind could "open its wings, & fly about in the *arabesques* of improvised conversation."[39] But he could not approve of Pacaud, or even stand by him; and the wrench made Laurier's heart ache.[40] He was forced to say in Quebec, on January 18, 1892, that the Baie des Chaleurs scandal was impossible to defend, and was to be condemned out of hand.[41] Things continued to go badly for Mercier in that bitterly cold provincial campaign. "A bas des voleurs!" was the cry. The Church came out against him. The news on March 8 was devastating: the Conservatives took fifty-two of the sixty-five seats. Mercier kept his own seat only with great difficulty. The Liberals were out. The damage done to Quebec by the Mercier scandal cannot be overlooked either. J. S. Hall, the new Treasurer, went over to London in June, 1893 to renegotiate a two-year loan of Fr.20,000,000. It had been floated at four per cent in 1891; the best Hall could get was seven and a half. Admittedly the money market was bad; admittedly the Paris banking houses were out for blood; but the legacy of Mercier's financial dealings brought Quebec close to default in 1893.[42]

For Mercier there was a sterner mandate. He was already ill with diabetes. The Conservative ministry blamed much on Mercier; but he denied to the last that he personally had ever touched a cent of public money. The scene in the Assembly at Quebec the night of December 28, 1893, almost passes belief. After Conservative accusations, Mercier got up with great effort and spoke with vehemence. The Conservatives were his executioners, he said; and walking to the Clerk's table, holding on to it with both hands, he looked directly with his dark blazing eyes at Taillon and the others a few feet away:

> Vous m'avez ruiné, vous avez voulu me déshonorer et vous voulez maintenant piétiner sur mon cadavre: eh bien! ce cadavre, le voici. Regardez-le en face, car il se dresse. . . .[43]

The Assembly was struck dumb. Taillon, without a word, got up and gave his hand to Mercier.

So too, a few months later, did Chapleau, who replaced Angers as Lieutenant-Governor in December, 1892. In September, 1894 he asked Mercier if he could visit him. Against all advice, Mercier agreed. There was a great reconciliation. They talked for twenty minutes about the struggles of the old days. When Mercier's exhaustion enjoined departure, the histrionic but susceptible Chapleau, leaned over Mercier, and in a thick voice said:

> "Nous nous sommes portés mutuellement de rudes coups. Nous avons été injustes l'un pour l'autre. Mais le plus injust n'a pas été toi. Mercier, j'ai voulu venir te demander pardon."
> Et il embrassa son ancien ennemi qui ne put répondre, car il éclatait en sanglots. A l'écart de la chambre, Dansereau, bouleversé, pleurait aussi.
> Il y a tres peu de gens méchants, vraiment méchants.[44]

Mercier died a month later.

Sir John Thompson had been Prime Minister since November, 1892. Abbott had done his duty; he accepted office knowing he was merely filling a gap, but privately he was tired and disgusted within a few months.[45] And it was difficult, as the Montreal *Star* insisted, to reconcile the Canadian public to a Senator prime minister.[46] Thompson could have assumed more authority than he did, but seems to have been punctilious in deferring to Abbott, and it is fair to say that Abbott was equally careful in dealing with Thompson. Thompson did much of the work.

Early in August, 1892, in the middle of the Sault Ste. Marie canal crisis with the United States, Abbott was suddenly taken ill at his office. It was weakening of heart and circulation and peremptory orders came from his doctor for instant stopping of work. Abbott was so weak he could scarce walk around the lawn at his house at St. Anne de Bellevue. Though disposed to carry on till new arrangements were made, he was determined to shirk as much work as he could.[47] He went to London where he decided, on the advice of Macdonald's old doctor, Sir Andrew Clark, that resignation was inevitable. He suggested Thompson for his successor,[48] and on November 24, Thompson was asked to form a Government.

Thompson was now just forty-eight, with seven hard years of parliamentary experience behind him. He had a solid reputation for probity, which even his partial covering for Langevin and Caron had not dissipated, a reputation as solid and portly as he was himself. His wife used to tell him to exercise, but being rowed up the Rideau Canal by young Tupper in the hot Ottawa summer sessions of 1891 and 1892 seems to have been as near to exercise as Thompson ever got. He had sound judgment and a fund of common sense. He also had a useful streak of belligerence. There were fissures in the party that Thompson had not been able to close. He lacked the common touch and any warmth of manner, and in a party so divided, probity was not enough to pull it together. It was not easy to love Thompson, however capable he may have been. With the two vital ingredients of party cement, soft sawder and boodle, Thompson was not very lavish, and he was probably too prone to believe that periodic doses of the latter were a substitute for the former. With Sir John Macdonald it had been the other way round. Not without reason was Thompson called Sir John the Less. Still, whatever his weaknesses, the party utterly depended upon him.

By this time, the Conservatives in Parliament were, on the surface at least, stronger than in March, 1891. They had survived the Langevin scandal, and had since won a remarkable series of bye-elections that had substantially increased their majority. Some fifty-five – the result of an extraordinary series of disputed ones – were held between December 1891 and January 1893. Of these ten Liberal and twenty-eight Conservative seats were unchanged. The Liberals took two from the Conservatives, but the Conservatives won eighteen from the Liberals, thereby increasing by thirty-two the Conservative majority in the House. This accounts for their confidence in 1892. Equally the Liberal party looked woebegone and gloomy. In later years they were to speak of "those dark days of '92" when the party suffered so much in the bye-elections that it was almost as if the devil sat upon their counsels.[49] "The oldest politicians," wrote *The Week's* Ottawa correspondent, "say they cannot account for the reverses which the [Liberal] party have met with in Ontario and elsewhere. . . ."[50]

Much of it was due to Liberal tariff policy, and moreover the Conservatives were also revising theirs. Sir John Macdonald, in April and May, 1891, was already writing Galt about an Imperial preference. Galt's reply, written from a transatlantic steamer off Cork, did not reach Macdonald before he died, but it sketches arrangements that both men seem to have had in mind.

> If you think 33 1/3 % too great a differential duty – make it 25% – it will not affect our Manufacturing interest – whose competition is mainly with the U.S. . . .
> I write this on board, not wishing to lose a day – But once more – I will [?] beg you to act *now*. Do not risk those fatal words "too late" – [51]

Abbott was apparently less sympathetic to the idea of an Imperial preference, and Thompson seems to have been uninterested.

The Canadian government was in fact still bemused with the hope of some sort of reciprocity treaty with the United States. The outcome of the 1891 negotiations had been postponement of the meeting of the Canadian government with Blaine until February 1892, when Thompson and Foster went to Washington to discuss the question. The Canadians were willing to extend reciprocity beyond the natural products of the 1854 treaty, perhaps even to something resembling Brown's draft treaty of 1874, the essence of which it will be recalled, was the willingness of Canada to discriminate against Great Britain. Blaine made this point abundantly clear. Great Britain was, in his view, America's chief competitor in nearly every line of manufactured goods. Americans expected to have "to compete with Canadian manufacturers in Canadian markets on even terms, but with no others." In fact, Blaine was obliging enough to add, the Canadian "tariff must be practically the tariff of the United States of America."[52]

These views quoted boldly by Foster in the Canadian House of Commons were a tremendous blow to the Liberal party. The wind was quite taken out of their sails.[53] In truth the Liberal party was at the end of its five-year flirtation with unrestricted reciprocity. There was no evidence that Cleveland's election in 1892 would make any substantial difference in the American position. W. S. Fielding, in Boston that December, got the impression that reciprocity was a long term hope of the Democratic party, and that the Liberals of Canada might well read in this signal that too much stress had been laid on it.[54] Even the Toronto *Globe* slacked off. Its editorials on reciprocity fell from two or three a day to two or three a month between 1891 and 1894.[55] The Liberal party sadly needed a boost to its morale which had been sagging badly since the beginning of 1892. It also needed to shift its ground on the tariff; and while this might have been managed by party caucus, it was much more useful to have a convention. It was largely John Willison's idea, and it was held in Ottawa in June 1893. Martin Griffin cheerfully remarked, from the precincts of the Parliamentary Library, that since the Ottawa River was in flood, there would be "no lack of opportunity for getting a bath for those who have not indulged since the last convention."[56] Every province but British Columbia was represented; Sifton came from Manitoba, Fielding from Nova Scotia. Mercier did not come; he was as conscious as Laurier of "l'hostilité féroce des Anglais" toward him. Laurier seems to have urged him, in the best interests of the party as a whole, to stay home.[57]

The convention watered down the enthusiastic continentalism that had branded the party for the past five years. Reciprocity was not dropped, but it was proposed within the framework of a policy to develop the natural resources of Canada, and with the frank recognition that the tariff was necessary for revenue. There was the expected condemnation of corruption in government, greater need for economy, a denunciation of the Franchise Act, and a declaration in favour of a plebiscite on prohibition.[58] And more than anything else the convention made it quite clear that Laurier had consolidated his hold on the party leadership, to a degree indeed that few would have thought possible six years before.[59]

Meanwhile, Sir John Thompson was making a significant contribution to the settlement of the Bering Sea controversy in Paris. This delightful essay in American aggrandizement cannot be rehearsed in detail. Suffice it that American seizures of Canadian schooners began in 1886, and after a great deal of indignation was generated in Canada, the arbitration in Paris in February, 1893 virtually accepted the British-Canadian case.

The only question remaining was that of compensation for the illegally seized vessels. This the United States was lamentably reluctant to pay. In 1894-95 authorization to pay damages was rejected by a jingoistic United States Senate. Eventually in 1898, the Americans paid $473,000, as settlement for the Canadian claims.

Another of Thompson's great efforts was not quite so successful, though it can be classed as a near-miss: that of bringing Newfoundland into Confederation. Had he been alive in the spring of 1895 it might have been managed. Newfoundland's relations with Canada since the decisive refusal of 1869 ran the gamut from the peacefulness engendered by distance and disdain, to acerbitic wrangling over fishing rights, or over relations with the United States. And there was some cussedness on both sides. Not all of Newfoundland's political leaders were the most tractable of diplomats or the most scrupulous of politicians. Thrown up by a tough, ignorant, and often pauperized electorate, many of them played political games at a level usually regarded as the diplomatic by other colonies. On the other hand many Canadians were belligerent and exploited their sense of outraged righteousness, like Sir Charles Hibbert Tupper. Mixed with this were the ordinary quarrels of fishermen each with their own interests and illusions. Relations were, in short, difficult on both sides; and complicating all other issues was the unswerving purpose of both Sir John Macdonald and Sir John Thompson to bring Newfoundland into Confederation if at all possible. Newfoundland politicians knew this; much of the tortuousness of diplomatic and political relations stemmed from this undercurrent, itself a reason why some Newfoundlanders, wanting to anchor their boat with an extra-heavy anchor, tried to choose, whenever possible on any issue, the best holding ground.

More obvious issues caused more immediate concern to Newfoundland. The French shore was a perpetual source of wrangling. The channels of communication between St. John's, London, and Paris seem choked with issues raised by the French fishing rights from Port aux Basques to Cape St. John. Was a lobster a fish? The issues that hinged upon that answer bedevilled French-English diplomacy, especially from 1886 to 1891. There was much that was exasperating in this three-cornered quarrel. Two things are obvious: one, the French government was determined to hold on to every right they possessed legally (itself an unanswered, and perhaps unanswerable question), and to insist on rights that they did not have as a measure of insurance; two, the Newfoundland government, by fair means or foul, was determined to acquire full control of her own western shoreline.

What caused the hardening of attitudes on the part of both Newfoundland and France was Newfoundland's Bait Act of 1887 which came into force at the beginning of January 1888. Changes in tastes, markets, and policies had all weakened the sales of Newfoundland dried cod in the main importing centres of southern Europe, Naples, Genoa, Barcelona, Valencia, Malaga. Superior Norwegian processing and French bounties (dating from 1881) on French caught fish exported to Italy and Spain, heavily undercut Newfoundland's market. Moreover the fishing of 1888-89 had not been good. Newfoundland was thus caught in the double squeeze, of shrinking markets and poor supply. It must be remembered here that the Banks of Newfoundland, despite the name, were international. Labrador was partly Newfoundland's, but could not be closed to Nova Scotians or Québecois, and her own coast was alienated partly to France, and partly to the Americans by the Convention of 1818. Not without reason did a weary Lord Salisbury describe Newfoundland as the "sport of historic errors."[60] About one-third of Newfoundland's coast line was shared by treaty arrangements with foreign countries, and the rest was shared by British subjects who were also competitors. What she did have was indispensable fresh bait, particularly in the big bays of the south coast, Fortune Bay and Placentia Bay, near the Banks. Nova Scotia, the Magdalen Islands (Quebec), and St. Pierre and Miquelon (France) had bait, but in nothing like the same profusion.

Thus a hard-pressed colonial government seized upon the one strong card they had to play, saying in effect to France: "We will sell you no more bait whilst you pay a bounty of three quarters of the value of the fish to drive us out of all the open markets of the world."[61] The Act prohibited the catching, sale, and export of bait without a special licence from the Receiver-General of Newfoundland. There was no specific guidance, however, for the Receiver-General's exercise of this vast discretionary power. It was clearly designed to control the French and American acquisition of bait. It was not clear whether the Act included Canadians. Moreover, it gave exceptional powers to stipendiary magistrates, who, without any regular legal procedure, could seize a vessel and its cargo for violation of the Act. And the informer was given half of the proceeds!

The Act exacerbated Newfoundland-Canadian relations. The Newfoundland government protested that Canadians were not included within its purview, that they were on precisely the same footing as Newfoundland fishermen, who had the right to take bait for their own use.[62] This, for the time being worked, although Americans soon complained that Newfoundland was not recognizing the licences issued by Canada to American ships under the *interim* arrangement of 1887.[63]

Then in 1890 came further complications. In April, Robert Bond, the Colonial Secretary in Whiteway's Liberal administration brought into effect, by proclamation, an 1889 revision of the Bait Act. It was brought in without the slightest warning, an action that Sir James Winter, leader of the Conservative opposition, condemned as "utterly, absolutely, wrong unwarranted and foolish, from *every* point of view. . . ."[64] The Bait Act would now apply to all vessels, except those registered in Newfoundland. Furthermore, in addition to a licence, a bond of one thousand dollars was to be posted to guarantee that the bait would be used for the vessel's own fishing needs. The ostensible reason for this was the charge that Canadian ships (and American ships under licence) were buying bait and selling it in St. Pierre and Miquelon to the French. That was true. But so in fact were the Newfoundlanders of the south coast, though Bond denied it. Despite the Imperial government's opinion that the new form of the Bait Act was *intra vires*, Canada protested vigorously.

That summer, while these protests were still echoing, Newfoundland received permission from the Imperial government to negotiate directly with the United States about a reciprocity arrangement. Bond went to Washington, and by the end of October a draft convention had been arranged, giving Amercan vessels the right to purchase bait and trade in Newfoundland waters, in return for free entry of Newfoundland sea products into the United States. Canada, of course, got wind of this almost at once, and proposed promptly that any ratification of a Newfoundland-American arrangement be delayed until a Canadian-American joint commission had considered a reciprocity treaty, a new fishery treaty and the Alaskan boundary, in other words, every outstanding issue between Canada and the United States except for the Bering Sea controversy.[65] Canada's representations to London were successful. The Bond-Blaine convention was blocked, and the Newfoundlanders were now angry. Canada then began the unsuccessful reciprocity talks with Blaine that were to lead directly to the Canadian general election of 1891.[66]

But no rational settlement of the issues raised by the Bait Act was easily possible; Newfoundland was in no mood to give up a lever against Ottawa. It was hinted if Canada withdrew her opposition to the Bond-Blaine convention, the Bait Act would not be enforced against her.[67] But Canada was determined to block the convention, and even added a protective tariff against Newfoundland fish. From November 9 to 15, 1892, a conference was held at Halifax where Whiteway, Bond, and the anti-confederate, A. W. Harvey met with Abbott, Thompson, and Chapleau. No solution emerged to the fisheries and reciprocity issues, though both Whiteway and Bond were interested in finding out Canadian terms for Confederation, if they could do so without committing themselves. So the unhappy impasse went on until 1893, when, after stormy debates in the Newfoundland legislature, the Bait Act was suspended. By this time the whole position of Newfoundland had altered for the worse.

Sir William Whiteway had managed the political leadership of Newfoundland from 1878 to 1897, except for Robert Thorburn's Conservative administration of 1885-89, and a few wild months following the colony's election of 1893. His great project had been the trans-Newfoundland railway, which was begun in 1881; but as time went on Newfoundland's financial position, never very good, became steadily more dangerous. By 1894 the full debt of the colony was nearly $16 million, with a population of only 207,000. Funded debt and other loans were $11.2 million, and $4.6 million had been spent on the railway. The service of this debt took half the annual revenue. Newfoundland revenue derived almost exclusively (95 per cent) from rather steep import duties, which, with an underpaid and understaffed customs service, encouraged a vast amount of smuggling, especially between St. Pierre and the south shore.

The colony's desperate financial plight was apparent as early as 1891 when the Government appealed to London for an Imperial guaranteed loan of £2 million. The Imperial government was willing only upon condition of a general commission of inquiry into all aspects of Newfoundland finance, an inquiry which Whiteway had good reason to avoid. So the colony staggered into the intractable problems of the early nineties, the first of which was the fire of July 8-9, 1892 which levelled three-quarters of the wooden city of St. John's. Abbott and Thompson at once sent a steamer with $10,000 in relief supplies.[68] This gesture, more than anything else, had probably made possible the discussions in Halifax four months later.

Throughout this tangled history there was always the question of Confederation. It came up again in the mid-1880's after fifteen years of quiescence. For the next decade the centre of Confederation agitation in Newfoundland was A. B. Morine, a Nova Scotian who had become a Conservative member in the Newfoundland Assembly, and was editor of the St. John's *Evening Mercury*. Morine, headstrong and enthusiastic, without much diplomatic sense, had little difficulty in alienating the Newfoundland Roman Catholics from both the Conservative party and Confederation. A delegation to Canada was promised in 1888 by the Thorburn Conservative government, after a visit by Sir Charles Tupper in 1887. But it was postponed and Whiteway's victory of 1889, with Catholic support, put a new complexion on matters. Whiteway himself was not averse to considering union, but he was playing a canny game, willing to talk about terms, but in effect only shopping.

A letter in 1891 to Lord Stanley's ADC remarked, "The Colony is drifting into Confederation or bankruptcy as fast as ever it can go."[69]

Another letter, in the St. John's *Evening Herald*, April 10, 1894 echoes the Confederation movement of the 1860's and anticipates 1933:

> Years ago I have heard the old folks say that the children yet unborn would curse the day Responsible Government was granted to this land of ours, and their prophecy has been fulfilled to the very letter. As a Crown colony we were a happy and prosperous people. No want, no starvation . . . no public debt, no political thieves . . . no political or sectarian ranks. . . . After 40 or 45 years of Responsible Government we are burthened with an enormous public debt, an empty exchequer. . . . Each year finds us settling down, deeper and deeper into the mire of debt, poverty and wretchedness. . . .[70]

Within nine months of that letter the Newfoundland crash came. The Commercial Bank failed, with a majority of the directors facing criminal charges. The Union Bank also went; both banks were indebted to the Newfoundland Savings Bank for about $1.5 million, and another $1.5 million of Savings Bank funds were invested in Newfoundland government bonds. This virtually stripped the institution of all its liquid cash, since Newfoundland bonds were unredeemable. The Bank of Montreal stepped in, opened a St. John's branch, and advanced the Government $400,000. Whiteway and the Liberal party had been temporarily out of power in the last critical months when a furious and unpleasant interregnum prevailed. But in January 1895 he was back in office, and at once cabled Sir Mackenzie Bowell for a Confederation conference. It was convened in Ottawa in April.

It failed. It is easy to blame Mackenzie Bowell – and he has been freely blamed – for being niggardly. Newfoundland was desperate, and Bowell knew she was. At the same time, 1894-95 had not been a particularly opulent time for Canadian government revenues either, and Newfoundland's debt looked formidable. The debt allowance would have required nearly $80 a head just to break even. Moreover Bowell's government was as shaky as Whiteway's had been. Therefore, the Canadian government suggested that the British government subsidize the marriage by dowering the penniless bride. The amount suggested made John Bull balk: £1 million sterling, or nearly $5 million. Not without a full investigation of the lady's financial delinquencies would the Lord Commissioners of the Treasury consider such an amount. The lady herself declined to be investigated, and was left with only her pride. Whiteway took an enormous gamble and won: Robert Bond made the rounds in Montreal and London, and got enough money to bail out the Savings Bank and save the Newfoundland government. Luck did the rest. 1895 was a good year for the fishing and the seal hunt; and Newfoundland survived intact. The opportunity for Confederation was lost again. And while the Newfoundlanders returned home from Ottawa, the Canadian government was drifting helplessly toward the vortex of the Manitoba school question.

It is possible that too much has been made of the Manitoba school question. Like the school questions in New Brunswick and Prince Edward Island, the Manitoba school question of 1890-97 (and after) was basically insoluble. The Roman Catholic position and that of the province of Manitoba were logically incompatible. A practical solution – that favourite Anglo-Saxon device – was at best a makeshift and really unacceptable to either side. No doubt it could have been if not solved, at least made reasonable, if there had been reasonableness available in Manitoba. But reasonableness there was not, until six years of war left both sides exhausted and willing to accept, though even then grudgingly, what was basically a shotgun peace. And the Roman Catholics got the worst of it.

What made the Manitoba school question so difficult and so intractable was its effortless metamorphosis from a provincial to a federal problem, made inevitable by the Manitoba Act, and at a subsequent stage by the invocation of the British North America Act. At the national level it was frightful for either party to contemplate. There would always be a few members of Parliament who afforded themselves what in a Canadian context was the luxury of firm political and religious convictions. But broadly speaking both the Conservatives and Liberals feared these difficult, divisive issues, and sought whenever possible to avoid them, or at least to emasculate their effect. There is no better evidence of this than the history of both parties when faced with the Manitoba school question.

That there were political possibilities in the issue no party doubted; but how to realize them without alienating a substantial section of one's party? With forty per cent of the country Roman Catholic, a Protestant coalition was unthinkable. This woolliness on points of principle, for that is what it is, is endemic in large national parties that cross a diversity of religions and races. Broadly speaking, there is no principle of cohesion save that of loyalty to friends, to a leader, to a tradition, or perhaps to some generalized social principle – conservatism perhaps – so diffuse as to be nearly devoid of positive content. So the Manitoba school question was to confound both political parties: the advantage for the Liberals was in being out of office, and thus not needing a policy; the disadvantage to the Conservatives, unhappily, was that they were in office, and had to have a policy, or to seem to have one.

The policy that guided the Conservative party at the beginning was suggested by Edward Blake. He introduced a motion in April 1890 that legality of provincial acts of education be left to the courts to decide.[71] This was accepted by Macdonald; in any case he was in no position to disallow the Manitoba legislation of 1890 even if he had wanted to, not in the face of the Government's acceptance of the Jesuits' Estates Act, even though he would have had much better ground for disallowing the former than the latter. It was Sir John Thompson's determination too that the issue should be settled by law, by constitutional and legal means, not by political means. This was sound. It was wise policy to put the issue to the courts. Unfortunately for the Conservatives, the courts failed to provide an answer. It may have been that the constitution on this point was too nebulous. It may have been that the courts were wrong-headed. But as a policy, it was to end in failure, and finally, after four years, the Manitoba school question came back to roost fairly with the Conservative government, where it had started, but at an extraordinarily difficult time.

It has often been said that McCarthy called this question into existence, with that speech in Portage la Prairie, August 5, 1889. And he has been duly criticized for it. But political storms do not simply arise from intemperate speeches. Unwise and intemperate McCarthy may have been, but there was going to be a Manitoba school question sooner or later. It had been quietly brewing even in the 1870's during the reaction against the ultramontane movement, at the time when the Manitoba Legislative Council was abolished. It had appeared again in the summer of 1889 as a result of the Jesuits' Estates Act agitation, in a speech by James Smart at Souris on August 1. Roman Catholics in Manitoba were a dwindling minority, and the French Roman Catholics even more so. The basic problem was that the Catholic schools were not very efficient, they consumed a disproportionate amount of the school money available,[72] and they seemed increasingly anomalous in a province where a growing proportion of the racial and religious spectrum was wildly heterogenous. Nothing was easier than to make a case against the Catholic schools.

It will be remembered that from 1889 on the Greenway Liberal government of Manitoba badly needed a good political issue. Disallowance had vanished in 1888; the government was rather a seamy enterprise, Greenway with his peccadilloes with maids in local hotels, Martin with his rabid and headlong policies; there was as yet little solid weight in the régime, and it was going badly. A first class issue that would appeal to a substantial majority of the Manitoba voters was just what was needed to keep them in power; and the school questions offered precisely that.[73]

Joseph Martin had been on the platform with McCarthy on August 5, 1889, pledging himself, and thus in some sense the Manitoba government, to the abolition, not only of the separate schools, but also of the official use of French in Manitoba. This made the animus of the Government apparent. But on the abolition of French, Greenway was being pulled, against his will, by Martin. Nevertheless, official use of French went by the board early in 1890, at the session of the Manitoba legislature, and with it went the right of a French Manitoban to trial by a jury at least half French-speaking. The famous Education Acts followed, virtually a copy of the School Act of Ontario with the provision for separate schools omitted. The public school system was in effect a system of non-denominational schools, with religious exercises permitted. It passed, after vigorous speeches against it by Roman Catholics, both French and English-speaking, by a vote of twenty-seven to eight.[74] And it was assented to by the Lieutenant-Governor, John Schultz, on April 1, 1890.

Whether the Acts were constitutional was a mighty question. Disallowance was urged strongly by Archbishop Taché of St. Boniface. His Catholic constituents even urged him to go to Ottawa to make a personal appeal to all Catholic M.P.'s.[75] He refused, chiefly because he was finally persuaded by Sir John Thompson that disallowance in these cases* was an impossible tactic for the government, and that the whole question was far better left to the courts. There was also a political consideration. W. B. Scarth, Macdonald's sturdy right arm in the West, wrote from Winnipeg in January, 1891:

> The feeling among lawyers here is that the decision of the full court here on Monday will be against the Catholics on the Separate School question & the feeling . . . is that if this is the case the disallowance of the Act would hurt instead of helping them, as it would keep Martin their Arch Enemy, as they think, in power for a long time.[76]

Scarth was often right, and he was right again, on both counts. Ottawa was not to disallow the Manitoba School Acts, and on Monday, February 2, 1891, the decision by the full Court of Queen's Bench did go against the Roman Catholics, in *Barrett vs. Winnipeg*.

Dr. John Kelley Barrett had made application in October 1890 before Justice Killam, of Queen's Bench, to quash two assessment bye-laws of the City of Winnipeg, that had been passed in July 1890, pursuant to the School Act. In Killam's view the case turned on Section 22 of the Manitoba Act of 1870, wherein the minorities of Manitoba should continue to have

* Two acts of Manitoba passed in 1890 were however disallowed: the Cattle Quarantine Act and the Public Companies Act.

after 1870 whatever educational rights they had "by law or practice" before 1870. Did "practice" mean anything at all? Killam thought not. "The position of affairs here before the Union was anomalous. Both the extent of the territorial jurisdiction of the Hudson's Bay Company and the nature of its authority had been regarded as very doubtful." Consequently, Killam chose to regard the addition of the words "or practice" as being natural in the absence of any specific law, and thus added nothing to the ordinary sense of the enactment. He found it more difficult to explain the change from the British North America Act to the Manitoba Act on the right of appeal of minorities, which in the British North America Act is given conditionally, and in the Manitoba Act absolutely. Nevertheless, he dismissed Barrett's case with costs.[77] Justice Killam's position is interesting for it anticipates virtually the whole position of the Privy Council. Whether both were right is, of course, another matter.

Barrett then appealed, (with full backing from Ottawa for his costs) to the full Queen's Bench, where it was argued on December 13, 1890. Barrett's counsel was J. S. Ewart, just then well into his remarkable career before the Bar, forty-one years of age, and well connected.* T. W. Taylor, the Chief Justice of Manitoba, agreed broadly with Killam, and by a 2-1 vote Barrett's case was once more thrown out. It then went to the Supreme Court of Canada, where the decision handed down on October 28, 1891, reversed the decision of the Court of Queen's Bench, and by 6-0 sustained Barrett. The decision was written by the Chief Justice of Canada, W. J. Ritchie, who had written the New Brunswick decision eighteen years before. Justice Ritchie denied any application of that decision to Barrett's case. There were no legal rights of which the New Brunswick Roman Catholics had been deprived:[78] but the case in Manitoba was very different. The Dominion Parliament in 1870 knew full well that in Manitoba there were no schools at all established by law. Was the court therefore to read the words "or practice" as having no meaning whatever?

> It is clear that at the time of the passing of the Manitoba Act no class of persons had by law any rights or privileges secured to them; so if we reject the words "or practice" as meaningless or inoperative we shall be practically expunging the whole of the restrictive clause from the statute. I know of no rule of construction to justify such a proceeding. . . . It is a settled canon of construction that no clause, sentence or word, shall be construed superfluous, void or insignificant if it can be prevented. . . . What absurdity, inconsistency, injustice, or contradiction is there in giving the words "or practice" a literal construction?. . . If the literal meaning is not to prevail I have yet to hear what other meaning is to be attached to the words "or practice."[79]

* Mowat's nephew by marriage. Oliver Mowat's wife was an Ewart.

These were strong words, cogent words, and his fellow judges concurred.

It was at this point that the Logan case was deliberately launched by the province of Manitoba to show the logical conclusion of the Supreme Court decision vis-à-vis an apparently unaggrieved minority, the Anglicans. The Manitoba Court of Queen's Bench now felt obliged to accept the Supreme Court's decision in Barrett, and upheld Logan against the City of Winnipeg. Both *Barrett vs. Winnipeg* and *Logan vs. Winnipeg* then went to the Privy Council where judgment was handed down on July 30, 1892. On the principle that "evidently the word 'practice' is not to be construed as equivalent to 'custom having the force of law,'" they threw out Barrett's contention. His appeal, and Logan's, were dismissed, with costs.[80]

This decision is one of the more curious in the tortured history of Privy Council decisions about Canadian law. One expected that in Manitoba the judges, subject to that kind of "hydraulic pressure before which even well-settled principles of law will bend,"[81] would declare for the obvious view of the majority of Manitobans. The Privy Council decision, after the unanimous one of the Supreme Court of Canada, can best be explained upon grounds of a strong *a priori* prejudice against separate schools, a prejudice which, it is fair to say, the clever appeal in *Logan vs. Winnipeg* did much to crystalize.[82] It is easy however, to read too much into "practice," and it may be that the Manitoba Act of 1870 simply did not translate into effective legislation what Parliament wanted. Edward Blake, no mean authority, seems to have been of the private opinion that those who wanted separate schools in Manitoba had not a legal leg to stand on.[83]

In any event, the Privy Council decision put the fat in the fire. Almost at once Manitoba Roman Catholics began to talk of remedial legislation based upon subsections 2 and 3 of Section 22 of the Manitoba Act. In Winnipeg the feeling against any remedial legislation was intense. Even Hugh John Macdonald was opposed. A. W. Ross, in writing Sir John Thompson in August 1892, made an accurate prediction. "The question will – I am satisfied [–] prove to be one of the very worst with which we have been compelled to deal in the House of Commons."[84] Sam Hughes, from his editorial desk in Lindsay, damned freely all clerics, Protestant and Catholic alike, and thought religion ought to be out of the schools altogether. But one thing he was certain of – he was always certain of everything – remedial legislation was impossible.

> Sir John, believe me from the bottom of my heart. It would never do. Even if the Grand Orange Lodge of Canada with all its masters and Chief Officers were to hold the Premiership and Cabinet positions, the public would not for one hour tolerate it. Mark what I tell you, it is the truth. Why even roman catholic *citizens*, not churchmen, do not want it.[85]

By the late summer of 1892 Roman Catholics and Protestants in Manitoba had moved so far apart as to lose any point of contact. The debate was out of the courts and into the papers. The legal question amplified, and now moved over to the British North America Act, Section 93, subsection 3, which said that where a separate school system was established *after* the union – the case in Manitoba – and such separate school system were destroyed, then would an appeal lie to the Governor General in Council. This new issue was broached in Parliament in March, 1893. On March 6, Israël Tarte moved an amendment going into Supply, that the House of Commons disapproved of the Government's handling of the Manitoba school question. Laurier accused the Government of having neither courage nor convictions. But the Government had already made its decision. It referred to the Supreme Court six questions, later known as the Brophy case; these turned upon whether an appeal did lie to the federal government under Section 93, subsection 3, and whether, if it did, the federal government had the power to make remedial legislation. Judgment was handed down by the Supreme Court of Canada on February 20, 1894, deciding all six questions by a narrow vote of 3-2 in the negative, in effect that no appeal either under the British North America Act or the Manitoba Act lay to the Ottawa government. Here the Supreme Court of Canada missed the firm grasp of Chief Justice Ritchie, who had died in September 1892. Chief Justice Strong was able to carry only two of his colleagues with him, in an awkward and curious decision. The six questions were then appealed to the Privy Council, under the name *Brophy vs. Attorney-General of Manitoba,* where the argument opened on December 11, 1894.

Then, the day after the argument began at the Privy Council in the Brophy case, Sir John Thompson died suddenly at Windsor Castle, December 12, 1894. The 1894 session had been a long, hard one, beginning in March, and going on into July. Thompson had gone to England late in October, partly for a rest, partly to be sworn in as a member of the Imperial Privy Council. He had already been warned that symptoms of heart disease were apparent, and was told to give up work entirely and spend the winter in a warm climate. He compromised by promising to cut down his work, and take a holiday in England and the Continent. This he duly did in November, in the process climbing all the steps to the top of St. Peter's, Rome. On his return to London he was immersed in the copyright question with the Colonial Secretary and then, with his old colleague and enemy, Sir Charles Tupper, had gone down to Windsor for his installation on December 12. There at one-thirty in the afternoon he was sworn in by the Queen. All went well until at lunch with some Cabinet members he complained of feeling faint. He was helped from the room, and after taking a bit of brandy and water recovered and insisted on going back to the table. The Queen's doctor was put beside him. Thompson complained that he had been suffering from chest pain for some time; the doctor turned away for a minute and when he looked again Thompson was insensible. He never moved or breathed again.

It is a measure of Thompson's probity in political life that his estate amounted to only $9,700; with a wife and five children, one of them a cripple, it meant also that his family were left virtually penniless. Among the most devastated by Thompson's sudden death were the Aberdeens. The new Governor General and his wife had come to Canada in September 1893, and almost from the beginning had taken up Thompson. He appealed to them both. His dignity was only the outward and visible sign of the man within, not put on as seeming to befit his station. What impressed Lady Aberdeen was "the combination of self control and accurate sound judgment."[86]

Thompson's funeral took place in Halifax, Thursday, January 3, 1895. He was buried with more pomp than he (or his widow) would have liked, in the Catholic cemetery a few blocks from where his wife had virtually pushed him from his home to take his election as Minister of Justice, not ten years before.[87] The Conservative government of Canada followed in the funeral train. Its motto might well have been an aphorism of Foster's, uttered the day the news of Thompson's death reached Ottawa. "Here we are, twelve of us, and every one of us as bad, or as good as the other – Jack is good as his master."[88] An interesting and apt comment; and within four weeks of Thompson's funeral came the Privy Council decision in the Brophy case, handing to a deeply divided, perplexed, and virtually leaderless Government, that awful poisoned chalice – action.

CHAPTER 13

The Fall of the Conservative Government 1895-1896

Few of the knights named to serve the Queen on New Year's Day, 1895 could have been more pleased than the pompous, ponderous, decent old newspaperman from Belleville, Ontario, who now rejoiced in the rotund appelation of Sir Mackenzie Bowell. He was seventy-two, ripe with whiskers, politics and vanity. He had represented Hastings County since 1867, had served faithfully as Minister of Customs from 1878 until he was given a minor portfolio and shipped thankfully up to the Senate by Sir John Thompson at the end of 1892. He was headed for the pasture when Thompson died. Bowell was not a bad man, but his talent for leadership was non-existent. He believed, of course, that he could follow the precepts of Macdonald; but stupidity usually imitates the worst.[1] Bowell could not be fastened down to anything, because he found it difficult to seize the point of a policy. So he was accused of shuffling or downright evasion, often by his colleagues, and not infrequently by the Governor General, all of which hurt him, because he was often unaware he was doing either. He was, in short, a little man in a big place, fatuous, petty, and on important matters untrustworthy.

How he came to be chosen Prime Minister is a curious comment on the characters of the Governor General, Lord Aberdeen, and, to a degree, that of Lady Aberdeen. Lord Aberdeen was a gentle soul, self-effacing, retiring, adaptable, tolerant, and by no means unintelligent. He had some industry but woefully little power of concentration.[2] That his wife supplied in abundance. She was a die-hard Liberal, passionate, energetic, and aggressive, with a confident, critical mind, the kind of woman who is apt in some circumstances to make a political martyr of her husband. She interpreted her duty as not so much to provide a serene private life for her husband – there was evidence that it was anything but serene – but rather to act as one who "thought and fought for him in all his affairs."[3] There is much peril in such a view. One is reminded of the decisions of Bishop Proudie in *Barchester Towers* that could be altered between bedtime and breakfast.

Lord Aberdeen seems to have been disposed to Bowell partly because he was the acting Premier. But it is fair to add that there was no clear choice among Thompson's cabinet. George Foster was able enough, but waspish and lacking the capacity to draw support. John Haggart, Minister of Railways, was a strong man in the House, partly because he was a good man at getting campaign funds. But he was lazy, and had developed a penchant for plump and available lady typists, unfortunate since it was all too often public knowledge. Foster would not serve under Haggart and *vice versa*. Sir Charles Hibbert Tupper, the Minister of Justice, was too self-willed and headstrong. T. M. Daly, perhaps the ablest man in the Government, was still unknown, having been Minister of the Interior only since 1892; Caron was discredited; Ouimet was considered hopeless; Angers was tired and old; W. B. Ives was more a liability than an asset; N. C. Wallace, Controller of Customs, was not in the Cabinet because of his strong Orange connections, and was ruled out as Premier for the same reason. Who was left? Old Sir Charles Tupper, in London, England.

In Joseph Pope's view, had Sir Charles been called the Conservative government might have been saved.[4] But Thompson's influence, and that of the strong-minded women behind the scenes who so admired him, made this choice difficult. Lady Thompson burst out to Lady Aberdeen, the day after Thompson's death, "if *he* [Sir Charles Tupper] were sent for, I should look upon it as an insult to my husband's memory. . . ." Lady Aberdeen assured her that Lord Aberdeen would never, if he could help it, allow Sir Charles Tupper back into Canadian politics.[5] The prejudice Lord Aberdeen had imbibed against old Tupper from Sir John Thompson had ample domestic reinforcement. Apparently no one in the Government, barring presumably his son, actively urged old Sir Charles upon an uncertain and weak Governor General. And if ever there were a case for a Governor General making up his own mind, it was now.

So Mackenzie Bowell was asked to form a government the day after Thompson died. It was entirely characteristic that his first action was to continue all but Sir John Carling of the old Cabinet in office. Including the three that were not of the Cabinet but in the Ministry (an innovation of Thompson's), eleven members of the Ministry kept the same portfolios they had had before. Three new ministers were added: A. R. Dickey, M.P. Cumberland, the son of Senator R. B. Dickey; Dr. W. H. Montague, M.P. Haldimand; and Senator Donald Ferguson of Prince Edward Island.

Within this Ministry there were at least four discernible factions: the French Canadians, Angers, Caron, and Ouimet, including at times John Costigan, the Irish Catholic representative; the Protestants, who comprised most of the Ontario ministers, John Haggart, J. C. Patterson, J. F. Wood, and N. C. Wallace, the latter two being outside the Cabinet; the trimmers, Bowell himself, W. B. Ives, and T. M. Daly (the only capable trimmer); and the tough-minded and resolute, with no sectarian axe to grind, G. E. Foster and C. H. Tupper. Some of these groups were split internally. Angers was an ultramontane; Ouimet was ultra-Ouimet, closer to Chapleau, by then Lieutenant-Governor of Quebec. Altogether it was, as Cartwright observed at Sarnia in March 1895, a menagerie, "birds and beasts, saints and sinners, orange and green, brewers and distillers and apostles of all sorts." And lest the two most energetic members of the menagerie escape, he singled them out for special attention. The late nineteenth century, said Cartwright (one can almost hear that stentorian voice), "is an age of sham and cram." Foster exhibited the latter. As for Charles Hibbert Tupper, he

> is a perfectly beautiful illustration of the great doctrine of heredity. . . . As for blaming Sir Hibbert Tupper for his hereditary preference for juicy fictions to dry facts, sir, I would as soon think of censuring an active and industrious young wolf for preferring to make his dinner off a lamb instead of a hay stack. . . . (Laughter.)
>
> He possesses no digestive apparatus suitable for the assimilation of dull, dry facts, and so if he is to speak at all he must be allowed a copious use of his imagination, and to do him justice I have never known it to fail him yet. (Laughter.)
>
> Take them for all and all, Mr. Foster and Sir Hibbert Tupper are a very pretty pair. . . .
>
> Two worthies in two neighbor countries born,
> New Brunswick and Nova Scotia did adorn;
> In cunning claptrap none the first surpassed,
> For cool effrontery few matched the last.[6]

One vital force missing from the government was, of course, D'Alton McCarthy. McCarthy was not exactly ultra-Protestant. Indeed, he distrusted the Orange Order, hence his bitter feud with N. C. Wallace. He distrusted the Protestant Protective Association (P.P.A.), a nativist American import that complicated Ontario and Dominion politics from 1892 to about 1896. Both groups were sufficiently bigoted and intolerant as to be more of a liability to his cause than an asset.[7] No, McCarthy's quarrel with Roman Catholicism was not over religion as such, but over its political and social ramifications. It would not stay put in what McCarthy regarded as its proper place, that is, as a religious solace to its adherents. He considered it mediaeval in its exclusiveness and in its claims upon political society. This needs to be emphasized, because French Canadians and Irish Catholics found it difficult to sort McCarthy out, equating him freely with Orangemen and P.P.A.'s. He was too intellectually self-contained, too austere, to be either.

His other quarrel was with the French language and what it meant for Canada. If anything his attitude had grown tougher since 1889:

> It would have been far better for me to have clung to the old party. I dare say I might have been Premier today. As it is, I suppose I never will be Premier, and may never hold office. . . .

> I stand here as an example, a warning to any man raising his voice in Parliament in opposition to the French-Canadian influences at Ottawa.[8]

In dealing with the Manitoba question the Liberal party's only advantage – no small one – was that it was in opposition and did not need to have a policy; otherwise, the Manitoba school question was as devastating for them as for the Conservatives. More so: their leader was, at least ostensibly, a Roman Catholic relying for much of his expectations upon substantial support from a Catholic province. Anything that might blight these hopes he regarded with no little suspicion. The position of Manitoba's Liberal government was quite clear. They would defend their new school system *coûte que coûte*; they would refuse concessions in order to promote the demise of a Conservative government at Ottawa. But as for making concessions to further the prospect of a Liberal government in Ottawa, that was probably impossible. J. D. Cameron, Manitoba's Provincial Secretary, told Willison frankly that his government was in no position to make any concessions. If Greenway did, he would be forced out of power by those who were prepared to fight it out.[9] Having called out the armies of resistance, Greenway could no longer get them home again, and the school system as a whole Manitobans would insist on retaining in principle. Laurier in this difficulty reached desperately for expedients. His speech at Massey Hall, February 5, 1895, suggests one. The Manitoba school question, he said, was "a question of fact and nothing else." He argued, as he had already done in Parliament, that if the Manitoba school system imposed Protestant schools, disguised as non-sectarian, upon Manitoba Roman Catholics, then that system was iniquitous. As to what the Liberal party would actually do, he was delightfully vague. "If the answer of the Government is just I will support them, if not I won't."[10]

Laurier had not much alternative, and he continued to be reluctant well into 1895 to abandon the Manitoba Roman Catholics. His long and anguished correspondence with John Willison makes this abundantly clear. Willison and the *Globe* were committed to the idea of provincial rights. Laurier wrote:

> Let me ask you: can there be here a question of Provincial Rights? How can this be pretended? . . . How is it possible to talk of provincial rights, when by the very letter of the constitution, jurisdiction is given to the Federal authorities to review & over-ride provincial legislation?
> What is the use of giving an appeal to the minority, if the appeal is only to be denied? . . .
> Let us bring back public opinion to the tariff.[11]

Laurier was supported in his view, not only by French-Canadian Liberals, but by David Mills[12] and Mowat, the latter having particular reason to be grateful for Roman Catholic support in Ontario. Moreover the Roman

Catholic bishops were vitally interested in Laurier's position, none more than Archbishop Adélard Langevin, who succeeded Alexandre Taché upon the latter's death early in 1895. Bishop Langevin had an interview with Laurier in May that year and gained the impression that Laurier's views were similar to his own. (This was possible in interviews with Laurier.) But even Laurier had to hedge on the question of the approval of the Remedial Order. Archbishop Langevin felt very strongly:

> A mon humble avis encore, quiconque infirme l'ordre-en-conseil nous fait un tort immense. . . .J'ai beaucoup regretté que vous n'ayez encore rien dit pour revendiquer nos droits et pour appuyer l'ordre-en-conseil.[13]

Laurier's reply is firm. "Ici je me permettrai de différer complètement d'avec Votre Grandeur. Je considère cet ordre-en-conseil aussi faible de fond, que violent de forme."[14]

The Remedial Order was the result of an anguished debate within the Conservative government that followed the Privy Council decision in the Brophy case. There were those who argued – D'Alton McCarthy and some Ontario Conservatives – that the Privy Council decision did not enjoin action upon the Conservative government. But the Government as a whole disagreed. Action was required. But what action was there to be, when should it be implemented, and when ought there to be a general election? For there had to be an election. It was now four years since the last one, and the necessary time in which to manoeuvre a controversial policy was none too long. Approval for a dissolution being secured from the Governor General in mid-February, 1895, the Government then decided to hear the appeal from the Roman Catholic minority of Manitoba, as the Manitoba Act and the British North America Act indicated.

The Cabinet had constituted itself as a judicial tribunal, a sort of Canadian Privy Council, for this purpose. The hearings concluded on March 7, and on March 19, Sir Charles Hibbert Tupper, as Minister of Justice, reported to Cabinet in favour of ordering Manitoba to restore Roman Catholic schools' rights, failure to do so authorizing, indeed requiring, the Dominion Parliament itself to act. The Remedial Order, as an Order in Council, was issued two days later authorized by the Governor General and twelve members of the Cabinet.[15] The appeal of the Manitoba minority was allowed. The Governor General in Council declared that "it seems requisite that the system of education (since 1890) . . . shall be supplemented by a Provincial Act or Acts which will restore to the Roman Catholic minority the said rights and privileges. . . ."[16]

In the meantime the Government had already agreed, apparently with the approval of a majority of the parliamentary caucus[17] that it would go to the country in May 1895. But again the Government hesitated. Sir Mackenzie himself, and some of the English-speaking ministers, thoroughly disliked the prospect of the plunge into that chilly water. Sir Charles Hibbert Tupper was, however, convinced that nothing could be gained by postponing a general election. Assuming that Manitoba would refuse to accept the Remedial Order, it would be wrong to legislate on the question without a popular mandate of approval. The Cabinet was, in his view, so hopelessly split that they could agree on nothing except upon doing nothing. "... you are like Micawber," he wrote to Daly, "– and rely on time."[18] Tupper resigned, March 21, 1895.[19]

There was probably more involved in dissolution than the Manitoba school question, vital though that was. One of Macdonald's old operating rules had been, that if a district were intractable, it could be made less so by putting a railway into it, or giving an existing railway a subsidy. The Hudson Bay Railway, or the Winnipeg Great Northern Railway, to give it its new title, had built all of forty miles on its way north to Churchill, and in March 1895, the Bowell Cabinet agreed by Order in Council to ask Parliament for a $2.5 million loan.[20] It was understood, so J. D. Edgar told Laurier (and Edgar often had access to good information) that ten per cent of the loan was to be set aside as Conservative election funds, besides a *pot-au-vin* for Caron.[21] In the House Laurier asked persistently for a copy of the Order in Council, but it was not forthcoming.[22] Then in the last days of the 1895 session, by use of the revived charter of a defunct company,* and a subsidy to the Winnipeg Great Northern that was transferable, the Government achieved much the same thing. With malodorous haste, the Winnipeg Great Northern Bill was put through the Commons, all three readings on the last day before prorogation and, with some difficulty through the Senate.

Great pressure was put upon Charles Hibbert Tupper to reconsider his decision, pressure in which both the Governor General and his wife joined in exercising, together with Sir Donald Smith and Senator George Drummond, vice-president of the Bank of Montreal and head of Canada Sugar Refining.[23] Tupper did agree to rejoin the Government, at the end of March 1895. Under the new arrangement, the Government would meet Parliament again in 1896, declare in favour of remedial legislation if it were still necessary, and then appeal to the country in a general election. Parliament opened three weeks later, to sit until July 22, with George Foster as leader of the House of Commons.

In the meantime the Remedial Order was solemnly read to the Manitoba legislature at the end of March, after which that body adjourned for a leisurely three months.

When the Governor General invited Greenway and Sifton to Ottawa in May, they were polite, but they were resolute. "We shall be compelled,"

* This company, the Lake Manitoba Railway, and Canal Company, became the basis of Mackenzie and Mann's success with the Canadian Northern.

wrote Greenway to Lord Aberdeen, "to discuss the matter upon the understanding that the discussion does not of itself admit of an intention to compromise." Nor would better terms help; "it will no doubt occur to Your Excellency that to adopt Sir Mackenzie's suggestion would in all probability lead to a mis-conception of the motives of both parties."[24] No doubt it would. Greenway and Sifton also refused to meet any of the Dominion ministers. Archbishop Langevin, also in Ottawa at the time, was just as stubborn, making "unwise fighting speeches, exhorting his listeners not to give way an inch."[25] All returned to Manitoba with matters where they were before, if anything with positions more solidly entrenched. Not that the Manitoba Liberals and the federal Liberals were in agreement. Greenway and Sifton were clearly still nettled by the attitude of some prominent Liberals, including Laurier and Mills. Greenway wrote to Charlton,

> I like the ring of your letter, but it is very different from some that I have received from some of your prominent friends whom I should have expected would have shared in the views which you express. We are doing everything we can to keep this important matter in proper shape. . . .[26]

Thus Manitoba went her own way, with the knowledge of increasing support from Ontario and from both sides of politics.

The Manitoba legislature met again on June 13, and a few days later announced the answer to the Remedial Order. It was clever, and bore the mark of Clifford Sifton and his long talks with D'Alton McCarthy.* Any modification of the school system would produce not just one set of separate schools but several. Moreover, there was not enough information available to the Dominion government when the Remedial Order was issued. Manitoba offered to "cheerfully assist in affording the most complete information available." If however, the Dominion government insisted on legislating for Manitoba schools, how would they administer such legislation?

However worded, there was little basis for compromise in the reply, except on that treacherous middle ground Manitoba so invitingly suggested: more information. The Dominion government in desperation decided to take a step in that direction. A majority in the Cabinet felt that the reply did not preclude further negotiations, a position which suited the English Protestants nicely, and which even the English-speaking Catholics, Sir Frank Smith, and John Costigan, accepted.[27] The Cabinet decided on the iron hand in the velvet glove. It would issue a statement indicating that a remedial bill would be passed in the next session of Parliament unless a settlement were reached in the meantime. But it also spoke of friendly negotiations that might very well obviate the necessity of remedial legislation at all.

* On June 28, 1895, Sifton was sent a bill for $2100 for McCarthy's services in connection with the Manitoba school question. (PAM, Sifton Papers.)

Had such negotiations been possible all would doubtless have been well. It was precisely this that Laurier achieved in 1896-97. But it was not possible. The Manitoba Liberal government were not really prepared to accept anything from an Ottawa Conservative government but complete surrender, and Manitoba now had Ottawa nearly on the ropes. As Lady Aberdeen remarked in her journal:

> It is rumoured that they [the Manitoba government] would be found more tractable if their own party with M. Laurier at its head were to be returned to power in the Dominion Government. Such is the prevailing idea. Whether there is any foundation for it remains to be seen. Certain it is that the leaders of the Liberal party seem very confident of being able to deal with the question satisfactorily, & that they are equally determined not to be drawn into announcing their policy whilst in Opposition.[28]

All this Senator Réal-Auguste Angers, Minister of Agriculture, knew perfectly well. He believed that Manitoba would do absolutely nothing, but would continue to hold out false hopes for a negotiated settlement. Many of the French Canadians felt the same. In Angers' view, the Government, if it was sincere about remedial legislation, was putting it off far too long. There was not enough time between January 1896 and expiry of Parliament in April to formulate and pass such a momentous piece of legislation. Angers was clear and adamant, and he resigned on July 9, 1895. With him went the other two French-Canadian ministers, Ouimet and Caron. Dejectedly Bowell told Lord Aberdeen on July 10, that whips had reported the government would be in a minority of seventeen the moment the French-Canadian ministers' resignations were effective.[29] But at the last moment, Caron and Ouimet withdrew their resignations, on the ostensible ground that the six-month delay was not tantamount to postponement. Laurier remarked to an amused House that the kittens had come back for the cream.[30]

Nevertheless the Liberals were not very outspoken. They were remarkably evasive. "The Grit party is dumb in this House," said Amyot, M.P. Bellechasse, with perfect justice.[31] Charles Hibbert Tupper said the same.

> . . . though he [Laurier] has spoken at a crisis in Canada's history, not for the second time . . . but dozens of times, neither the House of Commons nor the people of Canada know where he stands upon the Manitoba school today.[32]

Laurier had however devised, if not a policy, at least a graphic way of describing his lack of one. In a speech at Morrisburg, Ontario on October 8, he compared himself to the Duke of Wellington, behind the lines of Torres Vedras awaiting his opportunity to strike. His happier hit, in the same speech, about the contest between the north wind and the sun in Aesop's fables, is still worth quoting:

> They [the Government] have blown and raged, and threatened, but the more they have threatened and raged and blown the more that man Greenway has stuck to his coat. (Laughter and applause.) The Government are very windy. If it were in my power, and if I had the responsibility, I would try the sunny way.[33]

It was at about this point that the cabal against Bowell began to form. No one had been found to replace Angers. Chapleau would not come. The Jacques Cartier bye-election, November 30, made Bowell's difficulty worse. Désiré Girouard, Conservative member for Jacques Cartier since 1878, was made Supreme Court Judge in September, 1895. The bye-election was fought with clerical support for the Government.* Caron had urged Archbishop Langevin that if Jacques Cartier were lost, the position of all the Roman Catholic members of the Cabinet would be weakened.[34] Laurier, on the other hand, was confident; he believed that "were elections to come to-morrow, we would sweep everything in Quebec."[35] The election was fought straight upon the school question, between Liberal policy and Conservative policy, that is, between the velvet glove apparently without an iron hand, and the velvet glove apparently with one. And the Government lost.

By the end of the year, when the bye-election in Montreal Centre was fought on December 27, the Government's policy had become sharper. Clarke Wallace, the great anti-remedialist in the Ministry, resigned December 14. On December 20 Manitoba made it perfectly clear that only a full-scale investigation could answer for what the Bowell government called "friendly negotiations." There would be no substantial amendments to the school acts. A Manitoba provincial election, called for January, 1896, was to give resounding support to the Greenway government. For the Bowell government there was neither time nor desire for a full-scale investigation. Now everything depended upon the support of the Church, and here Quebec was going to be vital. Laurier was made more desperate by this increase in remedial pressure. Conservative papers in Quebec were already denouncing him as a traitor. He wrote to Willison in mid-December, "I am in terror as to this province. . . . What else than disasters am I to expect here?"[36] He was rather more cheerful with the news of the Government's defeat in Montreal Centre, but he warned that that victory came not because his policy of conciliation was more popular than the Government's, but because

> the Government by their bungling and double-dealing have created an impression of distrust, which no efforts on their part have yet been able to dispel.[37]

* The Government had also lost Antigonish in April, 1895, despite clerical support. There the Liberal was strong for remedial action, and so Catholic Liberals had no difficulty voting Liberal.

It was for reasons of this kind that the conspiracy against Bowell within the Government grew. As early as November, J. F. Wood, the Controller of Inland Revenue, told a friend that some morning Bowell would wake up to find the resignations of all his ministers on his desk. Haggart and Foster were working to bring him down.[38] Charles Hibbert Tupper was playing his own game, in private touch with Lady Aberdeen, and desperately uneasy about "a leader who does not lead! The school subject must soon be dealt with. Why we are waiting I do not know, but everything seems to be waiting."[39] Waiting to see if Chapleau would come, waiting to see if Chief Justice Meredith would come, waiting, waiting. And neither man would come, as it turned out.

By now Bowell was finding it impossible to get anyone from Quebec. Ouimet and Caron had no more influence. Bowell had got himself into the position where every prominent man knew about his efforts, and wanted nothing to do with him. Late in November his colleagues went to him in a body (all but two perhaps, Ouimet and Caron) and told him that unless the Government were strengthened it was inadvisable to meet Parliament or people. As Foster tells it,

> He promised to go to work. He did in his way. He peddled Cab. positions all about Quebec – everybody seeing what he was doing – getting a refusal each time & so lowering the credit of his Cabinet stock.[40]

The empty Quebec portfolio still remained, as J. T. Saywell put it, "the symbol of his incompetence."[41] He tried. He sent Father Lacombe to offer the portfolio to Senator Rodrigue Masson, who refused on grounds of bad health. That was on December 30. The Cabinet pressed him again the next day. Bowell said he had every hope of getting a good man, that it was "only a question of hours."[42] Desjardins promised an answer New Year's Day. The answer was no. The next day, Thursday, January 2, 1896, Parliament opened, and with it the announcement of the introduction of remedial legislation.

By this time old Sir Charles Tupper had been on the Ottawa scene for two weeks. Late in November Bowell had invited him back ostensibly on public business, to discuss a projected fast line of transatlantic steamers. Old Tupper gave a shrewd assessment to his son. "I still think Laurier will go against remedial legislation this coming session and that you will be defeated, but I may be wrong."[43] He arrived in Ottawa on December 15, and became at once, with what reluctance it is impossible to know, the prospective saviour of the party.

Within twenty-four hours of the opening of Parliament, it had to be adjourned until Tuesday, January 7. Bowell had a major Cabinet revolt on his hands. Seven members resigned, and urged the Governor General replace

Bowell by old Sir Charles Tupper.* Even T. M. Daly, though he did not resign, urged Bowell to give way. To add to dissatisfaction, there was also a quarrel between Haggart and Ouimet, and a bitter one between Caron and Montague, over anonymous letters in the papers, allegedly from Dr. Montague, maligning Caron.[44] And the quarrels within the Cabinet had been transferred to the ranks of the party. There was still that vacant Quebec portfolio. The Protestants in the Government now feared, from the bye-elections in Quebec, that in a general election they would be unable to recoup there the losses they anticipated in the English-speaking provinces.[45] "To go to business with the confession that from Quebec – on a main question of policy – we could get no one to enter the Cabinet would have [been] so ruinous that we would have received a death blow to our prestige." The story of what happened next is also told in Foster's words:

> Then commenced the fun. B.[owell] first told two of us that he would resign at once. Then Ouimet, Caron & Costigan, got around him, & knowing that their fortunes depended on it, advised fight. So he fought. He went to the G.G. with his version – on it the G.G. concluded that we were quite in the wrong – especially in sending in our resignations at the time we did &c. &c. B. told him that our resignations were the first intimations he had that we would not go to business without a complete cabinet. We found out this state of things at Govt. House – sent in a full statement & asked leave to state fully our position before the House. This opened the eyes of the G.G. and he came around to a full appreciation of the facts of the case. – Bowell was then told that he must either reform or resign if he failed to do so. He peddled Cab. positions to Tom, Dick and Harry – and in the end found not one man of respectable attainments who would go in with him.[46]

This statement is pretty accurate. It overlooks, however, the apparently successful attempts on the part of the rebel group to warn off prospective cabinet appointees by watching the railway stations and hotels for arrivals.[47] By January 6 as the Toronto *Globe* said, "The blackened ruins of the Cabinet edifice are still smoking from the effect of the political explosion. Premier Bowell, the struggling proprietor, has been all day going round with tools in hand trying to repair it."[48] However, the Governor General's pull finally filled the French vacancy. Senator Desjardins was now willing and on January 14 secured a formal promise from Bowell that the remedial bill would be brought down with no major concessions to its principles permitted to the rebels as the price for their return.

Foster continues:

> The proposition was then made by the Party – which remained remarkably steady all through – that a re-organization take place on certain lines – run

* The seven were, Foster. C. H. Tupper, Dickey, Ives, Wood, Haggart and Montague.

> the session through & that then a new head & a Govt should take charge & go to the Country. B. objected to me, Haggart & Montague. But at last he had to give in & here we are. The outcome is the best possible – faction is avoided [!], & the future provided for.
> As to the action of the "Rump" [*i.e.* those who stuck with Bowell] – no words can characterize. They took three of our staunch remedialists from the Commons & opened constituencies which are doubtful. They superannuated & apptd. right & left & raised complications innumerable. . . .[49]

The rump consisted of Bowell, Daly, Costigan, Smith, Caron, Ouimet, and Senator Ferguson. Most of them supported the rebels up to the resignation of the seven, then sustained Bowell, until the Conservative ship was nearly on its beam ends. Bowell's refusal to take back Foster, Haggart and Montague was nearly the end. Only the scarcely veiled threat of the Governor General to call upon Laurier forced Bowell into accepting the "traitors" back.

So the Conservative ship slowly righted itself, its rigging awry, its decks awash, its hull leaky, but nevertheless afloat, and with some sail still usable. The captain was discredited, though he was still nominally captain; but there was to be a new first mate. Old Sir Charles Tupper, that grizzled sailor, was to be leader in the Commons, and would take over as captain when the session was over.

Some of this time Parliament was sitting.[50] Bowell was even observed on January 7, as visitor from the Senate, talking to Liberals and pointing to the "nest of traitors" on the Government side. "Come over to us," said one cheerful Liberal, "and you find no treachery here."[51] With all of this Sir Richard Cartwright, with that magisterial sarcasm of his, made tremendous sport:

> . . . we are in the presence of the Royal Ottawa Low Comedy Troupe, and we should be grateful to them for the great benefit they have done us as a party, and for the amusement they have afforded. . . . What we have been listening to after all has been a series of rehearsals. We had number one rehearsal, for I can hardly count the episode of the member for Pictou (Sir Chas. H. Tupper) [in March, 1895] as one; . . . a sort of undress rehearsal in July, when three went out, one of whom being a person of some honour and respect [Angers] stayed out. (Laughter.) Then we have lately had what I call a full dress rehearsal, when seven go out, and practically seven come back, because the substitution of the senior [Tupper] for junior really hardly affects the situation. (Opposition laughter.) There is, however, and to this I call the attention of the House, in preparation a real performance, which will not be long delayed, when they all go out and none come back. (Opposition laughter.) Allow me to congratulate these gentlemen on the spectacular effects which they have produced, entirely regardless of expense.[52]

Two days later Cartwright was at it again, this time at Nova Scotia; he labelled it "arida nutrix leonum," which he translated as "the dry nurse of boodlers."[53]

It was there, on his old ground, that Sir Charles Tupper went for a seat in the House of Commons. A seat in Cape Breton was opened for him, and he began his campaign in mid-January.[54] Tupper used the coal tariff to argue the Conservative case, an argument that was to reappear in June. But he used more than that. All the familiar tactics of Cape Breton elections were available. Bishop Cameron interfered again. One private letter, reportedly sent for reading in church on Sunday, February 2, 1896, was published in a garbled extract; "among those hell-inspired hypocritical Catholics are to be found not a few who will vote against justice being done to their co-religionists. . . ."[55] But Tupper kept the Manitoba issue well into the background. After two weeks strenuous campaigning old Sir Charles won Cape Breton with a slightly larger majority than it had carried in 1891.

Tupper was given a tremendous reception when he arrived back in Ottawa on February 10. At an interview that day the Governor General pointedly said to Bowell, "Now you must not let me keep you, Sir Mackenzie. I know you have to leave at once to meet Sir Charles." All of Bowell's irascibility and stubborness was compressed into four short words: "I am *not* going," he said.[56]

Tupper was introduced to the House of Commons on February 11. Within a few minutes, A. R. Dickey, the new Minister of Justice,* and one of the ablest of the new ministers, moved first reading of the "Remedial Act of Manitoba." It was not yet even ready for distribution, but it was drafted substantially upon the lines of the pre-1890 legislation of Manitoba. It established a Board of Education for separate schools. Those who subscribed to the system were exempted from the school taxes of the province of Manitoba. It was assumed that the province would itself supply the legislative grant. The Board of Education was to be appointed by the province; failure to do so empowered the Dominion government to appoint.[57] In the eyes of shrewd Quebec clerics the bill was only a *trompe d'oeil*, so far had lack of faith in the Bowell government gone, Father Lacombe commented sadly.[58] Greenway's comment is instructive:

> There are many clauses in it which are simply monstrous. . . . It has always been said here by those who speak for the minority, that they do not want the old system re-introduced, but I regret that this bill is restoring the old system in all its worst features. . . . Of course it can never accomplish what it professes to do. . . . Many of its provisions are a complete farce.[59]

With all of this, the Winnipeg *Free Press*, no lover of Greenway, agreed. The Remedial Bill, it said, appeared "to meet no condition but the political

* It had been decided that in view of old Sir Charles' presence in Cabinet, Sir C. H. Tupper would have to be Solicitor-General and remain outside the Cabinet.

necessity of appeasing the demands of an influential vote. The interests of Manitoba are for the moment forgotten.[60]

In the meantime the Governor General had persuaded Sir Donald Smith to go to Winnipeg to see if anything could be accomplished. Apparently this was done without the knowledge or the consent of the Government. Bowell learned about it half an hour before Smith's departure. Hopes were held that some adjustment might be made. But that too was an illusion.

Far more serious were the effects of the Cape Breton election and the genesis on the Remedial Bill upon Laurier. Laurier, in January and in early February, was by no means sure he could oppose a remedial bill. Having urged the "sunny way" as long as he could, he now faced a hard decision, and his instinct was against combatting the full power of the Church. It was probably sometime late in January when Laurier, Willison, and the *Globe* had an agonized discussion on the subject. The *Globe* was put under the utmost pressure from Laurier and Mowat to turn its policy toward support of the Remedial Bill. G. W. Ross, Ontario Minister of Education, and the political representative of both the Dominion Liberal party and the Ontario government on the *Globe's* Board of Directors, even supplied a leading editorial making the curve "with infinite casuistry and temerity,"[61] as Laurier and Mowat wanted. John Willison resisted:

> . . . I resisted pressure from Ottawa and pressure from the Board of Directors and steadily and resolutely opposed interference with Manitoba. I was "ordered" to Ottawa by Laurier and while there had, I think, the most unhappy time I ever had with my political leaders. Among those who assailed me most bitterly as responsible for the ruin of the party were Fraser of Guysboro, Lister of West Lambton, and Casey of West Elgin. The only people who gave me open support were Mulock and Martin.[62]

Willison stuck to his guns and it was Laurier who changed. The responsibility for convincing Laurier that opposition was possible was mainly Israël Tarte's, who through 1895 and 1896,

> . . . was always resolute on one point, that whatever the Government's policy was he would take the opposite position trusting to Laurier's popularity and to the treachery in the Tory ranks which he had carefully organized through Chapleau to carry Quebec.[63]

Tarte was against coercion. For the same reason Laurier was worried about the tone of the French Liberal papers. He wrote Ernest Pacaud on February 5:

> . . . le ton de ta rédaction va produire une sensation contre nous, si nous sommes obligés de voter contre le Bill. Le ton de "*l'Electeur*" ne nous laisse pas d'autre alternative que de voter pour le Bill – ce n'est pas là qu'il faut faire. Ce qu'il faut faire c'est de pousser à la politique de conciliation que j'ai adoptée.[64]

There was little doubt in Laurier's mind after the Cape Breton bye-election that the clergy were going to back the Government, and there was going to be a new ecclesiastical war, reminiscent of the 1870's.[65] In fact, the Roman Catholic bishops were badly divided on the Manitoba school question. The Ontario bishops were most unhappy with the prospect of coercing Manitoba. The Quebec bishops were much more divided than their mandement of May 16 was to suggest.[66]

One prominent member of the clergy had no doubts, however. That was Father Lacombe. An outspoken and minatory letter on January 20 asked Laurier point blank to support the Remedial Bill. Lacombe said that Laurier's commission of inquiry was an illusion, and that if Laurier did not support the Remedial Bill the Government might very well fall. If that happened, "I inform you with regret that the episcopacy, like one man, united to the clergy, will rise to support those who may have fallen to defend us."[67] Father Lacombe was a blunt and honest man, with no guile. But it was an unwise and impolitic letter, and was condemned by at least one French Conservative paper as indiscreet.[68]

The letter was read in the House February 20, and published widely the next day; there then followed one of those Saturday night mass meetings of righteous indignation at Massey Hall, Toronto, with McCarthy, Wallace, Mulock, Martin, and others on the platform. The theme was "No coercion!" Laurier was most uneasy over that meeting, especially with Joseph Martin there. Martin was strictly enjoined to be careful. It was terribly easy for Liberals to suggest that if they were in power no federal coercion of any kind would be used. But neither Laurier nor the party caucus were willing to risk a statement of that kind. Dominion interference with Manitoba "as a last resort" was still Liberal party policy, even now.[69]

The Remedial Bill was given first reading on February 11. It then sat for three mortal weeks. Bishop Langevin did not like some aspects of the bill, even though it had been originally drafted by J. S. Ewart, and he had to be persuaded to accept it by Lacombe and others.[70] This may explain the delay. It was March 3, just after three o'clock, that Sir Charles Tupper finally rose to propose second reading.

The debate lasted almost without interruption until March 20. It was a good debate. What gave it its strength was the weight and the range of the issues involved. What gave it its cutting edge was the imminence of a general election. There were remedialists and anti-remedialists on both sides of the House. There were Liberals who believed the Remedial Bill went too far, and Liberals who believed it did not go far enough; Conservatives the same. That there were enormous pressures on both sides is undeniable. It was rumoured that C. A. Geoffrion (M.P. Verchères and son of old Félix) and Louis Lavergne on the Liberal side were drafting a remedial bill stronger than the Government's for private circulation to French Liberals. Laurier put that down. On the Conservative side there were promises to Ontario Conservatives to stand firm, and that if the Government were defeated they would be found some suitable haven rather than having to stand an election before their Ontario constituents.[71]

Laurier's speech in moving the six-month hoist to the Bill is well known, and justly so, but there is another question first. Why did he not move for a commission of inquiry? It was his favourite subject. It would have made it much easier for him in Quebec. Apparently his Ontario and Quebec followers disagreed, and there is some evidence that as a compromise he adopted D'Alton McCarthy's suggestion of the six-month hoist.[72] Thus Laurier's famous peroration to this speech has to sound a little hollow in the context of his long reluctance to oppose a remedial bill at all.[73]

Basically it was fencing, skilful, elegant, sharp, with a fine flourish at the end. The best speech came from George Foster. It came well on in the debate, with a great tangle of legal, constitutional lore preceding it. Foster's honest broadsword cut through much of this jungle, and laid open the ground so that all could see its configuration. The issue, he said, was not "hands off Manitoba." It would have been better expressed as "hands off the Manitoba minority." The point, he said, was a simple one. The constitution of Confederation had, rightly or wrongly, given to the Manitoba Roman Catholics certain privileges. These had been unconstitutionally taken away, and the Government had no alternative but to try to give them back. If the constitution was wrong, it could be revised in the future. In the meantime, what was guaranteed in 1867 to the Protestants of Quebec, to the Roman Catholics of Ontario, had also been guaranteed in 1870 to the Roman Catholics of Manitoba.

> The Government is attacked in this House and in the country for its action with reference to this question. Men meet me every day and say: Why did you raise this question at all? . . . I am speaking to that class of men now particularly, when I ask: Who raised this question? It was not raised, but settled, by the men of 1867, in the Confederation Act; it was not raised, but settled by the men of 1870 in the Manitoba Act. . . . There is an even harmony of peace, and of security, and of contentment, so far as that clause of the Act is concerned in its relation to the province, for all that period, broken but once, but broken in Manitoba, and broken by whom?[74]

Not by the Dominion government. Laurier's talk of investigation was an excuse. There was no use in appointing a commission of investigation unless some principle of action lay before it.

> On the other hand what is there? There is the genius and spirit of the constitutional compacts of this country. There is the splendid lesson of toleration and of compromise which has been read to you in that constitution. . . . There is the cry of the minority, small in the area of those who directly suffer, but large, let me tell you, in the area of those who sympathize with it in this country from one end to the other. There are the minorities in other provinces demanding of you where they shall stand. . . . There is the Parliament, Sir,

invested, knowingly, definitely, positively invested by the fathers of confederation in the constitution with the jurisdiction to maintain these rights, and to restore them if they are taken away.[75]

Foster's policy was all very well, but Cartwright pointed out the inadequacies of the bill that implemented the policy, with its forty pages and one hundred and twelve complex clauses. Even at the best of times joint jurisdiction was difficult.

> . . . what is it likely to be when we know from the very outset that the rival authorities are utterly and bitterly opposed? . . . this is a case in which a single, careless phrase, a single ill-turned sentence, may well produce a dozen years of costly litigation. If ever there was a Bill submitted to Parliament which needed the most careful drafting . . . it is the Bill which is sub mitted for our consideration to-day. . . . I take the Bill itself as it stands, and I can define it as nothing but a parliamentary scarecrow. Sir, this Bill is simply an imposture. There is no motive power in this bill whatever. It threatens what it cannot perform; it promises what it can never implement.[76]

The brutal fact was, said Cartwright, that physical coercion of Manitoba was impossible, and interference with the revenues of Manitoba, inevitably contemplated in the Bill, were to all practical purposes, equally impossible.[77]

There were however constitutionalists on the Liberal side. David Mills broadly supported Foster's argument.

> Provincial rights are not a species of squatter sovereignty. A province cannot acquire exclusive authority over a subject by usurpation.[78]

Tupper promptly said that if one wanted a complete vindication of the Government's position one had only to read David Mills' speech.[79] Mills however objected strongly to the Government's method of handling the issue. So did Joseph Martin, now M.P. Winnipeg. Martin said that nothing would be done by Manitoba, no negotiations would ever come to anything, unless the remedial order of 1895 were repealed.[80] Nicholas Davin interrupted Martin to ask if it were true that in 1890 all the Roman Catholic school districts and Boards of Trustees were abolished, and only the Protestant ones retained? Ha! said Martin triumphantly, does that not prove that the whole subject needs investigation before anything substantial can be done?[81]

Mills and Foster had both spoken of the rights of minorities in the British North America Act and in the Manitoba Act as compacts that could not be violated. McCarthy followed a principle suggested by Principal Caven of Knox College, Toronto, the year before; "The Manitobans of 1870 had no right to bind the Manitobans of 1895. The State is a living organism. . . . Each generation must make its own laws."[82] Does the past have the right to control the future? Times change: does a constitution change with the times, or are prescriptive rights, once established and guaranteed, to be permanent?

There is really no answer to such a question, it is as much philosophical as political, and therein lay the conflict over Manitoba.

The great difficulty for the Government was the practical implementing of what they believed, or professed to believe, was a constitutional policy. It would have been difficult enough at ordinary times; but March 1896, one month before Parliament was due to expire, was no ordinary time. And the Ontario papers were making the Government's position no easier. Of the major Toronto newspapers, only the *Mail and Empire* supported the Government's position.[83] And the Government was at one point even defeated in the House on a minor issue, the Chignecto Marine railway, on March 9.[84] Immediately after that Sir Charles Tupper announced that Greenway was still willing to consider negotiations, and that the Government would propose a conference with him immediately after second reading of the Remedial Bill carried.

Second reading did carry in the early hours of Friday, March 20. Laurier's motion for the six-month hoist was defeated by twenty-four votes, and the main motion passed by just eighteen. The Toronto *Mail and Empire* analyzed that vote as follows: of the 112 for second reading, there were 105 Conservatives and 7 Liberals; of the 94 against, 73 Liberals, 18 Conservatives and 3 independents.[85] The Bill went to Committee of the Whole, but only after several days further debate. Finally, on March 27, work in Committee started.

In the meantime, on March 23, the Government's commissioners, Sir Donald Smith, Senator Desjardins, and A. R. Dickey, left for Winnipeg, Smith's second trip within a month. The Dominion government clearly wanted a settlement. Equally, most Liberals preferred not to have one. There was talk of a bi-partisan commission; Dickey was strongly in favour, as was the Governor General. Whether Laurier would have accepted it is doubtful, but Sir Charles Tupper may have believed a settlement was in the making and preferred to have the Government get the credit.[86]

The Manitoba government were well briefed about how to handle such a commission. D'Alton McCarthy had seen to that. Sir Donald Smith was, McCarthy believed, in a position to force the Dominion government to accept any settlement he approved of. Manitoba's line, McCarthy suggested, was to try to have the Remedial Bill suspended; in any case, "*if conference likely to be a failure, it should be kept going as long as possible.*"[87]

On the other hand the Manitoba Catholics had reason to be accommodating. That narrow vote on second reading frightened J. S. Ewart and weakened even Archbishop Langevin's determination.[88] In fact, the Dominion government offered more concessions in March 1896, than Laurier finally gave the following autumn.[89]

The delaying tactics were effective. Greenway was not even in Winnipeg during the conference.[90] All the advances for an amicable settlement were clearly coming from the Dominion government. Sir Donald Smith confessed himself "completely disheartened."[91] Sifton said publicly three days later that "nothing had been accomplished." Greenway's paper, the Winnipeg *Tribune*, said that nothing less than separate schools had been insisted upon.[92] This was palpably false, but on April 4 the commissioners returned to Ottawa without a settlement.[93]

By this time the Remedial Bill was thoroughly bogged down in Committee of the Whole. D'Alton McCarthy wrote Sifton cheerfully:

> I note what you say as to your hope that the bill will not be allowed to pass and I think I may say to you that unless a change comes over the spirit of the Opposition that you may rely on it that the Bill will not pass.[94]

The obstructive tactics available to an opposition in the years before closure are well known; amendments, interminable points of order, and talk. Three opposition contingents worked eight hours each, on a diet of whisky and sleeplessness that made life in the Commons a shambles.

> When Mr. Casey rose [to speak, at 9:30 A.M. April 9] the chamber was still in a bedraggled and deserted state, not having received its refreshed day reinforcement. On the Treasury Benches the Minister of the Interior reclined upon two chairs, and the Controller of Inland Revenue [E. G. Prior] slept as peacefully as a child with the morning sunlight, which was shining through the glass roof, illuminating his ruddy countenance.[95]

Tupper did his best to wear down the Opposition. The House was kept in session almost continually from Monday, April 6 to Saturday, April 11, and again the following week. Finally, at 2:30 A.M. Thursday, April 16, after the Chairman had asked for the adoption of Clause 15, paragraph 2, (there were ninety-seven more clauses still to go) Tupper rose, excoriated the Opposition for their obstruction, and abandoned the Remedial Bill. There was but a week to get estimates through. On the evening of Thursday, April 23, came prorogation, and with it the announcement of an immediate dissolution.

Did the Government seriously intend the Remedial Bill to go through? That they seriously intended to make a vigorous demonstration of trying to get it through, there is no doubt. But there are some awkward facts. When the ministerial rebellion was over the House settled down to work, and the Address in Reply was passed; after some desultory business it went on to the Budget, postponed until January 31. The Budget took up all of February, and the motion for second reading of the Remedial Bill came only on March 3. When it appeared even its supporters admitted it was badly put together. "There is no united or symmetrical idea whatever in the Bill," said Davin when it was all about over.[96] Both Opposition and Government had a standing interest in delay. The Opposition's reasons are obvious. But the Government's method of proceeding allowed it to say to its Protestant friends, "It is not going to become law; don't be alarmed"; and at the same time to say to its Catholic friends, "We are ready to die for the Bill."[97] Both Government statements could be true, and it looked suspiciously as though the Government might have intended it that way.

It was inevitable that the Manitoba school question would be the subject of a great deal of talk on the hustings. But the public were saturated with the subject by this time. Hormidas Jeannotte, M.P. L'Assomption, remarked a week after the Remedial debate began in the House, "Mr. Speaker, if there be a subject which has been discussed to the very limit of human patience it is truly this everlasting question of the Manitoba separate schools."[98] A Winnipeg report of April 3 noted, "People here are sick and tired of the school question, and will be glad when the Parliament at Ottawa ends it."[99] Magistrate G. T. Denison said the same from Toronto, "The great mass of the people are disgusted over the wrangling about the school question."[100]

The new Prime Minister of Canada, Sir Charles Tupper, had long felt the force of these sentiments, and it influenced his new Cabinet formed upon the resignation of Sir Mackenzie Bowell on April 27, 1896. This came four days after prorogation. There was a brief movement, apparently strong, in favour of Sir Donald Smith as prime minister. But he did not want the task, preferring the High Commissionership in London, which he was to hold until his death in 1914 as Lord Strathcona.[101] There was still some reluctance, understandable perhaps, on the part of the Governor General to send for Tupper. But Tupper was called and formed his Cabinet. Out went the Bowell wing almost completely: Bowell himself, Ouimet, Caron, and Daly. Tupper made great efforts to get Chapleau. Mgr. Laflèche, Bishop of Three Rivers, wrote Chapleau (who was on holiday in the United States) urging him to join Tupper; Chapleau refused, for which he was not forgiven by leading French-Canadian Conservatives.[102] Dansereau wrote to Chapleau about this time, "Nous sommes dans le pendemonium. Un vrai bouquet de fleurs. Tout est à la farce, qui est d'une sincérité tragique."[103] Chapleau was in truth closer to Laurier now than to Tupper. Tupper did get, however, L.-O. Taillon, the Premier of Quebec. Thomas Chapais and A. R. Angers urged it upon Taillon as an essential duty that he could not refuse.[104] Angers himself returned to the Conservative cabinet, and there were also Senator Desjardins and J.-J. Ross. None of them carried much popular support in Quebec. Taillon, as premier, had imposed a hard régime of economy after the spendthrift régime of Mercier. Angers was thought of by many as the persecutor of Mercier. The French-Canadian ministers were strong with the church, not with the public.[105]

Tupper also added Hugh John Macdonald as Minister of the Interior. He was very reluctant to come, being convinced that remedial legislation of the kind of the Remedial Bill would never work. He told Tupper that it would "be resisted even to the extent of rebellion."[106] Tupper did his best. He promised a K.C.M.G.,* insisted upon Hugh John's duty to his country and his party, made it indeed a personal matter.[107] More important, Tupper made it clear after the failure of the Remedial Bill that remedial legislation proposed by the Tupper goverment in the future would follow completely new lines, indeed, that a settlement with Manitoba might be arrived at "without the matter coming before Parliament at all."[108] Hugh John finally agreed to come, though basically disliking the prospect of political life, and very doubtful that he could carry Winnipeg in the general election against Joseph Martin. (He did, however.)

It is commonly said that the election of 1896 was fought upon the Manitoba school question. So it was, but there were other issues as well, and in many parts of Canada the other issues were of more importance. The most important of these was the tariff. The bulk of the Liberal party, and the most important of its leaders, had moved a considerable distance from the tariff position of 1891. Many who voted Conservative in 1891 out of fear of unrestricted reciprocity, now felt, like Professor Archibald MacMechan in Halifax, that there was no such danger from Liberal trade policy in 1896.[109] In Nova Scotia the issue was put, even by Conservative papers, not upon the school question, but on trade policy. "The great issue in the approaching general election must, of course, be that same great issue which has divided the two political parties in Canada for twenty years and more, namely the trade issue.[110] Robert Borden, Conservative candidate for Halifax, making his first major political speech since 1882, remarked in Dartmouth,

> The time which has been devoted to it [the school question] both in Parliament and in the press is out of all proportion to its importance. . . . It is a question which should be settled by mutual forbearance. . . .[111]

Liberal tariff policy was not, however, sufficiently explicit to prevent the Conservative party's making a good deal of it. "How many bicycles would have been manufactured in Canada under free trade?" "The pretended science of free trade denies the principle of nationality." "The nation that begins exporting its raw materials ends by exporting its men." These were some of the mottoes that decorated the walls of Massey Hall for Tupper's speech of June 19, 1896.

The speech was virtually shouted down by an audience heavily laced with Liberal supporters. Tupper was famous for his "I this" and "I that"; there was a Bengough cartoon of him in the *Globe* as the "I Commissioner.[112] As soon as he used the word "I" it was echoed to the roof by Liberal *claqueurs* trying to drown him out. Hector Charlesworth recalled that even ten feet away from the platform it was nearly impossible to hear old Tupper.[113] He made a strong effort, nevertheless:

* Hugh John's knighthood had to await the Borden government. He was made Knight Bachelor in 1913.

> That question [the school question] is a very simple one. The people have been deluded into the belief that it is a question of forcing Separate schools on the majority of the people in Manitoba by the Government. (Cries of "So it is!") That I have no hesitation in saying is a palpable delusion, as I can show you in five minutes if you will give me an ear, and some of them are long enough in all truth. (Laughter and cheers.) I say the question is simply this: It is not a question of Separate schools at all. ("Hear, hear," and hisses.) It is not a question of the creation of Separate schools at all. (Uproar.) The Parliament of Canada have no more power to create a Separate school in Canada than they have to take charge of the Government of Russia, not a bit. (Cheers.) . . . You men who are making these interruptions are the most block-headed set of cowards that I ever looked upon. (Uproar.) . . . A voice – Rub it in, old man. (Cheers.)[114]

Tupper's campaign was dogged by incidents of a similar kind. And there was some personal unpleasantness. D'Alton McCarthy in a speech at Brockville referred to Tupper's remark that he (Tupper) was ashamed of having been McCarthy's political godfather. McCarthy replied that he, McCarthy, would be ashamed "to be numbered among the numerous progeny who claimed Sir Charles as father." He added slyly that there were other things he could not speak of in the presence of ladies.[115]

Tupper made much of the National Policy in places where it would do the most good, in southwest Ontario, in Montreal, and in Nova Scotia. On June 15, when he arrived in Berlin, Ontario, there was a great parade of working men illustrating their faith in the Conservative tariff: sixty from the Simpson Furniture Company, forty from the Williams, Green & Rome Shirt and Collar Company, sixty from the Berlin Felt Company, twenty from the Berlin Piano and Organ Company, and some 240 others from similar enterprises. Tupper gave his speech under the sign, "The N.P. is the life of the Town."[116] In London, Ontario, John McClary, owner of the McClary foundry, put in pay envelopes a circular which stated that the firm was forced to reduce staff or ask employees to work shorter time; "until the trade policy of the company is assured we may look for a waiting condition. . . ."[117]

But by no means were all the manufacturers Conservative. There was a definite shift from 1891. The C.P.R. was Conservative in 1891, and neutral in 1896. The manufacturers gave support to both parties in 1896. W. E. H. Massey, President of Massey-Harris, asked by the *Globe* about what Canada needs, replied, "Greater loyalty to Canada and Canadian institutions on the part of our people, and particularly on the part of some of our newspapers. . . ." He added especially, "Our manufacturing industries need a fair and *stable* trade and tariff policy, which our manufacturers can rely on not being tampered with every few months for political purposes."[118] In Western Ontario and in Nova Scotia the Manitoba school question was treated almost abstractly. The tariff was the burning question. The great free traders in the Liberal camp. Charlton and especially Cartwright, were kept largely muzzled by Laurier during the campaign. Cartwright wandered on the side lines and talked mainly in rural areas; not one major industrial centre did he visit.[119]

In Quebec of course, the issue was more clear-cut, though even here the tariff could not be neglected. Israël Tarte promised categorically to maintain in principle the protective tariff.[120] The presence of English-Canadian Liberals like R. R. Dobell, President of the Quebec Board of Trade, Robert Mackay, and Sydney Fisher from Brome, two of whom were later in Laurier's cabinet, gave solid weight to such promises. More important still was the announcement in the *Globe*, May 5, that Mowat would join any future Liberal government in Ottawa. This was an enormous help in Quebec; Mowat's generous treatment of Roman Catholics in Ontario was known and appreciated east of the Ottawa.[121]

The Manitoba school question in Quebec was a hard battle. It was not simply a struggle between Laurier and the Quebec bishops; there were ramifications that made the issue more complicated. Archbishop Langevin launched a crusade in Quebec for the Manitoba Roman Catholics; he urged that all candidates in Quebec be required to promise support, not for an inquiry, or some spurious principle of conciliation, but for a firm federal law. But the Quebec bishops were uneasy over strong statements like these; and Bishop Langevin was asked politely, but firmly, to keep quiet. The bishops were even more uncomfortable over the Conservative insistence on a strong collective mandement. It was not easy to get agreement; some bishops, it is true, wanted such a statement and were prepared to risk the consequences; but others, notably Bishop Emard of Valleyfield, would have been happier with a form of neutrality.[122] Thus the collective mandement of May 16, 1896 was a compromise:

> . . . tous les catholiques ne devront accorder leur suffrage qu'aux candidats qui s'engagent formellement et solennellement à voter, au Parlement, en faveur d'un législation rendant à la minorité catholique du Manitoba les droits scolaires qui lui sont reconnus par l'honorable Conseil Privé d'Angleterre.[123]

This would seem definitive. But it did not condemn the Liberal party as such, and it was possible, without too much ingenuity, for many Liberal candidates to subscribe to such a promise. All but two did. Mgr. Laflèche, however, had by no means exhausted his armoury. He published a sermon in which he cited Laurier's six-month hoist speech as affirming that same kind of liberalism that had been condemned so categorically by the Church. "Il [Laurier] formule une doctrine entièrement opposée à la doctrine catholique."[124] This was pounced upon, promptly and enthusiastically, by the Conservative papers, and tens of thousands of copies were issued as pamphlets.

A savage debate followed between Liberal and Conservative papers; Pacaud's *L'Electeur* was indignant. Tarte, however, in *Le Cultivateur*, was conspicuously moderate, merely claiming that if the Bishop had read Laurier's speech completely, he could not have given it the interpretation he did. But Tarte felt that the intransigeance of the bishops, especially of Mgr. Langevin, was compromising any real possibility of solution. Tarte retained not only his political adroitness, but all his deftness and precision at party organization. He was served by an exact and capacious memory, and always seemed to know where he could gain, if needed, a few more votes. He always believed that Laurier could win, never mind that the issue was, simply because he was Tarte, Laurier was Laurier, and the Quebec Conservatives hopeless.

Laurier had a marvellous talent for attracting the young, bright men to him. He liked youth himself, and he gathered together in 1896 "la plus brillant équipe que l'on puisse former, à cette époque, au Canada français."[125] Among these was a young grandson of Papineau, Henri Bourassa. Bourassa never shared the contempt of the Church accorded by some of the Liberals. There were religious principles as well as secular issues, and Bourassa was always a man who put principles before politics. Laurier accepted his ultramontane inclinations and made light of them. "Bourassa est un monstre; c'est un castor rouge; je n'en avais encore jamais vu."[126]

Laurier was not wholly without episcopal support. Bishop Emard made a firm statement of neutrality on Sunday, June 14. Now, toward the end of the campaign, Laurier was beginning to scent victory. John Willison recalled a conversation with Laurier on that same Sunday, in London, Ontario:

> I am sure I remember almost his exact words – he said to me, "I do not want to be too confident, but I think we will win. Whether we win or lose I want to say to you that if you had not driven us into the course we have taken I would not have a party left except in the Province of Quebec. I should have seen at once that the position of a Catholic leader with a Catholic policy tailing in behind Tupper would have been impossible. If we are beaten you will never find me complaining that you forced us into a wrong position."[127]

At about the same time Sir Leonard Tilley, that wily old veteran of many political wars, wrote to Tupper from Saint John. "You have not only religious prejudice to fight but the influence of five local Governments to contend with. And a divided Roman Catholic vote as well. If you succeed in defeating all these, and the influence of U States greenbacks as well, you will have accomplished wonders."[128] It was just about the last letter Tilley wrote. Full of good sense to the last, he died, three weeks later, on June 25, 1896. By the end of the campaign, it was virtually holy war in Quebec. On election eve *La Patrie* said openly, "Now we are going to see if Laurier is stronger than the bishops."[129]

He was. The election was held on Tuesday, June 23, 1896. Quebec returned forty-nine Liberals and sixteen Conservatives, in most cases by heavy majorities. It was a victory in Quebec of really astonishing magnitude. Angers, Taillon, Desjardins, Langevin were all defeated. In their place came newer men like Henri Bourassa and Rodolphe Lemieux. Some years later Tarte attributed the extent of the victory to tithes; that is, in a period of economic stringency the habitant resented the exactions of the Church, not to be able to buy farm machinery because of tithes; voting for Laurier was their chance to get even.[130] Rumilly is fair:

> Les chef conservateurs ont accompli un effort, au risque de s'aliéner des partisans ontariens, pour rendre justice aux catholiques et aux Canadiens français. La province de Québec leur a préféré le chef, déjà anglicisé de sentiments, mais canadien-français d'origine et de nom, qui avait entravé cet effort et qui ne promettait – et qui ne donnerait – rien pour l'avenir. La magie de Laurier étouffe l'appel des évêques.[131]

The vote elsewhere in Canada was divided, more or less evenly, between Liberals and Conservatives. Nova Scotia gave ten to each party, New Brunswick elected nine Conservatives and five Liberals, Prince Edward Island three Conservatives and five Liberals, Manitoba four Conservatives and two Liberals, British Columbia the reverse of Manitoba, Northwest Territories, one Conservative and five Liberals. Ontario was a surprise, for Laurier should have done better there: forty-three for each party, with three McCarthyites, who would probably vote Liberal, two Patrons, and an Independent. Tupper did well to concentrate his effort in Ontario. He had a good return for it. Doubtless fears about the National Policy contributed to the weakening of Liberal strength. Mowat had even asked Laurier late in May for an authentic statement on the trade question.[132] Although, however, Laurier could count on a majority of about thirty in the new House.

Archbishop Langevin wrote to Tupper the day after the election, "I can hardly realize this calamity."[133] That same day Laurier telegraphed to the Governor General, then at Quebec, asking to see him. It was to request that no new judges or Senators be appointed by the retiring ministry. Lord Aberdeen agreed that it would be undesirable, and at the same time replied ominously to Tupper that the election results would not render necessary any considerable discussion between himself and the defeated prime minister.[134] On Thursday, July 2 Tupper arrived at Government House, Ottawa:

> It was his birthday, & seemingly neither all his recent arduous fight nor its results, nor the extreme heat affected him. The plucky old thing came down blooming in a white waistcoat & seemingly as pleased with himself as ever. He did not at all appear as the defeated Premier come to render an account of his defeat & of its causes to the representative of the Sovereign. Not he![135]

Lord Aberdeen steadfastly refused to sanction last-minute appointments.

Tupper was bitterly angry and clearly intended to make an issue of it. All the Conservative newspapers were in full cry. Tupper resigned July 8. Laurier, willing to take full responsibility for the Governor General's "despotic" action, was asked on July 10 to form a government. He was sworn in the next day.

And so the Conservatives, fighting at the very last on their favourite ground, patronage, finally gave up the government of Canada after eighteen years. Without Sir Charles Tupper, the party would have been annihilated. He carried the great burden of the Conservative campaign upon his own broad shoulders, but he was "a bulldog without the guidance of a master," in Goldwin Smith's hard verdict.[136] Tupper himself probably never fully realized the magnitude of the difficulties before him. No one seemed to have told him the full truth, and the extent to which Tarte's organizing genius had undermined the party in Quebec.[137] Tupper's own explanation admits something of this:

> When I came to Canada last winter I found the Conservative party utterly demoralized, and was reluctantly compelled to consent to become its leader as the only hope of avoiding defeat. The fatal mistake had been made of refusing to dissolve immediately after the adoption of the remedial order. . . . Down to the last moment I confidently relied upon the accuracy of Mr. Angers' opinion that Quebec would give the Government a majority of 20.[138]

For everything depended upon carrying Quebec. Willison gave Laurier the right policy to hold at least half the rest of Canada. Tarte believed that Laurier could win Quebec no matter what the issue. The old Conservative, J. C. Patterson, now at Government House, Winnipeg, was right in a letter to Pope, "Laurier owes his success in Quebec to Tarte more than to any other man, or a dozen men!"[139] A cheerful epilogue to the campaign is John Charlton's, writing to Willison:

> The election returns were what I hardly dared at any period of the battle to hope for. God has in his mercy remembered this political Israel of ours. . . . Every few minutes in the course of the day my thoughts revert to that great great victory for the truth in Laurier's own Province. What gratification he must feel at the magnificent endorsation given him by his countrymen. It looks as though the French Canadian had made up his mind to stand an extra allowance of Purgatory rather than go back on a trusted and honored leader. No event in our political history impresses me as giving such promise for the future good of Canada.[140]

CHAPTER 14

Fin de Siècle

Canada in 1896: it is wrong to say that there was a new generation on the scene in 1896. There are always new generations on the scene. There were several thousands of them in Canada, every month of every year from 1874 to 1896. Life, and history, are a continuum, a seamless texture of future becoming present becoming past. So history is a false order imposed upon an immensely complicated reality; it is an arbitrary, and doubtless haphazard, selection of what really was.

Most of the men who had made Confederation were gone, and their work was in other hands now. Tupper, of course, lived on and on, until 1915 – to the crusty old age of ninety-four; but Tilley, Macdonald, Galt, Cartier, Dorion, Brown, had all gone. Edward Blake, whose happiest years in Canada, so he said, were 1888-90,[1] now represented an Irish constituency in the British House of Commons; he would return to Canada in 1907 and die in 1912. There were newer men now; Robert Borden was beginning his political career at the age of forty-two; Bourassa at twenty-six; Rodolphe Lemieux at thirty; W. S. Fielding, that "brisk, amiable, matter-of-fact Nova Scotian"[2] was starting his career in federal politics at forty-eight; so was Clifford Sifton, already experienced at thirty-five. R. B. Bennett was already in Calgary, on his way to fortune and later to fame. But continuity of past and present there was, as always there would be; the new House of Commons that was to meet in August 1896 was not so very different from the old, though its habits were gradually changing; under Laurier it was to become a little less raucous than it had once been.

The newspapers had a different complexion from twenty-five years before; they were now of pulp paper, thicker, bigger, rather like those of our own day. In the *Globe* of May 1896, Eddy's announced that they made twenty-eight thousand matches a day; J. A. Wilson advertised golf clubs; Cook's would take a Canadian to Europe and back, a sixty-day tour for $575.[3] A Saturday *Globe* had delightful pictures of skiing on the banks of the Ottawa, with the skiers all in ferociously portentous attitudes.[4] And with the late spring came the bicycles, not the penny-farthing kind of fifteen years earlier, but in the modern style, which dated from 1890 and used Dunlop's new pneumatic tire. By 1896 bicycles were perhaps the most obvious of the changes upon the Canadian scene; thousands of cyclists were to be seen, daily, "gliding along the streets and out in the suburbs of the city," pleased with the speed, the ease, and the grace with which they cover distance.[5] There was also talk of new horseless carriages, destined to make the streets virtually horseless within four decades.

These aspects of social change were themselves superficial in character, but they had implications of real significance. Canadian society would adjust, though slowly, to new ways of living and doing. W. L. Grant wrote in the *Queen's Quarterly*, July 1894, "The progress of discovery in electricity has been so rapid during the past fifteen years that it is possible only for the specialist to keep pace with it. It is within this period that electric lighting, electric railways, and the telephone have come into common use."[6] Manners and morals still lagged behind.

Much of what is often called "Victorian" morality was foreign to the age after which it was named. The full temperance experiment was still in the future; the Ross government of Ontario complained in 1897 of being between two fires, the temperance advocates on the one side and the liquor trade on the other. Drinking habits had changed in twenty-five years, but in this respect late Victorian Canada was still raw and lusty. James Edgar, from the depths of the Remedial Bill debate, wrote his wife that Moncrieff (of Imperial Oil) was speaking, but was drunk and getting drunker on gin and water. "He has knocked his tumbler over once & sent for more."[7] Two weeks later Davin wound up an impromptu Blackfoot dance in the Commons smoking room, by springing up on the long table, laden with bottles and glasses, and jigging down the centre, kicking over everything in sight.[8] But then Davin was notorious. Goldwin Smith, in a happier mood in 1880 than in 1896, described for Sir John A. Macdonald a delicious incident on a Toronto horse-car:

> You know Alderman Baxter – he is a leading Conservative. He was sitting in the street car when a lady getting in dropped her handkerchief on his knees. He could not see it fall for his stomach. The lady was too shy to take it. The eyes of the passengers were fixed upon him. At last his attention was directed to the handkerchief. He took it for a part of his shirt, and opening his nether garments in a great hurry, tucked it in, to the delight of the crowded car. This from an *eyewitness*.[9]

One can almost hear Macdonald chuckling over this. But Laurier did not like telling stories, nor did he like being told them; he neither drank, nor smoked, nor played games. Laurier's Canada was not to be Macdonald's.

Laurier was asked more than once, even before 1896, for permission to use his autograph on cigars. "Can these people be serious?" he asked Ernest Pacaud.[10] They were. This commercial ambience went right through Canadian society. Trade was always a decent way to make a living. Sara Jeanette Duncan's novel, *The Imperialist*, published a few years later, reflects these values:

> Dry goods were held in respect and chemists in comparative esteem; house furnishings and hardware made an appreciable claim, and quite a leading family was occupied with seed grains. Groceries, on the other hand, were harder to swallow . . . smaller trades made smaller pretensions; Mrs. Milburn could tell you where to draw the line. . . . Anything "wholesale" or manufacturing stood, of course, on its own feet; there was nothing ridiculous in molasses, nothing objectionable in a tannery, nothing amusing in soap.[11]

At election time these business men of the community were apt to be quiet fellows, with less sophistication and less polemic than their American counterparts, though no less expectant. They wore the air of being prosperous; but they were not prosperous enough for fancy doctrines, or indeed for doctrines of any kind. "Life was a decent rough business that required all their attention; there was time enough for sleep but not much for speculation."[12] They were democrats by instinct, but under a monarch; and what harm could she do overseas?

Not much. The Imperial Federation movement, as one recent study has concluded, was largely nationalist.[13] G. W. Ross remarked in 1900, "there is no antagonism between Canadianism and Imperialism. The one is but the expansion of the other."[14] Nevertheless, by the early 1890's a perceptible movement for independence was appearing. "From year to year," said the Montreal *Herald*, July 1, 1893, "their [Canadians'] pride in their native land is fed by the growth of her greatness."[15] *The Week* in 1892 taunted those who thought independence was the same thing as disloyalty. Was it disloyal for a son to leave his father's house and set up for himself?[16] Roberts' poem, which *The Week* had quoted in 1890, comes forcibly to mind:

> How long the ignoble sloth, how long
> The trust in greatness not thine own?
> Surely the lion's brood is strong
> To front the world alone!
>
> How long the indolence ere thou dare
> Achieve thy destiny, seize thy fame?
> Ere our proud eyes behold thee bear
> A nation's franchise, nation's name?[17]

In the twenty-three years since 1873, despite great inherent difficulties, much had been done; the physical strength, the muscular development of the fledgling of 1873 had been prodigious; the thin gangling frame had been filled out, strengthened with factories, western farms, Nova Scotian and British Columbian orchards; and with the arterial power of railways, there came an energizing circulation of trade between the Maritime provinces, central Canada, and the West; Canada was ready to sustain the massive weight thrown upon it by the great immigration of the Laurier years. It had not been easy; one is tempted again to say that nothing in Canada is easy. Canada's destiny was an arduous one achieved at tremendous cost; the immense capital and energy that went into transportation was a material symbol of a great political and perhaps moral price to Canada's people. It was easy to despair, easy to be faint-hearted; many did and many were; but even Sir Richard Cartwright, for all his blue ruin speeches of years past, made his amends to the House of Commons and Canada, in March, 1896;[18] and John Willison, writing from Calgary on his first trip west, in September, 1895 was even better:

> If we compare what has been accomplished with the predictions of the boom traders and political prophets we shall be disappointed. If we are content with reasonable expectations and take account of mistakes of policy and acquired knowledge of the characteristics and capabilities of the country we shall be encouraged and hopeful for the future. . . .

Canadians have sometimes forgotten, said Willison in that sensible way of his, "that this Confederation is not much more than a quarter of a century old . . . you cannot build a nation in a day."[19]

ABBREVIATIONS

A.P.Q.: Archives publiques de Québec, Québec.
B.C.H.Q.: British Columbia History Quarterly.
C.H.A.: Canadian Historical Association.
C.H.R.: *Canadian Historical Review.*
C.J.E.P.S.: *Canadian Journal of Economics & Political Science.*
C.M. & N.R.: *Canadian Monthly and National Review.*
C.P.S.A.: Canadian Political Science Association.
N.B.M.: New Brunswick Museum, Saint John.
P.A.B.C.: Public Archives of British Columbia.
P.A.C.: Public Archives of Canada.
P.A.M.: Public Archives of Manitoba.
P.A.N.S.: Public Archives of Nova Scotia.
P.A.O.: Public Archives of Ontario.
R.H.A.F.: *Revue d'histoire de l'Amérique française.*
R.S.C.: Royal Society of Canada.

NOTES TO CHAPTER ONE

1. Louis Hémon, *Maria Chapdelaine: récit du Canada français* (Paris, 1924), p. 23.
2. D. C. Scott (ed.), *Selected Poems of Archibald Lampman* (Toronto, 1947), p. 81.
3. P.A.O., Blake Papers, Edward Blake to David Mills, April 12, 1892.
4. P.A.C., Macdonald Papers, Vol. 197, Campbell to Macdonald, March 22, 1885.
5. *The Week*, Toronto, August 21, 1884.
6. *Ibid.*, March 27, 1884.
7. It is fair to say that while this description owes something to local observation, it owes more to Henry James's description of the Boston of 1884. *The Bostonians* [orig. 1885], Bodley Head, London, 1967), pp. 179-80.
8. Mary Fitzgibbon, *A Trip to Manitoba* (London, 1880), pp. 38-9.
9. Beckles Willson in the London (Eng.) *Daily Mail*, 1896, republished as *The Tenth Island* (London, 1897), p. 124.
10. George Ham, *Reminiscences of a Raconteur* (Toronto, 1921), pp. 176-7.
11. P.A.C., George Johnson Papers, Johnson to Grant, August 1, 1900.
12. See also O. J. Firestone, *Canada's Economic Development*, 1867-1953 (London, 1958), p. 84.
13. *Canada: House of Commons, Journals*, 1874. Third Report of Select Committee respecting prohibitory liquor law, p. 9. G. W. Ross, Chairman.
14. *The Nation*, Toronto, Dec. 10, 1874. The Crooks Act, passed by the Ontario Legislature in 1875, came into force in 1876, and at once reduced licensed taverns by 35 per cent.
15. Ottawa *Citizen*, April 1, 1874, described the bar in Parliament as a daily working disaster to the intellects and welfare of Canada's representatives in Parliament.
16. Guelph *Weekly Mercury*, April 18, 1878, London *Daily Advertiser*, April 16, 1878. Other sources are the Toronto *Globe*, Montreal *Herald*, Hamilton *Evening Times* of the same date, and Conservative papers to set against them. The whole matter was aired, on motion of privilege, on April 17, 1878. See *Debates*, 1878, pp. 2057-67.
17. Halifax *Evening Express*, Feb. 5, 1874. This has been brought to my attention by Professor K. G. Pryke of the University of Windsor.
18. D. G. Creighton, *John A. Macdonald, the Old Chieftain* (Toronto, 1955), pp. 124-5, 134; Bernard Ostry, "Conservatives, Liberals, and Labour in the 1870's," C.H.R. XLI, 2, June 1960, pp. 93-127.
19. P.A.C., Macdonald Papers, Vol. 524, Macdonald to Meredith, Jan. 14, 1882.
20. P.A.C., Macdonald Papers, Vol. 524, Macdonald to Rose, Oct. 12, 1880.
21. *Royal Commission on the relations of Labor and Capital in Canada*, Ottawa, Queen's Printer, 1889, "Our Factory System," p. 98, quoting a recent writer (unnamed).
22. Toronto, *Globe*, Jan. 6, 1881. See K. W. McNaught, *The Globe and Canadian Liberalism*, 1880-90. M.A. thesis, University of Toronto, 1946.
23. *Canada: Sessional Papers*, 1882, No. 42, "Report of Commissioners appointed

to enquire into the working of Mills and Factories of the Dominion and the labor employed therein," p. 3.

24. *The Week*, Toronto, July 29, 1886 "A trip to Newfoundland. I."

25. Beckles Willson, *The Tenth Island*, p. 15.

26. F. F. Thompson, *The French Shore Question in Newfoundland* (Toronto, 1961), p. 45.

27. See Frank Cramm, *The Construction of the Newfoundland Railway, 1875-1898*, M.A. thesis, Memorial University, 1961.

28. Figures for 1868-1875 of ship tonnage built in Canada:

1868	87,203	1872	114,065
1869	96,439	1873	140,370
1870	93,166	1874	174,404
1871	106,101	1875	188,098

See, Report of Select Committee on the causes of the Present Depression of the Manufacturing, Mining, Commercial, Lumber and Fishing Interests. David Mills, Chairman, Report dated April 11, 1876. *Canada: House of Commons, Journals* 1876, App. 3. iv-v.

29. Evidence of F. Killam, March 27, 1876. *Ibid.*, p. 165.

30. F. W. Wallace, *Wooden Ships and Iron Men* (London, 1924), p. 296.

31. Halifax *Morning Chronicle*, August 14, 1872. This has been brought to my attention by Mr. Colin Howell. See his "Repeal, Annexation and commercial union in Nova Scotia 1886-1888," M.A. thesis, Dalhousie University, 1967.

32. Barbara Fraser, "The political career of Sir Hector Louis Langevin" C.H.R. XLII, 2 (June, 1961), pp. 98-9.

33. The channel in Lake St. Peter was the critical point to the development of Montreal's sea-going traffic. In 1867 it had been dredged to 20 feet, and was 300 feet wide. By the autumn of 1878, the whole river from Quebec to Montreal was open to a depth of 22 feet. *Canada: Sessional Papers*, 1881, No. 6, App. 35, Memorandum of Harbour Commissioner of Montreal, dated March 31, 1879, p. 203.

34. *Canada: House of Commons, Journals*, 1874, app. 3. "Select Committee to enquire into the extent and condition of the Manufacturing Interests of the Dominion." p. 38. See *infra*, 76-7.

35. G. O. Rothney, "Political nationalism: Sherbrooke, 1866-1966," unpublished paper given at C.P.S.A., Sherbrooke, June 1966, pp. 11-12.

36. A. I. Silver, "French Canada and the prairie frontier, 1870-1890," C.H.R., Vol. L, No. 1, March 1969, p. 16.

37. *Ibid.*, p. 17.

38. *Ibid.*, p. 12.

39. Meteorogical observations for Winnipeg, Nov. 2, 3, 4, 5, all record below zero, and wind velocities up to 20 m.p.h. Dept. of Transport, Meteorlogical Branch, Toronto. Records for Nov. 1873.

40. As quoted by C. E. Denny, *The Law Marches West* (Toronto, 1939), p. 4.

41. *Canada: House of Commons, Debates* 1867-68, 225, Dec. 9, 1867.

42. P.A.C., David Laird papers, C. N. Bell to Alexander Morris, March 23, 1874 (copy).

43. There is a comprehensive return in *Canada: Sessional Papers*, 1877, No. 121, to an address of the Senate asking for copies of all instructions and O.I.C.'s of N.W.T.

44. P.A.M., Alexander Morris Papers, Rev. G. M. McDougall to D. A. Smith, from Edmonton, Jan. 8, 1874

45. *Ibid.*, J. F. Grahame to Morris, Jan. 6, 1875.

46. *Ibid.*, Morris to Minister of Interior, Dec. 4, 1873 (copy). (My italics)

47. The census of 1871 gives the British Columbia population as 36,247, including Indians. But the Indians were badly underestimated. Their numbers have been more accurately put at 81,600. Thus with the white population of 28,000 British Columbia would have a total population in 1871 of 109,600. See M. C. Urquhart and K. A. H. Buckley, *Historical Statistics of Canada* (Toronto, 1966), p. 4.

48. J. H. E. Secretan, *Canada's Great Highway* (London, 1924), p. 40.

49. *Ibid.*, p. 38.

50. Macdonald's phrase. Margaret Ormsby uses it as the title of her excellent chapter on British Columbia from 1871 to 1886. See *British Columbia: A History* (Toronto, 1958), pp. 259-292.

NOTES TO CHAPTER TWO

1. This description is based on two sources, the official meteorological observations at Ottawa for November, 1873, obtained through courtesy of the De-

partment of Transport; and a piece in *The Week*, Toronto, Nov. 18, 1886, "Afternoon Tea," by Garth Grafton.

2. P.A.M., Alexander Morris Papers, Alexander Campbell to Morris, Nov. 29, 1873, private and confidential.

3. A.P.Q., Collection Chapais, Papiers Langevin, H. Langevin to Bishop Edouard Langevin, 31 Oct. 1873.

4. Peter Mitchell to A. F. Gault, Oct. 7, 1893, published by A. L. Burt, "Peter Mitchell on John A. Macdonald," C.H.R., XLII, 3 (Sept. 1961), p. 216.

5. Toronto *Globe*, Nov. 5, 1873. There is no reason to think the *Globe's* report is incorrect.

6. The *Nation*, Toronto, Dec. 26, 1874; also see London *Times*, Nov. 12, 1873, an editorial written with fairness and by one who seems to have known the Canadian situation well.

7. A.P.Q., Collection Chapais, Papiers Langevin, Langevin to E. Langevin, 4 Nov. 1873, (privée). Also, *Perth Courier*, Nov. 7, 1873, report of Nov. 4, signed "Logograph."

8. The account that follows here is based on two sources that are in substantial agreement. The first is D. A. Smith's account given in the chaotic closing of the 1878 session. *Canada: House of Commons, Debates*, 1878, pp. 2558-2564. (May 9, 1878). The second is Peter Mitchell's account of 1893, in A. L. Burt's article, cited above.

9. On the dubious authority, however, of W. T. R. Preston, *The Life and Times of Lord Strathcona* (London, 1914), pp. 84-5.

10. *Perth Courier*, Nov. 14, 1873; also Marchioness of Dufferin and Ava, *My Canadian Journal*, 1872-78 (New York, 1891), p. 133; Fredericton *New Brunswick Reporter*, Nov. 12, 1873.

11. Ottawa *Daily Citizen*, Friday Nov. 7, 1873.

12. Dale Thomson, *Alexander Mackenzie: Clear Grit* (Toronto, 1960), pp. 3-9.

13. Dale Thomson, *Alexander Mackenzie*, p. 133.

14. Mackenzie's words, quoted by C. H. Mackintosh, *The Canadian Parliamentary Companion and Annual Register*, 1878, p. 147.

15. *Canada: House of Commons, Debates*, 1876, p. 1001 (April 1, 1876).

16. *Canada: House of Commons, Journals*, 1875. Select Standing Committee on Public Accounts. James Young, Chairman. App. 2, p. 42. Norman Ward has a most useful account of the work of this standing committee. See his *The Public Purse: A Study on Canadian Democracy*, (Toronto, 1962), pp. 56-69.

17. The authority for this is a statement of Holton's in P.A.C., Mackenzie Papers, Holton to Mackenzie, Feb. 6, 1876 (confidential).

18. P.A.N.S., Jones papers, Mackenzie to Jones, Nov. 10, 1873, private and confidential. The Mackenzie letters to Jones are published in P.A.N.S., *Report*, 1952. The reference here is p. 33.

19. John Costigan asserted this in 1891. *House of Commons, Debates*, 1891, p. 1178 (June 22, 1891).

20. Queen's University, Alexander Mackenzie Papers, Mackenzie to Charles Mackenzie (his brother), March 4, 1877.

21. Halifax *Witness*, Oct. 1876, in Carl Wallace, "Albert Smith, Confederation, and Reaction in New Brunswick, 1852-1882," C.H.R., XLIV, 4, (Dec. 1963), p. 307.

22. W. R.. Graham, "Sir Richard Cartwright and the Liberal Party, PH.D. thesis, University of Toronto, 1950, pp. 12-15.

23. P.A.O., Cartwright papers, Bowell to Cartwright, Oct. 9, 1869; also in Graham, "Cartwright," p. 32.

24. *Ibid.*, p. 56.

25. Queen's University, Alexander Mackenzie Papers, Aug. 15, 1876, private.

26. P.A.O., Cartwright papers, Brown to Cartwright, Jan. 7, 1878.

27. Ottawa *Citizen*, Feb. 23, 1874, quoting the London *Free Press*.

28. Mackenzie's statement, *Canada: House of Commons, Debates*, 1877, p. 176, (Feb. 20, 1877).

29. Fredericton *New Brunswick Reporter*, Nov. 12, 1873.

30. The question of the date of Tilley's appointment was argued over. It ought to be said the appointment was offered to A. J. Smith in June, 1873, and was refused. (N.B.M., Tilley Papers, Smith to Tilley, June 27, 1873, telegram.) Tilley seems to have opposed the appointment himself until almost the last minute. P.A.C., Macdonald papers, Vol. 276, Tilley to Macdonald, April 17, 1877 (private).

31. P.A.N.S., Jones Papers, Mackenzie to Jones, Nov. 10, 1873 (private and confidential); also same, Nov. 25, 1873. See P.A.N.S. *Report*, 1952, pp. 33-5.

32. There is an illuminating return on the whole subject of appointments in 1873 and their cancellation in *Canada: Sessional Papers*, 1877, No. 144, p. 35.
33. *Canada: House of Commons, Debates*, 1878, p. 2228, (April 27, 1878).
34. P.A.N.S., Jones Papers, Mackenzie to Jones, Nov. 10, 1873 (private and confidential).
35. Sir Richard Cartwright, *Reminiscences (Toronto*, 1912), p. 119.
36. *Canada: House of Commons, Debates*, 1878, p. 2235, (April 27, 1878).
37. P.A.C., Alexander Mackenzie Papers, Letter books. Mackenzie to Power in Halifax, Nov. 18, 1873.
38. P.A.N.S., Jones Papers, Mackenzie to Jones, Nov. 25, 1873.
39. *Canada: House of Commons, Debates*, 1878, p. 2229 (April 27, 1878).
40. In the election of 1872 Crawford had won the seat for the Conservatives by a 2-1 majority; the position was nearly reversed in December, 1873.
41. P.A.C., Macdonald Papers, Mackintosh to Macdonald, Jan. 20, 1874, quoted in D. G. Creighton, *John A. Macdonald: The Old Chieftain* (Toronto, 1956), p. 183.
42. I have taken Murray Beck's estimates in *Pendulum of Power* (Toronto, 1968), p. 29, rather than Norman Ward's in *Historical Statistics of Canada* (Toronto, 1966), p. 620. Most of the votes of the early years of Mackenzie suggests Beck's are closer; by 1876 Ward's would be more accurate.
43. Statistical information here is based on Murray Beck's work.
44. There are various estimates. The *Globe*, Feb. 1, 1874 claimed 146 seats for the Government, 40 for the Opposition and 7 independent with 12 seats still to come. These were mainly the western seats. The *Globe's* estimate would give Mackenzie at least 90 seats. Lord Dufferin estimated 60 or 70 or even more.
45. The Pacific Scandal, says Hector Charlesworth, "made *Grip*, for it was admitted that Bengough had contributed much to the Reform victory by his cartoons." (*The Canadian Scene* [Toronto, 1927], p. 128).
46. *Grip*, Toronto, Jan. 16, 1875. Carling went down, with Gibbs, in 1874. Gibbs was re-elected in a famous bye-election in 1876; Carling in the general election of 1878.
47. The *Nation*, Toronto, June 4, 1874.
48. Brown Papers, Mackenzie to Brown, Sept. 24, 1878, (confidential); Mackenzie Papers, Brown to Mackenzie, Oct. 1, 1878; Brown Papers, Mackenzie to Brown, Oct. 2, 1878.
49. C. W. de Kietwiet and F. H. Underhill, *Dufferin-Carnarvon Correspondence*, 1874-1878 (Toronto, 1955), 2, Dufferin to Carnarvon, Feb. 26, 1874.
50. This is based on the slender authority of Sir Joseph Pope's Memorandum on Brown, but it is suggestive. "It was commonly understood at that time that if he [Brown] was not a member of the Mackenzie Administration it was because Mr. Mackenzie could not afford to have him on any terms, so clearly was he recognized as a governmental impossibility." P.A.C., Pope Papers, Vol. 97.
51. C.M. & N.R., May, 1876, p. 4.
52. A comprehensive account of the negotiations that follow is in J. M. S. Careless, *Brown of the Globe: Statesman of Confederation, 1860-1880* (Toronto, 1963), pp. 312-22.
53. Dufferin to Carnarvon, June 10, 1874, from Quebec. *Dufferin-Carnarvon Correspondence*, pp. 46-7.
54. Brown gives details of his Senate speech. *Canada: Senate, Debates*, 1875, 102 (Feb. 22, 1875). Senate Debates in 1875 are numbered by columns, not by pages.
55. Dufferin to Carnarvon, June 10, 1874, *Dufferin-Carnarvon Correspondence*, p. 46.
56. *Canada: Senate, Debates*, 1875, 144-5 (Feb. 24, 1875). I have omitted Kaulback's italics. He does not give a date for the Boston *Post*.
57. P.A.C., Mackenzie Papers, Vol. 3, Letterbooks, Mackenzie to Charles Raymond of Guelph, April 8, 1874.
58. The *Nation*, Toronto, April 2, 1874.
59. *Ibid.*, Sept. 17, 1874. Caniff's letter is dated Sept. 14, 1874. For other comments on reciprocity see also Aug. 20, Sept. 10, 1874.
60. Brown went to Washington again in January, 1875, but even he returned pessimistic. In his Senate speech on Feb. 22, 1875 he recognized that the matter was for the present hopeless.
61. 37 Vic. cap. 9. Some of the details and intentions of the Act are given by Mackenzie in 1883. *Debates*, 1883, pp. 172-3 (March 12, 1883).
62. Mackenzie's statement might be quoted: ". . . I never was an advocate of vote by ballot. I accepted it as the will of

the people, declared by their representatives, but I have expressed an adverse opinion frequently." *Canada: House of Commons, Debates*, 1877, p. 215 (Feb. 22, 1877).

63. Toronto *Globe*, Sept. 11, 1876, reporting Mackenzie's speech at Watford, Ontario, Sept. 8, 1876.

64. Ottawa *Daily Citizen*, Feb. 4, 5, 1874.

65. A.P.Q., Langevin Papers, Langevin à Edmond Langevin, 12 mai 1873, privée. "Le scrutin secret ne me plaît pas plus qu'à toi, mais Le Parlement le reçut. Nous l'aurons donc, mais ça ne remédiera à rien."

66. P.A.C., Alexander Mackenzie Papers, Brown to Mackenzie, Nov. 13, 1875 (private and confidential).

67. Queen's University, Alexander Mackenzie Papers, Vail to Mackenzie, Jan. 24, 1878, from Digby.

68. *Ibid.*, Holton to Mackenzie, Feb. 21, 1874 (confidential).

69. See Margaret Ormsby, *British Columbia: A History* (Toronto, 1958), p. 248; W. L. Morton, *The Critical Years: The Union of B.N.A. 1857-1873* (Toronto, 1964), pp. 247-8.

70. Article II of the terms. Macdonald wrote Lord Lorne in 1883, "I must confess that the fixing of a period for the completion of the road was unwise. I am sure that had I been present I should have resisted the insertion of such a stipulation. . . ." P.A.C., Lorne Papers, Macdonald to Lorne, July 11, 1883 (private).

71. *Canada: Senate, Debates*, 1876, Vol. 153 (March 20, 1876) (original italics).

72. P.A.B.C., H. P. P. Crease Papers, Crease to Langevin, May 23, 1874 (private; copy).

73. Blake summed up this feeling very well in 1880, ". . . all that we can raise by taxes or by loans all that we can beg or borrow is to be sunk in the gorges of the Fraser." *Canada: House of Commons, Debates*, 1880, p. 1467 (April 16, 1880).

74. Sandford Fleming, C.P.R.: *report of progress on exploration and surveys up to January, 1874* (Ottawa, 1874), pp. 18-23.

75. *Canada: House of Commons, Debates* 1867-8, p. 305 (Dec. 16, 1867).

76. For the Intercolonial Railway, and general problems of government railway construction, see *infra*, pp. 54-7.

77. Queen's University, Mackenzie Papers, Holton to Mackenzie, Feb. 21, 1874 (confidential).

78. A.P.Q., Collection Chapais, Papiers Langevin, Macdonald to Langevin, July 13, 1873, telegram (private).

79. In 1875 Blake referred to this "notorious contract." Tupper, who spoke to Blake's remarks did not deny the existence of the arrangement. *Canada: Commons, Debates*, 1875, p. 543 (March 5, 1875). For the views of the Conservative government prior to 1873 see L. B. Irwin's interesting work, *Pacific Railways and Nationalism in the Canadian-American Northwest, 1845-1873* (Philadelphia, 1939).

80. Mackenzie gives an interesting perspective of his whole railway policy in the 1880 debates. *Canada: Commons, Debates*, 1880, p. 456 (March 5, 1880).

81. J. H. E. Secretan, *Canada's Great Highway: From the First Stake to the Last Spike* (London, 1924), p. 67.

82. *Canada: House of Commons, Journals*, 1877, App. 2, pp. 24-5, Fleming's evidence for the Select Standing Committee on Public Accounts.

83. Other, more northerly, contenders were the Pine River Pass (now used for the gas pipeline from Dawson Creek), and the Peace River Pass. The Kicking Horse Pass, to the south, was not mentioned.

84. *Report of progress on the explorations & surveys up to January, 1874* (Ottawa, 1874), pp. 194-6.

85. A letter to John Robson, of Victoria, B.C. makes it clear how determined Mackenzie was, at this stage at least, to stick to his guns. P.A.C., Mackenzie Papers, Letterbook 3, Mackenzie to Robson, Dec. 15, 1873.

86. Dufferin to Carnarvon, July 9, 1874, *Dufferin-Carnarvon Correspondence*, pp. 51-2.

87. P.A.C., Alexander Mackenzie Papers, Mackenzie to Galt, Dec. 25, 1873 (private).

88. P.A.O., Edgar Papers, Mackenzie to Edgar, Feb. 19, 1874 (confidential).

89. Edgar Dewdney's view. *Canada: House of Commons, Debates*, 1876, p. 1058 (April 5, 1876).

90. Edgar Dewdney's gossip, and almost impossible to verify, but it has a smack of authenticity about it. *Ibid.*, p. 1056 (April 5, 1876).

91. A.P.Q., Langevin Papers, Trutch to

Langevin, July 29, 1874, private, from Victoria.

92. P.A.B.C., Crease Papers, Crease to Langevin, May 23, 1874 (private). This interesting letter is quoted *in extenso* in M. A. Ormsby, *British Columbia*, pp. 265-6.

93. Nanaimo coal was already important. It was one reason for the British naval base at Esquimalt; and export of Nanaimo coal to San Francisco increased from 16,000 tons in 1871 to 51,000 in 1874. Toronto *Globe*, March 15, 1875, quoting Nanaimo *Free Press*.

94. M. A. Ormsby, *British Columbia*, p. 265; R. M. Stamp, "J. D. Edgar and the Liberal Party, 1867-96," C.H.R., XLV, 2 (June, 1964), 99.

95. Queen's University, Alexander Mackenzie Papers, Walkem to Mackenzie, Friday, Jan. [?] 1875, from Rideau Club, Ottawa.

96. See Dale Thomson, *Alexander Mackenzie*, pp. 212-13.

97. Dufferin to Carnarvon, Sept. 17, 1874 (private), in *Dufferin-Carnarvon Correspondence*, pp. 70-2.

98. There is some confusion about this vote. It has often been stated the bill was defeated by two votes, and it is so stated in the Senate *Debates*, 1875, col. 748. But the *Journals* record 24-21, with the Senators' names, among which one, McMaster's, is missing from the list in the *Debates*. It should probably be assumed the *Journal* is right. Senate, *Journals*, 1875, pp. 282-3.

99. *Senate: Debates*, 1876, 256 (March 31, 1876).

100. Margaret Ormsby, *British Columbia*, p. 290.

NOTES TO CHAPTER THREE

1. See *The Week*, March 6, 1884, 229, quoting a correspondent of the *New York Sun*.

2. G. W. Ross, *Getting into Parliament and After* (Toronto, 1913), pp. 143-4.

3. The *Nation*, Toronto, November 12, 1875.

4. P.A.O., Lindsey Papers, Goldwin Smith to Charles Lindsey, February 13, 1878 [?], quoted by Elizabeth Wallace, *Goldwin Smith: Victorian Liberal* (Toronto, 1957), p. 80.

5. P. D. Ross, *Retrospects of a Newspaper Person* (Toronto, 1931), pp. 50-1.

6. J. S. Willison, *Reminscences, Political and Personal* (Toronto, 1919), p. 141.

7. For the origins, development and character of Canada First see also W. L. Morton, *The Critical Years: Union of B.N.A. 1857-73*, pp. 235-7. G. M. Hougham, "Canada first, a minor party in microcosm," C.J.E.P.S., Vol. XIX, pp. 174-84 (May, 1953), is more detailed but now needs supplementing from the superb book of Elizabeth Wallace, *Goldwin Smith: Victorian Liberal* (Toronto, 1957). Hougham did not use the Coyne papers at the University of Western Ontario which has interesting material.

8. In 1879 the name was changed to *Rose-Belford's Canadian Monthly*, and it lasted until 1882. See Roy Daniells' attractive essay in Carl Klinck (ed.), *Literary History of Canada*, (Toronto, 1966), pp. 191-207.

9. Quoted, probably correctly, in the *Nation*, September 3, 1875.

10. The quotation is from "Absolom and Achitophel." The *Bystander*, Toronto, April, 1883, p. 86. This is also the locus of Goldwin Smith's remark, "The Father of Confederation was Deadlock. . . ."

11. *Nation*, August 6, 1874.

12. *Canadian Monthly*, November, 1874, "Current Events," written by Goldwin Smith. See also Blake Papers, Smith to Blake, October 5, 1874.

13. W. S. Wallace (ed.), "Edward Blake's Aurora speech" C.H.R. II, 3 (September, 1921).

14. *Canada: House of Commons, Debates*, 1880, p. 1467 (April 16, 1880).

15. Sir John Willison remarked that it was not possible to follow the comment the Aurora speech aroused "without sincere respect for the press of Canada forty-five years ago." J. S. Willison, *Reminiscences, Political and Personal*, p. 78.

16. Montreal *Gazette*, October 14, 1874. In an editorial on October 22, 1874 it argued some of the points Blake had made in more detail.

17. Toronto *Globe*, October 7, 1874.

18. *Ibid.*, October 17, 1874.

19. *Ibid.*, October 27, 1874.

20. *Ibid.*, November 7, 1874. Goldwin Smith's letter was dated November 5.

21. Queen's University, Alexander Mackenzie Papers, Brown to Mackenzie,

October 30, 1874 (private and confidential).

22. *The Week*, Toronto, July 17, 1884, by "Bystander." There is a clever sentence in the same sense in French: "Grattez un libéral, vous trouverez un réactionaire, grattez un conservateur, vous trouverez un actionaire." In J. Hamelin, J. Hust, M. Hamelin's series of articles, "Aperçu sur la politique canadienne au XIXe siècle," in *Culture*, XXVI. This quotation from Vol. 4, p. 438.

23. *Canada: House of Commons, Debates*, 1878, p. 14 (February 7, 1878).

24. Goldwin Smith was asked to edit it, but he had more than enough on his hands. John Cameron, of the London *Advertiser*, was brought to Toronto for the purpose.

25. Original estimates for working expenses were about $900 a week for the first year, and actually turned out to be $1400. The paper was taking in $700 a week. P.A.O., Blake Papers, Cameron to Blake, May 17, 1875.

26. There is an ironic twist to the end of the *Liberal*. George Brown was offered the whole plant at 25 per cent off, and in return offered to take it at 50 per cent: Brown's offer does not seem to have been accepted. P.A.C., Brown Papers, Vol. 10, Brown to Mackenzie, July 15, 1875, from Edinburgh.

27. The *Bystander*, Toronto, June 1880. This series was monthly.

28. P.A.O., Blake Papers, Smith to Blake, May 7, 1876 (private).

29. In a series called "The political destiny of Canada," *Fortnightly Review*, London, republished in C.M. & N.R., June, 1877. The series was published as a book in 1878.

30. The *Canadian Monthly* of 1877 said that although "the requiem of 'Canada First' has often been said," the purpose of the group was, and is, "to infuse a national spirit into the policy of our statesman [*sic*] and people." April, 1877.

31. P.A.C., Denison Papers, Mair to Denison, March 16, 1876. See also Mair to Denison, January 28, 1876. Both letters from Portage la Prairie.

32. See Blake's résumé in the 1880 *Debates*, p. 1429 (April 15, 1880).

33. The expression of faith, and the phrase, is the *Nation's*, May 28, 1875.

34. The *Nation*, June 11, 1875.

35. *Ibid.*, September 29, 1876.

36. David Farr, *Colonial Office and Canada*, 1867-1887 (Toronto, 1955), p. 116.

37. *Canada: House of Commons, Debates*, 1867-68 (Ottawa, 1967), p. 566 (April 27, 1868).

38. The source for this is a letter from Mme Chapais to her son Thomas, 27 October 1876, Julienne Barnard, *Mémoires Chapais*, 3 vols. (Montreal, 1961-64), III, 33.

39. "The forces of disunion [among Quebec Liberals] antagonisms and rivalries, personal and political - have acquired a momentum which cannot at once be arrested. . . ." C.M. & N.R., July, 1874.

40. *Canada: House of Commons, Debates*, 1875, p. 289 (February 22, 1875).

41. *Ibid.*, p. 935 (March 27, 1875). They felt however that the number of French-Canadian judges ought to be written in. *Ibid.*, p. 970 (March 30, 1875). It was not written in however.

42. Essential to the consideration of this issue are the legal niceties involved in it. Appeals reached the Privy Council in two ways: (1) as of right, *i.e.* the subject's right to appeal to the Throne; (2) by special leave from the Throne itself, *i.e.* of grace. Irving proposed to abolish the first method. See Farr, *Colonial Office and Canada*, 1867-1887, pp. 137-8.

43. *Canada: House of Commons, Debates*, 1875, p. 981 (March 30, 1875). Quoted also by David Farr in an excellent chapter on the whole subject, "Lord Chancellor and the question of appeals to the Privy Council," *Colonial Office and Canada*, pp. 133-65.

44. *Ibid.*, p. 286 (February 23, 1875).

45. In conversation with Lord Dufferin, Dufferin to Carnarvon, November 3, 1875 (private). *Dufferin-Carnarvon Correspondence*, p. 160.

46. *Canada: House of Commons, Debates*, 1875, p. 980 (March 30, 1875).

47. P.A.C., Mackenzie Papers, Blake to Mackenzie, August 9, 1876 (confidential).

48. *Canada: House of Commons, Debates*, 1880, p. 253-4 (February 26, 1880).

49. *Supra*, p. 7; see also W. L. Morton, *The Critical Years*, p. 269.

50. This summary is based upon Langevin's view, expressed in a long letter to his brother Edmond, Vicar-General of the diocese of Rimouski, which recounts letters between Archbishop Taschereau and Langevin. A.P.Q., Collection Chapais, Papiers Langevin, Hector Langevin to

Edmond Langevin, 12 mai, 1873 (privée).

51. The early reports of the Supreme Court of New Brunswick were collected by Wm. Pugsley. The legal citation is: I Pugsley, 279-92. J. J. Allen and Weldon concurred in the decision but wrote separate judgments.

52. The case is not reported in any Canadian collection I know of. The Privy Council reports mention it briefly. There is an account of the case in the Macdonald Papers, perhaps transcribed for him. P.A.C., Macdonald Papers, Vol. 303, Miscellaneous Papers, 1874-78.

53. P.A.C., Costigan Papers, Sweeney to Costigan, January 25, February 12, 1875.

54. Brown Papers, George Brown to Anne, March 9, 1875.

55. Mackenzie was very insistent on this point. He got Dufferin to reiterate it in the letter covering the despatch of the Commons resolution to England. Dufferin to Carnarvon, March 19, 1875, in *Dufferin-Carnarvon Correspondence*, p. 140.

56. *Canada: House of Commons, Debates*, 1875, pp. 609-34 (March 10, 1875).

57. Robert Rumilly, *Histoire de la province de Québec* (Montreal, n.d.), II, 37.

58. Lieutenant-Governor Morris subsequently cancelled the commission of the magistrate concerned. J. H. O'Donnell, *Manitoba as I Saw It: From 1869 to Date* (Toronto, 1909), p. 78.

59. Archives épiscopales des Trois Rivières, Taché to Leflèche, 9 mai 1874, in Rumilly, *Histoire de Québec*, I, 309.

60. L. O. David, Mes contemporains (Montréal, 1894), pp. 23-4, 271-5. See also, Castor, *Le Parti, le Pays, et le Grand Homme* (Montréal, 1882). For new lights on Chapleau see Jacques Gouin, "Histoire d'une amitié: correspondance intime entre Chapleau et DeCelles (1876-1898)." R.H.A.F. XVIII, 3 and 4, déc. 1964 and mars 1965, pp. 363-386, 541-565.

61. J.B. Proulx in *Annales térésiennes*, jan. 1882, in Rumilly, II, 11.

62. Chapleau explained the jury's verdict. "Pour comprendre ainsi facilement pourquoi les paroles du juge ont tant influé sur l'opinion des jurés. . . . ils ont cru devoir obéir aux instructions du juge plûtot qu'aux supplications de l'avocat. . . ." Rumilly, II, 14, from *Le Nouveau Monde*, probably 20 nov. 1874.

63. Toronto *Liberal*, February 8, 1875.

64. Dufferin to Carnarvon, December 4, 1874 (private), in *Dufferin-Carnarvon Correspondence*, p. 113. This is a long despatch summing up the whole Riel crisis, with admirable objectivity and perceptiveness.

65. Dufferin to Carnarvon, December 8, 1874, pp. 115-121.

66. G. F. G. Stanley, *Riel*, pp. 115-16.

67. A.P.Q., Collection Chapais, Papiers Langevin, Macdonald to Langevin, February 13, 1875, from Ottawa (private).

68. Stanley, *Riel*, pp. 240-1.

69. P.A.O., Blake Papers, Huntington to Blake, November 2, 1875.

70. Toronto *Globe*, September 15, 1875, letter of Joseph Doutre, September 13, 1875.

71. Blake Papers, E. G. Penny to Mackenzie, November 6, 1875 (private).

72. There is a full account of the funeral in the *Globe*, November 17, 1875.

73. This was admitted by Joseph Doutre in his letter to the Toronto *Globe* of September 13, 1875, in *Globe*, September 15, 1875.

74. Letter from Archbishop Lynch, dated April 8, 1876, replying to Galt's pamphlet against the church of 1876. Toronto *Globe*, April 10, 1876.

75. Rumilly, *Québec*, I, 322.

76. P.A.C., Gédéon Ouimet Papers, Irvine to Ouimet, June 24, 1874; July 15, 1874. P.A.O., Cartwright Papers, Galt to Cartwright, May 26, 1874 (confidential).

77. P.A.C., Macdonald Papers, Vol. 226, Ouimet to Macdonald, November 12, 1880.

78. Rumilly, *Québec*, I, 331.

79. A.P.Q., Collection Chapais, Papiers Langevin, Macdonald to Langevin, January 6, 1875; February 13, 1875 (private). Macdonald was writing in exactly the same sense, and at the same time to D'Alton McCarthy, P.A.C., Dalton McCarthy Papers, Macdonald to McCarthy, February 15, 1875 (private).

80. Charles Langelier, *Souvenirs Politiques, 1878 à 1900*, 2 vols. (Québec 1909), I, p. 29.

81. Cauchon as a source is not necessarily reliable, but there seems no good reason why he should lie in a private letter to Mackenzie. P.A.C., Mackenzie Papers, Cauchon to Mackenzie, January 28, 1876 (confidential).

82. Quoted in C.M. & N.R., February, 1876.

83. *Grip*, Toronto, October 13, 1877. There is an apt description of Cauchon

in the *Canadian Monthly*, January, 1876, "active, *exigeant*, and importunate, undaunted by repulse and unshaken by scruple. . . ."

84. It is curious to note that in this election of 2,882 eligible voters, only 1,683 voted, despite all the sound and fury, whereas in 1874 some 2,481 voted, 1,377-1,104.

85. *Mandements de Québec*, V, 403-14, in LaPierre, *Tarte*, p. 55. The effect of this 1876 *mandement* was somewhat mitigated by Taschereau's still formal adherence to the collective *mandement* of September 22, 1875. It was impossible to get all the bishops to agree to this second *mandement* and it issued from Taschereau alone.

86. See E. R. Norman, *Anti-Catholicism in Victorian England* (London, 1968).

87. See A. T. Galt, *Civil Liberty in Lower Canada* (Montreal, 1876).

88. Bishop Conroy was not then named; but an Archbishop was promised. This whole paragraph is based, I trust not unwisely, on a copy of a letter, in Vol. 1 of the Laurier Papers, from E. B. K. to Mackenzie, December 16, 1876 (private and confidential), written from Paris. I am assuming the "E.B.K." means Sir Edward B. Kenny, Irish Catholic Senator from Nova Scotia, who was once in the Macdonald government. In 1876 Kenny resigned his Senate seat for non-attendance.

89. P.A.C., Laurier Papers, Vol. 547, Laurier to Young, December 2, 1875, from Arthabaskaville. Some, but not all of this letter was published by Skelton. See Vol. I, p. 39.

90. Toronto *Globe*, October 31, 1874 had an editorial about him.

91. Laurier's reactions to his reading of Macaulay and G. O. Trevelyan's life of Macaulay, are vividly described in a letter to John Young. P.A.C., Laurier Papers, Vol. 547, Laurier to Young, October 31, 1876.

92. Charles Langelier, *Souvenirs politiques*, I, p. 41.

93. *Mandements de Québec*, VI, 44-53. Tarte in *Le Canadien*, especially in October, 1877 and January, 1878, condemned the work of Bishop Conroy. See Laurier LaPierre, *Tarte*, pp. 86-9.

94. P.A.M., Morris Papers, Dufferin to Morris, November 1, 1877, private: "We found things as dull as usual in Ottawa, but Laurier's defeat has a good deal startled the political world." Also P.A.C., Macdonald Papers, Vol. 79, Dufferin to J. A. Macdonald, October 31, 1877 (private).

95. P.A.C., William Miller Papers, Thompson to Miller, October 29, 1877, from Halifax.

96. A.P.Q., Collection Chapais, Langevin Papers, Macdonald to Langevin, November 5, 1877 (private and confidential).

97. At Langevin's request. P.A.C., Macdonald Papers, Vol. 226, Langevin to Macdonald November 8, 1877 (private and confidential).

98. Langevin Papers, Chapleau to Langevin, November 23, 1877. Chapleau after a week had but $500 from French sources and $500 from English.

99. P.A.C., Mackenzie Papers, Mackenzie to Charles Mackenzie, May 12, 1878 (private).

NOTES TO CHAPTER FOUR

1. In 1877 it was listed with grades of 110 feet per mile, the highest in Canada; curves with radius of 462 feet, the second sharpest in Canada. The gauge was 3 ft. 6 in. *Canada, Sessional Papers*, 1877, No. 143 which has a useful chart of the railways of Canada with miles of track laid and the respective gauges and types of rails.

2. See G. R. Stevens, *Canadian National Railways*, I. *Sixty Years of Trial and Error* (Toronto, 1960), pp. 188-92..

3. Mackenzie's evidence before Select Standing Committee on Public Accounts, April 12, 1875, James Young, Chairman. *Canada: House of Commons, Journals*, 1875, App. 2, p. 44. See also P.A.C., Mackenzie Papers, Mackenzie to Brydges, May 12, 1874 (private).

4. P.A.C., Mackenzie Papers, Mackenzie to Letellier, November 9, 1874. Letellier was in the Senate, but came from Kamouraska County, and thus had a standing interest in the Intercolonial.

5. A. W. Currie, *The Grand Trunk Railway of Canada* (Toronto, 1957), p. 158.

6. *Canada: Sessional Papers*, 1877, No. 6, Report of C. J. Brydges, pp. 196-7.

7. *Ibid.*, 1879, No. 8, Brydges report, p. 9.

8. *Ibid.*, No. 113.

9. *Ibid.*, 1881, No. 26.

10. P.A.C., Macdonald Papers, Joseph

Hickson to Macdonald, January 15, 1879.

11. *Canada: Sessional Papers*, 1881, No. 61.

12. One emigrant's baggage totalled 8500 lbs., one modest package of which weighed 750 lb. Toronto *Globe*, August 4, 1874.

13. Letter to *Globe* signed W. H. Carpenter & Co., *loc. cit.* The North West Mounted Police in October, 1873 did it in 13 days.

14. Toronto *Globe*, August 29, 1874, letter signed "Nor'Wester," dated August 3, 1874, from Kettle Falls.

15. P.A.C., Sandford Fleming Papers, Fleming to Mackenzie, February 14, 1874 (draft); Mackenzie to Fleming March 23, 1874. Fleming clearly was reluctant to give up the International so near to the end of it.

16. Mary Fitzgibbon, *A Trip to Manitoba* (London, 1880), p. 115.

17. *Ibid.*, p. 147. Nitro-glycerine would not always go off if handled that way; but you could not tell whether it would or it would not.

18. *Canada: Sessional Papers*, 1881, No. 12, report of W. C. B. Grahame, Canadian government agent in Duluth, December 31, 1880.

19. See the exchange between Blake and Tupper in 1875. *Canada: House of Commons, Debates*, 1875, pp. 543 (March 5, 1875).

20. *Canada: House of Commons, Debates*, 1878, pp. 1675-1696 (April 4, 1878).

21. *Canada: House of Commons, Debates*, 1878, p. 2556 (May 9, 1878). See Creighton, *John A. Macdonald*, II, 239-40.

22. *Guelph Herald*, December, 1878; quoted from the *Manitoba Free Press*, December 14, 1878, in Gilbert, *Stephen*, p. 56.

23. For the history of the Pembina branch see Heather Gilbert, *Awakening Continent: The Life of Lord Mount Stephen* (Aberdeen, 1965), I, (1829-1891), 55-62.

24. P.A.C., Macdonald Papers, Vol. 191, Brydges to Tupper, September 26, 1879.

25. *Canada, Sessional Papers*, 1881, No. 5, App. 4, report of Collingwood Schreiber, Chief Engineer of Canadian Government Railways.

26. *Ibid.*, 1882, No. 8, App. 3, report of Schreiber.

27. *Ibid.*, 1879, No. 43m. Fleming's report April 5, 1879.

28. Sir Albert Smith noted the profit of the Pembina branch and complained it was turned over to the C.P.R. without any consideration. *Canada: House of Commons, Debates*, 1880-81, p. 412 (January 12, 1881).

29. Toronto *Globe*, July 28, 1874, letter from its Winnipeg correspondent of July 18.

30. G. H. Ham, *Reminiscences of a Raconteur* (Toronto, 1921), p. 39.

31. J. L. Holmes, "Factors affecting politics in Manitoba: a study of the provincial elections, 1870-99," M.A. thesis, University of Manitoba, 1936, pp. 17-41.

32. Other causes were frequent failures of hay crops, the absence of cod around the shores, and the system of leasehold tenure. See, W. C. Krieger to Minister of Agriculture, May 25, 1876, from Reykjavik, *Canada: Sessional Papers*, 1877, No. 8, pp. 73-4.

33. *Ibid.*, John Taylor to Minister of Agriculture, June 1, 1877, from Gimli, 92 *et seq*. For further details of the settlement, W. Kristjansen, *The Icelandic People in Manitoba* (Winnipeg, 1965).

34. Evidence of John Lowe, Secretary to the Department of Agriculture (1871-1889), before the Select Standing Committee on Immigration and Colonization. Lowe visited the colony in September, 1877. *Canada: House of Commons, Journals*, 1878, App. 2, p. 16.

35. P.A.M., Morris Papers, Mackenzie to Morris, April 16, 1874 (confidential).

36. *Canada: House of Commons, Debates*, 1877, pp. 109-11 (February 19, 1877). Question of Joseph Ryan, M.P. for Marquette, and reply of David Mills, Minister of the Interior.

37. Chester Martin, *"Dominion Lands" Policy* (Toronto, 1938), pp. 238-9. Supplementary claims totalled 993.

38. In order to complete the 1/20, section 26 in every fifth township was also Hudson's Bay Company land. Altogether Hudson's Bay Company land totalled nearly 6,640,000 acres.

39. See map in W. A. Mackintosh, *Prairie Settlement: The Geographical Setting* (Toronto, 1934), p. 22.

40. Wallace Stegner, *Wolf Willow* (New York, 1962), p. 91.

41. *Canada: House of Commons, Journals*, 1876, App. 3, "Report of the Select Committee on the causes of the present Depression," David Mills, Chairman,

pp. 74-5, Evidence of William Lukes of Newmarket.

42. *Ibid.*, 1877, App. 6, "Report of Select Standing Committee on Immigration and Colonization," James Trow, Chairman, p. 163.

43. *Ibid.*, 1876, App. 3, *op. cit.*, p. 74.

44. *Canada: Sessional Papers*, 1881, No. 12, J. P. Sheldon's report. He was one of several tenant farmer delegates invited to Canada by Macdonald's Minister of Agriculture, J. H. Pope. He was two months in Canada, in September and October, 1880.

45. *Canada: House of Commons, Journals*, 1877, App. 6, "Report of Select Standing Committee on Immigration and Colonization," p. 162.

46. W. L. Morton, *Manitoba, A History* (Toronto, 1957), pp. 176-83.

47. 34 Vic. c 16. See L. H. Thomas, *The Struggle for Responsible Government in the North-West Territories, 1870-1897* (Toronto, 1956), p. 48.

48. *Ibid.*, p. 65.

49. See *ibid.*, 78n for the details on the passing of this 1877 amendment.

50. P.A.M., Morris Papers, Morris to Langevin, June 8, 1878 (private). See Thomas, *North-West Territories*, pp. 83, 83n.

51. Alexander Morris, *The Treaties of Canada with the Indians of Manitoba and the North-West Territories* (Toronto, 1880), p. 293.

52. Taylor to Seward, March 26, 1878, from Consular Despatches in Winnipeg, quoted by G. F. G. Stanley, *The Birth of Western Canada: A History of the Riel Rebellions* (Toronto, 1960 [orig. 1936]), pp. 214-15.

53. Morris, *Treaties of Canada with the Indians*. See, however, note 47, Chapter One.

54. Stanley, *Birth of Western Canada*, pp. 194-215 has a most useful chapter on Indian treaties.

55. Treaty No. 3 is a good example. See *Canada: Sessional Papers*, 1875, No. 8, pp. 19-22.

56. P.A.M., Morris Papers, Morris to Mills, March 27, 1877; also Morris to Mills, December 4, 1876, reporting the treaty.

57. Mills came west in the summer of 1877 and visited settlements in Manitoba.

58. "In the West there was no strong leader in command on either side, and with its small representation in Parliament its attitude was not considered important." G. W. Ross, *Getting into Parliament and After* (Toronto, 1913), p. 106.

59. J. P. Turner, *The North-West Mounted Police, 1873-1893* (Ottawa, 1950), 2 vols., I, 344-357.

60. *Supra*, 10-11.

61. Turner, *North-West Mounted Police*, I, 149.

62. Turner's history is strewn with references to Jerry Potts. A picture of him I, 158. See especially C. M. MacInnes' brief description, in his superb book on the history and life of southern Alberta, *In the Shadow of the Rockies* (London, 1930), pp. 96-7.

63. C. M. MacInnes, *In the Shadow of the Rockies*, p. 99.

64. Stegner, *Wolf Willow*, p. 134.

65. *Canada: House of Commons, Debates*, 1876, p. 730 (March 7, 1876).

66. Stegner, *Wolf Willow*, p. 101.

67. Denny, *Forty Years in Canada*, p. 83.

68. C. M. MacInnes, *In the Shadow of the Rockies*, p. 195.

69. University of Western Ontario, Mills Papers, Memo to Council, August 23, 1877.

NOTES TO CHAPTER FIVE

1. O. J. Firestone, *Caanda's Economic Development, 1867-1953: with special reference to changes in the country's national product and natural wealth* (London, 1958), Table 87, 88, pp. 276-80.

2. R. C. McIvor, *Canadian Monetary, Banking and Fiscal Development* (Toronto, 1961), p. 75. Some of this increase was owing to money coming out of socks and going into banks.

3. On the basis of 1935-1939, $1.00 = 100, the price index reads: 1870, 67.3; 1890, 62.1; 1900, 58.1. This is an implicit price index. See Firestone, *op. cit.*, p. 77.

4. G. W. Bertram, "Economic Growth in Canadian industry, 1870-1915: the staple model," in W. T. Easterbrook and M. H. Watkins, *Approaches to Canadian Economic History* (Toronto, 1967), Carleton Library, pp. 74-98.

5. Tax revenue amounted to 80-85 per cent of government revenue. I have omitted consideration of non-tax sources, such as the Post Office, since

they were offset by equivalent expenses. Urquhart and Buckley, *Historical Statistics of Canada* (Toronto, 1965), p. 198.

6. Alan Wilson, *John Northway: Blue Serge Canadian* (Toronto, 1963), pp. 28-69.

7. Merrill Denison, *Harvest Triumphant: The Story of Massey-Harris* (Toronto, 1948), p. 63.

8. G. W. Bertram "Economic growth in Canadian industry 1870-1915," *op. cit.*, 96 n.

9. William Kilbourn, *The Elements Combined: A History of the Steel Company of Canada* (Toronto, 1960), p. 15.

10. *Canada: House of Commons, Journals*, 1874, App. 3, "Select Committee to enquire into the extent and condition of the Manufacturing interests of the Dominion." A. T. Wood, Chairman, p. 38.

11. *Canada: House of Commons, Journals*, 1876, App. 3, "Report of the Select Committee on the causes of the Present Depression of the Manufacturing, Mining, Commercial, Shipping, Lumber and Fishing interest." David Mills, Chairman, pp. 118-21 (March 22, 1876). Also, p. 197 (March 30, 1876).

12. *Canada: Senate, Debates*, 1875, 82-3 (February 24, 1875).

13. The 1880 Act is 43 Vic. c. 13; the 1895, 58-59 Vic. c. 16. See McIvor, *Canadian Monetary, Banking and Fiscal Development*, 65n. Both Cartwright and Tilley offer some comments on their experience with the question of gold reserves between 1874 and 1885 in the 1885 debates. *Canada: House of Commons, Debates*, 1885, pp. 351-4 (March 4, 1885).

14. See the illuminating essay by the American economic historian, Bray Hammond, "Banking in Canada before Confederation, 1792-1867" from his *Banks and Politics in America from the Revolution to the Civil War* (Princeton, 1957), pp. 631-70. It has been reprinted in Easterbrook and Watkins, *Approaches to Canadian Economic History* (Toronto, 1967), pp. 127-68.

15. It was not quite as simple as it sounds. John Rose, in 1869 sought to follow the example of the United States in their National Bank Act of 1863. This had several disadvantages, the most well known of which was the inverse stringency principle. Canadian bankers, led by McMaster of the new Canadian Bank of Commerce, protested vigorously, and brought Rose's resignation. Francis Hincks fathered the 1871 Bank Act, built upon older Canadian practice, and for which he ought to be remembered more often than he is. See, Victor Ross, *History of the Canadian Bank of Commerce* (Toronto, 1920); G. P. de T. Glazebrook, *Sir Edmund Walker* (Toronto, 1933).

16. R. C. McIvor, *Canadian Monetary and Banking Development*, p. 68.

17. Of the six that went into liquidation, two were in Nova Scotia, and four were in Quebec. Total paid-up capital was about $3.5 million and liabilities to the public about $2.5 million. McIvor *op. cit.*, 73n.

18. The net debt increased in Mackenzie's time by about $40 million.

19. Mackenzie to Dufferin, February 15, 1876 (confidential), in *Dufferin-Carnarvon Correspondence*, pp. 193-4. See also Cartwright, *Reminiscences*, pp. 156-7.

20. Montreal *Herald*, January 27, 1876. This speech was cited in the debates by Mackenzie Bowell. *Canada: House of Commons, Debates*, 1876, p. 428 (March 3, 1876).

21. *Canada: House of Commons, Debates*, 1876 (March 7, 1876), p. 489.

22. *Canada: House of Commons, Journals*, 1874, App. 3, "Report of Select Committee to enquire into the extent and condition of the Manufacturing Interests of the Dominion," dated May 19, 1874, A. T. Wood, M.P. for Hamilton, Chairman.

23. *Ibid.*, 1876, App. 3. "Report of the Select Committee on the causes of the Present Depression of the Manufacturing, Mining, Commercial, Shipping, Lumber and Fishing Interests," David Mills, Chairman, Report dated April 11, 1876. Evidence of Edward Gurney of Hamilton, March 30, 1876, p. 180.

24. *Loc. cit.*, evidence of G. Boivin of Montreal, March 16, 1876, p. 92.

25. Merrill Denison, *Harvest Triumphant*, p. 65. Cf. however Massey's views in the 1890's, *infra*, 208.

26. P.A.O., Patteson Papers, Belford to Patteson, February 26 [1876], from Ottawa.

27. *Canada: House of Commons, Debates*, 1876, p. 259 (February 25, 1876).

28. *Ibid.*, p. 407 (March 3, 1876).

29. They supported Workmen and Mac-

donald's motions on protection in 1876. See *infra*, 81.

30. See especially Young's article in C.N. & M.R., August, 1875.

31. *Canada: House of Commons, Debates*, 1876, p. 590 (March 7, 1876).

32. University of Western Ontario, Coyne Papers, Casey to Coyne, March 15, 1877.

33. Toronto *Weekly Globe*, August 23, 1878.

34. *Canada: House of Commons, Debates*, 1876, p. 253 (February 25, 1876).

35. *Ibid.*, p. 262.

36. *Canada: House of Commons, Debates*, 1877, p. 146 (February 20, 1877).

37. *Ibid.*, 1878, p. 440-1 (February 22, 1878).

38. *Ibid.*, 1877, p. 336 (February 28, 1876).

39. Macdonald made use of it in the election of 1878. P.A.C., Macdonald Papers, Vol. 65, f.26336 has notes for speeches.

40. *Grip*, Toronto, April 15, 1876.

41. C.M. & N.R., May, 1876: "Those who talk idly of a 'Chinese Wall' seem to forget it has been already erected by our neighbours, and it even appears necessary to remind them that a wall has two sides, the inside and the outside."

42. *Canada: House of Commons, Debates*, 1877, p. 404 (March 2, 1877).

43. On March 7, 1876, prior to Macdonald's introduction of his own motion, Thomas Workman, Liberal M.P. for Montreal West (President of Sun Life and Vice-President of Molson's Bank) introduced a motion simply calling for protection for the manufacturing industry. Macdonald voted for this motion, but explained before hand that he intended to bring forward a more comprehensive motion. (*Debates*, 1876, pp. 496-7.)

44. V. C. Fowke, *Canadian Agricultural Policy: The Historical Pattern* (Toronto, 1946), pp. 259-61; also P.A.O., Blake Papers, Barr to Blake, July 5, 1882 (private and confidential).

45. F. W. Taussig's views are usefully compressed in his *Principles of Economics* (New York, 1939) 4th edition, 2 vols. I, 508-547. See however his more extended works, *The Tariff History of the United States* (New York, 1931) 8th edition, and *Some Aspects of the Tariff Question* (New York, 1931).

46. J. H. Dales launched his attack against the National Policy in "Some historical and theoretical comments of Canada's National Policy," *Queen's Quarterly*, Autumn, 1964, pp. 297-316; also, "Cost of protectionism in high international mobility of factors," C.J.E.P.S., (November, 1964), pp. 512-25; "Protection, immigration and Canadian nationalism," in P. Russell, ed., *Nationalism in Canada* (Toronto, 1966), pp. 164-77. These have been conveniently published as *The Protective Tariff in Canada's Development* (Toronto, 1966).

47. D. G. Creighton, *Macdonald: The Old Chieftain*, p. 120.

48. Queen's University, Douglas Library, *Notes*, (Winter, 1965), XIV, No. 1, 6, Macdonald to James Williamson (his brother-in-law), February 24, 1874.

49. P.A.C., H. H. Smith Papers, Macdonald to Smith, Nov. 1, 1882 (private).

50. Macdonald to Tupper, August 24, 1874, in E. M. Saunders, *The Life and Letters of the Rt. Hon. Sir Charles Tupper* (London, 1916), I, 234. See also P.A.C., Pope Papers, Andrew Holland to Pope, October 26, 1914.

51. The rule of the 1874 Act was that any candidate guilty of corrupt practice or aiding in it was to be disqualified for two full Parliaments, i.e. for approximately 8 to 10 years. Bribery by agents, acting (presumably) without the candidate's knowledge, voided the election.

52. This was Disraeli's view. Disraeli to the Queen, September 23, 1880. Robert Blake, *Disraeli* (London, 1966), p. 730.

53. Creighton, *Macdonald*, pp. 184-5.

54. C.M. & N.R., June, 1874. "Current Events" by Goldwin Smith.

55. *Ibid*, March, 1876.

56. A.P.Q., Collection Chapais, Langevin Papers, Macdonald to Langevin, May 7, 1874 (private).

57. E. M. Saunders, *Life and Letters of Sir Charles Tupper* (London, 1916), I, 134.

58. Creighton, *Macdonald*, p. 192. He quotes a good example from the 1875 *Debates*, p. 32 (February 11, 1875).

59. J. M. S. Careless, *Brown of the Globe* (Toronto, 1963), II, 340-2.

60. *Grip*, November 13, 1875.

61. A.P.Q., Collection Chapais, Langevin Papers, Macdonald to Langevin, January 11, 1877 (from Toronto; private).

62. Creighton, *Macdonald*, pp. 219-23.

63. C.M. & N.R., October, 1876.

64. *Ibid.*, July, 1877.

65. P.A.C., Macdonald Papers, Vol. 276,

Tilley to Macdonald, December 4, 1875; September 2, 1876 (private).

66. P.A.C., Tupper Papers (new additions), Tilley to Tupper, January 27, 1876 (private).

67. *Grip*, Toronto, April 5, 1879.

68. See the comments, not altogether unfriendly, of G. W. Ross, *Getting into Parliament and After* (Toronto, 1913), pp. 161-2.

69. See Colin Cameron's remarks, *House of Commons, Debates*, 1880, p. 702 (March 18, 1880).

70. Halifax *Morning Chronicle*, June 12, 1896. This little gem I owe to Kenneth McLaughlin. See his thesis, "The federal election of 1896 in Nova Scotia," M.A. thesis, Dalhousie University, 1967, p. 123.

71. A.P.Q., Collection Chapais, Langevin Papers, Hector Langevin to Edmond Langevin, 22 juillet, 1873. This was four days after the Montreal *Herald* had published the deadly telegrams and correspondence from J. J. C. Abbott's files.

72. The Liberals lost bye-elections to Conservatives in: Berthier, Chambly, Charlevoix, Digby, Drummond-Arthabaska, Huron South, Kamouraska, London, Middlesex East, Norfolk South, Ontario North, Ontario South, Queens (P.E.I.), Renfrew North, Toronto East, Toronto West, Two Mountains, Victoria North.

73. *Canada: House of Commons, Debates*, 1877, p. 1711 (April 23, 1877).

74. Dufferin to Carnarvon, April 27, 1877; May 3, 1877, in *Dufferin-Carnarvon Correspondence*, pp. 349-50.

75. Blake Papers, Blake to Mackenzie, November 5, 1877 (draft).

76. P.A.C., Mackenzie Papers, Mackenzie to Anglin, January 3, 1878 (confidential).

77. For the drunk, *supra*, p. 4; for the Letellier affair, *infra*, pp. 97-9.

78. Cartwright wished to expose Macdonald, and Preston to expose Donald Smith. Cartwright, *Reminiscences*, pp. 380-88; W. T. R. Preston, *The Life and Times of Lord Strathcona* (London, 1914), pp. 303-15.

79. The scene made quite an impression; it was noted in the House nine years later. *Debates*, 1887, p. 705, (June 1, 1887). Also, G. W. Ross, *Getting into Parliament and After*, p. 100. Cartwright adds that if Macdonald had succeeded in really hitting Smith there would never have been a C.P.R. Company with Smith in it.

80. Ottawa *Citizen*, May 21, 1874, quoting Hamilton *Evening Times*. See Norman Ward, "The formative years of the House of Commons, 1867-1891" for the ways, character, and methods of the House. In C.J.E.P.S., Vol. 18, no. 4 (November, 1952), pp. 431-451. For comment on saturnalia, pp. 432-4.

81. *Ontario Workman*, September 5, 1872, in Bernard Ostry, "Conservatives, Liberals and Labour in the 1870's," C.H.R., XLI, 2, (June, 1960), p. 117.

82. H. A. Logan, *Trade Unions in Canada* (Toronto, 1948), p. 44.

83. Shirley Ayer, "The locomotive engineers' strike on the Grand Trunk Railway in 1876-1877," M.A. thesis, McGill University, 1961, pp. 29-30.

84. See also Dufferin to Carnarvon, Oct. 29, 1875 (private). *Dufferin-Carnarvon Correspondence*, 159.

85. Edward Harrison, Captain of No. 1 company, Hastings Rifles, to Lt. Col. James Brown (M.P., West Hastings), Commanding Officer. Canada: *Sessional Papers*, 1877, No. 55, pp. 5-6.

86. Mackenzie to Hickson, January 2, 1877; Ayer, "Grank Trunk strike," p. 123.

87. A. W. Currie, *The Grand Trunk Railway of Canada* (Toronto, 1957), p. 153.

88. *Canada: House of Commons, Debates*, 1878, p. 2463 (May 6, 1878),

89. John White, M.P. for East Hastings, and Grand Master of the Orange Order for East Ontario, mentioned some of these tunes as being provocative. *Debates*, 1878, 2461 (May 6, 1878). Lillibulero dates from the Irish rebellion of 1689-91; the other two from 1798.

90. P.A.C., Mackenzie Papers, Hickson to Mackenzie, April 13, 1878 (private).

91. 41 Vic. c. 17.

92. Queen's University, Mackenzie Papers, John Cameron to Mackenzie, August 15, 1876.

93. *Canada: House of Commons, Journals*, 1874, App. 8. "Third Report of the Select Committee respecting a Prohibitory Liquor Law," G. W. Ross, Chairman, For some examples from the report of the committee see *supra*, p. 3.

94. It also allowed for local licences, granted under provincial law, to expire.

95. *Canada: House of Commons, Debates*, 1878, p. 2404 (May 3, 1878).

96. A.P.Q., Collection Chapais, Langevin Papers, Macdonald to Langevin, May 2, 1878, 8 P.M.

97. Cartwright is particularly stern here. *Reminiscences*, pp. 167-70.

98. *Canada: House of Commons, Debates*, 1887, pp. 941-2 (June 13, 1887). Dr. Bergin was not however in the Commons when the Act was first passed. He was elected in the 1878 election.

99. Counties and municipalities were: Nova Scotia 12, New Brunswick 10, Prince Edward Island 4, Quebec 3, Manitoba 2. By 1896 there were none in Ontario or British Columbia. See *Statistical Year Book of Canada for 1897* (Ottawa, 1898).

100. Firestone, *Canada's Economic Development*, p. 84.

101. C. R. W. Biggar, *Sir Oliver Mowat* (Toronto, 1905), I, 264-70.

102. John Willison, who was no Conservative, is quite firm on this point, and there is other contemporary evidence to support him. J. S. Willison, *Reminiscences* (Toronto, 1919), pp. 92-3.

103. P.A.O., Sir Alexander Campbell Papers, G. B. Boyle to John A. Macdonald, June 10, 1880 (private and confidential).

104. According to Cartwright, Macdonald said as much to Sir Albert Smith, with whom Macdonald maintained not unfriendly relations. Cartwright, *Reminiscences*, p. 185.

105. A.P.Q., Collection Chapais, Langevin Papers, Macdonald to Langevin, May 18, 1878 from Toronto (private).

106. Mackenzie Papers, Mackenzie to Brown, Saturday [May, 1878], (confidential).

107. Toronto *Mail*, August 27, 1878.

108. *Ibid.*, August 7, 1882, letter from David Blain. Blain was independent Liberal in Mackenzie's time but was, in 1882, a Conservative.

109. P.A.O., Edgar Papers, Mackenzie to Edgar, September 24, 1878 (confidential).

110. P.A.C., Mackenzie Papers, Mackenzie to Charles Black, October 15, 1878 (private). Black was an old Sarnia friend now living in Montreal.

111. P.A.C., Mackenzie Papers, Pelletier to Mackenzie, November 17, 1877.

112. *Grip*, Toronto, April 3, 1880.

113. P.A.C., Mackenzie Papers, Cameron to Mackenzie, October 28, 1878 (private). Cameron's view about the *Globe* and Brown must be taken with care; Cameron had after all been editor of the Toronto *Liberal*. But compare Toronto *Telegram*, September 20, 1878, ". . . the blunt fact remains that Mr. Brown and his newspaper are not popular and their assistance is most likely to prove disastrous than useful."

114. Ross, *Getting into Parliament and After*, p. 107.

115. P.A.C., Mackenzie Papers, Brown to Mackenzie, October 1, 1878 (private and confidential); October 3, 1878.

116. *Grip*, April 3, 1880, "An intercepted letter."

NOTES TO CHAPTER SIX

1. For Macdonald at Halifax see Creighton, *Macdonald*, pp. 248-9, 254-5.

2. Queen's University, Mackenzie Papers, Mackenzie to his daughter Mary, September 25, 1879.

3. *The Week*, Toronto, November 6, 1884. J. E. Collins, "Social life at Ottawa."

4. C. O. Ermatinger, *The second half-century of the Talbot settlement*, (1853-1903). Unpublished MSS in University of Western Ontario Library, Chapter XIII, p. 4.

5. His granddaughter's recollections of him, C.B.C. broadcast, January 11, 1966. Daisy Macdonald was Hugh John Macdonald's daughter.

6. *The Week*, Toronto, March 6, 1884, an account of Macdonald and Blake by the Ottawa correspondent of the *New York Sun*.

7. P.A.C., Macdonald Papers, Vol. 528, Macdonald to Stephen, August 7, 1888 (private and confidential).

8. University of British Columbia Library, Charles Hibbert Tupper Papers, *Reminiscences*. P.A.C., microfilm, M. 109.

9. J. Pope, *Day of Sir John Macdonald* (Toronto, 1920), p. 153.

10. *Canada: House of Commons, Debates*, 1883, p. 714-15 (April 19, 1883).

11. I have not found the original locus of this famous remark, but that it was common knowledge in Parliament is evidenced in the great 1885 debate on the Franchise Act. James Somerville (North Brant): "We want to know why

the hon. Minister of Agriculture has kept silent; he might have told us at least that 'there ain't nothing to it' . . ." *Canada: House of Commons, Debates*, 1885, p. 1550 (May 2, 1885). Willison says (*Reminiscences*, p. 196) he could never find out whether the remark was fact or fabrication.

12. P.A.C., Macdonald Papers, Vol. 88. Lansdowne to Macdonald, June 23, 1889, from Simla, India.
13. *The Week*, Toronto, April 5, 1889 has a short sketch of Pope.
14. Robert Rumilly, *Histoire de la province de Québec*, II, 155.
15. *Ibid.*, II, 182.
16. There is an excellent account of the Letellier affair in John T. Saywell, *The Officer of Lieutenant-Governor* (Toronto, 1957), pp. 113-119. Subsequent stages of the affair are, pp. 147-9, 234-48. See also Rumilly, *Québec*, II, 179-290.
17. Robert Rumilly, *Mercier* (Montréal, 1936), p. 94.
18. L. Pacaud (ed.), *Sir Wilfrid Laurier, letters à mon père et ma mère* (Arthabaska, 1935), p. 9, Laurier to Pacaud, March 5, 1878.
19. P.A.C., Macdonald Papers, Vol. 253, Mousseau to Macdonald, August 3, 1878 (confidential).
20. ". . . no officer of the Local Government should be independent of the Federal Government." *Canada: Senate, Debates*, 1867-68, 347 (May 20, 1868).
21. *Canada: House of Commons, Debates*, p. 651 (March 15, 1880).
22. Montreal *Gazette*, February 12, 1880 (parliamentary notes).
23. O. D. Skelton, *Life and Letters of Sir Wilfrid Laurier* [Orig. 1921], Carlton Library, 1965, 2 vols., I, 67. This is not footnoted in Skelton, and almost certainly derives from interviews between Skelton and Laurier.
24. *Canada: House of Commons, Debates*, 1880, p. 1815 (April 27, 1880). See Dale Thomson, *Mackenzie*, pp. 361-3; Mackenzie to Jones, May 3, 1880 (private). P.A.N.S., Jones Papers, *Report* 1952, pp. 61-2.
25. *Bystander*, Toronto, August, 1880.
26. *Canada: House of Commons, Debates*, 1880, p. 1468-9, (April 16, 1880).
27. P.A.O., Alexander Campbell Papers, Tilley to Campbell, September 14, 1889, gives an account of the provenance of the 1879 tariff.
28. *Canada: House of Commons, Debates*, 1879, p. 527 (March 18, 1879).
29. *Ibid.*, p. 528 (March 18, 1879).
30. *Canada: Statutes*, 1879. (42 Vic. c. 15).
31. *Canada: House of Commons, Debates*, 1879, p. 880 (April 1, 1879).
32. *Ibid.*, p. 1015 (April 4, 1879).
33. *Ibid.*, p. 528 (March 18, 1879).
34. *Canada: House of Commons, Debates*, 1880-1881, p. 1261 (March 8, 1881).
35. P.A.C., Minto Papers, J. S. Willison to Minto, July 18, 1903: "Both parties here fear the manufacturers and properly so, for they have been the controlling factor in every election since 1878."
36. For a short but comprehensive collection of documents on this subject, see *Canada: Sessional Papers*, 1881, No. 21K.
37. Macdonald's gloss upon the terms. P.A.C., Macdonald Papers, Vol. 279, Macdonald to Trutch, May 17, 1880 (confidential; draft).
38. *Loc. cit.* See also *House of Commons, Debates*, 1880-81, p. 114 (December 16, 1880).
39. For further details see Ormsby, *British Columbia*, pp. 281-5.
40. P.A.C., Sandford Fleming Papers, Vol. 47, contain some extraordinary and bitter letters from Marcus Smith. Smith to Fleming, December 7, 1877 (confidential and personal); December 28, 1877; February 25, 1878 (private); November 13, 1878 (strictly private). Also P.A.C., Macdonald Papers, Vol. 127, Smith to Macdonald, May 12, 1879 (private).
41. P.A.C., Willison Papers, Pope to Willison, May 4, 1922, refers to the breach between Macdonald and Tupper, from 1878 to 1881.
42. See Alan Wilson, "Sandford Fleming and Charles Tupper: the fall of the siamese twins, 1880," in John Moir, ed., *Character and Circumstance: Essays in Honour of Donald Grant Creighton* (Toronto, 1970), pp. 99-127.
43. *Canada: Report of the Royal Commission on the Canadian Pacific Railway* (Ottawa, 1882).

NOTES TO CHAPTER SEVEN

1. See *Rob Roy*, in the Everyman edition, pp. 97-8. W. T. R. Preston uses this quotation (at length) pejoratively to introduce his book on *Lord Strathcona*.

2. For Stephen's early history see Heather Gilbert, *Awakening Continent: The Life of Lord Mount Stephen* (Aberdeen, 1965), I, 1829-1891, pp. 1-33.
3. Macdonald Papers, Vol. 269, Stephen to Macdonald, September 2, 1882 (from Montreal; private).
4. Senator David Macpherson admitted his great energy and ability, but said that he was considered in London as "dangerously sanguine." P.A.C., Macdonald Papers, Vol. 249, Macpherson to Macdonald, June 2, 1884 (from London; confidential).
5. P.A.C., Macdonald Papers, Vol. 267, Stephen to Macdonald, October 18, 1880 (from Montreal; confidential).
6. P.A.C., Angus Papers, Angus to Ashworth, May 2, 1878 (private): "You will observe the general drift of the [cable] above is depreciation . . . of inducing the Dutchman to sell more freely."
7. W. T. R. Preston makes much of the unscrupulousness of the transaction (*The Life and Times of Lord Strathcona* [London, 1914], pp. 103-6), and he seems to have had access to at least some accurate information; but he must now be read against Heather Gilbert's account which is much more favourable to Stephen. (*Stephen*, pp. 34-54.) See also J. G. Pyle, *The Life of James J. Hill*, 2 vols. (New York, 1917); Beckles Willson, *The Life of Lord Strathcona* (Toronto, 1915), in part a reply to Preston's book.
8. Quoted by J. M. Gibbon, *The Romantic History of the Canadian Pacific* (New York, 1937), p. 197.
9. P.A.C., Macdonald Papers, Vol. 267, Stephen to Macdonald, July 9, 1880 (private and confidential). This most interesting letter is quoted fully in Gilbert, *Stephen*, pp. 63-5, and substantially in Gibbon, pp. 199-201.
10. *Canada: House of Commons, Debates*, 1880-81, p. 209, December 22, 1880.
11. J. B. Hedges, *Building the Canadian West: The Land and Colonization Policies of the Canadian Pacific Railway* (New York, 1939), p. 56.
12. See J. B. Hedges' remarks in *The Federal Railway Land Subsidy Policy of Canada* (Cambridge, 1934), p. 31.
13. Of the four Manitoba members of the House of Commons three were Conservatives, and the fourth, Joseph Ryan, M.P. Marquette, seems to have been unconcerned.
14. *Manitoba Assembly, Journals*, 1880, 16 (Dec. 21, 1880).
15. *Canada: House of Commons, Debates*, 1880-81, p. 494 (January 17, 1881); see also White's speech, *ibid.*, p. 577 (January 20, 1881).
16. *Bystander*, Toronto, October, 1880.
17. P.A.O., Blake Papers, Laurier to Blake, November 26, 1880 (private).
18. G. W. Ross, *Getting into Parliament and After*, p. 116. Ross was a Liberal, but was told this by a Conservative "whose word could not be doubted."
19. Edmonton *Bulletin*, December 13, 1880. This was the second of the new weekly's issues. The *Bulletin* tactfully omitted reference to the section between Kamloops and the eastern side of the Rockies.
20. *Canada: House of Commons, Debates*, 1880-81, p. 191 (December 21, 1880).
21. *Bystander*, Toronto, January 1881.
22. Montreal *Gazette*, December 16, 1880 (parliamentary notes).
23. *Canada: House of Commons, Debates*, 1880-81, p. 144 (December 17, 1880).
24. *Ibid.*, p. 105 (December 15, 1880). The italics are mine, since I felt it was important not to misconstrue Blake's words.
25. P.A.C., Macdonald Papers, Vol. 127, Memorial of Toronto Board of Trade to House of Commons, December 21, 1880.
26. *Ibid.*, Vol. 127, December 11, 1880.
27. *Canada: House of Commons, Debates*, 1880-81, p. 464 (January 14, 1881).
28. *Ibid.*, p. 479 (January 14, 1881).
29. *The Week*, Toronto, February 28, 1884; also in *Grip*, March 8, 1884.
30. Edmonton *Bulletin*, December 27, 1880.
31. P.A.C., Macdonald Papers, Vol. 191, Brydges to Macdonald, October 23, 1880 (private). See also *ibid.*, Vol. 127, D. MacArthur to Macdonald, December 24, 1880 (private).
32. December, 1880 rate per car, Montreal to Winnipeg, $293; actual breakdown of costs, Montreal to St. Paul, $120; St. Paul to Winnipeg, $173. On the basis of cost per mile Blake calculated that Montreal to Winnipeg freight cost 9.5 cents per mile per car; the rate from St. Paul to Winnipeg was 42.8 cents per mile per car. *Canada: House of Commons, Debates*, 1880-81, p. 10 (December 10, 1880).
33. P.A.C., Macdonald Papers, Vol. 256, Pope to Macdonald, August 24, 1882.

34. C. J. Brydges, reporting a conversation with J. J. Hill in St. Paul on December 4, 1880. P.A.C., Macdonald Papers, Vol. 127, Brydges to D. C. Macpherson, December 28, 1880 (from Montreal).
35. Toronto *Globe*, December 21, 1880, for example.
36. P.A.C., Macdonald Papers, Vol. 256, Stephen to Macdonald, August 27, 1881 (from Causapscal). Stephen had just returned from Winnipeg.
37. *Canada: House of Commons, Debates*, 1882, p. 1392 (May 8, 1882).
38. See R. M. Dawson, "The Gerrymander of 1882," C.J.E.P.S., I, 2 (May, 1935), pp. 197-221.
39. David Mills' information. *House of Commons, Debates*, 1882, p. 1391 (May 8, 1882).
40. *Ibid.*, p. 1409 (May 9, 1882).
41. *Ibid.*, p. 1489 (May 12, 1882).
42. London *Advertiser*, February 15, 1882.
43. Toronto *Globe*, May 24, 1879.
44. McLaren to Caldwell, April 12, 1880, cited by D'Alton McCarthy, *House of Commons, Debates*, 1882, p. 901 (April 17, 1882).
45. *Ibid.*, 1882, p. 922 (April 17, 1882), for Macdonald's reasons.
46. Order in Council of November 12, 1874. There are several collections of papers on this issue – a good one is the Ontario publication of 1882, *Ontario Boundary Papers*.
47. 42 Vic. c. 2.
48. *Canada: House of Commons, Debates*, 1880, p. 73 (February 18, 1880).
49. *Canada: House of Commons, Journals*, 1880, App. 1, XXVI.
50. P.A.C., Macdonald Papers, Vol. 34, G. W. Burbidge (Deputy Minister of Justice) to Macdonald, July 28, 1883 (telegram): reports telegram from Rat Portage, "twenty five Ontario constables here and fifteen Manitoban they are now arresting one another citizen[s] taking part on both sides a general riot expected. . . ."
51. *Ibid.*, Vol. 34, Fred White (Comptroller of North West Mounted Police) to Macdonald, July 25, 1883 (telegram from Winnipeg).
52. *Bystander*, Toronto, October, 1883.
53. Winnipeg, *Manitoba Free Press*, July 28, 1883.
54. P.A.C., Macdonald Papers, Vol. 35, Campbell to Macdonald, October 30, 1883 (from Montreal; confidential).
55. P.A.O., Alexander Campbell Papers, Mowat to Campbell, November 26, 1883 (private).
56. W. L. Morton, *Manitoba: A History* (Toronto, 1957), p. 219.
57. P.A.C., Macdonald Papers, Vol. 35, Macdonald to Norquay, March 13, 1885 (draft telegram); Norquay to Macdonald, March 13, 1885.
58. Hector Charlesworth, *Candid Chronicles* (Toronto, 1925), pp. 196-7.
59. P.A.O., Blake Papers, Joly to Blake, January 4, 1882 (personal). Joly's italics.
60. *Ibid.*, Mercier to Blake, 17 jan. 1882 (personelle). Mercier's italics.
61. P.A.O., Blake Papers, Laurier to Blake, June 3, 1882 (private).
62. *Ibid.*, Laurier to Blake, July 10, 1882 (private).
63. *Ibid.*, Pacaud to Blake, 14 sept. 1882 (from Québec).
64. Robert Rumilly, *Mercier* (Montréal, 1935), p. 144.
65. *Ibid.*, p. 94.
66. Rumilly, *Québec*, III, 184.
67. J. W. Longley, "Great Canadians I have known," *Canadian Magazine*, LVII, No. 1 (May, 1921), p. 65.
68. There is justice in the remarks of the Halifax *Morning Chronicle*, Liberal though it was: ". . . both in the house [of Assembly] and at the bar he showed himself to be a polished and graceful speaker and a plausible though not always fair and scrupulous debater." Halifax *Morning Chronicle*, September 1, 1885.
69. *The Week*, February 13, 1891. Article on Sir John Thompson, by "W."
70. P.A.O., Blake Papers, Fielding to Blake, January 23, 1882 (private).
71. See J. M. Beck, *The Government of Nova Scotia* (Toronto, 1957), p. 159, for a useful analysis of the effects upon political parties.
72. J. W. Longley, "Reminiscences, political and otherwise," *Canadian Magazine* (Nov. 1920), LVI, No. 1, 65.
73. Saint John *Daily Sun*, August 19, 1878.
74. *Ibid.*, December 22, 1881.
75. For Whiting's remarks to the Wood Committee of 1874, *supra*, p. 76.
76. P.A.O., Blake Papers, F. W. Glen to Blake, January 2, 1882.
77. *Ibid.*, Mercier to Blake, 17 jan. 1882 (personelle).
78. P.A.O., Blake Papers, Paterson to Blake, July 15, 1882 (from Brantford; private). Paterson was M.P. for Brant South.

79. P.A.C., Macdonald Papers, Vol. 65, "Elections."
80. There is an interesting opinion survey instituted in the 1882 session by the "Select Committee to inquire into the operation of the tariff on the agricultural interests of the Dominion." One question, was Canada in a better position to negotiate reciprocity with the United States with the new tariff? (Yes, 383 to 100.) Had the tariff increased the price of cottons? (No, 348 to 225.) *Canada: House of Commons, Journals*, 1882, App. 2, p. 16.
81. P.A.C., William Buckingham Papers, Mackenzie to Buckingham, September 23, 1881 (private).

NOTES TO CHAPTER EIGHT

1. P.A.C., Galt Papers, Vol. 8, Supplementary, Galt to his wife, March 1, 1882, from London, England.
2. University of Western Ontario, James Coyne Papers, George Casey to Coyne, January 17, 1882; Coyne to his wife, February 13, 1882. See also H. A. Stevenson, "James H. Coyne: his life and contributions to Canadian history," M.A. thesis, University of Western Ontario, 1960.
3. P.A.O., Cartwright Papers, Smith to Cartwright, August 3, 1882 (private); Cartwright to Donald Smith, August 5, 1882 (private).
4. P.A.C., Macdonald Papers, Vol. 331, Davin to Macdonald, November 22, 1889 (private and confidential).
5. This interesting point is made by James Armstrong, M.P. for South Middlesex (a Liberal), in *House of Commons, Debates*, 1884, p. 789 (March 11, 1884).
6. *Canada: House of Commons, Debates*, 1884, pp. 1148-9 (March 27, 1884).
7. This happy phrase is not mine but Augustus Bridle's, who has an attractive essay, "Sir William Van Horne," in a series of vignettes, *Sons of Canada* (Toronto, 1916). See page 196.
8. J. H. E. Secretan, *Canada's Great Highway: From the First Stake to the Last Spike* (London, 1924), pp. 104-5.
9. P.A.C., Macdonald Papers, Vol. 127, J. J. C. Abbott to Macdonald, December 20, 1881.
10. Heather Gilbert, *Awakening Continent: The Life of Lord Mount Stephen* (Aberdeen, 1965), pp. 85-6.
11. P.A.C., Galt Papers, Vol. 8, Supplemental, Galt to Macdonald, March 13, 1881 (draft).
12. Thomas White's recollection. *Canada: House of Commons, Debates*, 1884, p. 639 (March 4, 1884).
13. Walter Vaughan, *The Life and Work of Sir William Van Horne* (New York, 1920), pp. 83-4.
14. P. T. Bone, *When the Steel Went Through : Reminiscences of a Railroad Pioneer* (Toronto, 1947), p. 51.
15. P.A.C., Macdonald Papers, Vol. 267, Stephen to Macdonald, July 16, 1882, from St. Paul.
16. See L. H. Thomas, *North-West Territories, 1870-1897*, pp. 98-9, 107.
17. Winnipeg *Times*, January 5, 1883.
18. P.A.C., Macdonald Papers, Vol. 211, Dewdney to Macdonald, May 10, 1882 (from Qu'Appelle; private).
19. *Ibid.*, Dewdney to Macdonald, July 11, 1882, telegram in cipher from Winnipeg.
20. Walter Moberly, "Reminiscences of British Columbia," address to the Vancouver Canadian Club, March 13, 1907. P.A.C., MG 26, A 16.
21. J. H. E. Secretan, *Canada's Great Highway*, p. 186.
22. *The Week*, Toronto, Rev. George Grant's account, "The C.P.R., by the Kicking Horse Pass and the Selkirks," No. 10, May 1, 1884.
23. For the 1872 trip, see G. M. Grant, *Ocean to Ocean: Sandford Fleming's Expedition Through Canada in 1872* (Toronto, 1873). Sandford Fleming published an account of the 1883 trip, *England and Canada: A Summer Tour Between Old and New Westminister* (Montreal, 1884). Rev. George Grant's account of the 1883 trip is published in 10 parts in *The Week*, from December 1883 through to May, 1884. It is much the best of the two.
24. *The Week*, Toronto, April 3, 1884, Grant's "The C.P.R. by the Kicking Horse Pass and the Selkirk's," No. 9.
25. P.A.C., Fleming Papers, Vol. 48, Stephen to Fleming, "Want you to go B.C. soon as possible," June 27, 1883, (cable).

26. Fleming's report is not in the Stephen Papers; there are only Macdonald letters there. But Stephen's reply to a preliminary judgment is in the Fleming Papers, Vol. 48, Stephen to Fleming, October 13, 1883.
27. Katharine Hughes, *Father Lacombe, the Black-Robe Voyageur* (New York, 1914), p. 273.
28. P.A.C., Macdonald Papers, Vol. 267, Stephen to Macdonald, December 15, 1883 (confidential).
29. *Canada: House of Commons, Debates*, 1884, p. 127 (February 5, 1884). The authenticity of the *Star's* report was disputed; but it reads like vintage Van Horne.
30. P.A.C., Macdonald Papers, Vol. 267, Stephen to Macdonald, August 27, 1882.
31. See *supra*, p. 120.
32. Gilbert, *Stephen*, p. 113.
33. P.A.C., Stephen to Macdonald, Vol. 267, Macdonald Papers, December 3, 1883 (private).
34. P.A.C., Galt Papers, Vol. 8, Supplementary, Macdonald to Galt, January 8, 1883 (confidential).
35. P.A.C., Macdonald Papers, Vol. 270, Stephen to Macdonald, September 4, 1886 (private): ". . . in dealing with Galt, we departed from sound business principles and made a contract with him for five years' supply, and upon terms which we should never have thought of except that, he being the 'pioneer collier,' we wanted to get the business started."
36. P.A.C., Macdonald Papers, Vol. 190, Bowell to Macdonald, August 28, 1890 (from Lethbridge).
37. A very useful account of the Canadian Pacific Railway's postion is *Sessional Papers*, 1884, No. 31.
38. Blake argued in 1885 that of the original $25 million issue only $5 million was actually paid up; that the later issues went on an average of 46%; that $60 million of nominal capital had only yielded $24.5 million in actual cash. *Canada: House of Commons, Debates*, 1885, p. 2617 (June 17, 1885). Blake's argument is interesting, and may have real information behind it.
39. P.A.C., Macdonald Papers, Vol. 267, Stephen to Macdonald, December 23, 1883 (confidential).
40. Tupper Papers, Stephen to Tupper, December 28, 1883; January 5, 1884. See Creighton, *Macdonald*, pp. 364-6, which gives the atmosphere of crisis surrounding this loan.
41. *The Week*, Toronto, February 7, 1884.
42. P.A.C., Lorne Papers, Macdonald to Lorne, March 26, 1884 (private).
43. *Canada: House of Commons, Debates*, 1884, p. 13 (January 18, 1884).
44. *Ibid.*, p. 235 (February 12, 1884).
45. A.P.Q., Collection Chapais, Langevin Papers, Abbott to Langevin, January 8, 1885. Abbott was very close to the Canadian Pacific Railway, and gives an interesting summary of the Company's position since the 1884 loan.
46. Québec, *Le Canadien*, 4 mars, 1884.
47. Toronto *Mail*, February 20, 1884.
48. *Canada: House of Commons, Debates*, 1884, pp. 456-7 (February 20, 1884). It speaks much for the rapidity of transport that the Toronto morning paper was discussed in Parliament the evening of the same day.
49. *The Week*, Toronto, February 28, 1884. "Ottawa Notes," by Edward Ruthven.
50. Saint John *Daily Sun*, December 13, 1881; January 20, 1882. A good thesis on this whole subject is M. E. Angus, "The policies of the 'Short Line,'" M.A. thesis, University of New Brunswick, 1958; see p. 18-26.
51. This was added in Committee. See *Debates*, 1884, p. 1486 (April 10, 1884). Angus, "Short Line," p. 64.
52. *Ibid.*, p. 1540 (April 12, 1884).
53. *Ibid.*, p. 1529.
54. *Ibid.*, p. 1567 (April 14, 1884).
55. P.A.C., Stephen Papers, Macdonald to Stephen, February 18, 1884 (private).
56. P.A.C., H. H. Smith Papers, Macdonald to Smith, March 13, 1884 (private).
57. P.A.C., Stephen Papers, Macdonald to Stephen, July 24, 1884 (private).
58. *Supra*, p. 113.
59. Vaughan, *Van Horne*, p. 109.
60. J. G. Pyle, *The Life of James J. Hill* (New York, 1917), 2 vols., I, 322-3, Hill's papers are not open and will not be until 1981.
61. P.A.C., Macdonald Papers, Vol. 269, Stephen to Macdonald, August 2, 1884. Stephen was thinking of the possibility, remote though it was, of a Fenian raid.
62. Mackenzie to Stephen, August 18, 1884, quoted by Stephen in his letter to Macdonald of August 19, 1884. Vol. 269, Macdonald Papers. Mackenzie went out at Stephen's invitation. His impressions

are given in Thomson, *Mackenzie*, pp. 380-1.

63. P.A.C., Macdonald Papers, Vol. 269, Stephen to Macdonald, December 14, 1884 (confidential).
64. P.A.C., Stephen Papers, Macdonald to Stephen, July 18, 1884 (private).
65. P.A.C., Macdonald Papers, Vol. 269, Stephen to Macdonald, January 14, 1885 (private).
66. *Ibid.*, Stephen to Macdonald, January 17, 1885.
67. Vaughan, *Van Horne*, pp. 115-16.
68. P.A.C., Macdonald Papers, Vol. 197, Campbell to Macdonald, Sunday evening, 1885. (Sunday, January 17 is a possibility, here.)
69. *Canada: House of Commons, Debates*, 1885, p. 57 (February 9, 1885).
70. P.A.C., Tupper Papers, Macdonald to Tupper, March 17, 1885. Macdonald was also including the Short Line and the North Shore in the things he would like to be well out of.
71. *Canada: House of Commons, Debates*, 1885, p. 454 (March 10, 1885).
72. For nearly three weeks Parliament did not sit beyond 6 P.M., and no legislation of any importance was introduced.
73. I have collated primary sources with Vaughan's *Van Horne*, pp. 125-6, and made some educated guesses.
74. Creighton, *Macdonald*, p. 417.
75. Vaughan, *Van Horne*, p. 121.
76. See *infra*, p. 145.
77. References here are: B.C., Revised Statutes, 1877, c.66; Manitoba, Revised Statutes, 1880, c.3; Ontario, Revised Statutes, c.10; Quebec, 38 Vic. c.7; New Brunswick, Revised Statutes, c.4; Nova Scotia, Revised Statutes, 1873 Appendix A; Prince Edward Island, 41 Vic. c.14.
78. Ontario, 48 Vic. c.2. It is briefly described in Norman Ward, *The Canadian House of Commons: Representation* (Toronto, 1950), 216 n.
79. *Canada: House of Commons, Debates*, 1885, p. 1686 (May 7, 1885). James McMullen, M.P. North Wellington, a Liberal, makes some telling observations on this point.
80. *Ibid.*, pp. 1133-4 (April 16, 1885).
81. *Ibid.*, p. 1405 (April 27, 1885).
82. *Ibid.*, p. 1969 (May 19, 1885).
83. *Ibid.*, p. 1501 (May 1, 1885), as reported by Lewis Wigle, M.P. South Essex.
84. Toronto *Globe*, May 21, 1885
85. Blake seems to have taken no part in the discussion of the Franchise Bill between May 4 and May 26, and between June 6 and July 3. It was commented on by Ives, who added that Blake spent seven weeks working on his speech against the Canadian Pacific Railway loan. *Canada: House of Commons, Debates*, 1885, p. 2619 (June 17, 1885).
86. *Ibid.*, p. 1746 (May 11, 1885).
87. Norman Ward, *Canadian House of Commons*, pp. 221-2.
88. This letter of Stephen's is not in the Macdonald Papers.
89. P.A.C., Stephen Papers, Macdonald to Stephen, May 26, 1885 (confidential).
90. See the resolutions, proposed on June 15, 1885. *Canada: House of Commons, Debates*, 1885, p. 2531. Also Langevin's exposition of them, *Ibid.*, p. 2974 (July 1, 1885). Macdonald in a later memorandum to Hickson of the Grand Trunk gives the details. P.A.C., Macdonald Papers, Vol. 130, Macdonald to Hickson, August 25, 1885 (from Rivière du Loup).
91. P.A.C., Stephen Papers, Macdonald to Stephen, September 16, 1885 (private).
92. P.A.C., Macdonald Papers, Vol. 271, Stephen to Macdonald, September 3, 1889.
93. *Ibid.*, Stephen to Macdonald, January 30, 1889.
94. *Ibid.*, Stephen to Macdonald, September 3, 1889.
95. *Canada: House of Commons, Debates*, 1885, p. 2978 *et. seq.* (July 1, 1885).
96. Vaughan, *Van Horne*, *p.* 130.
97. P.A.C., Macdonald Papers, Vol. 269, Stephen to Macdonald, October 3, 1885, (from London; private and confidential): "*You* but only *you* know . . . only about one half of £3,000,000 [$15,000,000] were actually subscribed by the public, Barings and their friends taking the other half. . . . P.S. Don't give Pope even a hint of what I have said about the bonds, it would do harm."
98. *Ibid.*, Vol. 272, Stephen to Macdonald, November 22, 1890 (private).
99. *Ibid.*, Vol. 85, Lansdowne to Macdonald, October 6, 1885 (from Neilson's Store, British Columbia; telegram).
100. *Ibid.*, Vol. 269, Stephen to Macdonald, November 14, 1885 (private).
101. A.P.Q., Collection Chapais, Langevin Papers, Macdonald to Langevin, August 28, 1883 (private and confidential).
102. P.A.C., Macdonald Papers, Vol. 197, Macdonald to Campbell, September 12, 1885 (private).

103. *Canada: House of Commons, Debates*, 1885, p. 3474 (July 20, 1885).
104. P.A.C., Macdonald Papers, Vol. 197, Campbell to Macdonald, September 9, 1885.
105. *Ibid.*, Vol. 197, Macdonald to Campbell, September 12, 1885 (private).
106. P.A.O., T. C. Patteson Papers, Campbell to Patteson, August 8, 1885 (private and confidential). Patteson's reply ought perhaps to be quoted: "If Sir John is failing he naturally avoids labour [,] shirks going into the collar. He was always timid and yielding: & if he has ever taken a bold stand I think it was because he had a bold man at his elbow at the time." P.A.O., Campbell Papers, Patteson to Campbell, August 11, 1885 (private).

NOTES TO CHAPTER NINE

1. P.A.C., Denison Papers, Mair to Denison, April 16, 1884.
2. P.A.C., Macdonald Papers, Macpherson to Macdonald, November 3, 1883.
3. G. T. Denison, *Soldiering in Canada: Recollections and Experiences* (Toronto, 1900), pp. 262-4.
4. *Canada: House of Commons, Debates*, 1906, p. 4270 (May 31, 1906).
5. Open letter from Alexander Flemming and Clifford Sifton in the *Manitoba Daily Free Press*, July 17, 1884, addressed to A. M. Burgess, the Deputy-Minister.
6. Toronto *Mail*, February 2, 1886, report from James Grier of Oldman River.
7. *Ibid.*, January 13, 1886, reporting interview with John McDougall.
8. P.A.C., Tupper Papers, Martin Griffin to Tupper, July 28, 1884. This is part of new additional Tupper acquisitions interleaved with the old volumes. Griffin was made Librarian of Parliament in 1885, which post he held until 1920.
9. Stanley, *Birth of Western Canada* (London, 1936), p. 269 *et seq.*
10. P.A.C., Macdonald Papers, Vol. 107, Dewdney to Macdonald, [August], 1884 (private). My italics.
11. Denny's letter is quoted in Stanley, *op. cit.*, 272.
12. P.A.C., Macdonald Papers, Vol. 107, Dewdney to Macdonald, [August], 1884 (private).
13. *Ibid.*, enclosure, John Rae to Macdonald, July 5, 1884 (from Battleford; private).
14. Antoine Lose Brave to Riel, March 13, 1885, quoted in Stanley, *Birth of Western* Canada, p. 276, and from which pages much of the previous paragraph is due.
15. *Ibid.*, p. 217.
16. Grandin, "Les missions sauvages du nord-ouest" in *Missions des* O.M.I., XXI, 1883, pp. 126-7, quoted in Stanley, *op. cit.*, p. 177.
17. *Canada: Sessional Papers*, 1883, No. 5, "Report of Department of Indian Affairs," December 31, 1882, p. x.
18. *Canada: Sessional Papers*, 1884, No. 4, "Report of A. Macdonald, Indian Head (Treaty No. 4)," August 31, 1883, p. 75.
19. *Ibid.*, "report of C. E. Denny from Fort Macleod," July 10, 1883, pp. 77-8.
20. C. E. Denny, *The Law Marches West* (Toronto, 1939), p. 202.
21. *The Week*, Toronto, September 18, 1884. "Notes on the North-West," by Bystander.
22. P.A.C., Macdonald Papers, Vol. 113.
23. *Ibid.*, Vol. 212, Dewdney to Macdonald, October 29, 1884.
24. Stanley, *Birth of Western Canada*, pp. 262-6.
25. P.A.C., Macdonald Papers, Vol. 211, Hayter Reed to Dewdney, November 8, 1883 (from Carlton; private). Private correspondence was clearly not, with Dewdney, private, since this letter turns up in the Macdonald Papers.
26. *Prince Albert Times*, May 23, 1884, quoted in L. H. Thomas, *The Struggle for Responsible Government in the North-West Territories*, p. 112.
27. *Ibid.*, p. 130.
28. Edmonton *Bulletin*, quoted in *Prince Albert Times*, February 22, 1884, in Thomas, *op. cit.*, p. 123.
29. *Canada: House of Commons, Debates*, 1885, p. 3118 (July 6, 1885).
30. *Ibid.*, 1885, p. 2029 (May 20, 1885). Macdonald is replying to a question from Blake.
31. *Ibid.*, p. 3117 (July 6, 1885).
32. Burgess to Duck (Land agent at Prince Albert), October 21, 1882, in *Sessional Papers*, 1885, No. 13; it also is cited by Laurier in the *Debates*, p. 3126 (July 7, 1885).

33. See Stanley, *Birth of Western Canada*, pp. 258-9.
34. *Canada: Sessional Papers*, 1885, No. 13. *Debates*, 1885, p. 3126 (July 7, 1885).
35. *Canada: House of Commons, Debates*, 1885, p. 3103, (July 6, 1885).
36. E. R. Markson, Cyril Greenland, R. E. Turner, "The life and death of Louis Riel – a study of forensic psychiatry," *Canadian Psychiatric Journal*, Vol. 10, No. 4 (August, 1965), pp. 249-251.
37. Henry Jackson told Father Lacombe in Edmonton, in October, 1909, that Isbister and Dumont brought Riel letters from the leading white men of Prince Albert. Jackson also said he saw these letters burnt at the end after the rebellion was over to avoid incriminating the writers. Katharine Hughes, *Father Lacombe, the Black-Robe Voyageur* (New York, 1914), 294n.
38. P.A.C., Denison Papers, Mair to Denison, June 11, 1884 (from Windsor, Ontario; private).
39. Riel to J. Riel and L. Lavallée (his brother-in-law), n.d., 1884, P.A.M., Riel Papers, quoted in Stanley, *Birth of Western Canada*, pp. 279-80.
40. P.A.C., Macdonald Papers, Vol. 107, Forget to Dewdney, September 18, 1884, enc. in Dewdney to Macdonald, September 19, 1884 (private).
41. Stanley, *Louis Riel*, p. 291.
42. Apparently on the morning of Riel's execution, or possibly the night before, in reply to an inquiry of Rev. Charles McWilliams, a priest whom Riel had known since childhood, Riel made this assertion. Reported by the Regina correspondent of the Toronto *Mail*, in the *Toronto Daily Mail*, November 17, 1885.
43. Stanley, *Louis Riel*, p. 311.
44. *Ibid.*, p. 305.
45. Riel to Crozier, March 21, 1885, *Ibid.*, p. 310.
46. *Canada: House of Commons, Debates*, 1885, p. 2718 (June 19, 1885).
47. *The Week*, Toronto, March 25, 1886.
48. *Canada: House of Commons, Debates*, 1886, p. 177-8 (March 16, 1886).
49. So at least Vankoughnet informed Macdonald. P.A.C., Macdonald Papers, Vol. 213, Vankoughnet to Macdonald, February 2, 1886 (private).
50. *Ibid.*, Vol. 212, Dewdney to Macdonald, July 17, 1885 (private), enclosing Lacombe to Dewdney, July 11, 1885 (strictly confidential).
51. The *Bystander*, Toronto, July 1883, p. 210.
52. *The Week*, Toronto, July 23, 1885, G.B.E., "Canadianizing the North-West," pp. 533-4.
53. G. T. Denison, *Soldiering in Canada: Recollections and Experience* (Toronto, 1900), pp. 296-9; Stanley, *Riel*, p. 338.
54. According to John Thompson, Minister of Justice, *Canada: House of Commons, Debates*, 1886, p. 269 (March 22, 1886).
55. Battleford *Saskatchewan Herald*, April 23, 1885.
56. P.A.C., Macdonald Papers, Vol. 197, Campbell to Macdonald, May 21, 1885, reporting cipher telegram from Lt.-Gov. Aikens of Manitoba.
57. Manitoba *Statutes*, 1883, 195, Sec. 70 and 72. Campbell elucidated these points for Macdonald. P.A.C., Macdonald Papers, Vol. 197, Campbell to Macdonald, April 13, 1885.
58. P.A.C., Macdonald Papers, Vol. 197, Campbell to Macdonald, May 21, 1885.
59. *Ibid.*, Campbell to Burbidge, June 23, 1885 (copy).
60. See Hughes, *Lacombe*, 294n.
61. G. T. Denison, *Soldiering in Canada*, p. 319.
62. *The Week*, Toronto, September 10, 1885.
63. P.A.C., Campbell Papers, Macdonald to Campbell, May 18, 1885: "Look carefully at the Treason-felony Act. I think there may be some difficulty in applying the Statute to Riel's case. I hope we shall not be obliged to have recourse to the Statute of Edward [III]. The proceedings are complicated & perhaps can not be applied in the N-W."
64. Stanley, *Riel*, p. 345.
65. Stanley makes this point. *loc. cit.*
66. North-West Territories Act, 43 Vic. c.25, Section 74.
67. P.A.C., Macdonald Papers, Vol. 211, Dewdney to Macdonald, September 27, 1883 (private).
68. There are two sources, not mutually conflicting, about the jury, but I may have reconciled them with distortion. First, Blake's quotation of a letter from one of the jury, *Canada: House of Commons Debates*, 1886, p. 255 (March 19, 1886); second, Stanley's reference to statements made by the foreman's daughter, published in the *Globe & Mail*, July 22, 1955, Stanley, *Riel*, p. 357.
69. Toronto *Mail*, November 30, 1885,

Tarte's letter to the *Mail* was dated Quebec, November 26, 1885, and published in English in *Le Canadien*, 27 nov. 1885.

70. P.A.O., Blake Papers, A. E. Forget to Mercier, 23 nov. 1885 (from Council Chamber, Regina; copy).

71. D. G. Creighton has a useful summary of the McNaughten rule of 1843 in *Macdonald: The Old Chieftain*, pp. 434-6.

72. *Canada: Sessional Papers*, 1886, No. 43, p. 161.

73. Winnipeg *Manitoba Daily Free Press*, December 17, 1885; the rest of the quotation, however, was, "laudably condemned, and justly executed."

74. P.A.O., Blake Papers, Laurier to Blake, December 31, 1885 (private).

75. Langevin wrote his brother, "Maintenant si mes deux collègues Francais et moi nous étions rétirés du gouvernement sur cette question, qu'arrivait-il? Riel aurait été pendu, tout de même et nous aurons mis une barrière infranchissable entre le gouvernement actuel et les Canadiens Francais." A.P.Q., Langevin Papers, Langevin to Edmond Langevin, 20 nov. 1885.

76. Glenbow Foundation, Calgary, Dewdney-Riel Papers, Jukes to Macdonald, November 9, 1885 (draft), quoted by Stanley, *Riel*, p. 367.

77. Privately Jukes believed Riel was insane and ought not to be hanged. So reported Thomas White at second hand. P.A.C., Macdonald Papers, Vol. 296, White to Macdonald, November 7, 1885 (telegram from Winnipeg).

78. P.A.O., Blake Papers, Forget to Mercier, 23 novembre 1885, from Regina (copy).

79. Glenbow Foundation, Calgary, Dewdney Papers, Folder 72. This is an unmarked draft of a telegram, but bearing so close a resemblance to Valade's published telegram that, with Forget's remarks, I felt justified in assuming Valade's authorship.

80. *Canada: Sessional Papers*, 1886, No. 43, p. 1, Valade to Macdonald, November 8, 1885 (from Regina).

81. Glenbow Foundation, Calgary, Dewdney Papers, Macdonald to Dewdney, November 15, 1885 (private).

82. *Toronto Daily Mail*, November 17, 1885, report from Regina correspondent who had talked with Father André, report dated November 16.

83. Montreal *Gazette*, November 17, 1885, reports this.

84. P.A.C., Macdonald Papers, Vol. 107, Dewdney to Macdonald, November 16, 1885 (telegram).

85. Montreal *Gazette*, July 21, 1885.

86. *Canada: House of Commons, Debates*, 1886, p. 3445 (March 24, 1886), quoted by Chapleau.

87. Sir John Willison, "The correspondence of Sir John Macdonald," *Dalhousie Review*, II, 1 (April, 1922), p. 14.

88. Rumilly, *Québec*, III, 200.

89. See Rumilly, *Québec*, IV, 16-21; Neatby and Saywell, "Chapleau and the Conservative party in Quebec," C.H.R., XXXVII, No. 1 (March, 1956), pp. 6-7.

90. T. Chapais, to J. C. Taché, 25 mars 1884, from Quebec, in Barnard, *Memories Chapais*, (Montreal, 1962-4), 3 vols., III, 235-6.

91. Rumilly, *Québec*, IV, 128.

92. Charles Langelier, *Souvenirs politicques* (Quebec, 1909), I, 191.

93. It is unfortunate that historians have tended to avoid the moderate statements that exist in important French and English newspapers.

94. *Toronto Daily Mail*, August 3, 1885.

95. *Ibid.*, October 7, 1885.

96. Toronto *Globe*, November 21, 1885.

97. Montreal *La Minerve*, 12 août 1885, quoting a letter from Fathers André, Touse, Moulin, Fourmond, Vegreville and LeCoq, dated Prince Albert, 12 juin 1885.

98. Montreal *Le Monde*, 3 août 1885; 25 août 1885; 10 sept. 1885; 24 oct. 1885; 13 nov. 1885.

99. *Canada: House of Commons, Debates*, 1891, p. 5813, September 21, 1891.

100. Gosselin to Chapais, 2 déc. 1885 from Chicoutimi, in Barnard, *Memoires Chapais*, III, 305-6.

101. Québec *Le Canadien*, 22 déc. 1885, cited in Laurier LaPierre, "Joseph Israel Tarte," PH.D. thesis, University of Toronto, 1959, p. 165.

102. Tarte, *Procès Mercier*, p. 20. Also *Ibid.*, p. 161.

103. *Toronto Daily Mail*, November 20, 1885.

104. *Ibid.*, November 23, 1885. It is quoted also by Stanley, *Birth of Western Canada*, 400; Schull, *Laurier*, 178-9; Mason Wade, *French Canadians 1760-1945* (Toronto, 1955), 419. All three quotations omit the second paragraph, and all three omit the following sentences in the first: "We are free to confess that, in the early days (before 1840) . . . injustice was

often times done to them. . . . We challenge the press of Quebec and Montreal to point to a wrong wittingly done [since], or to name any country in the wide world where the rights of a minority have been more conscientiously respected."

105. P.A.C., Laurier Papers, Edgar to Laurier, October 5, 1885 (private and confidential). There was some discussion of Blake's resigning the leadership in both the *Globe* and *Mail* in October, 1885.

106. P.A.C. Laurier Papers, Vol. 1, Cartwright to Laurier, Nov. 13, 1885 (private).

107. *Ibid.*, Edgar to Laurier, November 18, 1885 (private and confidential).

108. This position is sketched out persuasively by R. W. Cox, "Quebec provincial election, 1886," M.A. thesis, McGill, 1948, p. 107.

109. P.A.C., Laurier Papers, Vol. 1, C. A. P. Pelletier to Laurier, 23 nov. 1885.

110. P.A.C., Macdonald Papers, Vol. 197, Alexander Campbell to Macdonald, Nov. 16, 1885.

111. Toronto *Globe*, January 15, 1886, reporting Blake's speech of January 14.

112. P.A.C., Thompson Papers, Vol. 29, Thompson to Annie Thompson, May 26, 1886.

113. St. Francis Xavier Library, Antigonish, Thompson Papers, Thompson to Annie Thompson, January 23, 1887. This is a typed copy of a letter that seems no longer to exist. Most, if not all, of the Thompson Papers at Antigonish are typed copies of letters in the Public Archives of Canada. This letter is the only one I have discovered that is not.

114. It opened late in order to give the Quebec Conservatives as much time as possible to allow the Riel agitation to cool down.

115. Landry himself almost invites this comment. He said in his speech, "It has been loudly stated . . . that there was an agreement between myself and the Government with regard to this motion. I deny the assertion." *Canada: House of Commons, Debates*, 1886, p. 73 (March 11, 1886).

116. *Ibid.*, p. 183 (March 16, 1886).

117. *Ibid.*, p. 237 (March 19, 1886).

118. This is also W. R. Graham's conclusion, "Sir Richard Cartwright," p. 122.

119. Willison, *Reminiscences*, 147-8.

120. *Canada: House of Commons, Debates*, 1886, p. 668 (April 13, 1886). Act was 49 Vic. c.26.

121. *The Week*, Toronto, July 22, 1886, "Jottings along the C.P.R."

122. *Ibid.*, July 12, 1888, "The North-West Farmers," by N. F. Davin.

123. *The Week*, Toronto, "Saunterings," by Sara Jeanette Duncan. November 25, 1886.

124. *Ibid.*, October 14, 1886, "Saunterings."

NOTES TO CHAPTER TEN

1. Peter H. Russell, *Leading Constitutional Decisions* (Toronto, 1965), pp. 65-6..

2. See Russell's useful headnote to this case, *ibid.*, p. 1.

3. R. A. Olmstead (ed.), *Decisions of the Judicial Committee of the Privy Council*, 2 vols. (Ottawa, 1954), I, 111.

4. *Canada: House of Commons, Debates*, 1887, p. 401. May 12, 1887. Tupper's budget speech.

5. *Royal Commission on the relations of Labour and Capital in Canada* (Ottawa, 1889), p. 17.

6. *Ibid.*, p. 8.

7. *Ibid.*, p. 116.

8. *Ibid.*, p. 118.

9. *Ibid.*, p. 37.

10. See also *supra*, p. 5.

11. *Ibid.*, App. O.

12. Anon., *Montreal by Gaslight* (Montreal, 1889), p. 32.

13. *The Week*, Toronto, May 13, 1886.

14. Hamilton *Palladium*, October 3, 1885, quoted in V. O. Chan, "Canadian Knights of Labor with special reference to the 1880's," M.A. thesis, McGill, 1949, p. 29.

15. H. A. Logan, *History of Trade Unions in Canada*, Toronto, 1939, p. 51.

16. *Ibid.*, pp. 165-76.

17. *Royal Commission on the relation of labour and capital in Canada*, "Our factory system," pp. 86-87.

18. The Perkins Bull collection.

19. *Canada: House of Commons, Debates*, 1885, p. 873 (April 11, 1885). Dr. Bergin, M.P. Cornwall and Stormont, was proposing second reading of Bill 85 on factory legislation.

20. D. C. Scott (ed.), *Archibald Lampman: Selected Poems* (Toronto, 1947), "The City at the end of things," pp. 173-5; "The City," pp. 153-5.
21. *Royal Commission in the relation of Labour and capital in Canada*, "Our factory system," p. 87.
22. *Canada: House of Commons, Debates*, 1881, p. 862 (February 7, 1881).
23. The *Bystander*, Toronto, September, 1890.
24. *Canada: House of Commons, Journals*, 1888, App. 3, p. 3.
25. *Canada: House of Commons, Debates*, 1888, p. 33 (February 29, 1888).
26. *Canada: House of Commons, Journals*, 1888, App. 3, p. 5.
27. *Canada: House of Commons, Debates*, 1889, p. 1111-1117 (April 8, 1889). 52 Vic. c.41, was entitled "An Act for the prevention and suppression of combinations formed in restraint of trade."
28. *Monetary Times*, Montreal, June 12, 1885, quoted in A. W. Currie, *The Grand Trunk Railway of Canada* (Toronto, 1957), p. 330.
29. *Canada: House of Commons, Debates*, 1886, p. 593 (April 8, 1886).
30. A useful summary of the Galt Commission's recommendations is given in Currie, *Grand Trunk Railway*, pp. 334-5.
31. *Nova Scotia: Assembly Journals*, 1886, App. 6, has a comprehensive short history of Nova Scotian coal production. Tupper gives figures for total Canadian production in *House of Commons, Debates*, 1887, p. 400 (May 12, 1887) slightly more complete and slightly lower than those in Urquhart and Buckley *Historical Statistics of Canada*.
32. *Loc. cit.*
33. *Canada: House of Commons, Debates*, 1887, p. 401 (May 12, 1887). Tupper here gives in his Budget speech, a long and interesting description of the Canadian coal and steel industry.
34. *United States: Department of State, United States Consulates*, Halifax, Phelan to Porter, August 15, 1885.
35. *Canada: House of Commons, Debates*, 1887, p. 768 (June 3, 1887).
36. R. L. Borden, *Memoirs*, I, 25 (Toronto, 1938).
37. *Supra*, p. 122.
38. Fielding became Premier in 1884 in most curious circumstances, owing to the dislike of other members of the Pipes cabinet to being displaced. There is a long and interesting letter from the Lieutenant-Governor, M. H. Richey to Macdonald about it, August 2, 1884 (confidential). P.A.C., Macdonald Papers, Vol. 117.
39. Beckles Willson, *From Quebec to Piccadilly and Other Places* (London, 1929), pp. 63-4.
40. *Nova Scotia: Assembly, Journals*, 1886, App. 12, Fielding to Macdonald, July 3, 1885.
41. *Nova Scotia: Assembly, Journals*, 1886, 147-9 (Saturday, May 8, 1886).
42. P.A.C., Macdonald Papers, Vol. 117, Richey to Macdonald, May 17, 1886 (private and confidential).
43. However, 4 Liberals and 1 Conservative were elected with less than a 50-seat majority.
44. P.A.C., Macdonald Papers, Vol. 117, J. W. Stairs to Macdonald, June 17, 1886 (confidential).
45. *Grip*, Toronto, June 26, 1886.
46. *The Week*, Toronto, May 20, 1886.
47. P.A.O., Blake Papers, Longley to Blake, February 25, 1887 (private).
48. J. W. Longley, "Reminiscences, political and otherwise," *Canadian Magazine*, November, 1920, LVI, No. 1, p. 64.
49. *Nova Scotia: Assembly Journals*, 1887, 103-4 (April 21, 1887). An amendment proposed by the Conservatives that the repeal agitation was productive of "great injury to the public welfare" was defeated 27-5, April 27, 1887; the main motion then passed, 24-8.
50. Halifax *Morning Herald*, April 29, 1887. This has been brought to my attention by Colin Howell. See his thesis, "Repeal, Reciprocity and Commercial union in Nova Scotian politics, 1886-1887," M.A. thesis, Dalhousie University, 1967.
51. R. W. Cox, "The Quebec provincial election of 1886," M.A. thesis, McGill University, 1948, p. 112.
52. Montreal *Witness*, September 30, 1886, quoted by Cox, p. 112.
53. Cox, 114.
54. P.A.C., Laurier Papers, Vol. 1, N. W. Trenholme to Laurier, October 24, 1883 (private).
55. P.A.O., Cartwright Papers, Cartwright to Blake, January 1, 1887 (private).
56. Cox, p. 303.
57. Québec, *Le Canadien*, 11 septembre 1886, in LaPierre, "Israël Tarte," p. 171.
58. *The Week*, Toronto, June 14, 1888. "Prominent Canadians," by H. Beaugrand, editor of *La Patrie*.

59. P.A.C., Thompson Papers, Vol. 289, Thompson to Annie Thompson, June 30, 1886.
60. *Ibid.*, Thompson to Annie Thompson, October 31, 1886.
61. *Ibid.*, Thompson to Annie Thompson, November 12, 1886. Thompson seems always to have retained a poor opinion of Lady Macdonald and of Macdonald's domestic life. His dislike was reciprocated.
62. *Ibid.*, Thompson to Annie Thompson, November 21, 1886.
63. *Loc. cit.*
64. *Ibid.*, Thompson to Annie Thompson, November 28, 1886 (from Toronto).
65. P.A.C., Macdonald Papers, Vol. 205, Chapleau to Macdonald, February 4, 1887; February 10, 1887.
66. *Ibid.*, Macdonald to Chapleau, February 13, 1887 (private; copy).
67. *Ibid.*, endorsement on Chapleau to Macdonald, February 14, 1887 (private).
68. P.A.C., Lansdowne Papers. Macdonald to Lansdowne, February 24, 1887.
69. Mowat's leadership had been suggested 18 months before: *Grip*, June 20, 1885.
70. P.A.O., Blake Papers, Blake's drafts of letters to Mowat of January 8, 1886 [7], January 9, 1887; January 11, 1887; January 12, 1887. See also M. A. Banks, "The change in Liberal party leadership, 1887," C.H.R., XXXVIII, No. 2 (June, 1957), pp. 109-128.
71. My gloss on Blake's speech.
72. Toronto *Globe*, January 24, 1887, reporting Blake's speech of January 22.
73. Tilley alleged however that the Conservatives lost 3 seats in Saint John city and county because of extension of Franchise to householders. February 28, 1887, private, from Fredericton, P.A.C., Tupper Papers, Additional.
74. P.A.O., Blake Papers, Laurier to Blake, February 24, 1887 (private).
75. J. S. Willison, *Reminiscences, Poltical and Personal*, p. 158.
76. *The Week*, November 11, 1886, quoting Cartwright's speech to the young Liberals at Seaforth, Ontario.
77. *Canada, House of Commons, Debates*, 1880-81, p. 496 (January 18, 1881); *Debates*, 1884, p. 529 (April 14, 1884), and p. 1570 (April 14, 1884).
78. Willison, *Reminiscences*, 151.
79. University of Western Ontario Library, David Mills' diary, June 3, 1887. This is also quoted in F. Landon, "When Laurier met Ontario," T.R.S.C., XXXV, Sec. 2, 1941, p. 7.
80. O. D. Skelton, *The Life and Letters of Sir Wilfrid Laurier* 2 vols., [orig. 1921], Carleton Library (Toronto, 1965), I, 103.
81. Toronto *Globe*, June 24, 1887.
82. J. S. Willison, *Reminiscences*, p. 164.
83. P.A.C, Macdonald Papers, Vol. 38, Davie to Macdonald, September 30, 1887 (private).
84. *Nova Scotia: Assembly, Journals*, 1888, App. 12, Macdonald to Mercier, October 4, 1887.
85. *Ibid.*, Davie to Mercier, October 10, 1887.
86. *Ibid.*, Sullivan to Mercier, October 7, 1887.
87. *Ontario: Assembly, Sessional Papers*, 1887, No. 51, 3. See also, J. A. Maxwell, *Federal Subsidies to the Provincial Government in Canada* (Cambridge, 1937), p. 97.
88. P.A.C., Macdonald Papers, Vol. 328, C. N. Skinner to Macdonald, July 1, 1888 (from Saint John). It is clear from this correspondence that Premier Blair was coquetting with the Conservatives; he told Skinner that he went to the Quebec conference because he had so far committed himself to pull out would do more harm than good.
89. *Maxwell, Federal Subsidies*, p. 100.
90. *Canada: House of Commons, Debates*, 1886, p. 1348 (May 18, 1886).
91. Winnipeg *Sun*, October 25, 1887.
92. P.A.C., Macdonald Papers, Vol. 270, Stephen to Macdonald, September 20, 1887.
93. *Ibid.*, Stephen to Macdonald, June 6, 1887 (confidential).
94. *Ibid.*, Stephen to Macdonald, August 6, 1887 (private).
95. Heather Gilbert, *George Stephen*, p. 213.
96. See H. A. Fleming, *Canada's Arctic Outlet: A History of the Hudson's Bay Railway* (Berkeley, 1957).
97. P.A.C., Macdonald Papers, Vol. 186 Aikens to Macdonald, November 12, 1887 (private); November 30, 1887 (private); December 28, 1887 (private).
98. See W. L. Morton, *Manitoba*, p. 237.
99. Winnipeg, *Manitoba Free Press*. October 27, 1888; *Toronto Daily Mail*, November 3, 1888, Van Horne's letter of November 3.
100. Morton, *Manitoba*, pp. 238-9.
101. P.A.C., Macdonald Papers, Vol. 528, Macdonald to Stephen, October 22, 1888.

This letter is quoted by Pope, but the reference to undermining Greenway he omitted.

102. *The Week*, Toronto, July 12, 1888, N. F. Davin, "The North-West Farmers."

NOTES TO CHAPTER ELEVEN

1. *Canada: House of Commons, Debates*, 1889, p. 178 (February 18, 1889).
2. *Imperial Federation Journal*, February 1888, in G. R. MacLean, "The Imperial Federation movement in Canada 1884-1902," PH.D. thesis, Duke University, 1957, p. 66.
3. See D. M. L. Farr's excellent chapter, "A Canadian Resident Minister in Great Britain," in *Colonial Office and Canada 1867-1877*, pp. 253-70.
4. *Canada: House of Commons, Debates*, 1891, p. 574, (May 29, 1891).
5. *Canada: House of Commons, Debates*, 1886, p. 12 (February 26, 1886).
6. Brebner briefly refers to this in his *North Atlantic Triangle*, but there is now a much more comprehensive account, R. C. Brown, *Canada's National Policy, 1883-1900: A Study in Canadian-American Relations* (Princeton, 1964), pp. 13-90.
7. *Canada: House of Commons, Debates*, 1888, p. 676 (April 10, 1888).
8. Tupper stressed this point in his report to Parliament in 1888, and it has been generally neglected.
9. Boston *Herald*, October 6, 1886, publishing letter of Captain Nathan F. Blake, of Schooner *Andrew Burnham* of Boston. Quoted by H. F. McDougall, M.P. Cape Breton, *Debates*, 1888, p. 864 (April 16, 1888).
10. See Brown, *Canada's National Policy*, pp. 28-34.
11. Bayard to Tupper, May 31, 1887, in *Caanda: Sessional Papers*, 1888; also quoted by Cartwright, *Debates*, 1888, p. 847 (April 16).
12. *The Week*, Toronto, October 22, 1885; November 12, 1885, "Is Confederation a success?" by J. W. Longley; Halifax *Acadian Recorder*, December 1, 1885; Willison, *Reminiscences*, p. 166.
13. John Charlton, M.P. North Norfolk, born an American citizen, defined what he understood to be commercial union in *House of Commons, Debates*, 1888, p. 211 (March 16, 1888).
14. Toronto *Globe*, December 28, 1887.
15. Both of these quotations were cited by J. C. Rykert, M.P. Lincoln, *Canada: House of Commons, Debates*, 1888, p. 430 (March 26, 1888).
16. See references *supra*, note 12.
17. *The Week*, January 28, 1886. See also September 15, 1887.
18. Willison, *Reminiscences*, p. 167.
19. G. Amyot, (M.P. Bellechasse) to Laurier, 5 août 1887 (personelle). P.A.C., Laurier Papers, Vol. 2.
20. Montreal *Star*, February 14, 1888, cited by James Edgar, *House of Commons, Debates*, 1888, p. 30 (February 14, 1888).
21. P.A.C., Laurier Papers, Vol. 2, Cartwright to Laurier, October 29, 1887 (confidential).
22. Toronto *Globe*, September 19, 1887, letter from James Young, of September 17. For an earlier letter in March, 1887, see Brown, p. 162.
23. P.A.O., Cartwright Papers, Mackenzie to Cartwright, September 27, 1887.
24. P.A.C., Laurier Papers, Vol. 2, Cartwright to Laurier, October 29, 1887 (confidential).
25. P.A.O., Edgar Papers, Laurier to Edgar, October 31, 1887 (private).
26. This is not my metaphor but Dr. C. F. Ferguson's, M.P. North Leeds and Grenville. *Canada: House of Commons, Debates*, 1888, p. 430 (March 26, 1888).
27. *Canada: House of Commons, Debates*, 1888, p. 183 (March 15, 1888). See also W. E. O'Brien's remarks, *ibid.*, p. 525 (April 4, 1888).
28. Telegram from Massey is quoted by J. C. Rykert, *ibid.*, p. 420 (March 26, 1888). For C. A. Massey's views in 1876 see *supra*, p. 80.
29. See also the views of Gurney Stoves Ltd., *ibid.*, p. 422 (March 26, 1888), quoted by J. C. Rykert.
30. *Ibid.*, p. 561 (April 5, 1888).
31. P.A.C., Laurier Papers, Vol. 2, Willison to Laurier, July 19, 1888.
32. *Ibid.*, Blake to Laurier, March 6, 1888 (from Florence; private and confidential). See also, F. H. Underhill, "Edward Blake, the Liberal party and unrestricted reciprocity," C.H.A., *Report*, 1939, 133-41. W. R. Graham, "Sir R. Cartwright, W. Laurier and Liberal Party Trade Policy." C.H.R., 1952, pp. 1-18.
33. *Canada: House of Commons, Debates*, 1889, p. 178-9 (February 18, 1889).

34. P.A.C., Laurier Papers, Vol. 2, Jetté to Laurier, 9 juin, 1888 (confidential).
35. No division was recorded in the *Journals;* Peter Mitchell now owner of the Montreal *Herald*, said that the two Protestants wanted a division, but without names; when Mercier insisted on names, it was carried unanimously. For Mitchell's comments, see *House of Commons, Debates*, 1889, p. 840 (March 26, 1889). See also R. C. Dalton, *The Jesuit Estates' Question, 1870-1888* (Toronto, 1968).
36. Joseph Pope, *The Day of Sir John Macdonald* (Toronto, 1915), p. 164.
37. I am grateful to Mr. James Miller for bringing these points to my attention.
38. *Toronto Daily Mail*, March 14, 1889. The editorials were written by Edward Farrer.
39. *Canada: House of Commons, Debates*, 1884, p. 907 (March 17, 1884).
40. See Creighton, *Macdonald*, pp. 518-19.
41. See for instance *Globe*, March 4, 1889, and March 16, 1889.
42. P.A.O., Blake Papers, E. W. Thomson to Blake, March 18, 1889 (confidential); Blake to Jaffray, March, 1889 probably March 19, 1889 (draft); Jaffray to Blake, March 20, 1889.
43. *Canada: House of Commons, Debates*, 1889, p. 874 (March 28, 1889).
44. *Ibid.*, p. 898 (March 28, 1889).
45. Macdonald sought opinion in London on the constitutionality of the act; see P.A.C., Macdonald Papers, Vol. 94, Blake to Macdonald, April 26, 1889 telegram). *Parliament: Sessional Papers*, 1890, No. 70, 7, Lord Knutsford to Lord Stanley, July 25, 1889 (telegram).
46. *Canada: House of Commons, Debates*, 1890, p. 42 (January 22, 1890).
47. *Toronto Daily Mail*, July 13, 1889, reporting McCarthy's speech of July 12.
48. J. Tardivel, *Pour la Patrie* (Montréal, 1895), p. 369. See the useful article of John Hare, "Nationalism in French Canada and Tardivel's novel, 'Pour la Patrie,'" *Culture*, XXII, 1961, pp. 403-12.
49. P.A.C., Macdonald Papers, Vol. 228, McCarthy to Macdonald, November 5, 1889.
50. See his own account, *Canada: House of Commons, Debates*, 1890, p. 847 (February 18, 1890).
51. Winnipeg *Manitoba Free Press*, August 7, 1889, reporting McCarthy's speech of August 5.
52. *Brandon Sun*, May 16, May 30, 1889, cited in Morton, *Manitoba*, pp. 242-3.
53. *Lethbridge News*, July 24, 1889; *Qu'Appelle Vidette*, July 25, 1889; Battleford *Saskatchewan Herald*, November 13, 1889; all cited in Thomas, *North-West Territories*, 185; also *Calgary Herald*, February 1, 1890.
54. Regina *Leader*, September 10, 1889.
55. *Canada: Parliament, Sessional Papers*, 1890, No. 33E.
56. Grandin to Cardinal Taschereau and the Quebec bishops, November 20, 1889, from St. Albert, quoted by Amyot, M.P. Bellechasse, *House of Commons, Debates*, 1890, pp. 119-20 (January 29, 1890).
57. *Ibid.*, p. 619 (February 13, 1890).
58. *Ibid.*, p. 674-5 (February 14, 1890); Blake is here checking the wording.
59. Creighton, *Macdonald*, pp. 534-9, a good discussion of the whole debate.
60. *Blake: House of Commons, Debates*, p. 678 (February 14, 1890); Macdonald, *ibid.*, p. 745 (February 17, 1890); Cartwright, p. 839 (February 18, 1890).
61. Willison, *Reminiscences*, p. 175.
62. *The Week*, Toronto, January 31, 1890.
63. *Mitchell: House of Commons, Debates*, 1890, p. 887 (February 20, 1890); Edgar, p. 900 (February 20, 1890).
64. New Brunswick Museum, Tilley Papers, Foster to Tilley, February 25, 1890 (private).
65. *Canada: House of Commons, Debates*, 1884, p. 309 (February 15, 1884).
66. Augustus Bridle, *Sons of Canada* (Toronto, 1916), p. 222; an excellent little piece.
67. *Ibid.*, p. 227.
68. See *House of Commons, Debates*, 1890, p. 1739 (March 11, 1890).
69. *Ibid.*, 1718 (March 11, 1890).
70. *Canada: House of Commons, Debates*, 1886, p. 1034-5 *et. seq.* (May 4, 1886).
71. L. L. LaPierre "J. I. Tarte and the McGreevy-Langevin scandal," C.H.A. *Report*, 1961, p. 49. For the later development of the scandal see *infra*, p. 230-3.
72. *Canada: House of Commons, Debates*, 1886, p. 620 April 9, 1886).
73. *Ibid.*, 1878, p. 1180 (March 15, 1878).
74. *Ibid.*, 1890, p. 1866 (March 13, 1890).
75. *Ibid.*, p. 1862 (March 13, 1890). David Mills is here quoting a Bowell speech of July 11, 1887.
76. See P.A.C., Macdonald Papers, Vol. 186, endorsement on letter of the four Toronto M.P.'s to Macdonald, November 1, 1880.

77. *Ibid.*, Vol. 286, C. H. Tupper to Macdonald, July 4, 1889.
78. *Ibid.*, Vol. 529, Macdonald to C. H. Tupper, July 8, 1889 (private).
79. *Ibid.*, C. H. Tupper to Macdonald, July 10, 1889; July 11, 1889; October 16, 1889.
80. University of British Columbia, Charles Hibbert Tupper Papers, "Reminiscences," also P.A.C., Microfilm 109.
81. Thompson Papers, Vol. 103, Cahan to Thompson, March 28, 1890 (private).
82. U.B.C., C. H. Tupper Papers, "Reminiscences"; P.A.C., M 109.
83. Creighton, *Macdonald*, p. 546; Halifax *Morning Herald*, October 2, 1890.
84. Halifax *Morning Herald*, October 4, 1890.
85. *Loc. cit.*
86. *Grip*, Toronto, December 5, 1890.
87. P.A.C., Macdonald Papers, Macdonald to Scarth, January 16, 1891 (confidential): "It is quite in the cards that we may have an election next summer altho that is *for your own information only.*"
88. The provenance is described, without specific dates, in R. C. Brown, *Canada's National Policy* (Princeton, 1964), pp. 206-7.
89. P.A.C., Macdonald Papers, Vol. 89, Stanley to Macdonald, January 31, 1891 (private).
90. Toronto *Globe*, February 18, 1891, letter from Farrer, February 17, 1891.
91. P.A.C., Macdonald Papers, Vol. 67. Also Brown, pp. 207-8; Creighton, pp. 554-5.
92. Toronto *Globe*, February 18, 1891, letter from Farrer, February 17, 1891.
93. Brown, p. 205; Creighton, p. 552.
94. Quoted by Charles Hibbert Tupper, *Canada: House of Commons, Debates*, 1891, 584 (May 29, 1891). See also T. G. Kenny's quotation from the *New York Tribune*, *ibid.*, 823 (June 5, 1891).
95. P.A.C., Laurier Papers, Vol. 5, Longley to Laurier, February 10, 1891.
96. This information comes to light as a result of the accidental opening of a letter addressed to Ritchie at Rossin House, Toronto, by the wrong Ritchie. P.A.C., Macdonald Papers, Vol. 44, Fred C. Denison to Macdonald, December 30, 1890 (private).
97. London *Railway News*, April 11, 1891, letter from Sir Henry Tyler of April 7; this was in reply to bitter denunciations from Tupper in the London *Times*, April 7, 1891, letter of Sir Charles Tupper, of March 26, 1891.
98. *Globe*, March 2, 1891.
99. P.A.C., Macdonald Papers, Vol. 288, Van Horne to Macdonald, February 28, 1891 (confidential).
100. University of Western Ontario, Fairbank Papers, J. H. Fairbank to C. O. Fairbank (son), February 11, 1891. See Edward Phelps, "A Liberal backbencher in the Macdonald regime: the political career of John Henry Fairbank of Petrolia," *Western Ontario Historical Notes* (Library, University of Western Ontario), XXII, No. 1, March, 1966, pp. 1-45.
101. P.A.C., Tarte Papers, Laurier to Tarte, 11 mars 1891.
102. *The Week*, Toronto, February 13, 1891.
103. Toronto *Empire*, February 18, 1891.
104. P.A.C., Laurier Papers, Vol. 5, Ellis to Laurier, March 7, 1891 (private). Cartwright's speech in Boston of January 30th, referred to "a new tier of northern states" as a result of unrestricted reciprocity. Halifax *Morning Herald*, February 13, 1891.
105. *Ibid.*, Davies to Laurier, March 27, 1891.
106. New Brunswick Museum, Tilley Papers, Bowell to Tilley, April 3, 1891.
107. From a signed statement, dated March 7, 1891, *Globe*, March 9, 1891. Also quoted by T. E. Kenny, *House of Commons, Debates*, 1891, p. 823 (June 5, 1891).
108. P.A.C., Laurier Papers, Vol. 5, Davies to Laurier, March 27, 1891.
109. Truro *Colchester Sun*, March 6, 1891. A Conservative paper, be it noted.
110. P.A.O., Edgar Papers, Laurier to Edgar, November 11, 1891 (private).
111. J. S. Willison, *Reminiscences*, p. 226.
112. P.A.O., Blake Papers, Laurier to Blake, February 2, 1891, (confidential).
113. Toronto *Globe*, March 6, 1891: also in Brown and Prang, *Confederation to 1949* (Toronto, 1966,) pp. 31-3.
114. Toronto *Globe*, March 12, 1891, letter from Blake of March 11. See also Willison, *Reminiscences*, p. 243.
115. *Grip*, Toronto, March 28, 1891.
116. P.A.O., Edgar Papers, Laurier to Edgar, November 11, 1891 (private).
117. P.A.O., Blake Papers, Blake to Longley, March 15, 1892 (private and confidential; copy).

118. P.A.O., Blake Papers, Blake to Mills, April 12, 1892. Also in Brown, *Canada's National Policy* (Princeton, 1964), p. 406.

119. *The Week*, Toronto, May 8, 1891.

120. *Ibid.*, May 15, 1891.

121. P.A.C., Mme Lavergne Papers, Laurier to Emilie Lavergne, May 17, 1891.

122. P.A.C., Edgar Papers, Edgar to his wife, June 14, 1891, reporting conversations with Sir John Abbott and Sir James Grant.

123. *The Week*, Toronto, June 5, 1891.

NOTES TO CHAPTER TWELVE

1. P.A.O., Edgar Papers, Edgar to his wife Matilda, May 31, 1891.
2. Toronto *Globe*, May 21, 1891. Lady Macdonald's preference for Tupper is well known; less known is her animus toward Thompson, one which was well reciprocated.
3. Edgar, though a Liberal, was well acquainted socially with J. J. C. Abbott. P.A.O., Edgar Papers, Edgar to his wife, June 14, 1891.
4. Creighton, *Macdonald*, pp. 568-9.
5. P.A.O., Patteson Papers, Patteson to John Thompson, June 9, 1891 (confidential).
6. P.A.O., Edgar Papers, Edgar to his wife, June 12, 1891.
7. St. Francis Xavier University, Thompson Papers, Thompson to his sons in England, July 6, 1891 (copy).
8. P.A.O., Patteson Papers, Thompson to Patteson, June 6, 1891 (private).
9. *Canada: House of Commons, Debates*, 1891, pp. 1123, 1137 (June 22, 1891). Also Saint John *Gazette*, June 11, 1891.
10. P.A.O., Patteson Papers, Abbott to Patteson, June 4, 1891.
11. *Canada: Senate, Debates*, 1211 (June 17, 1891).
12. P.A.C., Thompson Papers, Vol. 291, Thompson to his wife, July 9, 1891.
13. *Canada: House of Commons, Journals*, 1891, Vol. I, App. XXV (June 15, 1891).
14. P.A.C., Thompson Papers, Vol. 130, Osler to Thompson, June 17, 1891, (telegram).
15. *Ibid.*, Vol. 142, Tarte to Thompson, n.d., but probably late September, 1891.
16. *Canada: House of Commons, Journals*, Volume I, Appendix. "Reports of the Select Standing Committee on Privileges and Elections relative to certain statements and charges made in connection with tenders and contracts respecting the Quebec Harbour Works and the Esquimalt 'Graving Dock' (hereafter 'McGreevy-Langevin-inquiry,')," pp. 644-5. Robert McGreevy to Thomas McGreevy, January 14, 1889.
17. P.A.C., Thompson Papers, Vol. 134, Edward Moore to B. B. Osler, August 10, 1891, from Portland, Maine.
18. "McGreevy-Langevin inquiry," pp. 1131-3. Questions by L. H. Davies, August 12, 1891.
19. *Ibid.*, p. 179, Owen Murphy's evidence. Questions by Félix Geoffrion, June 26, 1891.
20. P.A.C., Thompson Papers, Vol. 291, Thompson to Annie Thompson, July 23, 1891.
21. A.P.Q., Langevin Papers, Boîte 7, Abbott to Langevin, July 28, 1891 (confidential).
22. *Ibid.*, Abbott to Langevin, September 5, 1891 (confidential).
23. "McGreevy-Langevin inquiry," ivnn. The minority report of Mills and Davies found the charges against Langevin fully proved. *Ibid.*, lxxxiimm.
24. *House of Commons, Debates*, 1891, p. 6124-5 (September 24, 1891).
25. P.A.C., Thompson Papers, Vol. 193, Martin J. Griffin to Thompson, December 18, 1893.
26. *House of Commons, Journals*, 1891, Volume II. Appendix. These inquiries are each paged separately. "Langevin Block inquiry," p. 37. Rousseau's evidence, July 24, 1891.
27. *Ibid.*, pp. 16-17, Fensom's evidence, July 21, 1891.
28. *Ibid.*, "Printing Bureau inquiry," 64, August 27, 1891, Perrott's evidence.
29. *Ibid.*, p. 213, Brown Chamberlain's evidence, September 25, 1891.
30. Sénécal claimed he was available for several weeks, but finally on doctor's orders had to rest. His letter is most interesting and claimed that the Civil Service Act did not prohibit "testimonials of esteem" from friends. *Ibid.*, 53, Sénécal to Clarke Wallace, August 24, 1891 (from Ottawa). He was dismissed.
31. *Canada: House of Commons, Debates*, 1891, p. 3835-6 (August 13, 1891).

32. "McGreevy-Langevin inquiry," 780-1, July 31, 1891.
33. I have translated this passage from the French. P.A.C., Honoré Mercier Papers, LeBoeuf to Pacaud, 23 avril 1889.
34. See *The Senate, Journals*, 1891, Appendix, "Report and evidence from the Select Committee on Railways, Telegraphs and Harbours, *in re* 'An Act respecting the Baie des Chaleurs Railway Company'" (hereafter "Baie Des Chaleurs inquiry").
35. P.A.C., Laurier Papers, Vol. 5, Laurier to Beaugrand, 17 août 1891 (personelle).
36. *Ibid.*, Davies to Laurier, December 20, 1891 (private).
37. Rumilly, *Québec*, VI, 246.
38. J. T. Saywell, *The Office of Lieutenant-Governor* (Toronto, 1957), 128, quoting Landry Papers, Mercier to Angers, December 17, 1891. Saywell has an excellent analysis of the political crisis.
39. P.A.C., Lavergne Papers, Laurier to Emilie Lavergne, August 4, 1891.
40. *Ibid.*, Laurier to Emilie Lavergne, September 3, 1891.
41. Rumilly, *Québec*, VI, 277.
42. P.A.C., Thompson Papers, Vol. 182, Hall to Thompson, June 9, 1893 (private); Hall to Thompson, June 26, 1893 (cable); J. M. Courtney to Thompson, June 30, 1893.
43. Charles Langelier, *Souvenirs politiques* (Québec, 1909), II, 220. Rumilly has a longer description of the same scene, but does not give his source, in *Mercier* (Montréal, 1936), pp. 526-7.
44. Rumilly, *Mercier*, pp. 531-2.
45. P.A.C., Tupper Papers, Vol. 10, Van Horne to Tupper, August 5, 1891.
46. Montreal *Star*, October 22, 1891. The *Star* was however opposed to Abbott on other grounds, mainly Abbott's preventing Hugh Graham from exposing swindles by Montreal City Council.
47. P.A.C., Thompson Papers, Vol. 160, Abbott to Thompson, Tuesday [August 9, 1892?].
48. *Ibid.*, Volume 166, Abbott to Thompson, November 10, 1892, (from London).
49. P.A.C., Laurier Papers, Vol. 11, W. S. Bletchey to Laurier, June 27, 1896, (from Port Hope).
50. *The Week*, Toronto, March 4, 1892.
51. Abbott Papers, Vol. 1, Galt to Macdonald, May 22, 1891.
52. Foster's recollection, *House of Commons, Debates*, 1892, pp. 330, 332 (March 22, 1892).
53. See, for example, C. H. Tupper's reply to Cartwright, *ibid.*, p. 358 (March 22, 1892).
54. Laurier Papers, Vol. 6, L. G. Power to Laurier, December 29, 1892.
55. G. R. MacLean, "The Imperial Federation movement in Canada, 1884-1902," PH.D. thesis, Duke University, 1958, p. 166.
56. Thompson Papers, Vol. 181, Griffin to Thompson, May 22, 1893.
57. Laurier Papers, Vol. 6, François Langelier to Laurier, 16 juin 1893.
58. Montreal *Herald*, June 23, 1893. See J. W. Lederle, "The Liberal convention of 1893" C.J.E.P.S., XVI, No. 1, Feb. 1950, 42-52.
59. *The Week*, Toronto, June 30, 1893.
60. Reported from a House of Lords speech in March, 1891, by the Toronto *Globe*, January 17, 1895.
61. F. F. Thompson, *The French Shore Problem in Newfoundland* (Toronto, 1961), p. 78.
62. *Canada: Sessional Papers*, 1892, No. 23C, 3-4, Attorney-General of Newfoundland to C. H. Tupper, April 20, 1887.
63. *Ibid.*, 19-21. Also Halifax *Morning Herald*, July 27, 1889.
64. P.A.C., Thompson Papers, Vol. 106, Winter to Thompson, April 30, 1890 (from Halifax).
65. Brown, *Canada's National Policy*, 199-200.
66. See *supra*, pp. 222-3.
67. Thompson Papers, P.A.C., A. B. Morine to Thompson, July 20, 1891 (confidential).
68. P.A.C., Abbott Papers, Vol. 1A, Daly to Abbott, August 5, 1892.
69. F. J. S. Hopwood to Major Colville, October 22, 1891, Thompson Papers, Vol. 139.
70. Enclosed in Vol. 206, C. C. Carlyle, of Harbour Grace to Thompson, April 18, 1894.
71. *Canada: House of Commons, Debates*, 1890, pp. 4086-94. (April 29, 1890).
72. Joseph Martin, in a letter to Laurier, said that the main point which told against the separate schools was that with 1/10 of the population they got 1/4 of the school money. He added, however, "This of course could have been remedied without changing the whole

system[.]" Laurier Papers. Vol. 7, Martin to Laurier, December 6, 1893.

73. Manitoba *Free Press*, July 8, 1892, cited in J. L. Holmes, "Factors affecting politics in Manitoba . . . 1870-99," M.A. thesis, University of Manitoba, 1936, p. 89.

74. W. L. Morton, *Manitoba: A History* (Toronto, 1957), pp. 244-9.

75. Thompson Papers, P.A.C., Vol. 107, Taché to Thompson, May 7, 1890.

76. *Ibid.*, Vol. 121, Scarth to John A. Macdonald, January 28, 1891.

77. *Manitoba Reports*, Vol. 7, 1891, 301.

78. *Supra*, pp. 40-1.

79. *Reports of the Supreme Court of Canada*, Vol. 19, 1892, pp. 383-6.

80. R. A. Olmstead (ed.), *Decisions of the Judicial Committee of the Privy Council Relating to the British North America Act, 1867* (Ottawa, 1954), I, 280.

81. Justice Holmes' dissent in U.S. v. *Northern Securities Company* (1904).

82. See the last page of their decision, Olmstead, 286.

83. Reported at least by Hugh John Macdonald. Thompson Papers, Vol. 173, Macdonald to Thompson, January 25, 1893 (private).

84. *Ibid.*, Vol. 160, Ross to Thompson, August 5, 1892.

85. *Ibid.*, Vol. 162, Hughes to Thompson, September 16, 1892.

86. J. T. Saywell (ed.), *The Canadian Journal of Lady Aberdeen, 1893-1898* (Toronto, 1960), pp. 169-70 (December 13, 1894).

87. *Lady Aberdeen's Journal*, p. 181 (January 2, 1895). This is also confirmed in Thompson's private correspondence with his wife in the 1880's.

88. *Ibid.*, p. 163 (December 13, 1894).

NOTES TO CHAPTER THIRTEEN

1. Toronto *Globe*, June 16, 1891, nastily described him as "a cheap monument to the Prince of Orange."

2. P.A.C., Minto Papers, Vol. 36, Bertie Elliott to Peter Elliott, December 25, 1898, relating Rideau Hall gossip.

3. Marjorie Pentland, *A Bonnie Fechter: The Life of Ishbel Marjoribanks . . .* (London, 1952), p. 44. Quoted in J. T. Saywell (ed.), *The Canadian Journal of Lady Aberdeen, 1893-1898* (Toronto, 1960), xv.

4. Maurice Pope (ed.), *Public Servant: The Memoirs of Sir Joseph Pope* (Toronto, 1960), p. 108.

5. *Lady Aberdeen's Journal*, p. 166 (December 13, 1894).

6. Toronto *Globe*, March 7, 1895, reporting Cartwright's speech at Sarnia, of March 2. The poem is a paraphrase of Dryden on Homer and Vergil.

7. E. J. Noble, "D'Alton McCarthy and the Election of 1896," M.A. thesis, University of Guelph, 1969, p. 52.

8. Toronto *Globe*, December 29, 1894, reporting McCarthy's speech at Picton on December 28.

9. P.A.C., Willison Papers, Vol. 13, J. D. Cameron to Willison, March 4, 1895.

10. Toronto *Globe*, February 6, 1895, reporting Laurier's speech of February 5.

11. P.A.C., Laurier Papers, Vol. 8, Laurier to Willison, March 30, 1895 (draft; private); also P.A.C., Willison Papers, Vol. 48, for the actual letter.

12. P.A.C., Laurier Papers, Vol. 9, Mills to Laurier, March 29, 1895.

13. *Ibid.*, A. Langevin to Laurier, 11 mai 1895 (from University of Ottawa; privée et confidentielle).

14. *Ibid.*, Laurier to A. Langevin, 14 mai 1895 (draft).

15. Sir Frank Smith and J. S. Patterson did not sign the Remedial Order presumably owing to inavoidable absence. Ministers not of the Cabinet did not sign.

16. See *Canada: Sessional Papers*, 1895, No. 20. But it is however conveniently available, with many other documents, in Lovell Clark, *The Manitoba School Question: Majority Rule or Minority Rights?* (Toronto, 1968), pp. 166-7.

17. University of British Columbia, Charles Hibbert Tupper Papers, Tupper to Daly, March 26, 1895 (copy). Also P.A.C., Microfilm 106.

18. *Loc. cit.*

19. P.A.C., Bowell Papers, vol. 14, Tupper to Bowell, March 21, 1895.

20. See H. A. Fleming, *Canada's Arctic Outlet: A History of the Hudson's Bay Railway* (Berkeley, 1957), pp. 22-49.

21. P.A.C., Laurier Papers, Vol. 9, Edgar to Laurier, March 28, 1895 (confidential).

22. *Canada: House of Commons, Debates*, 1895, p. 207 (April 24); 516-7 (May 3, 1895).
23. Saywell, *Lady Aberdeen's Journal*, xlviii.
24. P.A.M., Greenway Papers, Greenway to Aberdeen, May 11, 1895 (copy).
25. *Lady Aberdeen's Journal*, p. 235 (July 13, 1895).
26. P.A.M., Greenway Papers, Greenway to Charlton, Letterbook C, May 6, 1895 (private and confidential).
27. Saywell, *Lady Aberdeen's Journal*, li.
28. *Ibid.*, p. 234 (July 13, 1895).
29. *Ibid.*, p. 237 (July 13, 1895).
30. *Canada: House of Commons, Debates*, p. 4190 (July 11, 1895).
31. *Ibid.*, 4217 (July 11, 1895).
32. *Ibid.*, 4193-4 (July 11, 1895).
33. Toronto *Daily Mail and Empire*, October 9, 1895, reporting Laurier's speech of October 8. Lovell Clark, "The Conservative party in the 1890's," PH.D. thesis for the University of Toronto, 1966, pp. 88-9.
34. Saywell, *Lady Aberdeen's Journal*, lviii.
35. P.AC.,Willison Papers, Vol. 48, Laurier to Willison, November 19 1895 (private).
36. *Ibid.*, Laurier to Willison, December 17, 1895 (private).
37. *Ibid.*, Laurier to Willison, December 31, 1895 (private).
38. P.A.C., Laurier Papers, Vol. 9, F. L. Jones to Laurier, November 12, 1895.
39. University of British Columbia, C. H. Tupper Papers, Tupper to Lady Aberdeen, November 4, 1895; also P.A.C., Microfilm 106.
40. New Brunswick Museum, Tilley Papers, Foster to Tilley, January 23, 1896 (confidential). This is a long letter recounting the events since November.
41. Saywell, *Lady Aberdeen's Journal*, lvii.
42. N.B.M., Tilley Papers, Foster to Tilley, January 23, 1896 (confidential).
43. Tupper Papers, Tupper to C. H. Tupper, November 25, 1895, quoted in Saywell, lvii.
44. There is a comprehensive story of this affair in the Toronto *Daily Mail and Empire*, January 6, 1896. The Toronto *Mail* and Toronto *Empire*, the former a maverick Conservative, the latter an official Conservative paper, were merged in 1895.
45. *Ibid.*, January 8, 1896, quoting Montreal *La Minerve*.
46. N.B.M., Tilley Papers, Foster to Tilley, January 23, 1896 (confidential).
47. This was frequently alleged in the press. See also Costigan's view, Saywell, *Lady Aberdeen's Journal*, lxi.
48. Toronto *Globe*, January 7, 1896.
49. N.B.M., Tilley Papers, Foster to Tilley, January 23, 1896 (confidential).
50. On January 7, Caron who was leader of the House at the time, tried to get Laurier to agree to a two-week adjournment. Laurier refused, insisted on notice; on January 9, on division, it was agreed to adjourn until January 14, 1896.
51. Toronto *Daily Mail and Empire*, January 8, 1896, despatch from Ottawa of January 7.
52. I have taken this report from the *Daily Mail and Empire*, January 16, 1896, but it differs very little from the Debates, See *House of Commons, Debates*, 1896, pp. 75-6 (January 15, 1896).
53. This phrase does not occur in the *Debates* exactly, but Cartwright makes reference to it, and the Nova Scotian members took issue with it. *Ibid.*, 240 *et. seq.* (January 17, 1896). The phrase is however quoted in the *Daily Mail and Empire*, January 18, 1896, reporting Parliament for January 17.
54. Cape Breton constituency was then a dual one. D. C. Mackeen, one of the two Conservatives sitting members, resigned to make room for Tupper.
55. Halifax *Morning Chronicle*, February 4, 1896. It was reported later that this was garbled extract. (Antigonish *Casket*, February 6, 1896.) Both these references have been brought to my attention by Mr. Kenneth McLaughlin.
56. Saywell, *Lady Aberdeen's Journal*, p. 319 (February 10, 1896). Also P.A.C., Pope Papers, Vol. 43, Diary, February 10, 1896.
57. *Canada: House of Commons, Debates*, 1896, p. 1512-14 (February 11, 1896).
58. Katharine Hughes, *Father Lacombe: Black-Robe Voyageur* (Toronto, 1911), p. 370.
59. P.A.M., Greenway Papers, Greenway to M.C.Cameron,February 29, 1896. Liberal M.P. M. C. Cameron had been elected January 14, 1896 in a bye-election in West Huron, where the Government lost the seat previously held by J. C. Patterson, who had been made Lieutenant-Governor of Manitoba.

60. Winnipeg *Manitoba Free Press*, February 13, 1896. This reference has been brought to my attention by Mr. Kenneth McLaughlin.
61. Sir John Willison, *Reminiscences*, p. 248. For a much more comprehensive reference to this incident see the next note.
62. P.A.C., Willison Papers, Vol. 21, Willison to John W. Dafoe, March 7, 1923 (draft). This was a comment elucidated by a reading of Dafoe's *Laurier*, just published.
63. *Ibid.*, Dafoe to Willison, March 19, 1923. See also *Ibid.*, Willison to Dafoe, March 26, 1923 (copy).
64. P.A.C., Pacaud Papers, Laurier to Pacaud, 5 fév. 1896 (copy).
65. *Ibid.*, Laurier to Pacaud, 5 fév. 1896 (personelle).
66. Paul Crunican, "The Roman Catholic Church and the election of 1896," PH.D. thesis, University of Toronto, 1967.
67. Quoted by the Toronto *Globe*, February 21, 1896.
68. Montreal *La Presse*, 20, 24, 27, fév. 1896; in Clark, Chapter V, 130.
69. P.A.C., Willison Papers, J. D. Edgar to Willison, February 19, 1896. This has been brought to my notice by Mr. Kenneth McLaughlin.
70. See Paul Crunican, "The Manitoba School Question and Canadian federal politics: a study in church-state relations," PH.D. thesis, University of Toronto, 1968, pp. 226-7, 391, 409-12.
71. Saywell, *Lady Aberdeen's Journal*, p. 329 (March 19, 1896).
72. This was reported, as a matter of undoubted fact, by the Conservative Toronto *Mail and Empire*, April 4, 1896 report from Ottawa, of April 3.
73. *Canada: House of Commons, Debates*, 1896, p. 2759.
74. *Ibid.*, pp. 3490-4 (March 13, 1896).
75. *Ibid.*, pp. 3512-3.
76. *Ibid.*, pp. 3278-9 (March 11, 1896).
77. *Ibid.*, p. 3289.
78. *Ibid.*, pp. 3834-5 (March 18, 1896).
79. *Ibid.*, p. 3878.
80. *Ibid.*, p. 3026 (March 6, 1896).
81. *Ibid.*, p. 3033.
82. Toronto *Globe*, August 12, 1895, referring to Caven's speech at the Pavilion, Toronto, of March 11, 1895.
83. Referred to *ibid.*, p. 2926 (March 5, 1896), by Dr. Sproule, M.P. Grey East, a Conservative who crossed the floor of this issue, and whom Tupper read out of the party.
84. *Ibid.*, pp. 3097-8 (March 9, 1896).
85. Toronto *Daily Mail and Empire*, March 21, 1896.
86. Saywell, *Lady Aberdeen's Journal*, pp. 330-2 (Friday, March 20, 1896; Saturday, March 21, 1896).
87. P.A.M., Sifton Papers, Memorandum in D'Alton McCarthy's hand. No date. McCarthy's italics.
88. Toronto *Daily Mail and Empire*, March 31, 1896, report from Winnipeg, of March 30.
89. Saywell, *Lady Aberdeen's Journal*, lxviii.
90. He returned to Winnipeg only on March 31. Toronto *Globe*, April 1, 1896, report from Winnipeg March 31.
91. Toronto *Daily Mail and Empire*, March 31, 1896, report from Winnipeg of March 30.
92. *Ibid.*, April 3, 1896, report from Winnipeg of April 2.
93. See also *Canada: House of Commons, Debates*, 1896, p. 4932 (March 31, 1896).
94. P.A.C., Sifton Papers, Vol. 7, D'Alton McCarthy to Sifton, April 4, 1896.
95. Toronto *Globe*, April 10, report from Ottawa of April 9. Casey made some amusing comments on the character of the Bill. See *House of Commons, Debates*, 1896, pp. 5785-6 (April 9, 1896).
96. *Canada: House of Commons, Debates*, 1896, p. 6474 (April 15, 1896). Nevertheless Davin had supported the Bill on second reading.
97. This was J. F. Lister's view, M.P. Lambton West. *Ibid.*, p. 6489 (April 15, 1896).
98. *Ibid.*, p. 3223 (March 10, 1896).
99. Toronto *Daily Mail and Empire*, April 4, 1896.
100. P.A.C., Denison Papers, Denison to Lord Salisbury, May 2, 1896 (copy).
101. Saywell, *Lady Aberdeen's Journal*, pp. 339-340 (April 24, April 27, 1896).
102. Rumilly, *Histoire de la province de Québec*, VIII, 43.
103. P.A.C., Chapleau Papers, Dansereau to Chapleau, 1 mai 1896 (privée).
104. Rumilly, *Québec*, VIII, 44.
105. *Ibid.*, 46.
106. P.A.C., Tupper Papers Additional, Hugh John Macdonald to Tupper, January 17, 1896.
107. University of Western Ontario, J. H. Coyne Papers, Hugh John Macdonald to Coyne, May 19, 1896 (private).
108. P.A.C., Tupper Papers Additional,

Tupper to Hugh John Macdonald, April 15, 1896 (copy).
109. Halifax *Morning Chronicle*, May 29, 1896, letter from MacMechan. This and the next two references have been brought to my attention by Kenneth McLaughlin. See his M.A. thesis, "The federal election of 1896 in Nova Scotia," Dalhousie University, 1967.
110. Halifax *Morning Herald*, April 9, 1896.
111. Halifax *Morning Herald*, May 15, 1896. In 1882 Robert Borden supported his cousin, Dr. F. W. Borden, in the Liberal interest. His break with the Nova Scotia Liberals came over the repeal issue in 1886.
112. Toronto *Globe*, January 31, 1896.
113. Hector Charlesworth, *Candid Chronicles* (Toronto, 1925), pp. 206-7.
114. Toronto *Daily Mail and Empire*, June 20, 1896.
115. *Ibid.*, May 21, 1896, reporting McCarthy's speech of May 20. Tupper later used this speech at Brockville against McCarthy. *Ibid.*, June 10, 1896, reporting Tupper at Brockville, June 9.
116. *Ibid.*, June 16, 1896. Also noted by Elizabeth L. Eayrs, "The election of 1896 in Western Ontario," M.A. thesis, University of Western Ontario, 1950, p. 74.
117. *Ibid.*, June 4, 1896. See also Eayrs, "Election of 1896 in Western Ontario," p. 48.
118. Toronto *Globe*, May 1, 1896.
119. Alleged confidently by the Toronto *Daily Mail and Empire*, June 19, 1896.
120. Rumilly, *Québec*, VIII, 58-9.
121. Paul Crunican, "Manitoba School Question and Canadian federal politics," p. 511.
122. *Ibid.*, p. 523-36.
123. Rumilly, VIII, 61.
124. *Ibid.*, VIII, 64.
125. Robert Rumilly, *Henri Bourassa: la vie publique d'un grand canadien* (Montreal, 1953), p. 26.
126. *Loc. cit.*
127. P.A.C., Willison Papers, Vol. 21, Willison to Dafoe, March 7, 1923.
128. P.A.C., Tupper Papers Additional, Tilley to Tupper, June 3, 1896.
129. Rumilly, *Québec*, VIII, 84.
130. Hector Charlesworth, *Candid Chronicles*, p. 200, reporting his own conversation with Tarte.
131. Rumilly, *Bourassa*, p. 32.
132. P.A.C., Laurier Papers, Vol. 11, Mowat to Laurier, May 22, 1896 (private).
133. P.A.C., Tupper Papers, Vol. 11, Langevin to Tupper, June 24, 1896 (confidential).
134. *Ibid.*, additional, Aberdeen to Tupper, June 27, 1896.
135. Saywell, *Lady Aberdeen's Journal*, p. 351 (July 4, 1896).
136. P.A.C., Bourassa Papers, Goldwin Smith to Bourassa, February 8, 1900. This reference was brought to my attention by Professor Mary Hallett.
137. P.A.C., Pope Papers, Vol. 1, J. C. Patterson to Pope, June 29, 1896 (private).
138. Toronto *Daily Mail and Empire*, June 25, 1896, report from Ottawa of June 24, of an interview with Tupper.
139. P.A.C., Pope Papers, Vol. 1, J. C. Patterson to Pope, June 29, 1896 (private).
140. P.A.C., Willison Papers, Vol. 15, Charlton to Willison, June 25, 1896 from Lynedoch, Ontario).

NOTES TO CHAPTER FOURTEEN

1. P.A.O., Blake Papers, Blake to McMullen, Oct. 24, 1906.
2. Beckles Willson, *From Quebec to Piccadilly and Other Places* (London, 1929), p. 63.
3. Toronto *Globe*, May 1, 1896.
4. *Ibid.*, April 25, 1896.
5. *Ibid.*, April 18, 1896.
6. *Queens Quarterly*, Vol. II, No. 1 (July, 1894), 79.
7. P.A.O., Edgar Papers, Edgar to his wife, March 6, 1896.
8. Saywell, *Lady Aberdeen's Journal*, p. 330 (March 19, 1896).
9. P.A.C., Macdonald Papers, Vol.. 266, Goldwin Smith to Macdonald, Feb. 27, 1880.
10. P.A.C., Pacaud Papers, Vol 3, Laurier to Pacaud, 15 jan. 1894.
11. Sara Jeanette Duncan [Mrs. Everard Cotes] *The Imperialist* (London, 1904), pp. 67-8; New Canadian Library edition (Toronto, 1961), p. 47.
12. *Ibid.*, p. 329; New Canadian Library edition, p. 191.
13. G. R. MacLean, "The imperial federation movement in Canada, 1884-1902," PH.D. thesis, Duke University, 1958, p. 313.
14. R. J. D. Page, "The impact of the

Boer War on the Canadian general election of 1900 in Ontario," M.A. thesis, Queens University, 1964, p. 149; see also Carl C. Berger, "The vision of grandeur: studies in the ideas of Canadian imperialism," PH.D. thesis, University of Toronto, 1966, pp. 11, 302, 625, and *passim*.
15. Montreal *Herald*, July 1, 1893.
16. *The Week*, Toronto, Dec. 16, 1892, "An independent Canada," pp. 76-7.
17. *Ibid.*, May 23, 1890.
18. *Canada: House of Commons, Debates*, 1896, p. 3292 (March 11, 1896).
19. Toronto *Globe*, Sept. 4, 1895. "In the West," report from Calgary of Aug. 29, 1895.

SELECT BIBLIOGRAPHY

Regrettably, it has not been possible to list here all the sources used in this book. Specific references to points in the text are given in the notes.

MANUSCRIPTS

The manuscript sources for the period 1874-1896 are particularly rich and comprehensive. Of pre-eminent importance are the 500 volumes of the Macdonald Papers in P.A.C. Copies of Macdonald's own letters appear in his letterbooks; but he wrote frequently, without using letterbooks, and the best sources for his letters are in the papers of his innumerable correspondents. These are notably: the George Stephen Papers (P.A.C.), the T. C. Patteson Papers (P.A.O.), Sir Alexander Campbell Papers (P.A.O.), H. H. Smith Papers (P.A.C.), W. B. Scarth Papers (P.A.O.), Dewedney Papers (P.A.C. and Glenbow Foundation, Calgary), Galt Papers (P.A.C.), Joseph Hickson Papers (P.A.C.), D'Alton McCarthy Papers (P.A.C.), Sir John Thompson Papers (P.A.C.), Sir Charles Tupper Papers (P.A.C.), Sir Hector Langevin Papers (A.P.Q.), and Sir Leonard Tilley Papers (N.B.M.). Macdonald's correspondence with Governor Generals is especially valuable, for he often summarized the political and legal questions of the time for the Queen's representative. Here the most important are the papers of Lord Lorne and especially those of Lord Lansdowne. (Both on microfilm, P.A.C.)

The Alexander Mackenzie Papers (P.A.C.) are not inconsiderable, but they must be supplemented by the collection at Queen's University Library, of which there is a microfilm in P.A.C. There are also important Mackenzie letters in the George Brown Papers (P.A.C.), Blake Papers (P.A.O.), Wm. Buckingham Papers (P.A.C.), J. D. Edgar Papers (P.A.O.), A. G. Jones Papers (P.A.N.S. and published in the P.A.N.S. Report for 1953), Laurier Papers (P.A.C.), David Mills Papers (University of Western Ontario).

Sir John Thompson's Papers are also comprehensive, and are organized chronologically. His letterbooks are disappointing, but his wife collected many he wrote while away, and they will usually repay attention. They are in the Thompson Papers, as are those he addressed to his sons.

The J. J. C. Abbott Papers, and the Mackenzie Bowell Papers are also in P.A.C.

Other collections that should be consulted are: the Sir Adolphe Caron Papers (P.A.C.), H. P. P. Crease Papers (P.A.B.C.), Greenway Papers (P.A.M.), George Denison Papers (P.A.C.), Alexander Morris Papers (P.A.M. and P.A.C.), Sir Joseph Pope Papers (P.A.C.), Clifford Sifton Papers (P.A.M. and P.A.C.), and especially, the Willison Papers (P.A.C.). The R. B. Angus Papers (microfilm P.A.C.), Sir Sandford Fleming Papers (P.A.C.), Sir Henry Tyler Papers (P.A.C.), and Sir William Van Horne Papers, (P.A.C.), are all useful, not only for railways but for political inter-relations. Sir Charles Hibbert Tupper Papers are at the University of British Columbia but there is a microfilm of them (P.A.C.). The Joseph Trutch Papers are also at the University of British Columbia. The J. H. Coyne Papers, at the University of Western Ontario, have some letters from Hugh John Macdonald and from G. E. Casey. There are small collections of the papers of A. R. Angers, Adolphe Chapleau, Gédéon Ouimet and Ernest Pacaud at P.A.C. Mercier's papers there are disappointing.

SERIALS

The *Nation* (1874-76) is a mine of information; even more valuable is *The Week* (1883-96), which is really indispensable to a comprehensive inside look at the period, to which could also be added *Bystander* (1880-82, 1890-91). *The Week* does not maintain its high quality after 1891, however. *The Canadian Monthly and National Review* (1872-82) is valuable. The *Queen's Quarterly* starts in 1893, as does the *Canadian Magazine*. *Grip* (1873-94) is well known for its Bengough cartoons, but its writing ought to be better known. Uneven and often unreliable, it nevertheless offers much comment on the manners and morals of the time. *La Revue de Montréal* (1877-81) and *Le Canada Français* (1888-91) are useful French-Canadian periodicals.

NEWSPAPERS

No attempt can be made here to list the newspapers for the period 1874-96. There is a list of the more important newspapers of the period 1857-1900 in W. H. Kesterton, A *History of Journalism in Canada* (Toronto, 1967) pp. 35-7, whose whole chapter, "The third press period" can be read as a survey of newspaper life of the period.

PRINTED COLLECTIONS:

A. *Diaries and Letters*
Indispensable for the period 1893-96 is J. T. Saywell's edition of the *Canadian Journal of Lady Aberdeen* 1893-8 (Toronto, 1960) with a first-class introduction. J. Barnard has edited *Mémoires Chapais* (3 vols., Montreal, 1961-4). C. W. de Kiewiet and F. H. Underhill have edited the *Dufferin-Carnarvon Correspondence* (Toronto, 1955), essential for the Mackenzie régime. Lucien Pacaud has edited some of Laurier's letters, *Sir Wilfrid Laurier: Letters to my Father and Mother* (Toronto, 1935). Joseph Pope has published *The Correspondence of Sir John A. Macdonald* (New York, 1921).

B. *Reminiscences*
P. E. Bilkey, *Persons Papers and Things* (Toronto, 1940) has interesting recollections of an experienced newspaperman. R. L. Borden's memoirs should not be neglected for the period before 1896: H. Borden, (ed.), *Robert Laird Borden: His Memoirs*. 2 vols., Toronto, 1938. Richard Cartwright's *Reminiscences* is a famous and one-sided view of Canadian politics to 1896 (Toronto, 1812). Hector Charlesworth has some well-told recollections in *Candid Chronicles* (Toronto, 1925) and *More Candid Chronicles* (Toronto, 1928). On similar genre, and well done, are the vignettes of Augustus Bridle, *Sons of Canada* (Toronto, 1916). L. O. David has published *Biographies et portraits* (Montréal, 1876), *Mes contemporains* (Montréal, 1894), and *Laurier et son temps* (Montréal, 1905). George Tayler Denison also: *Recollections of a Police Magistrate* (Toronto, 1920); *Soldiering in Canada* (Toronto, 1900), and his better known study, *The Struggle for Imperial Unity* (London, 1909). G. H. Ham has a delightful series of stories, leaving one to wonder if they are all quite true, *Reminiscences of a Raconteur Between the* [18]*40's and the* [19]*20's* (Toronto, 1921). Charles Langelier, *Souvenirs politiques*, 1878 à 1900 (2 vols., Québec, 1909) is indispensable for Laurier and for Quebec. J. W. Longley's reminiscences on public life are in the *Canadian Magazine*, Oct. 1920 to Feb. 1821, as "Reminiscences, political & otherwise." Maurice Pope has edited *Public Servant: the Memoirs of Sir Joseph Pope* (Toronto, 1960), which well repays reading. W. T. R. Preston, *My Generation of Politics and Politicians* (Toronto, 1927) grinds Preston's usual axes, against Lord Strathcona and the Conservatives in general, and like most of Preston's works must not be trusted too far. G. W. Ross, *Getting into Parliament and After* (Toronto, 1913) is an engaging account by a Liberal who seems to have seen good in both sides of politics. P. D. Ross's story is a vivid reminder du temps perdu: *Retrospects of a newspaper person* (Toronto, 1931). Goldwin Smith's *Reminiscences* (New York, 1910), edited by Arnold Haultain, deals with his Canadian life only in the last 50 pages but is worth reading. Sir Charles Tupper's *Recollections of Sixty Years* (London, 1914) is, not surprisingly, uninformative. Best of all the reminiscences perhaps, the best written, and certainly the most important politically, is Sir John Willison's. *Reminiscences: Political and Personal* (Toronto, 1919).

James Young's *Public Life and Public Men in Canada* (2 vols., Toronto, 1912) is stodgy, but useful.

Two useful memoirs by railwaymen P. T. Bone, *When the Steel Went Through: Reminiscences of Railroad Pioneer* (Toronto, 1947), and especially J. H. E. Secretan, *Canada's Great Highway: From the First Stake to the Last Spike* (London, 1924).

There are also two valuable Mounted Police memoirs. C. E. Denny, *The Law Marches West* (Toronto, 1939), and S. B. Steele, *Forty Years in Canada: Reminiscences of the Great North-West* (London, 1915).

BIOGRAPHY

A. MAJOR FIGURES

Blake

There is no comprehensive biography of Blake. Margaret Banks has written *Edward Blake: Irish Nationalist* (Toronto, 1957), about Blake's career after 1892 as M.P. for Longford in the British House of Commons, and also about his renunciation of the leadership in 1887 (C.H.R., June 1957, pp. 109-28). The best work on Blake's Canadian career is still the excellent series of articles by F. H. Underhill: "Edward Blake," in *Our Living Tradition* (Toronto, 1957), Vol. I, pp. 3-28; "Edward Blake and Canadian liberal nationalism," in R. Flenley (ed.), *Essays in Canadian History in Honour of G.. M. Wrong* (Toronto, 1939), pp. 132-53; "Edward Blake, the Supreme Court Act and the appeal to the Privy Council 1875-6," C.H.R., Sept. 1938, pp. 245-63; "Edward Blake, the Liberal party and unrestricted reciprocity," C.H.A. *Report*, 1939, pp. 133-41; "Laurier and Blake," C.H.R., 1943, pp. 135-55.

Laurier

Laurier has not lacked biographers. Sir John Willison's *Sir Wilfrid Laurier and the Liberal Party* (2 vols., Toronto, 1905) is almost in the class of a primary source; O. D. Skelton's *Life and Letters of Sir Wilfrid Laurier* (2 vols., Toronto, 1921) is a solid work by an admirer; J. W. Dafoe's *Laurier* (Toronto, 1922), originated because of Skelton's book. Joseph Schull's *Laurier* (Toronto, 1966) is sensitive, well written, and good for the Laurier before 1896, if a little uncritical. Blair Neatby's PH.D. thesis, "Laurier and a Liberal Quebec" (University of Toronto, 1956), is valuable. Articles include: Marc La Terreur, "Correspondence Laurier-Mme Joseph Lavergne, 1891-3." C.H.A. *Report*, 1964, pp. 37-51; Paul Steven's article is revisionist in tendency, "Wilfrid Laurier, politician" in *The Political Ideas of the Prime Ministers of Canada* (Ottawa, 1969), pp. 69-83.

Macdonald

Macdonald's secretary, Sir Joseph Pope, published two books, *The Memoirs of Sir John A. Macdonald*, (2 vols., Ottawa, 1895), *The Day of Sir John A. Macdonald* (Toronto, 1915), sympathetic and sound; but they have both been made obsolescent by D. G. Creighton's biography, *John A. Macdonald: The Old Chieftain* (Toronto, 1955), which has set a standard for biography that has not yet been matched. An important primary source is Sir John Willison's review of Pope's edition of Macdonald's correspondence (see Printed collections), "The correspondence of Sir John A. Macdonald," *Dalhousie Review*, April 1922, pp. 5-25. Other studies: A. L. Burt, "Peter Mitchell on John A. Macdonald," C.H.R., Sept. 1961, pp. 209-27, which cannot be safely neglected; J. A. Roy, "John A. Macdonald, barrister, and solicitor," *Canadian Bar Review*, Feb. 1948, pp. 415-32; two studies by P. B. Waite, "The political ideas of John A. Macdonald," in *Political Ideas of the Prime Ministers of Canada* (Ottawa, 1969), pp. 51-67, and "Sir John A. Macdonald, the man", in H. L. Dyck and H. P. Krosby (eds.), *Empire and Nations: Essays in Honour of F. H. Soward* (Toronto, 1969) pp. 36-53; F. W. Watt, "Sir John Macdonald, the workingman, & proletarian ideas in Victorian Canada," C.H.R., Mar. 1959, pp. 1-26.

Mackenzie

Dale Thomson's *Alexander Mackenzie: Clear Grit* (Toronto, 1960) has largely superseded the older biography by Buckingham and Ross, *The Hon. Alexander Mackenzie:*

His Life and Times (Toronto, 1892). Mackenzie's adventures with the British Columbians are also described in Margaret Ormsby's, "Prime Minister Mackenzie, the Liberal party and the bargain with British Columbia," C.H.R., June 1945, pp. 148-73. See also T. A. Burke, "Mackenzie & his Cabinet, 1873-8," C.H.R., June 1960, pp. 128-48.

Thompson
Thompson is nearly as badly off for biographers as Blake. One study exists, J. Castell Hopkins, *Life and Work of Sir John Thompson* (Brantford, 1895), not without value but largely hagiography. A recent survey is unpublished, J. P. Heisler's "Sir John Thompson," PH.D. thesis, University of Toronto, 1955. Articles include, F. W. Bissett, "Rt. hon. Sir John Thompson," *Dalhousie Review*, Oct. 1945, pp. 323-30; D. H. Gillis has two articles based partly upon papers not yet available, "Sir John Thompson's elections," C.H.R., March 1956, pp. 23-45; and "Sir John Thompson and Bishop Cameron," Canadian Catholic Historical Association *Report*, 1955; Justice Russell, "The career of Sir John Thompson," *Dalhousie Review*, July, 1921, pp. 188-201, is reminiscences by a personal friend.

Tupper
Wily, clever and able, Tupper still eludes his biographers. E. M. Saunders has an official life, *The Life and Letters of Sir Charles Tupper* (2 vols., London, 1916), with a supplement by his son Sir Charles Hibbert Tupper (Toronto, 1926). There is a comprehensive PH.D. thesis, "The career of Sir Charles Tupper in Canada, 1864-1900" by A. W. MacIntosh, University of Toronto, 1960.

B. OTHERS

Brown: J. M. S. Careless, *Brown of the Globe, Vol. II The Statesman of Confederation, 1860-1880*. (Toronto, 1963).

Cartwright: It is regrettable there is no published biography of Cartwright. The best available, and it is very good, is W. R. Graham's "Sir Richard Cartwright," PH.D. thesis, University of Toronto, 1950. See also his "Sir Richard Cartwright, Wilfrid Laurier, & Liberal party trade policy," C.H.R., Mar. 1952, pp. 1-18.

Chapleau: H. B. Neatby and J. T. Saywell, "Chapleau and the Conservative party in Quebec," C.H.R., March, 1956, pp. 1-22: Jacques Gouin, "Histoire d'une amitié: correspondence intime entre Chapleau et De Celles, 1875-1898," R.H.A.F., déc. 1964, pp. 363-86; and mars 1965, pp. 541-65. F. Ouellet, "Lettres de J. A. Chapleau, 1870-96" *Rapport de l'Archiviste de la province de Québec*, 1959-60, pp. 25-118.

Fielding: D. C. Harvey, "Fielding's call to Ottawa," *Dalhousie Review*, Jan. 1949, pp. 369-85; Hon. B. Russell, "Recollections of W. S. Fielding," *Dalhousie Review*, Oct. 1929, pp. 326-40.

Fleming: L. J. Burpee, *Sandford Fleming, Empire Builder* (Oxford, 1915) can be supplemented with W. N. Sage, "Sandford Fleming, engineer," *Queen's Quarterly*, Autumn, 1950, pp. 353-61; and Alan Wilson's "Sandford Fleming and Charles Tupper: the Fall of the Siamese Twins" in John Moir (ed.), *Character and Circumstance: Essays in Honour of D. G. Creighton* (Toronto, 1970) pp. 99-127.

Foster: W. S. Wallace, *The Memoirs of the Rt. Hon. Sir George Foster* (Toronto, 1933); J. W. Dafoe, "The political career of Sir George Foster," C.H.R., June, 1934, pp. 191-5, which is a review article of Wallace's book; S. M. Scott, "Foster on the Thompson-Bowell succession," C.H.R.., Sept. 1967, pp. 273-6.

Galt: O. D. Skelton, *The Life and Times of Sir A. T. Galt* (Toronto, 1920).

Hill: J. G. Pyle, *Life of James J. Hill* (2 vols., New York, 1917).

Lacombe: Katherine Hughes, *Father Lacombe, Black-Robe Voyageur* (Toronto, 1911). P. E. Crunican, "Father Lacombe's strange mission: Lacombe-Langevin correspondence on the Manitoba School Question, 1895-6," Canadian Catholic Association, *Report*, 1959, pp. 57-71.

Langevin: Barbara Fraser, "The political career of Sir Hector Louis Langevin," C.H.R., June 1961, pp. 93-132. Newly published and too late for my use is, Andrée Desilets, *Hector Langevin* (Quebec, 1970).

Mair: Norman Shrive, *Charles Mair: Literary Nationalist* (Toronto, 1965). Not to be neglected.

Mercier: R. Rumilly, *Mercier* (Montréal, 1936).

Mitchell: Esther H. Greaves, "Peter Mitchell, a Father of Confederation," M.A. thesis, University of New Brunswick, 1958. Despite the title it covers Mitchell's career to his death in 1899, and is most useful.

Mowat: C. R. W. Biggar, *Sir Oliver Mowat* (2 vols., Toronto, 1905), is the standard biography; but see also, A. M. Evans, "The Mowat era, 1872-96; stability and progress," in Ontario Historical Society, *Profile of a Province* (Toronto, 1967), pp. 97-106: J. B. Kerr, "Sir Oliver Mowat and the campaign of 1894," *Ontario History*, March, 1963, pp. 1-14; J. C. Morrison, "Oliver Mowat and the development of Provincial rights in Ontario," Ontario Department of Public Records and Archives, *Three History Theses*, (Toronto, 1962). Morrison's is an M.A. thesis for University of Toronto, 1947.

McCarthy: Fred Landon, "D'Alton McCarthy & the politics of the later 'eighties,'" C.H.A., *Report*, 1932, pp. 43-50; E. J. Noble, "D'Alton McCarthy and the election of 1896," M.A. thesis, University of Guelph, 1969; J. F. O'Sullivan, "D'Alton McCarthy & the Conservative party, 1876-96," M.A. thesis, University of Toronto, 1949.

Riel: There are several biographies of Riel. The best one is G. F. G. Stanley, *Louis Riel* (Toronto, 1960), a more comprehensive study than his earlier *Birth of Western Canada* (London, 1936). Stanley has also two articles that can be consulted, "Louis Riel," R.H.A.F., juin 1960, pp. 10-26, and "Louis Riel," in *Our Living Tradition*, fifth series (Toronto, 1965), pp. 21-40. A good psychiatric analysis of Riel is E. R. Markson, Cyril Greenland and R. E. Turner, "The life and death of Louis Riel – a study of forensic psychiatry," *Canadian Psychiatric Journal*, Aug. 1965, pp. 244-64. Also Léon Pouliot, "Correspondence Louis Riel" – Mgr. Bourget, R.H.A.F., déc. 1961, pp. 430-2.

Ross: Margaret Ross, *Sir George W. Ross* (Toronto, 1924).

Sifton: J. W. Dafoe, *Clifford Sifton in Relation to His Times* (Toronto, 1931).

Smith, A. J.: Carl Wallace, "Albert Smith, Confederation, and Reaction in New Brunswick, 1852-82," C.H.R., Dec. 1963, pp. 283-312.

Smith, Goldwin: Elizabeth Wallace, *Goldwin Smith, Victorian Liberal* (Toronto, 1957). R. C. Brown, "Goldwin Smith and anti-imperialism," C.H.R., June, 1962, pp. 93-105; Malcolm Ross, "Goldwin Smith," *Our Living Tradition*, first series (Toronto, 1957), pp. 29-47.

Stephen: Heather Gilbert, *Awakening Continent: The Life of George Stephen* (Aberdeen, 1965).

Strathcona: Donald Smith, to give him his original name, has engendered a surprising amount of biographical controversy. W. T. R. Preston, *The Life and Times of Lord Strathcona* (London, 1914) is clearly out to run his quarry to earth. Rescue is performed by Beckles Willson, *The Life of Lord Strathcona and Mount Royal* (London, 1915).

Tarte: The field is dominated by the studies of Laurier LaPierre. Two published studies are, "Joseph Israël Tarte: relations between the French Canadian episcopacy and a French Canadian politician, 1874-96," Canadian Catholic Historical Association, *Report*, 1958, pp. 23-37; and "Joseph Israël Tarte and the McGreevy-Langevin scandal," C.H.A., *Report*, 1961, pp. 47-57. Of more importance are LaPierre's two theses for the

University of Toronto: his M.A. thesis, "Joseph Israël Tarte," 1957; his PH.D. thesis, "Politics, race and religion in French Canada: Joseph Israël Tarte," 1962.

C. H. Tupper: F. H. Patterson, "Some incidents in the life of Sir Charles Hibbert Tupper," Nova Scotia Historical Society, *Collections*, Vol. XXXV, 1966, pp. 127-62. Gossipy but informative account.

Walker: G. P. de T. Glazebrook, *Sir Edmund Walker* (Oxford, 1933).

Willison: A. H. U. Colquhoun, *Press, Politics and People: The Life and Letters of Sir John Willison* (Toronto, 1935), and R. T. Clippingdale, "J. S. Willison and Canadian Nationalism 1886-1902," C.H.A. *Historical Papers*, 1969, pp. 74-93.

LEGAL AND CONSTITUTIONAL HISTORY

Privy Council decisions relating to the B.N.A. Act are covered in R. A. Olmstead (ed.), *Decisions of the Judicial Committee of the Privy Council relating to the British North America Act, 1867*, Vol. I (Ottawa, 1954). Decisions relating to other acts, such as the New Brunswick School Act of 1871 *et seq.*, have to be sought in the Appeal Cases themselves. Supreme Court of Canada decisions, as those of the provincial Supreme Courts, are to be found in their respective *Reports*. A most useful compilation is Peter H. Russell's *Leading Constitutional Decisions* (Toronto, 1965), Carleton Library, which has excellent introductions and a good bibliography.

On disallowance, see W. E. Hodgins (ed.), *Correspondence, reports of the ministers of justice, and orders in Council, upon the subject of Dominion and provincial legislation* (Ottawa, 1922). See also the useful article by Eugene Forsey, "Disallowance of provincial acts, reservation of provincial bills, and refusal of assent by Lieutenant-Governors since 1867," C.J.E.P.S., Feb. 1938, pp. 47-59.

On the Lieutenant-Governors themselves the leading work is J. T. Saywell, *The Office of Lieutenant-Governor* (Toronto, 1957), with a bibliography that obviates detailed repetition here.

On subsidies and their tangled history, J. A. Maxwell, *Federal Subsidies to the Provincial Governments in Canada* (Cambridge, 1937), as well as W. Eggleston and C. T. Kraft, *Dominion-Provincial subsidies and grants*, Appendix to Royal Commission on Dominion-Provincial relations (Ottawa, 1940).

For studies of Parliament and its working, Norman Ward dominates the field: *The Canadian House of Commons* (Toronto, 1950); *The Public Purse: A Study of Canadian Democracy* (Toronto, 1962); "The formative years of the House of Commons, 1867-1891," C.J.E.P.S., Nov. 1952, pp. 431-52; "Electoral corruption and controverted elections," C.J.E.P.S., Feb. 1949, pp. 74-86. E. A. Forsey also: "Alexander Mackenzie's memorandum on the appointment of extra Senators, 1873-4," C.H.R., June, 1946, pp. 189-94; "Oaths of ministers without portfolio," C.J.E.P.S., May, 1948, pp. 246-7, mainly about the Bowell crisis of January, 1896.

ADMINISTRATIVE HISTORY

W. E. Bauer, "The Department of the Interior and Dominion Lands, 1873-1891: a study of administration," M.A. thesis, Queen's, 1953, defends the department, in particular, its senior civil servants. G. Blake, *Customs Administration in Canada* (Toronto, 1957), is particularly revealing for the early years after Confederation. A. W. Currie, "The Post Office since 1867," C.J.E.P.S., May, 1958 pp. 241-50.

On Indian administration: a useful and comprehensive retrospect is H. B. Hawthorn (ed.), *A Survey of the Contemporary Indians of Canada* (2 vols., Ottawa, 1966); T. R. L. MacInnes, "History of Indian administration in Canada," C.J.E.P.S., 1946, pp. 387-94. On the Treaties see G. F. G. Stanley, *Birth of Western Canada* (London, 1936). A contemporary account of 1880 is Alexander Morris, *The Treaties of Canada with the Indians of Manitoba and the North-West Territories* (Toronto, 1880), and since Morris negotiated many of them, he is worth listening to.

R. M. Dawson, *The Civil Service of Canada* (London, 1929) is the standard work on the civil service as a whole.

IMPERIAL RELATIONS

D. M. L. Farr, *The Colonial Office and Canada*, 1867-1887 (Toronto, 1955), is an excellent study, well written and carefully done. J. E. Tyler *Struggle for Imperial Unity*, 1868-95 (London, 1938) and Norman Penlington, *Canada and Imperialism*, 1896-1899 (Toronto, 1965) cover the broader ground. R. A. Preston covers *Canada & "Imperial Defense"* (Durham, 1967).

Leading articles: A. C. Cooke, "Empire unity and colonial nationalism, 1884-1911," C.H.R. *Report*, 1939, pp. 77-86; D. G. Creighton, "The Victorians and the Empire," C.H.R., June 1938, pp. 138-53; C. P. Stacey, "Canada and the Nile expedition of 1884-5," C.H.R., Dec. 1952, pp. 319-40, and also "John A. Macdonald on raising troops for imperial service, 1885," C.H.R., March, 1957, pp. 37-40; Alice Stewart, "Canadian-West Indian Union, 1884-1885," C.H.R., Dec. 1950, pp. 369-89, and "Sir John A. Macdonald and the Imperial Defence Commission of 1879," C.H.R., June, 1954, pp. 119-39.

On imperial federation there are two good theses: Carl Berger's "The vision of grandeur: studies in the ideas of Canadian imperialism," PH.D. thesis, University of Toronto, 1966, a searching analysis of the ideas of the 1890's and early 1900's; G. R. MacLean's "Imperial federation in Canada," PH.D. thesis, Duke University 1958 is more generally political in range.

CANADIAN-AMERICAN RELATIONS

Brebner's *North Atlantic Triangle* (New Haven, 1945) is still an admirable introduction. C. C. Tansill's *Canadian-American relations*, 1875-1911 (New Haven, 1943) is more detailed, and must now be supplemented by R. C. Brown's *Canada's National Policy, 1883-1900: A Study in Canadian-American Relations* (Princeton, 1964); A. C. Gluek, *Minnesota and the Manifest Destiny of the Canadian Northwest* (Toronto, 1966); and in a broader frame, D. F. Warner's uneven but interesting *The Idea of Continental Union: Agitation for the Annexation of Canada to the United States, 1849-93* (Lexington, 1960). Not to be neglected is C. C. Tansill's comprehensive study, *The Foreign Policy of Thomas Bayard, 1885-1897* (New York, 1940). It is a pity someone has not done the same for James G. Blaine.

POLITICAL HISTORY

A. *The 1870's*

W. R. Graham, "Liberal nationalism in the 1870's," C.H.A. *Report*, 1946, pp. 101-19; G. M. Hougham, "Canada first: a minor party in microcosm," C.J.E.P.S., May 1953, pp. 174-84; D. Lee, "Dominion general election of 1878 in Ontario," *Ontario History*, Summer, 1959, pp. 172-90; Bernard Ostry, "Conservatives, Liberals & Labour in the 1870's," C.H.R., June, 1960, pp. 93-127; F. H. Underhill, "Political ideas of Upper Canada Reformers, 1867-1878," C.H.A., *Report*, 1942, pp. 104-15; G. F. G. Stanley, "The 1870's" in J. M. S. Careless and R. C. Brown, *The Canadians*, 1867-1967 (Toronto, 1967), pp. 37-69.

B. *The 1880's*

W. S. MacNutt, *Days of Lorne* [1878-1883], (Fredericton, 1955); also his "The 1880's" in *The Canadians, 1867-1967*, cited above. Other articles: Margaret A. Banks, "Change in the Liberal party leadership, 1887," C.H.R., June, 1957, pp. 109-28. R. M. Dawson, "The Gerrymander of 1882," C.J.E.P.S., May, 1935, pp. 197-221; W. R. Graham, "Sir Richard Cartwright, Wilfrid Laurier and Liberal Party trade policy, 1887," C.H.R., March, 1952, pp. 1-18; Fred Landon, "The Canadian scene, 1880-1890," C.H.A. *Report*, 1942, pp. 5-18; Bernard Ostry, "Conservatives Liberals and labour in the 1880's," C.J.E.P.S., May, 1961, pp. 141-61. On the Ontario Boundary: M. Zaslow, "The Ontario boundary question," in Ontario Historical Society, *Profile of a Province* (Toronto, 1967), pp. 107-113.

The election of 1887: J. I. Cooper, "The Canadian general election of 1887," M.A. thesis, University of Western Ontario, 1933.

For Saskatchewan rebellion, see Regional history.

C. The 1890's

Lovell C. Clark, "The Conservative party in the 1890's," C.H.A. *Report*, 1961 pp. 58-74; a much more comprehensive study is Clark's PH.D. thesis for Toronto with the same title (1967); J. W. Lederle, "The Liberal convention of 1893," C.J.E.P.S., Feb. 1950, pp. 42-52; J. T. Saywell, "The 1890's," a particularly valuable essay in *The Canadians, 1867-1967*, cited above, and his "The Crown and the politicians: the Canadian succession question, 1891-1896," C.H.R., Dec. 1956, pp. 309-337; J. T. Watt, "Anti-Catholic nativism in Canada: the Protestant Protective Association," C.H.R., March, 1967, pp. 45-58.

The election of 1891: I. A. Hodson, "Commercial union and the background of the election of 1891," M.A. thesis, University of Western Ontario, 1952; K. A. MacKirdy, "The Loyalty issue in the 1891 federal election campaign, and an ironic footnote," *Ontario History*, Sept. 1963, pp. 143-54.

For the Manitoba school question see especially Lovell C. Clark, *The Manitoba School Question: Majority Rule or Minority Rights?* (Toronto, 1968), a compendium of documents, and his PH.D. thesis for Toronto, "The Conservative Party in the 1890's." J. S. Ewart, *The Manitoba School Question* (Toronto, 1890) is a contemporary pro-Catholic source. C. B. Sissons has a general discussion *Church and State in Canadian Education* (Toronto, 1959). An important new study is Paul E. Crunican's comprehensive, "The Manitoba School Question and Canadian federal politics: a study in church-state relations," PH.D. thesis, University of Toronto, 1968, and his "Bishop Laflèche and the Mandement of 1896," C.H.A., *Historical Papers*, 1969, pp. 52-61.

ECONOMIC HISTORY AND DEVELOPMENT

A. Transportation

A. W. Currie, *Economics of Canadian Transportation* (Toronto, 1954), and G. P. de T. Glazebrook, *History of Canadian Transportation* (2 vols., Toronto, 1938), are two important studies. R. Dorman, *A Statutory History of the Steam and Electric Railways of Canada, 1836-1937* (Ottawa, 1932) is pure fact and valuable, as is M. L. Bladen, "Construction of railways in Canada," a calendar in *Contributions to Canadian Economics*, in two parts, to 1885 Vol. V (1932), and 1885-1931 in Vol. VII (1934).

On the Grand Trunk Railway, A. W. Currie *Grand Trunk Railway of Canada* (Toronto, 1957) is a solid and well-made work; G. R. Stevens, *Canadian National Railways*, Vol. I *Sixty Years of Trial and Error* (Toronto, 1960) is more flamboyant, but written by a man who knows railroading. It is also more useful for the Intercolonial than Sandford Fleming's *The Intercolonial* (Montreal, 1876) which is sporadic, and unsatisfactory for the political background.

The Canadian Pacific Railway has been essayed several times. Probably the best, though heavily on the financial side, is still H. A. Innis, *A History of the Canadian Pacific Railway* (Toronto, 1923); J. M. Gibbon's *Steel of Empire: The Romantic History of the Canadian Pacific* (Toronto, 1935) is worth reading. E. J. Pratt's *Toward the Last Spike* (Toronto, 1952) is a long narrative poem, but it is still good history.

Other railway studies are, H. Fleming, *Canada's Arctic Outlet: A History of the Hudson's Bay Railway* (Berkeley, 1957). A valuable background for the western railway question is L. B. Irwin, *Pacific Railways and Nationalism in the Canadian-American Northwest, 1845-73* (Philadelphia, 1939).

Indispensable for ships and shipping are the works of Frederick William Wallace, especially *Wooden Ships and Iron Men* (Toronto, 1924). There has been remarkably little work done on this aspect of Canadian history. His "Ships of the timber trade," *Canadian Geographical Journal* (July, 1935), pp. 3-14, and P. Smith's "The passing of the sailing ship at Quebec," C.H.A. *Report*, 1923, pp. 65-71, deal with Quebec shipping. W. K. Lamb, "Pioneer days of the trans-Pacific service, 1887-1891," B.C.H.Q., July, 1937, pp. 143-64 is informative.

Lyn Harrington's "The Dawson route," *Canadian Geographical Journal*, Sept. 1951, pp. 136-43, is short but knowledgeable, as is Bruce Peel's "Steamboats on the Saskatchewan," *Alberta Historical Review*, Summer, 1968, pp. 11-21.

B. Economic growth and industrial development

An important, probably indispensable overall work is O. J. Firestone, *Canadian*

Economic Development 1867-1953 (London, 1953). Kenneth Buckley's *Capital Formation in Canada 1890-1930* (Toronto, 1955) has some relevance to the period, but more directly useful is J. Pickett, "Residential capital formation in Canada, 1871-1921," C.J.E.P.S., Feb. 1963, pp. 40-58, and G. W. Bertram, "Economic growth in Canadian industry, 1870-1915," C.J.E.P.S., May, 1963. H. C. Pentland has two articles, "The role of capital in Canadian economic development before 1875," C.J.E.P.S., Nov. 1950, pp. 457-74, and "Further observations on Canadian development," C.J.E.P.S., Aug. 1953, pp. 403-10.

C. Banking

A. B. Jamieson, *Chartered Banking in Canada* (Toronto, 1952) and R. C. McIvor, *Canadian Monetary, Banking and Fiscal Development* (Toronto, 1958) are standard works. Victor Ross, *A History of the Canadian Bank of Commerce* (2 vols., Toronto, 1922) is especially valuable for the role of Senator McMaster in the establishment of the Canadian Bank Act of 1871. Merrill Denison's *Canada's First Bank: A History of the Bank of Montreal* (2 vols., Toronto, 1967) is handsomely presented and uses some Bank of Montreal archives.

D. The Tariff

There are few more controversial subjects. J. H. Dales has been the leading critic of the national policy tariff. His "Canada's national policies," appeared in the *Queen's Quarterly* (Autumn, 1964) pp. 297-316; several articles have followed, all now included in his *The Protective Tariff in Canada's Development* (Toronto, 1966). O. J. McDiarmid's *Commercial Policy in the Canadian Economy* (Cambridge, 1946) is an overall study and a basic work. S. J. McLean, *The Tariff History of Canada* (Toronto, 1895) is factual and statistical, and is one of the first of the University of Toronto studies. Articles would include, S. D. Clark, "The Canadian Manufacturers Association and the tariff," C.J.E.P.S., Feb. 1939, pp. 19-39; J. I. Cooper, "Some early French Canadian advocacy of protection, 1871-3," C.J.E.P.S., Nov. 1937, pp. 530-40; V. C. Fowke, "National policy – old and new," C.J.E.P.S., Aug. 1952.

E. Business History

S. D. Clark, *The Canadian Manufacturers Association* (Toronto, 1939); Merrill Denison, *The Barley and the Stream: The Molson Story* (Toronto, 1955); also his *Harvest Triumphant: The Story of Massey-Harris* (Toronto, 1948). William Kilbourn, *The Elements Combined* (Toronto, 1960) is an excellent history of the Steel Company of Canada. Alan Wilson's *John Northway: Blue Serge Canadian* (Toronto, 1965), is a useful corrective to conventional views of business at the time.

F. Land Policy

J. B. Hedges, *Building the Canadian West: The Land and Colonization Policies of the Canadian Pacific Railway* (New York, 1939) is indispensable, as well as his less well known, *The Federal Railway Land Subsidy Policy in Canada* (Cambridge, 1934). Chester Martin's *"Dominion Lands" Policy* (Toronto, 1938) is in the same category. Important articles are: J. S. Galbraith, "Land policies of the Hudson's Bay Company, 1870-1913," C.H.R., March 1951, pp. 1-21; Chester Martin, "Our 'kingdom for a horse': the railway land grant system in western Canada," C.H.A. *Report*, 1934, pp. 73-9.

G. Prairie Settlement and Agricultural Production

Robert England, *Colonization of Western Canada* (London, 1936); V. C. Fowke's *Canadian Agricultural Policy: The Historical Pattern* (Toronto, 1946) is suggestive and compressed. W. A. Mackintosh has two good studies, *Prairie Settlement: the Geographical Setting* (Toronto, 1934), and with others, *Economic Problems of the Prairie Settlement* (Toronto, 1935). A. S. Morton's *History of Prairie Settlement* (Toronto, 1938) is indispensable. Articles include H. Michel, "Notes on prices of agricultural commodities in the United States and Canada, 1850-1934," C.J.E.P.S., May, 1935, pp. 269-79; E. H. Oliver's two articles on Saskatchewan settlement, "Economic conditions in Saskatchewan, 1870-1881," R.S.C., *Transactions*, Sec. 2 (1933), pp. 15-39, and "Settlement of Saskatchewan to 1914," R.S.C., *Transactions*, 1962, pp. 63-87; F. G. Roe, "Early opinions on the 'fertile belt' of western Canada," C.H.R., June, 1946, pp. 131-49. The last author has three articles on the buffalo: "The extermination of the buffalo in western Canada," C.H.R., March, 1934, pp. 1-23; "Buffalo and snow," C.H.R., June, 1936, pp. 125-46; "The numbers of buffalo," R.S.C., *Transactions*, Sec. 2 (1937), pp. 171-203. See also the articles listed under Regional History.

H. Immigration and Population

Norman Macdonald, *Canada: Immigration and Colonization, 1841-1903* (Toronto, 1966) is the major work in the field. Articles include, K. Buckley, "Historical estimates of internal migration," in C.P.S.A., Conference on statistics, 1960, *Papers* (Toronto, 1962); J. W. Grant, "Population shifts in the Maritime Provinces," *Dalhousie Review*, Oct. 1937, pp. 282-94; D. M. McDougall, "Immigration into Canada, 1851-1920," C.J.E.P.S., May 1961, pp. 162-75; R. Wilson, "Migration movements in Canada, 1868-1925," C.H.R., June, 1932, pp. 157-82.

I. Labour, Trade Unions, and Factory Legislation

There is a valuable bibliography in Sylvia Ostry and H. D. Woods, *Labour Policy and Labour Economics in Canada* (Toronto, 1962). H. A. Logan, *A History of Trade Unions in Canada* (Toronto, 1939) is still indispensable. R. N. Coats, "The Labour Movement in Canada" in *Canada and its Provinces*, Vol. IX, is old but good. D. R. Kennedy, *The Knights of Labour in Canada* (London, Ont. 1956) is a solid work and is too much neglected. Useful articles are: Eugene Forsey's "History of the labour movement in Canada," *Canada Year Book*, 1957-1958, and his "Note on the Dominion factory bills of the eighteen-eighties," C.J.E.P.S., Nov. 1947, pp. 580-5; Elizabeth Wallace, "Origins of the social welfare state in Canada," C.J.E.P.S., Aug. 1950, pp. 383-93.

LITERARY HISTORY

There seems no point in repeating the excellent bibliography in C. F. Klinck, *Literary History of Canada: Canadian Literature in English* (Toronto, 1965). A few highlights can be mentioned. The book just cited is probably the best place to begin. C. T. Bissell (ed.) *Our Living Tradition*, first series (Toronto, 1957) is followed by R. L. McDougall (ed.) *Our Living Tradition*, second, third, fourth and fifth series (Toronto, 1959-62) should be consulted for excellent essays both on poets and politicians. E. K. Brown, *On Canadian Poetry* (Toronto, 1943) is a masterpiece on the post-Confederation poets.

On French-Canadian literature see Gérard Tougas, *Histoire de la littérature Canadienne-français* (Paris, 4th edition, 1967), especially Chapter III. See also Marcel Dugas, *Un romantique canadien, Louis Fréchette* (Paris, 1934); for Arthur Buies, see Léopold Lamontagne, *Arthur Buies, homme de lettres* (Québec, 1957).

For Tardivel: Mathieu Girard, "La pensée politique de Jules-Paul Tardivel," R.H.A.F., déc. 1967, pp. 397-428, an admirable piece; John Hare, "Nationalism in French Canada and Tardivel's novel 'Pour la Patrie,'" *Culture*, 1961, pp. 403-12; P. Savard, "Jules-Paul Tardivel, un ultramontain devant les problèmes et les hommes de son temps," C.H.A. *Report*, 1963, pp. 125-40.

REGIONAL HISTORY

A. Newfoundland

St. John Chadwick, *Newfoundland: Island into Province* (Cambridge, 1967) is a recent new survey that only emphasizes how much work there is yet to be done. R. A. Mackay (ed.), *Newfoundland: Economic, Diplomatic and Strategic Studies* (Toronto, 1946) is a series of essays, uneven, but really indispensable. D. W. Prowse, *A History of Newfoundland* (London, 1895) is still valuable. F. F. Thompson, *The French Shore Controversy in Newfoundland* (Toronto, 1961) is important for this period. Articles: L. A. Harris, "Newfoundland, 1867-1921," in *Cambridge History of the British Empire*, VI, pp. 673-85, is short and good; Harvey Mitchell, "Canada's negotiations with Newfoundland, 1887-95," C.H.R., Dec. 1959, pp. 277-93, as well as his "Constitutional crisis of 1889 in Newfoundland," C.J.E.P.S., Aug. 1958, pp. 323-33; G. F. G. Stanley, "Further documents relating to the union of Newfoundland and Canada, 1886-95," C.H.R., Dec. 1948, pp. 370-86.

B. Nova Scotia

J. M. Beck, *Government of Nova Scotia* (Toronto, 1957) is a good historical survey. His recent *History of Maritime Union: A Study of Frustrations* (Fredericton, 1969) is useful for the repeal movement of the 1880's. There is very little secondary material available except in graduate theses. Among the more useful are: Colin Howell, "Repeal, annexation and commercial union in Nova Scotia, 1886-8," M.A. thesis, Dalhousie University, 1967; Kenneth McLaughlin, "The Canadian general election of 1896 in Nova Scotia," M.A. thesis, Dalhousie University, 1967.

C. New Brunswick

Hugh Thorburn, *Politics in New Brunswick* (Toronto, 1961) is the leading secondary source. On education see, K. F. C. McNaughton, *Development of the Theory and Practice of Education in New Brunswick, 1784-1900* (Fredericton, 1947). There are a number of good M.A. theses, among which, M. E. Angus, "The politics of the 'Short Line,'" M.A. thesis, University of New Brunswick, 1958; D. L. Poynter, "Economics and politics of New Brunswick, 1878-1883," M.A. thesis, University of New Brunswick, 1961.

D. Prince Edward Island

A. H. Clark, *Three Centuries and the Island* (Toronto, 1959) is historical geography; Frank Mackinnon *The Government of P.E.I.* (Toronto, 1951) is historical political science. Both are excellent.

E. Quebec

R. Rumilly, *Histoire de la province de Québec*, Vol. III to VIII (Montréal, n.d.) is detailed and comprehensive, written with verve and a few lively prejudices. He also gives no references for his sources. Mason Wade's *French Canadians 1760-1945* (Toronto, 1955) is helpful, but parts of it have to be used with care. J. I. Cooper's "French-Canadian conservatism in principle and practice, 1873-1896," PH.D. thesis, McGill University, 1938, is a good survey. Volume X, 2-3, 1969, of *Recherches Sociographiques* is devoted to "Idéologies au Canada Français 1850-1900."

On provincial elections see, J. Hamelin, J. Letarte et M. Hamelin, "Les élections provinciales de Québec" in *Cahiers de géographie de Québec*, Oct. 1959 - March 1960. There is an excellent account of 1886 by R. W. Cox, "The Quebec provincial election of 1886," M.A. thesis, McGill University, 1948.

The Jesuits' Estates history is given by R. S. Dalton, *The Jesuit Estates' Question 1760-1888* (Toronto, 1968), but it is useless for the agitation that followed, for which see J. R. Miller's forthcoming PH.D. thesis for the University of Toronto, "The Impact of the Jesuits' Estates Act on Canadian Politics, 1888-1891."

French-Canadian relations with the Northwest: L. Pouliot, "Le Nouveau Monde et la question du Nord Ouest," R.H.A.F., Dec. 1957, pp. 353-60, and an excellent and comprehensive article by A. M. Silver, "French Canada and the prairie frontier," C.H.R., March, 1969, pp. 11-36.

F. Ontario

G. P. de T. Glazebrook's *Life in Ontario: A Social History* (Toronto, 1968) is an introduction, but we need a comprehensive political history. Two volumes of *Canada and its Provinces* (23 vols., Toronto, 1913-17) are devoted to Ontario, Vols. 17 and 18; see especially W. S. Wallace's "Political history, 1867-1912," Vol. XVII, pp. 103-88. D. C. Masters, *Rise of Toronto, 1850-90* (Toronto, 1947) was a pioneering study, but it is now becoming out of date. A solid and interesting work is F. A. Walker, *Catholic Education and Politics in Ontario* (Toronto, 1964). Ross Harkness, *J. E. Atkinson of the Star* (Toronto, 1963) is a history of the paper from its founding in 1892. Articles and theses: E. L. Eayrs, "The election of 1896 in western Ontario," M.A. thesis, University of Western Ontario, 1950; W. E. Greening, "The Toronto *Globe* 1890-1902 and its policies," M.A. thesis, University of Toronto, 1939; K. W. McNaught, "The *Globe* and Canadian liberalism, 1880-1890," M.A. thesis, University of Toronto, 1946; G. R. Tennant, "The policy of the *Mail*, 1882-1892," M.A. thesis, University of Toronto, 1946.

G. Manitoba

W. L. Morton, *Manitoba: A History* (Toronto, 1957) is an excellent introduction. W. Kristjansen, *The Icelandic People in Manitoba* (Winnipeg, 1965) is an anecdotal chronicle but comprehensive. Articles and theses: J. L. Holmes, "Factors affecting politics in Manitoba: a study of provincial elections, 1870-99," M.A. thesis, University of Manitoba, 1936; J. A. Jackson, "The disallowance of Manitoba railway legislation in the 1880's: railway policy as a factor in the relations of Manitoba with the Dominion, 1878-1888," M.A. thesis, University of Manitoba, 1948; R. O. MacFarlane, "Manitoba politics and parties after Confederation," C.H.A. *Report*, 1940, pp. 45-55; J. A. Maxwell, "Financial relations between Manitoba and the Dominion, 1870-86," C.H.R., Sept. 1934, pp. 376-89.

H. The Northwest Territories (the present provinces of Alberta and Saskatchewan)

There are a number of excellent books, some of them works of literature in their own right. L. V. Kelly, *The Range Men* (Toronto, 1913); C. M. MacInnes, *In the Shadow of the Rockies* (London, 1930) is an excellent and sensible book, and indispensable for Alberta. Edward McCourt, *Saskatchewan* (Toronto, 1968) is evocative rather than comprehensive. Wallace Stegner, *Wolf Willow* (New York, 1962), although it does not specifically deal with the period, is perhaps the finest book about the west written since Butler's *Great Lone Land* of 1872, and is essential reading for the feel of the west. Paul Sharp's *Whoop-up Country 1865-1885* (Helena, 1960) is superb. G. F. G. Stanley *The Birth of Western Canada* (London, 1936) is indispensable for the two Riel rebellions and for Indian history. L. H. Thomas, *The Struggle for Responsible Government in the North-West Territories 1870-97* (Toronto, 1956), although it is heavily constitutional and political in orientation, is very well done by a careful scholar, and will well repay attention. J. P. Turner's *History of the North-West Mounted Police, 1873-1893*, (2 vols., Ottawa, 1950) is an official history, and tends to be fulsome.

Articles: R. C. Brown, "Canadian nationalism in western newspapers," *Alberta Historical Review*, Summer, 1962, pp. 1-7; H. A. Dempsey, "The Calgary-Edmonton trail," *Alberta Historical Review*, Autumn, 1959, pp. 16-21; Earl Drake, "Regina, 1882-1955," *Canadian Geographical Journal*, 1955, pp. 2-17; Wm. Pierce, "The establishment of national parks in the Rockies," *Alberta Historical Review*, Summer, 1962, pp. 8-17; R.. C. Russell, "The Carlton Trail," *Beaver*, Winter 1959, pp. 4-11.

There is a considerable literature on the Northwest rebellion of 1885. Stanley's work mentioned above, as well as his biography of Louis Riel, are vital, to which may be added, C. P. Stacey, "The military aspect of Canada's winning of the west, 1870-1885," C.H.R., March 1940, pp. 1-24, as general accounts. Three important primary accounts are: G. H. Needler (ed.), *General Sir Fredericton Middleton: Suppression of the Rebellion* (Toronto, 1948) and G. F. G. Stanley's review article of it is *Saskatchewan History*, Spring, 1949, pp.30-4; Stanley's "Gabriel Dumont's account of the Northwest rebellion, 1885," C.H.R., Sept. 1949, pp. 249-69; T. B. Strange, *Gunner Jingo's Jubillee* (London, 1894). But there are many others, among which: J. H. Archer, "North-West rebellion, 1885," *Saskatchewan History*, Winter, 1962, pp. 1-18; V. Lachance, "The diary of Francis Dickens," *Queen's Quarterly*, Spring, 1930, pp. 312-34; G. F. Stanley, "Le journal d'un militaire au Nord-Ouest canadien," R.H.A.F., Sept. and Dec. 1956, pp. 263-78, 416-30. H. M. Hitsman has a military piece, "Near disaster at Cut Knife Hill, 1885," *Canadian Army Journal*, July, 1959, pp. 62-74.

I. British Columbia

Margaret Ormsby, *British Columbia: A History* (Toronto, 1958) is an excellent work, with a good bibliography. W. N. Sage has published a number of articles, "British Columbia becomes Canadian 1871-1901," *Queen's Quarterly*, 1945, pp. 168-83; "Federal parties and provincial groups in British Columbia, 1871-1903," B.C.H.Q., April, 1948, pp. 151-69.

INDEX